Birnbaum's 94
Portugal

A BIRNBAUM TRAVEL GUIDE

Alexandra Mayes Birnbaum
EDITORIAL CONSULTANT

Lois Spritzer
Executive Editor

Laura L. Brengelman
Managing Editor

Mary Callahan
Senior Editor

Patricia Canole
Gene Gold
Jill Kadetsky
Susan McClung
Beth Schlau
Associate Editors

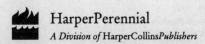

HarperPerennial
A Division of HarperCollinsPublishers

To Stephen, who merely made all this possible.

FIRST EDITION

ISSN 0749-2561 (Birnbaum Travel Guides)
ISSN 1055-5668 (Portugal)
ISBN 0-06-278111-1 (pbk.)

93 94 95 96 97 CC/CW 10 9 8 7 6 5 4 3 2 1

Cover design © Drenttel Doyle Partners
Cover photograph © Bob Krist

BIRNBAUM TRAVEL GUIDES

Bahamas, and Turks & Caicos
Berlin
Bermuda
Boston
Canada
Cancun, Cozumel & Isla Mujeres
Caribbean
Chicago
Disneyland
Eastern Europe
Europe
Europe for Business Travelers
France
Germany
Great Britain
Hawaii
Ireland
Italy
London

Los Angeles
Mexico
Miami & Ft. Lauderdale
Montreal & Quebec City
New Orleans
New York
Paris
Portugal
Rome
San Francisco
Santa Fe & Taos
South America
Spain
United States
USA for Business Travelers
Walt Disney World
Walt Disney World for Kids, By Kids
Washington, DC

Contributing Editors

David Baird
F. Lisa Beebe
Frederick H. Brengelman
Kevin Causey
Peter Collis
Thomas Fitzmaurice de la Cal
Martha de la Cal
Piers A. C. Gallie
Dwight V. Gast
Judith Glynn
Michael Hudec
Arline Inge
Donald A. Jeffrey
Robert Latona
Suzanne Lavenas

Charles Leocha
Jan S. McGirk
Jeanne Muchnick
Joan Kane Nichols
Clare Pedrick
Allan Seiden
Richard Slovak
Tracy Smith
Richard Swanson
Peter Webster
David Wickers
Mark Williams
Peter Wise
Maria Emília Zino

Maps

B. Andrew Mudryk

Contents

Getting Ready to Go

Practical information for planning your trip.

Useful Words and Phrases

The Cities

*Thorough, qualitative guides to each of the 5 cities
most often visited by vacationers and businesspeople.
Each section offers a comprehensive report on the
city's most compelling attractions and amenities —
highlighting our top choices in every category.*

Diversions

*A selective guide to a variety of unexpected
pleasures, pinpointing the best places in which to
pursue them.*

Exceptional Experiences for the Mind and Body

Directions

*The most spectacular routes and roads; most
arresting natural wonders; and most magnificent
castles, manor houses, and gardens — all organized
into 8 specific driving tours.*

Foreword

My first memory of Portugal is wrapped up in a whirl of shirtwaist dresses, hula hoops, getting the braces off my teeth, and preparing to celebrate my sixteenth birthday. I was on my first Grand Tour of the Continent, complete with parents and older sister. My father asked me where I would like to spend this momentous moment of my life, and although I later confessed to my husband Stephen Birnbaum that I had heard of Lisbon and possibly vaguely remembered some geography text relating to the Iberian Peninsula, that was the full extent of my expertise on things Portuguese. Yet for reasons unknown, I replied firmly, "Portugal." That long-ago granted birthday wish turned out to stand me in splendid stead.

Above all, I developed a fondness for Spain's understated and underrated Iberian neighbor Portugal that I never lost. In Portugal, a traveler first discovers, above all, that he or she is not visiting a suburb of Spain. Language, food, history, and music are all dramatically Portuguese, and despite its modest size, Portugal offers travelers tastes of its remarkable heritage that are both pungent and wonderfully pleasurable.

Obviously, any guidebook to Portugal must keep pace with and answer the real needs of today's travelers. That's why we've tried to create a guide that's specifically organized, written, and edited for the more demanding modern traveler, one for whom qualitative information is infinitely more desirable than mere quantities of unappraised data. For years, dating back as far as Herr Baedeker, travel guides have tended to be encyclopedic, much more concerned with demonstrating expertise in geography and history than with a real analysis of the sorts of things that actually concern a typical tourist. I think you'll notice a different, more contemporary tone to our text, as well as an organization and focus that are distinctive and more functional.

Early on, we realized that giving up the encyclopedic approach precluded our listing every single route and restaurant, a realization that helped define our overall editorial focus. Similarly, when we discussed the possibility of presenting certain information in other than strict geographic order, we found that the new format enabled us to arrange data in a way that best answers the questions travelers typically ask.

Travel guides are, understandably, reflections of personal taste, and putting one's name on a title page obviously puts one's preferences on the line. But I think I ought to amplify just what "personal" means. I don't believe in the sort of personal guidebook that's a palpable misrepresentation on its face. It is, for example, hardly possible for any single travel writer to visit thousands of restaurants (and nearly as many hotels) in any given year and provide accurate appraisals of each. And even if it were physically possible for one human being to survive such an itinerary, it would of necessity have to be done at a dead sprint, and the perceptions derived therefrom would probably be less valid than those of any other intelligent individual visiting the same establishments. It is, therefore, impossible (especially in a large, annually revised and updated guidebook *series* such as we offer) to have only one person provide all the data on the entire world.

I also happen to think that such individual orientation is of substantially less value to readers. Visiting a single hotel for just one night or eating one hasty meal in a random restaurant hardly equips anyone to provide appraisals that are of more than passing interest. We have, therefore, chosen what I like to describe as the "thee and me" approach to restaurant and hotel evaluation and, to a somewhat more limited degree, to the sites and sights we have included in the other sections of our text. What this really reflects is a personal sampling tempered by intelligent counsel from informed local sources, and these additional friends-of-the-editor are almost always residents of the city and/or area about which they are consulted.

In addition, very precise editing and tailoring keep our text fiercely subjective. So what follows is the gospel according to Birnbaum, and it represents as much of our own taste and instincts as we can manage. It is probable, therefore, that if you like your cities stylish and prefer hotels with personality to high-rise anonymities, we're likely to have a long and meaningful relationship.

I also should point out something about the person to whom this guidebook is directed. Above all, he or she is a "visitor." This means that such elements as restaurants have been specifically picked to provide the visitor with a representative, enlightening, stimulating, and above all pleasant experience. Since so many extraneous considerations can affect the reception and service accorded a regular restaurant patron, our choices can in no way be construed as an exhaustive guide to resident dining. We think we've listed all the best places, in various price ranges, but they were chosen with a visitor's enjoyment in mind.

Other evidence of how we've tried to tailor our text to reflect modern travel habits is most apparent in the section we call DIVERSIONS. Where once it was common for travelers to spend a foreign visit seeing only obvious sights, the emphasis today is more likely to be directed toward pursuing some special interest. Therefore, we have collected these exceptional experiences so that it is no longer necessary to wade through a pound or two of superfluous prose just to find unexpected pleasures and treasures.

Finally, I should point out that every good travel guide is a living enterprise; that is, no part of this text is carved in stone. In our annual revisions, we refine, expand, and further hone all our material to serve your travel needs better. To this end, no contribution is of greater value to us than your personal reaction to what we have written, as well as information reflecting your own experiences while using the book. Please write to us at 10 E. 53rd St., New York, NY 10022.

We sincerely hope to hear from you.

Alexandra Mayes Birnbaum

ALEXANDRA MAYES BIRNBAUM, editorial consultant to the *Birnbaum Travel Guides,* worked with her late husband Stephen Birnbaum as co-editor of the series. She has been a world traveler since childhood and is known for her lively travel reports on radio on what's hot and what's not.

Portugal

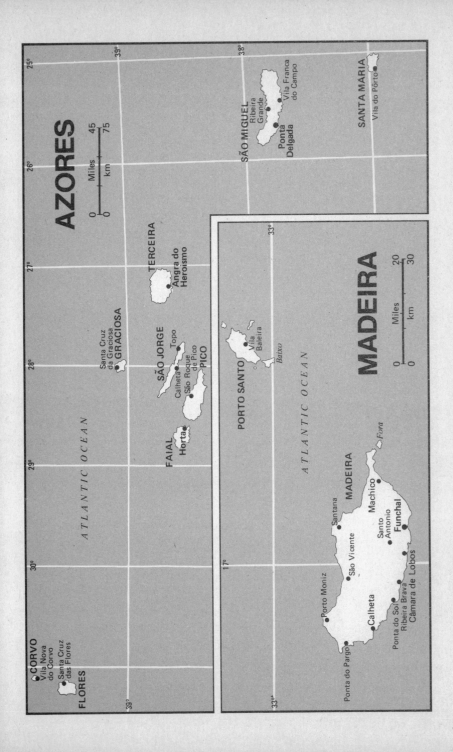

How to Use This Guide

A great deal of care has gone into the special organization of this guidebook, and we believe it represents a real breakthrough in the presentation of travel material. Our goal is to create a more modern generation of travel books, and to make this guide the most useful and practical travel tool available today.

Our text is divided into five basic sections in order to present information in the best way on every possible aspect of a vacation to Portugal. Our aim is to highlight what's where and to provide the basic information — how, when, where, how much, and what's best — to assist you in making the most intelligent choices possible.

Here is a brief summary of the five sections of this book, and what you can expect to find in each. We believe that you will find both your travel planning and en route enjoyment enhanced by having this book at your side.

GETTING READY TO GO

A mini-encyclopedia of practical travel facts with all the precise data necessary to create a successful trip to Portugal. Here you will find how to get where you're going, plus selected resources — including useful publications, and companies and organizations specializing in discount and special-interest travel — providing a wealth of information and assistance useful both before and during your trip.

USEFUL WORDS AND PHRASES

Though many hotels and restaurants in Portugal have English-speaking staff, a little knowledge of Portuguese will go a long way. This collection of often-used words and phrases will help you to make a hotel or dinner reservation, order a meal, mail a letter — and even buy toothpaste.

THE CITIES

Individual reports on the five Portuguese cities most visited by travelers and businesspeople offer a short-stay guide, including an essay introducing the city as a historic entity and a contemporary place to visit; *At-a-Glance* material is actually a site-by-site survey of the most important, interesting, and sometimes most eclectic sights to see and things to do; *Sources and Resources* is a concise listing of pertinent tourism information such as the address of the local tourism office, which sightseeing tours to take, when special events and holidays occur, where to find the best museums and theaters, where to hail a taxi, which are the shops that have the finest merchandise and/or the most irresistible bargains, and where the best golf, tennis, fishing, and swimming are to be found; and *Best in Town* lists our choices of the best places to eat and sleep on a variety of budgets.

DIVERSIONS

This section is designed to help travelers find the best places in which to engage in a variety of exceptional — and unexpected — experiences for the mind and body without having to wade through endless pages of unrelated text. In every case, our particular suggestions are intended to guide you to that special place where the quality of experience is likely to be highest.

DIRECTIONS

Here are eight itineraries that range all across Portugal, along the most beautiful routes and roads, past the most spectacular natural wonders, through the most historic cities and countrysides and the most idyllic islands. DIRECTIONS is the only section of this book that is organized geographically, and its itineraries cover the touring highlights of Portugal in short, independent journeys of 3 to 5 days' duration. Itineraries can be "connected" for longer sojourns or used individually for short, intensive explorations.

To use this book to full advantage, take a few minutes to read the table of contents and random entries in each section to get a firsthand feel for how it all fits together. You will find that the sections of this book are building blocks designed to help you put together the best possible trip. Use them selectively as a tool, a source of ideas, a reference work for accurate facts, and a guidebook to the best buys, the most exciting sights, the most pleasant accommodations, the tastiest food — *the best travel experience* that you can possibly have.

Getting Ready to Go

When to Go

Because of its proximity to the Atlantic, Portugal has a relatively temperate and damp climate, although the amount of rainfall varies considerably between regions. The eastern part of the country is the driest, with almost no rain in summer. In the coastal regions, the weather can be mild even in February and November, and throughout the country, frosts and snow are uncommon. On the other hand, summers in the Algarve can be hot.

Mid-May to mid-September generally is the peak travel period, but travel during the off-season (roughly November to *Easter*) and shoulder seasons (the months immediately before and after the peak months) also offers relatively fair weather and smaller crowds. During these periods, travel also is less expensive.

The *Weather Channel* (2600 Cumberland Pkwy., Atlanta, GA 30339; phone: 404-434-6800) provides current weather forecasts. Call 900-WEATHER from any touch-tone phone in the US; the 95¢ per minute charge will appear on your phone bill.

Traveling by Plane

SCHEDULED FLIGHTS

Leading airlines offering flights between the US and Portugal include *Air France, British Airways, Delta, KLM, Sabena, TAP Air,* and *TWA*.

FARES The great variety of airfares can be reduced to the following basic categories: first class, business class, coach (also called economy or tourist class), excursion or discount, and standby, as well as various promotional fares. For information on applicable fares and restrictions, contact the airlines listed above or ask your travel agent. Most airfares are offered for a limited time period. Once you've found the lowest fare for which you can qualify, purchase your ticket as soon as possible.

RESERVATIONS Reconfirmation is strongly recommended for all international flights. It is essential that you confirm your round-trip reservations — *especially the return leg* — as well as any flights within Europe.

SEATING Airline seats usually are assigned on a first-come, first-served basis at check-in, although you may be able to reserve a seat when purchasing your ticket. Seating charts often are available from airlines and are included in the *Airline Seating Guide* (Carlson Publishing Co., PO Box 888, Los Alamitos, CA 90720; phone: 310-493-4877).

SMOKING US law prohibits smoking on flights scheduled for 6 hours or less within the US and its territories on both domestic and international carriers. These rules do not apply to nonstop flights between the US and international destinations. A free wallet-size guide that describes the rights of nonsmokers is available from *ASH* (*Action on Smoking and Health;* DOT Card, 2013 H St. NW, Washington, DC 20006; phone: 202-659-4310).

SPECIAL MEALS When making your reservation, you can request one of the airline's alternate menu choices for no additional charge. Call to reconfirm your request 24 hours before departure.

BAGGAGE On a major international airline, passengers usually are allowed to carry on board one bag that will fit under a seat or in an overhead bin. Passengers also can check two bags in the cargo hold, measuring 62 inches and 55 inches in combined dimensions (length, width, and depth) with a per-bag weight limit of 70 pounds. There may be charges for additional, oversize, or overweight luggage, and for special equipment or sporting gear. Note that baggage allowances may vary for children (depending on the percentage of full adult fare paid) and on domestic and intra-European routes abroad. Check that the tags the airline attaches are correctly coded for your destination.

CHARTER FLIGHTS

By booking a block of seats on a specially arranged flight, charter operators frequently offer travelers bargain airfares. If you do fly on a charter, however, read the contract's fine print carefully. Charter operators can cancel a flight or assess surcharges of 10% of the airfare up to 10 days before departure. You usually must book in advance (no changes are permitted, so invest in trip cancellation insurance); also make your check out to the company's escrow account. For further information, consult the publication *Jax Fax* (397 Post Rd., Darien, CT 06820; phone: 203-655-8746).

DISCOUNTS ON SCHEDULED FLIGHTS

COURIER TRAVEL In return for arranging to accompany some kind of freight, a traveler may pay only a portion of the total airfare and a small registration fee. One agency that matches up would-be couriers with courier companies is *Now Voyager* (74 Varick St., Suite 307, New York, NY 10013; phone: 212-431-1616).

Courier Companies
Courier Travel Service (530 Central Ave., Cedarhurst, NY 11516; phone: 516-763-6898).
Discount Travel International (169 W. 81st St., New York, NY 10024; phone: 212-362-3636; and 940 10th St., Suite 2, Miami Beach, FL 33139; phone: 305-538-1616).
Excaliber International Courier (c/o *Way to Go Travel,* 6679 Sunset Blvd., Hollywood, CA 90028; phone: 213-466-1126).

F.B. On Board Courier Services (10225 Ryan Ave., Suite 103, Dorval, Quebec H9P 1A2, Canada; phone: 514-633-0740).

Halbart Express (147-05 176th St., Jamaica, NY 11434; phone: 718-656-8279).

International Adventures (60 E. 42nd St., New York, NY 10165; phone: 212-599-0577).

Midnight Express (925 W. High Park Blvd., Inglewood, CA 90302; phone: 310-672-1100).

Publications

Insider's Guide to Air Courier Bargains, by Kelly Monaghan (The Intrepid Traveler, PO Box 438, New York, NY 10034; phone: 212-304-2207).

Travel Secrets (PO Box 2325, New York, NY 10108; phone: 212-245-8703).

Travel Unlimited (PO Box 1058, Allston, MA 02134-1058; no phone).

World Courier News (PO Box 77471, San Francisco, CA 94107; no phone).

CONSOLIDATORS AND BUCKET SHOPS These companies buy blocks of tickets from airlines and sell them at a discount to travel agents or to consumers. Since many bucket shops operate on a thin margin, before parting with any money check the company's record with the Better Business Bureau.

Bargain Air (655 Deep Valley Dr., Suite 355, Rolling Hills, CA 90274; phone: 800-347-2345).

Council Charter (205 E. 42nd St., New York, NY 10017; phone: 800-800-8222 or 212-661-0311).

International Adventures (60 E. 42nd St., New York, NY 10165; phone: 212-599-0577).

Travac Tours and Charters (989 Ave. of the Americas, New York, NY 10018; phone: 800-872-8800 or 212-563-3303).

Unitravel (1177 N. Warson Rd., St. Louis, MO 63132; phone: 800-325-2222 or 314-569-0900).

LAST-MINUTE TRAVEL CLUBS For an annual fee, members receive information on imminent trips and other bargain travel opportunities. Despite the names of these clubs, you don't have to wait until literally the last minute to make travel plans.

Discount Travel International (114 Forest Ave., Suite 203, Narberth, PA 19072; phone: 215-668-7184).

Last Minute Travel (1249 Boylston St., Boston, MA 02215; phone: 800-LAST-MIN or 617-267-9800).

Moment's Notice (425 Madison Ave., New York, NY 10017; phone: 212-486-0500, -0501, -0502, or -0503).

Spur-of-the-Moment Cruises (411 N. Harbor Blvd., Suite 302, San

Pedro, CA 90731; phone: 800-4-CRUISES in California; 800-343-1991 elsewhere in the US; or 310-521-1070).

Traveler's Advantage (3033 S. Parker Rd., Suite 900, Aurora, CO 80014; phone: 800-548-1116 or 800-835-8747).

Vacations to Go (1502 Augusta, Suite 415, Houston, TX 77057; phone: 713-974-2121 in Texas; 800-338-4962 elsewhere in the US).

Worldwide Discount Travel Club (1674 Meridian Ave., Miami Beach, FL 33139; phone: 305-534-2082).

GENERIC AIR TRAVEL These organizations operate much like an ordinary airline standby service, except that they offer seats on not one but several scheduled and charter airlines. One pioneer of generic flights is *Airhitch* (2790 Broadway, Suite 100, New York, NY 10025; phone: 212-864-2000).

BARTERED TRAVEL SOURCES Barter is a common means of exchange between travel suppliers. Bartered travel clubs such as *Travel World Leisure Club* (225 W. 34th St., Suite 909, New York, NY 10122; phone: 800-444-TWLC or 212-239-4855) offer discounts to members for an annual fee.

CONSUMER PROTECTION

Passengers with complaints who are not satisfied with the airline's response can contact the US Department of Transportation (DOT; Consumer Affairs Division, 400 7th St. SW, Room 10405, Washington, DC 20590; phone: 202-366-2220). If you have a complaint against a local travel service, contact the Portuguese tourist authorities. Also see *Fly Rights* (Publication #050-000-00513-5; US Government Printing Office, PO Box 371954, Pittsburgh, PA 15250-7954; phone: 202-783-3238).

Traveling by Ship

Your cruise fare usually includes all meals, recreational activities, and entertainment. Shore excursions are available at extra cost, and can be booked in advance or once you're on board. An important factor in the price of a cruise is the location and size of your cabin; for information on ships' layouts and facilities, consult the charts issued by the *Cruise Lines International Association* (*CLIA;* 500 Fifth Ave., Suite 1407, New York, NY 10110; phone: 212-921-0066).

Most cruise ships have a doctor on board, plus medical facilities. The US Public Health Service (PHS) also inspects all passenger vessels calling at US ports; for the most recent summary or a particular inspection report, write to Chief, Vessel Sanitation Program, National Center for Environmental Health (1015 N. America Way, Room 107, Miami, FL 33132; phone: 305-536-4307). For further information, consult *Ocean and Cruise News* (PO Box 92, Stamford, CT 06904; phone: 203-329-2787). And for a free listing of travel agencies specializing in cruises, contact the *National Association of Cruise Only Agencies* (*NACOA;* PO Box 7209, Freeport, NY 11520; phone: 516-378-8006).

Cruise Lines

Crystal Cruises (2121 Ave. of the Stars, Los Angeles, CA 90067; phone: 800-446-6645).

Cunard (555 Fifth Ave., New York, NY 10017; phone: 800-5-CU-NARD or 800-221-4770).

P&O Cruises (c/o *Express Travel Services,* Empire State Bldg., Suite 7718, 350 Fifth Ave., New York, NY 10118; phone: 800-223-5799 or 212-629-3630).

Princess Cruises (10100 Santa Monica Blvd., Los Angeles, CA 90067; phone: 800-421-0522).

Royal Cruise Line (1 Maritime Plaza, Suite 1400, San Francisco, CA 94111; phone: 800-792-2992 in California; 800-227-4534 elsewhere in the US).

Royal Viking Line (95 Merrick Way, Coral Gables, FL 33134; phone: 800-422-8000).

Seabourn Cruise Line (55 Francisco St., Suite 710, San Francisco, CA 94133; phone: 800-929-9595).

Sun Line (1 Rockefeller Plaza, Suite 315, New York, NY 10020; phone: 800-468-6400 or 212-397-6400).

Traveling by Train

Companhia dos Caminhos de Ferro Portuguêses (CP), also known as *Portuguese National Railways,* serves most cities and towns across Portugal. *Inter-Regional (IR)* trains, which offer only basic amenities (snacks and drinks) and make numerous local stops, are the most common. The best trains are the *Rapidos,* which are similar to the *Inter-City (IC)* trains in use throughout Europe. They offer a full range of facilities, including lounges and restaurant and bar cars. Car-carrying trains, called *Auto-Expresos* in Portugal, are available on some routes (note that this service can be booked only in Europe).

Most Portuguese trains provide both first and second class cars. Meal service ranges from traditional dining cars to vendors dispensing sandwiches and beverages from a cart. Sleeping accommodations include *couchettes* (coach seats of a compartment converted to sleeping berths) and *wagons lit,* or sleepers (bedroom compartments providing one to three beds). Baggage often can be checked through to your destination or can be checked overnight at most stations. It is best to travel light — porters and self-service carts are hard to find.

You can buy your rail tickets before leaving the US either from travel agents or from *Portuguese National Railways'* North American representative, *Rail Europe* (226-230 Westchester Ave., White Plains, NY 10604; phone: 800-4-EURAIL). *Rail Europe* can make reservations for train trips of 3 hours or more in duration, including overnight excursions. Reservations, which can be made up to 2 months prior to the date of travel, are obligatory for those trains crossing the border, and advisable on all trains during the summer and other peak travel periods. Passage on some trains, such as the *Rapidos,* requires payment of a supplement. Various discount excursion tickets and rail passes also are available, including the Eurail-pass, which is good for train travel throughout much of Europe. Note that most rail passes must be purchased before you leave the US.

A company offering packaged rail tours is *Accent on Travel* (112 N. 5th St., Klamath Falls, OR 97601; phone: 503-885-7330 in Oregon; 800-347-0645 elsewhere in the US).

FURTHER INFORMATION

Rail Europe (address above) offers a *Travel Guide,* as well as various *Eurail* brochures. The *Thomas Cook European Timetable,* a compendium of European rail services, is available in bookstores and from the *Forsyth Travel Library* (PO Box 2975, Shawnee Mission, KS 66201-1375; phone: 800-367-7984 or 913-384-3440). Other useful resources include the *Eurail Guide,* by Kathryn Turpin and Marvin Saltzman (Eurail Guide Annuals, 27540 Pacific Coast Hwy., Malibu, CA 90265) and *Europe by Eurail,* by George Wright Ferguson (Globe Pequot Press, PO Box 833, Old Say-brook, CT 06475; phone: 203-395-0440).

Once you arrive in Portugal, rail information is available from the main office of *Portuguese National Railways* (Direção Comercial de Passageiros, Informação Publica, 66 Av. da Republica, Lisbon 1000), as well as from offices at the Santa Apolónia (phone: 1-87-6025) and Rossio (phone: 1-346-5022) train stations, both in Lisbon. Additional branch offices are located at train stations throughout the country.

Traveling by Bus

A map of Portugal's bus routes is not much different from a road map: If the way is paved, it's likely that some bus — express or local — is assigned to travel it.

Portuguese buses are run by numerous small regional lines under the auspices of *Rodoviaria Nacional, EP (RN;* 18 Av. Casal Ribeiro, Lisbon 1000; phone: 1-545439). This company can provide information on service to most cities and towns throughout the country. Schedule and fare information is available at the main bus terminal in Lisbon (18-B Av. Casal Ribeiro; phone: 1-577523) and from local tourist offices. From the US, information can be obtained from the Portuguese National Tourist Office or travel agents.

Seats cannot be reserved — tickets for a given trip are sold on a first-come, first-served basis at bus stations or (in towns where there are none) at local stores acting as ticket agents. The ticket generally is good only for that ride on that day. Toilet facilities are likely to be provided only on the newer buses on long-distance trips, and air conditioning, though common, is not universal — particularly on rural routes.

Although many American tour operators offer motorcoach tours (see listings below), *Rodoviaria Nacional, EP* (*RN Tours;* 38 Av. Fontes Pereira de Melo, Lisbon 1000; phone: 1-352-8683), which is the Portuguese affiliate of *Gray Line,* specializes in bus tours of Portugal.

Traveling by Car

Driving is the most flexible way to explore Portugal. To drive in Portugal, a US citizen needs a US driver's license. Although it is not required, an International Driver's Permit (IDP) — available from US branches of the *American Automobile Association (AAA)* — is strongly recommended. Proof of liability insurance also is required and is a standard part of any car rental contract. (To be sure of having the appropriate coverage, let the rental staff know in advance about the national borders you plan to cross.) If buying a car and using it abroad, you must carry an International Insurance Certificate, known as a Green Card (*Cartão Verde* in Portugal), which can be obtained from your insurance agent or through the *AAA*.

Driving in Portugal is on the right side of the road, and those coming from the right at intersections have the right of way. Pedestrians, provided they are in marked crosswalks, take precedence over all vehicles. (Unfortunately, such laws are not always observed.) Exceptions include priority roads, marked by a sign with a yellow diamond on it; these have the right of way until the diamond reappears with a black bar and the right of way reverts to those coming from the right. Pictorial direction signs are standardized under the International Roadsign System, and their meanings are indicated by their shapes: Triangular signs for danger; circular signs for instructions; and rectangular signs for information.

Distances are measured in kilometers (1 mile equals 1.6 kilometers; 1 kilometer equals .62 mile) and speeds are registered as kilometers per hour (kph) on the speedometer. On highways, the *minimum* speed is 50 kph (31 mph), and the speed limit is 120 kph (74 mph). On main roads outside of towns, speed limits usually are 90 kph (56 mph) for cars, unless they are towing trailers, in which case the speed limit is 70 kph (43 mph). On other roads, speed limits usually are 60 kph (about 38 mph). Pay attention to parking signs in large cities. If you park in a restricted zone, you may return to find a wheel "clamped," which renders the car inoperable and involves a tedious — and costly — process to get it freed. For additional information, consult *Euroad: The Complete Guide to Motoring in Europe* (VLE Ltd., PO Box 444, Ft. Lee, NJ 07024; phone: 201-585-5080).

MAPS

In the US, free maps can be obtained from the Portuguese National Tourist Office. The best road maps for touring are available from Michelin Guides and Maps (PO Box 3305, Spartanburg, SC 29304-3305; phone: 803-599-0850 in South Carolina; 800-423-0485 elsewhere in the US). Freytag & Berndt maps cover most major destinations throughout Europe;

they can be ordered from *Map Link* (25 E. Mason St., Suite 201, Santa Barbara, CA 93101; phone: 805-965-4402). The *American Automobile Association* (*AAA;* address below) also provides some useful reference sources, including an overall planning map of Europe, regional maps of Portugal, the *Travel Guide to Europe,* and *Motoring in Europe.*

AUTOMOBILE CLUBS AND BREAKDOWNS

To protect yourself in case of breakdowns while driving to and through Portugal, and for travel information and other benefits, consider joining a reputable automobile club. The largest of these is the *American Automobile Association* (*AAA;* 1000 AAA Dr., Heathrow, FL 32746-5063; phone: 407-444-7000). Before joining this or any other automobile club, check whether it has reciprocity with Portuguese clubs such as the *Automóvel Club de Portugal* (24 Rua Rosa Araújo, Lisbon 1200; phone: 1-793-6191).

GASOLINE

Gasoline is sold in liters (about 3.7 liters to 1 gallon). Leaded, unleaded, and diesel fuel are available.

RENTING A CAR

You can rent a car through a travel agent or international rental firm before leaving home, or from a local company once in Portugal. Reserve in advance.

Most car rental companies require a credit card, although some will accept a substantial cash deposit. The minimum age to rent a car is set by the company; some impose special conditions on drivers above a certain age. Electing to pay for collision damage waiver (CDW) protection will add to the cost of renting a car, but releases you from financial liability for the vehicle being rented. Additional costs include drop-off charges or one-way service fees. One way to keep down the cost of car rentals is to deal with a car rental consolidator, such as *Connex International* (phone: 800-333-3949 or 914-739-0066).

International Car Rental Companies

Auto Europe (phone: 800-223-5555).

Avis (phone: 800-331-1084).

Budget (phone: 800-472-3325).

Dollar Rent A Car (known in Europe as *Eurodollar Rent A Car;* phone: 800-800-4000).

Europe by Car (phone: 212-581-3040 in New York State; 800-223-1516 elsewhere in the US).

European Car Reservations (phone: 800-535-3303).

Foremost Euro-Car (phone: 800-272-3299).

Hertz (phone: 800-654-3001).

Kemwel Group (phone: 800-678-0678).

Meier's World Travel (phone: 800-937-0700).

National (known in Europe as *Europcar;* phone: 800-CAR-EUROPE).
Thrifty (phone: 800-367-2277).

Portuguese Car Rental Companies
Olivauto (phone: 1-893588).
Viata Rent A Car (phone: 1-293-3148).

Package Tours

A package is a collection of travel services that can be purchased in a single transaction. Its principal advantages are convenience and economy — the cost is usually lower than that of the same services bought separately. Tour programs generally can be divided into two categories: escorted or locally hosted (with a set itinerary) and independent (usually more flexible).

When considering a package tour, read the brochure *carefully* to determine what is included and other conditions. Check the company's record with the Better Business Bureau. The *United States Tour Operators Association* (*USTOA;* 211 E. 51st St., Suite 12B, New York, NY 10022; phone: 212-944-5727) also can be helpful in determining a package tour operator's reliability. As with charter flights, always make your check out to the company's escrow account.

Many tour operators offer packages focused on special interests such as the arts, nature study, sports, and other recreations. *All Adventure Travel* (PO Box 4307, Boulder, CO 80306; phone: 800-537-4025 or 303-499-1981) represents such specialized packagers; some also are listed in the *Specialty Travel Index* (305 San Anselmo Ave., Suite 313, San Anselmo, CA 94960; phone: 415-459-4900 in California; 800-442-4922 elsewhere in the US).

Package Tour Operators
Abreu Tours (317 E. 34th St., New York, NY 10016; phone: 800-223-1580 or 212-532-6550).
Adventure Golf Holidays (815 North Rd., Westfield, MA 01085; phone: 800-628-9655 or 413-568-2855).
Adventures in Golf (29 Valencia Dr., Nashua, NH 03062; phone: 603-882-8367).
Alternative Travel Groups (69-71 Banbury Rd., Oxford 0X2 6PE, England; phone: 800-527-5997 in the US).
American Express Vacations (offices throughout the US; phone: 800-241-1700 or 404-368-5100).
AutoVenture (425 Pike St., Suite 502, Seattle, WA 98101; phone: 800-426-7502 or 206-624-6033).
Bacchants' Pilgrimages (475 Sansome St., Suite 840, San Francisco, CA 94111; phone: 415-981-8518).
Blue Marble Travel (c/o *Odyssey Adventures,* 89 Auburn St., Suite 1199, Portland, ME 04103; phone: 800-544-3216 or 207-878-8650).
Cycling Through the Centuries (PO Box 877, San Antonio, FL 33576; phone: 800-245-4226 or 904-588-4132).

Dailey-Thorp (330 W. 58th St., New York, NY 10019-1817; phone: 212-307-1555).

Easy Rider Tours (PO Box 1384, E. Arlington, MA 02174; phone: 800-488-8332 or 617-643-8332).

Equitour (PO Box 807, Dubois, WY 82513; phone: 307-455-3363 in Wyoming; 800-545-0019 elsewhere in the US).

Extra Value Travel (683 S. Collier Blvd., Marco Island, FL 33937; phone: 800-336-4668 or 813-394-3384).

Fishing International (PO Box 2132, Santa Rosa, CA 95405; phone: 800-950-4242 or 707-539-3366).

FITS Equestrian (685 Lateen Rd., Solvang, CA 93463; phone: 805-688-9494).

Globus and Cosmos (5301 S. Federal Circle, Littleton, CO 80123; phone: 800-221-0090 or 800-556-5454).

Golfing Holidays (231 E. Millbrae Ave., Millbrae, CA 94030; phone: 800-652-7847 or 415-697-0230).

InterGolf (PO Box 500608, Atlanta, GA 31150; phone: 800-468-0051 or 404-518-1250).

ITC Golf Tours (4134 Atlantic Ave., Suite 205, Long Beach, CA 90807; phone: 800-257-4981 or 310-595-6905).

Marsans International (19 W. 34th St., Suite 302, New York, NY 10001; phone: 800-777-9110 or 212-239-3880).

Maupintour (PO Box 807, Lawrence, KS 66044; phone: 800-255-4266 or 913-843-1211).

Melia International (450 7th Ave., Suite 1805, New York, NY 10103; phone: 212-967-6565 in New York State; 800-848-2314 elsewhere in the US).

Mill-Run Tours (424 Madison Ave., 12th Floor, New York, NY 10017; phone: 212-486-9840 in New York State; 800-MILL-RUN elsewhere in the US).

Olson Travelworld (970 W. 190th St., Suite 425, Torrance, CA 90502; phone: 800-421-2255 or 310-354-2600).

Perry Golf (8302 Dunwoodie Pl., Suite 305, Atlanta, GA 30350; phone: 800-344-5257 or 404-641-9696).

Prospect Music and Art Tours (454-458 Chiswick High Rd., London W4 5TT, England; phone: 44-81-995-2151 or 44-81-995-2163).

Skyline Travel Club (376 New York Ave., Huntington, NY 11743; phone: 516-423-9090 in New York State; 800-645-6198 elsewhere in the US).

Spanish Heritage Tours (116-47 Queens Blvd., Forest Hills, NY 11375; phone: 800-221-2580 or 718-520-1300).

Sun Holidays (26 Sixth St., Suite 603, Stamford, CT 06905; phone: 203-323-1166 in Connecticut; 800-243-2057 elsewhere in the US).

TAP Air Portugal Discovery Vacations (399 Market St., Newark, NJ 07105; phone: 800-247-8686).

Thomas Cook (Headquarters: 45 Berkeley St., Piccadilly, London W1A

1EB, England; phone: 44-71-408-4191; main US office: 2 Penn Plaza, 18th Floor, New York, NY 10121; phone: 800-846-6272 or 212-967-4390).

Trafalgar Tours (11 E. 26th St., Suite 1300, New York, NY 10010-1402; phone: 800-854-0103 or 212-689-8977).

Travcoa (PO Box 2630, Newport Beach, CA 92658; phone: 800-992-2004 in California; 800-992-2003 elsewhere in the US; or 710-476-2800).

Travel Concepts (62 Commonwealth Ave., Suite 3, Boston, MA 02116; phone: 617-266-8450).

TWA Getaway Vacations (phone: 800-GETAWAY).

Value Holidays (10224 N. Port Washington Rd., Mequon, WI 53092; phone: 800-558-6850).

Wide World of Golf (PO Box 5217, Carmel, CA 93921; phone: 408-624-6667).

X.O. Travel Consultants (38 W. 32nd St., Suite 1009, New York, NY 10001; phone: 800-262-9682 or 212-947-5530).

Insurance

The first person with whom you should discuss travel insurance is your own insurance broker. You may discover that the insurance you already carry protects you adequately while traveling and that you need little additional coverage. If you charge travel services, the credit card company also may provide some insurance coverage (and other safeguards).

Types of Travel Insurance

Baggage and personal effects insurance: Protects your bags and their contents in case of damage or theft anytime during your travels.

Personal accident and sickness insurance: Covers cases of illness, injury, or death in an accident while traveling.

Trip cancellation and interruption insurance: Guarantees a refund if you must cancel a trip; may reimburse you for the extra travel costs incurred in catching up with a tour or traveling home early.

Default and/or bankruptcy insurance: Provides coverage in the event of default and/or bankruptcy on the part of the tour operator, airline, or other travel supplier.

Flight insurance: Covers accidental injury or death while flying.

Automobile insurance: Provides collision, theft, property damage, and personal liability protection while driving your own or a rented car.

Combination policies: Include any or all of the above.

Disabled Travelers

Make travel arrangements well in advance. Specify to all services involved the nature of your disability to determine if there are accommodations and facilities that meet your needs. Regularly revised hotel and restaurant guides, such as the *Michelin Red Guide to Spain and Portugal* (Michelin Guides and Maps, PO Box 3305, Spartanburg, SC 29304-3305; phone: 803-599-0850 in South Carolina; 800-423-0485 elsewhere in the US), use a symbol of access (person in a wheelchair) to point out accommodations suitable for wheelchair-bound guests.

Organizations

ACCENT on Living (PO Box 700, Bloomington, IL 61702; phone: 309-378-2961).

Access: The Foundation for Accessibility by the Disabled (PO Box 356, Malverne, NY 11565; phone: 516-887-5798).

American Foundation for the Blind (15 W. 16th St., New York, NY 10011; phone: 800-232-5463 or 212-620-2147).

Holiday Care Service (2 Old Bank Chambers, Station Rd., Horley, Surrey RH6 9HW, England; phone: 44-293-774535).

Information Center for Individuals with Disabilities (Ft. Point Pl., 1st Floor, 27-43 Wormwood St., Boston, MA 02210; phone: 800-462-5015 in Massachusetts; 617-727-5540 or 617-727-5541 elsewhere in the US; TDD: 617-345-9743).

Mobility International USA (*MIUSA;* PO Box 3551, Eugene, OR 97403; phone: 503-343-1284, both voice and TDD; main office: 228 Borough High St., London SE1 1JX, England; phone: 44-71-403-5688).

National Rehabilitation Information Center (8455 Colesville Rd., Suite 935, Silver Spring, MD 20910; phone: 301-588-9284).

Paralyzed Veterans of America (*PVA;* PVA/ATTS Program, 801 18th St. NW, Washington, DC 20006; phone: 202-872-1300 in Washington, DC; 800-424-8200 elsewhere in the US).

Royal Association for Disability and Rehabilitation (*RADAR;* 25 Mortimer St., London W1N 8AB, England; phone: 44-71-637-5400).

Society for the Advancement of Travel for the Handicapped (*SATH;* 347 Fifth Ave., Suite 610, New York, NY 10016; phone: 212-447-7284).

Travel Information Service (MossRehab Hospital, 1200 W. Tabor Rd., Philadelphia, PA 19141-3099; phone: 215-456-9600; TDD: 215-456-9602).

Tripscope (The Courtyard, Evelyn Rd., London W4 5JL, England; phone: 44-81-994-9294).

Publications

Access Travel: A Guide to the Accessibility of Airport Terminals (Consumer Information Center, Dept. 578Z, Pueblo, CO 81009; phone: 719-948-3334).

Air Transportation of Handicapped Persons (Publication #AC-120-32; US Department of Transportation, Distribution Unit, Publications Section, M-443-2, 400 7th St. SW, Washington, DC 20590).

The Diabetic Traveler (PO Box 8223 RW, Stamford, CT 06905; phone: 203-327-5832).

Directory of Travel Agencies for the Disabled and *Travel for the Disabled*, both by Helen Hecker (Twin Peaks Press, PO Box 129, Vancouver, WA 98666; phone: 800-637-CALM or 206-694-2462).

Guide to Traveling with Arthritis (Upjohn Company, PO Box 989, Dearborn, MI 48121).

The Handicapped Driver's Mobility Guide (*American Automobile Association*, 1000 AAA Dr., Heathrow, FL 32746; phone: 407-444-7000).

Handicapped Travel Newsletter (PO Box 269, Athens, TX 75751; phone: 903-677-1260).

Handi-Travel: A Resource Book for Disabled and Elderly Travellers, by Cinnie Noble (*Canadian Rehabilitation Council for the Disabled*, 45 Sheppard Ave. E., Suite 801, Toronto, Ontario M2N 5W9, Canada; phone: 416-250-7490, both voice and TDD).

Incapacitated Passengers Air Travel Guide (*International Air Transport Association*, Publications Sales Department, 2000 Peel St., Montreal, Quebec H3A 2R4, Canada; phone: 514-844-6311).

Ticket to Safe Travel (*American Diabetes Association*, 1660 Duke St., Alexandria, VA 22314; phone: 800-232-3472 or 703-549-1500).

Travel for the Patient with Chronic Obstructive Pulmonary Disease (Dr. Harold Silver, 1601 18th St. NW, Washington, DC 20009; phone: 202-667-0134).

Travel Tips for Hearing-Impaired People (*American Academy of Otolaryngology*, 1 Prince St., Alexandria, VA 22314; phone: 703-836-4444).

Travel Tips for People with Arthritis (*Arthritis Foundation*, 1314 Spring St. NW, Atlanta, GA 30309; phone: 800-283-7800 or 404-872-7100).

Traveling Like Everybody Else: A Practical Guide for Disabled Travelers, by Jacqueline Freedman and Susan Gersten (Modan Publishing, PO Box 1202, Bellmore, NY 11710; phone: 516-679-1380).

Package Tour Operators

Accessible Journeys (35 W. Sellers Ave., Ridley Park, PA 19078; phone: 215-521-0339).

Accessible Tours/Directions Unlimited (Lois Bonnani, 720 N. Bedford Rd., Bedford Hills, NY 10507; phone: 800-533-5343 or 914-241-1700).

Beehive Business and Leisure Travel (1130 W. Center St., N. Salt Lake, UT 84054; phone: 800-777-5727 or 801-292-4445).

Classic Travel Service (8 W. 40th St., New York, NY 10018; phone: 212-869-2560 in New York State; 800-247-0909 elsewhere in the US).

Dialysis at Sea Cruises (611 Barry Pl., Indian Rocks Beach, FL 34635; phone: 800-775-1333 or 813-596-4614).

Evergreen Travel Service (4114 198th St. SW, Suite 13, Lynnwood, WA 98036-6742; phone: 800-435-2288 or 206-776-1184).

Flying Wheels Travel (143 W. Bridge St., PO Box 382, Owatonna, MN 55060; phone: 800-535-6790 or 507-451-5005).

Good Neighbor Travel Service (124 S. Main St., Viroqua, WI 54665; phone: 608-637-2128).

The Guided Tour (7900 Old York Rd., Suite 114B, Elkins Park, PA 19117-2339; phone: 800-783-5841 or 215-782-1370).

Hinsdale Travel (201 E. Ogden Ave., Hinsdale, IL 60521; phone: 708-325-1335 or 708-469-7349).

MedEscort International (ABE International Airport, PO Box 8766, Allentown, PA 18105; phone: 800-255-7182 or 215-791-3111).

Prestige World Travel (5710-X High Point Rd., Greensboro, NC 27407; phone: 800-476-7737 or 919-292-6690).

Sprout (893 Amsterdam Ave., New York, NY 10025; phone: 212-222-9575).

Weston Travel Agency (134 N. Cass Ave., PO Box 1050, Westmont, IL 60559; phone: 708-968-2513 in Illinois; 800-633-3725 elsewhere in the US).

Single Travelers

The travel industry is not very fair to people who vacation by themselves–they often end up paying more than those traveling in pairs. Services catering to singles match travel companions, offer travel arrangements with shared accommodations, and provide useful information and discounts. Also consult publications such as *Going Solo* (Doerfer Communications, PO Box 123, Apalachicola, FL 32329; phone: 904-653-8848) and *Traveling on Your Own,* by Eleanor Berman (Random House, Order Dept., 400 Hahn Rd., Westminster, MD 21157; phone: 800-733-3000).

Organizations and Companies

Club Europa (802 W. Oregon St., Urbana, IL 61801; phone: 800-331-1882 or 217-344-5863).

Contiki Holidays (300 Plaza Alicante, Suite 900, Garden Grove, CA 92640; phone: 800-466-0610 or 714-740-0808).

Gallivanting (515 E. 79th St., Suite 20F, New York, NY 10021; phone: 800-933-9699 or 212-988-0617).

Globus and Cosmos (5301 S. Federal Circle, Littleton, CO 80123; phone: 800-221-0090 or 800-556-5454).

Insight International Tours (745 Atlantic Ave., Boston, MA 02111; phone: 800-582-8380 or 617-482-2000).

Jane's International and Sophisticated Women Travelers (2603 Bath Ave., Brooklyn, NY 11214; phone: 718-266-2045).

Marion Smith Singles (611 Prescott Pl., N. Woodmere, NY 11581; phone: 516-791-4852, 516-791-4865, or 212-944-2112).

Partners-in-Travel (11660 Chenault St., Suite 119, Los Angeles, CA 90049; phone: 310-476-4869).

Singles in Motion (545 W. 236th St., Riverdale, NY 10463; phone: 718-884-4464).

Singleworld (401 Theodore Fremd Ave., Rye, NY 10580; phone: 800-223-6490 or 914-967-3334).

Solo Flights (63 High Noon Rd., Weston, CT 06883; phone: 203-226-9993).

Suddenly Singles Tours (161 Dreiser Loop, Bronx, NY 10475; phone: 718-379-8800 in New York City; 800-859-8396 elsewhere in the US).

Travel Companion Exchange (PO Box 833, Amityville, NY 11701; phone: 516-454-0880).

Travel Companions (Atrium Financial Center, 1515 N. Federal Hwy., Suite 300, Boca Raton, FL 33432; phone: 800-383-7211 or 407-393-6448).

Travel in Two's (239 N. Broadway, Suite 3, N. Tarrytown, NY 10591; phone: 914-631-8301 in New York State; 800-692-5252 elsewhere in the US).

Older Travelers

Special discounts and more free time are just two factors that have given older travelers a chance to see the world at affordable prices. Many travel suppliers offer senior discounts — sometimes only to members of certain senior citizen organizations, which provide other benefits. Prepare your itinerary with one eye on your own physical condition and the other on a topographical map, and remember that it's easy to overdo when traveling.

Publications

Going Abroad: 101 Tips for Mature Travelers (Grand Circle Travel, 347 Congress St., Boston, MA 02210; phone: 800-221-2610 or 617-350-7500).

The Mature Traveler (GEM Publishing Group, PO Box 50820, Reno, NV 89513-0820; phone: 702-786-7419).

Take a Camel to Lunch and Other Adventures for Mature Travelers, by Nancy O'Connell (Bristol Publishing Enterprises, PO Box 1737, San Leandro, CA 94577; phone: 510-895-4461 in California; 800-346-4889 elsewhere in the US).

Travel Tips for Older Americans (Publication #044-000-02270-2; Superintendent of Documents, US Government Printing Office, PO Box 371954, Pittsburgh, PA 15250-7954; phone: 202-783-3238).

Unbelievably Good Deals & Great Adventures That You Absolutely Can't Get Unless You're Over 50, by Joan Rattner Heilman (Contemporary Books, 180 N. Michigan Ave., Chicago, IL 60601; phone: 312-782-9181).

Organizations

American Association of Retired Persons (AARP; 601 E St. NW, Washington, DC 20049; phone: 202-434-2277).

Golden Companions (PO Box 754, Pullman, WA 99163-0754; phone: 208-858-2183).

Mature Outlook (Customer Service Center, 6001 N. Clark St., Chicago, IL 60660; phone: 800-336-6330).

National Council of Senior Citizens (1331 F St. NW, Washington, DC 20004; phone: 202-347-8800).

Package Tour Operators

Elderhostel (PO Box 1959, Wakefield, MA 01880-5959; phone: 617-426-7788).

Evergreen Travel Service (4114 198th St. SW, Suite 13, Lynnwood, WA 98036-6742; phone: 800-435-2288 or 206-776-1184).

Gadabout Tours (700 E. Tahquitz Canyon Way, Palm Springs, CA 92262; phone: 800-952-5068 or 619-325-5556).

Grand Circle Travel (347 Congress St., Boston, MA 02210; phone: 800-221-2610 or 617-350-7500).

Grandtravel (6900 Wisconsin Ave., Suite 706, Chevy Chase, MD 20815; phone: 800-247-7651 or 301-986-0790).

Insight International Tours (745 Atlantic Ave., Suite 720, Boston, MA 02111; phone: 800-582-8380 or 617-482-2000).

Interhostel (UNH Division of Continuing Education, 6 Garrison Ave., Durham, NH 03824; phone: 800-733-9753 or 603-862-1147).

OmniTours (104 Wilmont Rd., Deerfield, IL 60015; phone: 800-962-0060 or 708-374-0088).

Saga International Holidays (222 Berkeley St., Boston, MA 02116; phone: 800-343-0273 or 617-262-2262).

Money Matters

The basic unit of Portuguese currency is the **escudo,** which is divided into 100 **centavos.** In expressing monetary values in Portugal, the dollar sign ($) serves the same function as the decimal point in US notation; thus, 5 escudos and 50 centavos would be expressed as 5$50 in Portugal. Coins are issued for 2$50, 5, 10, 20, 50, and 100 escudos. Bank notes are in denominations of 100, 500, 1,000, 5,000, and 10,000 escudos.

Exchange rates are posted in international newspapers such as the *International Herald Tribune.* Foreign currency information and related services are provided by banks and companies such as *Thomas Cook Foreign Exchange* (for the nearest location, call 800-621-0666 or 312-236-0042); *Harold Reuter and Company* (200 Park Ave., Suite 332E, New York, NY 10166; phone: 212-661-0826); and *Ruesch International* (for the nearest location, call 800-424-2923 or 202-408-1200). In Portugal, you will find the official rate of exchange posted in banks, airports, money exchange houses, hotels, and some shops. Since you will get more escudos for your US dollar at banks and money exchanges, don't change more than

$10 for foreign currency at other commercial establishments. Ask how much commission you're being charged and the exchange rate, and don't buy money on the black market (it may be counterfeit). Estimate your needs carefully; if you overbuy, you lose twice — buying and selling back.

TRAVELER'S CHECKS AND CREDIT CARDS

It's wise to carry traveler's checks while on the road, since they are replaceable if stolen or lost. You can buy traveler's checks at banks and some are available by mail or phone. Although most major credit cards enjoy wide domestic and international acceptance, not every hotel, restaurant, or shop in Portugal accepts all (or in some cases any) credit cards. (Some cards may be issued under different names in Europe; for example, *Master-Card* may go under the name *Access* or *Eurocard,* and *Visa* often is called *Carte Bleue.*) When making purchases with a credit card, note that the rate of exchange depends on when the charge is processed; most credit card companies charge a 1% fee for converting foreign currency charges. Keep a separate list of all traveler's checks (noting those that you have cashed) and the names and numbers of your credit cards. Both traveler's check and credit card companies have international numbers to call for information or in the event of loss or theft.

CASH MACHINES

Automated teller machines (ATMs) are increasingly common worldwide. Most banks participate in one of the international ATM networks; cardholders can withdraw cash from any machine in the same network using either a "bank" card or, in some cases, a credit card. At the time of this writing, most ATMs belong to the *CIRRUS* or *PLUS* network. For further information, ask at your bank branch.

SENDING MONEY ABROAD

Should the need arise, it is possible to have money sent to you via the services provided by *American Express* (*MoneyGram;* phone: 800-926-9400 or 800-666-3997 for information; 800-866-8800 for money transfers) or *Western Union Financial Services* (phone: 800-325-4176). If you are down to your last cent and have no other way to obtain cash, the nearest US Consulate will let you call home to set these matters in motion.

Accommodations

For specific information on hotels, resorts, and other selected accommodations, see *Best in Town* in THE CITIES, *Checking In* in DIRECTIONS, and *Pousadas and Manor Houses* in DIVERSIONS. The Portuguese National Tourist Office in the US offers a comprehensive guide to accommodations throughout the country called the *Portugal Hotel Guide,* which includes ratings of the facilities available in each establishment.

POUSADAS, MANOR HOUSES, AND FARMHOUSES

The *pousada* network of state-owned inns consists of historic buildings in scenic areas. *Pousadas* tend to be small, ranging from 6 rooms to a maximum of 55 in the largest (*Pousada de Santa Marinha da Costa,* near Guimarães). All have modern conveniences and restaurants. The *Turismo no Espaço Rural* (Tourism in the Country) program is an association of privately owned properties — from 16th- and 17th-century manor houses to rustic farmhouses — that accommodate paying guests. Like the *pousada* system, this association was formed to help preserve the country's historic and architecturally significant structures.

RENTAL OPTIONS

An attractive accommodations alternative for the visitor content to stay in one spot is to rent one of the numerous properties available throughout Portugal. For a family or group, the per-person cost can be reasonable. To have your pick of the properties available, make inquiries at least 6 months in advance. The *Worldwide Home Rental Guide* (369 Montezuma, Suite 297, Santa Fe, NM 87501; phone: 505-984-7080) lists rental properties and managing agencies.

Rental Property Agents

At Home Abroad (405 E. 56th St., Suite 6H, New York, NY 10022-2466; phone: 212-421-9165).

Europa-Let (92 N. Main St., Ashland, OR 97520; phone: 800-462-4486 or 503-482-5806).

Hideaways International (PO Box 4433, Portsmouth, NH 03802-4433; phone: 800-843-4433 or 603-430-4433).

Interhome (124 Little Falls Rd., Fairfield, NJ 07004; phone: 201-882-6864).

International Lodging Corp. (300 1st Ave., Suite 7C, New York, NY 10009; phone: 212-228-5900).

Rent a Home International (7200 34th Ave. NW, Seattle, WA 98117; phone: 206-789-9377).

Rent a Vacation Everywhere (*RAVE;* 383 Park Ave., Rochester, NY 14607; phone: 716-256-0760).

VHR Worldwide (235 Kensington Ave., Norwood, NJ 07648; phone: 201-767-9393 in New Jersey; 800-633-3284 elsewhere in the US).

Villas International (605 Market St., Suite 510, San Francisco, CA 94105; phone: 800-221-2260 or 415-281-0910).

HOME EXCHANGES

For comfortable, reasonable living quarters with amenities that no hotel could possibly offer, consider trading homes with someone abroad. The following companies provide information on exchanges:

Home Base Holidays (7 Park Ave., London N13 5PG, England; phone: 44-81-886-8752).

Intervac US/International Home Exchange (PO Box 590504, San Francisco, CA 94159; phone: 800-756-HOME or 415-435-3497).

Loan-A-Home (2 Park La., Apt. 6E, Mt. Vernon, NY 10552; phone: 914-664-7640).

Vacation Exchange Club (PO Box 650, Key West, FL 33041; phone: 800-638-3841 or 305-294-3720).

Worldwide Home Exchange Club (138 Brompton Rd., London SW3 1HY, England; phone: 44-71-589-6055; or 806 Brantford Ave., Silver Spring, MD 20904; phone: 301-680-8950).

HOME STAYS

The *United States Servas Committee* (11 John St., Room 407, New York, NY 10038; phone: 212-267-0252) maintains a list of hosts throughout the world willing to accommodate visitors free of charge. The aim of this nonprofit cultural program is to promote international understanding and peace, and *Servas* emphasizes that member travelers should be interested mainly in their hosts, not in sightseeing, during their stays.

Time Zones

Mainland Portugal and the island of Madeira are in the Greenwich Mean Time zone, which means that the time is 5 hours later than in east coast US cities. The time in the Azores is 1 hour earlier than in the rest of the country. Portugal moves its clocks ahead an hour in late spring and an hour back in the fall, although the exact dates of the changes are different from those observed in the US. Portuguese and other European timetables use a 24-hour clock to denote arrival and departure times, which means that hours are expressed sequentially from 1 AM.

Business Hours

Throughout Portugal, most businesses and shops are open Mondays through Fridays from 9 AM to 1 or 2 PM, and then from 3 or 4 PM until 7 or 8 PM. Many shops also are open on Saturdays from 9 AM to 1 PM. In small towns and villages, shops may close on a weekday at 1 PM, or simply not open at all on that day (usually Monday). Larger stores in shopping centers generally stay open through midday and may close as late as 9 PM; in shopping malls, some stores stay open until midnight.

In Portugal, weekday banking hours are from 9 AM to 3 PM. Certain banks (particularly in Lisbon) may remain open until 1 PM on Saturdays, and also may have late hours from 6 to 11 PM on weekdays. Major airport banks may be open 7 days a week.

Holidays

In Portugal, the public holidays are as follows:

New Year's Day (January 1)
Good Friday (April 1)
Liberty Day (April 25)
Labor Day or May Day (May 1)
Corpus Christi (June 2)
Portugal's and Camões Day (June 10)
St. Anthony's Day (June 13)
Assumption Day (August 15)
Republic Day (October 5)
All Saints' Day (November 1)
Restoration of Independence (December 1)
Immaculate Conception (December 8)
Christmas Day (December 25)

Mail

Most post offices in Portugal are open Mondays through Saturdays from 9 AM to 5:30 PM. Stamps *(selos)* can be bought at post offices and at authorized tobacconists *(tabacarias)*. Letters can be deposited in mail boxes (these are red, with the word *correio* printed on them) found on the street, but it is better to send letters (and certainly packages) directly from post offices. If your correspondence is especially important, you may want to send it via one of the international courier services, such as *Federal Express* or *DHL Worldwide Express*.

You can have mail sent to you care of your hotel (marked "Guest Mail, Hold for Arrival") or to a post office (c/o *Posta Restante,* the Portuguese equivalent of "General Delivery"). *American Express* offices also will hold mail for customers ("c/o Client Letter Service"); information is provided in their pamphlet *Travelers' Companion.* US Embassies and Consulates abroad will hold mail for US citizens *only* in emergency situations.

Telephone

Direct dialing and other familiar services are all available in Portugal. The number of digits in phone numbers varies somewhat throughout the country. The procedure for calling Portugal from the US is to dial 011 (the international access code) + 351 (the country code) + the area code (if you don't know this, ask the international operator) + the local number. To call the US from Portugal, dial 00 (the international access code) + 1 (the US country code) + the US area code + the local number. To make a call between Portuguese cities, dial 0 + the area code + the local number. To call a number within the same area code, just dial the local number.

Public telephones are widely available. The majority of these still take coins, but phones that take special phone cards are increasingly common. Phone cards are sold at post offices, national phone company offices, and by some tobacconists.

Long-distance telephone services that help you avoid the surcharges that hotels routinely add to phone bills are provided by *American Telephone and Telegraph (AT&T Communications,* International Information Service, 635 Grant St., Pittsburgh, PA 15219; phone: 800-874-4000), *MCI* (323 3rd St. SE, Cedar Rapids, IA 52401; phone: 800-444-3333), *Metromedia Communications Corp.* (1 International Center, 100 NE Loop 410, San Antonio, TX 78216; phone: 800-275-0200), and *Sprint* (offices throughout the US; phone: 800-877-4000). Some hotels still may charge a fee for line usage.

AT&T 's Language Line Service (phone: 800-752-6096) provides interpretive services for telephone communications in Portuguese. Also useful are the *AT&T 800 Travel Directory* (available at *AT&T Phone Centers* or by calling 800-426-8686), the *Toll-Free Travel & Vacation Information Directory* (Pilot Books, 103 Cooper St., Babylon, NY 11702; phone: 516-422-2225), and *The Phone Booklet* (*Scott American Corporation,* PO Box 88, W. Redding, CT 06896; phone: 203-938-2955).

Important Phone Numbers
Local and long-distance operator: 16.
International operator: 098.
Local and countrywide information: 16.
For emergency assistance: 115.

Electricity

Like most other European countries, Portugal uses 220-volt, 50-cycle alternating current (AC). Thus, travelers from the US will need electrical converters to operate the appliances they use at home, or dual-voltage appliances, which can be switched from one voltage standard to another. (Some large tourist hotels may offer 110-volt current for your convenience or may have converters available.) You also will need a plug adapter set to deal with the different plug configurations found in Portugal.

Staying Healthy

For information on current health conditions, call the Centers for Disease Control and Prevention's *International Health Requirements and Recommendations Information Hotline:* 404-332-4559.

Travelers to Portugal — and to Western Europe in general — do not face the same health risks entailed in traveling to many other destinations around the world. Tap water generally is clean and potable in metropolitan and tourist areas throughout the country. Ask if the water is meant for drinking, but if you're at all unsure, bottled water is readily available in stores. Do not drink water from freshwater streams, rivers, or pools, as it may be contaminated. Milk is pasteurized throughout Portugal, and dairy products are safe to eat, as are fruit, vegetables, meat, poultry, and fish. Because of Mediterranean pollution, however, all seafood should be eaten cooked, and make sure it is *fresh,* particularly in the heat of the summer, when inadequate refrigeration is an additional concern.

Portugal is famous for its beaches, but it's important to remember that the sea can be treacherous. When you are swimming, be careful of the undertow (a current running back down the beach after a wave has washed ashore), which can knock you down, and riptides (currents running against the tide), which can pull you out to sea. If you see a shark, swim away quietly and smoothly. Also beware of eels, Portuguese man-of-war (and other jellyfish), sea urchins, and razor-sharp coral reefs — although Portugal's coral reefs are not extensive. Though rare, bites from snakes, spiders, and — in southern Portugal — the occasional scorpion can be serious and should be treated immediately.

Portugal has socialized medicine and medical care is free (or relatively inexpensive) for Portuguese citizens, but this does not apply to travelers from the US. There are both public and private hospitals. *Policlinicas,* or clinics, are for less serious medical matters; however, the staff may not speak English, and you generally need an appointment. Ask at your hotel for the house physician or for help in reaching a doctor or contact the US Consulate. Pharmacies (called *farmácias* in Portugal) are identified by a red cross out front. There should be no problem finding a 24-hour drugstore in any major Portuguese city. Each pharmacy is part of a local network, so that there always should be a drugstore somewhere that is open. Closed pharmacies often have a sign in the window that provides the location of a pharmacy that is open — the name and address follow the words *farmacia de serviço.* A call to a local hospital also may produce this information.

In an emergency: Go directly to the emergency room of the nearest hospital, dial the emergency number given above, or call a local operator for assistance.

Additional Resources

International Association of Medical Assistance to Travelers (*IAMAT;* 417 Center St., Lewiston, NY 14092; phone: 716-754-4883).

International Health Care Service (440 E. 69th St., New York, NY 10021; phone: 212-746-1601).

International SOS Assistance (PO Box 11568, Philadelphia, PA 19116; phone: 800-523-8930 or 215-244-1500).

Medic Alert Foundation (2323 Colorado Ave., Turlock, CA 95380; phone: 800-ID-ALERT or 209-668-3333).

TravMed (PO Box 10623, Baltimore, MD 21285-0623; phone: 800-732-5309 or 410-296-5225).

Consular Services

The American Services section of the US Consulate is a vital source of assistance and advice for US citizens abroad. If you are injured or become seriously ill, the Consulate can direct you to sources of medical attention and notify your relatives. If you become involved in a dispute that could lead to legal action, the Consulate is the place to turn. In cases of natural disasters or civil unrest, Consulates handle the evacuation of US citizens if necessary.

The US Embassy is located at Av. das Forças Armadas, Lisbon 1600 (phone: 1-726-6600). The US Consulate is located at Av. D. Henrique, 9500 Ponta Delgada, Azores (phone: 9-622216).

The US State Department operates a 24-hour *Citizens' Emergency Center* travel advisory hotline (phone: 202-647-5225). **In an emergency, call 202-647-4000 and ask for the duty officer.**

Entry Requirements and Customs Regulations

ENTERING PORTUGAL

A valid US passport is the only document a US citizen needs to enter Portugal for a stay of up to 60 days as a tourist. Visas are required for study, residency, or work, and are good for up to 1 year. US citizens should inquire at the Portuguese Embassy or the nearest Portuguese Consulate well in advance of a proposed trip. Proof of substantial means of independent financial support during the stay is pertinent to the acceptance of any long-term–stay application.

You are allowed to enter Portugal with the following duty-free: 200 cigarettes or 250 grams of tobacco, 2 bottles of wine, and 1 bottle of liquor. Personal effects and sports equipment appropriate for a pleasure trip also are allowed.

RETURNING TO THE US

You must declare to the US Customs official at the point of entry everything you have acquired in Portugal. The standard duty-free allowance for US citizens is $400; if your trip is shorter than 48 continuous hours, or you have been out of the US within 30 days, it is cut to $25. Families traveling together may make a joint declaration. Antiques (at least 100 years old) and paintings or drawings done entirely by hand are duty-free.

A flat 10% duty is assessed on the next $1,000 worth of merchandise; additional items are taxed at a variety of rates (see *Tariff Schedules of the United States* in a library or any US Customs Service office). With the exception of gifts valued at $50 or less sent directly to the recipient, items shipped home are dutiable. Some articles are duty-free only up to certain limits. The $400 allowance includes 1 carton of (200) cigarettes, 100 cigars (not Cuban), and 1 liter of liquor or wine (for those over 21); the $25 allowance includes 10 cigars, 50 cigarettes, and 4 ounces of perfume. To avoid paying duty unnecessarily, before your trip, register the serial numbers of any expensive equipment you are bringing along with US Customs.

Forbidden imports include articles made of the furs or hides of animals on the endangered species list. In addition, you must obtain a permit from the *Instituto Português do Património Cultural* (Palácio da Ajuda a la Norte, Lisbon 1300; phone: 1-363-1677) to take archeological finds or other original artifacts out of Portugal.

For further information, consult *Know Before You Go; International Mail Imports; Travelers' Tips on Bringing Food, Plant, and Animal Products into the United States; Importing a Car; GSP and the Traveler; Pocket Hints; Currency Reporting;* and *Pets, Wildlife, US Customs;* all available from the US Customs Service (PO Box 7407, Washington, DC 20044). For tape-recorded information on travel-related topics, call 202-927-2095 from any touch-tone phone.

| DUTY-FREE SHOPS AND VALUE ADDED TAX | Located in international air- |

ports, duty-free shops provide bargains on the purchase of foreign goods. But beware: Not all foreign goods are automatically less expensive. You *can* get a good deal on some items, but know what they cost elsewhere.

Value Added Tax (VAT) — called *IVA* in Portugal — is a tax added to the purchase price of most goods and services, and visitors usually are entitled to a refund. For information about minimum purchase requirements and refund procedures, contact the Portuguese tourist authorities.

For Further Information

The **Portuguese National Tourist Office** in the US (590 Fifth Ave., 4th Floor, New York, NY 10036-4704; phone: 212-354-4403) is the best source of travel information. The office is open on weekdays, during normal business hours.

Useful Words and Phrases

Useful Words and Phrases

Unlike the French, who tend to be a bit brusque if you don't speak their language perfectly, the Portuguese do not expect you to speak their native tongue, but appreciate your efforts when you try. In many circumstances, you won't have to, because the staffs at most hotels, as well as at a fair number of restaurants, speak serviceable English, or at least a modicum of it, which they usually are eager to try. If you find yourself in a situation where your limited Portuguese turns out to be the only means of communication, take the plunge. Don't be afraid of misplaced accents or misconjugated verbs — in most cases you will be understood.

The list that follows is a selection of commonly used words and phrases to speed you on your way. Note that in Portuguese, nouns either are masculine or feminine, as well as singular or plural, and that the adjectives that modify them must agree in both gender and quantity. Most nouns ending in *o* in the singular are masculine; the *o* becomes *os* in the plural. Most nouns ending in *a* in the singular are feminine; the *a* becomes *as* in the plural. Nouns may have other endings.

You also might consider taking a course in Portuguese before you go. Language courses are offered at some adult education and community colleges. *Berlitz,* among others, has a series of teach-yourself language courses on audiocassette tapes. They are available for $15.95 from Macmillan Publishing Co., 100 Front St., Riverside, NJ 08075 (phone: 800-257-5755).

The list below of commonly used words and phrases can help get you started.

Greetings and Everyday Expressions

Good morning! (also, Good day)	*Bom dia!*
Good afternoon/evening	*Boa tarde/noite*
Hello	*Olá!*
How are you?	*Como esta?*
Pleased to meet you. (How do you do?)	*Muito prazer em conhecê-lo (-la).*
Good-bye!	*Adeus!*
So long!	*Até logo!*
Goodnight! (when leaving)	*Boa noite!*
Yes	*Sim*
No	*Não*

Please	*Se faz favor/Por favor*
Thank you	*Obrigado(a)*
You're welcome	*De nada*
I beg your pardon (Excuse me)	*Perdão*
I don't speak Portuguese.	*Não falo português.*
Do you speak English?	*Fala inglês?*
I don't understand.	*Não compreêndo.*
Do you understand?	*Compreênde?/Entende?*
My name is . . .	*Chamo-me . . .*
What is your name?	*Como se chama?*
miss	*senhorita*
madame	*senhora*
mister	*senhor*
open	*aberto/a*
closed	*encerrado(a)/fechado(a)*
entrance	*entrada*
exit	*saída*
push	*empurre*
pull	*puxe*
today	*hoje*
tomorrow	*amanhã*
yesterday	*ontem*

Checking In

I would like . . .	*Queria/Costaria . . .*
I have a reservation	*Mandei reservar*
a single room	*um quarto individual*
a double room	*um quarto duplo*
a quiet room	*um quarto tranquilo*
with bath	*com banho*
with shower	*com chuveiro*
with a sea view	*com vista para o mar*
with air conditioning	*com ar condicionado*
with balcony	*com varanda*
overnight only	*só uma noite*
a few days	*alguns dias*
a week (at least)	*uma semana (pelo menos)*
with full board	*com pensão completa*
with half board	*com meia-pensão*
Does that price include	*O preço está incluido*
breakfast	*café da manhâ*
taxes	*os impostos*
VAT (Value Added Tax)	*IVA*
It doesn't work.	*Não funciona*

Do you accept traveler's checks?   *Aceitam cheques de viagem?*

Do you accept credit cards?   *Posso pagar com cartão de*
         crédito?

Eating Out

ashtray	*um cinzeiro*
bottle	*uma garrafa*
(extra) chair	*uma cadeira (mais)*
cup	*uma chávena*
fork	*um garfo*
knife	*uma faca*
napkin	*um guardanapo*
plate	*um prato*
spoon	*uma colher*
table	*uma mesa*
beer	*uma cerveja*
hot cocoa	*um cacau*
black coffee	*um café*
coffee with milk	*café com leite*
cream	*creme*
milk	*leite*
tea	*um chá*
fruit juice	*um sumo de fruta*
lemonade	*uma limonada*
water	*água*
mineral water	*água mineral*
(carbonated)	*(com gás)*
(not carbonated)	*(sem gás)*
orangeade	*uma laranjada*
port	*vinho do Porto*
sherry	*vinho de Xerez*
red wine	*vinho tinto*
white wine	*vinho branco*
cold	*frio/a*
hot	*quente*
sweet	*doce*
(very) dry	*(extra) seco/a*
bacon	*bacon/toucinho Americano*
bread	*pão*
butter	*manteiga*
eggs	*ovos*
hard-boiled	*ovo cozido*
fried	*ovos estrelados*
omelette	*omeleta*
soft-boiled	*ovo(s) quente(s)*
scrambled	*ovos mexidos*

honey	*mel*
jam/marmalade	*doce de fruta/marmelada*
orange juice	*sumo de laranja*
pepper	*pimenta*
salt	*sal*
sugar	*açúcar*
Waiter	*Criado*
I would like	*Queria*
a glass of	*um copo de*
a bottle of	*uma garrafa de*
a half bottle of	*uma meia-garrafa de*
a carafe of	*um jarro de*
a liter of	*um litro de*
The check, please.	*A conta, por favor.*
Is a service charge included?	*E serviço incluido?*
I think there is a mistake in the bill.	*Creio que se enganou na conta.*

Shopping

bakery	*a padaria*
bookstore	*a livraria*
butcher shop	*o talho*
camera shop	*a loja de artigos fotográficos*
cosmetics store	*perfumaria*
delicatessen	*charcuteria*
department store	*o grande armazém*
grocery	*mercearia*
jewelry store	*a ourivesaria*
newsstand	*o quiosque a banca de jornais*
pastry shop	*a pastelaria*
pharmacy/drugstore	*a farmácia*
shoestore	*a sapataria*
supermarket	*o supermercado*
tobacconist	*a tabacaria*
inexpensive	*barato/a*
expensive	*caro/a*
large	*grande*
larger	*maior*
too large	*muito grande*
small	*pequeno/a*
smaller	*mais pequeno/a*
too small	*muito pequeno/a*
long	*comprido/a*
short	*curto/a*
old	*velho/a*

new	*novo/a*
used	*usado/a*
handmade	*feito/a à mão*
Is it machine washable?	*Pode lavar-se à máquina?*
How much does it cost?	*Quanto custa isto?*
What is it made of?	*De que é feito?*
camel's hair	*pêlo de camelo*
cotton	*algodão*
corduroy	*bombazina*
filigree	*filigrana*
lace	*renda*
leather	*couro/pele*
linen	*linho*
silk	*seda*
suede	*camurça*
synthetic	*sintético/a*
tiles	*os azulejos*
wool	*lã*
brass	*latão*
copper	*cobre*
gold	*ouro*
gold plate	*banho de ouro*
silver	*prata*
silver plate	*banho de prata*
stainless steel	*aço inoxidável*
wood	*madeira*

Colors

beige	*bege*
black	*prêto/a*
blue	*azul*
brown	*castanho/a*
green	*verde*
gray	*cinzento/a*
orange	*laranja*
pink	*cor de rosa*
purple	*roxo/a*
red	*vermelho/a*
white	*branco/a*
yellow	*amarelo/a*
dark	*escuro/a*
light	*claro/a*

Getting Around

north	*norte*
south	*sul*

east	*este*
west	*oeste*
right	*direita*
left	*esquerda*
Go straight ahead	*Vá sempre em frente*
far	*longe*
near	*perto*
gas station	*estação de serviço*
train station	*a estação de comboios*
bus stop	*a paragem do autocarro*
subway station	*estação de metrô*
airport	*aeroporto*
tourist information	*informações de turismo*
map	*mapa*
one-way ticket	*um bilhete ida*
round-trip ticket	*um bilhete ida e volta*
track/platform	*o cais/a plataforma*
first class	*primeira classe*
second class	*segunda classe*
no smoking	*não fumadores*
gasoline	*gasolina*
normal leaded	*gasolina normal*
super leaded	*gasolina super*
unleaded	*gasolina sem chumbo*
diesel	*diesel*
tires	*pneus*
oil	*o óleo*
Fill it up, please.	*Encha o depósito, por favor.*
Where is . . . ?	*Onde fica . . . ?*
Where are . . . ?	*Onde ficam . . . ?*
How far is it to . . . from here?	*A que distância estamos de . . . ?*
Does this bus go to . . . ?	*Este autocarro pára em . . . ?*
What time does it leave?	*A que horas parte?*
Danger	*Perigo*
Caution	*Cuidado*
Detour	*Desvio*
Do Not Enter	*Entrada Proibida*
No Parking	*Estacionamento Proibido*
No Passing	*Proibido Ultrapassar*
One Way	*Sentido Unico*
Pay Toll	*Pedagio*
Pedestrian Zone	*Pedestres*
Reduce Speed	*Afrouxe/Devagar*
Steep Incline	*Descida Perigosa*

Stop	*Alto*
Use Headlights	*Acender as Luzes*
Yield	*Dê Passagem*

Personal Items and Services

barbershop	*o barbeiro*
beauty shop	*o instituto de beleza*
dry cleaner	*a lavandaria a seca*
hairdresser (salon)	*o cabeleireiro*
launderette	*a lavandaria automática*
laundry	*a lavandaria*
post office	*correio*
aspirins	*aspirinas*
Band-Aids	*pensos rápidos*
condoms	*preservativos*
sanitary napkins	*pensos higiênicos*
shampoo	*um shampoo*
shaving cream	*um creme de barba*
soap	*um sabonete*
stamps	*selos*
tampons	*tampões*
tissues	*lenços de papel*
toilet paper	*papel higiênico*
toothbrush	*uma escova de dentes*
toothpaste	*pasta de dentes*
Where is the bathroom?	*Onde fica a casa de banho?*
The bathroom door will say:	
for the men's room	*Cavalheiros/Homens*
for the women's room	*Senhoras*

Days of the Week

Monday	*Segunda-feira*
Tuesday	*Terça-feira*
Wednesday	*Quarta-feira*
Thursday	*Quinta-feira*
Friday	*Sexta-feira*
Saturday	*Sábado*
Sunday	*Domingo*

Months

January	*Janeiro*
February	*Fevereiro*
March	*Março*
April	*Abril*
May	*Maio*
June	*Junho*

July	*Julho*
August	*Agosto*
September	*Setembro*
October	*Outubro*
November	*Novembro*
December	*Dezembro*

Numbers

zero	*zero*
one	*um/uma*
two	*dois/duas*
three	*três*
four	*quatro*
five	*cinco*
six	*seis*
seven	*sete*
eight	*oito*
nine	*nove*
ten	*dez*
eleven	*onze*
twelve	*doze*
thirteen	*treze*
fourteen	*catorze*
fifteen	*quinze*
sixteen	*dezesseis*
seventeen	*dezessete*
eighteen	*dezoito*
nineteen	*dezenove*
twenty	*vinte*
thirty	*trinta*
forty	*quarenta*
fifty	*cinquenta*
sixty	*sessenta*
seventy	*setenta*
eighty	*oitenta*
ninety	*noventa*
one hundred	*cem*
one thousand	*mil*
1994	*mil novecentos e noventa e quatro*

The Cities

Braga

The capital of the northern Minho province, Braga has been Portugal's religious center and the home of its archbishops since the birth of the nation in the 12th century. At the height of the Church's power, not even the nobility was allowed to own land inside the city walls, and all industries centered around the Church's needs. Today, with a reputed 300 churches and only 140,000 inhabitants, Braga boasts one of the highest church-to-resident ratios in all Christendom.

Now, at the end of the 20th century, the medieval walls have come down, the city's economic base has been diversified, and a sprawling, ugly metropolis is springing up around the old center. Yet despite these changes, the Old Quarter of Braga, with its ornate Renaissance and Manueline palaces, baroque churches, and narrow medieval streets, still charms the visitor and attests to the city's former glory.

The strategic location of Braga, in a fertile valley at the foot of three mountain ranges, always has made it ripe for occupation and development. The Goidelic Celts, also known as the Bracari, are believed to have founded the city and given it its name several thousand years ago. The Romans occupied it in 250 BC and made it the hub of five major roads, all leading to Rome. Through them Christianity and the first Bishops of Braga eventually came. The Suevians overran the city in AD 409, but were replaced in 485 by Visigoth invaders, who, in turn, were vanquished in 711 by a Moorish army. For more than 3 centuries, the Christians and the Moors jousted over Braga, until the Muslims were finally expelled at the end of the 11th century.

It was a Spanish king, Alfonso (VI of León and I of Castile), who, with the help of French Crusaders, succeeded in wresting this part of northern Iberia from the Moors. The bishops barely had returned to Braga when, in 1095, the king rewarded a French nobleman, Henry of Burgundy, with the hand of his daughter Teresa in marriage. "Portucale" — not yet the kingdom, but a smaller county to which Braga belonged — was part of her dowry, and Henry became Count of Portucale. The new masters of Braga arrived with its first archbishop, a French prelate eventually canonized as St. Gerald, and work began on the cathedral. Later, in 1112, Henry granted a city charter to another archbishop, Dom Maurício Bourdin, making him Lord of Braga, a title the archbishops continued to hold until the late 18th century.

In the mid-12th century, when the Count of Portucale, Henry's son Dom Afonso Henriques, broke away from León and Castile and established the kingdom of Portugal, Braga's archbishops were his allies. They became the spiritual heads of the new nation and waged their own war against their Spanish arch-rivals in Santiago de Compostela and Toledo.

But their energies ultimately were diverted to the business of driving out the Moors and, later, to evangelizing the new continents discovered by the Portuguese mariners of the late 15th century.

During the 16th century, a dynamic archbishop named Dom Diogo de Sousa used money from Portugal's new spice trade with India to embellish the city. Sousa imported artists from neighboring Spain, built a Renaissance palace, and commissioned the construction of new churches. The building boom came to an end soon after his death, however, as the same discoveries that had brought the country prosperity also drained it of manpower and cash. After the Portuguese king and a large part of the nobility perished in a disastrous campaign against Morocco in 1578, Philip II of Spain invaded his neighbor and put an end to Portugal's golden age.

Independence returned to the nation in the 17th century, and the euphoria of that event, heightened by the religious zeal of the Counter-Reformation and by the flow of gold from Brazil, breathed new life into 18th-century Braga. Two prelates, Dom Rodrigo de Moura Teles and Dom Gaspar de Bragança (son of King João V), used the newfound wealth to fund large construction projects. They turned Braga into the center of baroque art in Portugal (it was from the Portuguese word *barroco,* meaning "rough pearl," that the style got its name). The Palácio do Raio and elegant Câmara Municipal (Town Hall) were built during this prolific period, as was the impressive staircase leading to the church at Bom Jesus do Monte. Braga artists also popularized the use of *talha dourada,* heavily gilded, carved wood, in church interiors. The archbishops, at the zenith of their power, patronized the arts, dressed in satin and jewels, and even had their own private orchestra.

The social upheavals and revolutions that swept through Europe during the late 18th century, however, eventually reached Braga and eroded the power of the Church. In 1792, the archbishops were forced to give up their feudal title as Lords of Braga and to hand over control of the city administration to a growing bourgeoisie. In 1808, Napoleon's forces overran the city and sacked the churches. Finally, in 1910, church properties were confiscated by the first Portuguese Republic. Although some of these were later restored, the Church in Braga never regained administrative control of the city.

Today, Braga is enduring the growing pains of modernity, with all its motorized traffic and noxious fumes, industrial parks and shopping malls. New industries operate alongside traditional crafts, and chic cafés are popping up next to dowager coffeehouses. Church institutions such as the Catholic University are being forced to compete with modern counterparts. And for the first time since the Inquisition, the supremacy of Roman Catholicism is being challenged by religious sects such as the Mormons and Jehovah's Witnesses.

Yet despite the changes, Braga remains Portugal's Eternal City. Its numerous street altars and chapels are constantly lit with votive candles, and dozens of shops sell a vast assortment of religious artifacts to a constant influx of pilgrims from all over the world. *Holy Week* remains the most important event of the year here (see *Special Events*), and the people of Braga — serious, hardworking, and contemplative — are considered the most religious in the country. It is said no citizen of Braga makes a major decision without lighting a candle and praying to any one of hundreds of saints, many of whom, incidentally, also come from Braga.

Braga At-a-Glance

SEEING THE CITY

For a spectacular view of Braga and its surroundings, leave town by Avenida João XXI and drive east 5½ miles (9 km) on N103-3 via Bom Jesus to the Monte Sameiro sanctuary and park. The reward for a climb up 265 steps to the lantern tower in the cupola of the Santuario da Virgen (Sanctuary to the Virgin) at the park's summit is a breathtaking panorama of the Minho region. On a clear day, the Atlantic coastline can be sighted 20 miles to the west, and the Serra do Gerês and Serra do Marão peaks are visible to the northeast and southeast; closer are Braga itself to the west and the prehistoric city of Briteiros to the east. Feast on the marvelous view, then settle down to a meal at the *Sameiro* restaurant (see *Eating Out*), one of the area's best eating establishments. The sanctuary is open daily from 8 AM to 8 PM; admission charge for the tower.

The Torre de Menagem, in Braga on Largo de São Francisco, across from the tourist office, is also open to visitors. The crenelated tower, an 18th-century addition to the city's medieval fortifications and the only part of them to survive urban expansion, provides a nice view of the Old Town. It is open daily from 10 AM to noon and 2 to 6 PM; admission charge.

SPECIAL PLACES

Although Braga is a sprawling metropolis, the city center, which includes the historic section, is compact enough to explore on foot. Leave your car at the municipal parking lot on Praça Conde de Agrolongo, walk past the Torre de Menagem, and turn into Rua do Souto, a pedestrian walkway that is the site of the city's most elegant shops and picturesque outdoor cafés and which, together with Rua Dom Diogo de Sousa, cuts through the Old Town and the religious heart of the city. Before this east-west parallel ends its trajectory at the Porta Nova arch, it passes several of the city's major landmarks: the Largo do Paço fountain and square, and the Antigo Paço Episcopal (former Archbishops' Palace) to the north; and the Igreja da Misericórdia (Misericórdia Church) and the cathedral to the south. Nearby, to the northwest, are the Palácio dos Biscainhos (Biscainhos Palace), now a museum, and Braga's baroque Câmara Municipal, on the Praça do Município; to the southeast are two notable houses, the Casa dos

Coimbras and the Casa dos Crivos, both on São João de Souto Square, and the Hospital de São Marcos, in the adjoining square, Largo Carlos Amarante. A 5-minute walk southeast from the hospital leads to the striking Palácio Raio and, next door, the pre-Roman Fonte do Idolo (Fountain of the Idol); its cool and relaxing setting makes it an ideal place to unwind after a day's walking tour.

THE SÉ (CATHEDRAL) COMPLEX

SÉ (CATHEDRAL) When the Portuguese want to point out the antiquity of something, they say it's "as old as the cathedral of Braga." Work on the Sé was begun in the 12th century by Henry of Burgundy and his wife, Teresa, on a site previously occupied by a 6th-century church destroyed by the Moors and, before that, by a Roman temple built in AD 43. The present building has undergone changes and additions over the centuries; the charming south door and the arches over the west (main) door are two of the most notable remnants of its early, Romanesque period. During the 16th century, the Gothic portico was added to the west door by Biscayan artists imported from Spain by Archbishop Dom Diogo de Sousa, who also rebuilt the apse in a Flamboyant ogival style. Archbishop Dom Rodrigo de Moura Teles was responsible for the 18th-century bell towers and the building's baroque façade. Several chapels line the cloister and courtyard of the cathedral. The plan was to incorporate the area where the courtyard stands into a five-nave structure so the Sé could compete with the cathedral in Santiago de Compostela, Spain. But financial restraints forced the archbishops to pare down their ambitions.

Upon entering the cross-shaped cathedral, a visitor sees a baptismal font carved in the ornate 16th-century Manueline style immediately to the left, and a chapel with the bronze tomb of the Infante Dom Afonso (a brother of Henry the Navigator), the work of 16th-century Flemish artisans, to the right. Still at the cathedral's west end, the *coro baixo* (lower choir) is flanked by two magnificent 18th-century organs, richly decorated in brass, marble, and gilded wood, while the *coro alto* (raised choir), the gallery above it, contains 18th-century stalls in black wood that can be seen during the Treasury visit (see below). Look across the nave to the east end of the cathedral and the rib-vaulted chancel, its high altar carved in stone; above the altar is a statue of St. Mary of Braga, the patron saint of the city. To the right of the chancel is the Chapel of the Holy Sacrament, with a 17th-century polychrome wood altar representing the Triumph of the Church; to the left is the Chapel of São Pedro de Rates, the first Bishop of Braga, with 18th-century *azulejos* (glazed and painted tiles) depicting his life. Open daily.

TESOURO (TREASURY) The cathedral's treasury — otherwise known as the *Museu do Arte Sacra* (Museum of Sacred Art) — contains religious objects dating as far back as the 10th century and is well worth a visit. There are rooms filled with gold and silver embroidered vestments and chalices from the 15th and 16th centuries, including a silver monstrance (a vessel used during mass) encrusted with 450 precious stones that belonged to Dom Gaspar de Bragança. Other treasures include a 10th-century Hispano-Arab (Mozarabic) ivory casket, a 17th-century silver reliquary cross, an iron cross said to have been used in the first mass celebrated in Brazil, a working 17th-century traveling organ, a 17th-century saddle embroidered in gold and silver used in Corpus Christi processions, and huge 17th- and 18th-century liturgical books. Most amusing are the giant platform shoes used by the diminutive archbishop Dom Rodrigo de Moura Teles, who was only 3′11″ tall and needed the enormous heels to reach the altar. The treasury is open daily from 8:30 AM to 6 PM in summer; from 8:30 AM to 12:30 PM and 1:30 to 5:30 PM in winter. It can be seen by guided tours only. The admission charge covers the tour (conducted in Portuguese) and visits to the cathedral's *coro alto* (for a close view of the organ cases and the choir stalls) and to the three chapels listed below; visiting hours for the chapels are the same as the Tesouro.

CAPELA DOS REIS (CHAPEL OF KINGS) This Gothic-style structure off the cathedral's cloister contains the tombs of the founders, Dom Henrique (Henry of Burgundy) and Dona Teresa. Teresa is buried beside her husband, although she took up with a Galician count after his death; in the early 16th century, Dom Diogo de Sousa had her placed in the same tomb as her husband, but a later archbishop had it opened and the bones separated into adjoining tombs. The chapel also contains the embalmed remains of a 14th-century warrior archbishop, Dom Lourenço Vicente, who distinguished himself in the famous battle of Aljubarrota, where a small Portuguese force and British archers defeated a much larger Spanish army.

CAPELA DE SÃO GERALDO (ST. GERALD'S CHAPEL) The walls of this handsome Gothic chapel, located across the courtyard from the Chapel of Kings, are covered with *azulejos* depicting the life of St. Gerald, the first Archbishop of Braga. On December 5, the public brings baskets of fruit to the chapel as an offering to the saint. The tradition is said to derive from St. Gerald's first miracle — saving the life of a sick child by conjuring up fresh fruit in the middle of winter.

CAPELA DA GLÓRIA (CHAPEL OF GLORY) Next to St. Gerald's Chapel is a third elegant Gothic chapel, this one built by Archbishop Gonçalo Pereira as his burial chamber. Vestiges of Renaissance frescoes and Mudéjar paintings can be traced on one of the walls. The archbishop's finely sculptured tomb is set on six sleeping lions, its sides bearing reliefs of the Crucifixion, the Apostles, the Virgin and Child, and a "theory of deacons" chanting the

Litany of the Dead. The reclining statue of Dom Gonçalo looks up at an 18th-century ceiling of painted wood.

ELSEWHERE IN THE CITY

IGREJA DA MISERICÓRDIA (MISERICÓRDIA CHURCH) This Renaissance church next to the cathedral doesn't catch the eye, but its dazzling altarpiece does. The baroque wooden altar, intricately carved and gilded by Marcelino de Araújo, is considered one of the best — and certainly one of the most sumptuous — examples of *talha dourada* in Portugal. The two figures at the top, practically lost in this sea of swirls and lines, are Mary and her sister Elizabeth. Open daily from 8 AM to noon. Rua Dom Diogo de Sousa.

ANTIGO PAÇO EPISCOPAL (FORMER ARCHBISHOPS' PALACE) The former residence of the Archbishops of Braga is made up of wings from the 14th, 17th, and 18th centuries — although the latter burned at the end of the last century and was remodeled in the 1930s. The palace now serves as the city library and headquarters of the University of the Minho. Part of the 14th-century wing is used for university seminars and can be visited, as can the library reading room in the 18th-century wing, notable for its carved wood ceiling. The library houses over 300,000 volumes and is considered the second most important source of civil documents in Portugal, after Lisbon's Torre do Tombo. Its priceless parchments, some stored in wooden drawers inlaid with ivory in the Sala do Arcaz, date back as far as the 9th century and include detailed family genealogies, compiled during the Inquisition, of those persons who applied to enter church service. (Special permission is required to visit the rooms with these collections.) The lobby of the university rectory has a small but fine display of 17th- and 18th-century Portuguese tiles taken from various churches and homes in the region. The library is open weekdays from 9 AM to noon and 2 to 8 PM. No admission charge. Praça do Município (phone: 612234).

JARDIM DE SANTA BÁRBARA (ST. BARBARA'S GARDEN) The 17th-century garden behind the Antigo Paço Episcopal contains over 50 species of flowers, arranged in very original designs. A 17th-century fountain sits majestically in the midst of this sea of colors, and the medieval wing of the palace serves as a backdrop. Several stone arches from the interior of the palace, gutted by fire in the last century, have been placed in the garden along with Roman milestones retrieved from nearby archaeological sites. The setting is the most photographed in Braga. Always open; no admission charge. Rua Justino Cruz and Rua Eça de Queirós.

CHAFARIZ DO LARGO DO PAÇO (LARGO DO PAÇO FOUNTAIN) In the picturesque square between the Archbishops' Palace and the cathedral stands a fountain built in 1723 by Archbishop Dom Rodrigo de Moura Teles to glorify his family. The fountain's basin is supported by angels and encircled by the city's six towers; a seventh tower, prominently displaying the Moura Teles family coat of arms, serves as a base for a statue of St. Mary of Braga. Largo do Paço.

ARCO DA PORTA NOVA (ARCH OF THE NEW DOOR) The story behind this arch typifies the struggle between the church and the nobility for control of the city. In 1512, Archbishop Dom Diogo de Sousa had a door constructed to serve as the main gate to the city. In 1778, it was torn down and replaced by a wider structure on which, to the displeasure of the reigning archbishop, King José I placed his coat of arms. The situation was later resolved by the municipality, which simply added an episcopal hat on top of the royal coat of arms and encircled it with ecclesiastical tassels. Rua Dom Diogo de Sousa.

PALÁCIO DOS BISCAINHOS (BISCAINHOS PALACE) This nobleman's palace was built during the 17th century, but has undergone several alterations since then. It now serves as a museum, focusing on the lifestyle of the Portuguese nobility between the late 17th and the 19th centuries. Granite figures of pages welcome visitors to a spacious atrium leading to terraced gardens with interesting *casas de fresco* (cool houses) — large umbrella-shaped trees with square openings cut into them, which the nobility used to escape the hot sun. The Salão Nobre (Grand Salon) is lined with early-18th-century *azulejos* depicting the life of the leisure class (not always a life of ease, as can be seen in the painting on the ceiling portraying a missionary member of the household being burned at the stake in Japan in 1624). Several large rooms with ornate stucco ceilings contain elaborate Indo-Portuguese furniture, inlaid with ivory; handsome Portuguese, Chinese, and Dutch (Delft) pottery; glassware; silverware; and 18th- and 19th-century objets d'art. The salon of the Romantic period, with its rich reds and flamboyant furniture, provides a sharp contrast to the more austere elegance of the neo-classical dining room, while the 18th-century bedroom is decorated in the Queen Dona Maria style, which is characterized by its emphasis on religious decoration. Open for guided tours (in Portuguese) from 10 AM to 12:15 PM and 1:30 to 5:15 PM; closed Mondays. Admission charge except Sunday mornings. Rua dos Biscainhos (phone: 27645).

CÂMARA MUNICIPAL (TOWN HALL) The façade of this 18th-century building, attributed to the architect André Soares, is considered one of the best examples of baroque architecture in Portugal. Although its grand stairway is lined with tiles depicting the arrival in Braga of a new archbishop, Dom José de Bragança (the bastard brother of King João V), the building was constructed specifically as a Town Hall, demonstrating that secular power was already beginning to creep into the city. The reunion room drips with chandeliers, and its walls are hung with framed portraits of important religious and political figures. Open weekdays from 8:30 AM to noon and 2 to 5 PM for short guided tours (in Portuguese). No admission charge. Praça do Município (phone: 613371).

FONTE DO PELICANO (PELICAN FOUNTAIN) The water-spouting pelican at its center is the source of this lovely baroque fountain's name. Originally in the Antigo Paço Episcopal, it now graces a pleasant park in front of the Câmara Municipal.

CASA DOS CRIVOS (HOUSE OF SCREENS) Although at one time there were dozens of such houses, with exterior grilles and screens of Moorish design, this is the last of its kind in Braga. They were first built in the 16th century, during Dom Diogo's tenure, to allow cloistered nuns to look out onto the street without being seen. The present house dates from the 16th century. Restored inside, it is now a gallery for exhibitions of works by local artists and artisans. Open daily from 9:30 AM to 12:30 PM, 2:30 to 6:30 PM, and 9 to 11 PM. No admission charge. 45 Rua de São Marcos (phone: 76002).

CASA DOS COIMBRAS (HOUSE OF THE COIMBRAS) The handsome house and its chapel, built for Archbishop João Coimbra in 1525, are among the few remnants in Braga of the prolific and highly imaginative Manueline style of early-16th-century Portuguese architecture. Privately owned, the buildings are not open to the public, but they can be admired from the street. The house, which has suffered some unfortunate remodeling, has retained its ornate Manueline windows. Largo de São João de Souto.

HOSPITAL DE SÃO MARCOS (ST. MARCOS HOSPITAL) A functioning hospital known for its lively 18th-century façade by Carlos Amarante. At the top are large granite statues of martyrs and apostles. The figures are standing precariously on the ledge and gesticulating wildly, giving the impression that they are floating in mid-air. Largo Carlos Amarante.

PALÁCIO DO RAIO (RAIO PALACE) The 18th-century house — also called the Casa do Mexicano — was designed by André Soares, and is perhaps the finest example of a *solar,* or mansion, in Braga. Though the building is privately owned and is not open to the public, visitors can enjoy its best feature, the façade, an elegant blending of tile and stone, with unusually shaped windows accentuated by blue tiles. Rua do Raio.

FONTE DO IDOLO (FOUNTAIN OF THE IDOL) Despite the Roman inscriptions, it is generally believed that the fountain dates from pre-Roman times. Some historians have suggested it was an immersion fountain and/or an altar for offerings to the Lusitanian idol Tongenabiago. The structure collapsed at one time; what remains is a high-relief section with a bust of a human over the water spout and a figure beside it holding a child on its lap. The fountain is hidden behind a green iron gate, down some steps at 389 Rua do Raio.

ENVIRONS

BOM JESUS DO MONTE No visit to Braga is complete without a tour of this spectacular sanctuary set on a densely wooded hill 3 miles (5 km) east of town via N103-3. The complex is composed of a monumental baroque staircase, begun in the early 18th century by order of Archbishop Dom Rodrigo de Moura Teles, leading up to a neo-classical church, begun in the late 18th century and finished in the early 19th. The staircase, decorated with allegorical sculptures, fountains, and chapels, is the pièce de résistance of the sanctuary, and should be climbed in order to appreciate fully its wealth of detail. Those not relishing a hike can take the funicular up (it takes 3 minutes to ascend 380 feet on a 40° incline) and walk back down the stairs. There is also a winding road leading up to the church.

The staircase is divided into three sections. The first part, the Sacred Way, is bordered with chapels illustrating scenes from the Passion with life-size terra cotta figures. The second set of stairs, the Stairway of the Five Senses, pays homage to the senses through the use of fountains and figures. Before climbing this section, note the columns on either side of the base, entwined with snakes covered with the water that pours out of their mouths. Stand back and gaze up the stairs: Note how the central granite sculptures blend to form the shape of a chalice. Moving up the stairs, there is Sight, with water gushing from its eyes; Smell, with water dripping from its nose; Taste, with water pouring from its mouth; Touch, with water flowing from its hand; and Hearing, with water coming from its ears. The final section, the Stairway of the Three Virtues, evokes Faith, Hope, and Charity by using more fountains and allegorical figures. It gives way to a lovely circular terraced garden and fountain surrounded by manicured lawns with geometric flower beds. (There is also an equestrian statue of a saint; it is traditionally held that if a woman circles the statue three times, she will be married within the year.) At the top of the stairway, facing the church, are statues of the men who condemned Jesus, fountains dedicated to the Four Apostles, and, surrounding the main church, several chapels.

The Igreja do Bom Jesus (Good Jesus Church), designed by Carlos Amarante (who also designed the third staircase) and finished in 1811, contains an altar re-creating the final moments at Calvary with larger-than-life statues. Also of interest inside the church is the Altar das Relíquias (Altar of the Relics), practically buried under modern mementos from devoted pilgrims and tourists. Behind the church are several paths leading through grottoes and fountains to a small lake, where boats can be rented by the hour.

Those who have walked up the stairs may want to take the funicular down. Dating from the late 19th century, it is propelled by gravity and a tank of water — two carriages move in opposite directions at the same time, with the water in the carriage going down providing the weight to pull the other carriage up. It runs every half hour, or when its 20 seats are filled, from 8 AM until 8 PM, and costs about 75¢ for the 3-minute ride. Bom Jesus is open daily from 8 AM to 8 PM.

MONTE SAMEIRO The Santuario da Virgen at the summit of this green mountain is the most important center of devotion in Portugal after Fátima. Although the church itself (late 19th to early 20th century) is not particularly interesting, the view of the Minho region from the lantern tower of its cupola is breathtaking, and the size of the sanctuary grounds is also impressive. The courtyard outside the church is larger than a football field, and has held over half a million pilgrims at one time. (The main pilgrimages take place the first week of June and the third week of August.) A larger-than-life statue of Pope Pius XII, at the base of a staircase leading up to the courtyard, commemorates his visit in 1954, but the view up to the church from the stairway is obstructed by a large concrete stage used for outdoor masses. The woods and paths around the church are pleasant, and the *Sameiro* restaurant beside it (see *Eating Out*) is one of the best in the region. Monte Sameiro is located 5½ miles (9 km) east of Braga, 2½ miles (4 km) past Bom Jesus on N103-3. The sanctuary is open daily from 8 AM to 8 PM; there is a charge to climb the church tower.

SANTA MARIA MADALENA This granite church, which sits on the wooded heights of the Serra da Falperra, is one of the more unusual examples of baroque work in Portugal. André Soares, the same architect who designed the Palácio do Raio and the Câmara Municipal in Braga, focused on its façade, playing with curving lines to give the building a sense of depth and movement. The church is normally open only on Sundays from 9 AM to noon (although longer summer hours are contemplated), but even when closed, the interior is visible through a grille in the door at the front entrance. The surrounding woods were once used by a local Robin Hood called Zé de Telhado (and, in fact, there is a Portuguese saint, Santa Marta da Falperra, who is the patron saint of thieves). Santa Maria Madalena is 3 miles (5 km) east of Braga on N309; it also can be reached from N103-3 by passing Bom Jesus and, less than half a mile before Monte Sameiro, taking the signposted turnoff to Serra da Falperra. The church is 2½ miles (4 km) from the turnoff.

CAPELA DE SÃO FRUTUOSO DE MONTÉLIOS The chapel of São Frutuoso, believed to have been constructed in the 7th century by Bishop Frutuoso of Dume, was damaged by the Moors in 711 and rebuilt in the 11th century. In the shape of a Greek cross, it is one of the few remaining examples of Byzantine art in Portugal, and despite an advanced state of disrepair — only one of the four naves that made up the cross is still attached to the cupola — it retains the aura and dignity of age. To visit, apply to the priest or sacristan at the adjoining Igreja de São Francisco, itself interesting for its 16th-century stalls, which were removed from the cathedral of Braga in the 18th century. To reach São Frutuoso, 2½ miles (4 km) from Braga, take N201 northwest toward Ponte de Lima and turn right at Real.

| **EXTRA SPECIAL** | As elsewhere in Europe, whiling away the hours in a coffeehouse is an important part |

of life in Braga. Of the several historic cafés, the most famous is the 19th-century *Café Brasileira*. Its strategic location in the Largo do Barão São

Martinho, by the entrance to fashionable Rua do Souto, makes it the city's informal salon. It is here that most of the intellectuals and artists traditionally have met and lingered, and they still do. The marble tables and brass and copper fittings provide an Old World ambience; octogenarian waiters add timeless atmosphere. Patrons sit inside and stare out onto the street through large windows, which slide back in summer. In the arcade across from the tourist office are two other noteworthy coffeehouses, the refurbished *Café Astória* (phone: 22783) and *Café Vianna* (phone: 32694), with tables outside in fine weather. The latter is popular with the young, trendy crowd, who are attracted to the café's mix of Art Deco decadence, young waiters and waitresses, and "designer" snack and salad menu. The café doubles as a bar at night with live jazz and folk music.

Sources and Resources

TOURIST INFORMATION

The Municipal Tourism Board located in the center of town (1 Av. Central, at the corner of Av. da Liberdade; phone: 22550) offers advice and assistance in English. It is open daily from 9 AM to 7 PM (except Saturdays from October through April, when it is open from 9 AM to 12:30 PM and from 2 to 5 PM, and on Sundays during the same months, when it is closed entirely).

LOCAL COVERAGE The *Correio do Minho,* the local newspaper with the largest circulation, publishes a daily agenda listing events and other pertinent information, such as exchange rates, the weather forecast, and the schedules of trains and buses departing for major cities in Portugal and elsewhere in Europe. The *Diário do Minho,* another local paper, is also available. Newsstands in the arcade in front of the tourist office sell major European newspapers, and magazines and the European editions of American news magazines, but not the *International Herald Tribune.* A comprehensive English-language pamphlet describing the city, entitled *Braga,* is published by the Municipal Tourism Board and distributed free. Pick it up at the tourist office (address above).

TELEPHONE The city code for Braga is 53. If calling from within Portugal, dial 053 before the local number.

GETTING AROUND

Most of the major sights of the city are easily accessible by foot. In any case, do everything to avoid driving in town during the rush hours (from 8:30 to 10 AM and from 5 to 7:30 PM), particularly on the Avenida da Liberdade. There is a municipal parking lot on Praça Conde de Agrolongo, on the north side of the Old Town.

BUS Service is reasonable, but buses do get crowded during rush hours, and the frequency of their appearance drops off after midnight. Tickets are acquired on the bus (175 escudos — about $1.25 — within the city limits). The main bus station for long-distance arrivals and departures is the Central de Camionagem de Braga (Travessa da Praça do Comércio; phone: 616080). Intercity service is provided by the *Rodoviária Entre Douro e Minho* and *Resende* bus companies, which operate out of the same office in the station (phone: 616080). *Abreu,* a travel agency (171 Av. Central; phone: 613100/1/2/3), also handles reservations. The tourist office has lists of bus schedules to all destinations, and the *Correio do Minho* publishes a daily schedule of major runs.

CAR RENTAL *Avis* has a rental office beside the central bus station (28 Rua Gabriel Pereira de Castro; phone: 72520), and *Hertz* also has a local office (20 Largo Primeiro de Dezembro; phone: 616744).

TAXI There is a taxi stand in the Largo do Barão São Martinho, near the Municipal Tourism Board. You also can call for a cab (phone: 614019, 22009, or 23535).

TRAIN The main train station, Estação do Caminho de Ferro (phone: 22166 or 27001), on the west side of the city at the Largo de Estação, is a central rail hub for northern Portugal. The newspapers publish a daily schedule of trains to and from important destinations; the tourist office also has schedules.

SPECIAL EVENTS

Braga is famous for its religious processions, and though the crowds here may be smaller than those that gather for *Holy Week* in Seville, Spain, the enthusiasm is no less fervent.

FAVORITE FETE

Semana Santa (Holy Week) Not unexpectedly, this is the most important time of the year in Braga, a time when all commercial activity grinds to a halt and the city is transformed into a giant and sumptuous house of worship. Priceless gold and silver ecclesiastical relics are removed from church treasuries and paraded through town by the archbishop and his retinue, themselves clothed in diamonds and pearls. Balconies are decorated with luxurious drapes displaying the coats of arms of ancient families who fought in the Catholic armies to liberate Portugal from the Moors. The streets are festooned with lights and filled with the smell of burning wax and incense. Daily processions vent the religious fervor of the populace: In one procession, hundreds of penitents dressed in the black habit of gravediggers carry torches and walk somberly in front of the image of the Lord to the slow, martial cadence of a funerary tune. Hooded men add a dark and mysterious note to the events. At one time, these masked men went around with large torches pointing out the houses of suspected sinners. *Holy Week* events are held annually a week before *Easter Sunday,* a day that also marks the start of Portugal's bullfighting season.

From June 23 through 25, the city comes alive once again (and is again lit spectacularly) for the *Festas de São João* (Feast Days of St. John), a Christian holiday with roots in pagan rites celebrating the summer solstice. This is the time of year when the crops are beginning to blossom and the people of the Minho come out and rejoice. Parties go on until all hours of the night, the *vinho verde* flows freely, and the aroma of festive food invades the popular neighborhoods. Young women wear colorful regional dresses and ornate gold filigree, folk groups perform, and medieval dances are staged. Customs such as throwing herbs into large bonfires to make divinations or passing around pots of leeks with carnations attached to them are reminders of the ancient origins of the festivities.

In addition, the *vinho verde* fair is held in the late spring or early summer (the schedule varies). And at any time of the year, Braga is probably playing host to some industrial fair, convention, or congress at the Palácio Municipal de Exposições e Desportos (in Parque São João da Ponte, at the southern end of Av. da Liberdade).

MUSEUMS

In addition to those museums mentioned in *Special Places,* the *Museu Pio XII* and the *Museu Medina,* which share the same building, may be of interest. The former is the city's museum of antiquities, housing artifacts dating as far back as the Neolithic period (albeit arranged in a haphazard way); the latter consists of a collection of paintings by 20th-century Portuguese artist Henrique Medina, in which his predilection for naturalist settings and young virgins is evident. The remains of a Roman swimming pool are in the courtyard. The museums are open from 10 AM to noon and 3 to 6 PM; closed Mondays. There are separate admission charges. 8 Campo São Tiago (phone: 23370).

SHOPPING

Braga and its environs are known for their fairly large selection of moderately priced handicrafts — lace and embroidery, wicker and straw articles, earthenware goods, and religious artifacts. The best bargains can be obtained at the weekly Tuesday fair, held at the Palácio Municipal de Exposições e Desportos in Parque São João da Ponte. For those unable to attend the fair, there is the shop at the tourist office that carries a small selection of regional goods, including the Minho's famed filigree jewelry, at prices only slightly above those of the manufacturer. Shopping malls, or *centros comerciais,* have made their appearance here: They're largely restricted to Avenida da Liberdade, and are especially convenient because they stay open until midnight. Shoppers in search of quality, however, continue to patronize the shops on and around Rua do Souto. Stores are open from 9 AM to 1 PM and 3 to 7 PM; closed Sundays.

CASA EDEN A large selection of hand-embroidered linen and bedspreads (a damask bedspread can cost anywhere from $200 to $300). English is spoken. 140-144 Rua do Souto (phone: 22756).

CASA FÂNZERES The oldest religious artifacts shop in Braga both sells and restores religious objects. 132-134 Rua do Souto (phone: 22704).

HERDEIROS DE FRANCISCO JOSÉ FERREIRA Leather goods of quality — suitcases, briefcases, and women's handbags. 124 Rua do Souto (phone: 74574).

OURIVESARIA CONFIANÇA Fine silver and gold jewelry is sold and repaired. 1 Rua do Souto (phone: 23187).

SAPATARIA TERESINHA Top-quality leather shoes made in the region. 84-86 Rua do Souto (phone: 22943).

VADECA Typical handmade *viola braguesa,* or *cavaquinho* guitars, from which the ukelele was developed. 15 Largo do Barão São Martinho (phone: 71045).

SPORTS AND FITNESS

Braga has two major public sports facilities. The larger is the municipal sports complex (phone: 616788), which is part of the Parque Municipal de Exposições e Desportos, in the Parque São João da Ponte at the southern end of Avenida da Liberdade. The other is the Complexo Desportivo da Rodovia (Av. João XXI; phone: 76803). Both have parking facilities and can be reached by public transport.

BOATING Small rowboats can be rented at the lake above the Bom Jesus do Monte sanctuary.

FISHING Numerous rivers, lakes, and beaches in the vicinity provide diverse fishing opportunities. The huge reservoir at Peneda-Gerês National Park is only 30 miles (48 km) away. The *Braga Amateur Fisherman's Club* (112 Rua dos Chãos; phone: 26060) can be of assistance.

JOGGING The best place to run is the Parque São João da Ponte, which has both green spaces and a track.

SOCCER *Sporting Clube de Braga,* a first-division team, has its own stadium, *Estádio Primeiro de Maio,* in the Parque São João da Ponte. The season runs from September to May, and major league games are played on Sunday afternoons.

SWIMMING The Parque São João da Ponte has the largest public pool in town (phone: 24424), with restaurant and café service next door. The Complexo

Desportivo da Rodovia has both an indoor pool (phone: 76803) and an outdoor pool (phone: 616773).

TENNIS There is a tennis club at the Complexo Desportivo da Rodovia (phone: 611753).

THEATER

The *Cinema São Geraldo* (on Largo Carlos Amarante) and the *Cinema Avenida* (across the square from the tourist office) show films in their original language with Portuguese subtitles. The daily *Correio do Minho* publishes movie listings in its Roteiro section.

MUSIC

The Minho is Portugal's folklore center. On Saturday and Sunday evenings all summer long, regional folk groups, dressed in colorful costumes, take to the stage at the bandstand on Avenida Central, performing ancient songs and lively dances accompanied by small Minho fiddles, small Braga guitars, triangles, and bass drums. Keep an eye out for Braga's most famous group, the *Grupo Folclórico Dr. Gonçalo Sampaio.*

NIGHTCLUBS AND NIGHTLIFE

All the action unfolds between 9 PM and 2 AM. Discotheques currently in vogue are the *Discoteca Club 84* (beside the *Turismo* hotel at Praceta João XXI; phone: 76482) and *Coreto* (15 Av. Central; phone: 75814), a disco and pub catering to a younger and wilder set. The *Golden Bar* (in the *Turismo* hotel, Av. João XII; phone: 612200) serves tropical drinks and late-night snacks, while the *Latino Bar* in Old Town (56 Rua do Anjo; phone: 79127) is a warm and cozy spot with soft music for the romantically inclined. *Pub John Lennon* (28 Rua do Raio; phone: 26623) provides live music shows for the nostalgia crowd. *O Nosso Café* (Av. da Liberdade; phone: 23930) is popular with Braga's chic. The multipurpose complex, housed in a former theater, caters to all the senses. Guests can dine, or sip coffee and tropical drinks in the sleek, pastel-colored coffeehouse; listen to piano music daily, and live jazz and other types of music on the weekends; play chess, backgammon, or billiards in the suave *"T-Clube";* or let loose on the dance floor of *"Trignometria."* The brain behind this center is a former employee of Régine, the world-renowned socialite and club owner. The *Palácio de Dona Chica* (on N201 to Monção, 2½ miles/4 km north of Braga in Palmeiras; phone: 675114), a turn-of-the-century house with neo-Gothic and Arabic touches, is another multi-entertainment center and popular late-night watering hole with the old guard and newly chic. There is a pub, video lounge, Art Deco disco, and stylish snack bar with a large fireplace. The sprawling garden, with cedar, palm, almond, and other exotic trees, is a popular romantic spot. The center is also called *Investimentos Turísticos,* but locals know it by the name of its former resident.

Best in Town

CHECKING IN

Accommodations in the city don't live up to its monuments, so demanding travelers head for the hills to the more deluxe rooms around the Bom Jesus sanctuary. In Braga, the larger commercial hotels, catering to the business community, are located in the newer part of town, while smaller establishments — of which there are too few for summer demand — are in the quieter and more picturesque historic center. However, the number of moderate-priced establishments is growing as some inexpensive lodgings are refurbished and upgraded. Expect to pay $95 or more for a double room with continental breakfast at a place in the expensive category, between $60 and $80 at a moderate property, and less than $40 at an inexpensive one. Both *Semana Santa* and the *Festas de São João* (June 23 through 25) draw many pilgrims and visitors, so be sure to book well in advance. Reservations should be made at least a month in advance for summer traveling, and should be double-checked a week before departure. All telephone numbers are in the 53 city code unless otherwise indicated.

EXPENSIVE

Do Elevador On the grounds of the Bom Jesus sanctuary, this property is quite elegant, and tastefully decorated in classic Portuguese style. Its plush, Old World decor and efficient service make it a favorite of Lisbon and Porto society. The 25 rooms with baths (TV sets are available on request) face a manicured garden and have a sweeping view of Braga. The posh dining room (see *Eating Out*) commands a similar view and serves fine regional specialties. Parque do Bom Jesus do Monte (phone: 676611; fax: 676679).

Do Parque Also on the grounds of the Bom Jesus sanctuary, it has a turn-of-the-century look that has been retained despite refurbishing and modernization. The large sitting room is fashionably decorated in leather and wood; each of the 49 air conditioned bedrooms has a private bath, radio, and TV set. There is no restaurant, but meals can be taken at the sister *Do Elevador* hotel a few paces away. Parque do Bom Jesus do Monte (phone: 676607; telex: 33401).

MODERATE

Dona Sofia This former *pensão,* strategically placed near the Sé, has been upgraded thanks to a recent face-lift. All 34 double rooms offer modern comforts, including mini-bars and private baths. For a peaceful stay, ask for a room in the back. There's no restaurant. 68-90 Rua Dom Alfonso Henriques (phone: 71854; fax: 611245).

São Marcos Friendly service and 13 modern, clean, and simple rooms with private baths characterize this *pensão,* which is ideally located in a quiet pedestrian street in the Old Town. There's no restaurant or bar service. 80 Rua de São Marcos (phone: 77177).

Senhora-A-Branca Several minutes' walk from the historic center, Braga's newest and best bed and breakfast establishment sits on a quaint, cobbled square with orange trees and picturesque tiled houses. There are 18 rooms (some with French windows facing the square) and 2 suites with loggias (all with private baths), a comfortable lounge with a fireplace, and a breakfast room (but no restaurant). The private garage is a plus in a town with more cars than parking spaces. 58 Largo da Senhora-A-Branca (phone: 29938; fax: 29937).

INEXPENSIVE

Inácio Filho The Portuguese antiques, 8 clean rooms (some with private baths), and perfect location (in the heart of the Old Town) make this *pensão* an attractive bargain. No restaurant. 42 Rua Francisco Sanches (phone: 23849).

VERY INEXPENSIVE

Casa Santa Zita Run by a lay religious order, it provides functional, dorm-style accommodations (shared baths) at student rates. No restaurant. 20 Rua São João (phone: 23494).

Those wishing to get away from the conventional hotel circuit should note that Portugal's *Tourism in the Country* program — through which private homes take in paying guests — is particularly active in northern Portugal (see *Pousadas and Manor Houses* in DIVERSIONS for additional details and reservations information) and that many of the participating properties in the area are the very fine stately homes and manor houses belonging to the *Turismo de Habitação* network rather than the simpler houses of the *Turismo Rural* and *Agroturismo* networks. Among the participants in the Braga area is the *Casa dos Lagos,* a terraced house on the wooded hill at the entrance to Bom Jesus. The house has a cozy apartment with a bedroom, bathroom, sitting room, and kitchen. Contact Andrelina Pinto Barbosa (phone: 676738 or 24563), or write *Casa dos Lagos* (Bom Jesus, Braga 4700). Another participant, the *Casa da Pedra Cavalgada,* a 19th-century home a little over a mile northeast of Braga on N101, offers a pool, a garden, and a self-contained area with 2 spacious bedrooms and individual sitting rooms (but no private bathrooms). Contact Dr. José Mariz (phone: 24596), or write *Casa da Pedra Cavalgada* (Lugar do Assento, Palmeira, Braga 4700).

There also are several charming agricultural estates belonging to the *Turismo Rural* category in the hills northeast of Braga. The *Casa da Quinta da Fonte* sits amid vine-covered hills. There are 6 rooms with private bathrooms and views, a sitting room with a piano and a large fireplace, and a pool surrounded by trees. Meals, accompanied by the house wine, can also be prepared with advance notice. The house is 4½ miles (6 km) northeast of Braga off N205. Contact Maria Amelia Teles e Castro (*Casa da Quinta da Fonte,* Lago, Amares 4270; phone: 32780 or 31203). The *Quinta de São Vicente,* 8 miles (13 km) east of Braga off N103 to Chaves, is a more typical rural Minho farmhouse with sloping tiled roofs, granite exterior staircases, and a wood-lined loggia hung with bougainvillea. There are 4 tastefully decorated bedrooms (3 with private bathrooms) and 1 suite. The property forms a part of a larger agricultural estate. Meals are provided with advance notice, and horseback riding, fishing, swimming, and other aquatic sports are available nearby. Closed November through March. Contact Luís Veloso e Ferreira (*Quinta de São Vicente,* Lugar de Portas [Geraz do Minho], Povoa de Lanhoso 4830; phone: 632466). Each of the above is in the moderate price category. Most local *Turismo no Espaço Rural* (Tourism in the Country) properties require a minimum stay of 3 nights, though this is not rigidly enforced, particularly in the off-peak months.

EATING OUT

The cooking of Braga is rich and heavy, and the portions are generous. Pork, kid, and cod are the staple main dishes, and of the three, pork is the most common. Two pork dishes found frequently are *rojões de porco* (pork dumplings with maize) and *arroz de sarrabulho* (various meats stewed in pig's blood and rice). The *frigideiras de Braga* (pies filled with pork or other meat) are the traditional poor person's meal and are ideal for snacks and picnics. Roast *cabrito* (kid) is in season during the early summer, and *bacalhau* (dried salt cod), the most prized dish in the Braga repertoire, is consumed throughout the year — including at *Christmas* dinner. There are more than 300 ways to prepare cod — and each restaurant has its own recipe — but oven-baked codfish with cream is one of the better variations on the theme.

Braga is also known for its pastries. Not only are there more than 20 pastry shops — *pastelarias* — from which to choose, but most restaurants (in all categories) make their own pastries. Anyone with a sweet tooth should try the city's *pudim à abade de Priscos,* an extra rich pudding named after a corpulent prelate with a predilection for sweets. The recipe requires 15 egg yolks, in addition to port, lemon, and caramelized sugar.

Dining out in Braga, however, is not as popular as in other major Portuguese cities. Families tend to entertain at home, leaving restaurants for large celebrations, such as weddings and baptisms. The number of good restaurants is, therefore, limited, particularly in the expensive category. There are, however, several establishments on the Praça Conde de Agrolongo, near the municipal parking lot, serving simple, but tasty, dishes at modest prices for the merchant lunch crowd. A two-course meal for two, including *vinho verde* (green wine — referring to its age, not its color), brandy, and coffee, will cost $50 or more in a restaurant listed below as expensive, from $30 to $40 in a restaurant listed as moderate, and around $25 in an inexpensive one. All telephone numbers are in the 53 city code unless otherwise indicated.

EXPENSIVE

Do Elevador In the hotel of the same name, it offers elegant Old World charm, with views of box-hedged gardens and the Bom Jesus sanctuary. The set menu, which changes daily, balances regional fare with continental dishes. The typical three courses include fish and meat and may not leave much room for more, although the richly laden dessert cart will still be a temptation. When it arrives, try the homemade *bôlo de amêndoa* (almond cake). Open daily. Reservations advised. Major credit cards accepted. Parque do Bom Jesus do Monte (phone: 676611).

MODERATE

Abade de Priscos A simple, quaint restaurant upstairs, overlooking a tree-lined square next to the Catholic University. Good regional fare is served: Braga specialties and protein-rich dishes for the largely academic crowd that makes up its clientele. Closed Sundays. Reservations advised. No credit cards accepted. 7 Praça Mousinho de Albuquerque (phone: 76650).

O Cantinho do Campo das Hortas Lodged in a former townhouse overlooking the Campo das Hortas, this place is one of the best eateries in town, and attracts a strong and mixed following of city officials, clergy, and business-people. The no-frills, family-run establishment offers an à la carte menu and daily specials. Try the tender, mouth-watering *cabrito assado* (roast kid). Diners have the choice of eating in the wood-lined, sedate quarters upstairs, or in the bustling cellar dining room. Open daily. Reservations advised for lunch. No credit cards accepted. Largo da Senhora da Boa Luz (phone: 614003).

Casa Cruz Sobral What this ordinary-looking place lacks in decor and atmosphere, it makes up for in food and service. The owner and manager, son of the proprietor of the *Inácio* restaurant (see below), has taken the family recipes to a smaller locale next door, where he offers a traditional, seasonal menu, with special emphasis on roast meat. The *vitela assada à Cruz Sobral* (veal in a wine-based onion sauce with copious amounts of garlic, parsley, and cumin) and the *sarrabulho com rojões à moda do Minho* (pork with maize) are both tasty. Closed Mondays. Reservations unnecessary. No credit cards accepted. 7-8 Campo das Hortas (phone: 616648).

A Ceia Near the tourist office, this popular 14-table bistro offers friendly service, rustic decor, and a wholesome regional menu. Try the *bacalhau a Zé do pipo* (oven-baked purée of cod). Closed Mondays and the first 2 weeks in

September. No reservations. Major credit cards accepted. 331 Largo João Penha (phone: 23932).

Inácio The most popular restaurant in Braga proper. Family run, it is decorated with regional artifacts, divided into three cozy dining areas, and has stone walls, wooden beams, and an open kitchen to give it a rustic look that complements the menu. Cured hams hanging from the ceiling of the bar are consumed as appetizers with dry port. Some dishes worth noting are *cabrito no forno* (kid roasted over a wood fire), and *lampréia com arroz* (lamprey with rice). In the latter, the fish is marinated in wine and its own blood, which is used later to make the rice sauce; preparing this dish is time-consuming and labor-intensive, so have your hotel call in advance to order it. The wine cellar is well stocked with the best alvarinho green wines, as well as more modestly priced varieties such as Casal Garcia. Closed Fridays. Reservations advised. Major credit cards accepted. 4 Campo das Hortas (phone: 613235).

Sameiro Pilgrims visiting the shrine next door are not the only ones making tracks to this family-run restaurant beside the Sameiro sanctuary. Food connoisseurs as well are attracted by its excellent dishes and efficient service. The decor is as spartan as a monk's cell, but owner-chef Maria da Conceição has received several culinary awards for her regional cooking. Her wood-fired stoves add extra flavor to the dishes, which include lamprey with mayonnaise, and a soufflé of cod. The recipe for the squash-based *tarta de chila* is well guarded, but it appears to have been marinated in caramelized sugar, honey, and port. The house has its own *vinho verde*. Closed Mondays. Reservations advised. Major credit cards accepted. Monte Sameiro (phone: 675114).

INEXPENSIVE

Casa Pimenta A simple, family-run eating establishment that is a lunchtime favorite among local merchants and office workers. Open daily. Reservations unnecessary. No credit cards accepted. 24 Praça Conde de Agrolongo (phone: 22119).

Lusitana Despite its size, this small and bustling place manages to serve as a snack bar, tea shop, and pastry shop. Eat indoors or outdoors on the small esplanade inside the Jardim de Santa Bárbara, but if you plan to have lunch here, be sure to arrive before 12:30 PM to avoid the crowds. Combination platters include a succulent veal stew, and the Braga *frigideiras* (meat pies) are house specialties. This is also the most popular hangout in town for the tea and pastry set, since the establishment makes its own sweets, including traditional local delicacies such as *fatias de Braga* (square cakes made of almonds, eggs, and sugar), sweet Romeo and Juliet pastries, and the ultra-rich *pudim à abade de Priscos*. Closed Mondays. No reservations. No credit cards accepted. 127 Rua Justino Cruz (phone: 20690).

Coimbra

Sitting on the banks of the Mondego River, halfway between Lisbon and Porto, Coimbra is Portugal's third-largest city (pop. 97,000) — and its most romantic. The greatest Portuguese poets — including Luís de Camões, who wrote the national epic, *The Lusiads,* during the 16th century — lived in Coimbra and immortalized their city, some carving their romantic verses on its very stones. Coimbra is the home of Portugal's oldest university, and the town teems with young people. Indeed, the romantic image of Coimbra is one of students in black capes hurrying through the nearly perpendicular streets around the ancient university as the cathedral bells toll them to class. Or of the same students, armed with guitars, serenading the young women — *tricanas* — of Coimbra under their balconies.

Although the black capes worn by the students since the Middle Ages had almost disappeared, they are now returning. As in times past, they are pinned with a colored ribbon identifying the student's course of study — dark blue for letters, light blue for science, red for law, yellow for medicine — with a tear at the border for each romantic conquest.

There is no serenading under the balconies today, but Coimbra *fados,* the sweet, nostalgic songs dedicated to love or to the river or to the city itself and sung only by men, are still heard in student cafés and at festivals, or whenever students with guitars gather on the steps by the Sé Velha (Old Cathedral) at night. Many *fado* singers, among them doctors, lawyers, and judges — graduates of Coimbra University — are better known for their singing than they are in their professions.

The university is the dominant force in the life of Coimbra. In 1290, King Dinis (husband of Isabel of Aragon, celebrated as Santa Isabel or the Rainha Santa — Saintly Queen) founded a university in Lisbon. In 1308, he transferred it to Coimbra. It moved back and forth several times until 1537, when it was permanently located in the heart of Coimbra. The university became a renowned center for the study of philosophy, theology, law, and medicine, although it had its periods of stagnation, including one during this century, which prompted the dictator António Salazar, an alumnus and an ex-professor, to take action in the 1940s. Bent on having a really modern university, he tore down part of the historic Alta (Upper Town) surrounding the university — ancient narrow streets lined with 16th- and 17th-century houses and old churches — and to house his Universidade Nova (New University), erected some of the ugliest utilitarian buildings in Europe. Fortunately, the buildings in the adjoining Universidade Vehla (Old University) remain intact.

In the early days, only students, along with their servants, local nobility, and ecclesiastics, were allowed to live in the Alta section. Their lives and study habits were regulated by the ringing of the cathedral bells. There were strict rules for each class, particularly for the freshmen, who were often treated brutally and persecuted by the upperclassmen. Some of the ancient traditions persist. Students still live in *repúblicas* — houses passed down from one generation of students to another — where they share the household costs and chores. And they still celebrate the ancient ritual of burning their university ribbons at the end of the term in May to symbolize moving to an upper class (see *Extra Special*).

The other dominant force in Coimbra life is the Mondego River, often called the river of poets because so many poems and songs have been written about it. But the Mondego has done more than provide a romantic setting for the city. Long ago it made Coimbra an important port for trade with lands as far away as Phoenicia and Norway. Later, it was the dividing line between Christian and Moorish Portugal. The river also brought destruction. Over the centuries, silt buried a great part of the Baixa (Lower Town), where shopkeepers and artisans lived, and a good part of the Santa Clara area on the opposite bank. Old churches, convents, and other historic buildings disappeared forever before the Aguieira Dam tamed the river during this century.

Coimbra probably began as an Iron Age *castro* of Lusitanian and Celtic inhabitants on the Alta hilltop several hundred years before Christ. The Romans located their forum on the same hill, at the spot where the *Museu Nacional de Machada de Castro* (Machado de Castro National Museum) now stands, and called their settlement Aeminium. The Visigoths brought Christianity, and when the bishopric was moved from the old Roman town of Conímbriga nearby, the name came with it, eventually to be shortened to Coimbra. When the Moors came in 711, they built a set of walls around the hilltop city; one of its gates, the Almedina, still stands. The Christians recaptured the city, but in 987 the Moors again swept through and nearly razed it. In 1064, the city was taken once more and held for good under Ferdinand I, King of León and Castile.

Thus Coimbra became the capital of all the land between the Douro River to the north and Moorish-held territory to the south. Later, when Dom Afonso Henriques — son of Henry of Burgundy, to whom the Spanish king had given his Portuguese territory — defeated his mother and her Spanish allies and declared himself king of an independent Portugal, he, too, made Coimbra his capital.

A good number of Coimbra's monuments date from the 16th and 17th centuries. Besides the permanent establishment of the university, the 16th century saw the arrival of the Jesuits (who remained strong until the mid-18th century) and of many other religious orders, who founded schools and put up notable buildings. A famous school of sculpture was born when the Frenchmen Nicolas Chanterène, Jean de Rouen, and others set up studios to produce most of the statues and stone carvings that adorn the city's churches. The sculptors were influenced by the new methods and style of the Italian Renaissance, but they owed much of their art to the stone with which they worked — an exceptionally white, solid, granular limestone from the banks of the nearby Ançã River.

The spate of building during the 17th and 18th centuries was caused by the discovery of gold in Brazil. Buildings dating from this time — such as the Convento de Santa Clara-a-Nova (New Santa Clara Convent), the university library, and the Igreja de Santo António dos Olivais (Church of St. Anthony of the Olive Grove) — were literally covered with Brazilian gold. The 19th century brought a period of turmoil — the sack of the city by Napoleon's army during the Peninsular War and involvement in the War of the Two Brothers. In the latter, Coimbra sided with the liberal Pedro of Brazil, the victor, against his absolutist brother Miguel. A suppression of all religious orders in Portugal followed, drastically altering life on the banks of the Mondego. For the most part, the city's 33 monasteries, convents, and religious schools became army installations.

The fame of its ancient university and its monuments draws hundreds of thousands of foreign and Portuguese visitors to Coimbra each year. Yet its aura of romance and beautiful buildings are not its only attractions. There are the bohemian student haunts, including the little *tascas* (eating houses) offering all kinds of snacks (from spareribs, ham omelettes, and grilled sardines to boiled pigs' feet). The picturesque, narrow streets in the Baixa, with laundry, bird cages, plants, and balconies hanging over them, and with picturesque names like Terreiro da Erva (Herb Square) and Rua dos Gatos (Street of the Cats), are fun to explore. Browsers may come upon a curio or antiques shop in a cul-de-sac or a little alleyway, or an old workshop where they still make, in the traditional way, the famous guitars — roundish in shape and light in sound — that typify the city. Better yet, those seeking to be at one with the spirit of the place will track down a Coimbra guitar in use, in the hands of a very soulful singer of *fado*.

Coimbra At-a-Glance

SEEING THE CITY

From the hilltop above the Vale do Inferno (Valley of Hell), off the highway leading into Coimbra from Lisbon — turn left at the Miradouro Vale do Inferno sign about 2½ miles (4 km) before town — there is a panorama of Coimbra with its old churches and university buildings clustered around the Alta hill, modern buildings and green gardens sloping down to the river, and, as a distant backdrop, the peaks of the Serra da Lousã and the pine forests of Buçaco. In town, the patio of the Universidade Velha affords an impressive view of the city's rooftops, old buildings, and narrow streets leading down to the river. All of the countryside surrounding the city can be seen from Penedo da Saudade (Place of Nostalgia), a high rocky cliff southeast of the center. An isolated and romantic vantage point at the beginning of the century, it was a favorite haunt of students and poets, who carved verses on its stones. The place is still a nice garden with a view, but it is somewhat spoiled by encroaching modern construction.

SPECIAL PLACES

Coimbra is effectively divided into three districts. The Alta is the university quarter, as well as the original site of the Iron Age settlement and of the castles and forts of the Romans, Moors, and Portuguese kings. The Baixa is the part of the city that grew up by the river. Full of narrow streets and crowded with shops, banks, churches, cafés, and hotels, it is shaped roughly like a wedge, with the river on one side, Rua Ferreira Borges, Rua Visconde da Luz, and Rua da Sofia on the other, and Largo da Portagem at its point. Avenida Fernão de Magalhães is its main thoroughfare. The third district is the west bank of the Mondego, or the Santa Clara area, just across the Ponte de Santa Clara. Here, among other things, are the remains of an old convent associated with the saintly Queen Isabel and a newer one built as a replacement after the original began to give way to Mondego floodwaters. The bridge was not the first one to cross the Mondego. Parts of an 11th-century stone bridge can be seen from the present one when the water is low. It was torn down when the river silted up and caused the water level to rise too high for boats to pass under it.

The best way to see the sights is to take a taxi to the highest point of the Alta — the Universidade Velha — and walk down through its narrow streets, guided by one of the excellent maps available at the tourist office. To visit places beyond the Alta or the Baixa, go by car, taxi, or bus.

ALTA

UNIVERSIDADE VELHA (OLD UNIVERSITY) The entrance to the university is through the Porta Férrea (Iron Gate), a 17th-century triumphal arch surmounted by statues of King Dinis, who founded the university, and King João III, who donated his royal palace during the 16th century to house it. Inside the gate is the enormous University Patio, with a large statue of João III, looking very much like England's Henry VIII. (There is a large statue of King Dinis outside the university entrance in Praça Dom Dinis.) Beside the gate, to the left when entering, is a long, low palace wing that once contained suites for the princes and later served as the Colégio de São Pedro. It has a beautifully carved 18th-century baroque door in its façade.

The baroque Biblioteca Joannina (Joanine Library), the university's — and the town's — pièce de résistance, is in the far left-hand corner of the patio. Its three halls dazzlingly decorated with carved and gilded wood, its precious rosewood and jacaranda tables, and its trompe l'oeil ceilings qualify it as one of the most beautiful libraries in the world (although the books are not well preserved). A portrait of King João V, who had the library built between 1717 and 1728, hangs at the back. Next to the library, facing the Porta Férrea entrance, is the Capela de São Miguel, the university chapel, with an ornate 16th-century Manueline doorway. The sumptuous interior contains an intricately carved 18th-century baroque organ decorated with gilt panels and Chinese lacquerwork, a Mannerist main altar, rococo altars in the side chapels, and walls covered with beautiful 18th-century tiles. Installed in an annex to the chapel is the *Museu de Arte Sacra* (Museum of Sacred Art), with gold and silver pieces, furniture, vestments, paintings, and sculpture.

The university's 18th-century clock tower stands in the right-hand corner of the patio, dominating the Coimbra skyline. Next to it, on the patio's right side, is the main part of the Manueline palace donated by King João III. An exterior double staircase in stone leads to a colonnade known as the Via Latina (Latin Way), because all who walked there in the Middle Ages, when the university was at its zenith, spoke Latin. From it, another staircase leads to passageways that look down on the Sala dos Capelos (Salon of Cardinals' Hats), which has always been used for the awarding of degrees — its name derives from the fact that in the past cardinals usually presided at such ceremonies. Portraits of the Kings of Portugal, and 17th-century carpet tiles (rectangular panels of tiles that resemble upright rugs), adorn its walls, which rise to a notable 17th-century paneled ceiling. To the right of the Sala dos Capelos is the Sala das Armas (Arms Room), where old arms and standards used in the ceremonies are on display; to the left is a long portico, from which there is a breathtaking view of the Sé Velha, the Baixa, and the river. Downstairs again, a door at the end of the Via Latina opens to the Gerais, the cloister around which the old lecture rooms were located. The *Museu de Arte Sacra* is open from 10 AM to 12:30 PM and 2 to 5 PM; closed Mondays. The rest of the university opens daily at 9:30 AM. Admission charge for the library, the museum, the chapel, and the main hall. Tickets are available up the right staircase in the Reitoria (Rectory), the building on the right after the gate. Praça Dom Dinis (phone: 35448).

AQUEDUTO DE SÃO SEBASTIÃO (AQUEDUCT OF ST. SEBASTIAN) Though built during the 16th century to bring water to the Alta, it probably stands on the site of a more ancient Roman aqueduct. It originally had 20 arches, but part of it was torn down to make way for the Universidade Nova. The main arch is topped with images of São Roque and King Sebastião, during whose reign it was built. Arcos do Jardim.

JARDIM BOTÂNICO (BOTANICAL GARDEN) These pleasant gardens next to the aqueduct were begun by Prime Minister Marquês de Pombal during the late 18th century, and work on them continued into this century. Laid out on terraces and divided by tree-lined promenades and staircases, they contain trees and plants from all over the world. The terraces lead down to a large square with a lovely fountain; at the top, near the aqueduct, is an interesting fence of intricate 19th-century ironwork.

MUSEU NACIONAL DE MACHADO DE CASTRO (MACHADO DE CASTRO NATIONAL MUSEUM) Named after a major Portuguese sculptor of the 18th century, this is one of the most important museums in the country. It not only contains Portugal's finest collection of sculpture and gold and silver work, but it's housed in the former Paço Episcopal (Bishop's Palace), which is itself a work of art. The official residence of the Bishops of Coimbra from the 12th century until 1910, when it was transformed into a museum, it is constructed around a large courtyard, with a double-arched verandah on one side affording a good view of the river, the houses of the Alta, and the dome of the Sé Velha. Underneath it all, forming the foundation of the palace and part of the museum, is the cryptoportico — a series of vaulted underground passages and galleries built by the Romans beneath their forum, probably to serve as storerooms. One of the most interesting structures of its kind in existence, it holds the museum's collection of Roman sculpture, inscriptions, and other objects found on the spot.

Later sculpture in the museum collection ranges from 14th-century works from the atelier of Master Pero (who also carved the tomb of Queen Isabel in the Convento de Santa Clara-a-Nova) to 16th-century Renaissance art by Jean de Rouen and his followers of the Coimbra school (including an entire chapel by Jean de Rouen and a *Last Supper* by Philippe Houdart), as well as baroque works by Cipriano da Cruz and Claude Laprade. The museum's gold and silver objects, collected from the cathedral's treasury and other churches, cover all periods from the 12th century to the 19th, including articles that belonged to the saintly Queen Isabel. Flemish and Portuguese paintings of the 16th and 17th centuries (Josefa d'Obidos, a famous female painter of the 17th century, is represented), Oriental and Portuguese carpets, furniture, and a vast collection of faïence from the 16th century to the 19th are also on display. Although the museum was closed at press time for renovations (its opening date is uncertain), its new bar with a wonderful view of the city remains open. Call for new hours. Admission charge. Largo Dr. José Rodrigues (phone: 223727).

SÃO JOÃO DE ALMEDINA This church adjoining the museum once served as a chapel for the bishops. Founded during the 12th century, it was reconstructed during the late 17th and early 18th centuries. Its doorway came from an old west bank convent (Sant'Ana) that was virtually swallowed up by the river. Check with the tourist office for hours of operation. Largo Dr. José Rodrigues.

SÉ NOVA (NEW CATHEDRAL) Begun by the Jesuits during the late 16th century and finished during the mid-17th century, this church became Coimbra's cathedral only after the Jesuits were expelled a century later. It is a severe building, both inside and out, yet a forerunner of the baroque style — note that the façade becomes livelier as it ascends, and the top part, finished last, is rococo. Most impressive inside are the intricately carved and gilded baroque main altarpiece and the choir stalls and baptismal font brought from the Old Cathedral. Also of note are the neo-classical organs and the 17th-century altarpiece in the side chapels. Open Mondays and Wednesdays from 4:30 to 6:30 PM; the rest of the week from 9 AM to noon and 2 to 7 PM. Largo da Feira.

SÉ VELHA (OLD CATHEDRAL) Looking much like a fortress, this is considered the finest Romanesque church in Portugal. Its architects were French — Master Builder Robert and Master Builder Bernard — and its first stone was laid in the 12th century, during the reign of Afonso Henriques, Portugal's first king. The building has been modified since, particularly during the 16th century, and was totally restored during the 19th century. The portal in the west façade, decorated with columns, and the gigantic matching window above show signs of Islamic influence. The north façade's main portal was one of the first signs of the Renaissance in Portugal when it was added in 1530; one of the most important works of Jean de Rouen, it has a carved medallion of the Virgin and Child over it.

Inside, the cathedral is dominated by the gilded wood altarpiece at the high altar, a beautiful example of Flemish Gothic executed between 1498 and 1508 by the Flemish sculptors Oliver of Ghent and Jean of Ypres. To the right is the spectacular Capela do Sacramento (Chapel of the Sacrament), by Jean de Rouen. His beautifully sculpted figures are so filled with personality that they appear almost alive. To the left is the Capela do São Pedro, with a retable showing a scene (*Quo Vadis*) attributed to Nicolas Chanterène. The cathedral also contains the tombs of medieval bishops and a Byzantine princess and, via stairs on the south side, a notable Gothic cloister, added during the 13th century. Open from 9 AM to 12:30 PM and 2 to 5 PM; closed Mondays. Admission charge to the cloister. Praça Sé Velha (phone: 25273).

TORRE DE ANTO (ANTO TOWER) This 9th-century tower in the city wall was once the home of the famous 19th-century poet António Nobre. It now houses the nonprofit *Casa de Artesanato da Região de Coimbra* (Coimbra Region House of Handicrafts), displaying and selling a host of local products — ceramics, handwoven rugs, basketwork, wrought-iron objects, woodcarvings, hand embroideries, and starched laces; and sometimes artisans are invited to demonstrate their crafts. Open weekdays from 9 AM to 12:30 PM and from 2 to 5:30 PM. 45 Rua de Sobre-Ripas (phone: 36592).

PALÁCIO DE SOBRE-RIPAS (SUB-RIPAS PALACE) Some of the city wall is incorporated into the lower part of this palace, which dates from the 16th century and now serves as the Archaeological Institute (and is not open to the public). It has a Manueline door and windows, and walls covered with bas-reliefs and busts by Jean de Rouen. Rua de Sobre-Ripas.

CASA DA NAU (SHIP HOUSE) This house in the shape of a ship, built at the time of Portugal's New World discoveries, is now a students' *república*. It is not open to the public, but is worth viewing from the outside. Rua Joaquim António de Aguiar.

ARCO DE ALMEDINA (ALMEDINA ARCH) The Moors built a wall around Coimbra, and this is the only survivor of its three gates (*al-medina* is Arabic for "the city"). It is still the Alta's main entrance and exit, just down the fittingly named "step street," the Escadas de Quebra-Costas (Back Breaker Stairs).

BAIXA

PRAÇA 8 DE MAIO (8TH OF MAY SQUARE) At the southern end of Rua da Sofia, the square is named for the date Coimbra was liberated from the absolutist forces of Dom Miguel during the War of the Two Brothers. The eight streets of the Baixa meet in the square, which is lined with well-preserved 17th- and 18th-century buildings. The Câmara Municipal (Town Hall), housed in a wing of the Mosteiro de Santa Cruz (Holy Cross Monastery), is also in the square, its façade adorned with Coimbra's coat of arms.

IGREJA DE SANTA CRUZ (HOLY CROSS CHURCH) This monastery church is one of the most important monuments in the country, not only because of its historical interest, but also because of the artistic merit of its carvings and tiles. The cornerstone was laid in 1131 under the patronage of Dom Afonso Henriques, Portugal's first king, who is buried here along with his son, Sancho I, the country's second monarch. The church was reconstructed during the 16th century, although traces of the original — by the Frenchman known as Master Builder Robert — can still be seen in the walls near the entrance to the present structure. The Manueline façade that was imposed on the medieval one incorporates statues of the Apostles and churchmen by Nicolas Chanterène and of the Virgin, Isaac, and David by Jean de Rouen.

Inside, the church has a starred dome in its enormous, vaulted ceiling and lovely 18th-century tiles lining the walls. The intricately carved stone pulpit, in a transitional, Gothic-to-Renaissance style, is one of Chanterène's most important works, and he also sculpted the tombs of the two kings behind the main altar — Afonso Henriques on the left and Sancho on the right. The magnificent 17th-century sacristy, inspired by the architecture of the Vatican, is decorated with paintings by some of Portugal's most famous artists, including Grão Vasco. Beyond are the chapter house, with an interesting Manueline door and 16th-century tiles, and the adjoining 16th-century Manueline Claustro do Silêncio (Silent Cloister), with a lovely Renaissance fountain and bas-reliefs attributed to Chanterène around three of its four sides. Open daily from 9 AM to noon and 2 to 5

PM. Admission charge to visit the royal tombs, sacristy, chapter house, and cloister, but not for the church itself. Praça 8 de Maio.

JARDIM DA MANGA (MANGA GARDEN) The garden, behind Santa Cruz and once one of its cloisters, contains a unique Renaissance fountain. Its waters, symbolizing the rivers of Paradise or the word of God spreading to all corners of the world, flow out from a central temple with a pointed dome. (The gargoyles jutting out from the dome represent demons fleeing God's word.) The four chapels surrounding the temple were probably designed by Jean de Rouen, who sculpted the figures in their altarpieces. Rua Olimpio Nicolau Rui Fernandes.

IGREJA DO CARMO (CARMO CHURCH) Part of a theological college founded during the 16th century, this church has a single domed nave with a coffered ceiling, an enormous gilt altarpiece in typical Portuguese style, side chapels with rococo altarpieces, and an adjoining cloister paneled in rococo tiles. The college, one of several along a street whose name means Street of Learning, was at one time one of the most prestigious institutions in the city. Opening times vary according to the mass schedule. Rua da Sofia.

IGREJA DA GRAÇA (GRAÇA CHURCH) Another church founded during the 16th century as part of a school, it has a sober, classical façade. Inside are a high altar in Mannerist style, with carved, gilt frames surrounding panels depicting the life of the Virgin, and side chapels with rococo altarpieces and interesting 17th-century tiles in carpet designs. The cloister is classic Renaissance. Opening times vary according to the mass schedule. Rua da Sofia.

PRAÇA DO COMÉRCIO (COMMERCE SQUARE) Once known as Praça Velha (Old Square), this was the old marketplace where bullfights, *autos-da-fé,* and festivals were held. It is a large rectangle surrounded by shops and 17th- and 18th-century houses with lovely windows. There is a church at each end of the square and, in the center, a reconstructed pillory.

IGREJA DE SÃO TIAGO (ST. JAMES'S CHURCH) People condemned to death by the Inquisition were buried in the cemetery of this early-13th-century church, which has two interesting portals with ornamental molding and intricately carved columns and capitals. The façade was restored during this century. Opening times vary according to the mass schedule. Praça do Comércio.

IGREJA DE SÃO BARTOLOMEU (ST. BARTHOLOMEW'S CHURCH) Probably the oldest church in Coimbra, dating from the 10th century, although the present building was put up during the 18th century; the original church was destroyed by a Moorish invasion, reconstructed during the 12th century, then torn down 6 centuries later to make way for a new one. Archaeological remains can be seen in the floor. The main altar is typical Coimbra rococo. Opening times vary according to the mass schedule. Praça do Comércio.

LARGO DA PORTAGEM The large, busy square by the river, in front of the Santa Clara Bridge, is home to the tourist office. The statue is of Joaquim António de Aguiar, a 19th-century statesman born in Coimbra and known as the Mata Frades (Friar Killer), because he signed the proclamation expelling all religious orders from Portugal.

PARQUE DR. MANUEL BRAGA This park is south of Largo da Portagem, with the river running along one side of it and Avenida Emídio Navarro along the other. Besides the gardens, laid out in patterns resembling the emblem and coats of arms of Coimbra, it has a bandstand in ornate ironwork and, at one end, the *Museu de Transportes Urbanos* (Museum of Urban Transport; phone: 813222), containing a large collection of old streetcars. The museum is open daily from 2 to 5:30 PM; admission charge.

O CHOUPAL By the river at the north end of Coimbra, O Choupal was originally a grove of poplar trees (the translation of its name) planted to protect the riverbanks from floods. Most of the poplars have been cut down, but they've been replaced by eucalyptus, acacia, and other trees — as well as joggers. The park is more than a mile long and occupies the junction of the old and new courses of the Mondego — the two have existed since a plan to control floods was put into practice at the end of the 18th century. Inlets of the river cross it, spanned by wooden bridges. At one time, the Choupal was a place for romance, meditation, and serenades, and though less idyllic today, it is still a pleasant place to stroll.

SANTA CLARA AREA

CONVENTO DE SANTA CLARA-A-VELHA (OLD SANTA CLARA CONVENT) A convent for Clarissa nuns once stood here, but all that remains is a church — and not all of it, since the structure is partially buried in silt. When the convent was completed in 1330, floods from the Mondego were already threatening it, and by the 15th century, water had reached the doors. Finally, in 1677, the nuns moved out to their new convent, Santa Clara-a-Nova, on a nearby hill. Both Queen Isabel, the Rainha Santa (Saintly Queen), who spent the last years of her life here, and Inês de Castro (the mistress of Prince Dom Pedro, King Afonso IV's son), who was murdered nearby, were buried at the convent before their bodies were moved elsewhere, the former to Santa Clara-a-Nova and the latter to the Monastery of Alcobaça, near Nazaré. The old church is a fine example of Gothic architecture, with three very fine rose windows. Rua de Baixo.

PORTUGAL DOS PEQUENITOS (CHILDREN'S PORTUGAL) Interesting for adults, too, this is a wooded park containing reproductions of Portuguese houses from all provinces, of all of Coimbra's monuments, and of the principal monuments found throughout the country and its once far-reaching empire (Goa, Macao, Mozambique, Angola, and Guinea-Bissau). They're built on a small scale for children, most of them about 13 feet tall. Open daily from 9 AM to 7 PM from April through September (to 5:30 PM in winter). Admission charge. Rua António Augusto Gonçalves (phone: 441225).

CONVENTO DE SANTA CLARA-A-NOVA (NEW SANTA CLARA CONVENT) This hillside convent was built during the 17th century — although the cloisters and other buildings were not finished until the 18th century — to keep the Clarissa nuns high and dry as their old convent began to succumb to the continuous flooding of the Mondego. The installation has been likened to a barracks, and in fact, since religious orders were suppressed during the 19th century, most of the convent buildings have been occupied by the army. Only the church and cloister can be visited. The church has a domed, coffered ceiling, sides decorated with ornate false chapels (serving as enormous, intricately carved and gilded frames for portraits), and a sumptuous domed altar flanked with gilded pillars. The remains of Queen Isabel lie in the 17th-century silver-and-crystal urn behind the altar, which is also adorned with a statue of the queen and a bas-relief depicting scenes from her life. The most impressive sight in the church, however, is the magnificent 14th-century tomb, carved from a single block of Ançã stone, that the Saintly Queen had made for herself and in which she was originally buried. Located in the *coro baixo* (lower choir), it rests on six stone lions; pink, gold, and green carved statuettes of saints, Franciscans, Clarissa nuns, and other figures occupy niches on its sides; and on top is a reclining statue of the queen dressed in a nun's habit, complete with a pilgrim's staff and an alms bag such as those used by the pious on a pilgrimage to Santiago de Compostela in Spain. The actual pilgrim's staff that belonged to the queen can be seen in the *coro alto* (raised choir), which is a museum of religious objects and silver; the cloister, dating from the 18th century, is impressive for its size and massive architecture. Open daily from 9 AM to 12:30 PM and 2 to 5:30 PM. Admission charge. Calçada de Santa Isabel.

QUINTA DAS LÁGRIMAS (ESTATE OF TEARS) A 19th-century *palacete* (little palace) stands on the site where Prince Dom Pedro and his beautiful Spanish mistress, Dona Inês de Castro, lived and where their tragic love ended in her murder. Fearing that her powerful brothers in Spain would usurp the Portuguese throne for her illegitimate children, Dom Pedro's father, King Afonso IV, had Inês murdered. In the gardens at the back of the estate a spring gushes from the rocks into a wide pool. Local legend holds that the spring's waters are Dona Inês's tears and that the red spots on the plants growing there are her blood, the yellow ferns her hair. Verses by poet Luís de Camões, who immortalized the love of the unfortunate pair in *The Lusiads,* are carved in stone by the spring in this melancholy and haunted place. Open daily from 9 AM to 6 PM in winter; 9 AM to 8 PM in summer. Admission charge. Off Estrada das Lages; turn left on the road to Lisbon (Av. Inês de Castro) and turn right at the *Quintas das Lagrimas* sign (no phone).

PARQUE DE SANTA CRUZ An 18th-century archway off Praça da República (a gathering place for students, especially in the evening) is the entrance to this park. Beyond are fountains, pools, luxuriant vegetation, and paths lined with fragrant bay trees from Goa. An ornate portico with towers on both sides leads to a game area where, during the 17th and 18th centuries, girls played a ball game called *jogo de pela*. Also notable is the fountain, bedecked with statues of Triton and mermaids, at the top of a tall staircase that has pools and tile-backed stone benches on the landings. Stop for a drink at the terrace facing the park's large lake with a small island. Praça da República.

MOSTEIRO DE CELAS (CELAS MONASTERY) Founded in 1215 by King Sancho I's daughter, this convent was greatly modified later, particularly between the 16th and 18th centuries, and when the last nun died during the late 19th century, it was virtually abandoned. Today, only the church and cloister remain. Inside, the dark oak 16th-century choir stalls and Nicolas Chanterène's cloister door are noteworthy, and the cloister itself is of particular interest: Each of the 13th- and 14th-century capitals on the double pillars supporting the arches is carved with a different story from the lives of Christ and the saints. Open daily from 9:30 AM to 5 PM. Largo de Celas (ring the bell at No. 23 for the caretaker).

IGREJA DE SANTO ANTÓNIO DOS OLIVAIS (CHURCH OF ST. ANTHONY OF THE OLIVE GROVE) This is the only remnant of a Franciscan monastery that was founded during the 13th century and burned down 600 years later. It is named for St. Anthony of Padua, who taught here before going to Italy. Standing on the highest hill above Coimbra, the church, remodeled during the 18th century, is a typical sanctuary reached by a long flight of stairs flanked by chapels and representations of scenes from the Passion of Christ. The interior, covered with tile panels depicting the life of the saint, contains altarpieces from the 18th-century baroque Joanine period, as well as a sacristy richly decorated in gold leaf and finished with a painted, festooned ceiling. In the square at the bottom of the stairs is a small 16th-century chapel containing a Christ on the cross by Jean de Rouen. Open daily from 9:30 AM to 12:30 PM and 2 to 6 PM. Rua Brigadeiro Correia Cardoso.

EXTRA SPECIAL The *Queima das Fitas* (Burning of the Ribbons) is a collective student letting-off-of-steam that goes on for a week at the end of the school term in May and culminates when the fourth-year students burn their class ribbons in chamber pots and put on the wider ones of senior class members (university study in Portugal is 5 years). The celebration begins at midnight on a Thursday with a serenade of *fado* and guitar music on the steps of the Sé Velha. Each day thereafter is dedicated to a different faculty and a different class and ends with a musical evening by the riverside. There are balls, theatrical and sports events, and car races, plus a mock bullfight in Figueira da Foz on Sunday. The most colorful day, however, is Tuesday, when the actual burning of the ribbons takes place and the fourth-year students parade through the streets on top of flower-adorned cars. They are followed by freshmen with painted faces and funny clothes, second-year students in black suits and gowns, and upperclassmen in top hats. Coimbra is very crowded, so anyone planning a visit at this time (the exact week varies according to the school calendar) should make hotel reservations far in advance.

Sources and Resources

TOURIST INFORMATION

The Coimbra Tourist Office (Largo da Portagem, the main square in front of the Santa Clara Bridge; phone: 23886 or 33028) is open weekdays from 9 AM to 7 PM and weekends from 9 AM to 12:30 PM and 2 to 5:30 PM from May through September; weekdays from 9 AM to 6 PM the rest of the year. Staff members offer advice and assistance in English as well as other languages and hand out excellent folders and maps in several languages. They will also make hotel, train, and bus reservations. Multilingual guides are available for about $70 for a half day of sightseeing, about $120 for a full day.

LOCAL COVERAGE The local daily newspaper is the *Diário de Coimbra,* published on Sundays as *Domingo.* The *Jornal do Coimbra* is a weekly. The *International Herald Tribune* is available at newsstands in the better hotels, as are some of the British dailies and English-language news magazines. The newsstand near the *Tivoli* movie theater (Av. Emídio Navarro) is another source of English-language newspapers.

TELEPHONE The city code for Coimbra is 39. If calling from within Portugal, dial 039 before the local number.

GETTING AROUND

Coimbra is best seen on foot or by public transportation. Travel by car is difficult because of the narrow streets, horrendous traffic jams during rush hours, and limited parking space.

AIRPORT The tiny local airport (phone: 947235), at which only small private planes can land, is in Cernache, 5 miles (8 km) southwest of town via the main highway to Lisbon.

BUS Getting around by bus is fast and easy. There are no general maps of the routes, but each bus stop has a map. Among the most useful for tourists are bus No. 1, which goes to the Universidade Velha and the *Museu Nacional Machado de Castro;* No. 3, to the Jardim Botânico and Penedo da Saudade; No. 46, which goes over the river to the Santa Clara area, with the Santa Clara convents and Portugal dos Pequenitos (from which it is a short walk to reach Quinta das Lágrimas); and No. 7, to the Mosteiro de Celas, the Igreja de Santo António dos Olivais, and the camping parks. Tourist passes for 4 days or a week of unlimited travel are available at *Rodoviária* bus company kiosks throughout the city. All city buses leave from Largo da Portagem. For the Roman ruins in Conímbriga (see *Lisbon to Porto* in DIRECTIONS), buses leave from Largo da Portagem weekdays at 9:05 and 9:35 AM; weekends at 9:35 AM. The main bus station for long-distance buses is on Avenida Fernão de Magalhães (phone: 27081).

CAR RENTAL Six major companies operate here: *Hertz* (133 Av. and 221 Av. Fernão de Magalhães; phone: 37491), *Avis* (in the Coimbra A train station, Largo das Ameias; phone: 34786), *Beira Centro* (in the *Oslo Hotel,* 23-25 Av. Fernão de Magalhães; phone: 23664), *Hervis* (94 Rua João Machado; phone: 24062 or 33489), and *Auto Turística Central de Coimbra* (23 Rua Dr. Manuel Rodrigues; phone: 29815).

TAXI Coimbra's metered black-and-green taxis pick up riders anywhere. You can also call for a cab (phone: 28045 or 28049). Rides are inexpensive.

TRAIN There are two railway stations: Coimbra A (phone: 34998), at Largo das Ameias, beside the *Bragança* hotel, and Coimbra B (phone: 34998), beyond Choupal Park at the junction of the Porto and Figueira da Foz highways. Regional trains to Figueira da Foz and Aveiro on the coast and to Luso and other towns in the mountains leave from the A station. Through trains to Lisbon, Aveiro, and Porto leave from the B station. A special fast train — the *Alpha* — connects Coimbra B with Lisbon (2 hours), Aveiro, and Porto. Advance reservations are required.

SPECIAL EVENTS

In addition to the *Queima das Fitas* (see *Extra Special*), the *Festa da Rainha Santa* (Feast of the Saintly Queen) is Coimbra's other big event. This holiday commemorates the beatification of Queen Isabel in 1516 and takes place at the beginning of July in even-numbered years. On a Thursday night, the statue of the saint from the altar of Santa Clara-a-Nova is carried to Largo da Portagem by a procession of penitents; all lights in the city are turned off when it arrives, the better to see the spectacular fireworks display over the river. Another procession returns the statue to the church on Sunday afternoon.

MUSEUMS

In addition to those mentioned in *Special Places,* museums of interest include the following:

MUSEU BISSAYA BARRETO (BISSAYA BARRETO MUSEUM) Beautiful furniture and porcelain in a house once owned by the man who built Portugal dos Pequenitos. Open from 3 to 5 PM; closed Mondays and holidays. Admission charge. Arcos do Jardim (phone: 224868).

MUSEU MILITAR (MILITARY MUSEUM) Weapons, uniforms, and photographs from military actions after 1850, housed in a wing of the New Santa Clara Convent. Open daily from 10 AM to noon and 2 to 5 PM. Admission charge. Convento de Santa-Clara-a-Nova, Calçada de Santa Isabel (phone: 26459).

MUSEU NACIONAL DA CIÊNCIA E DA TÉCNICA (SCIENCE AND TECHNOLOGY MUSEUM) One part is dedicated to the life and works of Madame Curie and another to Leonardo da Vinci. Open weekdays from 10 AM to noon and 2 to 5 PM. Admission charge. 23 Rua dos Coutinhos (phone: 24922).

SHOPPING

Coimbra has beautiful handicrafts, examples of which are exhibited and sold in the *Casa de Artesanato da Região de Coimbra* in the historic Torre de Anto (see *Special Places*). Coimbra faïence, made as far back as the 12th century and revived during the 17th and 18th centuries, is again produced by several factories. The lovely, hand-painted pieces available in local shops run the gamut of local styles — multicolored Hispano-Arabic designs of the 15th century, Oriental designs of the 16th century, Delft-inspired blue and white designs of the 17th century, and pastel flora and fauna designs of the 18th century. Hand-embroidered bedspreads and tablecloths, and wool and linen blankets, are also worth buying, as are examples of traditional Coimbra wrought-iron work, artistic tinware, and basketry, still made in the same way they have been for hundreds of years. Shops also carry some fine leather goods, footwear, and jewelry. Rua Ferreira Borges, which leads north from Largo da Portagem, and Rua Visconde da Luz, its continuation, are the main shopping streets. Stores are open weekdays from 9 AM to 1 PM and 3 to 7 PM; Saturdays from 9 AM to 1 PM. Shopping centers are open daily from 10 AM to midnight. A big open-air market, selling everything from fish to video equipment, takes place daily from 6 AM to 2 PM at the end of Avenida Sá da Bandeira, near the Jardim da Manga. Other stores to explore:

AGATA JOALHARIA Fine jewelry, beautifully mounted at reasonable prices. 2 Escadas de São Tiago (phone: 22361).

CERAMICA DE CONÍMBRIGA Reproductions of old ceramics typical of Coimbra are produced here. On EN1 in Faia-Condeixa (phone: 942254).

CHARLES A large selection of Portuguese-made, fashionable shoes for men and women. 113 Rua Ferreira Borges (phone: 23264).

CRISLEX Home decorations, porcelain, and good crystal. 187 Rua Ferreira Borges (phone: 26801).

JORGE MENDES Some of the finest copies of 15th- to 17th-century porcelains and ceramics in Coimbra. Two locations: 19 Praça do Comércio (phone: 22620) and 9 Praça do Comércio (phone: 25646).

LOJA DAS ARTES MANUAIS A good selection of all regional handicrafts. 1-9 Rua Fernandes Tomás (phone: 33136).

PATRÃO JOALHEIROS One of the oldest and most respected jewelers in Coimbra, offering lovely Portuguese filigree, silver salvers, and silver tea and coffee services. 104 Rua Visconde da Luz (phone: 23096).

RENASÇENÇA A big, upscale shop selling fashionable shoes and other leather goods. 104 Rua Visconde da Luz (phone: 35050).

SPORTS AND FITNESS

BOATING A popular pastime on the Mondego in the summer; pedal boats and kayaks can be rented in the Choupal Park just across the Santa Clara Bridge. For about $25 you can rent a kayak, be paddled 16 miles (25 km) up the river, and spend the day paddling back to Coimbra. Tours leave daily from 10 AM to 3 PM in May through October from Parque Manuel Bragaga by the Santa Clara Bridge (phone: 478385).

SWIMMING The municipal indoor swimming pool is next to the *Estádio Municipal* (on Rua Dom Manuel; phone: 701695). It is open daily from 9 AM to 8:30 PM from July until mid-September; 12:30 to 1:30 PM the rest of the year.

MUSIC

Coimbra's music is the *fado* — haunting, sweet ballads sung to the accompaniment of Coimbra guitars. Unlike Lisbon *fado,* which is sung by men and women, *fado de Coimbra* is sung by men only, and by students, lawyers, doctors, and others, rather than by professional entertainers. Coimbra *fado* grew out of the student custom of singing in the streets at night and serenading Coimbra women; its themes range from unrequited love and homesickness to the city, the river, the university, and social issues. Some songs have become classics, among them the "Balada da Despedida" (Farewell Ballad), sung at graduation by medical students, and the "Balada de Coimbra" (Coimbra Ballad), which closes all serenades, including the beautiful and impressive midnight *serenata* on the steps of the Sé Velha at the opening of the *Queima das Fitas* celebrations. Although Coimbra *fado* is normally sung only at such special celebrations or for private entertainment, it is possible to hear it in two places in the city. One is the *Diligência* (on the narrow Rua Nova, off Rua da Sofia; phone: 27667), a very small, typical local bar, where the singing is spontaneous and often catch-as-catch-can. The other is the *Trovador* restaurant (see *Eating Out*), which presents *fado* on Fridays and is somewhat touristy.

NIGHTCLUBS AND NIGHTLIFE

Neither very lively nor sophisticated, nightlife here tends to center around student activities or nights out with the whole family. There are, however, a number of pubs and discotheques for dancing. The biggest and best dance spot, closed Mondays, is *Broadway* (in suburban Pedrulha, about 2 miles/3 km north of town; phone: 36330). It's not much to look at, but it has its own orchestra that plays fox-trots and Sinatra oldies from 10 PM to midnight; after midnight, the loud disco music takes over. Three others, all closed Sundays, are *Scotch* (Quinta da Insua; phone: 813136), just across the Santa Clara Bridge in a nice old house, with a quiet bar apart from the disco; *States* (Praça Machado Assis; phone: 27067), decorated in red, white, and blue with stars and catering to young people with lots of loud music; and *Coimbra B* (Monte Formoso; phone: 28919), small, but with two separate floors, a bar, and lots of flashing lights.

Quebra Costas (Escadas de Quebra-Costas; phone: 34724) is a small bar on the stairs in front of Praça Sé Velha; in summer, devotees stand on the stairs with their drinks, some with their guitars. *Sacristia* (phone: 24804), at the top of the stairs, is another small bar; it has live music at times, but people mostly just stand around and talk. Other pubs and bars include *Romisch* (102 Rua dos Combatentes; phone: 72172), a piano bar; *Briosa* (Rua Venancio Rodrigues; phone: 29642), decorated to look like an English pub; and *Sing Sing* (11 Rua Castro Matoso; phone: 32433), with an attractive white-and-yellow interior, and good music.

Best in Town

CHECKING IN

Coimbra suffers from a definite dearth of good hotels, although several new hostelries are being built. Those that exist tend to be very old or purely functional. Most are right downtown, which makes them convenient for sightseeing, but noisy. A number of clean, comfortable pensions supplement the pickings. Expect to pay $70 to $90 for a double room with breakfast at a hotel listed as expensive, from $55 to $70 at places in the moderate category, and under $50 at an inexpensive place. Reservations for rooms during July and August, or during the *Queima das Fitas* celebrations in May, should be made at least a month in advance. All telephone numbers are in the 39 city code unless otherwise indicated.

EXPENSIVE

Astoria Built in the 1920s, in the style of that period, this hotel features cupolas, arches, pillars, and wrought-iron balconies. The 64 rooms have baths and telephones; there is a TV salon, a bar, and a restaurant serving typical regional dishes. The hotel is shaped like a triangle to fit between two streets that converge at Largo da Portagem, and is consequently a bit noisy. 21 Av. Emídio Navarro (phone: 22055; fax: 22057).

Coimbra Jardim In the heart of the city, this hostelry offers 100 air conditioned rooms (including 10 suites), all with mini-bars, satellite TV, and telephones. Also on the premises are a restaurant, meeting rooms, and a health club boasting an indoor pool, a sauna, Turkish baths, a gym, and massage service. 4-5 Rua João Machado (phone: 26984; fax: 26827).

Dom Luís This hotel occupies a high hill by the highway to Lisbon, across the river from Coimbra and a little over a mile (2 km) from the center of town. All of the 105 rooms and suites have private baths, telephones, mini-bars, and TV sets. A panoramic restaurant (with good food and service) and a solarium with a terrace on the roof, plus plenty of parking space, help justify the distance. Banhos Secos (phone: 442510; fax: 813196).

MODERATE

Bragança Unpretentious and modern, it's on a busy street by the Coimbra A train station and the river. The 83 rooms, all with baths, are simple and functional. A bar, TV room, private parking lot, and large restaurant serving Portuguese and French food are among the facilities. 10 Largo das Ameias (phone: 22171).

Dona Inês Conveniently located in the center of town, near the train station and Choupal park, this new hotel has 72 rooms and 12 suites with private baths, air conditioning, direct-dial telephones, and satellite TV. Other features include a restaurant, bar, tearoom, and conference rooms. Rua Padre Estevão Cabral (phone: 25791; fax: 25611).

Oslo This simple, small place (30 rooms with private baths) on a busy street in the center of town, not far from the Coimbra A train station, has an upstairs bar and restaurant with a good view. 23-25 Av. Fernão de Magalhães (phone: 29075; fax: 20614).

INEXPENSIVE

Casa Residencial A downtown *pensão* with 13 rooms (4 with private baths) furnished in antiques. There is private parking, but no restaurant. 47 Av. Emídio Navarro, 2nd Floor (phone: 22444).

Residencia Antunes In the Old Town near the university, this *pensão* has 28 rooms, 20 with private baths and telephones, and some with TV sets. No restaurant. 8 Rua Castro Matoso (phone: 23048).

Among the local participants in Portugal's *Turismo no Espaço Rural* (Tourism in the Country) program — privately owned homes, even palaces, that take in paying guests (see *Pousadas and Manor Houses* in DIVER-SIONS) — is the *Casa dos Quintais,* a member of *Turismo Rural* set on a hill overlooking Coimbra about 4 miles (6 km) from downtown. The house, endowed with a swimming pool, has 3 double bedrooms (with private baths) for rent, and is in the moderate price category. To reach it, take the Lisbon highway south and turn left onto N110-2 toward the town of Assafarge. For information contact *Casa dos Quintais,* Carvalhais de Cima, Assafarge, Coimbra 3000 (phone: 438305 or 28821; in Lisbon, 1-670321).

EATING OUT

The food in Coimbra's better restaurants is imaginative and delicious, if a bit heavy for some tastes. Some typical dishes include *chanfana,* kid braised in wine; *lampreia à moda de Coimbra*, lamprey (eel) Coimbra-style; *leitão assado,* roast suckling pig; and the very special *boucho* — ox stomach stuffed with meats, sausages, and herbs and then roasted. Restaurants serving international cooking are also easy to find, as are many snack bars. Meals go down best with the fine, fruity bairrada wines that have been made in the region since the 10th century. They tend to be somewhat tannic when very young, so it's best to drink them aged. Some names to look for are Frei João, Caves Aliança, Souselas, Porta Férrea, Angelus, and Fundação. Also try some of the sweets made from old convent recipes. As elsewhere in Portugal, when religious orders were suppressed during the 19th century, the nuns turned to baking in order to support themselves, and many of the confections still eaten today take their names from their convent of origin, such as *pastel de Santa Clara,* made of sugar, eggs, and almonds. Some other favorites are *arrufadas,* arc-shaped puff cakes, and *chilas,* made of squash. Expect to pay $70 or more for a meal for two with wine and coffee at a restaurant listed as expensive, from $35 to $40 at a moderate place, and about $25 at an inexpensive one. Note that Coimbra's restaurants tend to be packed with families on Sundays. All telephone numbers are in the 39 city code unless otherwise indicated.

EXPENSIVE

Dom Pedro Decorated in classic Portuguese style, with interesting tiles on the walls and a fountain splashing in the middle of the room, this place serves well-prepared Portuguese and international dishes. Open daily. Reservations necessary. Major credit cards accepted. 58 Av. Emídio Navarro (phone: 29108).

Espelho d'Agua An elegant, refined restaurant in a beautiful setting — it's in the middle of a garden, with a lovely, glass-enclosed terrace. Excellent Portuguese dinners are served — by candlelight in the evening. Open daily. Reservations necessary. Major credit cards accepted. Parque Dr. Manuel Braga (phone: 20634).

Piscinas Although this place is over the municipal swimming pool, don't judge it by the unprepossessing exterior. It has some of the best regional cooking in the city — the *chanfana* and *boucho* are delicious. Closed Mondays. Reservations essential on weekends. Major credit cards accepted. Piscinas Municipais, Rua Dom Manuel (phone: 717013).

Trovador Probably the best dining place in town (or at least the most expensive). The ambience is elegant, the service excellent, the Portuguese and international fare very good. Near the Sé Velha, so it's a good place to dine after sightseeing. On Fridays there is *fado* music, and it's possible to drop in after 10 PM and listen to it over a drink. Closed Mondays. Reservations essential. Major credit cards accepted. 15-17 Praça Sé Velha (phone: 25475).

MODERATE

O Alfredo Always full of people and noise, this restaurant across the river serves good Portuguese food. Open daily. Reservations advised. Major credit cards accepted. 32 Av. João das Regras (phone: 441522).

Crep's Grill Pierrot Variety reigns here — pizza, plus French, American, and Italian food. The decor is simple (pine furniture and blue sofas); there is a snack bar downstairs. Open daily. No reservations. Major credit cards accepted. 25 Praça da República (phone: 33569).

Jardim da Manga A self-service eatery offering regional fare, but its location allows for dining in the beautiful gardens for which it is named. Closed Saturdays. No reservations. No credit cards accepted. Rua Olimpio Nicolau Rui Fernandes (phone: 29156).

Joaquim dos Leitões Roast suckling pig, as well as other dishes typical of the area, are served here. The dining room is decorated in regional style, its walls covered with tiles. Closed Sundays. Reservations advised. No credit cards accepted. 3 Rua do Arnado (phone: 33935).

Lanterna This large eatery occupying 2 floors in the Old Town serves good Portuguese and international fare. Open daily. Reservations advised. Major credit cards accepted. 6-7 Largo da Sota (phone: 26729).

Real das Canas Under the same management as *Piscinas* (see above), it's across the river in the Santa Clara area. The decor is simple, but the view of Coimbra from its windows is spectacular, and it serves good Portuguese food. Closed Wednesdays. Reservations advised. Major credit cards accepted. Vila Mendes, Santa Clara (phone: 814877).

A Taberna Very cozy, with a fireplace, it serves good Portuguese food in the main dining room and pizza in the restaurant downstairs. Closed Saturdays. Reservations advised. Major credit cards accepted. 86 Rua dos Combatentes (phone: 716265).

O Verde Minho In the eastern part of town, 10 minutes by car from the city center. Good Portuguese food, and some special French and African dishes, are served in a cozy atmosphere. Closed Mondays. Reservations advised. No credit cards accepted. Casal do Lobo, Mata do Vale de Canas (phone: 718163).

INEXPENSIVE

Calado e Calado A typical, roomy Portuguese eatery with a large and varied menu, specializing in regional fare, with such local favorites as kid in a casserole and rice with shellfish. Closed Sundays. No reservations. No credit cards accepted. 14 Rua da Sota (phone: 27348).

Evora

One of the oldest cities on the Iberian Peninsula, Evora is the Alto Alentejo's traditional capital, the capital of the Evora district, a "museum town," and a work of art all rolled into one. With its cobbled streets, dazzling whitewash, and splashes of southern color, Evora is in many respects the quintessential Alentejo town. For any connoisseur of Portugal's relatively untrodden south, that is recommendation enough. But Evora has another dimension: It stands out for its exceptionally large heritage of well-preserved historical buildings, over 30 of which are classified as national monuments.

Evora's earliest origins are lost in time, but all the archaeological clues indicate a city of extreme antiquity. It was already a fortified town of some importance when the Romans captured it from the Lusitanians during the 2nd century BC. Within a couple of centuries, it had become a prosperous imperial outpost, a *municipium* with the right to mint coins and a population that enjoyed most of the privileges of Roman citizenship. Just as it is today, Evora was a center of agriculture during the Roman era, noted for grain production. Pliny the Elder, who for a while held an official post in the region, referred to it, in his *Natural History,* as Ebora Cerealis.

At the beginning of the 5th century, as the Roman Empire crumbled, the city came under Visigothic rule. Then, in 713, it lay in the path of the Muslims sweeping up from North Africa and across the Iberian Peninsula. Under them, Evora grew considerably in military, economic, and cultural importance, so that the city described by the Moorish geographer Idrisi in 1154 is not much different — apart from its size — from the modern one. Evora, he said, is "large and populous, surrounded by walls, and with a strong castle and a mosque. The surrounding territory is of a singular fertility, producing cattle and all kinds of vegetables and fruit."

More than 400 years of Islam left an indelible imprint on the city's architecture and personality, but its most famous legend stems from the time of its recapture by the Christians. Several attempts had been made to win Evora back from the Moors, all of them unsuccessful or, like an assault in 1159, only briefly successful. Then, in October 1165, a Christian warrior chief called Geraldo Sem Pavor (Gerald the Fearless) scaled the walls under cover of darkness by driving lances into spaces in the masonry and using them as a ladder. After killing the surprised sentinels, Geraldo let in his men, took the castle, and conquered Evora. He presented his valuable prize to Portugal's first king, Afonso Henriques, who was engaged at the time in driving the Moors from the Alentejo, and in recognition of his feat was appointed *alcaide,* or governor.

Throughout the Middle Ages and the Renaissance, Evora grew steadily in importance and wealth. Already an occasional seat of the early kings of the House of Burgundy, it became one of the main royal residences after the succession of the Avis dynasty in 1385. In 1481, with Portugal poised on the threshold of its golden era of maritime expansion, Evora was the scene of an incident that was to be decisive in the evolution of the nation. After a long period of fractious struggle with the nobility, King João II put down a conspiracy against him and executed its leader, his ambitious brother-in-law, the Duke of Bragança. The square where Bragança was beheaded, now the Praça do Giraldo, was later the arena where heretics and other victims were burned during the Inquisition, one of the skeletons in Evora's historical closet.

In 1637, during the unpopular Spanish monarchy, another grass-roots revolt — the so-called Manuelinho uprising — convulsed Evora and sent shock waves rippling throughout the kingdom. For 5 days, the townspeople ransacked the houses of the Castilian-appointed officials they hated and burned their belongings in a huge bonfire in the main square. This was the first major rebellion in Portugal against the Spanish domination, and just as Evora's ire had been instrumental 250 years earlier in bringing about a change in command, so it was again. Three years later, the Spanish monarchy was ousted and independence from Spain was permanently secured.

In 1808, during the Peninsular War, Evora was sacked by the French; many buildings were damaged and a number of works of art lost forever. Then a long period of provincial somnolence ensued, from which Evora seemed to awaken only in 1974, with the April 25 revolution that paved the way for a return to democracy in Portugal. The city became the center of the agrarian reform movement in which the Communist party made a partially successful attempt to create an alternative to the Alentejo's residual feudalism. In addition, the university, founded in 1595 and one of the oldest in Europe, was reopened (it had been closed in 1795 by the Marquês de Pombal, Portugal's autocratic prime minister). Attention was paid to promoting the arts and preserving the city's architectural heritage, festivals were organized, and social services and infrastructure were improved. In short, Evora moved into the 20th century.

In addition to Evora's historic and artistic credentials, the art of restaurant cooking has progressed rapidly here in recent years — there is no better place than this once-provincial town to sample good Alentejo cuisine. And hotel accommodations are good and remarkably varied for a city with a population of slightly more than 50,000, making Evora an ideal stop for the traveler.

Evora At-a-Glance

SEEING THE CITY

Early drawings show Evora rising out of the flat Alentejo landscape with the uncluttered simplicity of a child's sandcastle on a beach. Making some allowance for the inevitable urban sprawl, that image is remarkably like the view of the city seen today from the top of the Alto de São Bento, a 1,094-foot hill 2 miles (3 km) out of town on the road to Arraiolos. From this vantage point, the three towers of the cathedral dominate the skyline, and it is apparent that Evora still remains tightly enclosed by its nearly unbroken girdle of 14th-century walls. Legend has it that Evora's Christian reconqueror, Gerald the Fearless, had his castle here on the São Bento hill, but what stands here today is the 13th-century Convento de São Bento de Castris, which is thought to be the first convent founded in Portugal. It has a fine 16th-century cloister, which unfortunately is not normally open to visitors (but you can try ringing the bell). Follow the little road past the convent up to the three ruined windmills for the view.

SPECIAL PLACES

Like all Alentejo towns, Evora is built on a hill. The cathedral occupies the highest point, and the rest of the Old City spreads out from it down to the encircling walls. The cathedral is thus a perfect reference point. It is nearly always visible if you crane your neck a bit, and practically everything there is to see lies within easy strolling distance of it. The old walled city — the "historical nucleus," as it is sometimes called — is divided into three sections: the Judiaria (Jewish Quarter), the Mouraria (Moorish Quarter), and the Zona Residencial dos Nobres (Quarter of the Nobles). Given the small size of Evora, however, it is easier to divide it into two simple parts: inside the walls and outside. In addition to nearly all the sights, the most worthwhile shops and restaurants are within the inner city.

Besides the sights listed below, several prehistoric sites in the vicinity are worth a short excursion. The Alto Alentejo region was a center of the megalithic culture that flourished on the Iberian Peninsula between 4000 and 2000 BC, and there are a number of imposing dolmens and menhirs within easy reach. The tourist office publishes a folder giving the principal sites and their locations. The cromlechs, or religious circles, at Almendres and Xarez are particularly impressive.

IN THE CITY

TEMPLO ROMANO (ROMAN TEMPLE) This structure is something of a trademark for Evora, and with good reason. It wears its age so gracefully that it looks as if it had been built just as it is for a Romantic 19th-century stage set. Popularly called the Temple of Diana — although it was probably not dedicated to Diana at all — it is Evora's oldest surviving building, dating from the 2nd or 3rd century. It is also one of the best-preserved Roman temples on the Iberian Peninsula, largely because it was bricked up in the Middle Ages and subsequently used as a storehouse. This practical use may have been inappropriate for such an elegant building, but it saved the structure from almost certain destruction. When the protective shell of bricks and rubble was removed in 1871, 14 of the 26 Corinthian columns that originally formed the peristyle were still standing. Twelve of the granite columns still have their Estremoz marble capitals. A large piece of the architrave remains in place, along with fragments of a frieze, but the rest has disappeared, perhaps incorporated into later structures in the area. Largo Conde de Vila Flor.

CERCA VELHA (OLD WALLS) The upper part of the city where the Roman temple stands is Evora's acropolis. It was once dominated by an old castle (the one that Gerald the Fearless took and that the angry populace of Evora largely destroyed in 1383–84), and was circled by Roman and Visigothic walls with a circumference of about 3,545 feet. Most of the old wall has disappeared, but some interesting fragments remain, including two of the five original gates: the Arco de Dona Isabel, a Roman archway opening onto Largo Alexandre Herculano, a block west of the Roman temple; and the twin towers that stand in Largo das Portas de Moura, on the southern side of the old perimeter. Bits of the old wall also can be seen incorporated into the façades of two palaces (neither is open to the public) in the former acropolis area: the Palácio dos Duques de Cadaval, across the square from the Roman temple, and the Solar dos Condes de Basto, behind the cathedral and near the old university.

PALÁCIO DOS DUQUES DE CADAVAL (PALACE OF THE DUKES OF CADAVAL) This rather severe, mainly 16th-century building, with two sturdy rectangular towers topped by Moorish-style battlements, was the palace of the Melo family, one of Portugal's oldest noble families. It includes part of a northwest section of the old castle, which King João I awarded to Martim Afonso de Melo in 1390 for his prowess in the Battle of Aljubarrota. The Duke of Bragança was held in the south tower before his execution by João II in 1484. Largo Conde de Vila Flor.

SOLAR DOS CONDES DE BASTO (MANOR HOUSE OF THE COUNTS OF BASTO) Originally a Moorish castle, this *solar* is one of Evora's oldest noble residences. It was given to the monks of the order of São Bento de Calatrava by King Afonso Henriques in 1167, after the city's reconquest from the Moors; it became crown property during the 13th century, and thereafter served as a royal residence on several occasions. It's now mainly a 15th- and 16th-century structure, but the base of the outer wall on the north side, facing Largo dos Colegiais, incorporates part of Evora's old wall. Largo dos Colegiais.

SÉ (CATHEDRAL) This very imposing church, dating from the 12th and 13th centuries, is one of Evora's most interesting buildings. Its plan is Romanesque, but in its structure and decorations, the building that rose was Gothic, and additions made up to the 18th century left it with a mixture of styles. On several occasions the cathedral has lived up to its fortress-like appearance. It was from the terraces of this building that the townspeople supporting monarchy for João of Avis in the late 14th century launched an incendiary assault on the old castle held by the unwanted regent, Queen

Leonor. And it was in the cathedral's great naves that the townspeople took refuge during the height of the killing when the French were sacking the city during the early 19th century.

Part of the massive Romanesque-Gothic façade dates from the 12th century, but the two oddly dissimilar towers flanking the deeply recessed Gothic portal — one topped with a tile-covered cone, the other with a series of turrets — are from the 16th century. The Apostles standing guard on either side of the church entrance are 14th-century works, probably southern Portugal's first notable pieces of Christian sculpture. Inside, the three naves are the longest in Portugal. They are early Gothic (though the tasteless white pointing applied to the granite columns is modern), but the side chapels and transept date from the 16th century, and the splendid neo-classical chancel and high altar at the end are from the 18th century, designed by Johann Friedrich Ludwig, the German architect of the great monastery-palace at Mafra. The little polychrome stone statue of the Virgin set in a carved baroque altar at the beginning of the central nave is a 12th-century representation of Our Lady of O, the pregnant Virgin. Be sure to climb the stairs to the *coro alto* (above the west end of the central nave). The 16th-century carved wooden stalls are worth the effort: Panels behind the seats are full of vivid secular scenes of day-to-day country life in the Alentejo, as well as biblical scenes.

The early-14th-century cloister on the south side of the church is a magnificent example of the austere beauties of Evora's transitional Gothic. Its founder, a 14th-century bishop, lies in the carved marble sepulcher in a chapel in the cloister's southeast corner. The cathedral is open daily from 9 AM to noon and 2 to 5 PM. Admission charge to the cloister. Largo da Sé.

MUSEU DE ARTE SACRA (MUSEUM OF SACRED ART) The collection, installed in the cathedral's south tower, contains fine ecclesiastical paintings, sculpture, vestments, gold, silver, and furniture. The ivory and polychrome stone figures of the 14th and 15th centuries are especially interesting — above all, the rare little ivory statue of the Virgin holding the infant Jesus, which opens up to form a triptych decorated with high-relief scenes from her life. The original head of this nearly unique figure is missing; the present wooden one dates from the 16th century. Open from 9 AM to noon and 2 to 5 PM; closed Mondays. Admission charge. Largo da Sé (phone: 26910).

MUSEU DE EVORA (EVORA MUSEUM) In the former Bishop's Palace, a 16th-to-early-18th-century building next door to the cathedral and facing the Temple of Diana, this museum has an extremely interesting collection of archaeological pieces, paintings, and sculpture. Among several fine works is the series of 13 paintings on the life of the Virgin that once graced the high altar of the cathedral; an anonymous 14th-century Flemish work from the Bruges school, the series alone makes a visit worthwhile. Another work not to be missed is the little 16th-century Limoges enamel triptych of the Crucifixion that was recently restored. The museum's archaeological section contains several exquisite fragments from Evora's antiquity. The 3rd-century marble relief of a maenad, her skirt twirling around her as she dances wildly, is particularly haunting. Open from 9 AM to noon and 2 to 5 PM; closed Mondays. Admission charge. Largo Conde de Vila Flor (phone: 22604).

BIBLIOTECA PÚBLICA (PUBLIC LIBRARY) Just across from the *Museu de Evora,* this is one of Portugal's outstanding libraries, with more than 500,000 manuscripts and 250,000 printed works, including a rare-book section containing over 500 incunabula (books printed before 1501), among other priceless early works. The collection is particularly noted for its codices connected with Portugal's maritime feats of the 15th and 16th centuries. Except for occasional exhibitions, the library's treasures are not on display. Visitors who wish to consult books must show their passports or other credentials to get a reader's card; the process normally takes 24 hours. Open weekdays from 9 AM to 12:30 PM and 2 to 8 PM. Largo Conde de Vila Flor (phone: 22369).

IGREJA E CONVENTO DOS LÓIOS (LÓIOS CHURCH AND MONASTERY) The monastery building has become a state-owned inn, or *pousada* (see *Checking In*), but the church, although privately owned, is open to the public. Dedicated to São João Evangelista (St. John the Evangelist), it was built in Gothic style between 1485 and 1491, but the main façade, with the exception of the Flamboyant portal, was rebuilt after the 1755 earthquake that destroyed Lisbon (and damaged several buildings in Evora). The single Gothic nave is lined with 18th-century *azulejos* (glazed tiles) depicting the life of St. Lawrence Justinian (a 15th-century patriarch of Venice). The church was founded by the nobleman Rodrigo Afonso de Melo to be his family's mausoleum. The chapterhouse belonging to the church has a particularly beautiful and curious doorway, with Manueline columns supporting two Moorish arches. Open daily from 9 AM to noon and 2 to 5 PM. Largo Conde de Vila Flor.

UNIVERSIDADE DO ESPÍRITO SANTO (UNIVERSITY OF THE HOLY GHOST) At the bottom of the hill, east of the cathedral, the Universidade was founded by Cardinal Henrique for the Jesuits in 1559. The classical-baroque building is a notable piece of architecture with an especially handsome cloister, and it is profusely decorated with 16th-, 17th-, and 18th-century tiles. The university closed in 1759 when the Jesuits were expelled from Portugal by Prime Minister Marquês de Pombal; it reopened in 1975. There are no regular visiting hours, but most parts of the building can be seen upon request. Largo do Cardeal Rei (phone: 25572).

LARGO DAS PORTAS DE MOURA This small, picturesque square is a few blocks south of the university (walk along Rua do Conde da Serra da Tourega, following, more or less, the line of the old Roman wall). The two square towers on its north side mark the site of the south gate through the old wall. The Renaissance fountain in the center, built with funds donated by the people of the neighborhood and by Dom Jaime, Duke of Bragança, was inaugurated with festivities on November 4, 1556. On the square's south side is the verandah of the 16th-century Casa Cordovil. Six slender columns support Moorish arches and a little conical dome, forming a structure that conveys the essence of Evora's mixed cultural history.

IGREJA NOSSA SENHORA DA GRAÇA (CHURCH OF OUR LADY OF GRACE) The magnificent façade of this semi-ruined 16th-century church, one of the most striking examples of Renaissance architecture on the Iberian Peninsula, inevitably invites comparison with the architecture of Michelangelo because of its dramatic composition of triangles, circles, and columns. It was almost certainly designed by Diogo de Torralva, the architect of the Claustro dos Filipes in Tomar. The four heroically muscular but rather graceless figures supporting the spheres on the corners of the façade actually symbolize the four rivers of faith, but local people call them, ironically, the *meninos da Graça,* the children of Grace. The vault of the church collapsed in 1884, and most of the contents were taken to other churches, including the Igreja de São Francisco (see below). The adjacent convent building is now occupied by the military. Opening times vary according to the mass schedule. Rua da Graça.

IGREJA DE SÃO FRANCISCO (CHURCH OF ST. FRANCIS) This 16th-century Moorish-Gothic church, about 2 blocks west of Nossa Senhora da Graça, has several outstanding architectural features, including a Gothic vault of unusual proportions over the single nave. But what everybody remembers it for is its curious Capela dos Ossos (Chapel of Bones). The walls of this macabre room are lined with bones and skulls laid out in intricate and sometimes ingenious patterns. The intention was to induce contemplation and instill a proper sense of mortality in the spirit of any Franciscan monk who might feel tempted toward frivolity. "We bones lie waiting here for yours," warns the Latin inscription over the door. The two mummified corpses hanging at the end of the chapel are said to be father and son, victims of an embittered wife's deathbed curse. (The woman's rather unusual malediction was that the flesh should never fall from their bones.) The chapel is open daily from 9 AM to 12:30 PM and 2:30 to 6 PM. Admission charge to the chapel. Praça Primeiro de Maio.

JARDIM PÚBLICO (PUBLIC GARDEN) Just south of São Francisco church, these charming gardens are enclosed by a section of the city wall. In the center is a fine old wrought-iron bandstand, where concerts are given in summer.

PRAÇA DO GIRALDO A short walk up Rua da República leads to this square, named after the city's Christian liberator. It has been the geographic center and focal point of life in Evora since its beginnings as the forum of the

Roman city. Until 1570, a triumphal arch stood at its northern end, where the parish Igreja de Santo Antão stands today. The Renaissance fountain in front of the church was built in 1571 (and paid for by the Cardinal-King Dom Henrique, the founder of the university), to replace an earlier one that was demolished along with the triumphal arch. The white marble benches ringing the fountain were placed there in 1970.

IGREJA DE SANTO ANTÃO (CHURCH OF ST. ANTÃO) This rather sober church, built during the 16th century by the local architect Manuel Pires, is worth a look inside. It has some fine carved and polychromed altars and, on the front of the high altar, a very rare low-relief marble panel of the Apostles, dating from the 14th century. The piece was saved from the Templars Church of Santo Antoninho, the predecessor of the present church. Opening times vary according to the mass schedule. Praça do Giraldo.

CERCA NOVA (NEW WALLS) The approximately 9,840 feet of so-called new walls that once girdled the city are still nearly intact today, although much restored. The new walls were begun during the first half of the 14th century, in the reign of King Afonso IV, and were finished between 1384 and 1433, during the reign of King João I. Originally, there were 40 towers and 10 gates, but most of these have long since fallen prey to time and to cannibalization by stone-hungry builders. One that still remains much as it was during the 14th century is the tower guarding the Porta de Alconchel (Alconchel Gate), at the bottom of Rua Serpa Pinto. A good road, the Estrada da Circunvalação, follows the path of the walls all the way around the city.

OUTSIDE THE WALLS

ERMIDA DE SÃO BRÁS (CHAPEL OF ST. BLAISE) Built during the late 15th century, this is an excellent early example of the battlemented church that is so characteristic of the Alentejo region. Fourteen cylindrical buttress-turrets give the little building its unique, bellicose aspect. Inside, the green-and-white diamond-pattern tiles covering the barrel vault over the nave are from the 16th century. Open daily from 9 AM to noon and 2 to 5 PM. Rua da República.

AQUEDUTO DA PRATA (PRATA AQUEDUCT) This outstanding work of engineering was built between 1532 and 1537, during the reign of King João III, to bring water from a spring at Graça do Divor, 11 miles (18 km) away. It cost quite literally a king's fortune at the time, but Evora has always suffered a shortage of water, and King João's court spent a lot of time in the city. The road around the city walls passes under the aqueduct at the point where it enters Evora, but the most monumental section lies between the walls and São Bento de Castris, 2 miles (3 km) away on the road to Arraiolos.

| EXTRA SPECIAL | Wander through the narrow streets and alleys of the Old City with a dictionary in hand, and you will discover wonderfully sonorous and evocative street names everywhere. Some commemorate local "celebrities" or simply local "characters" — Rua do Malbarbado (Street of the Unshaven One), Rua do Matamouros (Street of the Bully), Rua do Alfaiate da Condessa (Street of the Countesses' Tailor), and Rua da Ama do Cardeal (Street of the Cardinal's Maid). Residence near, or ownership of, an olive grove may have commended Manuel to posterity (Rua Manuel do Olival), and Master Resende de Alvaro (Rua Mestre Resende de Alvaro) may have won renown as a teacher, but the reasons for the immortalization of Beatriz de Vilhena (Rua Beatriz de Vilhena), the Cogominhos family (Travessa dos Cogominhos), or even the Dark Ladies (Rua das Morenas) are less obvious and probably long forgotten. Other names refer to features of the streetscape: Rua da Cozinha de Sua Alteza (Street of His Highnesses' Kitchen); Rua das Pedras Negras (Street of the Black Stones), an old street name often found in southern Portugal and Spain; and Rua das Casas Pintadas (Street of the Painted Houses), where Vasco da Gama's house is located — it has rooms decorated with frescoes of exotic wildlife (but is not open to the public). Some of the names may require a knowledge of Portuguese to appreciate their full flavor, but for beginners, this is a good way to pick up a little of the language, even if some of it is a bit archaic.

Sources and Resources

TOURIST INFORMATION

The Town Hall Tourism Department has an information office (73-74 Praça do Giraldo; phone: 22671) with an English-speaking staff. It is open daily from 9 AM to 7 PM from April through September; 9 AM to 12:30 PM and 2 to 5:30 PM the rest of the year. Guides can be hired by writing in advance to *Evora City Tours* (8 Rua da Corredoura, Evora 7000; phone and fax: 23616). This company can also arrange jeep safaris, hunting and fishing trips, and even hot-air balloon flights over the city and into the surrounding countryside.

LOCAL COVERAGE The daily *Diário do Sul* and the weekly *Notícias de Evora* are the leading regional newspapers. English-language newspapers such as the *International Herald Tribune* can be bought at *Tabacaria Genesis,* a tobacco and stationery shop (150 Rua João de Deus; phone: 22677). The *Guide to the Megalithic Monuments of the Evora Region* is a useful, English-language, illustrated guide to Evora's prehistoric sites; it is available at the tourist office.

TELEPHONE The city code for Evora is 66. If calling from within Portugal, dial 066 before the local number.

GETTING AROUND

The best way to see Evora is to walk. It is a small city, distances between places of interest are never very great, and the narrow streets make driving difficult, if not impossible, in the Old City. Parking spaces can usually be found in the squares, for those who do decide to drive across town.

AIRPORT The closest commercial airport is Lisbon's Portela de Sacavém (phone: 1-802060), about 93 miles (149 km) away. The nearby tiny airport in Campo de Aviação (phone: 22263) is for small private charters.

BUS The inner-city bus service is of limited use to the visitor, but the *Rodoviária do Alentejo* bus company has daily departures to Lisbon and points south. The buses are quite comfortable and inexpensive. Tickets should be bought in advance at the bus station (131 Largo da República; phone: 22121), or from *RN Tours–Viagens e Turismo,* a travel agency (131 Rua da República; phone: 24254).

CAR RENTAL *Hertz* is at 7 Rua Dona Isabel (phone: 21767).

TAXI Taxis are fairly plentiful. The best places to find one are the city cabstands, especially the centrally located ones at Praça do Giraldo, Largo das Portas de Moura, and Largo Luís de Camões. You also can call for a cab (phone: 32220 or 32222). Taxis can be hired by the kilometer for tours in the surrounding area.

TRAIN The station (phone: 22125) is a little over a half-mile south of the city. There are two or three trains a day to Lisbon (the trip takes about 3 hours) and also connections to Spain, the Lower Alentejo, and the Algarve. Those going to Lisbon should remember that trains do not cross the Tagus River. (The train takes passengers as far as Barreiro, on the south bank of the Tagus, where they ferry across to the river station on Lisbon's Praça do Comércio; the price of the ferry ride is included in the train ticket.)

SPECIAL EVENTS

Every second Tuesday of the month — June excepted — a market is held in the Rossio de São Brás outside the walls. These monthly markets are important events in all Portuguese country towns, and Evora's is especially so because it is held in a district capital. But Evora's biggest market gathering is the *Feira de São João* (St. John's Fair), held annually during the last 2 weeks of June. This major event is an enjoyable combination of country market, agricultural fair, and folk festival, and it draws huge crowds from all over the district. Open stalls sell everything from handicrafts to hair restorer, there is folk dancing and singing, and improvised restaurants serve tasty local dishes.

MUSEUMS

Evora's major museums are discussed in *Special Places*. In addition, the following may be of interest:

MUSEU DE ARTE SACRA (SACRED ART MUSEUM) Not to be confused with the *Museu de Arte Sacra* in the cathedral, this museum of religious art is a branch of the *Museu de Evora;* it's located in the Igreja das Mercês (Church of Mercy). Open from 9 AM to noon and 2 to 5 PM; closed Mondays. No admission charge. Rua do Raimundo (phone: 22604).

JOÃO CUTILEIRO Just outside the city walls, the studio of Evora's internationally known sculptor can be visited by appointment; his works can be purchased or commissioned. 13 Estrada de Viana do Alentejo (phone: 23972).

SHOPPING

This is the sort of provincial city whose inhabitants would probably do their shopping in Lisbon if they could. The local stores are fine for run-of-the-mill household needs; for travelers, the best buys are handicrafts. The main shopping areas are Praça do Giraldo and its side streets, as well as the arcades that run the length of the east side of Praça do Giraldo and continue down Rua João de Deus to Largo Luís de Camões. Most of the best regional handicraft shops are on Rua 5 de Outubro, the street that goes from the cathedral to Praça do Giraldo. The *Centro Comercial Eborim,* a modern shopping center (Rua Eborim; phone: 22260), has practically everything under one roof. The *Mercado Municipal* (Municipal Market; Praça Primeiro de Maio), open every morning except Mondays, is not only the best place for fresh food and delicacies such as the excellent local cheeses and cured sausages, but also a colorful place to visit. Handicrafts, including good, brown-glazed oven pots, are sold from stalls outside, along with the omnipresent plastic goods. Three handicraft shops worth noting:

CASA SILVA One of the best sources for the increasingly rare painted *alentejano* furniture. 11 Rua do Cano (phone: 23456).

CONDESTAVEL The famous Arraiolos woolen carpets in many designs. 66 Rua 5 de Outubro (phone: 42219).

TEOARTIS Hand-painted tiles, original or reproductions, made to order and available from stock. 78 Rua 5 de Outubro (phone: 22736).

SPORTS AND FITNESS

BULLFIGHTING The *Praça de Touros* is just outside the walls, along the Estrada da Circunvalação. Several bullfights are held during the season, which runs from May to sometime in October, but programming is irregular. Check with the tourist office:

SOCCER The two local teams are not major league, but they have strong support, and, as everywhere in Portugal, soccer is the top spectator sport. The season begins in September and ends in May. Games are played on Sundays in the *Estádio Sanches de Miranda* just outside town (phone: 22200).

SWIMMING An excellent complex of five *piscinas municipais* (municipal swimming pools) is set among lawns on the edge of town, 1¼ miles (2 km) from the city center. The facilities include an Olympic-size pool, a diving pool, a learners' pool, and two pools for children, plus two restaurants and a bar. The complex (phone: 32324) is open daily from 9 AM to 8 PM (1 to 8 PM on Mondays, to allow for cleaning).

TENNIS Good clay courts can be rented at either of two sports clubs: *Lusitano Ginásio Clube* (Estrada das Alcaçovas; phone: 22844) and *Juventudes Sport Clube (Estádio Sanches de Miranda;* phone: 22200). Bring your own gear.

THEATER

The *Teatro Garcia de Resende* (Praça Joaquim António de Aguiar; phone: 23112) is the biggest theater in the south of Portugal — the only one for miles around, in fact. It was built between 1881 and 1892 and reserved rather snootily for opera, recitals, and concerts only, but it was not a great success. In 1975 the theater was handed over to the Centro Cultural de Evora, which since then has operated a theater school in it. Check with the tourist office for possible shows and concerts.

MUSIC

The Câmara Municipal (Town Hall) sponsors classical music, jazz, and pop concerts, but there is no regular program. Check with the tourist office for upcoming events. Concerts take place in the *Teatro Garcia de Resende* (see above) and in other venues such as the Palácio de Dom Manuel, or even in old houses. Brass-band concerts are held in the Jardim Público in summer. Visitors interested in music should also ask the tourist office about the possibility of taking in a performance of *cantares alentejanos* (Alentejo songs). *Cantares* are folk songs of remote origin, sung (chanted might be a better word) by groups of men. The singers stand together in a tight group or sometimes march along slowly, swaying in unison as they sing. The *Feira de São João* (see *Special Events*) is a good occasion to hear them.

NIGHTCLUBS AND NIGHTLIFE

Evora is the perfect place to enjoy the benefits of early nights without feeling like an old fogey. It has virtually no nightlife, other than a few discotheques or the innocent pleasures of sitting on a café terrace or strolling through the town looking at the lighted monuments. Among the most popular discos are *Brown's* (54 Rua Serpa Pinto; phone: 20545) and *Slide* (135 Rua Serpa Pinto; phone: 28272).

Best in Town

CHECKING IN

Accommodations are limited in quantity, but they range fairly widely in style, from luxury to plain, comfortable economy. At the expensive end of the scale — and there is only one luxury establishment in Evora — expect to pay from $110 to $150, depending on whether it is high season or low, for a double room with breakfast. In the moderate range, expect to pay from $55 to $100, and in the inexpensive range $30 to $40. All telephone numbers are in the 66 city code unless otherwise indicated.

For an unforgettable Evora experience, we begin with our favorite *pousada,* followed by our cost and quality choices of urban hostelries, small inns, and *pensãos* — listed by price category.

SPECIAL HAVEN

Pousada dos Lóios This 32-room luxury establishment is one of the best of the state-owned *pousadas.* In the converted and restored Convento dos Lóios, built in 1485 by the nobleman Rodrigo Afonso de Melo, it occupies the site of Evora's old castle. Most of the rooms are in the old monks' cells, with period furnishings, but the essential modern services are adequate. There is an open-air pool and a restaurant serving regional food (see *Eating Out*). The location — next door to the Roman temple and right in the center of everything — is perfect. Largo Conde de Vila Flor (phone: 24051; 212-686-9213 in the US; fax: 27248).

MODERATE

Evorahotel The newest of Evora's lodgings, this hostelry is also the largest, offering guests a choice of 114 rooms, all with private baths, TV sets, direct-dial phones, and mini-bars. There's also an outdoor swimming pool and an excellent restaurant (see *Eating Out*). On the road to Montemor and Lisbon, 1 mile (1.6 km) west of town. Quinta do Cruzeiro, on N114 (phone: 734801; fax: 734806).

Monte das Flores This *estalagem,* or inn, occupies a converted farm 2½ miles (4 km) west of Evora on N114. The 17 rooms are all furnished attractively and comfortably in period rustic, and all have private baths. A pool and tennis courts are among the facilities; there's also horseback riding. The restaurant serves good regional dishes. Monte das Flores (phone: 25018; fax: 27564).

Planície One of Evora's busiest hotels and generally considered the top establishment in its price range, it has 33 well-equipped rooms with baths, TV sets, and direct-dial telephones. Spacious public rooms and a highly regarded restaurant add to the attractions. The location and service are first-rate. 40 Largo de Alvaro Velho (phone: 24026; fax: 29880).

Riviera In line with all establishments in its *pensão residencial* category, it lacks a few of the regular hotel services (there's no restaurant or bar). But its 22 rooms all have air conditioning, private baths, and color TV sets, and it is well located between the cathedral and Praça do Giraldo. 49 Rua 5 de Outubro (phone: 23304; fax: 20467).

Santa Clara An unpretentious but first-rate modern hostelry in the heart of the Old City, west of Praça do Giraldo. The 30 rooms (with baths) are comfortably appointed, the service is attentive, and there is a large and very good restaurant. All in all, an unbeatable value. 19 Travessa da Milheira (phone: 24141; fax: 26544).

Solar Monfalim Ideally located in the Old City, this former royal mansion has 24 rooms and 1 suite, all with private baths, color TV sets, and direct-dial telephones. There are lovely tiles and stones throughout, a cozy bar, and a breakfast room (no restaurant). 1 Largo da Mesiricórdia (phone: 22031; fax: 742367).

Vitória A modern *albergaria* (another category of inn), it's comfortable and very well equipped, although without a restaurant. All 48 rooms have private baths, color TV sets, air conditioning, and phones. The location, about 300 yards outside the city walls to the south, means easy parking. Rua Diana de Lis (phone: 27174; fax: 20974).

INEXPENSIVE

Diana A small, 15-room *pensão* in the center of town, modest but well regarded. The rooms are small, but all have baths and phone. There's no bar or restaurant. 2 Rua Diogo Cão (phone: 22008).

EATING OUT

With a couple of notable exceptions, Alentejo restaurants have not always scored well on finesse. However, the last few years have seen a welcomed revival of local culinary arts. This has unearthed country flavors and skills long-buried in home cookbooks, and caused gastronomes to reconsider their judgments. Happily for the visitor, Evora is the capital of this culinary renaissance, and good regional dishes are beginning to outnumber "international" choices on the menus of its best restaurants.

Bread, heavy, crusty, and delicious, is an important part of all meals, and even finds its way into the soup. The most basic of these, *sopa alentejana,* is in fact mostly bread and water, flavored with a lot of garlic and olive oil, and topped with a poached egg. *Carne de porco* (pork), *borrego* (lamb), and game are the staple meats. In one of the few local dishes that has acquired a wider fame, *carne de porco à alentejana,* small pieces of pork are blended tastily with clams. Pork is also a basic ingredient in popular bean dishes such as the various versions of *feijoada alentejana,* a substantial mixture of pork meats, fresh and cured, and white beans. Lamb and *cabrito* (kid) are most commonly eaten in *ensopados* (stews) or *assado no forno* (roasted in the oven). All meat dishes are inclined to be heavy in the Alentejo — and be warned that restaurant servings are never tailored to the needs of weight watchers.

Evora's desserts reflect their Moorish and medieval convent background. The people of the Alentejo have inherited a collective sweet tooth, and their traditional *doçaria* (sweetmeats) tend to err in this direction. Most of the favorites, such as *queijo conventual* (convent "cheese") or *toucinho do céu* (bacon from heaven), have an egg base and are flavored with almond. The great Alentejo cheese, serpa, is made near the town of that name not far from Evora. The salty little cheeses made in Evora from cured sheep's milk are good as appetizers.

Most of the best Alentejo wines come from the regions of Borba, Redondo, Reguengos de Monsaraz, and Vidigueira, all close to Evora, and from the Portalegre area to the north. Some labels to look out for are esporão, granja, and cartuxa. Expect to pay from $60 to $100 for a dinner for two with wine at those restaurants listed below as expensive, from $35 to $50 at places in the moderate range, and under $35 at spots in the inexpensive range. All telephone numbers are in the 66 city code unless otherwise indicated.

For an unforgettable dining experience, we begin with our local culinary favorite, followed by our cost and quality choices, listed by price category.

DELIGHTFUL DINING

Fialho Evora's most celebrated restaurant, it serves genuinely traditional food — it's not unknown for gastronomes from Lisbon to drive out here for lunch, especially during game season. Little plates of delicious *petiscos* (appetizers) precede the main meal. The *borrego assado no forno* (roast mutton) is justifiably renowned, and so is the *favada real da casa,* a monumental bean dish. It boasts the best and most authentic *carne de porco com amêijoas* (their version of the famous pork and clam stew) in Evora, and *sopa de cação,* a rich, aromatic soup made with shark, bread, garlic, vinegar, and coriander. In the game season, *perdiz, lebre,* and *javali* (partridge, hare, and wild boar, respectively) are specialties. Egg, almond, and pumpkin desserts provide a sweet touch, while the region's soft sheep cheeses, the creamy serpas, are an equally rewarding finale. Meals can be accompanied by Evora's estate-bottled cartuxa white wine, or other Alentejo greats such as the light, dry white esporão or tinto da anfora red. The restaurant's bar and two dining rooms are tastefully decorated with regional handicrafts and paintings; stuffed game mounted on the walls reflects the hunting fervor of the region. Closed Mondays and the first 2 weeks of September, but open throughout the day otherwise, with no break between lunch and dinner. The place is always thronged, and it's not large, so reservations are advised. Major credit cards accepted. 16 Travessa das Mascarenhas (phone: 23079).

EXPENSIVE

Luar de Janeiro One of Evora's top dining establishments, and it also stays open later than most — until 2 AM. For many true Alentejo gastronomes, the whole experience is summed up in the chef's highly acclaimed *lebre com grao e nabos* (hare cassarole with chick-peas and turnips). Closed Thursdays. Reservations advised. Major credit cards accepted. 13 Travessa de Janeiro (phone: 24895).

Pousada dos Lóios The commendable switch recently from bland international fare to good regional cuisine is one reason to dine here; try the chef's award-winning *perdizes de escabeche* (partridge in vinaigrette sauce), if it's in season. The other draw is the lovely dining room itself — once the refectory of this 15th-century former monastery. In good weather, tables and chairs are set up around the equally attractive cloister. Open daily. Reservations advised. Major credit cards accepted. Largo Conde de Vila Flor (phone: 24051).

MODERATE

Evorahotel This hotel restaurant, owned by the celebrated Fialho brothers, among others, has become a gastronomic attraction on its own. *Cabrito frito com migas de grelos* (fried kid with greens) is one of the Alentejo specialties, complemented by a well-chosen regional wine list. Comfortably spacious, it features panoramic views of the surrounding countryside. Open daily. Reservations advised. Major credit cards accepted. One mile (1.6 km) west of town, on the road to Quinta do Cruzeiro, N114 (phone: 734801).

Guião One of Evora's top traditional eateries in its price range. It's large (3 rooms) and comfortable, with an old-fashioned decor. The *borrego assado no forno* (roast mutton) vies with *Fialho*'s. Closed Mondays. Reservations unnecessary. Major credit cards accepted. 81 Rua da República (phone: 23071).

1/4 P'ras 9 The odd-looking name of this restaurant specializing in charcoal grills and seafood actually means a quarter to nine. The *açorda de marisco* (a difficult-to-describe mixture of bread and seafood) is excellent. Closed Wednesdays. No reservations. Major credit cards accepted. 9A Rua Pedro Simões (phone: 26774).

INEXPENSIVE

A Gruta On the basis of value for money, this is one of Evora's most popular restaurants. No frills, but the food is good. The specialty is oven-roasted kid. Closed Saturdays. No reservations. No credit cards accepted. 2 Av. General Humberto Delgado (phone: 28186).

Lisbon

Lisbon is a bit like the heroine of an old movie who faces the gravest of perils in every reel — but emerges in the end still beautiful. During its more than 2,000 years of history, the city has undergone devastating earth-quakes, plagues, fires, floods, invasions by barbarians, sackings, revolutions, and, more recently, the incursion of ugly urban development and pollution. But the wear and tear of centuries has become part of the charm of this hilled city of pastel perspectives.

Legend says that Lisbon was founded by Ulysses, who gave it the name Olisipo. A less romantic and probably more likely theory is that the name was Phoenician in origin, from the words "alis ubbo" (pleasant bay), and that the city started as a trading post, with its safety-conscious inhabitants residing on the hill where the Castelo de São Jorge stands today in order to avoid raiders.

Whatever its origins, the ancient settlement grew quickly after the Romans arrived in 137 BC. By Julius Caesar's time, Lisbon had acquired an honorary imperial title, Felicitas Julia, and its citizens had been awarded rights similar to those held by Romans. By the time the Roman Empire crumbled, Lisbon had become an important hub of a vital road network, a city with a theater, baths, and a 6-mile long aqueduct (not the one standing today).

After a somewhat obscure period under the Visigoths in the 5th century, Lisbon began to flourish again during the occupation of the Moors from 714 to 1147. During this time, it not only grew considerably in size but also became a renowned center of Islamic learning. A few years after proclaiming himself Portugal's first king, Dom Afonso Henriques (with an army of crusaders from northern Europe) recaptured the city for the Christians after an epic 17-week seige. Lisbon became the capital of the Christian realm in 1260, and by the 14th century it had spread well beyond the Roman and Moorish boundaries and had nearly 4 miles of walls, with 77 towers and 33 gates.

The city's greatest glory came in the 15th and 16th centuries, during the Age of Discovery. At a time when the world's seas were uncharted and darkness and superstition ruled people's imaginations, Lisbon was sending forth caravels (sailing ships) into the unknown. After Vasco da Gama sailed from Lisbon in 1497 and returned 2 years later from his trip to the Indies, the subsequent trade in spices between India and Portugal ushered in a period of enormous wealth, and the beginning of Lisbon's golden era. By the middle of the 16th century, the city had become a great commercial and maritime power, the "Queen of the Tagus," and sovereign of the sea trade routes to the East.

In 1580, Philip II of Spain annexed the country and became Philip I of

Portugal. Persecution of Jews began during the late 15th century, and the Inquisition was introduced during the early 16th century and endured some 200 years. Thousands were tortured in the Palace of the Inquisition in the Praça Rossio, and many others died in the autos-da-fé held in the public squares of the city. Spanish rule lasted until 1640, when the Spanish governor of Lisbon was deposed by a group of Portuguese noblemen. Lisbon then revived its profitable trade with the rest of the world, and a spate of new building began. As a result of the discovery of gold in Brazil during the late 17th century, the city's growing opulence was mirrored in the splendidly ornate baroque architecture of the time (it is possible that the name of the baroque style may have come from *barroco*, the Portuguese word for an irregularly shaped pearl). The reign of João V (1706–50) was known for its magnificence.

Then, on the morning of *All Saints' Day*, 1755, while most of its residents were at mass, one of the worst earthquakes ever known shook Lisbon. A 40-foot tidal wave rose on the Tagus River and slammed into the city. Fires, begun by tapers lighted in the churches for the feast day and fanned by a violent windstorm, burned what the quake had left intact, and as many as 40,000 people perished. Within minutes, two-thirds of the city was in ruins.

The Marquês de Pombal, Portugal's prime minister, quickly and efficiently set out to rebuild Lisbon. The stately plan of the city's classical squares and boulevards was traced out, and the straight lines and 18th-century proportions of the quarter called the Baixa (lower town) appeared, parallel streets lined with nearly uniform 5-story buildings replacing the previous medieval jumble.

For all the prime minister's remarkable achievements, however, political instability and turmoil marked the rest of the 18th century and continued into the beginning of the 20th century. In 1908, King Carlos I and his son were assassinated in Praça do Comércio; the successor to the throne, King Manuel II, was forced into exile 2 years later, when radical republicans overthrew the monarchy. The political turbulence of the ensuing democratic republic gave way to dictatorship in 1926 and the rise to power of António de Oliveira Salazar, a professor of economics from Coimbra University, who ruled Portugal until 1968. He put the country's finances in order and kept Portugal out of World War II, but during the nearly half century he and his successor, Marcello Caetano, remained in power, Portugal gradually became a police state.

In 1974, a group of young officers staged a coup in Lisbon and helped set up a democratically elected government. It was a revolution in which few lives were lost, but it altered the face of the capital as nearly a million refugees poured into the city. Within a few years, the situation stabilized. The refugees were absorbed into the life of Lisbon and helped make it a more dynamic place. The city's beauty began to reemerge as some of its more important buildings were renovated and repaired.

Portugal joined the European Economic Community (Common Market) in 1986, bringing in new investment funds and new products for Lisbon's shelves. The city itself also has changed in recent years. Many of the streets in the Baixa have been closed to traffic and turned into pedestrian malls paved with cobblestones. Musicians entertain the strollers, and sidewalk artists sketch inexpensive portraits. Artisans offer jewelry, leatherwork, embroidery, and other wares from little stalls.

More than 1.6 million people live in Lisbon and its environs today, and yet this westernmost capital of Europe is still in some ways a small town. The *lisboetas,* accustomed to foreigners, are tolerant of their visitors' ways and their inability to speak Portuguese. They make Lisbon a truly hospitable place, perhaps even more so this year because the city has been named Europe's Cultural Capital for 1994.

Lisbon At-a-Glance

SEEING THE CITY

A city built on hills, Lisbon frequently surprises visitors with lovely views that emerge without warning around unexpected corners. It has 17 natural balconies — called *miradouros* — from which to view the city. Foremost of these is the hilltop on which the ruins of Castelo São Jorge stand. All of the squares are laid out beneath: Praça do Comércio by the banks of the Tagus; the Rossio with its fountains and flower stalls; Praça da Figueira, the bustling market square; Práça dos Restauradores with its monument to Portugal's independence; the circular Praça Marquês de Pombal at the end of the broad Avenida da Liberdade; and beyond that, the lovely Parque Eduardo VII. On a clear day, it is possible to see the castles of Sintra far to the west. Another vantage point that's worth a pause is Largo de Santa Luzia, in the Alfama district, between the castle and Lisbon's cathedral. Although the view from here — over the Alfama's red-roofed buildings down to the port — is less broadly panoramic than the one from the castle, the esplanade is charming, lined with *azulejos* (glazed tiles), and endowed with flower beds and a trellis-topped colonnade. (For those who prefer not to walk, take one of Lisbon's picturesque, vintage *eléctricos,* or trams — the No. 28.) A third *miradouro* is the terrace on Rua de São Pedro de Alcântara, on the opposite hill across the city in the Bairro Alto. From here there is a picture-postcard view of the castle, with the Alfama district spread down the slopes below its walls.

Another breathtaking view is from the bridge across the Tagus, known since the 1974 revolution as Ponte 25 de Abril, but previously named for Salazar, who built it in the 1960s. The third-longest suspension bridge in the world, it is particularly spectacular at night, when its cables, the ships in the river, and the city are all brightly lit. On the other side, there is a marvelous panorama of the Tagus estuary from the top of the statue of

Cristo Rei (Christ the King), a gift to Portugal from Brazil. (Open daily from 10 AM to 6 PM; there is an admission charge, and an elevator takes visitors up.) Those without a car can cross the river by ferry from Praça do Comércio and take a bus from Cacilhas to the statue.

One excellent way to see the city is to join a 3-hour "Lisbon Walk" sponsored by the *Centro Nacional de Cultura* (National Culture Center; 68 Rua António Maria Cardoso; phone: 346-6722), whose regularly scheduled guided tours — in English and Portuguese — take in the Chiado, Alfama, and Belém districts.

SPECIAL PLACES

In ancient times, and later under the Moors, Lisbon was contained within walls that surrounded the hill where the Castelo São Jorge now stands. Today, that area is the Alfama, the oldest part of the city, where traces of the picturesque Judiaria (Jewish Quarter) and Mouraria (Moorish Quarter) still can be seen, along with Roman remains. The Alfama has been destroyed several times by earthquakes, but it always was rebuilt along the same plan, its tortuous, narrow streets spiraling down from the top of the hill to the Baixa below. The Baixa, to the west of the Alfama, is the main shopping and commercial district of Lisbon. Built after the earthquake in a grid fashion, it stretches northward from Praça do Comércio by the river to the top of the Rossio, one of the city's main squares, and includes such aptly named streets as Rua Aurea (its official name — confusingly, it's generally known and shown on most maps as Rua do Ouro, which means the same thing: Gold Street) and Rua da Prata (Silver Street), which are lined with fine jewelry stores and banks. Up the hill and west of the Rossio is the part of the Baixa known locally as the Chiado — not much more than 10 square blocks. This also is a popular shopping district dotted with coffeehouses and outdoor cafés, but a disastrous fire in 1988 destroyed a great number of the shops — including two of Europe's oldest department stores — and other landmarks. Happily, most of the façades of the burned buildings remained standing after the flames were put out, even though the interiors were gutted, and rebuilding plans call for restoration of the district, rather than wholesale modernization.

Higher up is the Bairro Alto, or High Quarter, above and to the west of Praça dos Restauradores and the Rossio. At one time a wealthy (and later a seedy) residential district, it has been taken over by the avant-garde and become the center of nightlife in downtown Lisbon, with fine restaurants, typical *tascas* (taverns or small eating places), and *fado* houses, where sad, Portuguese folk songs are sung. West of the Bairro Alto are the Madragoa and Lapa districts, residential areas where restaurants, government buildings, embassies, and several museums and art galleries also can be found. Modern Lisbon, with museums, the zoo, and contemporary housing, stretches to the north and east of the downtown area.

The Belém quarter is along the riverbank west of all of the above.

Because it suffered very little in the 1755 earthquake, many of its fine palaces and monuments are still standing. Belém also is home to several museums, as well as many restaurants.

CASTELO DE SÃO JORGE AND THE ALFAMA

CASTELO DE SÃO JORGE (ST. GEORGE'S CASTLE) Built on one of Lisbon's highest hills, this castle with ten towers is considered the cradle of the city. An Iron Age *castro,* or fortified hilltop town, probably was located here, succeeded by Roman fortifications (Roman walls and other remains are being excavated), a fortress built by the Visigoths during the 5th century, and later, a Moorish fortified town. The present castle was built during the 12th century. Within the grounds are lovely gardens where peacocks roam free, the remains of an Arabian palace where the Kings of Portugal lived from the 14th to the 16th century, and a restaurant, the *Casa do Leão* (see *Eating Out*). The views of Lisbon are extensive from the terrace on the south and west sides and from the walk around the towers. Open daily from 9 AM to 9 PM (to 7 PM from October through March). No admission charge. Rua Costa do Castelo.

ALFAMA This Old Quarter slopes downhill from São Jorge. A cobbled labyrinth with some streets so narrow that pedestrians must walk in single file, it is one of the most colorful spots in Europe. Its streets are overhung with balconies ablaze with scarlet geraniums and lined with little taverns decorated with strings of peppers, garlic, and cheese. By day, caged canaries on the balconies sing in the sun; at night, wrought-iron lamps light the scene; and on wash days, the buildings are strung with clotheslines and drying laundry. Although some medieval mansions and Moorish buildings exist, most of the houses date from the late 18th century, after the earthquake. The best times to see the Alfama are in the morning when the markets are open, late in the afternoon when the streets and squares are alive with people, or on a moonlit evening. The quarter stretches north to south from the castle to the banks of the Tagus, and west to east from the cathedral to the vicinity of the church of São Vicente de Fora.

SÉ (CATHEDRAL) Lisbon's oldest church, built just after the Christian reconquest in the 12th century, suffered enormous earthquake damage in 1755, but was rebuilt during the 18th century and restored during this one. It is a typical fortress-church of solid, massive construction, with battlements and towers. The plain façade is Romanesque, the ambulatory chapels and the cloister are pure Gothic, and the choir is baroque. In the *azulejo*-lined enclosure just inside the door is the baptismal font of St. Anthony of Padua, Portugal's patron saint, who was born here (although he spent much of his life in Italy), and in the chapel to the left is a *presépio* (Nativity scene) by Joaquim Machado de Castro. Relics of St. Vincent, patron saint of Lisbon, also are in the cathedral, but are brought out only on special occasions. There is a collection of religious vestments and ecclesiastical gold, which can be seen only by prior arrangement. The church is open daily from 8 AM to 8 PM. The cloister is open from 9 AM to 1 PM and 2 to 4 PM; closed Mondays. Admission charge to the cloister. Largo da Sé (phone: 886-6752).

MUSEU-ESCOLA DE ARTES DECORATIVAS (MUSEUM-SCHOOL OF DECORATIVE ARTS) Located just around the bend from the Largo de Santa Luzia *miradouro* and housed in a 17th-century palace that survived the earthquake, this museum contains collections of Portuguese porcelain, silver, crystal, paintings, tapestries, and furniture, mostly of the 17th and 18th centuries, all beguilingly arranged as the furnishings of an aristocratic Lisboan home of yesteryear. The objects once were the property of a banker, Dr. Ricardo Espírito Santo Silva, who set up a foundation both to create a museum and to preserve the skills and tools of traditional Portuguese craftsmanship. The foundation runs a school and workshops (phone: 872429) for the reproduction and restoration of antiques. Visitors may tour the workshops, which are adjacent to the museum, but an appointment is required. The museum is open Tuesdays through Saturdays from 10 AM to 1 PM and 2:30 to 5 PM. Admission charge. 2 Largo das Portas do Sol (phone: 886-2184).

IGREJA DE SÃO VICENTE DE FORA (CHURCH OF ST. VINCENT OUTSIDE THE WALLS) From Largo das Portas do Sol, follow the *eléctrico* tracks down Escadinhas de São Tomé and then up again to this church, which was built during the late 16th and early 17th centuries by Filippo Terzi and sports a mannerist façade. A remnant of an old monastery, it is notable for its cloisters, lavishly lined with 18th-century *azulejos*. Beyond, set up in the old monastery refectory, is the Panteão Real (Royal Pantheon), the mausoleum of the Bragança family, which ruled Portugal from 1640 to 1910. Most of the Bragança kings and queens, including Portugal's last monarchs, are buried here. Open from 9 AM to 12:30 PM and 3 to 6:30 PM; closed Mondays. Admission charge to the cloisters and pantheon also gains entrance to an ornate sacristy, lined with inlaid marble. Largo de São Vicente (phone: 876470).

IGREJA DE SANTA ENGRÁCIA (CHURCH OF ST. ENGRÁCIA) Begun during the 17th century but not completed until 1966, when it also was restored, this church gave rise to a Portuguese expression, *"obras de Santa Engrácia,"* used to describe a seemingly never-ending task. The grandiose structure, with a baroque façade and an interior richly decorated in marble, now serves as the Panteão Nacional (National Pantheon), containing the tombs of three Portuguese presidents and three writers, as well as memorials to other famous figures — including Prince Henry the Navigator, Luís de Camões, and Vasco da Gama — who are not buried here. This is within easy walking distance of São Vicente, but on Tuesdays and Saturdays you may be detained by the flea market that's set up on the street between the two. Open from 10 AM to 5 PM; closed Mondays. Admission charge. Campo de Santa Clara (phone: 871529).

MUSEU MILITAR (MILITARY MUSEUM) Housed in an 18th-century arsenal (the huge, saffron-yellow building in front of the Santa Apolónia train station), it contains cannon, guns, swords, armor, and uniforms, as well as paintings, sculptures, coin collections, and other mementos of Portugal's wars. One room is dedicated to the discoveries of Vasco da Gama. Open Tuesdays through Saturdays from 10 AM to 4 PM; Sundays from 11 AM to 5 PM. Admission charge. Largo dos Caminhos de Ferro (phone: 886-7131).

IGREJA DA MADRE DE DEUS (CHURCH OF THE MOTHER OF GOD) Although the convent complex here was founded in 1501, most of what is seen today was built during the 18th century. The church is resplendent with ornate, gilded baroque woodwork, oil paintings, and *azulejos,* but the church is only part of the attraction, because the *Museu Nacional do Azulejo* is installed in the convent complex, and it's a must-see for tile lovers. Exquisite examples of the art, both Portuguese and foreign, from the 15th century to the present, are displayed in rooms around two cloisters, one of them a small gem. In addition to its other treasures, the museum possesses a long tile frieze dating from approximately 1730 that depicts a panorama of Lisbon before the earthquake. There's also a pleasant cafeteria, decorated with 19th-century kitchen tiles. Open from 10 AM to 1 PM and from 2 to 5 PM; closed Mondays. Admission charge. Bus No. 104 from Praça do Comércio goes to the convent. Rua da Madre de Deus (phone: 814-7747).

IGREJA DA CONCEIÇÃO VELHA (CHURCH OF THE CONCEPTION) Built during the early 16th century on the site of Lisbon's ancient synagogue, this church was completely devastated in the 1755 earthquake, but its original Manueline portal survived. The beautiful doorway, richly carved with limestone figures, was retained for the new church, which, however, has little of note inside. Rua da Alfândega.

CASA DOS BICOS (HOUSE OF POINTED STONES) When it was built during the 16th century, this house belonged to the family of Afonso de Albuquerque, a famous Portuguese viceroy to India. The earthquake reduced the 4-story structure to only several feet of foundations, but it was completely rebuilt. The façade is covered with pyramidal stones, similar to the Casa de los Picos in Segovia, Spain, and the Palazzo dei Diamanti in Ferrara, Italy. The house is open to the public only when there are special exhibitions. Rua dos Bacalhoeiros (no phone).

BAIXA

PRAÇA DO COMÉRCIO This impressive riverside square, laid out after the earthquake by the Marquês de Pombal, is edged on three sides by arcaded neo-classical buildings. It's also known as Terreiro do Paço (Palace Square), after the royal palace that stood here in pre-earthquake days, and, to the English, as Black Horse Square, after the bronze equestrian statue of King José I by the 18th-century sculptor Joaquim Machado de Castro that stands in the middle. The triumphal arch on the north side of the square, leading to Rua Augusta and the rest of the Baixa, was finished during the late 19th century. The square was the scene of the assassination of King Carlos I and his son in 1908.

ROSSIO Officially called Praça de Dom Pedro IV, after the 18th-century king who is the subject of the statue in the center, this is the heart of the city and the northern limit of the Baixa. As early as the 13th century, this square was the city's marketplace, but like Praça do Comércio and the rest of the Baixa, it was destroyed by the earthquake of 1755; the *praça* was then newly laid out by Pombal. On the north side is the 19th-century *Teatro Nacional de Dona Maria II* (see *Theater,* below), standing on the site of a onetime royal palace that during the 16th century became the seat of the Inquisition. The square is much cheerier now, graced with flower stalls, fountains, and open-air cafés.

ELEVADOR DE SANTA JUSTA (SANTA JUSTA ELEVATOR) This lacy gray iron structure — often erroneously attributed to Alexandre-Gustave Eiffel — was designed by Raoul Mesnier, a Portuguese engineer of French descent, and erected in 1898. It not only spares visitors the climb from Rua do Ouro (Rua Aurea) to Largo do Carmo in the Chiado, but also provides a panoramic view of the city from the top, and as you exit, you pass under a flying buttress of the Igreja do Carmo. The elevator runs from 7 AM to 11 PM (from 9 AM on Sundays). Rua do Ouro.

IGREJA DO CARMO (CARMO CHURCH) Built during the 14th century, this was an imposing, majestic structure that overlooked the city until it was largely destroyed by the 1755 earthquake. The shell, with Gothic arches and doorway, remains, and is floodlit at night. The ruins have been turned into the *Museu Arqueológico do Carmo,* containing prehistoric, Roman, Visigothic, and medieval artifacts, as well as medieval sculpture, *azulejos,* and inscriptions. Open from 10 AM to 6 PM from July through September; from 10 AM to 1 PM and 2 to 5 PM the rest of the year; closed Sundays year-round. Admission charge. Largo do Carmo (phone: 346-0473).

BAIRRO ALTO

SOLAR DO VINHO DO PORTO This comfortable bar run by the Port Wine Institute is a good place to sample Portugal's most famous wine — called port in English and *vinho do Porto* in Portuguese — without making a trip to the northern city. It's stocked with all types and vintages of port (over 200 different kinds, although the whole list is rarely available), which visitors can order by the glass. Take the funicular streetcar from Praça dos Restauradores. Open daily from noon to 11:30 PM. 45 Rua de São Pedro de Alcântara (phone: 347-5707).

IGREJA DE SÃO ROQUE (CHURCH OF ST. ROCH) This 16th-century church has a flat wooden ceiling painted to look like a vaulted one, but it's best known for the baroque Capela de São João Baptista, the fourth chapel on the left. The chapel was commissioned during the mid-18th century by King João V, and designed, assembled, and blessed by the pope in Rome. It was then dismantled, shipped to Portugal, and rebuilt at its present address. The lapis lazuli, porphyry, marble, alabaster, ivory, and other precious and semi-precious building materials cost the king dearly, but the workmanship is impeccable. Note the *Baptism of Christ,* which looks like an oil painting but is actually an exquisitely fine mosaic. The *Museu de São Roque* adjoining the church contains paintings and liturgical objects and richly embroidered vestments. The museum is open from 10 AM to 5 PM, closed Mondays; admission charge. The church remains open after the museum closes. Largo Trindade Coelho (phone: 346-0361).

NORTHERN AND WESTERN LISBON

PARQUE EDUARDO VII (EDWARD VII PARK) Downtown Lisbon's largest green space is this formally landscaped park at the northern end of Avenida da Liberdade, just beyond Praça Marquês de Pombal. From the esplanade at the top of the park, the view extends over the lower town to the Tagus. In the northwest corner is the charming Estufa Fria (Cold Greenhouse), where plants and flowers from across the globe grow in luxuriant abundance along pathways, tunnels, streams, goldfish ponds, and waterfalls. A slatted roof protects them from the extremes of summer and winter and filters the sun's rays, suffusing the greenhouse with a magically soft light. Within the Estufa Fria is the Estufa Quente, a hothouse filled with tropical plants. Open daily from 9 AM to 6 PM (to 5 PM in winter); the Estufa Quente closes a half-hour earlier. Admission charge (phone: 682278).

MUSEU CALOUSTE GULBENKIAN (GULBENKIAN MUSEUM) When the Armenian oil tycoon Calouste Sarkis Gulbenkian died in 1955, he left most of his estate and his enormous art collection to Portugal, the country to which he had fled during World War II and where he spent the last years of his life. The result was the Calouste Gulbenkian Foundation, a modern complex that houses not only this museum, but also auditoriums, a library, and exhibition space. Don't miss the museum, a repository of 50 years of astute collecting — 6,400 pieces, including works Gulbenkian bought from the *Hermitage Museum* in the 1920s when the Soviet Union needed foreign currency. The treasures include fine European paintings, sculpture, 18th-century French furniture, Chinese vases, Greek coins, medieval ivories, illuminated manuscripts, Middle Eastern carpets and ceramics, and more.

There also is a marvelous collection of small Egyptian pieces and a unique collection of Art Nouveau jewelry by René Lalique. Open from 10 AM to 5 PM from June through November; winter hours are the same except the museum opens at 2 PM and closes at 7 PM on Wednesdays and Saturdays; closed Mondays year-round. Admission charge. 45 Av. de Berna (phone: 797-4167).

CENTRO DE ARTE MODERNA (MODERN ART CENTER) In the gardens behind the *Museu Calouste Gulbenkian,* it has an impressive collection of 19th- and 20th-century Portuguese paintings and sculpture, including works by José de Almada Negreiros, as well as a permanent exhibition of contemporary British art. There also are frequent temporary exhibits. A sinuous sculpture by Henry Moore and the oversize tapestries of the Portuguese Modernist José de Almada Negreiros are among the permanent fixtures. A cafeteria overlooks the gardens. The hours are the same as those of the *Museu Calouste Gulbenkian.* Admission charge. Rua Dr. Nicolau de Bettencourt (phone: 793-5131).

JARDIM ZOOLÓGICO (ZOO) Set in a 65-acre park, the zoo is home to some 2,000 animals, including an elephant who rings a bell for money. Other amusements include pony rides for children, rowboats, and a small train. Open daily from 9 AM to 8 PM from April through October (to 6 PM the rest of the year). Admission charge. Parque das Laranjeiras (phone: 726-8041).

PALÁCIO DOS MARQUESES DA FRONTEIRA (PALACE OF THE MARCHESSES OF FRONTEIRA) West of the zoo, on the edge of the Parque Florestal de Monsanto, is an interesting palace built during the second half of the 17th century and originally used by its aristocratic owners as a hunting lodge. It's notable for the great number of *azulejos* that cover its walls — both inside and outside in the formal gardens — many of them depicting historical events. The palace still is privately owned, but a public tour is offered at 11 AM daily except Sundays and holidays. Admission charge. 1 Largo de São Domingos de Benfica (phone: 778-2023).

AQUEDUTO DAS AGUAS LIVRES Built during the first half of the 18th century to bring water from Caneças (11 miles/18 km northwest of Lisbon) to a reservoir near the present-day *Amoreiras Shopping Center,* the Aguas Livres Aqueduct miraculously survived the 1755 earthquake and still supplies the city with drinking water. A quarter of the aqueduct runs underground, and there are 109 stone arches aboveground. The most impressive stretch, with one arch 214 feet high, is the section that crosses the Alcântara Valley on the edge of the city. It is visible as you cross the viaduct out of town on the road (N7) that leads to Estoril and Sintra. To learn more about the aqueduct, stop in at the *Museu de Agua* (Water Museum; 12 Rua de Alviela; phone: 813-5522), which chronicles the history of Lisbon's water supplies, going back to Roman times. At press time, it was uncertain whether the inside of the aqueduct, with its fountains and statuary, would be open to the public; the museum, however, is open Tuesdays through Saturdays from 10 AM to 12:30 PM and 2 to 5 PM; admission charge.

BASÍLICA DA ESTRELA (ESTRELA BASILICA) Built by Queen Maria I between 1779 and 1790, it fulfilled a vow she had made while petitioning God to grant her a son. The dome is one of Lisbon's landmarks; the tomb of the founder is inside. This church reflects the style of the school of sculpture founded at Mafra by the Italian sculptor Alessandro Giusti; one of Giusti's Portuguese pupils, Joaquim Machado de Castro, was responsible for the manger figures here. Open daily from 7:30 AM to 1 PM and 3 to 8 PM. Praça da Estrela.

MUSEU NACIONAL DE ARTE ANTIGA (NATIONAL MUSEUM OF ANCIENT ART) One of the most important of Lisbon's museums, it is housed partly in a 17th-century palace that once belonged to the Marquês de Pombal and partly in an adjacent 20th-century building. Although it contains numerous foreign works, such as a celebrated Bosch triptych, *The Temptation of St. Anthony,* the museum is most notable for its paintings of the Portuguese school, especially of the 15th and 16th centuries. The prize in this group — perhaps the most famous painting in Portugal — is the six-panel polyptych known as the *Panéis de São Vicente de Fora* (St. Vincent Panels), a masterpiece by Nuno Gonçalves, the most important Portuguese painter of the 15th century. The polyptych is precious not only for its artistic merit (and because it's the only Gonçalves painting still extant), but also because it constitutes a document of Portuguese society of the time. Also in the museum are sculptures; Portuguese, European, and Oriental ceramics; objects in silver and gold; jewelry, furniture, and tapestries; and the entire gilt-and-tile-laden St. Albert Chapel, an architectural leftover from a Carmelite convent that once occupied the spot. Worthy of special attention are the Japanese painted screens portraying the first Portuguese visitors to Japan. Open from 10 AM to 5 PM; closed Mondays. Admission charge. 95 Rua das Janelas Verdes (phone: 397-2725).

BELÉM

MOSTEIRO DOS JERÓNIMOS (HIERONYMITE MONASTERY) One of Lisbon's great landmarks, this white marble monastery was founded in 1502 by King Manuel I to give thanks for the successful return of Vasco da Gama's fleet from the Indies and to commemorate all the great voyages of Portugal's explorers during the Age of Discovery. Because Vasco da Gama had sailed from Belém, the site of a small mariners' chapel here seemed a fitting one for the memorial, said to have been "built by pepper" because it was funded by the lucrative spice trade. The sea motifs — seashells, ropes, anchors, and other symbols — that are carved throughout in great profusion are the characteristic decorative elements of Manueline architecture, a uniquely Portuguese style that represented a transition from Gothic to Renaissance and took its name from the king, Dom Manuel. The monastery is considered the country's finest example of the Manueline style: The two portals, the extremely slender columns and characteristic network vaulting of the church, and the richly sculpted 2-story cloister are exceptionally beautiful. King Manuel I and several other monarchs are buried in the church, as is Vasco da Gama, whose tomb, just inside the entrance, is marked by a caravel. Opposite it, marked by a lyre and quill pen, is a monument to Luís de Camões, Portugal's most famous poet, whose bones may or may not be inside (he died in Africa, and the wrong bones may have been brought back). The long galleries to the west of the monastery, neo-Manueline from the 19th century, contain the *Museu Nacional de Arqueologia e Etnologia* (National Museum of Archaeology and Ethnology; phone: 362-0000; open daily from 9 AM to noon and 2 to 5 PM; admission charge) and, around the corner, the *Museu de Marinha* (see below). More modern annexes across the courtyard from the entrance to the Naval Museum contain its collection of boats and the *Planetario Calouste Gulbenkian,* which has presentations several days a week (times are posted outside; admission charge; phone: 362-0002). The monastery is open from 10 AM to 6:30 PM from July through September (to 5 PM the rest of the year); closed Mondays year-round. Admission charge to the cloister. Praça do Império (phone: 362-0034).

MUSEU DE MARINHA (NAVAL MUSEUM) In the 19th-century galleries attached to the monastery, plus a modern extension to handle the overflow, this museum contains small models of boats from all eras of Portuguese history, from the earliest caravels of the Age of Discovery to warships, trading ships, and submarines — along with naval uniforms and other marine paraphernalia. Real boats are exhibited in the hangar-like extension. Of them, the late–18th-century *galeota,* or galley, built for the wedding of Crown Prince João (who became João VI) to a Spanish princess and rowed by 71 red-coated figures, is the star. Examples of traditional boats from various regions include a *rabelo* boat from the Douro River, a *moliceiro* from the Ria de Aveiro, and fishing boats from the Algarve. Open from 10 AM to 5 PM; closed Mondays. Admission charge. Praça do Império (phone: 362-0010).

MUSEU NACIONAL DOS COCHES (NATIONAL COACH MUSEUM) Probably the finest coach collection in the world, housed in a building that was once the riding school of the Palácio de Belém (which was formerly a royal palace and is now the presidential palace). The collection contains coaches from the 16th through 19th centuries, and although a few are simple (such as the one that carried Philip III of Spain when he came to claim the throne as King Philip II of Portugal), most are beautifully carved, gilded works of art suitable for transporting royal personages or their emissaries (note the three Italian-made 18th-century baroque extravaganzas used by the Portuguese Ambassador to the Holy See). It also houses an important collection of livery, harnesses, and bullfighting costumes. Open daily from 10 AM to 1 PM and 2:30 to 5 PM. Admission charge. Praça Afonso de Albuquerque (phone: 363-8022).

PADRÃO DOS DESCOBRIMENTOS (MONUMENT TO THE DISCOVERIES) On the river in front of the monastery, this modern monument was put up in 1960 to commemorate the 500th anniversary of the death of Prince Henry the Navigator. It's shaped like the prow of a Portuguese caravel, with the prince as a figurehead leading a sculptured frieze of the personages of the time seaward. Inside there's exhibition space and an elevator to a belvedere on top, from which the view extends up and down the Tagus and over formal green lawns to the Mosteiro dos Jerónimos and the rest of Belém. Outside is a marble mosaic on the ground that represents a compass; in the center is a map of the world. Open Mondays from 9 AM to 2 PM; Tuesdays through Sundays from 9 AM to 7 PM (to 6 PM from October through February); admission charge to the belvedere. Praça do Império.

TORRE DE BELÉM (TOWER OF BELÉM) This quadrangular, 5-story tower, which looks like a huge chess piece, stands on the banks of the Tagus, west of the Padrão dos Descobrimentos. The Portuguese consider it a symbol of their brave past, and its image often is used on official papers. Built during the 16th century to protect the river from pirates (the tower was at one time surrounded by water, but land has been reclaimed from the river since then), it later functioned as a prison. This is another example of Manueline architecture, richly decorated with sea motifs, statues, stone tracery, and Moorish balconies. There are temporary exhibitions inside. Visitors may climb to the top for a view of the Tagus from the outside terrace. Open from 10 AM to 6:30 PM (to 5 PM from October through May); closed Mondays year-round. Admission charge. Off Avenida Marginal (phone: 616892).

PALÁCIO NACIONAL DA AJUDA In the hills behind Belém, this former royal palace was built during the early 19th century and is full of furniture, paintings, sculpture, and objets d'art left much as they were when royalty still occupied the premises. The widow of King Luís, Maria Pia of Savoy, who died in 1911, was its last royal inhabitant, but the palace is still used occasionally by the Portuguese government for state dinners. Open from 10 AM to 5 PM; closed Mondays. Admission charge. Largo da Ajuda (phone: 363-7095).

ENVIRONS

ESTORIL This seaside suburb about 15½ miles (25 km) west of Lisbon became internationally famous during World War II when both Allied and Axis spies were tripping over each other here, notably at the *Palácio* hotel. Since Portugal was neutral, there was a gentlemen's agreement: Allied diplomats could play golf at the local clubs on certain days, Axis diplomats on others. Immediately after the war, Estoril became home for numerous members of Europe's exiled royalty, giving it a touch of glamour. The crowned heads are gone now, but Estoril, with its bars, cafés, and gambling casino, is still a glamorous place. Its large turn-of-the-century mansions, hidden away behind spacious lawns and gardens flanking winding, hilly streets and wide avenues, lend it a decidedly Old World air. The Parque do Estoril, a lovely garden of stately palm trees and purple-red bougainvillea, faces the seaside esplanade and the beach. The modern, elegant *Casino Estoril* (phone: 268-4521) sits at the top of the park. The residential district of Monte Estoril is west of the park, tending to merge with Cascais. By train, Estoril can be reached easily from Lisbon's Cais do Sodré station. By car, take either the beach highway (Estrada Marginal — EN 6) or the A5 toll highway that links Lisbon with Cascais and the towns in between. The tourist office is located on Arcadas do Parque (phone: 468-0113).

CASCAIS Once a simple fishing village whose picturesque, brightly painted boats headed out to sea each morning, Cascais (pronounced Kash-ka-*ish*) evolved during this century into a beach resort and the home of thousands of European — especially British — expatriates and, like Estoril, deposed royalty and dictators. Today, the fast-growing town, just west of Estoril, makes its living largely from tourism, although fishermen remain and the sight of fish being auctioned off (on weekday evenings) at the market by the beach is worth seeing. Cascais has few monuments to detain sightseers: There is one important church, the Manueline Nossa Senhora da Assunção (Largo da Assunçao), notable for its 18th-century *azulejos* and for its paintings by Josefa d'Obidos; the Cidadela (Estrada da Boca do Inferno), a 17th-century fortress overlooking the sea (closed to the public); and the *Museu-Biblioteca Condes de Castro Guimarães* (Av. Rei Humberto de Italia; phone: 483-0856), with paintings, sculpture, furniture, and objets d'art set up in an old mansion (open from 10 AM to 5 PM; closed Tuesdays; no admission charge). The town has plenty of other distractions, however. The bullfights held on summer Sundays at the *Monumental de Cascais* (Bairro do Rosario) attract many visitors. Water sports and sailing are available from its beaches; there are also riding stables, tennis courts, and golf courses in the vicinity. The town (and the coast around it) is famous for its seafood restaurants, many of which overlook the bay and the sea. There is no dearth of nightlife, either, as Cascais is full of bars and discos. Along the coast west of town is the Boca do Inferno (Mouth of Hell), a set of rocky cliffs full of caves and smaller cavities through which the sea storms and rages. Farther along the coast road, 5½ miles (9 km) from Cascais, is Praia do Guincho, an immense stretch of sand between two promontories where the wind howls (*guincho* means "shriek"), the sea is rough, and the undertow dangerous; it is popular with brave surfers. Still farther along is a headland, Cabo da Roca, the westernmost point of continental Europe, where there is a lighthouse. Cascais can be reached by train from Lisbon's Cais do Sodré station. A tourism kiosk is in the town's center (Av. Marginal; phone: 486-8204); it is open Mondays through Saturdays from 9 AM to 7 PM; Sundays and holidays from 10 AM to 6 PM.

QUELUZ This town 7½ miles (12 km) northwest of Lisbon on the road to Sintra is known for its lovely pink rococo Palácio Nacional, where official guests of the Portuguese government usually are housed. The palace was begun in 1747 by the Infante Dom Pedro, who became Pedro III, consort of Queen Maria I, who lived here after going mad following the deaths of both Pedro and her oldest son. Designed by Mateus Vicente de Oliveira, a pupil of the architect of the Mafra Monastery, the royal residence took decades to finish and was restored after being partially destroyed by fire in this century. Its rooms are filled with Portuguese furnishings and tapestries, Italian glassware and marble, Dutch tiles, Chinese screens, Austrian porcelain, and other exquisite antiques; its gardens are laid out to resemble those of Versailles (Queen Maria had been engaged to Louis XV), with fountains, statuary, and *azulejos*. Among the more striking rooms are the Throne Room, the Hall of Mirrors, the Hall of the Ambassadors, the Music Salon, and the Queen's Dressing Room. In the summer, cultural events intended to re-create the ambience of the 18th-century court of Queen Maria — costumed dances, chamber music concerts, equestrian exhibitions, and even games in which visitors can take part — are staged here. The palace is open from 10 AM to 1 PM and 2 to 5 PM; closed Tuesdays. Admission charge (phone: 435-0039). Queluz can be reached by train from Lisbon's Rossio station.

EXTRA SPECIAL   The beauty of Sintra, a town on the north slope of the Serra de Sintra about 17½ miles (28 km) northwest of Lisbon, has been sung through the ages, most notably by poet Luís de Camões in *The Lusiads,* and by Lord Byron, who called it a "glorious Eden" in "Childe Harold's Pilgrimage." The town has an enchanting setting, swathed in towering trees, dense ferns, and plants and flowers of every description brought by the Portuguese from all corners of their once far-flung empire — all kept green by springs gushing from the rocks and little waterfalls tumbling everywhere down the mountain. Mists from the nearby Atlantic often envelop its heights and lend the town an ethereal air (giving it a pleasant climate in summer while, on occasion, obscuring its majestic views). Among the oldest towns in Portugal, it was occupied by the Moors, who built two castles, one of them winding around the side of the mountain from pinnacle to pinnacle and the other in the center of the present town. After Sintra was taken from the Moors in the 12th century, it became a favorite summer residence of the Portuguese monarchs. Over the centuries, they built the imposing Palácio Nacional de Sintra in town on the site of one of the Moorish castles and the whimsical, *Disneyland*-like Palácio da Pena on the very peak of the mountain, where it can be seen from as far away as Lisbon and the Arrábida Peninsula.

The Palácio Nacional de Sintra, in the main square, was built by King João I in the late 14th century and added to by King Manuel I in the early 16th century. It received still further additions later, making the enormous structure a survey of styles from Moorish through Mudéjar, Gothic, Manueline, and Renaissance to baroque. Besides the twin conical chimneys that dominate the town, the most notable feature of the palace's exterior are the characteristic Manueline windows. Inside, its most important features are the *azulejos* facing its walls throughout, some of the finest to be seen in the country. One of the most interesting rooms is the Sala dos Brazoës (Hall of the Coats of Arms), built during Manuel's reign; its ceiling is an octagonal wooden cupola whose painted panels show the coats of arms of the king, his 8 children, and the 72 noble familes of Portugal at the time. In the Sala das Pêgas (Hall of the Magpies), the ceiling is decorated with 136 magpies — painted, so the story goes, on the orders of João I after his wife, Philippa of Lancaster, caught him kissing one of the ladies-in-waiting. (There were 136 ladies-in-waiting at court, and the idea was to put an end to gossip among them.) The palace is open from 10 AM to 1 PM and 2 to 5 PM; closed Wednesdays. Admission charge (phone: 923-0085).

The Palácio Nacional da Pena, standing on the highest peak above Sintra, is reached via a spectacular road of hairpin curves through beautiful parks and woods. After religious orders were expelled from Portugal in 1832, Ferdinand of Saxe-Coburg-Gotha, consort of Queen Maria II, bought a small 16th-century monastery that stood on this spot and commissioned a German architect, Baron Eschewege, to create a new medieval palace around it. Inspired by the Bavarian castles in his own country, the architect combined their styles with Moorish, Gothic, and Manueline elements to create a fantastic building complete with gold-topped domes, turrets, crenelated walls, parapets, and a drawbridge. The cloister and chapel of the monastery were preserved; the latter has a black alabaster and marble altarpiece executed in the 16th century by Nicolas Chanterène, although its stained glass windows are 19th-century German. The rooms of the palace proper are a delightful mixture of Indo-Portuguese and Sino-Portuguese furnishings, and are particularly noteworthy because they have been left much as they were when last occupied by the royal family, who used the palace as their summer home before they fled into exile in 1910. The views from the palace verandahs are spectacular, and the Parque da Pena surrounding it, planted in the 19th century, also is impressive, containing plants and trees from all over the world. The palace is open from 9 AM to 6 PM (to 5 PM in winter); closed Mondays. Admission charge (phone: 923-0227).

The Castelo dos Mouros, or Moorish Castle, is located off the same road that leads to the Palácio Nacional da Pena, about halfway up the mountain. It was originally built by the Moors in the 8th or 9th century and was restored after the Christian reconquest in the 12th century and later by King Fernando I. It has five rather dilapidated towers, a keep, and long walls that undulate over a great part of the mountain; always open. About 2 miles (3 km) from Sintra via N375 is the Quinta de Monserrate, a palace and park built by a 19th-century Englishman, Sir Francis Cook. The palace is an odd-looking, three-domed structure, but the wonderful gardens, landscaped on a steep slope, are the prime attraction here (open daily from 9 AM to sunset; admission charge). Another interesting sight is the 16th-century Convento dos Capuchos, 4 miles (6 km) from town via N247-3. The monks' cells are carved out of rock and lined with cork to keep out the dampness. (Ring the bell and the caretaker will open the door.) Still another of Sintra's palaces, the *Palácio dos Seteais,* has been turned into a luxury hotel (see *Checking In*).

Sintra is very crowded in summer and on weekends. It can be reached by car on N117 and N249 or by train from the Rossio station. Those who come by train can take a taxi to visit the palaces that are located at some distance from the center; the tourist office at 3 Praça da República (phone: 923-1157) provides maps for those who want to walk. There also are horse-drawn carriages that take visitors sightseeing around town. Good restaurants and hotels abound, as do excellent shops selling handicrafts, especially rugs, porcelain, and straw goods. The *Feira de São Pedro de Sintra,* a market that takes place on the second and fourth Sundays of every month, sells everything imaginable. During the *Sintra Music Festival,* held from mid-June to mid-July, concerts featuring internationally known performers are held in the palaces and other public buildings.

Sources and Resources

TOURIST INFORMATION

Maps, brochures, shopping guides, listings of monthly events, and other information can be obtained from the Postos de Turismo (Tourist Posts) run by the Direcção-Geral do Turismo (Directorate General for Tourism), headquartered at 86 Av. António Augusto de Aguiar. A tourist post is located at the same address (phone: 575086); open weekdays from 9 AM to 12:30 PM and 2:30 to 6 PM. The most convenient post in downtown Lisbon is at Palácio Foz (Praça dos Restauradores; phone: 346-3624); open daily from 9 AM to 6 PM. There also is a tourism post at Portela de Sacavém Airport (phone: 893689) for arriving passengers only. The posts have

English-speaking staff members available to answer questions and help make hotel reservations. It is possible to hire English-speaking guides through the tourist offices or by calling the guides union, the Sindicato Nacional da Actividade Turística, Tradutores e Intérpretes (phone: 342-3298).

The US Embassy is on Avenida das Forças Armadas (phone: 726-6600).

LOCAL COVERAGE The leading daily is the *Diário de Notícias,* a morning paper. *Semanario* and *Expresso* are two of the most prestigious weekly papers. English-language newspapers and magazines are sold at most newsstands.

TELEPHONE The city code for Lisbon is 1. If calling from within Portugal, dial 01 before the local number.

GETTING AROUND

Although various sections of the city, such as the Alfama, are ideal for strolling, remember that Lisbon is built on hills; visitors probably will want to ride from one section to another. Parking is problematic, so public transportation and taxis are the best bet.

AIRPORT Lisbon's airport for both domestic and international flights, Portela de Sacavém (phone: 802060), is only 5 miles (8 km) northeast of the center, a 15- to 30-minute drive, depending on traffic. The *Linha Verde* (Green Line) express bus runs between the airport and the Santa Apolónia train station, stopping at major downtown points. The local office of *TAP Air Portugal* is at 3A Praça Marquês de Pombal (phone: 386-1020). *TAP*'s subsidiary, *Linhas Aéreas Regionais* (*LAR;* phone: 848-8509 or 848-0367) has flights to many cities in Portugal, as does the independent company *Portugalia* (170 Rodrigues Sampaio; phone: 352-5336).

BOAT Ferryboats, carrying both passengers and cars, cross the Tagus every few minutes from the Praça do Comércio and Cais do Sodré ferry terminals for Cacilhas, Barreiro, and other points. Short cruises on the Tagus take place from April through October. For information, contact the tourist office.

BUS City buses are run by *CARRIS (Companhia Carris de Ferro de Lisboa).* Maps and other information can be obtained at the window at the side of the Elevador de Santa Justa, just off Rua do Carmo. Get on by the front door, buy a ticket from the driver, and cancel it in the machine. Tourist passes for 4 or 7 days of unlimited travel by bus, tram, subway, ferryboat, and the Elevador de Santa Justa can be bought at the Praça dos Restauradores and Praça Marquês de Pombal subway stations, at the Elevador de Santa Justa, and at *CARRIS* kiosks throughout the city. Long-distance bus service is provided by *Rodoviária Nacional,* whose terminal is at 18 Avenida Casal de Ribeiro (phone: 545439).

CAR RENTAL Most major firms have offices in Lisbon and at the airport: *Avis* (12C Av. Praia da Vitória; phone: 346-2676 or toll-free in Portugal, 500-1002; at the airport; phone: 849-4836; at the Santa Apolónia train station; phone: 876887; and at the *Ritz Inter-Continental* hotel; phone: 692020), *Hertz* (central reservations phone: 941-1090; 10 Av. 5 de Outubro; phone: 579077; 10 Av. Visconde Seabra; phone: 797-2944; at the *Novotel Hotel*, 1642 Av. José Malhoa; phone: 726-7221; and at the airport; phone: 849-2722), and *Budget* (central reservations phone: 89-803490; 6 Av. Fontes Pereira de Melo; phone: 537717; and at the airport; phone: 801785 or 803981).

ELEVATOR The Elevador de Santa Justa takes passengers from Rua do Ouro (Rua Aurea) in the Baixa to Largo do Carmo in the Chiado. The Portuguese also refer to several streetcars that travel a steep route as "elevators," among them the Elevador da Glória, running from Calçada da Glória, on the west side of Praça dos Restauradores, to the Bairro Alto. The unlimited-travel tourist pass is valid on elevators; individual rides cost 140 escudos.

SUBWAY The underground system serving Lisbon is called the *Metropolitano*. A large aboveground "M" designates the stations — Rossio and Restauradores are the most central ones. The fare is 65 escudos — slightly less if bought in a machine — to any point. The unlimited-travel tourist pass is valid underground. Beware of pickpockets.

TAXI Cabs are metered and inexpensive. For trips outside Lisbon, a set rate per kilometer is charged beyond the city limits. Taxis can be hailed on the street or picked up at cabstands conveniently scattered around town. (Note that by law, passengers must get in and out on the sidewalk side, not the street side. Also by law, drivers may charge extra for luggage.) To call a cab, dial 825060 or 825422.

TRAIN Frequent, fast electric trains connecting Lisbon with Belém, Estoril, and Cascais leave from the Estação Cais do Sodré (phone: 347-0181), by the river near Praça do Comércio. Trains to Queluz and Sintra operate from the Estação do Rossio (phone: 877092), just off the Rossio. (It's the 19th-century building with the charming, elaborately carved neo-Manueline façade just across from the side of the *Teatro Nacional*. Confusingly, it's hardly ever referred to by its real name, Estação Central, which is carved in neo-Manueline letters around its circular doors.) Trains for most of the rest of Portugal and elsewhere in Europe leave from Estação Santa Apolónia (phone: 876025), which is located along the river east of the Alfama district, not within walking distance of the center — take a bus or tram. The station for trains to the Algarve is Estação Sul e Sueste (phone: 877179), on the river at Praça do Comércio. These southbound trains actually leave from Barreiro, on the south bank of the Tagus, but tickets include the price of the ferry ride from the station. Trains between Lisbon,

Porto, and Faro have air conditioned coaches with bar and restaurant service. For information on all trains except those leaving from the Estação Cais do Sodre, call 888-4025.

TRAM Also run by *CARRIS,* Lisbon's trams are not only vintage vehicles and picturesque in themselves, but many go through the more historic parts of the city, providing an inexpensive way to take a tour. No. 28 is a particularly picturesque ride across the city to the Alfama district. *CARRIS* also offers two 2-hour tours from Praça do Comércio — a "Hills of Lisbon" circuit that goes through the city, and the "Tagus Line" tour that goes to Belém. Contact *CARRIS* (phone: 363-9343) for information.

SPECIAL EVENTS

The ancient celebrations of the summer solstice have been subsumed here by the *Festas dos Santos Populares* (Feasts of the Popular Saints), Christian rites in honor of São João (St. John), São Pedro (St. Peter), and Santo António (St. Anthony). The latter feast day is the highpoint of Lisbon's social calendar.

FAVORITE FETE

Festa de Santo António (Feast of St. Anthony) Although most people associate St. Anthony (of Padua) with Italy, he was actually born in the Alfama, and people here make much ado about it. The *Festa de Santo António,* June 13 and the night before, is a bit like *New Year's Eve* and *New Year's Day.* The Old Quarter comes alive on the eve: Dances are held in streets festooned with colored lanterns, and throughout the night gallons of good, rough wine are drunk to wash down mountains of sardines roasted on open barbecues. The saint is a powerful matchmaker. This is the night when the city's young women hope to meet their future husbands and street stalls sell little pots of a spicy-smelling green herb called *manjericão* (a variety of sweet basil), each pot holding a message of advice or consolation for lovers. In the Baixa, members of neighborhood associations bedecked in traditional costumes parade down Avenida da Liberdade, each attempting to outdo the display of the others.

For the *Festa de São João,* on June 23 and 24, people make bonfires sprinkled with scented herbs and thistles and jump over them to show their daring, an ancient rite connected with fertility. The final celebration is the *Festa de São Pedro,* on June 29. In little towns around Lisbon, such as Montijo, there is a running of the bulls and a blessing of ships on this day.

The international *Feira de Artesanato* (Handicrafts Fair) is held for 10 days during July. One of the finest fairs of its kind in Europe, it features lace, wicker, pottery, jewelry, hand-knitted items, ceramic and copper dishes, embroidered tablecloths, crystal, the famous Arraiolos rugs, and much more. It takes place in the *Feira Internacional de Lisboa* building, Praça das Indústrias (phone: 362-0130).

MUSEUMS

In addition to those discussed in *Special Places,* the following museums may be of interest. Many that ordinarily have an admission charge are free on Sundays.

MUSEU DA CIDADE (CITY MUSEUM) Maps, engravings, and other objects telling Lisbon's history, set up in an 18th-century palace. Open from 10 AM to 1 PM and 2 to 6 PM; closed Mondays. Admission charge. 245 Campo Grande (phone: 759-1617).

MUSEU NACIONAL DO TEATRO (NATIONAL THEATER MUSEUM) Costumes, scenery, drawings, programs, posters, and other theatrical memorabilia. Open from 10 AM to 1 PM and 2:30 to 5 PM; closed Mondays. Admission charge. 10-12 Estrada do Lumiar (phone: 757-2547).

MUSEU NACIONAL DO TRAJE (NATIONAL COSTUME MUSEUM) Changing exhibitions of Portuguese and foreign costumes, accessories, and fabric, in a lovely old suburban house located about a mile north of the *Museu da Cidade.* Open from 10 AM to 1 PM and 2:30 to 5 PM; closed Mondays. Admission charge. 5 Largo São João Baptista, Parque de Monteiro-Mor, Lumiar (phone: 759-0318).

MUSEU RAFAEL BORDALO PINHEIRO Devoted to the works of the 19th-century caricaturist, ceramist, and painter of the same name. Open from 10 AM to 1 PM and from 2 to 6 PM; closed Mondays. Admission charge. 382 Campo Grande (phone: 795-0816).

SHOPPING

The most important shopping area in Lisbon is the Baixa, the zone between the Rossio and the river, with the mosaic-paved, pedestrian street Rua Augusta as its backbone. Another shop-heavy street, Rua do Carmo, leads from this area to the part of the Baixa known as the Chiado, where many fashionable shops still are located, even though some of the more famous ones, along with two department stores, burned down when fire ravaged much of this area in 1988. The damaged blocks are being rebuilt, but at present shoppers either take the Elevador de Santa Justa to the Chiado or make their way from Rua do Carmo to Rua Garrett, the backbone of the area, via temporary scaffolding erected over the debris. Antiques row also is located in this part of the city: Rua Dom Pedro V, in the Bairro Alto, is the heart of it, but shops also congregate along Rua do Alecrim, Rua da Misericórdia, Rua São Pedro de Alcântara, and Rua da Escola Politécnica. Outside Lisbon, in São Pedro, near Sintra, antiques shops are open all day at the market on Largo Primeiro de Dezembro.

Shops in Lisbon's downtown area are open weekdays from 9 AM to 1 PM and 3 to 7 PM, Saturdays from 9 AM to 1 PM. Many *centros comerciais* (shopping centers) stay open until midnight, although not all of the shops in the complexes stay open that late. The most famous shopping center, with sophisticated stores and boutiques of all kinds — more than 300 of them — is the *Centro Comercial das Amoreiras* (Av. Engenheiro Duarte Pacheco; phone: 692558), a post-modernist complex with huge towers in pinks and greens and glass, designed by architect Tomás Taveira. *Centro Comercial Fonte Nova* (497 Estrada de Benfica; phone: 714-4654), just outside the city, has 80 shops, including excellent leather goods and home-decoration stores. The 45 shops at *Centro Comercial Alvalade* (Praça de Alvalade; phone: 848-0224) offer a classy assortment of giftware, clothing, shoes, and general shopping-mall merchandise. New to Lisbon are hyper-markets — enormous emporiums that stock everything from car parts to shoes. They are usually open from 10 AM to 10 PM; closed Sundays. The two hypermarkets where Lisboans flock to spend their escudos are *Pão Açúcar* on EN 117 toward Sintra and *Continente* on EN 240 in the direction of Amadora.

Also offering a wide variety of goods is the *Feira da Ladra* (Thieves' Market), a flea market selling everything from collectors' items to ready-to-wear. It's held Tuesdays and Saturdays on Largo de Santa Clara, at the edge of the Alfama. Bargaining begins at sunrise, and though the market is open until noon, the best buys are gone long before that, so come early. Portuguese Gypsies peddle closeout items and discontinued, secondhand, overrun, and leftover stock from many top Portuguese clothing manufac-turers and boutiques here; they also sell the apparel from stands on street corners throughout the week.

Among the best buys in Lisbon are gold, silver, and jewelry — rela-tively inexpensive, and the guaranteed content of the gold and silver makes many pieces a bargain. Rua da Prata and Rua Augusta are two of the better streets for jewelry. There has been a renaissance in painting, tapestry making, and ceramics, with the accompanying opening of many new gal-leries. A revival in tile making, often reproducing 17th- and 18th-century designs, also has taken place, and many of the stores selling these *azulejos* will pack and ship. Hand-stitched rugs from Arraiolos, lace from Madeira, beautiful glass and crystal, copperware, fishermen's sweaters, and baskets are other good buys, along with fashionable clothing, shoes, and leather goods. Note that many of the shops below have branches in the *Amoreiras Shopping Center*.

Some stores may provide shipping for their customers. In addition, the *American Visitors Bureau* (61 Rua Castilho; phone: 534879) will arrange to send purchases by air mail, parcel post, or freight.

A. CHAVE DE PRATA Well-stocked shelves of porcelain and glass giftware and some interesting bronze objects. 174 Rua da Prata (phone: 877915).

ALMORÁVIDA A wide variety of regional crafts, pottery, and filigree jewelry plus an extensive collection of Portuguese-style, custom-made rugs. 10-14 Rua do Milagre de Sto. António (phone: 862261).

ANA Antique *azulejos* and small 18th-century plaques. *Ritz Inter-Continental Hotel,* 88 Rua Rodrigo da Fonesca (phone: 658767).

ANA SALAZAR Clothes by Portugal's most famous avant-garde designer for women, who draws artistic inspirations from the turn of the century and the 1940s. 87 Rua do Carmo (phone: 347-2289).

ANTÓNIO CAMPOS TRINDADE Antique Portuguese, English, and French furniture, as well as Chinese porcelain and paintings. 18 Rua do Alecrim (phone: 342-4660).

ARTESANATO ARAMEIRO A wide variety of regional handicrafts — lace, rugs, ceramics, copperware, and filigree. 62 Praça dos Restauradores (phone: 342-0236).

ATLANTIS Fine crystal tableware from Alcobaça. *Amoreiras Shopping Center* (phone: 693670).

CASA DOS BORDADOS DA MADEIRA Embroidery and lace from Madeira, and a wide selection of other Portuguese handicrafts. 135 Rua Primeiro de Dezembro (phone: 342-1447).

CHARLES A very wide selection of shoes — it's the only store in Portugal that makes women's half sizes. It also specializes in Italian designer brands. 105 Rua do Carmo (phone: 347-7361) and 109 Rua Augusta (phone: 347-7360).

CHARLOT Considered a very fashionable boutique, with designer labels from Portugal, Italy, and France. 28 Rua Barata Salgueiro (phone: 573665).

DIADEMA Lovely gold and silver jewelry. 166 Rua do Ouro (phone: 342-1362).

ESCONDIPEL Known for its fine leather goods and fur creations. 9 Rua Ramalho Ortigão (phone: 542275).

FÁBRICA DE CERÂMICA VIÚVA LAMEGO Makes and sells reproductions of *azulejos* from the 15th through the 18th centuries; its bird and animal motifs are famous. It also makes high-quality modern designs, as well as a variety of planters, dishes, lamp bases, and pottery. 25 Largo do Intendente Pina Manique (phone: 315-2401).

GALERIA COMICOS A good gallery showing avant-garde paintings. 1B Rua Tenente Raul Cascais (phone: 677794).

GALERIA 111 The longest established of Lisbon's art galleries, selling the best of today's Portuguese artists. 111 Campo Grande (phone: 797-7418).

GALERIA SESIMBRA Lisbon's second-oldest art gallery, known for hand-stitched Agulha tapestries, made from designs by leading contemporary Portuguese artists. 77 Rua Castilho (phone: 387-0291).

HELIO Top-quality shoes for men and women. 93 Rua do Carmo (phone: 342-3171).

JALCO A good place for beautiful antique Arraiolos rugs. 44 Rua Ivens (phone: 342-8095).

THE KING OF FILIGREE Silver filigree items made in Porto. Some are also dipped in gold. 58 Rua da Prata (phone: 877441).

LIVRARIA BUCHHOLZ A large stock of foreign and Portuguese books. 4 Rua do Duque de Palmela (phone: 547358).

LUVARIA ULISSES Quality leather gloves. 87 Rua do Carmo (phone: 342-0295).

MADEIRA GOBELINS Embroidery, woven tapestries, and carpets from Madeira. 40 Rua Castilho (phone: 356-3708).

MADEIRA HOUSE Lisbon's oldest shop dealing in genuine Madeira embroidery and lace, it also sells less expensive embroidered linen. 137 Rua Augusta (phone: 342-6813).

MADEIRA SUPERBIA A fine selection of high-quality linen from Madeira and Viana do Castelo. 75A Av. Duque de Loulé (phone: 537968).

O MUNDO DO LIVRO Original maps and lithographs from the 16th through the 18th centuries at one of Lisbon's oldest and most famous bookstores. 11 Largo da Trindade (phone: 346-9951).

OURIVESARIA ALIANÇA Antique silver trays and tea service sets. 50 Rua Garrett (phone: 342-3419).

OURIVESARIA DIADEMA Gold, filigree, and souvenirs. 166 Rua do Ouro (phone: 342-1362).

OURIVESARIA PIMENTA Fine jewelry, watches, and silver. 257 Rua Augusta (phone: 342-4564).

PRÍNCIPE REAL ENXOVAL Specializes in handmade embroidery from one of the best factories in Madeira. 12 Rua da Escola Politécnica (phone: 346-5945).

QUINTÃO Beautiful handmade Arraiolos rugs that are works of art. 30 Rua Ivens (phone: 346-5837).

SANT'ANNA Founded in 1741, this store carries fabulous reproductions of 17th- and 18th-century *azulejos,* made in the shop's own factory. 95 Rua do Alecrim (phone: 342-2537). The factory, at 96 Calçada da Boa Hora, can be visited, but call first (phone: 363-8292).

SOLAR The largest selection of antique Portuguese *azulejos,* arranged by century, beginning with the 15th, as well as a fine collection of pewter and furniture. 68-70 Rua Dom Pedro V (phone: 346-5522).

VIDRARIA DA MARINHA GRANDE One of the largest selections of glass and crystal in the country. 38 Rua de São Nicolau (phone: 342-1840).

VISTA ALEGRE The makers of Portugal's finest porcelain, from dinnerware to figurines. Some of the samples and discontinued designs sold downstairs at the shop on the Chiado are great values. 52-54 Rua Ivens (phone: 342-8581) and 18 Largo do Chiado (phone: 346-1401).

W.A. SARMENTO Antique and modern gold jewelry. 251 Rua do Ouro (phone: 342-6774).

SPORTS AND FITNESS

BULLFIGHTING Portuguese bullfighting, quite different from the Spanish version, is more a spectacle of horsemanship than a fight. Bulls are never killed in the ring here, and the fighting is done mostly on horseback, with the *cavaleiros* wearing magnificent 18th-century costumes as they ride against the bulls. Although there is a bullfight at *Easter,* the season begins in earnest in June, and generally runs through September, with contests usually held on Thursdays, Sundays, and holidays. The most important fights take place at the 8,000-seat *Praça de Touros do Campo Pequeno* (Campo Pequeno Bullring; Av. da República; phone: 793-2093), a mosque-like structure with minarets all around its walls, and at the *Monumental de Cascais* (Bairro do Rosario).

FISHING Boats for deep-sea fishing can be rented from local fishermen at Sesimbra, a fishing village 27 miles (43 km) south of Lisbon, or at Cascais.

FITNESS CENTERS Branches of *Health Club Soleil,* a chain, are at the *Amoreiras Shopping Center* (Av. Engenheiro Duarte Pacheco; phone: 692907), and in the *Lisboa Sheraton* hotel, the *Palácio* in Estoril, and the *Estoril-Sol* in Cascais (see *Checking In*).

GOLF There are several prime golf courses within easy reach of Lisbon; visitors are generally welcome on weekdays, but gaining admission on weekends can be more difficult.

TOP TEE-OFF SPOTS

Aroeira Clube de Campo de Portugal Located 11 miles (18 km) from Lisbon on the Setúbal Peninsula, this 18-hole course, designed by Frank Pennink, stretches across rolling hills. Highlights are the 11th and 14th greens, both surrounded by seemingly unavoidable lakes and bunkers. Quinta da Aroeira, Fonte da Telha (phone: 297-1314).

Clube de Golfe do Estoril Opened in 1928 and expanded in 1945, the club features 27 holes in a compact layout that winds through pines, eucalyptus, and mimosa, and offers wonderful views of the sea, the rolling countryside, and the Sintra mountains. To score low on this course, players must drive the ball well. The accent here is on accuracy rather than distance. The well-trapped greens offer plenty of birdie opportunities. The 9th hole has to be seen to be believed — a highway runs between the tee and the green. The course is administered by the elegant *Palácio* hotel. On the weekends, only 9 holes are open to non-members. Av. da República, Estoril (phone: 468-0176).

Clube de Golfe da Marinha Carved out of a thick umbrella pine forest, this 18-hole, par 72 course designed by Robert Trent Jones, Sr. is the center-piece of a deluxe 330-acre residential resort complex. Sea-washed rock outcroppings and windblown dunes are visible along its 6,684 yards. The 14th hole features both the sea and a deep rocky gorge, which separates the tee and the plateau including the green. The 10th hole presents two large lakes joined in a figure eight by a narrow isthmus of land. Cascais (phone: 486-9881).

Estoril-Sol Golf Club In the Sintra Mountains 20 miles (32 km) from Lisbon, this course moves through pines, eucalyptus, and acacias, with the fairy-tale Palácio da Pena perched above. Although it is a short course (4,644 yards), offering 9 holes with 18 tees, it presents numerous chal-lenges — among them the second green, which lies 33 feet above a sheer drop. Estrada da Lagoa Azul, Sintra (phone: 923-2461).

HORSEBACK RIDING Equestrians can be accommodated at the *Clube da Marinha* (at Cascais; phone: 289282), at the *Clube de Campo de Lisboa* (south of Lisbon; phone: 226-1802 or 226-1060), at the *Pony Club Cascais* (Quinta da Bicuda; phone: 284-3233), and at the *Clube de Campo Dom Carlos I* (Estrada Areia, Praia do Guincho; phone: 285-1403). Nuno Veloso, in Cascais (phone: 486-9084), organizes riding circuits and can provide de-tails on watching horse-jumping competitions.

JOGGING Attractive as it may seem, jogging in Lisbon's central Parque Eduardo VII is not recommended, especially alone or at night. Instead, run along the riverside between the Ponte 25 de Abril and Belém. Another good place is the fitness circuit in the *Estádio Nacional* (National Stadium) area on the outskirts of the city on the way to Estoril, where the track winds through pleasant pine woods. (But do not jog alone.) The park in Estoril and the seafront in Cascais are also good, as is the jog down the median strip of Avenida da Liberdade from the Praça Marquês de Pombal toward the Baixa.

SOCCER This is Portugal's most popular sport by far, and it's ruled by a triumvi-rate of three top clubs: *Sporting* and *Benfica,* from Lisbon, and *Porto,* from the northern capital of Porto. Any game in which one of these teams takes part should be worth watching, as the rivalries are very intense. (Note that the crowds are not unruly, and hooliganism is unknown here.) The season runs from August until the end of June, and matches are played on Sundays at various stadiums; tickets can be obtained with the help of your hotel desk.

SWIMMING The entire coast west of the city (see "Estoril" and "Cascais" in *Special Places*) and south of it across the river is banded with sandy beaches, and many hotels have private swimming pools. However, water pollution is a problem on some of the beaches between Lisbon and Estoril, so check first about possible health hazards. (Don't go in the water unless the blue safety flag is flying.) In Estoril, the *Tamariz* restaurant, on the beach, has changing rooms.

TENNIS Although most of Portugal's tennis courts are in the south, there are a few in the Lisbon area. Here are two aces:

CHOICE COURTS

Clube de Tenis de Estoril This recently opened complex has some of the best facilities in the country. In addition to the 4 hard and 14 clay courts (11 are floodlit for night playing), instruction is offered, and there is a restaurant and a bar. Guests from the area's hotels receive special rates. Av. Conde de Barcelona, Estoril (phone: 466-2770 or 468-1613).

Quinta da Marinha Within view of the Atlantic on the aristocratic Estoril coast west of the city, this country club development offers privacy amid splendid, pine-studded surroundings. Villas and townhouses blend in with the landscape. Three of the 6 tennis courts are floodlit. Cascais (phone: 486-9881).

There also are a few public courts at the *Clube de Campo Dom Carlos I* (Estrada Areia, Praia do Guincho; phone: 285-2362) and at the *Estadio Nacional* (National Stadium; Estrada Marginal — EN 6, Cruz Quebrada; phone: 419-7212).

THEATER

Although theater takes a back seat to music in Lisbon, one place stands out.

CENTER STAGE

Teatro Nacional de Dona Maria II Some of the most important classical and contemporary plays are staged here year-round (except during July). All performances are in Portuguese. The theater stands on the site of a onetime royal palace that, during the 16th century, became the seat of the Inquisition. The square is much cheerier now, graced with many flower stalls, fountains, and open-air cafés. Praça Dom Pedro IV (phone: 347-1078).

Also check the publications listed in *Tourist Information,* above, for the increasing number of other theatrical possibilities, including the *revista,* or revue. This popular Lisbon tradition, which embraces topical sketches, satire, music, and dancing in a way reminiscent of old-fashioned vaudeville, can make for a lively evening even for those who don't understand the language.

MUSIC

Much of the country's cultural activity centers around *fado*, the country's unofficial national ballad, which pours out of the city's nightspots (see *Nightclubs and Nightlife*, below). Equally important, however, are the many opera and ballet performances that take place in the city. The following are a few recommended venues:

HIGH NOTES

Grande Auditorium de Fundação Calouste Gulbenkian This performing arts center presents orchestral, choral, and solo works next to the museum that houses the formidable art collection of the late Armenian financier Calouste Gulbenkian. The foundation also supports its own ballet company that performs both classical and modern dance, an orchestra, and a choir. 45 Av. de Berna (phone: 793-5131 or 793-4167).

Teatro Municipal de São Luís Located in the Chiado district, this theater is the site of *National Ballet Company* and *Portuguese National Broadcasting Station Orchestra* performances. Symphony and chamber music concerts and plays also are presented here. Rua António Maria Cardoso (phone: 342-7172).

Teatro Nacional de São Carlos Ensconced in the Chiado district, this is the city's principal concert hall and opera house. Built in the 18th century, it is one of Europe's prettiest, with an apricot-colored interior set off by touches of green and gold. Performances include operas by such greats as Verdi, Rossini, and Mozart. The season runs from mid-December until May. The *National Ballet Company* also performs here, along with the theater's own symphony orchestra and choir. 9 Rua Serpa Pinto (phone: 346-5914).

NIGHTCLUBS AND NIGHTLIFE

A good place to begin an evening with a pre-dinner glass of dry, white port is *A Brasileira* (122 Rua Garrett), one of Lisbon's traditional old cafés. Take a seat at one of the tables outdoors and watch the world go by; the bronze gentleman occupying the bronze table flanked by bronze chairs is the poet Fernando Pessoa (1888–1935) — this statue of him was placed here on the 100th anniversary of his birth. A second old café popular among the old guard is *Café Nicola,* on the Rossio.

Lisbon's popular *fado* houses — restaurants with *fado* music — are scattered throughout the Alfama and Bairro Alto districts. *Fado,* which means "fate" or "destiny," is the name given to the anecdotal, satirical, sentimental, or occasionally happy songs performed, usually by a woman swathed in black (the *fadista*), to the accompaniment of one or more 12-stringed guitars. Although *fado* has become commercialized and many restaurants beef up their shows with folk dancing and popular music, a visitor may be lucky enough to hear the real thing. Do not make a sound during the singing — neither the singers nor the spectators permit it. Some particularly good spots are *Senhor Vinho* (18 Rua do Meio à Lapa; phone: 397-2681), where the *fado* is pure; *O Faia* (54 Rua da Barroca; phone: 342-1923), one of the best known; *Adega Machado* (91 Rua do Norte; phone: 346-0095), entertaining because it offers spirited folk dancing in addition to moving renditions of *fado; Lisboa à Noite* (69 Rua das Gáveas; phone: 346-8557); and *A Severa* (51-61 Rua das Gáveas; phone: 346-4006). All are in the Bairro Alto, except *Senhor Vinho,* which is in the Lapa district west of the Bairro Alto. Those who are not dining should go after 10 PM. Reservations are essential.

Fado still draws its loyal fans, but over the years discotheques have become the most popular spots for Lisbon's midnight-oil burners. The clientele is cosmopolitan, and the action goes on into the wee hours of the morning. On busy nights, the more conservative top discotheques are sometimes difficult to get into for all but regular customers (they're often frequented by local socialites). Provided there's room, though, a properly dressed (no shorts or jeans) traveler should have no trouble gaining admission. Among the longest-established (and starchiest) of the Lisbon haunts in downtown Lisbon are *Stones* (1 Rua do Olival; phone: 396-4545) and *Ad Lib* (18 Rua Barata Salgueiro; phone: 356-1717). For the trendy, the scene is a dockside area close to Alcântara just west of the center, clustered around Avenida 24 de Julho. The current favorites here include *Alcântara Mar* (11 Rua da Cozinha Económica; phone: 362-1226), *Kapital* (68 Av. 24 de Julho; phone: 395-5963), and *Kremlin* (5 Escadinhas da Praia; phone: 608768). In a category of its own is the very fashionable *Bar Bairro Alto* (50 Travessa dos Inglesinhos; phone: 342-2717), featuring shows and other special events. For fans of African music, *Clave di Nos* (100 Rua do Norte; phone: 346-8420) is a bar-restaurant in the Bairro Alto that has live music from the Cape Verde Islands, with food to match. Good bars for a pre-disco or pre-dinner drink include the antiques- and curio-filled *Pavilhão Chines* (89 Rua Dom Pedro V; phone: 342-4729), on the edge of the Bairro Alto; *Procópio* (21 Rua Alto de São Francisco; phone: 652851), a pub-like hangout for artists, writers, theaterfolk, and politicians; and *Cerca Moura* (4 Largo das Portas do Sol; phone: 874859) in the Alfama, with an outdoor terrace with splendid views of the city.

Bars to try in Estoril include the *Founder's Inn* (11D Rua Dom Afonso Henriques; phone: 468-2221) and the *English Bar* (Estrada Marginal, Monte Estoril; phone: 468-0413). And don't miss a night at the world-famous *Casino Estoril* (phone: 268-4521), a shiny, modern building in the

Parque Estoril. The gaming rooms are open daily (to those over 21 endowed with a passport) from 3 PM to 3 AM, and have all the classic European and American games: roulette, baccarat, chemin de fer, blackjack, French bank, slot machines, and bingo. The roulette stakes are higher than in Portugal's other casinos, and the slot machines sometimes spit out jackpots of more than $200,000. But gambling is only one of the attractions. The glittering restaurant-nightclub resembles the *Lido* in Paris, with balconies and a main floor seating 800 and the only really international show in the country.

Cascais has a spirited nightlife, with many bars and cafés such as the *John Bull* (32 Praça Costa Pinto; phone: 483-3319), an English-style pub; *Tren Velho* (Av. Duquesa de Palmela; phone: 486-7355), a converted train coach sitting beside the station; *Bar 21* (1A Travessa da Misericórdia; phone: 486-7518), an attractive cocktail lounge; and *Cutty Sark* (6 Travessa da Ressureição). The list of popular discos includes *Coconuts* (7 Boca do Inferno; phone: 284-4109), with an outdoor terrace by the sea; *Julianas* (10 Av. 25 de Abril; phone: 486-4052); and the very snooty *Van Gogo* (9 Travessa da Alfarrobeira; phone: 483-3378). For *fado* in Cascais, try *Forte Dom Rodrigo* (Estrada de Birre; phone: 285-1373) or *Picadeiro Maria d'Almeida* (Quinta da Guia, Torre; phone: 486-9982).

Best in Town

CHECKING IN

A visitor's primary decision will be whether to stay right in Lisbon, to commute (with thousands of *lisboetas*) from Estoril or Cascais via the clean, inexpensive trains that run into the city about every 20 minutes, or even to stay in Sintra. Whichever your choice, a double room with a private bath will cost from $210 to $350 a night in a hotel in the expensive category, from $100 to $200 in the moderate range, and less than $100 in the inexpensive range. Reservations are necessary, and most places include breakfast in the room rate. Most of the major hotels in Lisbon, Estorial, Cascais, and Sintra have complete facilities for the business traveler. Those hotels listed below as having "business services" usually offer such conveniences as an English-speaking concierge, meeting rooms, photocopiers, computers, translation services, and express checkout, among others. Call the hotel for additional information. All telephone numbers are in the 1 city code unless otherwise indicated.

LISBON

EXPENSIVE

Altis This 9-story ultramodern hotel has 307 rooms, a nice view from its rooftop grill, a heated indoor pool, and 24-hour room service. It's located about halfway between the Rossio train station and Parque Eduardo VII. Business services. 11 Rua Castilho (phone: 522496; fax: 548696).

Lapa A handsomely converted palace surrounded by gardens and with a harmoniously designed modern annex, it has 102 rooms (including 8 suites), with views over the old Lapa embassy quarter and the Tagus River. All rooms have satellite TV, direct-dial telephones, and fax machines on request; 24 of them have Jacuzzis. Among the pluses are 24-hour room service, 2 pools, a fitness center, and a good restaurant with a Swiss chef who specializes in French fare. Business services. 4 Rua Pau da Bandeira (phone: 395-0005; fax: 395-0665).

Meridien This sparkling modern luxury hotel with 350 rooms overlooks Parque Eduardo VII. The decor runs to chrome, marble, and splashing fountains, and the restaurants feature French cooking, hardly unusual in a hotel run by a subsidiary of *Air France*. Business services. 149 Rua Castilho (phone: 690900; 800-543-4300 in the US; fax: 693231).

Ritz Inter-Continental On a hill overlooking Parque Eduardo VII, next door to the *Meridien,* this luxury establishment is contemporary on the outside (built in the 1950s), but traditional within. The appointments are dazzling — silks, satins, and suedes — and some of the 260 rooms and 40 suites are furnished with reproductions of antiques. There's a lovely piano bar overlooking the park, fine shops, a tearoom, 24-hour room service, a coffee shop, and a beauty parlor, as well as the *Ritz Grill Room.* Bedrooms are air conditioned, soundproofed, and equipped with mini-bars, TV sets, radios, and in-house movies; some have balconies overlooking the park. Business services. 88 Rua Rodrigo da Fonseca (phone: 692020; 800-327-0200 in the US; fax: 691783).

MODERATE

Carlton This small, charming hostelry is only a block away from the *Museu Gulbenkian.* There are 72 rooms, all with satellite TV, safes, mini-bars, hair dryers, and a marble-based decor. It has no restaurant, but guests may breakfast in the pleasant indoor patio, dominated by a spreading palm tree. There's an English-speaking concierge. 56 Av. Conde Valbom (phone: 795-1157; fax: 795-1166).

Diplomático Well situated near Parque Eduardo VII, it has 90 rooms equipped with air conditioning, mini-bars, and TV sets, plus a restaurant, a bar, 24-hour room service, and private parking. Business services. 74 Rua Castilho (phone: 386-2041; fax: 386-2155).

Dom Rodrigo A centrally located apartment-hotel, it features 9 twin-bed studios, 39 suites, and 9 penthouses. All accommodations are air conditioned and well soundproofed, and have fully equipped kitchenettes and satellite TV. The outdoor pool is an added asset, making this a viable alternative to a standard downtown hotel. For those who prefer to stay out of the kitchen, there is a coffee shop — but no restaurant. Business services. 44-50 Rua Rodrigo da Fonseca (phone: 386-3800; fax: 386-3000).

Flórida It has 120 air conditioned rooms with all the facilities (private baths, telephones, TV sets, radios); no restaurant, but there's a bar, a gift shop, and a hairdresser. Business services. Near Praça Marquês de Pombal, at 32 Av. Duque de Palmela (phone: 576145; fax: 543584).

Lisboa Plaza Centrally located off Avenida da Liberdade and redecorated by a leading Portuguese designer, this elegant, family-owned and -operated property has 94 rooms and 12 suites, all with air conditioning, sound-proofing, mini-bars, and TV sets. In addition to the *Quinta d'Avenida* restaurant, there is 24-hour room service, and the bar is a popular meeting place. Business services. 7 Travessa do Salitre (phone: 346-3922; fax: 347-1630).

Lisboa Sheraton One of the best of the chain in Europe, this 400-room high-rise offers comfortable accommodations, marble bathrooms, and elegant public areas and lounges. All rooms are air conditioned, and there is a heated, open-air pool, plus several restaurants (including the 29th-floor *Panorama*), 24-hour room service, bars, shops, and a health club. Business services. It's located a bit away from the city center, a few blocks north of Praça Marquês de Pombal. 1 Rua Latino Coelho (phone: 575757; 800-334-8484 in the US; fax: 547164).

Rex Modern, with 70 rooms, this establishment is on the edge of Parque Eduardo VII, near the more prestigious *Ritz* and *Meridien* hotels. Each room has air conditioning, a TV set, and a radio; half have balconies overlooking the park. There are 2 restaurants (one with a panoramic view) and a bar. Business services. 169 Rua Castilho (phone: 388-2161; fax: 388-7581).

Tivoli Right on the main avenue downtown, this hotel has 350 rooms and suites. Because it's so convenient, the lobby is a popular meeting place for businesspeople as well as travelers (and the excellent bar just off the lobby is a favorite of local journalists). There is a restaurant, 24-hour room service, plus a popular rooftop grillroom, a small pool set in a garden, and tennis courts. Business services. 185 Av. da Liberdade (phone: 530181; fax: 579461).

Tivoli Jardim On a quiet street behind its sister *Tivoli* hotel, this property is much quieter. It has 120 rooms (each with a private bath and many with balconies), a restaurant, 24-hour room service, a bar, and a parking lot. The service is first rate, and guests have access to the *Tivoli*'s pool and tennis courts. Business services. 7-9 Rua Júlio César Machado (phone: 539971; fax: 355-6566).

York House Like *Senhora do Monte* (below), this is an insider's inn. It is one of the most attractive places to stay in Lisbon, although it is some distance west of the heart of the city, close to the *Museu Nacional de Arte Antiga.* Housed in a 17th-century building that was once a convent, this lovely, antiques-filled *pensão* has a restaurant and a nice bar with tables in the garden — a particular favorite of British visitors, writers, and embassy personnel. Across and down the street a bit, in an 18th-century house (No. 47) that once belonged to the writer Eça de Queirós, there's an equally old-fashioned and aristocratic 17-room annex, making a total of 62 rooms (not all with private baths). Business services. 32 Rua das Janelas Verdes (phone: 396-2435; fax: 397-2793).

Zurique In an excellent location, near the *Campo Pequeno* bullring, this modern place has 252 rooms with a full range of services, including a pool, a restaurant, and a bar. Business services. 18 Rua Ivone Silva (phone: 793-7111; fax: 793-7290).

INEXPENSIVE

Dom Carlos A comfortable place to stay at Praça Marquês de Pombal. The 73 rooms are air conditioned and equipped with private baths, TV sets, and mini-bars. No restaurant, but there is a breakfast room and a bar. Business services. 121 Av. Duque de Loulé (phone: 539071; fax: 352-0728).

Príncipe Northeast of Parque Eduardo VII, it has 70 air conditioned rooms — each with a private bath, a TV set, and a telephone — plus a restaurant and bar. 201 Av. Duque de Avila (phone: 536151; fax: 534314).

Senhora do Monte This small place is a real find. Located up in the old Graça quarter northeast of Castelo São Jorge, it has good views of Lisbon from some of its 27 rooms (all with private baths). It's not the best location for access, but old hands swear by it. 39 Calçada do Monte (phone: 886-6002; fax: 877783).

Torre Modern and attractive, this little place is a 15-minute taxi ride from the center of Lisbon, but convenient for sightseeing in Belém, where it's right beside one of Lisbon's best-known sights — the Mosteiro dos Jerónimos. There are 50 rooms with private baths, a bar, and a restaurant. 8 Rua dos Jerónimos (phone: 363-7332; fax: 645995).

ESTORIL

EXPENSIVE

Palácio Imagine Allied and Axis spies peeping around pillars during World War II and the jewels of exiled royalty glinting in the light of crystal chandeliers; that's the essence of this gracious Old World hotel by the park. The public rooms are majestic; the staff is the sort that seems to remember everyone who has ever stayed here; and the 200 rooms and suites, with traditional and contemporary furnishings, are air conditioned. In addition to the dining room, there is the adjoining, superlative *Four Seasons Grill* (see

Eating Out), and 24-hour room service. A heated pool and cabañas are in the lovely gardens behind the hotel; the beach on the Atlantic is a 5-minute walk away. Temporary membership in the nearby *Clube de Golfe do Estoril* is available (hotel guests get a 60% discount on greens fees); there are tennis courts at a private club next door (special rates available for hotel guests). Business services. Parque Estoril (phone: 468-0400; fax: 468-4867).

MODERATE

Alvorada A modern hostelry, near the casino, it has 51 rooms, each with private bath and a balcony. There's no pool, but there is a solarium on top, and the hotel is only 200 yards from the beach. There's a breakfast room and a bar; no restaurant. Business services. 3 Rua de Lisboa (phone: 468-0070; fax: 468-7250).

Atlántico In the pleasant residential district of Monte Estoril, this is a modern spot on the sea (or rather, nearly on the sea, since the electric train tracks run between it and the beach). There are 175 air conditioned rooms (some with balconies overlooking the Atlantic), a terrace with a large saltwater pool, an excellent restaurant, a bar, a nightclub, and a billiards room. Business services. Estrada Marginal, Monte Estoril (phone: 468-5170; fax: 468-3619).

Grande On a hill overlooking the sea in Monte Estoril, this is a modern establishment with 73 rooms with private baths (some with balconies), a bar, a restaurant, and a covered pool. Av. Sabóia, Monte Estoril (phone: 468-4838; fax: 468-4834).

Inglaterra A charming, turn-of-the-century private home-turned-hotel, set in gardens near the *Palácio*. Inside, the 45 rooms (each with a private bath) are spare and contemporary, rather than old-fashioned in style; there's a bar, a restaurant, and a pool. Business services. 1 Rua do Porto (phone: 468-4461; fax: 468-2108).

Lennox Country Club A hillside *estalagem* (inn) standing in a garden setting overlooking the coast. There are 32 rooms with private baths, some in the main building, which was once a private home, and some in modern additions, plus a very good restaurant with excellent service, and a kidney-shape, heated outdoor pool. The inn emphasizes golf — golfing memorabilia decorate it, and free transportation is provided to courses in the area. 5 Rua Engenheiro Alvaro Pedro de Sousa (phone: 468-0424; fax: 467-0859).

INEXPENSIVE

Founder's Inn British-owned and also known as the *Estalagem do Fundador,* it has 10 pleasant rooms, each furnished differently; all have private baths, satellite TV, and direct-dial telephones. The restaurant serves excellent international fare; there's also a bar. A freshwater pool is on the grounds, which are on a hillside, set back from the beachfront. 11 Rua Dom Afonso Henriques (phone: 468-2221; fax: 468-8779).

Lido Very comfortable and modern, this hostelry is in a quiet spot on a hillside away from the beach, but not far from the casino and park. The 62 rooms and suites all have private baths and balconies, telephones, and radios; there is a restaurant, a bar, a large pool, a solarium, and a terrace with a view of the ocean. Business services. 12 Rua do Alentejo (phone: 468-4098; fax: 468-3665).

Pica-Pau A good inn in a nice old white-painted villa with a red tile roof, near the *Lido* and the *Founder's Inn*. The 48 rooms with private baths are completely modern; there is a bar, a restaurant, and a pool. Other amenities include an English-speaking concierge. 48 Rua Dom Afonso Henriques (phone: 468-0803; fax: 467-0664).

Smart A *pensão* in a very large old house, it has 16 rooms — most with TV sets and private baths (the rest have washbasins) — a breakfast room (no restaurant), and a garden with palm trees. It's not far from the beach. There's also an English-speaking concierge. 3 Rua José Viana (phone: 468-2164).

CASCAIS

EXPENSIVE

Albatroz A luxury property perched on the rocks at the water's edge. The location is choice, which is not surprising since the core of this hotel was built during the 19th century as a villa for the royal family. Between the original building and a newer balconied addition, there are 40 rooms with private baths, satellite TV, and mini-bars. An excellent restaurant (see *Eating Out*) and bar, both surrounded by windows overlooking the sea, and a pool with plenty of room for sunbathing are further attractions. Business services. 100 Rua Frederico Arouca (phone: 483-2821; fax: 484-4827).

Estalagem Muchaxo Set on the high cliffs above Guincho Beach, this charming inn has views of Cabo de Roca — the westernmost point in Europe. In addition to 63 air conditioned rooms (all with TV sets and mini-bars), there is an excellent panoramic restaurant, *Muchaxco,* which specializes in seafood (see *Eating Out*), a seawater pool, a sauna, squash courts, and a conference room. Praia do Guincho (phone: 487-0221; fax: 487-0444).

Estoril-Sol The biggest on the coast, this property has 317 air conditioned rooms and suites, all with satellite TV and mini-bars. It's east of town, between the center of Cascais and Monte Estoril, and is separated from the water only by the electric train tracks (an underground passage leads directly to the beach). There is a large, panoramic rooftop restaurant, 24-hour room service, 5 bars, a disco, and shops. Sports facilities include an Olympic-size pool on the roof and set in gardens, a children's pool, a health club, a sauna, and squash courts; guests have privileges at a nearby 9-hole golf course. Business services. Parque Palmela (phone: 483-2831; 800-843-6664 in the US; fax: 483-2280).

Guincho The waves crash on three sides of this restored 17th-century fortress that looks out to sea from a rocky promontory 5½ miles (9 km) northwest of Cascais. The location is spectacular, with beach on both sides, although walking on the beach is recommended over going in the water, due to the treacherous undertow here, near the westernmost point of continental Europe. The 36 rooms and suites in this elegant establishment all have private baths, old brick-vaulted ceilings, telephones, mini-bars, and TV sets, and some have balconies. There is a bar and a panoramic restaurant (see *Eating Out*). Business services. Praia do Guincho (phone: 487-0491; 800-843-6664 in the US; fax: 487-0431).

MODERATE

Baia Right on the beach, in the heart of town, where the local fishermen tie up their painted boats. There are 113 renovated rooms, most with balconies, all with air conditioning, satellite TV, and mini-bars. A restaurant, terrace bar, and pool round out the amenities. Business services. Av. Marginal (phone: 483-1033; fax: 483-1095).

Cidadela Near the center of town, with 140 rooms and some apartments, each with its own seaview balcony. Facilities include a good restaurant, a bar, and a pool set amid attractive gardens. Business services. Av. 25 de Abril (phone: 483-2921; fax: 486-7226).

Farol A charming *estalagem* (inn) in a building that was once the private house of an aristocratic family. It's located by the sea, just west of the center along the road to Boca do Inferno and Praia do Guincho. Each of the 15 rooms has a bath, TV set, mini-bar, and direct-dial telephone. There also is a pool, a tennis court, a bar, a snack bar, and a restaurant that overlooks the water. There's an English-speaking concierge. 7 Estrada da Boca do Inferno (phone: 483-0173; fax: 284-1447).

INEXPENSIVE

Dom Carlos In the center of Cascais, this *pensão* occupies a restored house built in 1640, and the breakfast room and chapel maintain the decorations of that period. There are 18 rooms with private baths, a TV salon, and a tree-filled garden. 8 Rua Latino Coelho (phone: 486-8463; fax: 486-5155).

Valbom An *albergaria* (inn) also in the center of Cascais, near the train station, it's better-looking inside than from the outside. There are 40 rooms with private baths and a bar (but no restaurant), and an English-speaking concierge. 14 Av. Valbom (phone: 486-5801; fax: 486-5805).

EXPENSIVE

Palácio dos Seteais One of the loveliest and most romantic hotels in Europe. Built at the end of the 18th century for the Dutch consul in Lisbon, it was sold to the fifth Marquês de Marialva and was often visited by royalty. Marble gleams underfoot and murals line the walls of the public rooms; the 29 guestrooms and 1 suite are beautifully decorated with antiques, handwoven rugs, and tapestries, but there are no TV sets and no mini-bars to destroy the neo-classical illusion. Located just outside Sintra, the hotel does have a TV lounge, a bar, and a well-known restaurant (see *Eating Out*) overlooking spacious gardens, a formal, windowed salon with views of the Sintra Valley, and a pool and tennis courts. Business services. 8 Rua Barbosa do Bocage (phone: 923-3200; fax: 923-4277).

MODERATE

Tivoli Sintra The best in town, it is situated off the main square of Sintra, right by the Palácio Nacional de Pena. The modern building has all the modern conveniences, along with traditional Portuguese touches in the decor. There are 75 air conditioned rooms with private baths, balconies, TV sets, and telephones. *Monserrate,* a highly regarded restaurant with a view (see *Eating Out*), 24-hour room service, lounges, bars, and a garage are among the amenities. Business services. Praça da República (phone: 923-3505; fax: 923-1572).

INEXPENSIVE

Central Located on the main square in front of the palace, this place is short on rooms (only 14, 11 with private baths), but long on charm. There is a pleasant restaurant with a terrace for lunch in the summer and a tearoom. 35 Praça da República (phone: 923-0063).

Sintra In São Pedro de Sintra, a 10-minute walk from downtown. This *pensão* has 10 rooms, a pool, a TV room, and a breakfast room (no restaurant). There is an English-speaking concierge. Travessa dos Avelares, São Pedro de Sintra (phone: 923-0738).

Portugal's *Tourism in the Country* program — a network of elegant old aristocratic estates and manor houses (categorized as *Turismo de Habitação* properties), simpler but still fine country homes (*Turismo Rural*), and farmhouses (*Agroturismo*) that take in small numbers of paying guests — is most active in the rural north, but travelers interested in this type of accommodation do have some choices in the Lisbon area. Among them is the charming *Casal de São Roque,* by the sea in Estoril. Built at the beginning of the century and furnished accordingly, it has 6 rooms for guests, 4 with private baths; the hosts will serve meals upon request.

Contact Casal de São Roque (Av. Marginal, Estoril 2765; phone: 268-0217). In the center of Cascais, there's the *Casa da Pérgola* (13 Av. Valbom, Cascais 2736; phone: 284-0040), set in lovely gardens, offering a luxurious suite and 5 bedrooms with private baths.

Sintra has four properties: The *Quinta de São Tiago* (Sintra 2710; phone: 923-2923) is an imposing noble house several centuries old, surrounded by vast lawns with a pool, near the *Palácio dos Seteais.* There are 7 double bedrooms, luxuriously furnished with antiques; the owners (an Englishman and his Spanish wife) serve meals on request. The *Quinta da Capela* (Estrada de Monserrate, Sintra 2710; phone: 929-0170) is another impressive old noble house surrounded by gardens, located beyond Seteais and the Quinta de Monserrate. One suite and 4 beautifully furnished bedrooms with private baths — or 2 independent apartments — are available. The *Vila das Rosas* (2-4 Rua António Cunha, Sintra 2710; phone: 923-4216) is a large, white 19th-century house with a red tile roof on the northern outskirts of Sintra; 4 double rooms with bath, a suite of 3 rooms with a private bath, and a cottage in the garden are available. In summer, breakfast is served in the cool wine cellar; other meals are served on request. Finally, the *Casa da Tapada* (Sintra 2710; phone and fax: 923-0342) is a 19th-century country mansion situated on a mountaintop, with a view of the Pena and Mouros palaces from the front. There are 5 large rooms, all with private baths. Dinner can be arranged upon request. The *Quinta de São Tiago* and the *Quinta da Capella* are in the expensive price category; the remaining two are in the moderate range. Reservations for the houses above can also be made through certain central booking agencies (also see *Pousadas and Manor Houses* in DIVERSIONS).

EATING OUT

Portuguese food offers a surprising variety of tastes. Over the centuries, this seagoing nation's cuisine has come under the influence of far-flung countries in Asia, Africa, and the Americas, as well as neighboring Spain and nearby France. Lisbon's restaurants reflect this heritage (and all its regional permutations). Fish and seafood abound and usually are fresh and delicious. Those who want to splurge should order steamed lobster or grilled prawns, or dishes such as *arroz de marisco* (rice with shellfish). Stuffed crab and boiled sea spider (eaten by cracking it open with a wooden mallet) are flavorful, and codfish is a great local favorite — it's said the Portuguese have as many ways to prepare it as there are days in the year, one of the best being *bacalhau à Gomes de Sá,* named for a Porto restaurant owner. The best restaurants serve delicious smoked swordfish, sliced very thin, with lemon and capers, but for something uniquely Portuguese, sample the charcoal-grilled sardines sold in the street. Although Lisbon's meat is best grilled, typical dishes such as *cozido à portuguesa* (a stew of boiled vegetables, sausages, and different types of meats, popular in the north) and *iscas à portuguesa* (thin slices of calf's liver marinated in wine, garlic, and bay leaves, and cooked in a shallow earthenware dish) are worth trying. Desserts, mostly based on eggs, sugar, and almonds, may be too sweet for some palates; if so, there are good cheeses — queijo da Serra, from northeastern Portugal, and serpa, from the Alentejo, are among the best. Wines from all over the country appear on the city's wine lists. The rule is to choose those that are more than 5 years old (except for northern *vinhos verdes,* which should be less than 2 years old). Pungent, fruity bairrada wines, mellow, woody dão wines, and flowery douro wines are all good. Bucelas is an excellent white from a small demarcated zone north of Lisbon.

Dinner for two, with a local wine, averages from $90 to $110 at restaurants listed below as expensive, from $50 to $70 at moderate establishments, and from $30 to $50 at inexpensive restaurants. Customary dining time is no earlier than 7:30 PM, but many restaurants close their kitchens at 11 PM. Lunch is served between noon and 2:30 PM. All telephone numbers are in the 1 city code unless otherwise indicated.

For an unforgettable dining experience, we begin with our culinary favorites (the first two in Lisbon, the third in Queluz), followed by our cost and quality choices, listed by price category.

DELIGHTFUL DINING

Aviz When the elegant, turn-of-the-century *Aviz* hotel closed its doors during the early 1960s, its chef and maître d' joined forces and started a new restaurant — same name, same furnishings — in a former tailor's shop. Legend has it that the Armenian oil millionaire Calouste Sarkis Gulbenkian, a frequent client of the hotel, may have contributed to the venture. Today, the restaurant's clients continue to be captains of industry, who like its subdued intimacy, refined Belle Epoque look, and flawless service. Guests have a choice of dining rooms: the cozy silk-lined *salão verde* (green room) or the lighter *salão amarelo* (yellow room), decorated with old musical instruments. Parties of 14 to 18 persons can retire to the intimacy of a private salon under the watchful eye of a 19th-century wooden statue of Pocahontas. Other attractions are the wooden pub-like bar and the tile-lined marble staircase. The chef's enticing culinary creations — smoked swordfish, gratinéed cod *Conde de Guarda*-style, rack of lamb with ground herbs, and chilled *bôlo de ananás* (pineapple cake) — help make the restaurant one of Portugal's dining landmarks. Closed Saturdays at lunch, Sundays, and holidays. Reservations advised. Major credit cards accepted. 12B Rua Serpa Pinto (phone: 342-8391).

Tágide This is a favorite with businesspeople and government officials, including the president. A beautiful staircase leads from the small dining room on the first floor to a second-floor dining area where picture windows afford a great view of the Tagus. The white walls, leather chairs, and 18th-century tiles depicting mythological characters give the dining room a classical elegance. Other attractions are a large wine list of over 70 vintages, spanning Portugal's eight main wine regions, and the fish delicacies, including the house salmon pâté and *cherne no forno com coentros* (oven-baked stone bass with coriander). Meat lovers can savor the succulent *churrasco de cabrito* (grilled kid) or *carne de porco à alentejana* (pork Alentejo-style), an ingenious dish of pork and clams prepared with wine, garlic, red pepper, coriander, and oil. The fruit and almond crêpes, topped with vanilla sauce, have been known to seduce the most ardent dieters. Closed weekends. Reservations necessary. Major credit cards accepted. 18 Largo da Biblioteca Pública (phone: 342-0720).

Cozinha Velha The name means "Old Kitchen" — and this is the former royal kitchen of the Palácio Nacional at Queluz, now turned into a restaurant with considerable atmosphere (and air conditioning). It has high stone arches, a 15-foot-long marble worktable, a walk-in fireplace, enormous spits, and walls lined with copper pots and utensils, many of them originals and bearing the royal seal. Wood-vaulted ceilings, red tile floors, iron lamps, refined service, and soft, piped-in music provide an elegant backdrop for such delectables as *terrina de casa* (veal pâté), *linguado suado* (steamed sole) served in a delicate onion, carrot, mushroom, and sour cream sauce, and souffléed, oven-baked *bacalhau espiritual* (codfish). The latter takes 40 minutes to prepare and should be ordered in advance. Guests have a choice of wines from all over the country and neighboring Colares, which produces the light-bodied tavares rodrigues. The restaurant's pièces de résistance are its desserts, fashioned from ancient convent recipes. Try the *doce real* (royal sweet), which comes stamped with the Portuguese royal seal in confectionery sugar and is made of squash, eggs, and nuts. Closed May 1. Reservations necessary. Major credit cards accepted. Palácio Nacional de Queluz (phone: 435-0232).

LISBON

EXPENSIVE

Casa da Comida This discreetly elegant restaurant is in a converted house, with tables set around a charming enclosed garden and an adjoining period bar. The food is delicious and beautifully presented; specialties include pheasant and shellfish dishes. Closed Saturdays at lunch, and Sundays. Reservations advised. Major credit cards accepted. 1 Travessa das Amoreiras (phone: 388-5376).

Casa do Leão A spectacular view of the city and the Tagus River are two drawing cards to this restaurant in the Castelo de São Jorge. The dining room was part of the living quarters of Portugal's first king, Dom Afonso Henriques, and is decorated with 17th-century tiles. Try Chef João Santos's monkfish with lemon, and beef filet with shrimp and cheese sauce. The menu changes in the summer and winter. Open daily. Reservations advised. Major credit cards accepted. Castelo de São Jorge (phone: 875962).

Club dos Empresarios–António Clara Located in a 19th-century, Art Nouveau mansion that is now a municipal monument, this dining spot specializes in Portuguese fare and fine fish dishes. It also boasts a good wine cellar, and a piano bar that is open until 2 AM. Closed Sundays. Reservations necessary. Major credit cards accepted. 46 Av. de República (phone: 796-6380).

Conventual The menu is based on old Portuguese convent and monastery recipes, some of which go back to the 17th century, and objects from churches decorate the premises. Typical dishes include *bacalhau com coentros* (cod with coriander) and *ensopado de borrego* (lamb stew). Closed Saturdays at lunch, and Sundays. Reservations advised. Major credit cards accepted. 45 Praça das Flores (phone: 609196).

Michel The owner, a well-known cook on television in Portugal, specializes in nouvelle cuisine, Portuguese-style, although traditional French dishes also are served. Handsomely decorated, this place is in the Alfama, just below the Castelo São Jorge. Closed Saturdays at lunch, and Sundays. Reservations necessary. Major credit cards accepted. 5 Largo de Santa Cruz do Castelo (phone: 886-4338).

Restaurante 33 Good food and a pleasant atmosphere prevail in this well-appointed eatery behind an elegant clapboard façade. Closed Sundays. Reservations advised. Major credit cards accepted. 33 Rua Alexandre Herculano (phone: 546079).

Sua Excelência Knock on the door to gain entry, and the attentive owner will read out the entire menu in English, if so desired. He serves a very good *açorda* (a sort of "dry" soup, or stew, a combination of seafood, bread, eggs, and coriander) and Mozambique prawns with a peppery sauce. In the Lapa district, near the embassy residences. Closed Wednesdays, weekends at lunch, and September. Reservations advised. Major credit cards accepted. 42 Rua do Conde (phone: 603614).

MODERATE

Caseiro A good restaurant among the many near the Mosteiro dos Jerónimos in Belém. It is typically Portuguese, specializing in regional dishes and seafood, and attractively decorated. Closed Sundays. Reservations advised. Major credit cards accepted. 5 Rua de Belém (phone: 363-8803).

Gondola A long-established Italian eatery near the *Museu Gulbenkian,* and a favorite with visitors. Portuguese dishes are also on the menu. There's a lovely vine-covered garden for summer dining. Closed Saturdays for dinner, and Sundays. Reservations advised. Major credit cards accepted. 64 Av. de Berna (phone: 797-0426).

Laçerda Also near the *Gulbenkian,* this small place used to be a butcher shop and is still devoted to meat (choose a cut from the hook by the door). Photos of celebrities who have dined here decorate the walls, and strings of garlic and onions hang from the ceiling. Closed Sundays and holidays. Reservations unnecessary. No credit cards accepted. 36 Av. de Berna (phone: 797-4057).

Varina da Madragoa An old tavern turned into a blue-and-white tiled restaurant, near Parliament. Good Portuguese food, including excellent *bacalhau.* Closed Saturdays at lunch and Mondays. Reservations unnecessary. Major credit cards accepted. 36 Rua das Madres (phone: 396-5533).

INEXPENSIVE

Bomjardim Considered tops in preparing *frango na brasa,* chicken that's charcoal-broiled on a rotating spit and accompanied by *piri piri* (a fiery chili sauce) if desired. This is one of Lisbon's most popular — and least expensive — culinary delights. There are two *Bomjardim* restaurants facing each other just off Praça dos Restauradores. They're both noisy and crowded at lunchtime; open daily. No reservations. No credit cards accepted. 10-11 Travessa de Santo Antão (phone: 342-7424).

Bota Alta Traditional Portuguese cooking, served in a cheery bistro atmosphere. It's in the midst of all the Bairro Alto nightlife, and usually very busy. Closed Sundays. Reservations advised — or go early. Major credit cards accepted. 35-37 Travessa da Queimada (phone: 342-7959).

ESTORIL

EXPENSIVE

Casino Estoril The glittering, balcony-lined restaurant here is known for its international show at 11:30 PM every night, but it's also commendable for the excellent food and service. It has a long menu listing Portuguese and international dishes. Open daily. Reservations advised. Major credit cards accepted. Parque Estoril (phone: 468-4521).

Choupana On a cliff overlooking the sea a bit over a mile (2 km) east of Estoril, this eatery specializes in seafood, but has a varied menu of other dishes as well. The dining room is large, panoramic, and air conditioned. Later at night, there is a show and music until all hours. Closed Mondays. Reservations advised. Major credit cards accepted. Estrada Marginal, São João do Estoril (phone: 468-3099).

English Bar This brown-and-white building overlooks the water, with windows all around. It's cozily decorated in the English manner (and has a popular bar), but serves very good Portuguese and international dishes. Closed Sundays. Reservations unnecessary. Major credit cards accepted. Estrada Marginal, Monte Estoril (phone: 468-0413).

Four Seasons Grill A very elegant place for the finest dining in Estoril. The long menu of Portuguese and international dishes changes seasonally, as does the china, the decor, and the waiters' uniforms. It is run by the *Palácio* hotel next door. Open daily. Reservations advised. Major credit cards accepted. Rua do Parque, Estoril (phone: 468-0400).

A Maré By the sea with a lovely panoramic view and a varied menu. There is a large air conditioned dining room and, in summer, an outside barbecue. Open daily. Reservations unnecessary. Major credit cards accepted. Estrada Marginal, Monte Estoril (phone: 468-5570).

MODERATE

Ferra Mulinhas An unusual mix of good Portuguese and Hungarian cooking is featured here. Open for dinner only; closed Sundays. Reservations unnecessary. Major credit cards accepted. 5A Rua Viveiro (phone: 468-0005).

CASCAIS

EXPENSIVE

Albatroz The dining room of the hotel of the same name is set on rocks at the edge of the sea (the picture windows afford wonderful views). It's known for a varied menu, including the paella and good seafood. There is piano music nightly and harp and flute music on weekends. Open daily. Reservations necessary. Major credit cards accepted. 100 Rua Frederico Arouca (phone: 483-2821).

Baluarte By the sea, with 2 air conditioned dining rooms featuring splendid views. It specializes in seafood, but also has many other Portuguese and international dishes. Open daily. Reservations advised. Major credit cards accepted. 1 Av. Marechal Carmona (phone: 486-5471).

Hotel do Guincho The restaurant here, in a cliff-top hotel that was once a fortress guarding continental Europe's westernmost extremity, is surrounded by windows looking onto the crashing Atlantic. The location alone makes it a wonderful lunch or dinner spot for those on a day's outing along the coast, but the excellence of the food — with emphasis on seafood — and of the service would recommend it even without the view. Located 5½ miles (9 km) northwest of Cascais. Open daily. Reservations advised. Major credit cards accepted. Praia do Guincho (phone: 487-0491).

Muchaxo In an *estalagem* of the same name, this is one of the most famous seafood spots on the Lisbon coast. The inn is by the sea, so there is a marvelous view over the water. Open daily. Reservations unnecessary. Major credit cards accepted. Praia do Guincho (phone: 487-0221).

Pescador A charming place near the fish market, it is decorated with a nautical motif. Fish and seafood are very good here. Open daily. Reservations advised. Major credit cards accepted. 10B Rua das Flores (phone: 483-2054).

MODERATE

O Batel Nicely decorated in a rustic fashion, this is another good seafood restaurant, near the fish market. Closed Wednesdays. Reservations unnecessary. Major credit cards accepted. 4 Travessa das Flores (phone: 483-0215).

Beira Mar One of the longest established of the seafood eateries near the fish market. Decorated with blue and white tiles, it serves international fare in addition to good seafood. Open daily. Reservations unnecessary. Major credit cards accepted. 6 Rua das Flores (phone: 483-0152).

John Bull A well-known English pub with a good little restaurant attached; international fare is served. Open daily. Reservations advised. Major credit cards accepted. 31 Praça Costa Pinto (phone: 483-3319).

Morgados By the bullring, it is large and air conditioned, and specializes in grilled meat. Closed Mondays. Reservations unnecessary. Major credit cards accepted. Praça de Touros (phone: 486-8751).

O Pipas A smart seafood spot in the center of town, near the fish market, it consists of a small air conditioned dining room decorated with wine barrels and hanging garlic braids and sausages. Open daily. Reservations advised. Major credit cards accepted. 18 Rua das Flores (phone: 486-4501).

INEXPENSIVE

Galegos Near the center of town, this simple place specializes in Portuguese and seafood dishes. Closed Wednesdays. Reservations unnecessary. Major credit cards accepted. 3 Av. Valbom (phone: 483-2586).

SINTRA

EXPENSIVE

Monserrate The floor-to-ceiling windows of this air conditioned hotel restaurant afford a panoramic view of the valley below Sintra. The menu features international dishes. Open daily. Reservations necessary. Major credit cards accepted. *Tivoli Sintra Hotel*, Praça da República (phone: 923-3505).

Palácio dos Seteais An 18th-century palace makes a lovely setting for lunch on a sunny day, especially when the garden terrace is open. This very elegant restaurant, with tall windows that overlook the valley, serves well-prepared Portuguese and international dishes. Open daily. Reservations necessary. Major credit cards accepted. Located outside Sintra, in the hotel of the same name. 8 Rua Barbosa do Bocage (phone: 923-3200).

MODERATE

Adega do Saloio The rustic decor, the braids of onions and garlic hanging from the ceiling, the fireplaces, and the open kitchen tell visitors that this "countryman's winery" is aptly named. Meat, fish, and seafood grilled on the spit are the specialties. Located at the entrance to Sintra from Lisbon or Estoril. Closed Tuesdays. Reservations unnecessary. No credit cards accepted. Chão de Meninos (phone: 923-1422).

Café Paris On the square facing the palace, this old-fashioned café/restaurant is one of the best dining places in the center of town; meat and fish dishes are featured. There is alfresco dining in the summer on the terrace. Open daily. Reservations unnecessary. Major credit cards accepted. Praça da Republica (phone: 923-2375).

Cantinho de São Pedro Also in São Pedro de Sintra, this rustic restaurant has 3 large dining rooms and a wine cellar. Try it for seafood, game, or one of the many French dishes on the menu. Closed Mondays. Reservations advised. Major credit cards accepted. 18 Praça Dom Fernando II, São Pedro de Sintra (phone: 923-0267).

Dos Arcos Typical Portuguese dishes are served in an attractive setting that includes a waterfall. In an old part of town, a 10-minute walk from downtown. Closed Wednesdays at dinner, and Thursdays. Reservations unnecessary. Major credit cards accepted. 4 Rua Serpa Pinto, São Pedro de Sintra (phone: 923-0264).

Galeria Real Above a gallery of antiques shops in São Pedro de Sintra, this is a lovely dining room, filled with antiques. The menu features Portuguese and French food. Open daily. Reservations unnecessary. Major credit cards accepted. Rua Tude de Sousa, São Pedro de Sintra (phone: 923-1661).

Solar de São Pedro Two large dining rooms with fireplaces and a menu of French and Portuguese selections keep this place busy. Closed Tuesdays at dinner, and Wednesdays. Reservations advised. Major credit cards accepted. 12 Praça Dom Fernando II, São Pedro de Sintra (phone: 923-1860).

Tacho Real Located in what once were the stables and coach house of a mansion in the historic center of town, this place exudes atmosphere. Try the *caldeirada à Tacho Real* (their rendition of the traditional fish stew) or the beefsteak with shrimp sauce. Closed Wednesdays, Thursdays at lunch, and from mid-October to mid-November. Reservations unnecessary. Major credit cards accepted. 14 Rua Ferraia, Vila Velha de Sintra (phone: 923-5277).

TEA SHOPS

A tradition almost as hidebound as London's, Lisbon's handsome tea shops provide a firsthand view of one of the city's long-standing ties to

England (as well as a relatively inexpensive snacking alternative). Every weekday around 5 PM, the city's tearooms fill up with clerks taking a break from work; families and friends getting together to discuss the latest news; housewives chatting and nibbling sticky cakes; students doing homework; and shoppers giving their feet a much-needed rest. Most tea shops offer a variety of snacks, from chocolate croissants and *pastelaria crema fina* (cream cake) to *pastéis de bacalhau* (codfish balls) and *folhados com salsicha* (sausage bread). The grande dame of the bunch — going strong for more than 60 years — is the high-ceilinged, chandelier-and-mirror-filled *Versailles* (15A Av. da República; phone: 546340), whose formal, immaculately uniformed waiters serve customers from old silver-plated tea services. Even older is *Pastelaria Bénard,* in the Chiado shopping area (104 Rua Garrett; phone: 347-3133). *Pastelaria Ferrari* (2 Calçada Nova de São Francisco; phone: 346-2741) is temporarily located around the corner from its former site (the old building was destroyed in the 1988 fire). Some of the country's best pastries are made by *Pastéis de Belém* (84 Rua de Belém; phone: 363-7423), an Old World place famous for its delicious offerings sprinkled with cinnamon. Most tea houses are closed on Sundays, except for the *Versailles,* which is open daily from 7:30 AM to 10 PM.

Porto

Few cities can boast of having a wine, a language, and a country named after them. And many would rest on these laurels alone. But not Porto (Oporto in English). The city is simply too busy doing business. The solid gray buildings of Porto's financial district and the sprawl of the city and the industrial belt surrounding it attest to the impact and importance of commerce in this metropolis. But deep inside the modern jungle is an old city, where Gothic elegance harmonizes with baroque flair, houses cling precariously to terraced slopes like the vines that produce the region's celebrated wine, and the soft pastels of crumbling riverside houses shimmer in the misty morning waters of the golden Douro River.

Portugal's second-largest city, with a million inhabitants, Porto may currently play second fiddle to Lisbon, but it hasn't always. Proud *portuenses* claim their city is the country's hereditary capital, more quintessentially Portuguese than their southern rival. After all, it was the fiercely independent people of Porto who helped give the nation its start, who played a key role in freeing Lisbon from the Moors, and who financed and built the bulk of the Portuguese armadas. In return, the city became known as the *capital do trabalho,* the work capital, and its burghers became the unofficial guardians of the nation's values and traditions.

Porto's prime location at the estuary of the Douro has always made it attractive to traders and settlers. The Phoenicians, drawn by the region's metal deposits, came to the mouth of the river to trade. By the time the Romans arrived in the 3rd century BC, a city already existed on the north bank of the Douro. The Romans fortified it and called it Portus (port or harbor), and built an urban metropolis on the south bank, which they named Cale. The twin cities became the major military and commercial center of Portus Cale, from which the name, language, and nation of Portugal were later derived.

Porto proved its mettle in the 9th century by being one of the first urban centers in Iberia to shake off the Moorish yoke. At the end of the 11th century, when Teresa, the daughter of the King of León and Castile, married Henry of Burgundy, the city, along with the rest of the county of Portucale, was part of her dowry. She, in turn, handed over the town charter to its powerful bishops. For centuries thereafter, the bishops, aristocrats, and merchants of Porto struggled for control of the city, and in the 14th century, the merchants claimed a major victory: The crown, in return for the merchants' support against powerful rivals, issued a decree barring the nobility from taking residence in the city's commercial district.

In the 15th century, Porto's most famous son, Prince Henry the Navigator, put the merchants' wealth and shipyards to use: The city built the bulk of the ships used in Portugal's voyages of discovery and reaped many of the profits that came with them. The 16th century was bleak, however. Porto was hit hard by the loss of the country's spice monopoly and the general economic and military decline, which culminated in Portugal's humiliating annexation by Spain in 1580. When the country reclaimed its independence in 1640, João of Bragança was crowned in Porto as King João IV.

By the 18th century, the resilient city was back on top, buoyed by wealth from Portugal's Brazilian colony and a considerable increase in port wine exports following the signing of the Treaty of Methuen with England. Under its terms, English cloth received favored status in Portugal, and Portuguese wine was accorded similar treatment in Britain. British wine merchants set up shop in Porto and went on to play a major role in the success of port wine and the city's subsequent history.

But not all went well for the British. In the mid-18th century, to curb their growing influence in the port wine trade, the powerful Marquis of Pombal set up the Alto Douro Company, giving it monopolistic control of wines from the Upper Douro region. But the company's strict rules and pricing policies annoyed producers and British shippers alike and led to violence when a supposedly drunken mob set fire to the company offices in what came to be known as the *revolta dos borrachos,* or "drunkards' revolt." Pombal's reprisal was vicious — public hanging of 25 participants. Eventually, however, the British merchants found ways to work with the Portuguese company, and to this day their descendants flourish in Porto.

In the early 19th century, Porto was occupied twice by Napoleonic armies. The first invasion, in 1808, ended when the British, alarmed at the prospect of having their coveted supplies of port cut off, sent troops under the command of Sir Arthur Wellesley, later named the Duke of Wellington. Wellesley expelled the French but had to return a year later to repel a second French force.

Porto played a major role in the social struggles of the 19th century. In 1820, liberal army officers with merchant connections formed an alliance in the city to curb the powers of the crown. The movement spread to Lisbon, where, 2 years later, a representative *cortes* drafted a liberal constitution putting an end to feudal rights. King João VI accepted the constitution, but when Miguel I, his son, dismissed it in 1828 and went on to rule like an absolute monarch, Porto rebelled. This caused Miguel's brother, Pedro of Brazil, to abdicate his own throne and return to Portugal to restore the liberal order. Pedro's forces landed north of Porto in 1832 and marched on the city, forcing Miguel to abandon it. Before the War of the Two Brothers was over, however, the Miguelites laid siege to Porto for a year — during which the populace was reduced to eating cats and dogs. The siege was finally lifted with Miguel's definitive defeat south of Lisbon, and Pedro returned to Porto to thank its citizens for their support. When he died 4 months later, leaving his daughter, Maria da Glória, on the Portuguese throne, he bequeathed his heart (encased in gold) to the city.

With the 20th century and the downfall of the monarchy came the triumph of the republicanism for which Porto's merchants had worked so hard, along with a new era of economic development and public works. While two metal bridges have spanned the Douro gorge since the late 19th century, linking Porto with Vila Nova de Gaia (formerly Cale) and the rest of the country, two more bridges (one a railway bridge) and a series of dams have been added in the past 3 decades. The dams produce hydroelectricity, make the river navigable, and control flood waters. In addition, a difficult sandbar at the river's mouth can now be bypassed, thanks to the new artificial port of Leixões, which was built north of the city, between the town of Leça da Palmeira and the onetime fishing village of Matosinhos, now a suburb of Porto. Today, the city's economic emphasis has shifted from the river to this area, where fish canning, oil refining, wood processing, and shipping thrive, and the Exponor exhibition center regularly hosts trade fairs.

The Old City, for better or worse, has been left to age in peace. It is weathered, somewhat tattered, and no stranger to poverty, but it's also teeming with life. Venture into the picturesque Barredo quarter, with its narrow alleyways and stone stairways that meander down to the river, and you will encounter a rich and vibrant world of tiny houses stacked against each other, fanned by the colorful morning wash, and of old women in black leaning over wrought-iron balconies and listening to the laughter of young children echoing off ancient walls. Stroll along the Ribeira, where the sweet smell of flowers emanates from quayside stalls and fish mongers exhibit their wares. Dine at a riverside tavern and gaze out at the south bank, where the city's wine treasure is stored and its handsome *rabelo* boats are docked. This is vintage Porto. Like the venerated wine, it should be savored slowly to be truly appreciated.

Porto At-a-Glance

SEEING THE CITY

Porto is built on several hills, so the city offers more than one panoramic vantage point. The best view is from the former Convent of Nossa Senhora da Serra do Pilar, on the south bank of the river in Vila Nova de Gaia, just across one of the city's two 19th-century bridges, the Ponte de Dom Luís I. Here, a tree-lined terrace looks down at the 2-tiered metal bridge and across to the Old City, the remains of the 14th-century Fernandina wall (which at one time encircled Porto but was torn down during 18th-century expansion), and the towers of the cathedral and the Clérigos church. The latter tower, the Torre dos Clérigos, located on the north bank, provides an alternative view: Climb its 225 steps and be rewarded with a sweeping panorama that includes the sea to the west and the south bank's wine lodges. (For admission information, see the Igreja dos Clérigos below.)

SPECIAL PLACES

Porto is vast, but monumental Porto — extending roughly from the 20th-century Câmara Municipal (Town Hall) at the northern end of the wide Avenida dos Aliados to the riverfront Praça da Ribeira — is fairly concentrated and can be explored on foot. Within this area is the old, or medieval, city. It begins at the southern end of the Avenida dos Aliados, at Praça da Liberdade, where the old Fernandina wall and an entrance to the city once stood, but which is now the heart of the Baixa, Porto's commercial and shopping district. South of the square is the cathedral — the nucleus of the medieval town — sitting at the crest of the Pena Ventosa, a steep hill or cliff overlooking the Douro and Vila Nova de Gaia on its south bank. The terrain suddenly drops sharply south of the cathedral, forcing houses in the Barredo quarter right below it to cling precariously to the slopes, as narrow cobbled streets and granite stairways make their way down to the quayside Ribeira quarter. Thus, there are two levels to Porto, the upper level stretching northward from the edge of the cliff and the lower level along the river.

Four bridges join Porto proper to its Vila Nova de Gaia suburb. The Ponte Dona Maria Pia, the easternmost bridge, was designed by Alexandre-Gustave Eiffel and built in 1877 (a new railway bridge has been built adjacent to it). Not too far to the west is the Ponte de Dom Luís I, built in 1886, a 2-tiered structure that ingeniously joins both the upper and lower parts of the city on both sides, and was the brainchild of an Eiffel disciple. Still farther west is the Ponte da Arrábida, dating from 1963, which stretches 885 feet across the Douro in a single reinforced-concrete span.

DOWNTOWN

SÉ (CATHEDRAL) The twin-towered, fortress-like 12th-century cathedral, with its 17th- and 18th-century modifications, is perched on a hill overlooking the Old Town. Outside, a 13th-century Romanesque rose window stands above the highly stylized baroque doorway. Inside, in the Chapel of the Holy Sacrament, is the church's famous 17th-century silver altar, which was painted over for a period during the French occupation to save it from marauding troops. Also of note are three marble stoups (basins for holy water) in the nave and a bronze relief of the baptism of Christ in the baptistery to the left of the entrance. The sacristy off the south transept contains a gold-carved retable dating from 1610, as well as the crypt of the Bishops of Porto. A door on the south side of the south transept leads to a 14th-century Gothic cloister decorated with *azulejos* (glazed tiles) depicting the life of the Virgin and Ovid's *Metamorphoses*. Open daily from 9

AM to noon and 2 to 5 PM. Admission charge to the cloister. Terreiro da Sé (phone: 319028).

TERREIRO DA SÉ (CATHEDRAL SQUARE) Bordering the cathedral is an imposing 14th-century tower; beside it is the Bishop's Palace, an 18th-century building with a Flamboyant baroque façade. From the square, you can gaze upon the Douro — or thread your way down to it via a maze of alleys leading to the *cais,* or quay.

IGREJA DOS GRILOS (GRILOS CHURCH) The first building owned by the Jesuits in Porto. The 17th-century structure, laid out in the form of a cross with a vaulted dome, has a handsome baroque wooden altar representing the Presentation of Jesus in the temple. More formally known as São Lourenço, the church is open only for services, weekdays from 7 to 9 AM, Saturdays from 3 to 5 PM, and Sundays from 9:30 to 11 AM. Largo do Colégio (phone: 200-8056).

IGREJA DE SANTA CLARA (ST. CLARA CHURCH) East of the cathedral, this basically Romanesque church was founded in the early 15th century but underwent later transformation. The door is a mix of Gothic, Manueline, and Renaissance stonework, while the interior is covered from top to bottom with gilded woodwork. The ceiling is Mudéjar in style. Open weekdays from 9:30 to 11:30 AM and 3 to 7:30 PM; Sundays from 9:30 AM to 12:30 PM. No admission charge, but contributions are suggested at the small museum inside. Largo Primeiro de Dezembro (phone: 314837).

ESTAÇÃO DE SÃO BENTO (ST. BENEDICT STATION) The interior walls of Porto's commuter train station are covered with *azulejos* done in 1930 by Jorge Colaço. They depict scenes of the development of the train and other historic events such as the capture of Ceuta by João I in the 15th century. Praça de Almeida Garrett.

IGREJA DOS CLÉRIGOS (CHURCH OF THE CLERICS) This 18th-century baroque church with an unusual, oval shape was designed by the Italian architect Niccolò Nasoni. It is flanked by the Torre dos Clérigos, a 250-foot-high bell tower that dominates the Porto skyline. The 225-step climb to the top of the tower provides a panoramic view of Porto, the Atlantic Ocean, the Douro, and the wine lodges at Vila Nova de Gaia (see below). The church is open daily from 7:30 to 9 AM, 10 AM to noon, and 6 to 8 PM; the tower is open from 10 AM to noon and 2 to 5 PM; closed Wednesdays. Admission charge for the tower. Rua dos Clérigos (phone: 200-1729).

IGREJA DO CARMO (CARMO CHURCH) Another 18th-century church, this one designed in an elaborate rococo style and dedicated to Our Lady. The outer eastern wall, covered with 20th-century glazed tiles depicting important events of the age of discovery and expansion, faces the lovely Fountain of the Lions. Open weekdays from 7:30 AM to noon and 2 to 5 PM; weekends, open mornings only. No admission charge. Rua do Carmo (phone: 200-8113).

MUSEU NACIONAL SOARES DOS REIS (SOARES DOS REIS NATIONAL MUSEUM)
The most interesting museum by far in Porto is housed in an 18th-century palace (the Palácio dos Carrancas, a former residence of the Portuguese royal family) and contains art from the 16th century on. There are paintings by such 16th-century Portuguese masters as Vasco Fernandes, who was known as Grão Vasco (Great Vasco), and Gaspar Vaz; also represented are 19th-century naturalist painters Silva Porto and Henrique Pousão, as well as Columbano Pinheiro, the 19th- and 20th-century portraitist and still life painter. There also are sculptures by António Soares dos Reis, the 19th-century *portuense* for whom the museum is named; local pottery; gold and silver liturgical objects; a set of 16th-century Limoges enamels representing the life of Christ; and a sword that belonged to the first King of Portugal, Dom Afonso Henriques. Open from 10 AM to 12:30 PM and 2 to 5 PM; closed Mondays. Admission charge. 56 Rua Dom Manuel II (phone: 200-7110).

MUSEU ROMÂNTICO (ROMANTIC MUSEUM) Art objects and furniture from the 19th century are featured at this museum lodged in a 19th-century house overlooking the river on the far side of Porto's Pavilhão Rosa Mota exhibition center (formerly the Palácio de Cristal). See the museum and then go down to the basement to the *Solar do Vinho do Porto,* a comfortable wine bar run by the Port Wine Institute, the body that has supervised and certified the quality of port wine since 1935. The museum (phone: 609-1131) is open Tuesdays through Saturdays from 10 AM to 12:30 PM and 2 to 5:30 PM; Sundays from 2 to 5:30 PM. Admission charge on weekdays. The bar (phone: 697793) keeps later hours, opening at 10 AM weekdays (at 11 AM on Saturdays) and closing at 11:30 PM (10:30 PM on Saturdays); closed Sundays. 220 Rua de Entre Quintas.

CASA TAIT Next door to the *Museu Romântico,* this is the administrative center for the city's chain of museums. Featured here are changing exhibitions of painting, sculpture, and photography, as well as gardens famous for having the largest tulip trees in Europe. Open weekdays from 10 AM to noon and 3 to 7 PM. No admission charge. 219 Rua de Entre Quintas (phone: 606-6207).

PALÁCIO DA BOLSA (STOCK EXCHANGE) The 19th-century granite building is known for its impressive marble staircase and its dazzling oval Arab Room, whose arabesques and stained glass windows imitate the highly decorative style of the Moorish Alhambra in Granada. Open for guided tours weekdays from 9 AM to 11:30 AM and 2 to 5:30 PM. From May through September, the building is also open on weekends from 9 AM to 12:30 PM and 2 to 5 PM. Admission charge. A statue of Prince Henry the Navigator stands in the square in front of the building. Rua Ferreira Borges (phone: 200-4497).

IGREJA DE SÃO FRANCISCO (ST. FRANCIS CHURCH) Originally a Gothic church, it has a fine rose window at its entrance. The church interior, however, is the most dramatic and lavish in all of Porto, the result of remodeling in the 17th and 18th centuries. Walls, vaulting, and pillars are generously covered with carved and gilded wood vines, grapes, birds, angels, and cherubs; a forest of carved, gilded wood covers the high altar. About the only object not dressed in sumptuous gold is the polychrome granite statue of St. Francis in a 13th-century chapel. Open from 9 AM to 12:30 PM and 2 to 5 PM; from 9 AM to 5 PM in March through September; closed Sundays year-round. Admission charge. Praça Infante Dom Henrique (phone: 200-8441).

CASA DO INFANTE Prince Henry the Navigator was born in this 14th-century house, or so it is traditionally — and dubiously — held. The building was a customs house up to the 19th century. Now restored, it serves as Porto's *Arquivo Histórico* (Historical Archive), containing artifacts and documents pertinent to the city's history. Open weekdays from 8:30 AM to 5 PM. No admission charge. Rua da Alfândega (phone: 316025).

IGREJA DA CEDOFEITA (CEDOFEITA CHURCH) Porto's oldest church dates from the 12th century. A 5-minute cab ride northwest of the city center, it has a simple and elegant Romanesque exterior; inside, a single-vaulted nave rests on three arches. Open Mondays from 6 to 8 PM; Tuesdays through Saturdays from 9 AM to 12:30 PM and 4 to 7 PM; Sundays from 9 AM to 12:30 PM. 193 Rua Anibal Cunha (phone: 200-5620).

MUSEU DE ARTE MODERNA (MUSEUM OF MODERN ART) Porto's newest museum, in the Casa Serralves, a former private mansion of the 1930s, is notable for its changing exhibitions of modern art, as well as for its fine, traditional Portuguese garden. Open Tuesdays through Fridays from 2 to 8 PM, and weekends from 10 AM to 8 PM (gardens open until sunset). Admission charge (except Thursdays). 977 Rua de Serralves (phone: 618-0057).

PORT WINE CELLARS

No visit to Porto would be complete or entirely satisfying without a tour of one of the wine "lodges," or cellars, where port wine from the Douro Valley is stored and aged. There are some 50 or so wine lodges in the area, located at Vila Nova de Gaia, on the south bank of the Douro. Some say they're kept at this safe distance from the city in order not to interfere with the sober requirements of business. But experts cite more practical reasons: The lodges are on the south side of the river, facing north, to take advantage of the greater humidity and cooler temperatures, which reduce the wine's evaporation in the cellars.

Most of the houses offer free guided tours, in English, which can be arranged through the tourist office (see *Sources and Resources*) or hotels, or by calling the lodges directly. Tours generally include a courtesy tasting; bottles also can be purchased. To reach the wine lodges at Vila Nova de Gaia, walk or drive across the lower level of Ponte de Dom Luís I and turn right. A stop at one of the several outdoor cafés on an esplanade by the quay is certainly in order — from here you can admire Porto proper across the river, as well as the old wine barges docked at the river's edge. These elegant, Egyptian-looking boats, Porto's characteristic *rabelos,* are the last of their kind, remnants of a pre-dam era when wine from the Upper Douro production area traveled downstream to the lodges by boat, rather than by truck and train. The following are some of the better-known wine lodges that welcome visitors:

COCKBURNS SMITHES Established in 1815 and now owned by the Allied-Lyons group, this firm maintains a high quality throughout their range of ports. Of traditional construction, the lodge has high, pine-beamed roofs and earthen floors. Allow at least 1 hour for the unusually comprehensive and personalized tour, which includes visits to the cooperage (where the casks are made), and to the dust- and cobweb-covered cellars where the wine is stored and aged. Open weekdays from 9:30 to 11 AM and 2 to 4 PM. Rua D. Leonor de Freitas, Vila Nova de Gaia (phone: 379-4031).

FERREIRA One of the largest Portuguese port wine companies, it has a long and colorful history. In the early 19th century, its founder, Dona Antónia Adelaide Ferreira, expanded the family holdings from 3 vineyards to 30 large estates stretching all the way up the Douro to the Spanish border. She became the richest woman in Portugal and endeared herself to the local population — who affectionately nicknamed her "Ferreirinha" (little Ferreira) — by building roads, school nurseries, and hospitals. Open weekdays from 10 AM to 12:30 PM and 2 to 5:30 PM; Saturdays from 10 AM to noon from mid-April through mid-October; open weekdays from 9:30 AM to noon and 3 to 5 PM the rest of the year. 19 Rua da Carvalhosa, Vila Nova de Gaia (phone: 370-0010).

SANDEMAN The lodge is housed, in part, in a former 16th-century convent. It holds about 20 million liters of port in bottles and oak barrels, as well as a small museum of tools and other implements used in the wine industry as early as the 18th century. The oldest section has an interesting floor of soft wood "stilts," placed upright as a cushion to prevent damage to the wine barrels as they are rolled over it. Sandeman was established in 1790 by the Scotsman George Sandeman, and the founder's family continues to supervise the company, although it now is owned by Seagrams of Canada. Open weekdays from 9:30 AM to 12:30 PM and 2 to 5 PM. 3 Largo Miguel Bombarda, Vila Nova de Gaia (phone: 370-6814).

TAYLOR, FLADGATE & YEATMAN One of the last privately owned English wine companies and still considered to produce some of the best ports. The tour is lively and informative; the view over the lodges and river, impressive. Open weekdays from 10 AM to 6 PM. 250 Rua do Choupelo, Vila Nova de Gaia (phone: 304505).

Other wine lodges include *Cálem* (26 Av. Diogo Leite, Vila Nova de

Gaia; phone: 379-4041), open from 9 AM to 12:30 PM and 2 to 5 PM, closed Sundays; and *Dow's, Graham, & Warre* (10 Travessa Barão Forrester, Vila Nova de Gaia; phone: 379-6063), open weekdays from 9 AM to 12:30 PM and 2 to 5 PM; also open Saturdays from 9 AM to 1 PM April through September. Most wineries are closed on local or national holidays; call in advance to check.

EXTRA SPECIAL For centuries before the arrival of the railroad, roads, and dams, the Douro was the lifeline of the people of Porto and the other towns lining the river. Its quicksilver waters carried the handsome, square-sailed *rabelo* boats with their precious cargos downriver from major wine producing and storage centers such as Régua. It is now possible to cruise up the river and admire the terraced slopes that rise like pyramids from the river's edge and surround the stately *quintas* — farms — of the wine families. *Endouro Turismo* (49 Rua da Reboleira, Porto 4000; phone: 324236; fax: 317260) operates a week-long trip on the 46-cabin *Altodouro* along the Douro, where the landscape changes from the lush green of Entre-os-Rios where the Douro and Tamega rivers meet to the stark and rugged beauty of the Alto Douro. Included are daily bus trips to historic towns, monuments, and palaces. The cruise leaves every Saturday from April through October from the quay at Praça da Ribeira and costs about $2,500 for two; reserve well in advance.

The most popular of several other options offered by *Endouro Turismo* is a 15-mile cruise as far as Crestuma, but longer trips, to Régua, Pinhão, and Barca D'Alva, can also be booked. Prices for two people range from about $220 to $460; advance reservations are necessary. There are no cruises from November through most of February. The boats also leave from the Ribeira dock. Another possibility from *Endouro Turismo*, especially for visitors on a tight schedule, is a 1-hour cruise under the city's four bridges. The boat leaves every hour on the hour from the quay in front of the Ferreira wine lodge at Vila Nova de Gaia. It costs about $25 for two and runs weekdays from 10 AM to 6 PM (except at 2 PM); Saturdays from 10 AM to 1 PM from mid-April through mid-October.

Sources and Resources

TOURIST INFORMATION

The Porto Tourist Board (25 Rua Clube Fenianos; phone: 312740) is open weekdays from 9 AM to 5:30 PM (until 7 PM from May through September); Saturdays from 9 AM to 4 PM; and Sundays from 10 AM to 1 PM from July through September only. It provides information on the city and the region, including a monthly booklet (in Portuguese) with information about cultural events in Porto. They also have a handy red pamphlet, in English, called *Oporto/Portugal,* complete with a map of the town showing bus routes, a brochure containing pictures of the city's sights, and a guide to port wine and its history. The office will make hotel reservations within Porto, and lists of manor houses in the area that take in guests also are available. A branch of the national tourist office (43 Praça Dom João I; phone: 317514) also has information on the city and the region. It is open weekdays from 9 AM to 7 PM; Saturdays from 9 AM to 2 PM; and Sundays from 10 AM to 2 PM. The Vila Nova de Gaia Tourist Office (located next to the Sandeman winery, at 242 Av. Diogo Leite; phone: 301902) provides information on the port lodges and other local points of interest. It also features several rooms exhibiting arts and crafts. Open weekdays from 9 AM to 7 PM; Saturdays from 10 AM to 4 PM.

LOCAL COVERAGE The *Jornal de Notícias* is one of Portugal's oldest dailies; *Publico,* one of the newest, has the largest circulation. The *International Herald Tribune* can be purchased the day after publication at the airport, at major hotels, and at the larger newsstands around Praça da Liberdade.

TELEPHONE The city code for Porto is 2. If calling from within Portugal, dial 02 before the local number.

GETTING AROUND

Central Porto can and should be seen on foot, but a car or public transportation is necessary for suburban areas and the environs.

AIRPORT Porto's Aeroporto Francisco Sá Carneiro (phone: 948-2141; for flight information: 948-2144), 9½ miles (15 km) northwest of the city along N107, handles both domestic and international traffic. The No. 56 bus provides regular service to Praça da Lisboa in the center of town. *TAP Air Portugal* has a local office (105 Praça Mousinho de Albuquerque; phone: 608-0200) and an office at the airport (phone: 948-2291); *British Airways* has an office at the airport (phone: 948-1989). The regional shuttle airline, *Linhas Aéreas Regionais (LAR;* phone: 948-3245), flies over the Douro Valley and connects Lisbon to northern tourist spots such as Bragança and Vila Real.

BUS, TRAM, AND TROLLEY These cover the city. Booklets of discount tickets or unlimited-travel tourist passes (good for 4 or 7 days) can be purchased from the *Serviço de Transportes Coletivos do Porto (STCP;* 806 Av. da Boavista; phone: 606-4054) weekdays from 8 AM to 7:30 PM. An interesting trip can be taken aboard the No. 1 tram — from Praça do Infante

Dom Henrique (opposite the Igreja de São Francisco) along the river past suburban Foz do Douro and right through to Matosinhos. (On Sundays, the route is covered by bus.) *Rodoviária Nacional (RN)*, the national bus company (629 Rua Sá da Bandeira; phone: 200-1109), provides sightseeing tours aboard special buses with English-speaking guides.

CAR RENTAL The major international firms represented include *Hertz* (899 Rua de Santa Catarina; phone: 312387; and at the airport; phone: 948-1400); *Avis* (125 Rua Guedes de Azevedo; phone: 315947; and at the airport; phone: 948-1525); and *Europcar* (1158 Rua de Santa Catarina; phone: 317737; and at the airport; phone: 948-2452).

TAXI They can be hailed on the street or picked up at a cabstand — there is a large stand at Avenida dos Aliados (no phone). Or call *Radio Taxi* (phone: 489898). Meters are not used beyond the city limits, so if you are going a long distance, be sure to ask the hotel concierge for an estimate and discuss the amount with the cab driver before setting off.

TRAIN There are three train stations. The main one, Estação de Campanhã (Rua da Estação; phone: 564141), on the eastern outskirts of the city, serves most of the country and foreign destinations. Estação de São Bento (Praça de Almeida Garrett in the city center; phone: 200-2722) is a commuter station. The third station, Estação de Trindade (at the end of Rua António Sardinha; phone: 200-5224), near the tourist office, serves the northern part of the country.

SPECIAL EVENTS

The enterprising side of the city can be seen throughout the year at a host of industrial fairs, conventions, and congresses, the largest of which is the *International Industrial Machines Exhibition* in October. But there are also more colorful events, such as the *International Folk Dance Festival*, sponsored by City Hall in August, and the popular festivals of *São João* (St. John) and *São Bartolomeu* (St. Bartholomew). The *Festa de São João*, which takes place on June 23 and 24, is a mix of pagan and Catholic rituals celebrating the summer solstice and involves curious customs such as passing around leeks and buying small earthenware pots of marjoram. The population stays up all night drinking *vinho verde* and eating roast kid, and lovers leap over huge bonfires. The *Festa de São Bartolomeu*, held on the third Sunday in August, has evolved into a *cortejo de papel*, or "paper parade," in which people dress in paper costumes to satirize public personages and politicians. They follow a float carrying Neptune and sirens to the beach, where they battle "pirates" from the sea; the battle ends with all the participants and some of the onlookers rushing into the water for a holy bath, a practice no doubt related to the old superstition that a dip in the sea can cast out the devil.

MUSEUMS

Besides those mentioned in *Special Places,* the following museums may be of interest:

CASA-MUSEU TEIXEIRA LOPES (TEIXEIRA LOPES HOUSE-MUSEUM) A collection of this well-known Portuguese artist's work, plus pieces by other contemporary sculptors. Open Tuesdays through Saturdays from 9 AM to 12:30 PM and 2 to 5 PM. No admission charge. 32 Rua Teixeira Lopes (phone: 301224).

MUSEU DE ARQUEOLOGIA E PRÉ-HISTÓRIA (ARCHAEOLOGY AND PREHISTORY MUSEUM) Local artifacts dating as far back as 4,000 years. Open weekdays from 9 AM to noon and 2 to 5 PM. No admission charge. Praça de Gomes Teixeira (phone: 310290).

MUSEU MILITAR (MILITARY MUSEUM) Small and heavy arms are exhibited here, plus a collection of 10,000 toy soldiers. Open from 2 to 5 PM; closed Mondays. No admission charge. Rua do Heroismo (phone: 565514).

SHOPPING

Porto and its environs are known for their elaborate gold and silver filigree work, embroidery, lace, leather goods (shoes, purses, wallets, belts), ceramics, tapestry, glass, and crystal. The Baixa, on either side of Praça da Liberdade, is the main shopping district — among the best shopping streets here are Rua de Santa Catarina (gift shops), part of which is an open-air pedestrian mall; Rua 31 de Janeiro (leather goods and shoe stores); nearby Rua da Cedo Feita (shoes); Rua das Flores (silver and gold, including some jewelry); Rua das Carmelitas (ceramics); and Rua dos Clérigos (fabrics). There are some good boutiques and shops along Avenida da Boavista, near the *Meridien* hotel. Several popular markets carry regional handicrafts such as wooden model boats and ox carts, wicker articles, and pottery at bargain prices, as well as clothing and shoes at below store prices. The *Bolhão* market (Rua de Sá da Bandeira) is in the Baixa district, while the more popular *Bom Sucesso* market is in the square of the same name on the western side of town. Both function weekdays from 7 AM to 5 PM; Saturdays from 7 AM to 1 PM. The outdoor *Vandoma* fair, a small flea market near the cathedral, specializes in antiques and knickknacks and is in operation on Saturdays from 7 AM to 1 PM. Regular shops are open weekdays from 9 AM to 12:30 PM and 2 to 7 PM, and Saturdays from 9 AM to 1 PM, but some shopping centers stay open weekends from 10 AM to 12 PM. *Dallas* (1588 Av. da Boavista), a huge center with 500 stores on 5 levels, is the best place in town to buy handicrafts and jewelry. The *Centro Comercial Brasília* (113 Praça Mousinho de Albuquerque) is a mini-mall with everything from gift and shoe shops to pastry shops and hairdressers; underground parking is available. The nearby Rua de Júlio Dinis has a good selection of shoe stores. Individual shops of note include the following:

CÂNDIDO JOSÉ RODRIGUES Many antique jewelry pieces, as well as the shop's own creations, including some interesting silver animal figurines, all of superior quality. 275 Rua das Flores (phone: 200-1840).

CASA DOS LINHOS A family-run firm specializing in the sale of linen and embroidery for over a century. 660 Rua de Fernandes Tomás (phone: 200-0044).

CENTRO DE ARTES TRADICIONAIS Arts and crafts are for sale, including plasterwork, pottery, and woodcarving. 37 Rua de Reboleira (phone: 320076).

CRISAL Producers and sellers of fine Atlantis crystal. In the Foco residential complex, at 301 Rua Eugénio Castro (phone: 695805).

DAVID ROSAS Portugal's largest manufacturer of silver animals, many life-size (and expensive!). This sleek shop also specializes in custom-made silver frames. 1471 Av. da Boavista (phone: 606-8464).

GALERIAS DE VANDOMA An antiques shop and auction house. 181 Rua Mouzinho da Silveira (phone: 200-1286).

JOSÉ ROSAS Antique and modern jewelry. In the Foco residential complex, at 282 Rua Eugénio Castro (phone: 695785).

LUIZ FERREIRA & FILHOS A small shop featuring chic and expensive jewelry and giftware. Its own designs mix sterling silver with interesting stones. 9 Rua Trindade Coelho (phone: 316146).

NANNI STRADA This Milan designer designs and manufactures a hot line of men's and women's clothes here. 1533 Av. da Boavista (phone: 609-2745).

ROSIOR Manufacturers of traditional and modern jewelry. In the Foco residential complex, at 263 Rua Eugénio Castro (phone: 606-8134).

VINCENT Top-quality leather jackets, pants, and coats sold in a wonderful antique interior. 174 Rua 31 de Janeiro; phone: 200-2478).

VISTA ALEGRE Fine handmade porcelain from the town of Vista Alegre; the shop can handle shipping. 18 Rua Cândido dos Reis (phone: 200-4554.)

SPORTS AND FITNESS

GOLF Two golf clubs within easy reach of Porto are the *Clube de Golfe de Miramar* (phone: 762-2067), which has a 9-hole course near the beach at Praia Miramar, 7½ miles (12 km) south of town off N109 (the road to Espinho), and the *Oporto Golf Club* (phone: 722008), with an 18-hole course beside the beach about 3 miles (5 km) south of Espinho and 14 miles (22 km) south of Porto. The latter was opened in 1890 by British wine shippers, and the atmosphere of a British club continues to prevail in its wood-paneled clubhouse. Equipment rental, caddies, and classes are available throughout the year at both clubs; guests of the *Praia do Golfe* hotel in Espinho may use the greens free of charge.

JOGGING Try the gardens (admission charge) of the Pavilhão Rosa Mota, the old exhibition center on Rua Dom Manuel II, or take the No. 18 bus 3 miles (5 km) west to suburban Foz do Douro, at the mouth of the river, and jog along the long esplanade by the beach.

SOCCER The season runs from September through June. Porto's two major clubs are the *Futebol Clube do Porto* (Av. de Fernão de Magalhães; phone: 481738), based at the *Estádio das Antas,* and the *Boavista Futebol Clube* (Rua 1 de Janeiro; phone: 690975), which plays at the *Estádio do Bessa.*

SQUASH The *Clube de Squash do Porto* (164 Rua João Branco; phone: 606-6771) is one possibility; the *Sheraton* (see *Checking In*) also has a squash court.

SWIMMING For a tan and a swim, go out of the city to Espinho, 10½ miles (17 km) south.

THEATER

Classic Portuguese plays and *revistas,* lighthearted political and social satires, can be seen at the *Teatro Municipal Rivoli* (see above).

MUSIC

The symphony orchestras of both Porto and Lisbon play at the elegant *Auditório Nacional Carlos Alberto* (Rua das Oliveiras; phone: 200-4540) and at the *Teatro Municipal Rivoli* (Praça Dom João; phone: 200-3782).

NIGHTCLUBS AND NIGHTLIFE

Porto has a varied nightlife. *Swing* (766 Praçeta Engenheiro Amaro de Costa; phone: 609-0019) attracts the well-heeled, who like its pub (upstairs) and disco (downstairs) combination. *Twins* (1000 Rua do Passeio Alegre; phone: 618-5740), in the affluent suburb of Foz, 3 miles (5 km) west of the center, has a similar setup, but it also provides intimate, continental dining. (It's a members-only club, but this rule is not strictly enforced.) The *Olympia* in the *Meridien* hotel (see *Checking In*) is a discotheque frequented by the business community, while the younger set flocks to *Griffon's* (Centro Comercial Brasília; phone: 606-6091), which is somewhat smaller and noisier.

It is possible to avoid the glitz and fast pace of the disco crowd, however. Although the *fado* tradition did not take hold north of the Douro, you can hear it sung nightly except Saturdays from 9:30 PM to 4 AM at the *Taberna São Jorge* (35 Passeio das Virtudes; phone: 318230). A night of *fado* will cost about $85 for two; reservations advised. The *Mal Cozinhado* (13 Rua do Outeirinho; phone: 208-1319) also has *fado* daily except Sundays from 9:30 PM (reservations necessary; see *Eating Out*). Several pubs in the Ribeira district have live music: *Postigo do Carvão* (26-34 Rua da Fonte Taurina; phone: 200-4539), in a refurbished warehouse by the river, is an animated restaurant and piano bar, and *Aniki-*

Bobo, next door, offers a jazz and folk repertoire popular with the college crowd. *Bela Cruz* (5458 Av. da Boavista; phone: 618-0891) is a pub in an old fort, the Castelo do Queijo, by the sea at Foz.

A final option: At Espinho, there's the *Casino Solverde* (phone: 724045), open from 3 PM to 3 AM, with roulette, slot machines, and bingo, as well as dining, dancing, and a floor show. Portuguese law requires foreigners to show their passports at the door; there's a small entrance fee to the gambling room.

Best in Town

CHECKING IN

Until fairly recently, Porto suffered from a lack of topnotch accommodations. The situation has been remedied with the addition of several deluxe hotels and the refurbishing of some older establishments, but because the newer establishments are in the suburbs (en route to the airport), the supply of recommendable accommodations in the historic part of the city is still limited. It is essential to choose carefully and make reservations well in advance, particularly for the summer months. Expect to pay $200 or more for a double room in the top hotels listed as expensive, from $140 to $180 in those listed as moderate, and under $120 for those listed as inexpensive. All telephone numbers are in the 2 city code unless otherwise indicated.

EXPENSIVE

Infante de Sagres Porto's most luxurious hotel — whose guest list has included the British royal family — is tucked away in a small, quiet square near the center of town. Built during the early 1950s, it has an Old World appearance, thanks to several centuries of antiques and a rich endowment of carved wood paneling, stained glass, and wrought iron. The 79 rooms are spacious and plush, the service is efficient and friendly. There is a bar, and its restaurant (see *Eating Out*) is the most elegant eating place in the city. 62 Praça Dona Filipa de Lencastre (phone: 200-8101; 800-528-1234 in the US; fax: 314937).

Ipanema Park Porto's newest first class hotel is stylish, with 281 spacious rooms that overlook the estuary. Although the design of the building is ultramodern, antique rugs add a nice classical touch. On the premises are 2 bars, the deluxe *Winter Garden* restaurant (see *Eating Out*), the best health club in town, 2 pools, 16 conference rooms, and underground parking for 200 cars. 124 Rua de Serralves (phone: 610-4174; fax: 610-2809).

Tivoli Porto Atlântico This medium-size place (58 rooms) just off the Avenida da Boavista has both outdoor and indoor swimming pools, a sauna, a mini-gym, a bar, and the *Foco* restaurant next door (see *Eating Out*). 66 Rua Afonso Lopes Vieira (phone: 694941; fax: 667452).

MODERATE

Batalha Ideally located in the commercial hub of the city, this Best Western affiliate has 150 rooms, a restaurant (see *Eating Out*), and a bar. 116 Praça da Batalha (phone: 200-0571; 800-528-1234 in the US; fax: 200-2468).

Castelo de Santa Catarina Built in the early 1900s, this charming fairy-tale castle has 25 rooms, complete with period furniture (but no restaurant). Ask for No. 22, or No. 41 at the very top. Parking is available. 1347 Rua de Santa Catarina (phone: 495599; fax: 410-6613).

Meridien A modern 232-room hotel located in the commercial zone en route to the airport, about a 10-minute bus or cab ride to the center. A favorite of young executives, who like the spacious conference facilities and the efficient communications system, it has most of the amenities of a chain hotel, including a French restaurant of the same name (see *Eating Out*), a piano bar, a health club (there is a charge), and a discotheque. 1466 Av. da Boavista (phone: 600-1913; 800-543-4300 in the US; fax: 600-2031).

Sheraton Newer than the nearby *Meridien,* this 253-room establishment provides all the familiar comforts of the chain, including a heated indoor swimming pool, a squash court, and a health club that guests may use for an extra charge. There is a piano bar, and the *Madruga* restaurant (see *Eating Out*) offers both regional and continental food. Free parking. 1269 Av. da Boavista (phone: 606-8822; 800-397-3535 in the US; fax: 609-1467).

INEXPENSIVE

Boavista Small and cozy, and about 3 miles (5 km) west of the center of town in the affluent suburb of Foz do Douro. The building seems a cross between a French château and an English country inn, and most of the 39 rooms, furnished with pine furniture, command views of the Douro estuary and Foz fortress. There's a bar and a dining room (see *Eating Out*), a small patio with a fountain, and terraces for sunning. For an extra payment, guests may use the *Oslo Health Club* in the basement, which has a small indoor swimming pool, a Jacuzzi, a Turkish bath, a sauna, and a massage room. Parking in front. 58 Esplanada do Castelo, Foz do Douro (phone: 618-0083; fax: 617-3818).

Grande Hotel do Porto A classic old hotel on a pedestrian street in the heart of the shopping district. Another Best Western affiliate, it has a charming *fin de siècle* look to it; the splendor and details of the salons and *Porto,* its dining room (see *Eating Out*), recall past glory. All 100 guestrooms were recently refurbished and have air conditioning, TV sets, and direct-dial telephones. There's adjacent parking. 197 Rua de Santa Catarina (phone: 200-8176; 800-528-1234 in the US; fax: 311061).

Novotel A modern place on the south bank of the river by the Arrábida Bridge, convenient for visiting the port wine lodges. There are 93 rooms (about half with a view of the Douro estuary), a bar adjacent to *Le Grill* restaurant (see *Eating Out*), a small outdoor pool, tennis courts, and parking facilities. Lugar das Chas, Afurada (phone: 781-4242; 800-221-4542 in the US; fax: 781-4573).

EATING OUT

Porto's native dish is tripe. The preference began of necessity in the 15th century, when the city's residents slaughtered all their animals to feed the armada of Prince Henry the Navigator on its way to North Africa and were left with only the offal for themselves. They invented various ways to cook it and earned themselves the nickname *tripeiros* (tripe eaters). Ingredients for the most typical dish — *tripas à moda do Porto* (tripe, Porto-style) — include tripe, chopped bits of pig's ear and pig's snout, bacon, sausages, white beans, onions, carrots, parsley, bay leaves, cumin seed, salt, and pepper. Served with rice, its advocates swear it is quite tasty. Before trying the tripe, however, sample the *caldo verde* (green soup), a northern Portuguese dish made with green cabbage, puréed potatoes, and spicy sausage. Other popular dishes are *bacalhau à Gomes de Sá,* a casserole of salt cod, onions, and potatoes attributed to a Porto restaurant owner, and the local version of *caldeirada,* a steamy stew of many different kinds of fish cooked in a tomato, onion, and herb sauce. Desserts are rich in eggs, almonds, and sugar, and have religious names, such as *barrigas de freira* (nuns' bellies), because they originally were made in convents. A word of caution for shellfish eaters: Lobster and shrimp are prohibitively expensive (up to $70 for a lobster). A delicious, more reasonably priced alternative is *arroz de marisco,* which contains several kinds of shellfish and is Portugal's juicier answer to Spanish paella.

Accompany the meal with the region's *vinho verde* (green wine — but young rather than actually green) or with mature red and white Douro wines. Begin with an extra-dry white port accompanied by a small plate of cheese and cured ham, and finish with a vintage port or an *aguardente velha,* an aged cognac-style brandy that goes well with coffee. Expect to pay anywhere from $70 to $90 for a meal for two (with wine) at a restaurant listed as expensive, from $50 to $65 in a moderate one, and from $30 to $45 in an inexpensive place. All telephone numbers are in the 2 city code unless otherwise indicated.

For an unforgettable dining experience, we begin with our culinary favorite, followed by our cost and quality choices, listed by price category.

DELIGHTFUL DINING

Portucale This landmark is favored by executives for its varied menu of Portuguese and continental dishes, attentive service, and sweeping view of the city and countryside. Wood paneling, leather chairs, and colorful modern tapestries serve as the backdrop for such house specialties as artichokes au gratin, lobster and rice stew, pheasant stuffed with almonds, chateaubriand with mushroom sauce, and wild boar, as well as tripe, Porto-style. Open daily. Reservations necessary. Major credit cards accepted. 598 Rua da Alegria, 13th Floor (phone: 570717).

EXPENSIVE

Conde de Leça On the second floor of an old townhouse, this restaurant in the suburb of Leça da Palmeira has a light and airy ambience. Specialties include fresh fish dishes; try the *caldeirada,* a stew of eel and fish in a tomato sauce. Closed Sundays. Reservations unnecessary. Major credit cards accepted. 110 Rua Pinto Araujo (phone: 995-8963).

Don Manoel Housed in a pleasant seaside villa overlooking the Atlantic Ocean, the food here is traditionally Portuguese and consistently topnotch, particularly the fish dishes and the multi-fish *caldeirada* stew. Closed Sundays. Reservations advised. Major credit cards accepted. To reach the restaurant, turn left at the end of Avenida da Boavista. 384 Av. de Montevideu (phone: 617-0179).

Escondidinho This popular place serves the best regional food in the city. Tiles, marble, and local crafts decorate it inside, while outside it has been designed to look like a typical country house — which makes it stand out in the otherwise modern urban street. Closed Sundays. Reservations advised. Major credit cards accepted. 144 Rua Passos Manuel (phone: 200-1079).

Flor do Castelo A small and cozy tavern that boasts excellent local dishes, such as freshly caught, grilled *salmão, tamboril,* and *robalo grelhado* (salmon, monkfish, and sea bass, respectively). Closed Sundays. Reservations advised. Major credit cards accepted. In the suburb of Leça da Palmeira, at 102 Rua Santa Catarina (phone: 995-1651).

Foco This place serves a range of both regional and international dishes as well as a buffet lunch on Sundays. Open daily. Reservations advised. Major credit cards accepted. 82 Rua Afonso Lopes Vieira (phone: 606-7248).

Infante de Sagres The poshest place in town, in the hotel of the same name. The game dishes are excellent, the wine cellar large, and the service ultra-professional. The decor — from the crystal chandeliers to the mirrors and wood-paneled walls — is the height of 19th-century elegance. Open daily. Reservations advised. Major credit cards accepted. 62 Praça Dona Filipa de Lencastre (phone: 200-8101).

Madruga This spacious eating spot, located in the basement of the *Sheraton* hotel, offers both regional and continental fare. A buffet lunch is served every day, and there's brunch on Sundays. A band plays in the evenings. Open daily. Reservations advised. Major credit cards accepted. 1269 Av. da Boavista (phone: 606-8822).

Mal Cozinhado A fairly large and busy restaurant near the Ribeira, it's also known for *fado* singing. Try their special codfish dishes. Open for dinner only; closed Sundays. Reservations necessary. Major credit cards accepted. 13 Rua do Outeirinho (phone: 208-1319).

Meridien Another hotel dining room, it offers a choice of traditional French cooking or nouvelle cuisine. Large plants and wicker furniture create a garden-like atmosphere. A businessperson's lunch is served weekdays, a buffet dinner is available on Fridays, and a family buffet is served on Sundays. Open daily. Reservations advised. Major credit cards accepted. 1466 Av. da Boavista (phone: 600-1913).

Winter Garden Situated in the deluxe *Ipanema Park* hotel, it offers superlative international and regional cooking in a sophisticated setting. Among the standouts is *linguado à Ipanema* (oven-baked sole with seafood sauce). Open daily. Reservations advised. Major credit cards accepted. 124 Rua de Serralves (phone: 610-4174).

MODERATE

Batalha This place in the hotel of the same name specializes in traditional local dishes including *bacalhau* (cod) and *tripas à moda do Porto*. It's worth reserving a table near the window for the fine view of Old Porto, the cathedral, and the Igreja dos Clérigos. Open daily. Reservations advised. Major credit cards accepted. 116 Praça da Batalha (phone: 200-0571).

Boavista The candlelit ambience and the views of the Foz fortress and the Douro estuary make this glass-enclosed verandah, the main dining room of the *Boavista* hotel, a good choice for a romantic evening. Fondue and chateaubriand, steak tartare, pepper steaks, and grilled sole are among the specialties. Closed Sundays. Reservations advised. Major credit cards accepted. 58 Esplanada do Castelo, Foz do Douro (phone: 618-0083).

Churrascão Gaucho This popular lunch spot specializes in Brazilian food and offers specials daily. Try the *alcatra* (roast beef). Closed Sundays and August. Reservations advised. Major credit cards accepted. 313 Av. da Boavista (phone: 609-1738).

Green's Elegant dining in a restaurant with the atmosphere of a private club. Try two of its specialties — steak *au poivre* (pepper steak) and *filetes de pescada com camarão* (filets of hake with shrimp). Closed Saturdays at lunch and Sundays. Reservations advised. Major credit cards accepted. 1086 Rua Padre Luís Cabral (phone: 618-5704).

Le Grill Ensconced in the *Novotel*, this modern-looking dining spot overlooks the pool and offers an à la carte menu of international fare. Open daily. Reservations unnecessary. Major credit cards accepted. Lugar das Chas, Afurada (phone: 781-4242).

Porto Elaborate stucco ceilings, crystal chandeliers, and flowers contribute to the turn-of-the-century elegance that endears this hotel dining room in the

Grande Hotel do Porto to an older, sedate crowd. Grilled ox steaks and grilled turbot are good menu choices. Open daily. Reservations unnecessary. Major credit cards accepted. 197 Rua de Santa Catarina (phone: 200-8176).

Porto Fino A fairly small dining spot, it's set upstairs in a Foz do Douro house. The pleasant atmosphere and the range of fish specialties — try the *linguado grelhado* (grilled sole) or the *lulas gratinadas* (squid gratiné) — have made it popular with the city's social set. A buffet lunch is served weekdays. Closed at lunch on Saturdays. Reservations advised. Major credit cards accepted. 103 Rua do Padrão, Foz do Douro (phone: 617-7339).

Tripeiro A popular, no-frills eatery that serves fine regional cooking and fish specialties. Try the *linguado grelhado* (grilled sole) or *filetes de pescada* (hake). Closed Sundays. Reservations unnecessary. Major credit cards accepted. 195 Rua Passos Manuel (phone: 200-5886).

INEXPENSIVE

A Brazileira This bustling café-restaurant, built at the turn of the century, is a felicitous marriage of Art Nouveau decor and a flamboyant Brazilian sensibility. The fare is Portuguese, and the adjoining *confeitaria* sells deliciously aromatic blends of coffee. Closed Sundays. Reservations unnecessary. Major credit cards accepted. 61 Rua Sá da Bandeira (phone: 200-7146).

Chez Lapin A pleasant, typical Ribeira restaurant lodged in a centuries-old arcade by the river. The walls and ceilings of this tiny but cozy tavern are filled with hunting and kitchen utensils, its busy kitchen is open, and there are two floors for dining. The house specialty is *coelho* (rabbit) in red wine sauce, but for fish lovers, there is tender, black swordfish. Open daily. Reservations advised. Major credit cards accepted. 40 Rua dos Canastreiros (phone: 200-6418).

Downing Street A pleasant family-run place located in a former warehouse in the Ribeira district. On the street level, there's a bar; for dining, there's an intimate, candlelit, tiled cellar or an upstairs room that's decorated with old photos of Porto and looks out onto a picturesque square of colorful houses. Try the *arroz de tamboril* (monkfish and rice stew). Open daily. Reservations unnecessary. Major credit cards accepted. 10 Praça da Ribeira (phone: 380-6777).

Taverna Bebodos The most authentic of several waterfront taverns serving typical regional dishes. Closed Sundays. Reservations advised. No credit cards accepted. 24 Cais da Ribeira (phone: 313565).

Diversions

Divertions

Exceptional Experiences for the Mind and Body

Quintessential Portugal

Despite the assumption on the part of many foreigners that it's just an extension of Spain, Portugal boasts a variety of unique qualities. There is the blend of Mediterranean weather, the variety of its landscapes — where colors can change in the space of a few miles from misty greens to sun-baked ochers — and the abundance of spas and history-packed cities. There is the endless variety of seafood, from the hearty, flavorful *caldeiradas* (fish stews) of the western coast and the aromatic clam dishes prepared in copper *cataplanas* in the Algarve to the sine qua non of a Portuguese summer — charcoal-broiled sardines washed down with rustic red wine. And there is the melodic and melancholy sound of the *fado,* the romance of the Azores and Madeira islands, and the stirring history of the Portuguese explorers.

Portugal's variety comes from its ability to assimilate. Over the centuries, Africa, the East, and other parts of Europe have all contributed to the rich patchwork of Portuguese life. The New World sent the old one tomatoes, potatoes, coffee, and the gold that enriched Portugal's churches and made Lisbon one of the most powerful cities in Europe. From the remnants of the Roman Empire to the Moorish aspect of a southern village to the ubiquitous café and the evening gathering around the motor scooter in a small town square, this mixed heritage is pervasive and consistently intriguing.

Here are several experiences that capture the special spirit of this strip of land, and provide a visitor with an insight into its irresistible personality.

SIPPING THE EARTH'S NECTAR: PORT AND MADEIRA After a long day of sightseeing, nothing goes down more smoothly than a glass of that Portuguese potable, port. Find yourself a comfortable spot in a bar or cozy restaurant and try one of the dryer types such as white or tawny, preferred as an aperitif, along with a chunk of cheese, and let the inviting aroma and soothing texture wash your worries and sore feet away. If you're at its source in Porto, a trip to one of the lodges to sip the wine at first hand will further enhance the experience. As the nectar swirls in your glass, imagine yourself back in the British colonial days when port was the Englishman's wine (it was the British who in the 18th and 19th centuries developed port).

For still more honeyed wine, wait until after your meal, and sip the nutty-sweet taste of madeira. The sweeter varieties, such as bual and malmsey, are ideal with dessert — some fresh strawberries or a pastry. Or try the light verdelho and sercial, both good alternatives to a dry sherry — appropriate before or between meals. If you're actually on the eponymous island of Madeira, you might mistakenly think you're in paradise, enjoying the sun and the rich taste of this ambrosial, molasses-colored liquid.

FADO FANTÁSTICO, Lisbon A visit to Portugal would not be complete without an evening listening to the soulful sounds of the Portuguese *fado*. Sit back in a darkened tavern, and as the musicians strum their guitars, a black-cloaked singer wails a mournful tale of love and abandonment or an ode to the city of Lisbon. If you're in Coimbra, it's the male students from the city's university singing the blues, as *fado* here becomes a ballad of the broken-hearted lover or a paean to the Mondego River, which flows through the city. To experience the pure, unadulterated strains of this melancholy music, book a table at *Senhor Vinho* at Rua do Meio à Lapa in Lisbon and hold someone's hand.

MID-ATLANTIC HONEYMOON, Flores, Azores Somewhere between Lisbon and New York, the Azores roll like a cluster of billiard balls in the pool-table-green waves of the Atlantic. One of the islands, Flores, is the ideal spot to spend a week or two in what will seem like another century, to kick up your heels or kick off your shoes and wade through the wildflowers that give this remote fleck of land its name. It is the westernmost island of this westernmost outpost of Europe, but still close enough to the New World to have been the site of a battle between Confederate and Union gunboats during the Civil War. Yet Flores and the other eight islands of this velvet archipelago, brilliantly embroidered with azaleas, hydrangeas, and lemon-yellow 16th-century churches, may be more Portuguese than mainland Portugal itself. Here, where windmills and bell towers still define the skyline, devotion is even stronger, the waterfalls even clearer, the hairpin curves even hairier. While the quaintness of mainland towns may now be somewhat packaged for the benefit of foreigners, the economy of Azorean villages is still tied to the land and sea.

CLIMBING THE BEANSTALK TO SINTRA After a day spent among the gritty realities of Lisbon, it's just a whoosh up north to the mist-shrouded fairyland of Sintra. This town that floats above the mortal world sports a glorious mishmash of extravagant styles, from the time-torn towers of an ancient Moorish castle to the lacy Mudéjar and frilly baroque of the Palácio Nacional de Sintra and the eccentric turrets and domes of the Bavarian-kitsch Palácio Nacional da Pena. You can sleep, dine, or just have a drink in the *Palácio dos Seteais,* once the country retreat of the Dutch consul and later of the fifth Marquês de Marialva; its marbled floors and muraled halls are a fine example of 18th-century Dutch Diplomatic–Deco. The eclectic architecture of Sintra narrates the passing of peoples through Portugal, and, as if the country had also been colonized by a series of foreign plant kingdoms, the Parque da Pena is the meeting place for an international crowd of shrubs, trees, and flowers, all kept moist and luxuriant by the fine spray from the obliging Atlantic down below.

THE EARLY BIRD CATCHES THE FISH, Algarve Dawn breaks and with the crisp, fresh air the fisherman returns home. In the tiny coastal villages in southern Portugal, there's nothing quite like rising with the sun to witness the weather-worn fishermen bringing in the day's catch. As their brightly colored, sea-beaten boats bob in the surf, the fishermen drag their nets ashore filled with shark, tuna, sardines, and *bacalhau* (cod). The lines on the fishermen's faces hold as many stories as the boats' hulls hold barnacles. Watch as workers on the beach skillfully clean the fish with sharp knives, aware of the awaiting merchants and housewives who are ready to pick and choose for the midday and evening meals. Near the resort areas of Faro, Vilamoura, Lagos, and Portimão, arrangements can be made for visitors to join a fishing boat on its break-of-day outing.

VISIONS OF ALMOND BLOSSOMS, the Algarve and Trás-os-Montes April showers bring almond flowers, and there's no better land to see and smell the fluffy white and pink blossoms than in the Algarve, in the south, or Trás-os-Montes, in the north. The air is perfumed with their sweet scent. Walking through the almond orchards at blossom time is like walking through a bakery just as a sheet of sugar cookies comes out of the oven. In the Algarve, the trees' fruit is captured in a confectionery delight called *amendoa,* almond and honey candies that come in the shape of vegetables, animals, and flowers. One sugary-sweet bite will bring back the sensation of springtime in bloom. Savor the flavor of this popular nut in a glass of *amendoa amarga,* a liqueur that captures the almond taste and aroma in one delectable swallow. Try it chilled on ice.

EXPLORING THE END OF THE WORLD, Sagres, Algarve Here, where navigators once thought land ended and the ocean dropped into nothingness, it is worth trying to catch both ends of the day. Get up early, while the lighthouse at the tip of Cabo de São Vicente still beams its comforting nightlight out to exotic pleasure boats and local trawlers. Go sit on the sharp, pointy rocks beneath Henry the Navigator's cliff-top fortress at Sagres, where fishermen cast their lines into the surging froth, and watch the sun's first beams light up the ancient trade routes to the Orient. When the cool air begins to vibrate with the summer heat, head a few miles north to stretch out on the beach at Carrapateira, wide enough so that there is no need to stake out shoreline turf in meager deck-chair widths even in the highest season. On this wind-cooled coast, your skin may burn before you feel it, so as the sun rises higher, drive into the wooded hills of Monchique and up to the nearly 3,000-foot peaklet of Fóia, from which, if you squint a little, you can convince yourself that you see the Moroccan coast. Spend the hottest part of the day napping under a cypress tree, or sipping a glass of *vinho verde* in the shaded main square of Caldas de Monchique. But make it back to the coast in time to curl your toes in the sand and watch the blood-orange sun slip off the edge of the earth. Then end the day with a platter of grilled sardines or tuna in one of the small, smoky restaurants in which the owner is also both waiter and chef.

Pousadas and Manor Houses

No visit to Portugal is complete without a visit or an overnight stay in a *pousada* or a manor house. Imagine sleeping where kings and queens slept, walking corridors and chambers where Franciscan monks walked, and dining in elegant rooms where nobles and aristocrats sat down to countless formal meals over the centuries. The Portuguese people pride themselves on their rich sense of tradition, and have impeccably restored and converted ancient landmarks into magnificent hotels, offering travelers a return to the past, complete with modern — and sometimes luxurious — facilities.

Many of the *pousadas* in Portugal are restored palaces, castles, and convents; some have retained their original furnishings and antiques. On the way to your room you might pass coats of armor, stone statues, and grand staircases. *Pousadas,* however, are not for everyone. Some double rooms only have two twin beds (double beds are harder to find), and many of the rooms have neither TV sets nor radios. But if you're willing to settle for a bit less luxury (in a contemporary sense), these spots are lovely reprieves from large, impersonal hotels.

The country began its *pousada* program in 1940, and today there are 35 government *pousadas.* Their sizes range from 6 to 55 rooms. All are meticulously clean and decorated with attractive furnishings from various centuries, and all have restaurants that emphasize regional foods and wines. Rates for a double room, including continental breakfast, range from $60 to $180 per night, depending on category and season. Low season runs from November through March, shoulder seasons are from April through June and all of October, and high season is from July through September. There is a 3-night maximum-stay policy (exceptions are permitted in some cases) throughout the *pousada* network.

The Portuguese tourist authority distributes an illustrated booklet — *Pousadas de Portugal* — that provides background information on the individual inns, details of the facilities at each, and prices. Since *pousadas* are very popular, reservations are strongly recommended, particularly during the high season. For more information, contact *Enatur* (10A Av.

Santa Joana a Princesa, Lisbon 1100; phone: 1-848-1221; fax: 1-805846); the *Portuguese National Tourist Office* (590 Fifth Ave., New York, NY 10036; phone: 212-354-4403); or the *pousada* network's US representative, *Marketing Ahead* (433 Fifth Ave., New York, NY 10016; phone: 212-686-9213).

Another option is to sleep in a manor house, perhaps the *casa, solar,* or *quinta* of one of the country's oldest families. Such aristocratic accommodations are the province of Portugal's *Turismo no Espaço Rural* (Tourism in the Country) program, a network of privately owned rural properties that take in paying guests. Begun in the 1980s, the program includes three types of properties. Manor houses and country estates of recognized architectural or historical merit are gathered under the heading of *Turismo de Habitação.* Less imposing — although equally traditional — houses or rustic farmhouses are billed as either *Turismo Rural* or *Agroturismo* properties. Happily, the top-of-the-line manor houses are in the greatest supply, particularly in northern Portugal. In most cases, the owner lives in the house with his or her family, but can no longer keep up with the great expense of running such an estate. (Some simply enjoy the company of foreign travelers.)

A manor house can offer as few as 1 or 2 double or single rooms or as many as 10, usually with private baths. Guest quarters are almost always separate and private, sometimes in apartments and adjoining cottages. Some properties have a swimming pool and tennis courts, while others have stables for horseback riding. The majority of the owners speak English, as well as other languages, and many assist visitors with sightseeing arrangements.

A complete listing of houses is available from the Portuguese National Tourist Office. A 2-month advance notice for booking is usually required. Prices range from approximately $60 to $125 for two people per night, breakfast included, depending on the type of lodging. The availability of other meals varies from house to house, at the discretion of the owner.

For more information, contact *Direcção-Geral do Turismo* (86 Av. António Augusto de Aguiar, Lisbon 1000; phone: 1-575086; fax: 1-556917). Bookings can be made directly with the houses or through the central booking offices of three owners' associations in Portugal. One of them, the *Associação de Turismo de Habitação* (*Turihab;* Praça da República, Ponte de Lima 4990; phone: 58-942729; fax: 58-741444), handles houses in the northern Minho region only. The two others, representing properties throughout the country, are the *Associação de Casas em Turismo* (*ACT;* Alto da Pampilheira, Torre D2 8A, Cascais 2750; phone: 1-486-7958; fax: 1-284-2901), whose marketing arm, *PIT* (phone: 1-286-7958), books the properties; and the *Associação Portuguesa de Turismo de Habitação* (*Privetur;* 10 Rua João Penha, Lisbon 1000; for reservations call 1-654953), whose reservations are also handled by a travel agency,

Feriasol, Viajens e Turismo (phone: 1-286-8232). A minimum stay, 3 nights in the case of *Turihab*, 2 or 3 nights elsewhere, usually is required.

Promoções e Ideias Turisticas (*PIT*) also handles bookings for a limited number of the Minho's manor houses. *PIT* houses can also be reserved in the US through *E & M Associates* (211 E. 43rd St., Suite 1404, New York, NY 10017; phone: 212-599-8280; fax: 212-599-1755).

We have highlighted exceptional *pousadas* in the country's major urban centers in the individual city reports in THE CITIES. Our other favorite Portuguese *pousadas* and manor houses, listed below, are located along the coastline, in the countryside, or in small towns or villages.

POUSADA DO INFANTE, Sagres, Algarve At the western end of the sunny, sandy Algarve coast is this 39-room *pousada* — so popular that rooms must be booked months in advance — named for Prince Henry the Navigator. The guestrooms in the main house have balconies overlooking a grassy terrace and the sea, which is often dotted with small fishing boats. On cool winter nights, guests gather in front of the fireplace in the circular lounge. The restaurant offers a variety of well-prepared fish dishes, and features an extensive Portuguese and international wine list. Information: *Pousada do Infante,* Sagres 8650 (phone: 82-64222; fax: 82-64225).

CASA DA PALMEIRA, Reguengos de Monsaraz, Alto Alentejo Located near the Spanish border in the southeast, this turn-of-the-century house has 8 guestrooms, a sitting room, and a dining room, all characteristic of the era. There is also a lovely garden. Information: *Fernando Nunes Gonçalves, Casa da Palmeira,* Praça de Santo António 7200 (phone: 66-52362).

QUINTA DA PONTE, Faia, Beira Alta An imposing 18th-century manor house in a river valley 9 miles (12 km) from Guarda, it has lovely gardens and a pool. There are 5 guestrooms and 1 suite (all furnished in antiques) in the main house, and 7 rooms in a separate building facing the gardens. All the guestrooms have private baths. This is a good base from which to explore the Serra da Estrela. Information: *Mary Alvim, Quinta da Ponte,* Faia, Guarda 6360 (phone: 71-96126; in Lisbon, phone and fax: 1-691508).

POUSADA DO CASTELO, Obidos, Costa de Prata If Portugal ever had fair maidens scanning the horizons for their returning heroes, surely they sat in the towers of this former castle, located in the picture-perfect village of Obidos. About 60 miles (96 km) north of Lisbon, the town was a traditional wedding gift of the King of Portugal to his bride. An ideal transformation of one wing of the castle has created a 9-room *pousada,* including 3 tower suites. The cobblestone courtyard, thick granite stairways, and antique furnishings (including medieval armor) are all evocative of its storybook history. There also is an excellent restaurant and a bar. Outside, the views of the surrounding farmlands are breathtaking. Information: *Pousada do Castelo,* Obidos 2510 (phone: 62-959105).

POUSADA DE SÃO BENTO, Caniçada, Costa Verde The ambience of a Swiss chalet and the surrounding mountain wilderness make this *pousada* a perfect country haven. In the Peneda-Gerês National Park, on a hilltop overlooking the Caniçada dam, this modern building has balconies with spectacular views of the Cávado River and the mountains. Bringing its guests close to the nature of Portugal, the 30-room *pousada* offers a swimming pool, as well as outdoor sports activities with local campers, hunters, riders, and mountain climbers; daily trips to the surrounding villages and the city of Braga also are available. Information: *Pousada de São Bento,* Caniçada, Vieira do Minho 4850 (phone: 53-647190; fax: 53-647867).

POUSADA DE SANTA MARINHA DA COSTA, Guimarães, Costa Verde One of the largest of all the country's *pousadas,* on a mountain overlooking Guimarães, it was once a 14th-century Augustinian monastery. It changed owners repeatedly through the centuries until finally it was sold to a family (as a game, they often rode horses throughout the long hallways) that kept it until the 1940s. Abandoned, and then almost destroyed by fire, it was eventually taken over by the government, restored, and transformed into a *pousada.* Guests have a choice of 50 rooms, ranging from monastic cells to suites furnished with objects from the former royal palace of Ajuda in Lisbon. At the end of one hallway is a terrace that overlooks the entire town. There is a huge garden, which stretches endlessly, a restaurant, and a bar. Conventions are held in its amphitheater, which holds 200. The *pousada* tends to attract tour groups, especially on the weekends. Information: *Pousada de Santa Marinha da Costa,* Estrada da Penha, Guimarães 4800 (phone: 53-514453; fax: 53-514459).

CASA DO ANTEPAÇO, Ponte de Lima, Costa Verde This restored stone manor house combines the qualities of the past with the comforts of the present and provides a peaceful atmosphere in rural surroundings. There are 4 large double rooms, a living room with a fireplace, a library, a garden, and a terrace offering superb views of the Lima River. Information: *Dr. Francisco de Abreu Lima, Casa do Antepaço,* Ponte de Lima 4990 (phone: 58-941702; reservations 58-942729; fax: 58-741444).

CASA DO AMEAL, Viana do Castelo, Costa Verde The long aristocratic pedigree of this manor house explains its almost museum-like collection of antiques and memorabilia. It has 4 double rooms and 2 apartments (each can accommodate four people) with private baths, sitting rooms, and pleasant gardens and grounds. Information: *Maria Elisa Araújo, Casa do Ameal,* Meadela, Viana do Castelo 4900 (phone: 58-22403).

CASA DE CORTEGAÇA, Viana do Castelo, Costa Verde A historic 16th-century manor house on the left bank of the Lima River, it offers the ultimate in modern comforts, in a setting steeped in tradition. The 3 double rooms (all with private baths) and tower suite are tastefully appointed with family heirlooms. There are several sitting and dining rooms, a lovely garden, a farmhouse, and plenty of rippling streams to stroll along. Romantic, candlelit meals in the sumptuous family dining room can be arranged. Information: *Maria Filomena de Abreu Coutinho, Casa de Cortegaça*, Subportela, Viana do Castelo 4900 (phone: 58-971639).

QUINTA DE SANTO ANDRÉ, near Lisbon Just up the Tagus, outside Vila Franca de Xira, about 20 miles (32 km) from Lisbon, this lovely estate is in the midst of horse and cattle country, where Portugal's fighting bulls are raised. There are 5 guestrooms, numerous sitting rooms, and a swimming pool. Information: *Karl Gerhard Brumm, Quinta de Santo André,* Estrada de Monte Gordo, Vila Franca de Xira 2600 (phone: 63-22776 or 63-22143).

POUSADA DE SÃO FILIPE, Setúbal, near Lisbon This former 16th-century castle sits atop a hill and overlooks a busy, picturesque waterfront. Inside, its chapel walls boast hand-painted blue tiles depicting scenes from the life of São Filipe and the Virgin Mary. Just an hour's drive from Lisbon, this recently renovated 14-room *pousada* is popular with weekend travelers. It's installed in a fortress built during the late 16th century by King Philip I (Philip II of Spain) to defend the "invincible" armada he had assembled in Portugal against a possible English attack. The town of Setúbal is itself worth exploring; it was once an important center of Catholicism, with as many as 13 convents and monasteries. Information: *Pousada de São Filipe,* Setúbal 2900 (phone: 65-523844; fax: 65-532538).

Satisfying Spas

The spas of Portugal are a slightly different breed from those of the US. Unlike their American counterparts, which are predominantly exercise- and fitness-oriented, Portuguese spas take more of a therapeutic approach. They are health resorts in a purer sense, and are monitored by the country's National Health Association.

The spas are generally more primitive than those in the US, and don't offer much in the way of facilities. Most have been built around the many mineral and thermal springs of the northern and central regions of the country. Their charm lies in the fact that they aren't overcommercialized commodities, but places where one can bathe in soothing waters and find peace with nature. Full details are available from the *Associação Nacional dos Indústrias de Aguas Minero-Medicinais e de Mesa* (93 Rua de São José, Lisbon 1100; phone: 1-347-5623) and from the *Direcção-Geral de Turismo* (86 Av. António Augusto Aguiar, Lisbon 1000; phone: 1-575086). Additionally, many US travel agencies specialize in spa vacations. Two of the best are *Spa-Finders Travel Arrangements* (91 Fifth Ave., Suite 301, New York, NY 10003; phone: 212-924-6800 or 800-255-7727) and *Spa Trek International* (475 Park Ave. S., New York, NY 10016; phone: 212-779-3480 or 800-272-3480).

LUSO, near Buçaco, Costa de Prata Set near the pristine Buçaco woods, this is one of the most renowned spas in Portugal. The mild climate and natural conditions of the region make for excellent physical and mental recuperation. The famous Luso waters rise in the São João spring in the center of town. Treatments include immersion baths, mud applications, and underwater massages. There is also a swimming pool, tennis courts, a sauna, a gymnasium, and ample opportunities for hiking. Information: *Sociedade das Aguas do Luso,* Rua Alvaro de Castelões, Mealhada 3050 (phone: 31-93044; fax: 31-930168).

CURIA, near Coimbra, Costa de Prata Portugal's most famous and most recommended spa, it's located in the Bairrada region amid the freshness, peace, and shade of the forest of Buçaco. Well known for its medicinal waters and its treatments for rheumatism, hypertension, gout, kidney ailments, gastric disturbances, and stress, the spa offers immersion baths and massages, among other therapies. There is also a gymnasium, a sauna, a swimming pool, tennis courts, fishing, boating, and a beach. The old-fashioned spa town of Luso and the glittering nightlife of Figueira da Foz are nearby. Information: *Sociedade das Aguas da Curia,* Anadia 3780 (phone: 31-521856; fax: 31-515838).

MONTE REAL, near Leiria, Costa de Prata Near the coast, halfway between Lisbon and Porto, Monte Real features some of Portugal's most famous ruins, and offers a varied range of activities. There are nearby beaches at São Pedro de Muel, Pedrogão, and Vieira. There is also a swimming pool, tennis courts, and fishing on the premises. The spa features Old World charm and a wonderful view of the poetic green fields of the Lis and Lena valleys. Information: *Termas de Monte Real,* Monte Real 2425 (phone: 44-62151).

VIMEIRO, Torres Vedras, Costa de Prata The Vimeiro village, which dates back to the first French invasion in 1808, is today a much-frequented spa, known for its perfect climate. Activities include horseback riding, golf, fishing, swimming, and tennis. Vimeiro's famous waters are recommended for liver, kidney, and skin ailments. Information: *1876 Empresa das Aguas do Vimeiro,* Av. Conselheiro Fernando de Sousa, Lisbon 1000 (phone: 1-680568 or 1-651445).

CALDAS DO GERÊS, near Braga, Costa Verde One of Portugal's most picturesque spas, it's situated in an unspoiled valley on the left bank of the Gerês River and inside the Peneda-Gerês National Park. The spa features immersion baths, bubble baths, and underwater massages, said to aid in curing liver and kidney ailments and hypertension. The water here supposedly has the highest fluoride content in Europe. In addition to the natural springs, guests can enjoy swimming, tennis, fishing, boating, and hiking. Information: *Empresa das Aguas do Gerês,* 114 Praça da Liberdade, Sala E, Porto 4000 (phone: 2-313587).

SÃO PEDRO DO SUL, north of Viseu The waters here — one of Portugal's most popular spa areas — lay claim to a variety of curative powers in the treatment of asthma, bronchitis, a variety of other respiratory infections, and rheumatism. The ultramodern, 64-room *Hotel das Termas,* which overlooks the Vouga River, offers all sorts of amenities, including its own health club with a gymnasium, sauna, massage, solarium, and beauty center. A swimming pool, tennis, archery, and canoeing also are available to guests. Information: *Hotel das Termas,* Termas São Pedro do Sul 3660 (phone: 32-72333; 800-528-1234 in the US; fax: 32-71011).

VIDAGO, near Chaves, northern Portugal A cosmopolitan resort whose springs produce most of the fresh water consumed in the country. Treatments include intramuscular injections of mineral water and medicinal baths. Located in a peaceful forest, the resort also has a swimming pool, sauna, horseback riding, tennis courts, golf, hunting, fishing, and a nightclub. Information: *SOVIPE,* Km 2 on EN 6, Alfragioe, Amadora 2700 (phone: 1-4715331).

Shopping Spree

No matter where the dollar stands relative to the escudo, the temptation to shop in Portugal is almost irresistible. Small roadside stalls along the Algarve coast offer a dazzling array of ceramics, and small antiques shops in cities like Lisbon and Porto are like mini-museums, with a fine assortment of items dating back to the 15th century. Although great bargains are now rare, the quality is high and the choice wide: leather goods, embroidery, jewelry, and fine porcelain.

Lisbon is a logical choice for most things, and Porto is worth a visit, particularly for silver. Madeira is known for its embroidery. Portuguese artisans mold earthenware and ceramics into works of art, as do modern Portuguese manufacturing plants, producing whimsical pottery, elegant porcelain, and gleaming crystal befitting any table. Tiles are everywhere: on churches, restaurants, palaces, storefronts, homes, and shops. They capture the bright colors and sunny vistas that are so much a part of Portugal's landscape and heritage. Handwoven rugs, both designer-quality and functional, as well as hand-knit sweaters and intricate embroidery symbolizing a national pride lovingly worked at for centuries, can be found throughout the country.

Portuguese shops are generally open weekdays from 9:30 AM to 1 PM and 3 to 7 PM; Saturdays from 9:30 AM to 1 PM (except in December, when they remain open until 7 PM). In addition to small shops and traditional outdoor markets, Portugal also has modern Centros Comerciais (shopping malls) and hypermarkets (large general stores). Most malls are open daily, including holidays, from 10 AM to midnight; hypermarkets generally close at 10 PM. Many shops throughout the country are closed in August.

Although store hours are generally observed, shops sometimes close unexpectedly or, when open, leave shoppers waiting for service. Many shopkeepers speak English. Note that many stores in Portugal still *don't* accept credit cards.

Portugal's *saldos* (sales) are held only twice a year — in January and February and again in September and October. In general, almost everything in Portugal is reasonably priced; in fact, Lisbon remains one of the most reasonably priced of Europe's shopping capitals.

Below we offer a description of some uniquely Portuguese products. See the *Shopping* entries in the individual city reports in THE CITIES for recommendations of specific stores.

BEST BUYS

ANTIQUES Portugal is an excellent, if increasingly pricey, hunting ground for antiques, with a wide range of dealers, auction houses, and non-commercial institutions that offer many items at bargain prices.

BOOKS AND MAPS While most visitors will not be able to read Portugal's treasured old books, it's still fun to browse. Many bookstores have dozens of booths and stalls filled with books from around the world, both old and new; some stores specialize in reduced-rate and secondhand books, old editions, and rare titles.

CERAMICS AND TILES A wide array of Portuguese ceramics, both antique and modern, awaits collectors and gift seekers. Arabic roots can be seen in many of the designs, but later styles — Dutch, English, and Chinese — predominate, and the result is a wide diversity of patterns. Glazed tiles, called *azulejos* in Portuguese for the color blue, are found throughout the country in many colors and designs.

EMBROIDERY AND LACE In Portugal, embroidery prices are determined by the intricacy of the stitch, not by the size of the item. Look carefully: Stitches made by a human hand cannot duplicate themselves over and over, and will therefore lack consistency; the more perfect the stitch, the more likely that an item was machine-made. Lace and embroidery come from Madeira; crocheted items come from the Azores. Regions such as Viana do Castelo produce a coarse, embroidered linen. In order to protect their handicraft industry, the government of Madeira attaches a small lead tag to each piece of Madeira embroidery sold on the island, on mainland Portugal, or anywhere else in the world. Madeira embroidery, while slightly higher in price than other kinds, is a timeless heirloom.

FOOD AND WINE Although packaged food is more and more becoming the norm, food shopping in Portugal is still a pleasure, because of the big central markets that overflow every morning with fresh country produce. Portugal also is famous for its wines — its *vinhos verdes,* ports, and madeiras.

GIFTWARE Travelers can go crazy buying giftware in Portugal. The country is famous for its Atlantis brand crystal, which ranks in quality and design with Waterford and Baccarat. Vista Alegre for porcelain giftware and dinnerware is another safe bet. It is exported worldwide to better stores; New York's *Metropolitan Museum of Art* sells famous reproductions. Portuguese silver products are also well known and range from place settings to elaborately hammered-out soup tureens.

HANDICRAFTS Manual arts are ubiquitous in Portugal. Among the traditional handcrafted items available are lace, rugs, ceramics, copperware, wicker, pottery, hand-knitted clothing, ceramic and copper dishes, embroidered tablecloths, plasterwork, and woodcarvings.

JEWELRY There are excellent jewelry bargains in Portugal, especially on pieces made of silver or gold. All Portuguese gold jewelry, by law, must contain at least 19.2 karats. Look for filigree earrings, necklaces, and bracelets, made with delicate silver threads.

LEATHER GOODS Most leather in Portugal comes from sheep and lambs; cows produce a heavier-quality skin that's made into jackets and coats. There are hundreds of stores selling leather jackets, coats, gloves, pocketbooks, wallets, and other items. Generally speaking, shoppers can tell the quality of the leather by the feel. The softer it is, the more expensive. The country's selection concentrates on leather accessories and shoes.

MUSICAL INSTRUMENTS Who can resist listening to the haunting sounds of Portuguese music? In addition to recordings, you can buy the typical handmade *viola braguesa,* or *cavaquinho* guitar, from which the ukelele was developed, in the city of Braga.

RUGS AND TAPESTRIES Rugs from Arraiolos, a small town near Evora, are reminders of the Moorish occupation of the Iberian Peninsula centuries ago. Today, local women still do needlepoint on these rugs in small workshops. They use 100% wool in the small petit point and the larger *ponto largo* stitch to create animals, birds, and even elaborate scenes. Depending upon the design and its intricacy, prices vary per square foot. Most establishments welcome special orders. The rugs can be found in stores all over the country, even tourist souvenir shops, and there are many suppliers in Arraiolos itself. Prices in the US, in some cases, are three to four times higher.

SHOES Portuguese styles are fashionable, and the leathers used are soft and durable. Women's shoes rarely come in half sizes, but men's do. Many shoe stores also carry leather accessories.

Antiques and Auctions

Antiques bargains abound in Portugal for the careful, tireless shopper. The country is particularly notable for its antique jewelry (especially filigree), old books, needlepoint rugs, *azulejos* (glazed tiles), and ceramics, although much that is antique has already been sold. Although Portugal remains one of the least expensive European destinations, antiques prices have skyrocketed as their supply has dwindled. Nevertheless, the ardent antiques hunter still will find a variety of pleasures in Lisbon and, to a lesser extent, in other Portuguese cities. For specific shops, antiques centers, and markets in the metropolitan centers, see the *Shopping* sections of the individual chapters in THE CITIES.

The Fundação Ricardo Espírito Santo Silva in Lisbon (2 Largo das Portas do Sol; phone: 1-862184) is dedicated to Portugal's decorative arts, and is a good source of information on Portuguese auctions.

A REPERTOIRE OF ANTIQUES SOURCES

SHOPS AND ANTIQUES CENTERS There are basically three different types of places in Portugal to hunt for antiques. At the low end of the scale are the flea markets, where those willing to sift through piles of miscellanea may uncover a true gem, or at least a good bargain. Auction houses are another option that can often yield a good find or two. Antiques shops, however, are usually the best bet. They are convenient; the dealer already has made the rounds through the markets and has purchased the cream of the crop. These shops do tend to be on the expensive side, but the quality is excellent and the selection can't be beat. Antiques hunters are practically guaranteed to find something of interest in one of these shops.

Outside Lisbon, there are some interesting buys in small villages around Porto, or in the Alentejo area east of Lisbon. The towns of Borba, Estremoz, and Evora are also good for antiques hunting.

FLEA MARKETS The heady mixture of rubbish and relic affords collectors the chance to find that special, unrecognized rarity. Try to arrive early, as markets quickly get crowded with other people who have the same idea.

AUCTIONS As any auction addict knows, this is a sport that combines the fanaticism of the stock market, gambling casino, and living theater. The Portuguese word for auction is *leilão,* and unlike auctions in New York, which usually are quite specialized, a Portuguese *leilão* offers an assortment of many kinds of objects. To find auctions in Portugal, inquire among antiques dealers and hotel concierges. Also check newspapers.

Auctions are the perfect answer to rainy day blues, although neophytes might want to keep in mind the following advice:

Don't expect to make a killing. Even Chinese peasant children are hip to the art market today, it seems. But chances of unearthing a real find are better for those who shop at smaller auctions.

Buy the catalogue before bidding. Catalogues often include a list of estimated prices. Those prices are not a contractual commitment, but they do act as a guide for prospective buyers. An elaborate stylistic code hints at the conviction the house may have about the age or authenticity of an item. The use of capital letters, of artists' full names, and of words like "fine," "rare," and "important" all carry positive connotations. The use of a last name only and of words like "style" and "attributed" should serve as warnings.

Visit the pre-sale exhibition carefully, thoroughly, and even repeatedly. There is the pleasure of browsing in a store without a hovering clerk. Even more important is the prospective buyer's chance to examine the offerings. *Caveat emptor* is the prevailing rule at any auction. Serious buyers should have paintings taken down from the wall and ask to handle objects under lock and key. Those who can't be at the sale can leave a commission bid with the auctioneer, or even place a bid by telephone, but if they can't be at the exhibition they should be wary of buying.

Decide on a top bid before the auction begins, and don't go beyond it. Bidding has its own rhythm and tension. The auctioneer becomes a Pied Piper, with buyers winking, blinking, and nodding in time to his or her music. This situation arouses unusual behavior in some people. Suddenly their self-worth is at stake, and they'll bid far beyond what the item is worth — or even what they can afford. A bid may be canceled by promptly calling out "Withdrawn." *Note:* In determining their top price, bidders should remember to add the house commission, which is generally 10% but can be more, plus any Value Added Tax.

RULES OF THE ROAD FOR AN ODYSSEY OF THE OLD

Buy for sheer pleasure and not for investment. Treasure seekers should forget about the supposed resale value that dealers habitually dangle in front of amateur clients. If you love an object, you'll never part with it. If you don't love it, let someone else adopt it.

Don't be timid about haggling. That's as true at a posh shop as at a market. You'll be surprised at how much is negotiable — and the higher the price, the more it has to fall.

Buy the finest example you can afford of any item, in as close to mint condition as possible. Chipped or tarnished "bargains" will haunt you later with their shabbiness.

Train your eye in museums. Museums that specialize in items you collect are the best of all.

Peruse art books and periodicals — preferably before you go auction hunting. Unfortunately, however, there is a lack of English-language reading material available.

Get advice from a specialist when contemplating a major acquisition. Major auction houses have fleets of resident specialists available for consultation. The Portuguese tourist offices may also be able to offer some assistance.

Museums, Monuments, and Ruins
Off the Beaten Track

A series of conquests, losses, and clever marriages left Roman ruins, Moorish castles, medieval turrets, and sinuous spires sculpted out of the land all over Portugal. Preserved and renovated, or ruined and crumbling, they stand as reminders of a turbulent and fascinating past.

Portugal also preserves its past, as well as its present culture, in its museums. Although the country lacks a vast international collection on the scale of the *Louvre* or the *Prado,* there are many small museums, which have all the virtues that reduced size can bring. In addition, since Portuguese Old Masters such as Nuno Gonçalves and Vasco Fernandes are rarely seen abroad, a visit to a museum here is a unique event.

The country's most important urban museums, monuments, and ruins are described in the individual chapters of THE CITIES; the two historic structures described below are off the usual tourist track and well worth the detour.

PALÁCIO NACIONAL DE MAFRA, Mafra This enormous monastery-palace is one of the largest historic monuments in Europe. The imposing structure, often compared to the Escorial in Spain, was constructed from 1717 to 1735, after Franciscan monks convinced King João V that his wife would produce a long-awaited heir if he built them a monastery. The first of the royal brood was soon born, and with gold pouring in from Brazil, the king spared no expense in showing his appreciation. Johann Friedrich Ludwig, an Italian-trained German architect, was commissioned to build a monastery for 13 friars (a number that quickly grew to 300), as well as a palace for the entire royal family and the court.

The resulting edifice, consisting of the palace, the monastery, and a basilica, covers 10 acres, with a main façade 725 feet long, and some 4,500 doors and windows. Rife with pink, white, and black marble from the nearby quarries of Pero Pinheiro and with exotic woods from Brazil, the embellishments caused so many foreign artists to gather here that the project became a training ground for an entire generation of Portuguese artists. It eventually gave rise to the famous Mafra school of sculpture, founded in mid-century under the Italian master Alessandro Giusti.

The basilica, predominantly Italian neo-classical and German baroque in design, occupies the middle of the façade, flanked by two majestic bell towers. Together, the towers contain 100 Flemish-made bells — the carillon of Mafra. Inside, the church is noted for its elegant proportions and its breathtakingly high, richly carved dome, as well as for the side chapels, which contain beautiful Carrara marble altarpieces with bas-reliefs carved by artists of the Mafra school. Note also the six early-19th-century organs and the plethora of brass chandeliers, candlesticks, crosses, and beautiful wrought-iron work.

The remainder of the building is an overwhelming maze of interminable corridors, vast staircases, and living quarters for the royal family and the monks. Most worthwhile are the Throne Room, with 19th-century paintings, and the marble-vaulted Benediction Room, with its beautifully patterned mosaic floor and, in the center, a bust of João V by Giusti. From the windows of this austere but impressive space, the royal family looked down into the basilica to hear mass. Other rooms have richly painted ceilings and murals, and there is an odd dining room with furniture made of the antlers and skins of deer from the palace's royal preserve. Gamerooms, a pharmacy, the kitchen, monks' cells, and a rich collection of religious art and vestments are also worth seeing, as is the largest single library room in Europe — 290 feet long. In all, there are some 40,000 16th- to 18th-century volumes, covered in white leather and gold. Information: *Pôsto de Turismo,* Av. 25 de Abril, Mafra 2640 (phone: 61-52023).

TOMAR, Ribatejo The striking monuments of the medieval town of Tomar attest to its former status as the headquarters of the Knights Templars, warrior-monks who first set up residence here during the 12th century. The town's imposing fortress-palace, the Convento de Cristo, was built by the Templars and their successors, the Knights of Christ, from the 12th to the 17th century. Its rich design and effusive decorations express a triumphant Christianity during a time of Portuguese exploration and conquest. The exotic oceanic iconography associated with that era is evident here. Tomar also was the home of a thriving Jewish community during the 15th century; its remains are preserved at the *Luso-Hebraic Museum of Abraham Zacuto* (73 Rua Dr. Joaquim Jacinto). This small museum, set up in the old Synagogue of Tomar, contains an assortment of tombstones with Hebrew inscriptions, collected from various sites. Information: *Pôsto de Turismo,* Av. Dr. Cândido Madureira, Tomar 2300 (phone: 49-313237).

Best Festivals

The calendar year in Portugal is a kaleidoscope of celebration, a constant whirl of dancing, drinking, and devotion. There are festivals to honor saints, bulls, horses, flowers, grapes, and shellfish. There are symphony orchestras and blaring local bands, dancers in ballet slippers and on stilts, and evenings lit by chandeliers or fireworks. Each festival bears the trademark of its town, and most fall on Catholic holidays or holy days — *Carnaval, Corpus Christi,* and *Holy Week* are celebrated everywhere — but many still show traces of their pagan roots. On the *Feast of St. Bartholomew* (April 21–23), for example, women in the town of Esposende dress in white, bathe in the ocean, and then sacrifice a black chicken to exorcise the devil. For a complete listing of events, contact the *Portuguese*

A word of caution to those planning to hurl themselves into the merriment at one of Portugal's frothiest celebrations: Everyone loves a party, so be prepared for crowded hotels, crowded restaurants, crowded streets, and crowded auditoriums. Advance planning will mitigate much of the discomfort — so reserve rooms ahead of time — but still be ready to be jostled, to wait in long lines, and to pay $2 or more for a can of warm cola — all part and parcel of festival going.

For details on the most important festivals in Portugal's major cities, see the *Special Events* sections in the individual reports in THE CITIES. The following festivals, held in smaller Portuguese towns, are worth a long detour.

NOSSA SENHORA DA AGONIA, Viana do Castelo, Costa Verde A dawn serenade of bursting rockets and pounding drums awakens this seaside town for the joyous *Feast of Our Lady of Suffering.* For 3 days at the end of the third week in August, the city is transformed, with thousands of lights glowing, food and *vinho verde* sold at hundreds of small stalls, and the sounds of singing and dancing echoing through the night. Mythical giants of the forest — *gigantones* — roam, and the statue of the Virgin is followed along a carpet of flowers by reverent revelers wearing giant heads with shiny red noses and toothy grins. The women deck themselves in golden heirlooms and the men strut in waistcoats, vests, and colored cummerbunds worn once a year for generations. At the conclusion, the statue is carried to the harbor to bless the fishing fleet, where the festival culminates in a blaze of fireworks. Another highlight is the selection of pottery and porcelain for sale at the outdoor market. Information: *Pôsto de Turismo,* Rua do Hospital Velho, Viana do Castelo 4900 (phone: 58-822620; fax: 58-829798).

FÁTIMA, near Tomar, Ribatejo Twice a year, the desolate land around Fátima teems with pilgrims who ride, walk, and drag themselves to where three children tending their sheep said they saw the Virgin Mary in 1917. Unlike most pilgrims, however, these worshipers come in modern clothes, without pomp or pageants or flowered carts, unorganized by any festival committee. This *romaria* (pilgrimage) is a mass commemoration of a 20th-century front-page story. Up to 1 million people converge on this tiny town on the eves of May 13 and October 13 to memorialize the reported appearances of the Virgin; the first witnessed only by the three young shepherds, the last by a crowd of 70,000 people. In the final appearance, the throng saw the sun break through a stormy day and appear to spin toward earth, but only the children saw the Virgin.

On the anniversaries, mass is celebrated on a huge esplanade where torch-lit processions also take place. At the edge of the promenade is a neo-classical basilica that contains the tombs of two of the children, Francisco and Jacinta Marto, who died of influenza in 1919 and 1920 (the third, Lúcia, dos Santos, still lives as a Carmelite nun in Coimbra). The Chapel of the Apparitions, marking the spot where the Virgin was said to have appeared, is at the far end of the esplanade. Information: *Direcção-Geral do Turismo,* 86 Av. António Augusto de Aguiar, Lisbon 1000 (phone: 1-575086), *Pôsto de Turismo,* Av. Dr. Cândido Madureira, 2300 Tomar (phone: 49-313237), or *Pôsto de Turismo,* Av. Dom José Alves Correia da Silva, Fátima 2495 (phone: 49-531139).

Great Golf

The British brought golf to Portugal around the turn of the century, but it was another 50 years before the game acquired any degree of popularity — and then it remained an activity of only the very social or the very rich. Today, an increasing number of foreign golfers have discovered that Portugal's courses offer the perfect formula for a golfing vacation: a beautiful natural setting, ideal climate almost year-round, and some rather challenging layouts. American visitors will find little problem adjusting to Portuguese course configurations, which tend to be designed in the American mold — target golf, with fairly narrow fairways leading to greens surrounded by bunkers and trees.

There are some 30 courses scattered across the mainland and the islands of Madeira and the Azores. Among them are the popular championship courses — some of the finest on the Continent — in the southern Algarve; perfect climate and increasing numbers of courses have made the region a magnet for golfers. Some of the best in that area and one in central Portugal are listed below. Our recommended courses around the capital are described in *Lisbon* in THE CITIES.

Golf fees vary at most Portuguese resorts. Expect to pay at least $50 during the week, and 15–20% more on weekends. Greens fees usually are included in the room rate for guests staying at a golf hotel. Club rentals start at $20 per half-set, handcarts at $10, gas or electric carts at $35. Lesson costs vary according to the reputation of the pro and the price level of the resort. Some courses require a valid US handicap certificate. Information: *Direcção-Geral do Turismo,* 86 Av. António Augusto de Aguiar, Lisbon 1000 (phone: 1-575086; fax: 1-530519), or the *Federação Portuguesa de Golfe,* 39 Rua Almeida Brandão, Lisbon 1300 (phone and fax: 1-397-4658). For US tour operators that offer golf trips and other packages to Portugal, see GETTING READY TO GO.

QUINTA DO LAGO, Almansil, Algarve Four different 9-hole combinations are possible on these 36 holes, featuring several doglegs and lakeside tees. The holes are spread over some 600 acres, and all were designed by Americans; one by Joe Lee, and the others by the late William Mitchell. These layouts are considered among the best courses in Europe by *Golf Digest* and are most popular with British golfers, which makes English the prevalent language here. The surrounding resort is a city within a city, featuring a shopping complex, a nightclub, and various restaurants, as well as other non-golf activities such as horseback riding, swimming, and tennis. Information: *Quinta do Lago,* Almansil 8135, Algarve (phone: 89-394529; fax: 89-394013).

SAN LORENZO GOLF CLUB, Almansil, Algarve Designed by Joe Lee in 1988, this 18-hole course is set against the dramatic backdrop of Rio Formosa National Park, a nature and wildlife preserve. The 17th hole is a particularly challenging par 4, and the 6th, 7th, and 8th holes go down slender greens to the estuary of the park, beyond which the wild waves of the Atlantic crash. It has been ranked among Europe's top 50 courses by *Golf World* magazine. Information: *San Lorenzo Golf Club,* Almansil 8135, Algarve (phone: 89-396534; fax: 89-396908).

PENINA GOLF CLUB, Penina, Algarve In the heart of the Algarve, here are three courses that surround the large *Penina Golf* hotel. Designed by three-time *British Open* champion Henry Cotton, the courses have managed to overcome the disadvantage of being set on very flat terrain. Literally hundreds of thousands of trees and shrubs were planted to provide a frame for the golf holes, and this former rice field is now a fine test of golfing skill. The south course has been a frequent venue for championships and tournaments, with 18 holes ranging from easy to difficult. The 13th hole, a 190-yard par 3 that doglegs to the right around a lake to a tightly guarded green, requires a tee shot of 190 yards in order to avoid the aquatic wildlife. There also are two 9-hole courses, which are said to "separate the men from the boys." Information: *Penina Golf Club,* PO Box 146, Penina, Portimão 8500, Algarve (phone: 82-415415; 800-225-5843 or 800-223-6800 in the US; fax: 82-415000).

PARQUE DA FLORESTA, Salema, Algarve This development, just inland from the little coastal fishing village of Salema (15 minutes from Lagos), provides the ideal environment for golfers yearning to get away from it all. The unspoiled 318-acre estate features an 18-hole course designed by Pepe Gancedo, the Spanish architect responsible for the *Torrequebrada* course on Spain's Costa del Sol. The 564-yard-long 1st hole curves gracefully into the horizon, while the short 5th hole is a mere 120 yards, with no place to go except on or over the green. The 17th hole, surrounded by lakes, gives way to the 18th, which climbs past a magnificent pine to the green set in an amphitheater below the clubhouse terrace. Information: *Parque da Floresta,* Vale do Poço, Budens, Vila do Bispo 8650, Algarve (phone: 82-65333; fax: 82-65436).

VALE DO LOBO GOLF CLUB, Vale do Lobo, Algarve Rugged and beautiful, this is perhaps Portugal's most scenic course. Located 20 minutes from Faro, the

27 holes here were designed by three-time *British Open* champion Henry Cotton. The famous 7th hole, perched atop sandstone cliffs at the edge of the ocean, is among the most photographed in Europe. There is also a driving range. This self-contained resort also offers the *Roger Taylor Tennis Clinic* (see *Tennis,* below) and a full range of water sports. Information: *Clube de Golfe,* Vale do Lobo, Loulé 8100, Algarve (phone: 89-394444; fax: 89-394713).

VILAMOURA GOLF CLUB, Vilamoura, Algarve The three courses here are set among umbrella pines and gentle slopes in sight of the sea. *Vilamoura I,* designed by Frank Pennink, plays to par 73, and its 6,923 yards add up to one of the best courses in the Algarve. The 6th hole is by far the most spectacular: an excellent par 3 with a narrow fairway cut through wild pine trees. Another feature favored by golfers is that the 5th, 9th, and 15th greens are close to the clubhouse, convenient for frequent stops at the "19th hole." *Vilamoura II* is a newer course, designed by Robert Trent Jones, Sr. *Vilamoura III,* the club's latest layout and also designed by Robert Trent Jones, Sr., has 18 holes and a barrage of water hazards. One of the largest private resort developments in Europe, the complex features villas, hotels, restaurants, tennis courts, horseback riding, water sports, and shopping near the esplanade of the Algarve's only yachting marina. Numerous international tournaments are held here, and it is one of the most popular resorts in the Algarve. Information: *Vilamoura Golf Club,* Vilamoura, Quarteira 8125, Algarve (phone: 89-302976; fax: 89-302976).

TRÓIA GOLF CLUB, Setúbal This club is on the Tróia Peninsula, about 20 minutes from Setúbal by ferry, and a 30-mile (48-km) drive from Lisbon. A challenging Robert Trent Jones, Sr. creation, it offers fine views of the sea, sand dunes, and pines. Be careful of the 3rd hole, a long par 4 that runs along the beach, and the 14th, where a sharp dogleg to the left demands a good drive. Amenities include a bar and restaurant, a private beach, a swimming pool, tennis courts, and a variety of water sports. Information: *Tróia Golf Club,* Setúbal 2900 (phone: 65-44112; fax: 65-44162).

Tennis

In Portugal, tennis usually takes a back seat to golf. But many hotels and resorts have tennis facilities, and beginners and experts alike will find plenty of places to play. Racquets, balls, and courts are easily rented, and single players will have no trouble tracking down opponents. Actual tennis-oriented resorts and clubs, however, are concentrated mainly in the Algarve, with its many small, seaside residential developments clustered around sports facilities. So far, only the British and wise Americans have truly "discovered" this area, and thanks in part to their inroads, almost everyone speaks English. There are a number of exclusive areas, listed below, where the tennis enthusiast can enjoy a vacation amid sandy beaches and warm waters. Our recommended tennis spots near the Lisbon metropolitan area are described in *Lisbon* in THE CITIES.

Most Portuguese tennis courts have either an asphalt or a clay surface, and traditional tennis whites are preferred — often required. Expect to pay about $7 per hour for court time, which, in most cases, must be reserved in advance. There is also an emphasis on the social aspects of tennis here, and many hotels sponsor weekly tournaments and "get acquainted" parties where tennis enthusiasts can meet and mingle. In addition, there are a variety of members-only tennis clubs spread among the major cities and resort areas where, for a small additional fee, guests are permitted to play. Also keep in mind that tennis can be fun to watch, and tennis as a spectator sport is catching on in Portugal. The country hosted its first *ATP* (*Association of Tennis Professionals*) tournament in 1989, in Estoril. For more information on tennis tournaments in Portugal, contact the *ATP*, 200 ATP Tour Blvd., Ponte Vedra Beach, FL 32082 (phone: 904-285-8000).

CARVOEIRO CLUBE DE TÊNIS, Praia do Carvoeiro, Algarve Perched atop a mountain development overlooking the small fishing village of Carvoeiro, this private resort community and racquet club commands a breathtaking view of the Atlantic and the whitewashed town below. Five of the 10 hard courts are floodlit for night play, and there is a half-size children's court — all adjacent to the racket-shaped swimming pool. Other pluses include a pro shop, various social activities, and frequent tournaments. Information: *Carvoeiro Clube de Tênis,* Apartado 231, Lagoa Codex 8400, Algarve (phone and fax: 82-357847).

ROGER TAYLOR TENNIS CLINIC, Vale do Lobo, Algarve Roger Taylor is to the Algarve what Lew Hoad is to Spain's Costa del Sol. Built amid the very planned, very developed, and very neatly organized Vale do Lobo complex, this 12-court (6 floodlit) facility has earned a reputation as one of Europe's top tennis centers. There is a 5-hour clinic daily that starts off with a jog along the sea. The club hosts special amateur tennis weeks in June and November. Facilities include a pro shop, a swimming pool, and a bar/café. Information: *Roger Taylor Tennis Center,* Vale do Lobo, Loulé, 8100 (phone: 89-394779), or *Roger Taylor Tennis Holidays,* 85 High St., Wimbledon SW19 5EG, England (phone: 44-81-947-9727).

Horsing Around

There's nothing quite as delightful as seeing the countryside from the back of a horse or sure-footed native pony, heading through narrow trails, along abandoned train beds, and down wide sandy beaches — and staying away from the trekking center for up to a week at a time. Post trekking, or trail riding, as this activity is called, is not generally recommended for riders without experience, as it usually involves good horses and a fast enough pace to cover about 25 miles (40 km) a day. Usually a warm camaraderie develops among riders en route, as they traverse the rural miles. Post trekking is also a practically worry-free holiday: There are guides to keep riders going at a reasonable pace, to make sure the group doesn't get lost, and to arrange for the rider's luggage to be transported from one hostelry to the next.

Our recommended riding spots in the Lisbon area are described in *Lisbon* in THE CITIES; a favorite equestrian center in the country's south is described below. The *Portuguese National Tourist Office* (590 Fifth Ave., New York, NY 10036; phone: 212-354-4403) can provide further details on horseback riding. For a list of US tour operators that offer horseback riding trips and other packages in Portugal, see GETTING READY TO GO.

Southern Portugal's cork forests and beaches are within easy access of the Quinto do Lago estate, where Englishwoman Beverly Gibbons takes groups of riders out on elegant Lusitano steeds to tour the dunes and lagoons of the Algarve. For information, contact *Centro Hípico,* Quinto do Lago, Almansil 8100, Algarve (phone: 89-394369 or 89-396468).

Best Beaches

With nearly 50% of its periphery edged by water, Portugal's shoreline has been a source of attraction as well as a gateway to the rest of the world for centuries. The variety of sea, sand, and landscape ranges from the shivering shocks of the Atlantic surf, to the wild isolation of the Azores, to the lively excitement of the Algarve.

One way to choose a beach in Portugal is by its lack of reknown. Since many of the country's most popular beach resorts are now being overrun by tourists, visiting them is as much of a return to nature as going to lunch at a salad bar. Many visitors, therefore, carefully seek out remote and undiscovered ocean paradises, far removed from the hordes of basking vacationers. Many others, however, head straight for the crowds. For those unable to avoid the large resorts, but wishing to escape the masses, a visit in late August or September is recommended. Or visit the less-than-torrid Costa Verde during May, when it's quiet. The tradeoff is paler tans and cooler waters for the luxury of a private beach.

Our recommended beaches in the capital area are described in *Lisbon* in THE CITIES. Listed below are some of our favorite sandy stretches elsewhere in the country.

ALGARVE, Tavira The white stucco town of Tavira is still unspoiled by tourism. Fishing boats depart daily and return loaded with tuna and sardines for the evening's grill. The spacious beach is on the long, sandy island of Tavira, where shoreline space is abundant, so much so that on Sundays in July there's even room for an oceanside game of touch football. The pallid be warned — the water is warm and the waves gentle, but the Algarvian sun is deceptively wind-cooled and burningly fierce. Information: *Região de Turismo do Algarve,* 100 Rua Ataíde de Oliveira, Faro 8000 (phone: 89-803-3667); in Tavira, at the tourist office on Praça da República (phone: 81-22511).

NAZARÉ, Costa de Prata In some respects a typical tourist beach town, it nonetheless retains some of its ancient customs and traditional garb. Men typically wear plaid pants rolled up to their knees and stock their tobacco, matches, and lighters in their black caps. Women often wear seven petticoats and clean and salt the fish along with the men. The Praia quarter, the area near the beach, affords glimpses of colorful fishing boats and fishermen mending nets (although the numbers have diminished in recent years). The Atlantic is in all its glory here — large waves crash along the shore, making swimming possible only for the daring. The beach itself is long and crescent-shaped, ending in a high cliff on the north end, where the Sítio — the Old Town — and the Igreja de Nossa Senhora da Nazaré are located. The church's small black image of the Virgin is carried down to the sea during the town's annual *romaria,* in September. Information: *Pôsto de Turismo,* 23 Rua Mouzinho de Albuquerque, Nazaré 2450 (phone: 62-561194).

Gone Fishing

With mile after mile of sun-soaked Atlantic coastline, over 150 varieties of fish, and mostly unpolluted waters, Portugal is truly a fishing paradise. Deep-sea enthusiasts can wrestle year-round with swordfish, ray, tuna, shark, trout, and snapper, while freshwater anglers can cast for tench, salmon, carp, trout, pike, bass, barbel, and chub. But while there are plenty of places to wet a line, Portugal also has numerous fishing regulations designed to protect and maintain its fish population. There are no restrictions on deep-sea fishing, but there are limits on where and when freshwater fishing is permitted, as well as various catch limits. These laws are often so dizzying that the effort to obtain permits and satisfy restrictions may not be worth the day on the river or lake. Consequently, many of the best — and most convenient — outings are organized through marinas and the various resorts along the water.

Nearly all game fishing waters in Portugal are tightly controlled by the various local and regional governments. Some regions do not allow foreigners to fish in their waters, period. Those that do require the appropriate licenses and permits, and they enforce catch limits, as well as strict rules regulating minimum sizes, bait and tackle, and Sunday fishing. Sea angling in Portugal is very common, and no license is required.

Because of Portugal's mild climate, fishing tends to be good year-round. More than 200 species can be found here; some, such as the scabbard fish, which averages 6 feet in length, are unique to Portuguese waters.

There are three species of trout native to Portuguese waters: rainbow trout, found only in lagoons and dams in the northern and central regions of the country; *fareo* trout, common in almost every river and stream; and sea trout, found in the Minho and Lima rivers. Black bass is found in lagoons and dams throughout the country, especially in the Algarve, as well as in the natural lagoon in Pateia de Fermentelos, near Agueda, about 25 miles (40 km) north of Coimbra. Salmon appears only in the Minho and Lima rivers. The best spot to catch it is in the north end of the Gadanha, a Minho tributary, near Monção. Portugal also boasts a variety of shellfish, namely dog whelks, rock and giant lobsters, crabs, and spider crabs. Sports anglers consider Peniche the center of Portuguese big-game fishing. In the north, cold-water fish such as skate, grouper, tope, shark, and bass predominate. The coast between Moledo and Porto (encompassing Vila Praia de Ancora, Esposende, Ofir, Póvoa de Varzim, Viana do Castelo, Vila do Conde, and Espinho), Figueira da Foz, and the towns of Nazaré and São Martinho do Porto are among the best areas, and are especially good for visitors because of the abundance of fishing boats. The Algarve is noted for deep-sea fishing. US companies that offers fishing trips and other packages in Portugal are listed in GETTING READY TO GO.

ALGARVE It is truly an experience of a lifetime to hook and finally bring in a mako or a hammerhead shark. The warm southeastern currents provide this area with a prolific and varied marine life. For many years, only fishing villages existed along Portugal's southern coast, and today the extreme ends of the Algarve remain much as they always were. The sun-roughed skin of fishermen, their hands tough and calloused, their character lines smooth and telling, will make arrangements for visitors who decide to venture out on their own. In between, near the resort areas of Faro, Vilamoura, Lagos, and Portimão, visitors are better off taking an organized tour out to sea. Big-game fishing is the sport here. Spectators are welcome, and there are sun decks and bar service to keep them occupied. Information: *Luz Bay Sea Sport Are,* Praia da Luz, Lagos 8600 (phone: 82-789538), or *Algarve Seafaris,* Vilamoura, Loulé 8100 (phone: 89-315666).

AZORES The nine-island Azorean archipelago, called the stepping-stones between the Old and New worlds, offers astounding results for big-game anglers. Much of the sea surrounding the islands — especially São Miguel, Faial, and Terceira — is virtually untouched and undiscovered. From May through July, millions of large fish such as Allison tuna roam the surface, feeding on smaller fish. White and blue marlin, broadbill swordfish, and bluefin tuna also have been spotted here on a regular basis. For the light caster, the Azores present a fascinating array of amberjack, bluefish, barracuda, tuna, mackerel, and jack crevalle. Information: *Pescatur,* 1 Largo Francisco Tavares, Ponta Delgada, São Miguel, Azores 9500 (phone: 96-24757).

COSTA VERDE The Minho River and its tributaries, particularly the area between Valença and Melgaço, are ideal for game fishing. The Lima and Homen rivers near Gerês, and the rivers near Trás-os-Montes, are excellent spots for trout and bass. A good base for a Costa Verde fishing trip is Viana do Castelo. Once a Roman outpost, this small, pleasant town offers easy access to the bucolic Lima River and the coast. Information: *Pôsto de Turismo,* Rua do Hospital Velho, Viana do Castelo 4900 (phone: 58-822620).

NAZARÉ, Costa de Prata This little village lives for the sea. Its people spend the day either on the water, cleaning and salting fish, or preparing bait. Once known only to diehard fisherfolk, Nazaré has become a very popular, rather touristy beach resort, but its fishing tradition remains intact. Information: *Pôsto de Turismo,* 23 Rua Mouzinho de Albuquerque, Nazaré 2450 (phone: 62-561194).

PENICHE, Costa de Prata Long dependent on the fishing industry, the city of Peniche, some 30 miles (48 km) from Obidos, is often ignored by tourists on their way to the Ilhas Berlengas (Berlenga Islands). It is a bustling fishing port whose colorful fleet can be seen unloading the daily catch by the tons and where seafood restaurants are plentiful (the local version of *caldeirada* is famous). Information: *Pôsto de Turismo,* Rua Alexandre Herculano, Peniche, Leiria 2520 (phone: 62-79571).

TOMAR, Ribatejo Mix with the locals at Tomar's *Clube dos Amadores de Pesca* and hook up with a fisherman familiar with the ways of the famous Nabão River, which crosses through the town. The Alva River and the Alge riverside, north of Tomar, are also good spots for catching trout and bass, among other fish. Information: *Pôsto de Turismo,* Av. Dr. Cândido Madureira, Tomar 2300 (phone: 49-313237).

Freewheeling by Two-Wheeler

Because of the mild climate in Portugal, touring by bicycle is easy and the itinerary possibilities are nearly inexhaustible. Visitors who pedal through the Portuguese countryside will get to know parts of the country that most people never see. Leisurely bicycle rides pass through tiny fishing villages and medieval towns occasionally dotted with Moorish ruins. A variety of terrain exists in Portugal, although there is much flat land. The roads tend to be narrow, and cyclists almost always share them with farmers riding their mules; it is not uncommon for riders to have to stop to let shepherds cross the road with their flocks.

Those who have traveled around Europe by bicycle before will find that a cycling vacation in Portugal is slightly more primitive than in most other Western European countries. There is hardly an abundance of sophisticated repair shops, except in the major cities, nor even the guarantee of well-surfaced secondary roads. Bicycle rentals are available, but not omnipresent. Intermediate and diehard cyclists will want to bring their own bicycles and gear. Airlines will generally transport bikes as part of passengers' personal baggage, but they may insist that the entire bike be crated; check with the airline before departure. Also be sure to confirm insurance coverage.

Some cyclists choose to travel alone through Portugal. Others, however, team up with fellow cyclists and soon become fast friends. The natives are so friendly they will practically apologize if they cannot accompany a rider to his or her destination (many riders often wind up staying in one place longer than they had planned). It does help, however, to have a rudimentary understanding of Portuguese, especially when touring the rural routes, as most people in the countryside do not speak English. A pocket dictionary is heartily recommended. Also take along a basic set of tools and spares — including a tire pump, puncture repair kit, tire levers, spoke key, oil can, batteries and bulbs, rag, extra spokes, inner tubes and tires, pliers, and odd nuts and bolts — and a good map (Michelin generally has the best). Traveling with a minimal amount of cash and a credit card is advised.

If the thought of biking alone is less than a satisfactory vacation idea, there are numerous organized bicycle tours in Portugal. Companies offering such packages are listed in GETTING READY TO GO.

When cycling in Portugal, always remember that it is more relaxing and enjoyable to take it slowly and enjoy the country's sights and sounds. After choosing a region, consult the local tourist literature. Then plot out the tour on a large-scale highway map of the country. Base daily mileage on what usually is covered on the road at home, but be sure to allot time for en route dawdling — chats with the locals, walks through ruined castles, wine and cheese at the local bar.

ALGARVE Portugal's coastal resort area provides some of the country's best cycling. The roads are fairly flat, the temperatures remain moderate year-round, the towns are very attractive and well spaced, and the landscape is a lyrical mixture of blue sky, fine golden sand, and crystalline water. This circuit begins in Vale do Lobo or the Quinta do Lago area, the center of activity in the Algarve and the point from which cyclists can choose to ride either east or west. Ride out to Sagres, the southwesternmost point of Europe, and watch the sun set like a ball falling off the edge of the earth. The region between Faro and the Spanish border is the least developed and most undiscovered, and makes for a very tranquil and leisurely ride. Information: *Pôsto de Turismo,* 8-12 Rua da Misericórdia, Faro 8000 (phone: 89-803604).

ALTO ALENTEJO This is the northern part of Portugal's plains region, flat and largely unpopulated. For cyclists looking to escape the city, this is a perfect route. Begin in the walled town of Elvas, conveniently situated some 20 miles (32 km) west of the Spanish border, and known throughout Portugal for its sugarplums. The tour passes through large farms and whitewashed hamlets, where olive and cork trees dot the countryside, to Evora, a medieval university town filled with reminders of the 15th and 16th centuries. Information: *Pôsto de Turismo,* 73-74 Praça do Giraldo, Evora 7000 (phone: 66-22671).

COSTA VERDE This aptly named green region in the northwestern corner of the country extends from the Douro River to Porto and up to the Minho River near the Spanish frontier. The route offers a close look at Porto, home of Portugal's famous port wines, and continues into the rolling hills and elegant parks of Braga, as well as the wine region of Viseu. The terrain here is challenging, but the roads are in good condition and very quiet. Information: *Pôsto de Turismo,* 25 Rua Clube Fenianos, Porto 4000 (phone: 2-312740).

Great Walks and Mountain Rambles

Almost any walker will say that it is the footpaths of a country — not its roadways — that show off the local landscape to its best advantage. Closer to earth than when in a car, those on foot notice details that might not otherwise come to their attention: valleys perfumed with almond blossoms, hillsides dotted with villages, sheep gamboling in the shade of fig and cork oak trees, and the sun glinting off leaves and making the hilltops glisten.

Portugal's topography makes walking here a pleasurable pastime. There is agreeable terrain for walkers and hikers of all abilities. The hills of northern and central Portugal and the sandy beaches of the Algarve all make for peaceful, pleasant strolls or climbs. There are a number of national parks to explore, while visitors less attracted to wilderness will find villages perched on high, with cobblestone streets, mansions, churches, ruins, and shops that are guaranteed to hold their interest and challenge their feet. Add to this a climate that is generally benign (Portugal is often referred to as the California of Europe), friendly locals, and good food, and you have all the ingredients necessary for a perfect expedition.

Before choosing a specific area of the country for hiking, look at a road map that shows physical characteristics, so as to choose terrain that meets your level of fitness. To make the outing safe and pleasant, it is imperative for hikers to know their own limits. Unless they are very experienced, hikers always should stick to the defined areas — and *always* let someone know the planned destination and time of expected return (leave a note on the car if hiking alone). Those who prefer going as part of an organized tour should contact a local hiking club, a travel agent, or one of the many tour packagers specializing in hiking tours. Companies offering such packages are listed in GETTING READY TO GO.

Since hot weather is not necessarily a welcome companion on a walk, it's best to avoid the southern regions in midsummer. And since it can get warm almost anywhere in Portugal from May through September, the wise walker will get most of a day's journey done before midday. Basic hiking essentials should include a sturdy pair of shoes and socks, long pants if headed into heavily wooded areas, a canteen, a hat, sunblock, rainwear, and something warm, just in case. It is always best to dress in layers. Also make sure to wear clothes with pockets, or bring along a pack so that both hands can remain free. Some useful but often overlooked tools include a jackknife, waterproof matches, a map, a compass, and snacks. In the more remote areas, a backpack, sleeping bag and pad, stove, food, and other gear are required.

Portugal's least strenuous treks are in the coastal regions, where there are numerous enjoyable trails through countrysides laden with natural beauty. Best bets include the Algarve, the Costa Verde, and the Costa de Prata. Inland, the terrain becomes more mountainous, and the walks more spectacular. The toughest mountain hikes are in the central Estrela range, where the country's highest peak — the Malhão (Tower), 6,532 feet high — is found.

ALGARVE This is one of the most ideal places for hiking, because the weather is always just right — visitors are practically guaranteed clear skies and steady breezes that keep the temperatures bearable all summer. One of the most interesting places to walk along Portugal's southern coast is in the vicinity of Sagres, at the extreme southwestern corner of the country, and once considered the end of the world. The sunsets alone make a visit here worthwhile. Some 40 miles (64 km) inland to the east is Porto de Lagos, on the road to Monchique. The town of Silves is 6 miles (10 km) east of Porto de Lagos, and between the two is a circular hiking route that skirts groves of orange trees and an irrigation ditch as it follows the course of the Arade River and Ribeira de Odelouca. Where the two meet, the Arade estuary, islands, and rice fields are visible. The village of Monchique and the hills surrounding it are also worthy hiking country. After perusing the village streets, follow a track of stone pavement that leads through the woods to an old convent, where there is a wonderful view over the valley. Return to Monchique's main square and follow Rua do Porto Fundo, located at the top of the square, up the slope. Upon reaching Rua Dr. Bernardino Moreira, turn right and continue to follow the road up, along Rua da Igreja, through Praça Alexandre Herculano, and along Rua Costa Gerdo, until finally reaching the Largo de São Gonçalo de Lagos, a small square. The street becomes steep here, but the reward is the scenic old convent in the distance. There are many walking tours of this region, and most can be found with the help of each town's tourist office. Information: *Pôsto de Turismo,* 8-12 Rua da Misericórdia, Faro 8000 (phone: 89-803604).

ALTO ALENTEJO Lonely little villages set between olive and cork trees are the treasures that await hikers in Portugal's plains region. The city of Portalegre, in the northern part of the region, lies in the foothills of the Serra de São Mamede, only 30 miles (48 km) from the Spanish border. This is a charming area, full of history. Sights include homes emblazoned with ageless family crests, as well as Moorish ruins. There are numerous footpaths between the villages surrounding Portalegre, and this is an idyllic place to escape the tourist traps of the coastal areas and truly savor the traditions of the Portuguese. Information: *Pôsto de Turismo,* Convento de Santa Clara, 25 Estrada de Sant'ana, Portalegre 7300 (phone: 45-21815).

COSTA DE PRATA, near Coimbra The Silver Coast of Portugal offers hikers some of the country's most diverse terrain. Among the region's many scenic towns is a wide variety of magnificent mountain ranges, poetic green valleys, and high dunes. The Buçaco Forest, situated just outside the university town of Coimbra, is a highlight of the region. Rocky paths shaded by luxurious foliage have drawn solitary hikers to this enchanted forest for centuries. The forest contains over 700 varieties of flora, including exotic plants from Asia and the Far East, brought by the first Portuguese explorers. Wandering freely among the forest's many paths can be confusing, so pick up a map at the refreshment stand, located next to the palace. Information: *Região de Turismo,* Largo da Portagem, Coimbra 3000 (phone: 39-33028; fax: 39-25576).

COSTA VERDE, near Porto This region has been called the cradle of the Portuguese nation. Originally inhabited by the Celts some 3,000 years ago, it remains rich in tradition, natural beauty, and wonder. A trek through the Costa Verde passes the historical monuments that dot the countryside, and vineyards where the famous *vinho verde* wine is produced. Begin in Braga, one of Portugal's oldest Christian towns, surrounded by rolling green hills and elegant parks. Nearby is the Peneda-Gerês National Park, a splendidly unspoiled expanse of mountains, lakes, vegetation, and wildlife. Hiking routes between the main village of Gerês and Pedro Bela skirt crashing waterfalls and natural pools. Information: *Pôsto de Turismo,* Av. Manuel Francisco da Costa, Gerês 4845 (phone: 53-65133).

TRÁS-OS-MONTES The Marão and Alvão ranges are among the mountains separating Portugal's northern coastal area from the more remote reaches of the Trás-os-Montes region. While difficult to reach, the fertile fields and rocky slopes of this zone are both challenging and rewarding to the dedicated and experienced hiker. Vila Real is the usual starting point. Information: *Região de Turismo da Serra do Marão,* 94 Av. Carvalho Araújo, Vila Real 5000 (phone: 59-322819).

Directions

Introduction

All too often, people mistake Portugal for a mere extension of its neighbor Spain. It is not until you actually land on Portuguese soil that the unique and varied qualities of this small but diverse country can truly be appreciated. In many ways Portugal still represents — in its unspoiled hills and pristine shores — the final frontier of Europe, and although prices are rising, it remains one of the few Western European countries that is still affordable.

This is a country rich in history and grounded in tradition and culture. As small as Portugal may be, it played an enormous role in the discovery of the world. Portugal's native sons — Prince Henry the Navigator, Bartolomeu Dias, Magellan, and Vasco de Gama — helped to widen the world's scope and usher in the Age of Discovery.

As you travel from one end of Portugal to the other, you will be delighted with the ever-changing landscape and the wealth of folklore and customs. Cities like Lisbon and Porto, situated on the Atlantic Ocean, are centers of business and industry. Lisbon is the gateway to the New World, and Porto gives us its fine port wine. Inland regions such as the Alentejo are agricultural areas filled with the lovely green of olive trees and the sweet aroma of almond orchards. Visitors who head south will find the Algarve, a popular tourist destination, drawing crowds to its beaches, golf courses, and nightlife. Offshore, hundreds of miles into the Atlantic, are the rustic and unspoiled islands of the Azores and Madeira — perfect for travelers in search of peace, solitude, and natural beauty.

On the following pages, we have outlined what we think are the best driving routes throughout the country. We have chosen roads and paths that best show off what Portugal has to offer, taking you through small villages and farmlands, to the bigger cities, and along the coast. The *Checking In* and *Eating Out* sections offer suggestions for the best hotels, *pousadas,* small *pensões,* and restaurants along the way.

The new highways in Portugal are excellent, and more roads are being built and improved all the time. Some of the smaller roads are slow-going and in less than good repair, but they will take you through some of the less-often-seen parts of the country. Each route is planned to last for approximately 3 days. Depending on your timetable and interests, however, travelers can mix and match the routes to fit their own needs. For each region, we have developed a single itinerary that we think best represents the area, so if time limits you to only one or two routes, you'll be certain to see the best that there is.

Lisbon to Porto

The road from Lisbon to Portugal's second-largest city — about a 197-mile (315-km) trip if approached in a direct fashion — proves that there is more to Portugal than the 500 miles of beaches that customarily take pride of place in the tourist brochures. Beaches are certainly not lacking here; the Costa de Prata (Silver Coast), which bridges the gap between the Lisbon and Estoril coasts and northern Portugal's Costa Verde (Green Coast), is one long succession of them. But the two Portuguese provinces that this coastline borders — Estremadura and Beira Litoral — contain much more than distractions for the aquatic sports enthusiast and the sunbather.

For the historian, there are the remains of *castros* — ancient, fortified hilltop towns — from the Bronze and Iron Ages, as well as old Roman roads, bridges, and a whole Roman city, Conímbriga, to be seen. There are fortresses — which have repelled attacks by everyone from the Moors to the troops of Napoleon — and Portugal's first capital, Coimbra, to be explored.

Lovers of art and architecture will be impressed by the profusion of fine Romanesque, Gothic, and baroque buildings, not to mention structures carved with the entwined ropes, seashells, nets, waves, and anchors characteristic of Portugal's own Manueline style. Three of Europe's greatest buildings — the monasteries at Mafra, Alcobaça, and Batalha — are here, and everywhere there are carvings in marble and golden Ança stone by sculptors of the Mafra and Coimbra schools. Intricate gilt carvings and beautiful 17th- and 18th-century tiles adorn churches, as do some fine paintings.

Nature lovers will appreciate the vast pine forest between Leiria and the sea, and the wildlife preserve in the sand dunes by the Ria lagoon at Aveiro. In fact, the entire misty, rather eerie Ria is a restful place outside the summer season — only the birds and high-prowed, painted fishing boats seem to disturb the peace. Those concerned about their health may want to spend time at the spas of Vimeiro, Luso, or Curia, reputed to cure all manner of complaints. (Also see *Satisfying Spas* in DIVERSIONS.)

And then there are the beaches. Those who would like to sun themselves on a deserted strand or in a secluded cove between high cliffs have only to follow one of the many little roads that lead off the main route down to just such private worlds by the sea. Those who prefer something more domesticated can head for one of the area's numerous popular beach resorts, such as Figueira da Foz, which has a beach that is more than 1,500 feet wide. Scuba divers might be lucky enough to discover one of the old treasure ships said to be submerged here, and enthusiasts of other water sports will find plenty to keep them busy. The less adventuresome who prefer pools to the sea will find them at most hotels and, because the surf can be rough along this Atlantic coast, in some of the beach towns themselves.

The giant lobsters and crabs that abound in the chilly coastal waters are a delight for food connoisseurs. (Such treats can be washed down with the fine wines of the Bairrada region around Coimbra and Aveiro or the not-quite-so-high-caste, but very good, wines of Torres Vedras.) The route's visual pleasures include the brightly painted boats in the harbors and on the beaches at Ericeira, Peniche, Nazaré, and Aveiro; the sturdy white windmills twirling on the hilltops; and the mountains that climb up from the coast. Finally, a vast number of visitors who come this way are the devout, drawn by the miracle that is believed to have occurred at Fátima early in this century.

The history of this region is that of all of northern Portugal. Lusitanians, probably Celtic in origin, were the first inhabitants of whom there is historical evidence; they were succeeded by Romans, waves of barbarians, Moors, and, during the 11th century, conquering Christian kings. In 1385, the famous battle of Aljubarrota, between a Portuguese and a Spanish pretender to the Portuguese throne, led to a Portuguese victory and to the building of the beautiful monastery at Batalha (Battle) — a monumental token of thanksgiving. From 1580 to 1640, however, the area — along with the rest of Portugal — was ruled by Spanish kings. Napoleon's armies invaded during the early 19th century; the two lines of fortifications built from the Tagus to the sea in the vicinity of Torres Vedras and Mafra were paramount in expelling the French. Before that happened, however, the invasion caused King João VI to flee to Brazil, taking most of the portable riches of the Palace of Mafra with him.

Political chaos characterized the rest of the 19th century and the beginning of this one. Portugal's last king, Manuel II, left for exile in England in 1910 from the Estremaduran fishing port of Ericeira. In 1932, a former economics professor at Coimbra University, António de Oliveira Salazar, became Prime Minister of Portugal and installed a dictatorship that lasted until 1974, when a coup ushered in the present democratic regime.

Today, there are increasing numbers of chemical, cellulose, textile, and shoe factories in Estremadura and the Beira Litoral, but many of the old ways of making a living, such as fishing, seaweed gathering, wine making, and cattle raising, persist. Tourism is growing rapidly, although this coastal region can still be considered underexplored and its people remain hospitable. Almost every town has a well-signposted tourist office with a multilingual staff.

The route outlined below begins in Lisbon and runs north, zigzagging between inland and coastal towns to Porto. The first major monument, the monastery-palace in the inland town of Mafra, is encountered almost immediately, followed by the first of the Costa de Prata beach towns, Ericeira. The route then takes in Torres Vedras on the way to the ancient fishing village of Peniche, from which an excursion to the island of Berlenga can be made. The lovely walled town of Obidos comes next, then Caldas da Rainha and its hot springs, the fishing port and beach resort of Nazaré, and Alcobaça and Batalha. After visits to Fátima, to Leiria (with its impressive hilltop castle), and to the popular beach resort of Figueira da Foz, the itinerary leads to the ancient university town of Coimbra. (Our driving route through the mountains to the east begins and ends in Coimbra — see *The Beiras* in DIRECTIONS.) The final leg of the route detours to the Roman ruins of Conímbriga and then proceeds to explore Aveiro and its misty lagoon, before pulling into Porto.

Towns are very close together, so more than one can be visited in a day. Some, such as Obidos, Nazaré, and Aveiro, however, are each worth an entire day or more, and Coimbra is so rich in history and monuments that 2 or 3 days are needed to see it all. The area's beach resorts and spas can be pleasant places for rest and relaxation or, since they are close to the historical sites, convenient headquarters for touring. But be warned that with the exception of the toll highway between Lisbon and Porto, the roads in this area are not very good — narrow, potholed, and full of trucks.

Hotels are scarce in some places, so visitors should make reservations far in advance — sometimes as much as 6 months. Compared with Lisbon and the Algarve, however, hotel prices are reasonable. A double room with a private bath and breakfast in a hotel listed as expensive will generally cost from $90 to $140 in summer (although the *Pousada do Castelo* in Obidos charges as much as $180 for a very expensive room in season); in a hotel listed as moderate, from $60 to $80; and in an inexpensive place, less than $60. Rates can drop by as much as 25% off-season. Most of the restaurants here specialize in fish and seafood; happily, lobster and other such delicacies cost less on this rocky coast than they do in the Lisbon and Algarve areas. Expect to pay $70 or more for a meal for two with wine at a restaurant listed as expensive, from $35 to $40 at a moderate spot, and around $20 in an inexpensive place. For each location, hotels and restaurants are listed alphabetically by price category.

En Route from Lisbon Leave the city on the A7 highway west toward Estoril, turning right onto N117 toward Sintra and Queluz. After 2½ miles (4 km), turn right again at the signposts for Sintra and Queluz. Take this connecting roadway a short distance to N249. Follow N249 for 19½ miles (31 km) to Sintra; Mafra is 14½ miles (23 km) north of Sintra on N9. Alternatively, leave Lisbon on the A7 highway and head west toward Estoril for 5 miles (8 km), where it becomes A5. Take A5 for 7 miles (11 km) to the turnoff for Sintra, and continue on to Mafra.

MAFRA Built in the early 18th century, the Palácio Nacional de Mafra, King João V's enormous monastery-palace, is one of the largest historic monuments in Europe. For a detailed description, see *Museums, Monuments, and Ruins* in DIVERSIONS. The monastery-palace (phone: 61-52332) is open daily from 10 AM to 1 PM and 2 to 5 PM; closed Tuesdays; admission charge. (The basilica, visited separately at no charge, is open daily.) It is best to buy a map and guidebook at the entrance. The tourist office (Av. 25 de Abril; phone: 61-812023) can supply information on other sights in Mafra. Pottery — off-white and trimmed in pale blue — is made in the region and is sold in local shops.

CHECKING IN

Castelão A modern hotel on the main street, not far from the monastery-palace. It has 34 rooms with private baths, mini-bars, and satellite TV. There also is a glassed-in restaurant and a bar. Av. 25 de Abril, Mafra (phone: 61-812050; fax: 61-51698). Moderate.

EATING OUT

Frederico Good Portuguese dishes are served in this modest restaurant, whose windows look out on the monastery. Closed Tuesdays. No reservations. Visa accepted. Terreiro D. João V, Mafra (phone: 61-52089). Inexpensive.

Pateo Built around an interior courtyard — hence its name — this eatery serves up fine renditions of local specialties. Closed Mondays. No reservations. Major credit cards accepted. 19 Rua Serpa Pinto, Mafra (phone: 61-811137). Inexpensive.

En Route from Mafra Head northwest on N116 to Ericeira, 7 miles (11 km) away.

ERICEIRA A simple fishing village popular with the Portuguese as a summer resort, Ericeira sits on cliffs above the Atlantic. There is a small beach in town, where colorful fishing boats are drawn ashore, and another larger beach outside town, where the water can be rough. Small restaurants, bars, and shops abound. Among the sights is the chapel of Santo António, which has tiles portraying the royal family's departure into exile from the port of Ericeira in 1910. North of town is the ruined São Isidro fort, built to protect the coast against pirates. About three-quarters of a mile (1 km) south of town, on the road to Sintra, is a big flashy disco called *Sociedade Anônima* (Foz do Lizandro; phone: 61-62325), which features an esplanade, a gameroom, and several bars. The Ericeira Tourist Office (33 Rua Dr. Eduardo Burnay; phone: 61-63122) is open weekends in winter.

CHECKING IN

Turismo A sprawling white building roofed in green tiles and set in gardens atop the cliff, it has 250 rooms with baths and telephones. What it lacks in decorative taste, it makes up for with views of the sea, as well as its 3 seaside swimming pools, private beach, restaurants, bar, and disco. Rua

Porto de Rezés, Ericeira (phone: 61-864045 or 61-864408; fax: 61-63146). Expensive.

Vilazul A charming blue-and-white inn in the center of town, only 5 minutes from the sea. It has 21 rooms with baths and TV sets, 2 bars, a rooftop lounge, and a restaurant. 10 Calçada da Baleia, Ericeira (phone: 61-864101; fax: 61-62927). Expensive.

Morais This blue-trimmed hotel on a quiet side street has a lovely inner garden graced with trees, flowers, and a swimming pool (around which lunch is served in summer). It also has 40 modern, clean rooms with baths. Reserve far in advance. 3 Rua Dr. Miguel Bombarda, Ericeira (phone: 61-864200; fax: 61-864308). Moderate.

Pedro o Pescador A pretty place with pointed dormer windows, on the main street. White marble floors and blue-and-white decorations make it seem light and airy. Besides its 25 rooms with private baths, it has a small garden patio off the bar, air conditioned lounges, and a dining room. 22 Rua Dr. Eduardo Burnay, Ericeira (phone: 61-864302; fax: 61-62321). Moderate.

Vinos A restored old mansion featuring 10 rooms (all with baths). No restaurant, but there is a bar on the premises. 25 Rua Prudêncio Franco de Trindade, Ericeira (phone: 61-63830; fax: 61-63686). Inexpensive.

EATING OUT

César An enormous panoramic restaurant on the cliffs north of town. Lobsters swim in an indoor fountain, and beneath the restaurant is a huge vivarium filled with baroque-decorated tanks of shellfish. There is a bar, and music for dancing in summer. Closed Tuesdays. Reservations advised. Major credit cards accepted. On N247, Km 1 (phone: 61-62926). Expensive to moderate.

O Barco A highly recommended dining place on a narrow, cobbled street, down the stone steps that lead to the fishing harbor. Try the *arroz de marisco* (rice with seafood), the *arroz de polvo* (rice with octopus), the *caldeirada de enguias* (eel stew), or the curried shellfish while enjoying the sea view. Closed Thursdays in winter. Reservations advised. Major credit cards accepted. Rua Capitão João Lopes, Ericeira (phone: 61-62759). Moderate.

Parque dos Mariscos In a big, white building on the main street, this dining room has green lattices and plants decorating its red brick walls. As expected, *arroz de marisco* is a specialty; so is *linguado* (sole). Open daily. Reservations advised. Major credit cards accepted. 28 Rua Dr. Eduardo Burnay, Ericeira (phone: 61-62162). Moderate.

Parreirinha Seafood is featured on the extensive menu at this eatery with a glassed-in terrace upstairs. Open daily. No reservations. Major credit cards accepted. 12 Rua Dr. Miguel Bombarda, Ericeira (phone: 61-62148). Inexpensive.

En Route from Ericeira A good road, N247, leads north into the Costa de Prata. It runs along the tops of cliffs, with spectacular views of rough seas smashing onto rocks below, and little roads lead down from it to inlets and indented beaches — Praia de São Sebastião, Praia de São Lourenço, and Porto da Calada. A number of windmills — some billed as "working windmills" — can be visited. The road then meets N9 and turns eastward across a flat plain beside the Sizandro River to Torres Vedras, 16½ miles (27 km) from Ericeira. Before town, there's a turnoff to the right (over an unpaved road) for Castro do Zambujal, the ruins of an important fortified hilltop town of the Iron and Bronze Ages, which has walls and towers still standing from 2500 BC. The many artifacts discovered here are in the *Museu Municipal* in Torres Vedras.

CHECKING IN/EATING OUT

Dom Fernando This *pensão* sits in solitary splendor on a cliff above the Atlantic 7 miles (11 km) north of Ericeira on N247. Originally a private house, it has a lovely garden and terrace over the sea, access to the beach below as well as a pool, a restaurant, and 14 rooms and suites, all with private baths, lovely views, and furnished with elegant reproductions of antiques. Quinta da Calada, Talefe (phone: 61-855204; fax: 61-855264). Moderate.

TORRES VEDRAS An old town that has been inhabited by Celts, Visigoths, Romans, and Moors, Torres Vedras is most famous as the headquarters for the defense of Lisbon from Napoleon's troops during the early 19th century. The Linhas de Torres Vedras were two lines of earthen battlements incorporating fortresses and castles that English and Portuguese troops under the command of Arthur Wellesley (later to become the Duke of Wellington) raised clear across the peninsula jutting from the coast to the Tagus River. The more northerly line began at the mouth of the Sizandro on the Atlantic and ended just south of Vila Franca de Xira, passing through Torres Vedras. The southern line crossed the peninsula at a point just north of Mafra. To see the remains of the lines, turn left at the entrance to town, where the sign points upward. The ruins of the São Vicente fort, built as part of the lines (many of its round towers were disguised as windmills to fool the French), stand at the top of a nearly perpendicular hill commanding a wide view of the countryside. Inside the courtyard there are reconstructions of the earthen battlements, but nothing of the original fort remains except the walls and an empty dome.

Torres Vedras today is a modern town with little of its ancient character, except for the Old Quarter, which has narrow, cobblestone streets winding steeply up to the old castle on the hill opposite the São Vicente fort. The castle was badly damaged when it was wrested from the Moors during the 12th century, and again in the earthquake of 1755, but it, too, became part of Wellington's lines. The Igreja de Santa Maria do Castelo, within its walls, has two Romanesque portals, numerous paintings, and 17th-century *azulejos,* but São Pedro, with its Manueline portal, opulent gilt work, and baroque tiles, is the most important of the town's many churches. Also to be seen are a Gothic fountain (the Chafariz dos Canos) and the *Museu Municipal* (in the Convento da Graça, Largo da Graça; phone: 61-321001), where, in addition to items dug up at the prehistoric Castro do Zambujal site, silver crowns, coins, paintings, and ceramics are on display. It's open from 10 AM to 1 PM and 2 to 6 PM; closed Mondays. There's an admission charge. The tourist office is on Rua 9 de Abril (phone: 61-314094).

CHECKING IN

Império Built in post-modernist style, it is in the center of town and is charming, light, and cheerful. Some of the 47 rooms have balconies with views of the town and the Graça church; there is a restaurant, a bar, and a café. Praça 25 de Abril, Torres Vedras (phone: 61-314232; fax: 61-321901). Inexpensive.

EATING OUT

Barrete Preto The most elegant restaurant in town, wood-paneled and carpeted, with an extensive menu. Specialties include codfish with cream, roast kid, and grilled meat and fish. There is an adjoining pub decorated in regional style with tiles and antique lanterns. Closed Thursdays. Reservations advised. Major credit cards accepted. 25 Rua Paiva de Andrade, Torres Vedras (phone: 61-22063). Moderate.

O Diamante A charming dining place featuring roast codfish, squid on a spit, and beef with cream. Closed Sundays. Reservations advised. No credit cards accepted. 32A Rua António Leal da Assunção, Torres Vedras (phone 61-25988). Moderate.

Pateo An old house has been turned into a very attractive modern restaurant, with white walls and a pale pink and green decor. Dishes featured include *arroz de pato* (duck with rice), *porco recheado* (loin of pork stuffed with cheese and ham), and *sopa conventual* (shrimp and vegetable soup). Closed Sundays. Reservations advised. Major credit cards accepted. 1B Rua José Eduardo César, Torres Vedras (phone: 61-311496). Moderate.

En Route from Torres Vedras Take N8-2 north through high hills covered with vineyards and pine woods. Proceed directly to Lourinhã, 12 miles (19 km) away, or, after about 4½ miles (7 km), turn left to the spa town of Vimeiro (another 4 miles/6 km along a not-so-good road) and the wide sandy beach of Praia do Porto Novo (still another 2½ miles/4 km west); then backtrack through Vimeiro to rejoin N8-2 north. Lourinhã, a flat and medieval-looking town beside the sea, is the gateway to many of the region's beaches, and it has several interesting churches, such as the 14th-century Gothic Igreja Matriz (Parish Church); the Igreja of Nossa Senhora da Annunciação (Church of Our Lady of the Annunciation), which is part of a Franciscan monastery founded in 1598; and the Misericórdia church, with a Manueline door. North of town about 2½ miles (4 km) is the shell-shaped beach of Praia da Areia Branca, with several hotels and restaurants, and a tourist office (phone: 61-422167). Still farther along is the fishing port of Peniche, at the tip of a peninsula jutting out to sea 12 miles (19 km) from Lourinhã.

CHECKING IN

Golf Mar Its beautiful, dramatic, solitary setting amid landscaped gardens very high above the rocky coast at Praia do Porto Novo gives guests the feeling of being suspended between the sky and the sea. Half of the 300 rooms have terraces overlooking the water, and the hotel has a 9-hole golf course, 2 outdoor pools and a heated indoor pool, horseback riding, tennis, a panoramic restaurant and bar, shops, a discotheque, a gameroom, a hair-dresser, and lounges. Praia do Porto Novo (phone: 61-984157; fax: 61-984621). Expensive.

Areia Branca Modern and near the beach, this *estalagem* (inn) has 29 rooms with private baths, a good restaurant, a bar, and a pool. Praia da Areia Branca (phone: 61-412491; fax: 61-413143). Moderate.

Apartamentos Turísticos São João This modern complex of 36 well-furnished apartments offers a swimming pool, tennis, a bar, and a discotheque. Praia da Areia Branca (phone: 61-422491; fax: 61-422491). Inexpensive.

EATING OUT

O Chalé French fare is the specialty here. Open daily. No reservations. No credit cards accepted. Largo Mestre Anacleto Marcos da Silva, Lourinhã (phone: 61-423003). Moderate.

Frutos do Mar At Porto das Barcas, south of Lourinhã, this eatery specializes in lobster — in fact, it has the largest vivarium in Portugal. Closed Tuesdays. No reservations. Major credit cards accepted. Agua Doce, Porto das Barcas (phone: 61-422774). Moderate.

PENICHE This is a bustling fishing port with many seafood restaurants. (The local version of *caldeirada,* fish stew, is famous.) On a mile-long peninsula jutting out to sea, Peniche was once an island — silt deposited over the centuries built up the sand isthmus that now joins it to the mainland. In earlier times, the island was the last refuge of Lusitanian warriors fleeing Roman invaders and a port of call for Phoenicians, Crusaders, and pirates.

The massive, sprawling fortress that dominates the harbor was built during the 16th century and later enlarged until its moats, walls, bastions, cisterns, and towers occupied 5 acres. Used as a political prison during the Salazar regime and later as a camp for refugees from Angola, it now houses the *Museu Municipal* (Campo da República; phone: 62-781848), a repository of prehistoric artifacts and articles pertaining to ships, fishing, and lace making (the ancient art of *bilros,* or bobbin lace, still flourishes in Peniche), as well as relics from its days as a prison. It's open from 9 AM to noon and 2 to 5 PM (to 7 PM from July through September); closed Mondays. There's an admission charge. Several of the town's churches are also worth a visit, among them the Misericórdia, where the walls are covered with beautiful 17th-century tiles and the ceiling is painted with New Testament scenes. In all there are about 100 paintings in the church, five of them by Josefa d'Obidos. The Church of Nossa Senhora do Socorro (Our Lady of Succor) has paintings attributed to Josefa's father, as well as interesting glazed tiles and gilt carving. São Pedro has an enormous baroque altarpiece and paintings of the life of the saint, and Nossa Senhora da Conceição is completely covered with 18th-century tiles. Peniche's Tourist Office is on Rua Alexandre Herculano (phone: 62-789571).

The coast of the Peniche Peninsula is lined with giant rock formations in the sea, many in fantastic, surreal shapes, as well as with caves, grottoes, and wide sandy beaches. At the tip of the peninsula is Cabo Carvoeiro, with another church, the tiny sanctuary of Nossa Senhora dos Remédios, which is completely covered with tiles attributed to the 18th-century master António de Oliveira Bernardes; nearby is an 18th-century lighthouse. The church is the focal point of one of Peniche's traditional festivals, the *Romaria da Nossa Senhora dos Remédios* (Pilgrimage of Our Lady of the Remedies), held in October, when the image of the Virgin is carried from the church down to the sea. Another local festival, also sea-related, is the *Festas da Senhora da Boa Viagem* (Festival of Our Lady of the Good Voyage), held the first week in August and marked by a procession of boats.

Cabo Carvoeiro provides smashing views of the surf-pounded coast and, in the distance, of Berlenga, the main island of an archipelago (the Ilhas Berlengas) whose rocks, caves, and coves are home to migratory birds and rare flora and fauna. From June through September, boats run from Peniche to Berlenga (for schedules, call *Empresa Víamar;* phone: 62-782153), making the trip in about an hour. During the 16th century, the island was inhabited by monks, who abandoned it after constant attacks by pirates. Today, a few fishermen and lighthouse keepers live here. The lighthouse stands on the highest point of the island, above the 17th-century São João Baptista fort, which is set on an islet connected to Berlenga by a winding stone bridge.

CHECKING IN

Praia Norte This modern place at the entrance to town has 103 rooms and suites (all with TV sets), a swimming pool, a discotheque, a bingo room, and a restaurant and grillroom. On N114, Praia Norte, Peniche (phone: 62-781161; fax: 62-781165). Expensive.

Felita A small *pensão* with 9 rooms (each with private bath), near the town gardens. 12 Largo Professor Franco Freire, Peniche (phone: 62-782190). Inexpensive.

Pavilhão Mar e Sol On Berlenga Island, this comfortable, 5-room residence is run by the Peniche municipal government. Open from June through mid-September, it has a pleasant restaurant — the only one on the island, in fact. Ilha Berlenga (phone: 62-789731). Very inexpensive.

EATING OUT

Os Corticais On the sea with its own little beach, this place specializes in seafood and has its own large vivarium that can be visited. Totally enclosed in glass, the dining room has lovely views. Closed Mondays. No reservations. Major credit cards accepted. Rua Corticais, Porto da Areia Sul, Peniche (phone: 62-782462). Moderate.

Praia Mar On the beach, this place specializes in fish and seafood and has windows looking out to sea. Open daily. No reservations. No credit cards accepted. Molhe Leste, Peniche (phone: 62-782523). Moderate.

Marisqueira Mili Near the fishing port, this eatery also specializes in seafood. Open daily. No reservations. No credit cards accepted. Rua José Estevão, Peniche (phone: 62-782278). Inexpensive.

En Route from Peniche Head east on N114, passing through Atouguia da Baleia, an interesting little town with São Leonardo, a 13th-century Romanesque-Gothic church and, facing the church, a Manueline pillory. In the square in front of the massive baroque church, Nossa Senhora da Conceição, are the rough stone remains of a bull stall built by King Pedro I during the 14th century — evidence that bullfighting is very old in Portugal. Continue east on N114, turning north onto N8 to the beautiful walled town of Obidos, 15 miles (24 km) from Peniche.

OBIDOS This small town set on a high hill is rightly called a "museum town." Its medieval atmosphere remains intact, and so many of its houses and other buildings are of historic or artistic significance that it has been declared a national monument. A picture-postcard town today, with flower-covered balconies, whitewashed houses, and narrow cobblestone streets — all surrounded by Moorish walls and dominated by an equally old castle — it was evidently just as pretty during the Middle Ages. The Saintly Isabel admired it so much during a 13th-century visit with her new husband, King Dinis, that he gave it to her as a wedding present. Obidos later became the property of Leonor Teles, wife of King Fernando; Philippa of Lancaster, the English wife of King João I; Leonor of Portugal, wife of João II; and Catherine, wife of King João III. Thus it became known as the Casa das Rainhas (House of Queens).

Pass through the double-arched gateway to the town (Porta da Vila) and follow the narrow main street, Rua Direita, to the Praça de Santa Maria, where there are a few tree-shaded parking spaces. The Igreja de Santa Maria is a beautiful 17th-century church (on the foundations of a Visigothic temple that later became a Moorish mosque), virtually paved with blue-and-white *azulejos* inside. The paintings over the main altar are by João da Costa, while those of St. Catherine over the altar in a chapel to the south (right) were signed by Josefa d'Obidos in 1661 (the great 17th-century painter, born in Seville, Spain, lived most of her life in Obidos and is buried in another town church, São Pedro). Note, too, the large paintings of biblical scenes, attributed to her father, Baltazar Gomes Figueira, as well as the exquisitely carved Renaissance tomb of a governor of Obidos. More works by Josefa d'Obidos are in the *Museu Municipal,* on the same square (phone: 62-959263), along with other paintings, sculpture, furniture, archaeological artifacts, and exhibits devoted to the Peninsular War. The museum is open daily from 9 AM to 12:30 PM and 2 to 6 PM; admission charge, except on Wednesdays. In the center of the square is a 15th-century pillory donated by Queen Leonor, the wife of João II. It bears the royal coat of arms and the *camaroeiro* (shrimp net) that became her symbol after her son drowned in Santarém and his body was recovered in a fisherman's net.

Built by the Moors, the walls enclosing the town are nearly a mile in circumference, with a wide walkway along the top that makes it possible to circumnavigate the crenelated battlements and take in a spectacular view of both the town and the countryside. There are only two interruptions in the circuit: one at the town gateway, the other at the castle, which began as a fortress, was turned into a royal palace during the 16th century, and has now been transformed, in part, into a *pousada* (see *Checking In*).

Outside the walls, there are several churches and chapels, but the most interesting is the unfinished hexagonal Church of Senhor da Pedra, which sits alone in a field to the north of town via N8; inside the 17th-century baroque building is an early Christian stone cross. To the south of town is the 16th-century aqueduct, a nearly 2-mile structure of double arches ordered built by Queen Catherine to feed water into the town's various fountains. The tourist office is on Rua Direita (phone: 62-959231).

During July and August in odd-numbered years, Obidos is the site of the *Biennale de Obidos,* an international art exhibition of paintings, sculpture, and ceramics. The works are displayed throughout the town.

CHECKING IN

Pousada do Castelo A rustically elegant, government-owned inn in the castle of Obidos, with 9 rooms and suites (all with private baths) and an excellent restaurant. For additional details, see *Pousadas and Manor Houses* in DIVERSIONS. Paço Real, Obidos (phone: 62-959105; 212-686-9213 in the US; fax: 62-959148). Very expensive.

Do Convento Just outside the walls, it was built during the early 19th century to cloister nuns, and it has been delightfully converted into an *estalagem* offering every modern convenience while maintaining its character. There are 24 rooms with private baths, a bar, and a beamed restaurant with a stone fireplace (and a garden patio for summer dining). Rua Dom João de Ornelas, Obidos (phone: 62-959217; fax: 62-959159). Expensive.

Mansão do Torre Just over a mile (2 km) from town is this recently remodeled mansion with its original old stone tower. There are 41 rooms with baths and satellite TV, a large pool surrounded by gardens, and a restaurant. Casal do Zambujairo (phone: 62-959247; fax: 61-959051). Expensive.

Josefa d'Obidos An *albergaria* (inn) in an old house just outside the walls at the entrance to town, it has 42 nicely furnished rooms with baths, a typical restaurant, a bar, and a weekend discotheque. Rua Dom João de Ornelas, Obidos (phone: 62-959228; fax: 62-959533). Moderate.

Rainha Santa Isabel Another *albergaria,* on the main street of Obidos. Formerly a private home, it's decorated with tiles and has 20 rooms with baths, as well as a bar and several lounges. Rua Direita, Obidos (phone and fax: 62-959115). Moderate.

EATING OUT

A Ilustre Casa de Ramiro The shell of this building outside the walls is very old, but the interior was designed with an Arabic motif by the contemporary architect José Fernando Teixeira. Among the specialties on the extensive menu are *arroz de pato* (rice with duck) and grilled codfish; wines are from the Obidos region. Closed Wednesdays. Reservations advised. Major credit cards accepted. Rua Porta do Vale, Obidos (phone: 62-959194). Expensive to moderate.

Alcaide On the main street in the center of town, with lovely views of the countryside. Try the tuna, Azores-style. Closed Mondays and November. Reservations advised. Major credit cards accepted. Rua Direita, Obidos (phone: 62-959220). Moderate.

En Route from Obidos Drive 4 miles (6 km) north on N8 to Calsa da Rainha.

CALDAS DA RAINHA This sprawling agricultural town has two claims to fame: hot springs and ceramics. The town's name means "the Queen's hot springs" — referring to the 15th-century Queen Leonor, wife of João II. Passing through on her way to Batalha, she noticed peasants bathing in some local pools and, upon learning that the waters were good for rheumatism, did the same. So effective was the therapy that the queen pawned her jewels to establish a hospital and lay out a park, both of which still bear her name. (It's still possible for visitors to steep themselves in the sulfurous waters at the Rainha Dona Leonor Hospital Spa.) The Igreja de Nossa Senhora do Pópulo, which was the chapel of the hospital, is a Gothic and Manueline structure noted for its *azulejos* and a fine 16th-century triptych.

Caldas has been a pottery-making center since ancient times. The ceramics fair that takes place here each July draws thousands of visitors, but for those who miss it, the local pottery (the cabbage leaf bowls are a typical item) and other crafts can be seen at the Saturday market on Praça da República, the main square. One of the most famous Caldas potters was Rafael Bordalo Pinheiro, a 19th-century ceramist, cartoonist, and painter who established a studio here and created brightly colored caricatures of people that are still copied today. The *Museu José Malhoa* (Parque Rainha Dona Leonor; phone: 62-831984) displays a fine collection of ceramics by Bordalo Pinheiro, along with paintings by the late-19th- and early-20th-century artist after whom the museum is named. It's open from 10 AM to 12:30 PM and 2 to 5 PM; closed Mondays; admission charge, except on Sunday mornings. More ceramics can be seen at the far end of the park in the *Museu da Cerâmica* (phone: 62-23157), which has a tiled garden. The museum is open from 10 AM to noon and 2 to 5 PM; closed Mondays; admission charge, except on Sunday mornings. More of Bordalo Pinheiro's work can be seen nearby at the *Faianças Artísticas Bordalo Pinheiro* (Bordalo Pinheiro Faïence Factory), which maintains a small museum (closed weekends). For more information on Caldas da Rainha, contact the tourist office (Praça da República; phone: 62-34511).

CHECKING IN

Caldas International This very modern hotel has 83 rooms with baths, satellite TV, mini-bars, and air conditioning. There is an outdoor pool, a bar, and a restaurant. 45 Rua Dr. Figueiroa Rego, Caldas da Rainha (phone: 62-832307; fax: 62-844482). Moderate.

Malhoa There are 113 rooms with baths in this modern hostelry, whose amenities also include a swimming pool, a sauna, a restaurant, and a discotheque. 31 Rua António Sérgio, Caldas da Rainha (phone: 62-842180; fax: 62-842621)). Moderate.

Dona Leonor A *pensão* with 30 rooms, each of which has a private bath, TV set, and telephone. There is a bar and restaurant. 6 Hemiciclo João Paulo II, Caldas da Rainha (phone: 62-842171; fax: 62-842172). Inexpensive.

Europeia Pension This very modern place has 50 rooms and 2 suites with private baths, phones, refrigerator/bars, and TV sets. There is a restaurant and 3 cafés in the *Rua das Montras* shopping mall where it is located. Rua Almirante Cândido dos Reis, Caldas da Rainha (phone: 62-34781; fax: 62-832680). Inexpensive.

EATING OUT

Pateo da Rainha Good regional cooking and attentive service prevail. Specialties of the house are rice with monkfish, codfish, and *cozido à portuguesa,* or Portuguese boiled dinner. Open daily. No reservations. Visa accepted. 39 Rua de Camões, Caldas da Rainha (phone: 62-35658). Moderate.

En Route from Caldas da Rainha Take N8 north 7½ miles (12 km) to Alfeizerão and then turn west onto N242. São Martinho do Porto, on a quiet bay, with some interesting 19th-century buildings among the more modern ones of a beach resort, is only 3 miles (5 km) from the turnoff. After São Martinho, N242 heads north to Nazaré, 18 miles (29 km) from Caldas da Rainha.

CHECKING IN

Apartamentos Turísticos São Martinho A tourist complex offering 160 apartments with kitchenettes, plus a restaurant, a bar, a swimming pool, and a discotheque. It's near the beach, and water sports are available. 31 Rua Dr. Rafael Garcia, São Martinho do Porto (phone: 62-989335; fax: 62-989343). Expensive.

São Pedro All 25 rooms in this *albergaria* (inn) near the beach have private baths; there also is a bar. 7 Largo Vitorino Frois, São Martinho do Porto (phone: 62-989328; fax: 62-989327). Moderate.

EATING OUT

O Viveiro A good seafood restaurant near the quay. Open daily. No reservations. Visa accepted. Rua Cândido dos Reis, São Martinho do Porto (phone: 62-989691). Moderate.

NAZARÉ This fishing village is a very popular, rather touristy beach resort, but some of its customs remain, including the wearing of traditional costumes — full skirts with up to seven petticoats for the women, and long, black, plaid-lined capes and black stocking caps for the men. There are two parts to Nazaré. The Praia quarter, along the beach, is the lower, newer part of town, while the older Sítio, or Upper Town, is atop a cliff to the north, reachable by car or by an old funicular. The sea once covered what is now the Lower Town, but it suddenly receded during the 17th century, after which fishermen from Sítio built huts on the beach and eventually made Nazaré the premier fishing town along the coast — an impressive feat, since it has no natural harbor and, until fairly recently, had no real port facilities. The fishermen launched their boats from the beach and used oxen and later tractors to pull the nets back to shore. Given the strong currents, it was a dangerous occupation, but today there is a sheltered port for the boats — which are long and narrow, with bright eyes painted on the pointed prows, highly suggestive of the Phoenicians from whom it is believed the people of Nazaré are descended. The Praia area is now full of hotels and restaurants, but visitors can still see women drying fish and men mending nets, even though only a few fishermen remain on the beach.

At one time, the Sítio quarter was all there was to Nazaré. There is a spectacular view from the belvedere here; it takes in all the town below, the beach tents and umbrellas, the boat shelter at the far end of the beach, and the distant coastline. On the main square is the Igreja de Nossa Senhora da Nazaré, rich in marble and gilt carving; the church's little black image of the Virgin, said to have been brought from the Holy Land after the death of Emperor Constantine, is carried down to the sea during the annual *Romaria da Nossa Senhora de Nazaré,* a festival held in early September. The tiny white Capela da Memória, built into the side of the cliff by the square, commemorates a 12th-century miracle performed by the Virgin. According to the legend, a very religious man was hunting on the cliffs when his horse jumped over the edge after a deer. The man prayed to the Virgin, who miraculously set him and his horse back on terra firma, after which he built the chapel on the very spot. The present chapel, dating from the 17th century, is covered with 17th-century *azulejos.* Another Sítio landmark is the São Miguel fort, built during the 16th century to protect the town from pirates and now turned into a lighthouse. The tourist office in Nazaré (23 Rua Mouzinho de Albuquerque; phone: 62-561194) is in the Praia section of town.

CHECKING IN

Maré Small (36 rooms, all with TV sets and private baths) and convenient, it's in the heart of the Praia, about a block from the beach, with a restaurant and a bar. 8 Rua Mouzinho de Albuquerque, Nazaré (phone: 62-561122; fax: 62-561750). Expensive.

Da Nazaré In a little square several blocks back from the beach in the Praia quarter, its 52 rooms all have baths, mini-bars, and air conditioning. There is a restaurant, and a place next door — *Mar Alto* — to take in some folk music and dancing. Largo Afonso Zuquete, Nazaré (phone: 62-561311; fax: 62-561238). Moderate.

Dom Fuas This hotel at the southern end of the Praia section has 32 well-furnished rooms, all with TV sets and private baths, as well as a restaurant, a bar, and a snack bar. Av. Manuel Remígio, Nazaré (phone: 62-551351; fax: 62-561351). Moderate.

Praia On a main street near the beach, this modern place has 40 rooms with baths, air conditioning, and TV sets. It also has a restaurant, a bar, a sauna, and a disco. 39 Av. Vieira Guimarães, Nazaré (phone: 62-561423; fax: 62-561436). Moderate.

EATING OUT

Paulo Caetano Named after a famous Portuguese bullfighter and decorated with bullfighting pictures and posters, this Sítio restaurant specializes in seafood. Open daily. No reservations. Major credit cards accepted. Largo Reitor Baptista, Nazaré (phone: 62-552011). Expensive to moderate.

Ribamar In a *pensão* on the beach in the center of town — a white building with yellow balconies and windows — it has a lovely view of the sea. Fish, seafood, and typical regional dishes are the specialties. Open daily. No reservations. Major credit cards accepted. Av. da República, Nazaré (phone: 62-551158). Expensive to moderate.

O Caselinho Comfortable and traditional, this famous local culinary veteran specializes in grilled fish and seafood. The decor is typically Portuguese-provincial, with a nautical motif. Open daily. No reservations. Major credit cards accepted. 7 Praça Sousa Oliveira, Nazaré (phone: 62-551328). Moderate.

A Petisqueira Run by three brothers, this yellow, glassed-in restaurant, at the far end of the beach by the fishing boat shelter, serves nine different variations of *caldeirada da Nazaré* (fish stew). Open daily. No reservations. Visa accepted. Av. Manuel Remígio, Nazaré (phone: 62-551594). Moderate.

En Route from Nazaré Take N8-4 8½ miles (14 km) southeast to Alcobaça.

ALCOBAÇA At the confluence of the Alcoa and Baça rivers, this small town is completely dominated by the enormous white limestone Cistercian abbey — the Mosteiro de Santa Maria. Once the home of Portugal's most prosperous religious community, the monastery is still one of the country's most important architectural landmarks. King Afonso Henriques granted land to St. Bernard of Clairvaux, the influential French Cistercian who had championed the Portuguese cause against the Moors. The monks began to build in 1178, and set to work farming their vast domain, recruiting lay brothers to help them and introducing new agricultural techniques (which accounts for the superior quality of the Alcobaça vineyards and wines).

The style of the monastery church, the largest church in Portugal, marks the transition from Romanesque to Gothic, although the façade, with its rose window and two bell towers, is a result of 17th- and 18th-century baroque alterations. Inside, the spacious church is, in accordance with Cistercian austerity, devoid of adornment, with two notable exceptions: the exquisite, intricately carved 14th-century Flamboyant Gothic tombs of King Pedro I and his beloved mistress, Dona Inês de Castro, the most famous lovers in Portuguese history. As a prince, Pedro had fallen in love with the beautiful Spanish aristocrat, but his father, fearing Spanish interference with the Portuguese throne, ordered her murder (which took place in Coimbra in 1355). Dom Pedro had his revenge when he ascended the throne. Besides executing some of Inês's murderers, he exhumed her body, dressed her in royal robes and a crown, and forced all of the nobility to kiss her hand. Whether the monastery church at Alcobaça was the scene of this "coronation" is open to question, but both Pedro and Inês are buried here, in tombs placed on opposite sides of the transept, so that their first sight upon opening their eyes on Judgment Day will be of each other.

Behind the ambulatory of the church is the sacristy, preceded by an ornate, 16th-century Manueline doorway, and just off the church nave is the beautiful 14th-century Claustro do Silêncio (its upper story, added later, is Manueline). Around the cloister range other monastic spaces, including the Sala dos Reis (Kings' Hall), an 18th-century addition with terra cotta statues of the Kings of Portugal surmounting an *azulejo* frieze, and the impressive kitchen, which has a branch of the Alcoa running through it — an early labor-saving device that allowed the monks to catch fish for their dinner and to wash the dishes, too. The monastery (phone: 62-43469) is open from 9 AM to 7 PM (to 5 PM from October through March); closed *Christmas* and *New Year's Day*. Admission charge, except on Sunday mornings. Oenophiles might want to stop at the *Museu do Vinho* (Museum of Wine; on the road to Leiria right outside town). On exhibit are many types of utensils used by the monks through the centuries to make wine. Open weekdays from 9 AM to noon and 2 to 5 PM; no admission charge.

The Alcobaça Tourist Office is on Praça 25 de Abril (phone: 62-42377).

CHECKING IN

Quinta do Campo Built around the same time as the Mosteiro de Santa Maria, this comfortable manor house has 8 rooms, all with baths. There also is a swimming pool, a tennis court, and horseback riding, but no restaurant. Located 2½ miles (4 km) from Alcobaça on N84 (phone: 62-577135; fax: 62-577555). Expensive.

Santa Maria This modern white building with a tiled roof sits in the gardens directly in front of the monastery. There are 31 rooms with baths (some rooms have balconies), plus a nice, wood-paneled bar, but no restaurant. Rua Dr. Francisco Zagalo, Alcobaça (phone: 62-597395; fax: 62-596715). Moderate.

EATING OUT

Frei Bernardo Behind the Art Nouveau exterior is a nice bar and a very large dining room specializing in *frango na púcara* (chicken in a pot), *chanfana* *de borrego* (lamb stew), grilled fish, and *açorda de marisco* (a stew or "dry" soup made of seafood and other ingredients). There's a show of folk dancing and singing and a band that plays Portuguese music on request for groups. Open daily. Reservations advised. Major credit cards accepted. 17-19 Rua Dom Pedro V, Alcobaça (phone: 62-42227). Moderate.

Trindade The region's most typical dishes — *frango na púcara, açorda de marisco,* and fish — are the specialties here. There also is a snack bar and a small bar; original 18th-century tiles are part of the decor. Closed Saturdays in winter and from mid-September through the first week in October. No reservations. Visa accepted. 22 Praça Dom Afonso Henriques, Alcobaça (phone: 62-42397). Moderate.

En Route from Alcobaça The town of Aljubarrota is 4 miles (6 km) north along N8, not far from the place where the armies of two pretenders to the Portuguese throne — one Portuguese and one Castilian — faced each other on August 14, 1385. The Portuguese pretender, whose forces were vastly outnumbered, vowed he would build a great monastery if he defeated the Spaniards. The battle was brief and won by the Portuguese, thereby assuring the country's independence and the right of João I to occupy its throne. The enduring monument he constructed is farther up the road, 6 miles (10 km) along N8 and then 2½ miles (4 km) along N1, in Batalha.

CHECKING IN

Casa da Padeira (House of the Baker) Named after a baker who fought the Spaniards with a wooden shovel and pushed them into her oven, this modern manor house has 8 rooms with baths, and a swimming pool. There is no restaurant; the bar is set in ample gardens. Estrada N8, Aljubarrota, Alcobaça (phone: 61-48272). Moderate.

BATALHA The monastery that João I raised to the Virgin Mary in thanks for his decisive victory at Aljubarrota is probably the most beautiful monument in Portugal, despite the discoloration and pollution damage inflicted by passing traffic. Begun in 1388, worked on by several architects throughout the 15th century, and left unfinished early in the 16th century, the Mosteiro de Santa Maria da Vitória (Monastery of Our Lady of Victory; phone: 44-96497) is a masterpiece of Portuguese Gothic, often cited as an example of how the country's builders were able to absorb various foreign influences to forge their own national style. Outside, it's trimmed with gargoyles, flying buttresses, pinnacles, and lacy balustrades (the west front is particularly suggestive of the English Perpendicular style, which is not surprising since the founder's wife, Philippa of Lancaster, was English). Inside, while the church nave is stark and soaring, cloisters and chapels are richly decorated with the delicate curves of Flamboyant Gothic and the florid details of the transitional, Gothic-to-Renaissance, Manueline style.

Be sure to see the Capela do Fundador (Founder's Chapel), off an aisle to the right, where King João I, Queen Philippa, and their children (including Prince Henry the Navigator) are buried beneath a star-shaped vault. The tomb of the king and queen is topped with reclining figures of the pair, their hands joined. The Claustro Real (Royal Cloister), on the other side of the church, mixes Gothic with Manueline (note the pearls, shells, and coils carved on the columns). Just off it is the Sala do Capítulo (Chapterhouse), which has a vaulted ceiling without intermediate supports — its construction was such a dangerous engineering feat that condemned criminals did the actual work. Another cloister, the Claustro de Dom Afonso V, is beyond the Royal Cloister. From here, visitors can walk around to the Capelas Imperfeitas (Unfinished Chapels), seven chapels radiating around a rotunda that was meant to be topped with a dome. The incomplete pillars are encrusted with Manueline carving, and the doorway to the chapels is a Manueline tour de force. The Batalha monastery is open daily from 9 AM to 6 PM (to 5 PM from October through May); closed *Christmas* and *New Year's Day*. There's an admission charge. Batalha's Tourist Office is on Largo Paulo VI (phone: 44-96180).

CHECKING IN

Pousada do Mestre Afonso Domingues Formerly a privately owned *estalagem,* this government-owned *pousada* in the square by the monastery is unlike most of the chain — it's of modern construction. Named after the first of the monastery's architects, it has 20 rooms with baths, a good restaurant, and a small bar. Largo Mestre Afonso Domingues, Batalha (phone: 44-96260; 212-686-9213 in the US). Expensive.

Quinta do Fidalgo This totally restored 17th-century house in front of a monastery is surrounded by acres of woods and gardens. It has 26 rooms with private baths. Breakfast only is served. In front of the monastery, Batalha (phone: 44-96114). Moderate.

Residencial Batalha Located in the historic center of Batalha, this new, modern hotel has 22 rooms with baths, air conditioning, and satellite TV. There is a bar, a terrace, and a handicraft shop. Largo da Igreja (phone: 44-767500; fax: 44-767467). Moderate.

São Jorge A motel up the hill on the road to Lisbon, it has 10 rooms with private baths, tennis courts, a large swimming pool amid lawns and trees, and a regional-style restaurant. On N1, Batalha (phone: 44-96210 or 44-96186; fax: 44-96313). Moderate.

EATING OUT

Mestre de Avis A large restaurant above a café near the monastery square. Decorated in blue and white, it has bay windows offering a good view of the monastery, as well as a terrace for summer dining. Open daily. No reservations. Major credit cards accepted. Largo Dom João I, Batalha (phone: 44-96427). Moderate.

En Route from Batalha Leiria is only 7 miles (11 km) north on N1, but for those with time to spare and an interest in the phenomenon that made it famous, Fátima — in the mountains 12½ miles (20 km) east of Batalha along the A1 toll road — is worth a side trip.

FÁTIMA On May 13, 1917, a vision of the Virgin Mary, standing above a small oak tree, appeared to three peasant children who were tending their sheep here. The apparition returned five more times — on the 13th of each succeeding month — and by the time of the last appearance, a crowd of 70,000 people had gathered at the spot. Fátima has since become a world-famous Roman Catholic shrine, and to this day, pilgrims arrive — some crawling on their knees for miles — to hear mass on the 13th of each month from May through October. For more information, see *Best Festivals* in DIVERSIONS.

Those who decide to visit Fátima should note that roads leading to it are jammed to capacity on the 12th and 13th of pilgrimage months, and that while hotels are not in short supply, they are equally jammed on those days, since they cater mainly to pilgrims who make reservations months in advance. The Fátima Tourist Office is located on Avenida Dom José Alves Correia da Silva (phone: 49-531139).

CHECKING IN

Dom Gonçalo A 43-room *estalagem*, with private baths, a TV set in each room, a good restaurant and bar, and gift shops. 100 Rua Jacinta Marto, Fátima (phone: 49-532262; fax: 49-532088). Moderate.

EATING OUT

Grelha One of the very few independent restaurants in Fátima, it specializes in Portuguese cooking, especially grilled meat. The dining room has a fireplace, and there's a good bar. Closed Thursdays. Reservations unnecessary. Major credit cards accepted. 76 Rua Jacinta Marto, Fátima (phone: 49-531633). Moderate.

En Route from Fátima Backtrack to Batalha and from there take the road north to Leiria or the A1 toll road. Alternatively, return to Batalha by making a circuit southwest of Fátima via N360 and N243 and the towns of Mira de Aire and Porto de Mós. Several *grutas* (caves) are located in this area, among them the São Mamede, Moinhos Velhos, Santo António, and Alvados caves. Of these, the last two — the Grutas de Santo António and the Grutas de Alvados — are probably the most interesting. At the former (phone: 49-84876), there is an enormous chamber of nearly 5,000 square yards, plus rooms of dramatically lighted stalactites and stalagmites. A restaurant and snack bar are also at the site. The latter contain a succession of halls with giant columns and lakes, all well lighted. The caves are open daily year-round. There's an admission charge (a combined ticket can be bought for both caves).

LEIRIA An attractive, clean town at the confluence of the Liz and the Lena rivers, Leiria consists of an old medieval quarter and a new town of pleasant gardens and wide avenues. Crowning the whole is a dramatic hilltop castle, which was wrested from the Moors during the 12th century. An Iron Age *castro* and a Roman fortress preceded the castle, whose Moorish foundations are still visible, even though the structure was rebuilt by King Sancho II during the 13th century and later by King Dinis, who, with Saintly Queen Isabel, used it as a residence. Inside the castle walls are the ruins of the Gothic chapel of Nossa Senhora da Pena, roofless but with tall arches; the royal palace of King Dinis, which has an arched loggia with a good view; and the keep of the castle, built by the same king and affording an even better view. The castle is open daily from 9 AM to 6 PM in summer; to 5:30 PM in winter; admission charge. Other monuments in the town include the 12th-century Romanesque Church of São Pedro and the Sé (Cathedral), a large, 16th-century building in pale stone.

On the hill opposite the castle is the Santuário de Nossa Senhora da Encarnação, built during the 17th century and full of tiles from that period. Dedicated to the patron saint of Leiria, it is approached by a staircase of 172 steps. Leiria's Tourist Office (phone: 44-823773) is in the Jardim Luís de Camões, a large park in the center of town graced with cafés and beer gardens. Here, too, is a statue of a man and a woman, representing the two rivers that meet in Leiria and continue on as one. An open-air market takes place in Leiria on Tuesday and Saturday mornings in Campo Gimnodesportivo, the main square.

CHECKING IN

Dom João III Modern, comfortable, and conveniently located, with 64 rooms (with TV sets and telephones), a bar, a restaurant, and gift shops. Av. Heróis de Angola, Leiria (phone: 44-812500; 800-528-1234 in the US; fax: 44-812235). Expensive.

Euro-sol A modern high-rise, nicely landscaped. Together with its sister hotel next door, the *Euro-sol Jardim,* it offers 134 rooms with TV sets, mini-bars, and air conditioning, an enticing outdoor swimming pool on a terrace, a top-floor bar and restaurant with a view, a discotheque, and a shopping center. 1 Rua Dr. José Alves Correia da Silva, Leiria (phone: 44-812201; fax: 44-811205). Expensive.

São Luís A simple, cozy place in a modern building located in the town center, it has 46 rooms with private baths and TV sets; the 8 suites also have mini-bars. There is a pleasant bar and breakfast room. At the corner of Rua Henrique Sommer and Rua Beatris Machado (phone: 44-813197; fax: 44-813897). Moderate.

Lis Attractive and in a renovated building, it has 42 rooms with baths, and a bar, but no restaurant. Largo Alexandre Herculano, Leiria (phone: 44-31017; fax: 44-25099). Inexpensive.

EATING OUT

Tromba Rija An eatery in regional style, typically decorated with onions and garlic hanging from the ceiling and located in a village more than a mile (2 km) north of town. The codfish and steak dishes are delicious. Try one of the homemade desserts and an almond liqueur. Closed Saturday nights for dinner, Sundays, holidays, and 3 weeks in August. Reservations advised. Major credit cards accepted. Marrazes (phone: 44-32421). Expensive to moderate.

O Casarão Located 3 miles (5 km) southwest of town via the road to Nazaré (N1), this is an excellent regional restaurant with a cozy fireplace. There's a garden for summer dining. Closed Mondays. Reservations advised. Visa accepted. Cruzamento de Azóia (phone: 44-871080). Moderate.

Solar do Alcaida Brazilian dishes are among the many international choices offered at this elegant restaurant. Closed Mondays. Reservations advised. Major credit cards accepted. Rua 25 de Avril, Leiria (phone: 44-35248). Moderate.

Tia Elvira Regional food is served in this rustic place — to the accompaniment of *fado* music on Fridays in summer and Saturdays year-round. Open daily. No reservations. No credit cards accepted. It's about 2 miles (3 km) from the center of town. 14 Rua do Pinhal Grosso, Marinheiros (phone: 44-854171). Moderate to inexpensive.

Esplanda Jardim A good, modern place, in the large garden in the center of town by the tourist office, it is especially recommended for outdoor dining in summer. Closed the first 2 weeks of October. Reservations advised. Major credit cards accepted. Jardim Luís de Camões, Leiria (phone: 44-27259 or 44-32514). Inexpensive.

En Route from Leiria Figueira da Foz is 34 miles (54 km) north on N109 or A1, but a side trip to the coast from Leiria is worthwhile to visit the famous old glassmaking town of Marinha Grande and the beach resort of São Pedro de Moel. Take N242 west, passing through the Pinhal do Rei, the pine forest that King Dinis planted almost 700 years ago to control the shifting sands; it later provided timber to build Portugal's fleet. In Marinha Grande, 7½ miles (12 km) from Leiria, there are more than 40 crystal and glass factories. Check with the tourist office (Av. José Henriques Vareda; phone: 44-591542) for those that can be visited; some also have showrooms with pieces for sale. São Pedro de Moel, an ancient fishing village turned charming resort, is another 6 miles (10 km) west. It boasts a wide, sandy beach set between cliffs below the pine woods and an enormous saltwater swimming pool by the sea (which is fairly rough here).

Return to Leiria and head north on N109 or the toll road A1 to Figueira da Foz. Just to the west about 8½ miles (14 km) up the road is Monte Real, a spa with a ruined castle and Belle Epoque houses set in shady gardens. Beyond, the road continues north through beautiful pine forests, skirting Atlantic beaches, only 6 or 7 miles (10 or 11 km) away.

FIGUEIRA DA FOZ The most popular bathing resort and one of the most important fishing ports on the Portuguese Atlantic is endowed with an exceedingly long, wide sandy beach, plus a full complement of hotels, restaurants, and discos, a Belle Epoque gambling casino, a bullring, and facilities for golf, tennis, and water sports. Cross the soaring bridge, turn left, and follow the Centro (Center) and Praias (Beaches) signs to the tree-lined esplanade along the seafront, where there are modern hotels and shops facing the beach and turn-of-the-century houses decorated with tiles and wrought-iron balconies. The old Santa Catarina Fort (with a lighthouse on top) guards the river's mouth.

Most visitors to Figueira spend their time on the 2-mile-long, approximately 1,600-foot-wide beach; indeed, the town has little to detain sightseers, but the enormous *Casa do Paço* (Rua 5 de Outubro; phone: 33-22159), built by a bishop during the 17th century, is well worth the time spent away from the sun. The walls of this old house, now a museum, are decorated with several thousand tiles, many of them Delft, constituting the largest collection in Portugal. It's open weekdays from 9 AM to 12:30 PM and 2 to 5 PM; admission charge. Another museum, the *Museu Municipal Dr. Santos Rocha* (Av. Calouste Gulbenkian; phone: 33-24509), contains archaeological artifacts, ceramics, coins, furniture, sculpture (religious and African), and contemporary Portuguese and other paintings. It's open from 9 AM to 12:30 PM and 2 to 5:30 PM; closed Mondays; no admission charge. Figueira's Tourist Office (Av. 25 de Abril; phone: 33-22610 or 33-22126) has information on other sights, which include the parish Church of São Julião and the Misericórdia and Santo António churches. The fish auction is held in the port in the morning when the fleet comes in from May through December, and is well worth getting up early to see. As in other fishing towns, seafood of all kinds is on local restaurant menus, and Figueira has its own typical *caldeirada,* or fish stew.

Housed in a Belle Epoque building is the *Grande Casino Peninsular* (on Rua Bernardo Lopes; phone: 33-22041). There are international floor shows in the large dining room, and food is also served in the piano bar. The casino is open daily from 4 PM to 3 AM; the slot machine room is open daily from 3 PM to 3 AM.

The old fishing village of Buarcos, 1¼ miles (2 km) along the coast northwest of Figueira (in the direction of Cabo Mondego), represents a change of pace from its larger, more worldly neighbor. Very rich during the 17th century, but always subject to attacks by pirates, the town has a ruined castle and long, sandy beaches with colorful *bateiras* (flat-bottomed fishing boats) drawn up on shore.

CHECKING IN

Atlântico This very tall tower is an apartment-hotel with 70 fully equipped units, as well as a bar, TV lounge, and shopping center. The rooms have spectacular views of the beach and the Mondego. Av. 25 de Abril, Figueira da Foz (phone: 33-20245; fax: 33-22420). Expensive.

Clube Vale do Leão A luxurious tourist complex on a hill above Buarcos, on the road to Vaís. It has 17 villas and 6 rooms, all with private baths, furnished with antiques, and endowed with lovely views. Amenities include a restaurant serving international and regional food, a piano bar, a pub, a tearoom, a pool by the sea, and a health center. Vaís, Serra da Boa Viagem (phone: 33-33057; fax: 33-32571). Expensive.

Estalagem da Piscina Named for the Olympic-size swimming pool that's next door and shared with the *Grande Hotel da Figueira* (see below), this 20-room inn with private baths is modern and comfortable, with a restaurant overlooking the pool and the beach. Closed from November through April. 7 Rua de Santa Catarina, Figueira da Foz (phone: 33-22146; fax: 33-22420). Expensive.

Grande Hotel da Figueira This hostelry on the seafront is the best in Figueira da Foz. There are 91 rooms with baths (those in the front have balconies), an excellent restaurant, and a bar. Guests enjoy free admission to the casino's international floor show. Av. 25 de Abril, Figueira da Foz (phone: 33-22146; fax: 33-22420). Expensive.

Costa de Prata There are two modern hotels by this name, *Costa de Prata I* and *Costa de Prata II,* with 66 and 120 rooms respectively, close to each other and both close to the beach. Neither has a restaurant. 1 Largo Coronel Galhardo, Figueira da Foz (phone and fax: 33-26610), and 59 Rua Miguel Bombarda, Figueira da Foz (phone: 33-22082; fax: 33-26610). Moderate.

Tamargueira Modern and functional, with 87 rooms and suites, and a panoramic restaurant and bar. It's on the harbor in the village of Buarcos. Marginal do Cabo Mondego, Buarcos (phone: 33-32514; fax: 33-21067). Moderate.

EATING OUT

Sereia do Mar Good seafood is the highlight at this modern place, decorated in blue and white, on the esplanade near the sea. Closed Mondays. Reservations advised. Major credit cards accepted. 59 Av. do Brasil, Figueira da Foz (phone: 33-26190). Expensive to moderate.

Teimoso Located just outside Buarcos, on the road to Cabo Mondego, this fish restaurant is as good a place as any to try *caldeirada*. Open daily. Reservations advised. Major credit cards accepted. Estrada do Cabo Mondego, Buarcos (phone: 33-32785). Expensive to moderate.

Caçarola II Right in front of the casino, with a snack bar downstairs and a restaurant upstairs. The seafood is especially good. Open daily until 4 AM. No reservations. Major credit cards accepted. 85 Rua Bernardo Lopes, Figueira da Foz (phone: 33-24861 or 33-26930). Moderate.

O Pateo Decorated in typical regional style, this eatery is in an old part of town above the beach and specializes in grilled meat and fish dishes. There is a patio with fruit trees for summer dining. Closed Mondays. No reservations. Major credit cards accepted. 31 Rua Dr. Santos Rocha, Figueira da Foz (phone: 33-26657). Moderate.

Quinta da Santa Catarina On the edge of town, this restaurant is in a tree-filled garden with a pool. The seafood is especially good — the *açorda* (shrimp and rice with shellfish) is a standout. Closed Mondays. No reservations. Major credit cards accepted. Rua Joaquim Sotto Maior, Figueira da Foz (phone: 33-22178). Moderate.

En Route from Figueira da Foz Take N111 east along the Mondego. The road descends into a valley and then climbs through forests of pine, chestnut, and oak trees, passing water mills and little white churches. After 10 miles (16 km), one of the biggest and most beautiful castles in Portugal is seen standing dramatically above the little town of Montemor-o-Velho. Although the site has been fortified for more than 4,000 years, the castle dates mainly from the 14th century; the church within, Santa Maria da Alcaçova, built during the 11th century, is now mostly Manueline in style. Continue along N111 the remaining 18 miles (29 km) to Coimbra.

COIMBRA For a detailed report of the city, its sights, hotels, and restaurants, see *Coimbra* in THE CITIES.

En Route from Coimbra Before continuing north toward Aveiro, take a short detour to visit the Roman ruins of Conímbriga, 9½ miles (15 km) southwest of town. Cross the bridge over the Mondego and take N1 south to Condeixa, then follow the signs.

CONÍMBRIGA The most important Roman site in Portugal, Conímbriga was inhabited as far back as the Iron Age, but it was the Romans who made it a monumental city, with an aqueduct, forum, temple, public baths, shops, and houses with beautiful mosaic floors. Situated along the Roman highway between Olisipo (Lisbon) and Bracara Augusta (Braga), the city was at its height during the first part of the 3rd century. Unfortunately, barbarian invasions began during the latter part of the century, forcing the inhabitants to build a new defensive wall, which encompassed only half of the city (stones from buildings outside, funerary stones, bits of statuary, and the old wall were used to construct the new one). The Suevians captured the city during the mid-5th century, and the Visigoths later moved to the nearby, more easily protected Aeminium, also Roman in origin. Aeminium grew at Conímbriga's expense and eventually took its new name — Coimbra — from Conímbriga.

Visitors can see remains of the old wall and the aqueduct before entering the site via the main gate in the new defensive wall. On the right are the ruins of the 3rd-century House of Fountains, which was partially destroyed to make way for the wall. The layout of the rooms, several with mosaic pavements, is clearly visible. Beyond are other houses, shops, and public baths; the 5th-century House of Cantaber, with private baths beside it; and the forum, including the temple, market, and tribunal. The *Museu Monográfico* at the site (phone: 39-941177) displays objects unearthed here — coins, pottery, cloth, lamps, games, jewelry, sculpture, murals, and mosaics. The museum is open from 9 AM to 1 PM and 2 to 6 PM from June through September (to 5 PM the rest of the year); closed Mondays. The site itself is open daily from 9 AM to 1 PM and 2 to 8 PM from June through September (to 6 PM the rest of the year). There are admission charges to both the ruins and the museum; there also is a restaurant (closed Mondays) with a panoramic terrace.

En Route from Conímbriga Return to Condeixa and take the A1 toll highway 37½ miles (60 km) north (bypassing Coimbra) to the junction with N235, which leads to Aveiro. Along the way, watch for turnoffs to points of interest such as Luso, a very ancient spa town on a mountainside (for a description of Luso and its hotels, see *The Beiras* in DIRECTIONS), and Curia, another spa town, famous not only for its waters, but also for its bairrada wines, among the best in Portugal. The bairrada wine producing area extends all the way north from Coimbra to Aveiro.

CHECKING IN/EATING OUT

Palace Hotel da Curia This was the most elegant and fashionable hotel in Portugal when it opened in 1922, and it's still a beautifully kept, Old World hostelry, surrounded by lovely woods and formal gardens. It has 114 rooms, a restaurant, a bar, an Olympic-size swimming pool, tennis courts, and a deer park. A stay here among the stained glass windows, marble statues, and Art Nouveau tables will be memorable. Closed from October to *Easter*. Parque da Curia, Anadia, Curia (phone: 31-52131; fax: 31-55531). Expensive.

AVEIRO Intersected by several canals, Aveiro was once a port on the Atlantic, at the mouth of the Vouga River. But ocean currents built up a coastal sandbar and the river deposited silt in the estuary, so that by the time a giant storm in 1575 closed the natural channel through the sandbar, Aveiro was left occupying the eastern side of an enclosed lagoon. The ancient port that had traded with the Phoenicians, and from which only a short time before ships had set sail on voyages of discovery and on fishing expeditions to the cod banks of Newfoundland, was left without an outlet to the sea. It was not until the early 19th century that a canal was cut through the sandbar (stones from the town's 15th-century walls were used in the construction), restoring a measure of prosperity.

Aveiro's shallow saltwater lagoon — the Ria de Aveiro — stretches nearly 30 miles from north to south, though it is only a few miles wide. The lagoon provides fish, salt, seaweed for fertilizer, and, in the parts above sea level, fertile farmland. It is picturesque, too, dotted with islands, bordered by salt flats, and full of impressive conical mountains of white salt, as well as a variety of boats. Of these, the most beautiful are the seaweed gatherers' flat-bottomed, square-sailed *moliceiros,* their high, curved prows brightly painted with Ria scenes. Their numbers have dwindled, but they can still be spotted throughout the lagoon or gathered together on special occasions, such as Aveiro's *Festa da Ria,* which takes place in late July and early August. A *moliceiro* regatta (departing from Torreira, a fishing village to the north, and arriving in Aveiro the same day) and a race of *moliceiros* and other boats are part of the festivities.

Aveiro itself is a lovely town — its canals are crossed by interesting carved wooden bridges, and in the middle of town, the Central Canal is lined with charming, colorful houses. The Convento de Jesus is the first stop for most visitors. Founded during the 15th century, but mainly baroque following later remodeling, the convent was for almost 2 decades the home of Infanta Dona Joana, the daughter of King Afonso V, who entered it after refusing to marry several kings. She died here in 1490, and her marble tomb can be seen in the convent church, which is decorated with 18th-century baroque woodwork so intricately carved and gilded it looks like filigree. Now the *Museu de Aveiro* (Praça do Milenário; phone: 34-23297), the convent contains works of art gathered from churches and monasteries throughout the region after the expulsion of religious orders during the 19th century, as well as works originally made for use here. There are valuable collections of sculpture, gold and silver work, vestments, and paintings (the most famous is one of Infanta Santa Joana in 15th-century court dress). The museum is open from 10 AM to 12:30 PM and 2 to 5 PM; closed Mondays. There's an admission charge, except on Sunday mornings.

Across from the convent is the Church of São Domingos, founded during the 15th century as a monastery church but now serving as the Sé (Cathedral) of Aveiro; its baroque door is the result of an 18th-century renovation. Not far away, in Praça da República, is the Misericórdia, a 16th-century church covered with *azulejos* inside (from the 17th century) and out (19th century). The 17th-century Igreja das Carmelitas, to the south (near the post office), is worth a stop to see more *azulejos;* beyond it is the 16th-century Santo António, known for its interesting barrel-vaulted ceiling and carved gilt work. On the north side of the Central Canal, near the fish market, is the Chapel of São Gonçalinho, the patron saint of salt workers. Still farther north, not far from the railroad station, is the 18th-century chapel of Senhor Jesus das Barrocas, an octagonal building with a rectangular chancel; magnificent woodcarvings adorn the interior, along with modern paintings of the lives of the saints, commissioned by the devout fishermen of Aveiro.

A variety of water sports — sailing, windsurfing, water skiing, and swimming — can be enjoyed in the Aveiro area, and several excursions can be made in the vicinity. From mid-June to mid-September, a boat tour of the Ria leaves from Aveiro daily at 10 AM; it stops for lunch at Torreira, and returns to Aveiro at 5 PM. The tourist office, in a beautifully restored Art Nouveau building on the Grande Canal (8 Rua João Mendonca; phone: 34-23680; fax: 34-28326), can supply information. Visitors should also make an effort to visit Vista Alegre, about 4½ miles (7 km) south of Aveiro via N109. The world-famous Vista Alegre porcelain factory (Fábrica de Porcelana da Vista Alegre; phone: 34-325365), founded in 1824, is located here, with the *Museu Histórico da Vista Alegre* on its grounds. The museum has a large collection of the stoneware and crystal that the factory produced in its early years, plus vases, lamps, and porcelain dinnerware from all periods, including examples of valuable pieces made for European royalty. It's open from 9 AM to 12:30 PM and 2 to 4:30 PM; closed Mondays; no admission charge. A further attraction is the showrooms, where porcelain can be purchased.

CHECKING IN

Barra Located 5 miles (8 km) from Aveiro, between the Atlantic and the lagoon, this modern hotel has 64 rooms with baths and TV sets. There is also a salt-water pool, sauna, bar, panoramic restaurant, and nightclub. 18 Av. Fernandes Lavrador, Praia da Barra, Ilhavo (phone: 34-369156; fax: 34-360007). Expensive.

Afonso V In a quiet residential district not far from the canals and monuments, it has 80 rooms with private baths and all the modern comforts, a pub-style bar, a discotheque, and the *Cozinha do Rei* restaurant (see *Eating Out*). 65 Rua Dr. Manuel das Neves, Aveiro (phone: 34-25191; fax: 34-38111). Moderate.

Imperial A big, modern hotel (107 rooms) in the center of town, with views over the canals and river. There are 3 bars, a solarium, and a very good, very big restaurant, with windows all around. Rua Dr. Nascimento Leitão, Aveiro (phone: 34-22141; fax: 34-24148). Moderate.

Arcada This lovely old hotel is right in the center of town, on the Central Canal. All 52 rooms have TV sets and telephones; 48 of them have private baths. There is a good bar, but no restaurant. 4 Rua Viana do Castelo, Aveiro (phone: 34-23001). Moderate to inexpensive.

EATING OUT

Cozinha do Rei This place is unquestionably the best restaurant in town. Fountains, plants, and the pink-and-white decor make the large dining room in the *Afonso V* hotel a pleasant spot, and the *sopa do rei* (king's soup), with fish and lobster, really is fit for a king. Open daily. Reservations advised. Major credit cards accepted. 65 Rua Dr. Manuel das Neves, Aveiro (phone: 34-25191). Expensive to moderate.

Centenario Restaurant Famous for its seafood soup, this large restaurant is the oldest in town. Open daily. No reservations. Major credit cards accepted. Praça do Mercado (phone: 34-22798). Moderate.

Taverna Dom Carlos Attractive, oak-beamed, with old bairrada wine bottles around the walls and even old wine bottling machinery on the premises, it serves good grilled meat and seafood. There is *fado* music after 10:30 PM on Fridays. Closed Sundays. No reservations. Major credit cards accepted. 46-48 Rua Dr. Nascimento Leitão, Aveiro (phone: 34-22061). Moderate.

En Route from Aveiro Porto is 42 miles (67 km) north of Aveiro via the A1 toll highway, but for a closer look at the Ria, the salt pans, and the *moliceiro* boats, take N109-7 west 5 miles (8 km) to Barra. The canal through the sandbar is located here, as are two beaches and houses with pointed roofs, tiled fronts, and brightly painted doors. Turn left and drive south along the Ria to Costa Nova, where there are rows of houses with red-and-white, green-and-white, or blue-and-white stripes, as well as little beaches, cafés, and restaurants. Farther south, at Vagueira, travelers may see trawlers launching their boats into the Atlantic and pulling back the nets with yoked oxen. Retrace the route to Aveiro or return by way of the opposite margin of the Ria.

To visit the northern part of the Ria, take N16 east out of Aveiro, turn onto N109 toward Estarreja, and then onto N109-5 to Murtosa. (The roads are not very good and full of trucks.) Murtosa has an interesting 18th-century parish church, but its port — Cais do Bico — with *moliceiros* gathering or unloading seaweed is the real attraction. Continue on N109-5 and, at the end of the causeway, turn onto N327 to Torreira, where a *moliceiro* race is part of a local festival, the *Romaria de São Paio da Torreira,* held the first week of September. Still on N327, continue south through sand dunes and pine forests to São Jacinto. On the right is the Reserva Natural de São Jacinto nas Dunas, a nature and wildlife preserve in pine-wooded dunes. Paths, elevated walks, and observation towers have been built so visitors can see the birds and animals, and there are two marked trails, one beginning by the preserve headquarters (phone: 34-331282) at its southern end.

Return north 14 miles (22 km) to the turnoff for Ovar, a town famous for its *pão de ló* (sponge cake); its yearly carnival enlivened by masked revelers, flower battles, and allegorical floats; and its *Holy Week* processions. The tile-faced parish church and two chapels (Calvário and Nossa Senhora da Graça) are worth a visit. Ovar is at the northern tip of the Ria, about 28 miles (45 km), via the A1 toll highway, from Porto, Portugal's second-largest city. To reach the highway, take N327 east for 4 miles (6 km). Or, if one last dip in the sea is desired, take N109 to Porto, passing through the popular, modern Costa Verde beach resort of Espinho.

CHECKING IN/EATING OUT

Pousada da Ria This beautiful, waterside state-owned *pousada* has verandahs where guests can sit and watch the Ria boats; its 19 rooms (all with private baths) also have private balconies overlooking the water. There is a pool and a restaurant with a terrace and a panoramic view. Fish and seafood are served — fishermen deliver the catch to the *pousada* at 8 every morning. Open all year, but very full from April through September; make reservations at least a month in advance. On N327 between Torreira and São Jacinto (phone: 34-48332; 212-686-9213 in the US; fax: 34-48333). Expensive.

Riabela All 35 rooms at this modern *estalagem* at the water's edge have private baths. There also is a very good restaurant, glassed in on three sides with views of the Ria, as well as a swimming pool, tennis courts, and a bar. Torreira (phone and fax: 34-48147). Moderate.

The Minho

This northwest corner of Portugal, bordered by the Minho River and Spain to the north, the Douro region to the south, the Atlantic Ocean to the west, and high mountains to the east, is the emerald in Portugal's crown. Of all the Portuguese regions, Mother Nature was most generous with the Minho, gracing it with an eternally green and varied landscape, dense forests, fertile valleys, rolling hills, majestic peaks, golden beaches, and thermal springs. People, in turn, went on to decorate it with picturesque granite villages, fortified castles, elegant manor houses, and a green mantle of vines.

This is a fairy-tale land shrouded in mist. Lush and verdant, the Minho has the highest level of rainfall in Portugal during the winter. Clouds coming in from the Atlantic are blocked from the interior by mountain ranges, or *serras,* such as Peneda, Gerês, and Padrela, and are forced to unload their precious cargo before reaching the high plains of the neighboring Trás-os-Montes region. The temperature is mild, the air somewhat humid, the light soothing to the eye.

Signs of human habitation here have been found dating as far back as 5,000 years. Vestiges of *castros,* fortified granite hamlets built on high ground by Celtic tribes who settled here about 3000 BC, still dot the landscape. The Phoenicians and Greeks, attracted by the area's rich metal deposits, traded actively with the inhabitants during the Bronze and Iron Ages. The Romans encountered stiff resistance during the 3rd century BC and never totally subjugated the Minho, but they did manage to introduce vine growing techniques and an extensive road system. The Suevians, a Germanic farming tribe, replaced the Romans and introduced the iron plow and the practice of cultivating small land holdings detached from villages. The Visigoths, who arrived next, embraced Catholicism. The Moors invaded from North Africa during the 8th century, but they, like the Romans before them, encountered resistance in the Minho and were forced out — after several generations.

The region claimed its independence during the 12th century when Afonso Henriques of Guimarães, ruler of an entity known as the county of Portucale and as such a vassal of the King of León and Castile, broke away from his feudal lord and had himself crowned King of Portucale. The Portuguese nation was thus born in the Minho, which provided leadership until Portugal's New World discoveries shifted the political focus south to Lisbon. Even then, it continued to play a large economic role, and today, it is one of the principal cattle raising, wine making, and textile manufacturing areas of the country.

A large part of the Minho, particularly the rural interior, retains much of its original beauty and charm and many of its age-old traditions, including a strong community spirit. During the harvest, for example, neighbors help each other husk the corn, singing elaborate traditional songs and drinking wine liberally as they work. This is also an occasion for the young to meet prospective partners, and for maidens who find a rare red ear, the *milho rei* (king corn), to kiss their young suitors. The *minhotos* are friendly, hardworking, and devoutly religious. They also know how to enjoy life — witness their lively folk dances, the *viras* and the *malhão*, and their colorful traditional clothing. The warm, hospitable character of the region is best summed up by its symbol, the heart.

The food in the Minho is diverse. There are game, kid, and pork dishes in the mountain areas, lamprey and trout in the river valleys, fish stews, shellfish, cod, and sardines in the coastal areas, and steaks in major livestock centers around Braga and Guimarães. Meals are accompanied by *pão de milho*, delicious, rich corn bread, and the region's *vinho verde*, or green wine. The wine, drunk chilled, takes its name from its relative youth rather than its color (which is usually white). The British, who began importing green wines during the 16th century, called them "eager wines" because of their natural effervescence. The best are the whites from estates such as Palácio de Brejoeira and Solar das Bouças, which have a slightly higher alcohol content than the more common wines such as casal garcia and gaitão. The vines are trained aboveground on concrete *pérgulas* (trellises) and *cruzetas* (crosses) and cling to wires strung over roadways and telephone poles — sometimes at heights of 30 to 40 feet. This frees the land for other crops and keeps the grapes from overripening on the warm soil. The result is a wine that is low in alcohol, not too sweet, and extremely refreshing, but one that doesn't age well. Green wines should be drunk within the first 2 years after bottling.

Allow 9 to 10 days for the leisurely tour outlined below. The route begins in Guimarães, the cradle of the nation, and moves on to Braga, the religious capital of Portugal. It then proceeds north into the heart of the Minho to Ponte de Lima and from there follows the bucolic Lima River past monasteries, Roman bridges, manor houses, and rustic farms, crossing paths with oxen whose highly decorated yokes are carved with Celtic inscriptions. The itinerary includes a visit to the Peneda-Gerês National Park before cutting across an impressive mountain pass into the spa-haven of Monção. From there, it makes its way west along the picturesque left bank of the Minho River, past a string of fortresses guarding Portugal's border with Spain. The region's Atlantic coast is explored during the final leg of the journey, as the route moves south past multicolored fishing villages, stops off at Viana do Castelo (known as the capital of Portuguese folklore), detours briefly inland to Barcelos for a dazzling display of pottery, then returns coastward for a final swing through the beach resorts of Póvoa de Varzim and neighboring Vila do Conde.

During July and August, the main coastal roads become congested with tourists and Portuguese vacationers, although some congestion has been eased by the new four-lane IP1 highway, which runs through the center of the region northeast of Porto to Braga. Try to avoid traveling on weekends, and move from town to town between 1 and 3 PM, when most of the population is eating, working, or at the beach. Better yet, schedule a visit for late May and early June, or mid-September and the first 2 weeks of October, to catch the grain and grape harvests. At all times, try to avoid driving at night, particularly on mountain roads. They tend to be winding and not well marked.

Whenever possible, reserve rooms in advance for the summer season, which runs from June through September. In addition to choosing from among hotels, *pousadas,* and other types of accommodations, travelers in the Minho can opt to stay in a variety of private houses that take in paying guests as part of Portugal's *Turismo no Espaço Rural* (Tourism in the Country) program. A great many of the participating properties along the route are the manor houses and other stately homes of *Turismo de Habitação,* while a few are the simpler rural houses and farmhouses of *Turismo Rural* and *Agroturismo.* For additional details and reservations information, see *Pousadas and Manor Houses* in DIVERSIONS. Expect to pay from $95 to $150 for a double room in a hotel listed below as expensive, approximately $60 to $80 for one in the moderate category, and $40 or less for one in the inexpensive category. A meal for two with house wine will cost $50 and up in a restaurant listed as expensive, from $30 to $40 in a moderate place, and less than $25 in an inexpensive one. For each location, hotels and restaurants are listed alphabetically by price category.

GUIMARÃES The birthplace of the first Portuguese king and the cradle of the nation lies at the foot of a mountain range about 30 miles (50 km) northeast of Porto via the new four-lane IP1 highway. For a more scenic route, take the smaller N105-2 and N105 roads. A note of warning: The latter turns into a bottleneck at morning and evening rush hours, and the fumes from trucks can ruin the ride.

Founded during the 10th century, the city came into prominence in 1095, when the King of León and Castile awarded the hand of his daughter, Teresa, to a French nobleman, Henry of Burgundy, who had assisted the Spanish king in driving the Moors out of northern Iberia. The county of Portucale (roughly, the land between the Minho and the Douro, including the city of Porto) was part of Teresa's dowry, and the couple chose Guimarães as their court. Teresa bore Henry a son, Afonso Henriques, and 2 years later, when Henry died, she became regent for the child. She soon incurred the wrath of her subjects, however, by taking up with a Galician count and allying herself with the Spanish overlords. When Afonso came of age, he revolted against Teresa's forces outside Guimarães, in 1128, and in 1139 dealt the Moors a severe blow near Santarém. As a result of these victories, Afonso broke his ties with León and Castile and crowned himself King of Portucale in 1139. Spain recognized the new kingdom in 1143.

Guimarães was also the birthplace of Gil Vicente (1470?–1540?), the founder of Portuguese theater. A goldsmith by trade, he nevertheless found time to entertain the courts of João II and Manuel I with his farces and tragicomedies, and he also wrote religious dramas. Gold- and silversmithing continue to thrive today, as do other crafts such as embroidery and linen weaving, but they are less important than the manufacture of textiles, shoes, and kitchenware. These industries keep Guimarães prosperous, but take their aesthetic toll. The medieval quarter, however, is being slowly restored. For the full medieval treatment, be here for the *Festas Gualterianas,* a large folk fair that takes place the first Sunday in August. The townspeople dress in medieval attire, there's singing and dancing, and all Guimarães returns to the 15th century.

Begin a tour of the city at Largo da Oliveira, a square in the heart of the medieval quarter. On the northwestern side is the Antigo Paço do Conselho (Old Town Hall), an arcaded and crenelated 16th-century building that's now a public library. On the eastern side is the former convent of Nossa Senhora da Oliveira (Our Lady of the Olive Tree). The convent church marks the spot where the 6th-century Visigothic warrior Wamba was confirmed as king. (According to legend, he said he would accept the charge if his staff sprouted olive leaves when he drove it into the ground, and it did.) During the 10th century, a primitive church was built on the site; virtually nothing remains of the original, but the church's main entrance, where a 14th-century doorway is surmounted by a Gothic pediment, and the Gothic porch in front are impressive. The convent's 13th-century Romanesque cloister and grounds house the *Museu Regional de Alberto Sampaio* (phone: 53-412465), with a collection of priceless 14th- to 17th-century works from various churches and convents — tiles, paintings by Portuguese masters, tapestries, statues, and a treasure in ecclesiastical plate. Note the Manueline monstrance attributed to Gil Vicente and the magnificent 35-pound silver cross. Open Mondays and Tuesdays for guided tours from 10 AM to 12:30 PM; Tuesdays through Sundays from 10 AM to 12:30 PM and 2 to 5:30 PM; admission charge. A tour of the square and museum can be topped off with a visit to the *Garrefeira Santa Maria* wine shop on the western end of the square, where an impressive array of Portuguese and regional wines are exhibited and sold to the public. The shop is open weekdays from 9 AM to 1 PM and 3 to 7 PM; Saturdays from 9 AM to 1 PM.

Walk west along Rua da Rainha to the *Museu Arqueológico da Sociedade Martins Sarmento* (Rua Paio Galvão; phone: 53-415969), housed partly in the cloister of the Igreja de São Domingos. Named for the 19th-century archaeologist who excavated the Iron Age cities of Briteiros and Sabroso near Guimarães, the museum contains items from these sites and elsewhere. Most impressive are the stone finds from Briteiros — the

Pedra Formosa, a huge carved granite slab that could have been the entrance to a Celtic crematorium, and the Colossus of Pedralva, a 10-foot-high granite idol that took 24 pairs of oxen to drag to its present home. The museum is open for guided tours from 9:30 AM to noon and 2 to 5 PM; closed Mondays; admission charge.

Return to Largo da Oliveira and walk north along the cobbled Rua de Santa Maria, lined with handsome 14th- to 17th-century aristocratic residences decorated with coats-of-arms, iron grilles, and statuary. The road slopes upward to the 15th-century Paço dos Duques de Bragança (Palace of the Dukes of Bragança). The massive complex was built by the first duke, Dom Afonso, who was the bastard son of King João I — his status mandated the tilt to the left of the family coat of arms at the entrance to the palace courtyard. The third duke was beheaded by King João II, but the resilient and Machiavellian family returned in style in 1640, when the Duke of Bragança was crowned King João IV, beginning a dynasty that furnished Portugal with kings until the country became a republic in 1910. In more recent times, the palace was restored by the late dictator António de Oliveira Salazar, who turned it into an official northern residence for the Portuguese president as well as a museum (phone: 53-412273). Inside is a collection of 15th- to 17th-century Persian carpets, copies of French and Flemish tapestries, Portuguese furniture, Chinese porcelain, paintings by Portuguese, Italian, and Dutch masters, and an armory with 15th-century chain mail. Note the chestnut wood ceilings of the dining and banquet halls, shaped like the hull of a Portuguese caravel in honor of the country's maritime exploits. Guided tours (in Portuguese only) take place from 10 AM to 5:15 PM, except on holidays. There's an admission charge, except on Sundays until 2 PM.

At the top of the hill overlooking the town is the 10th-century castle, with its eight flanking towers and large central keep, the inspiration for the country's coat of arms. Afonso Henriques, Portugal's first king, was born here; he was baptized, it is said, in the lovely, tiny 12th-century Igreja São Miguel do Castelo, set on the green between the castle and the ducal palace. Besides the baptismal font, the church contains a stone basin where parishioners placed offerings of grain; the floor is covered with the graves of Portuguese grandees. The castle has been restored and is open to the public from 9 AM to 9 PM; closed Mondays. There's no admission charge.

The Guimarães Tourist Office is in the southern part of town (83 Largo 28 de Maio; phone: 53-412450). Nearby, and worth a visit if time permits, is the Igreja de São Francisco (phone: 53-412228), a collage of 15th-, 17th-, and 18th-century architecture, rich in gilt and *azulejos.* The church is open from 10 AM to noon and 3 to 5 PM; closed Mondays; no admission charge. Ask the sacristan for permission to see the fine coffered ceiling in the sacristy. The surrounding countryside is also worthwhile, especially the forested Serra de Santa Catarina southeast of town. The road winds up the mountain to the 20th-century pilgrimage Church of Nossa Senhora da

Penha (Our Lady of the Rock, the patron saint of travelers) at the summit, where there are also restaurants, cafés, a simple hotel, and a breathtaking view of the region. Leave the city via N101 east and turn right after Mesão Frio; return to Guimarães via N101-2 by bearing left at the esplanade by the sanctuary.

CHECKING IN

Casa dos Pombais High walls and a large wooden gate protect this handsome 17th-century manor house from encroaching urban development in the western corner of Guimarães. Its 2 spacious rooms with private baths are decorated with antique family heirlooms and have fine views of a manicured garden. The patrician home is frequently rented out on weekends for weddings and other formal functions to which lodgers often are invited. Closed September. Av. de Londres, Guimarães (phone: 53-412917). Expensive.

Casa do Ribeiro This large Minho estate with its own woods and streams is a *Turismo de Habitação* participant. About 3 miles (5 km) west of town off N206, it has 3 rooms and 1 suite (all with private baths), but no central heating. Guests are served breakfast in a 15th-century stone kitchen. Open March through November. São Cristovão do Selho (phone: 53-532881). Expensive.

Casa de Sezim Set in a vine-covered valley (the estate's wine is award-winning), this palatial 14th-century manor and member of *Promoções e Ideias Turisticas* (*PIT,* a manor house booking agent) has been the ancestral home of the Pinto de Mesquita family for over 22 generations. Dom António, the present inhabitant, is a former ambassador to the US. The 5 bedrooms and 1 suite are filled with antiques, including four-poster beds, and have private baths. Be sure to note the 19th-century wallpaper in the sitting rooms, which depicts scenes of India, Boston Harbor, and the Hudson River. The majestic portico, emblazoned with the family crest, welcomes visitors after their drive up a long, mimosa-lined avenue. There is horseback riding, tennis, and a spring-fed swimming pool; guests also may visit the wine cellar. Three miles (5 km) southwest of Guimãres off N105, Nespereira, Guimarães (phone: 53-523000; fax: 53-523196). Expensive.

Paço de São Cipriano An elegant country manor house with a crenelated tower and a swimming pool, 6 miles (4 km) south of town off N105. Another *Turismo de Habitação* participant, it has 5 guestrooms with private baths. Closed in winter. Taboadelo (phone: 53-481337). Expensive.

Pousada de Santa Maria da Oliveira On a quaint narrow street in the heart of the medieval town beside the church of the same name, this is ideal for travelers in search of the service and elegance of old Portugal. Made up of converted townhouses, it has 16 rooms (all with private baths), furnished with Portuguese antiques. Wood floors and ceilings, embroidered quilts, and large, opulent beds are some of its attractive features. The 3 suites are large and luxurious, with marble-and-tile baths. There is a cozy bar; the fine restaurant is in a large granite kitchen with a huge central fireplace. Succulent specialities include *pato no forno* (roast duck) and tender *filetes de congro* (conger eel filets in butter sauce). Rua de Santa Maria, Guimarães (phone: 53-514157; 212-686-9213 in the US; fax: 53-514204; 212-686-0271 in the US). Expensive.

Pousada de Santa Marinha da Costa One of Portugal's most luxurious *pousadas* and a favorite of those looking for peace and quiet, it is about 1¼ miles (2 km) out of Guimarães via N101-2. There are 50 rooms with private baths, and a dining room in its former kitchen (see *Eating Out*). For additional details, see *Pousadas and Manor Houses* in DIVERSIONS. Estrada da Penha, Guimarães (phone: 53-514453; 212-686-9213 in the US; fax: 53-514459; 212-686-0271 in the US). Expensive.

Palmeiras This modern *albergaria* (bed and breakfast inn) with 22 rooms, private baths, a pub, a bar, and a small terrace, is located in a shopping center in the newer part of town. *Centro Comercial das Palmeiras,* Guimarães (phone: 53-410324). Moderate.

EATING OUT

Pousada de Santa Marinha da Costa Fine Portuguese cooking is served in the splendor of a former medieval monastic kitchen, lined with pillars and arches. Located about 1¼ miles (2 km) from town via N101-2. Open daily. Reservations advised. Major credit cards accepted. Estrada da Penha, Guimarães (phone: 53-514453). Expensive to moderate.

Jordão A lively and popular restaurant with regional decor and some of the best local food in town. Closed Monday for dinner and Tuesdays. Reservations unnecessary. Visa accepted. 55 Av. Dom Afonso Henriques, Guimarães (phone: 53-516498). Moderate.

Solar da Rainha This family-run establishment is ideal for a simple, unpretentious lunch. Closed Mondays. Reservations unnecessary. Visa accepted. 133 Rua da Rainha, Guimarães (phone: 53-413519). Moderate.

El Rei A comfortable, romantic little bistro in the medieval quarter, facing the back of the former Town Hall and the *Pousada de Santa Maria da Oliveira.* Gracing the walls are local works of art for sale. Closed Sundays. Reservations unnecessary. Visa accepted. 20 Praça de São Tiago, Guimarães (phone: 53-419096). Moderate to inexpensive.

Castelo No frills and home-style cooking make this place a bargain worth the short walk north from the castle. Closed Saturdays. Reservations unnecessary. No credit cards accepted. 47A Rua Dona Teresa, Guimarães (phone: 53-412218). Inexpensive.

En Route from Guimarães Head 4 miles (6 km) north on N101 to the town of Taipas, renowned at one time for its Roman baths. From here, continue directly to Braga, 10 miles (16 km) away, or take a more scenic and historic route — an extra 8 miles (13 km) or so — and visit the ruins of Citânia de Briteiros, an Iron Age settlement perched on a 1,112-foot hillock overlooking the valley of the Rio Ave. To reach Briteiros, turn right onto N310 toward Póvoa de Lanhoso, then turn left onto N309 toward Braga. The road climbs to the archaeological site, which is the largest and most important pre-Roman hill town discovered in Portugal, with remains of some 200 granite huts, streets, sewers, and a subterranean cistern. Two of the huts were reconstructed by Dr. Francisco Martins Sarmento, the 19th-century archaeologist who excavated the site. On the southwestern corner of the town is a carved granite slab believed to have been part of a Celtic reincarnation ritual. Small objects unearthed here can be seen in the *Museu Arqueológico da Sociedade Martins Sarmento* in Guimarães. The site is open daily from 9 AM to sunset; admission charge.

Continue climbing north on N309 through a forest of pine, oak, and eucalyptus trees. As the road ascends, the lantern tower of the Santuario da Virgen (Sanctuary of the Virgin) at the crest of Monte Sameiro comes into view through the treetops; after Sobreposta, the road becomes N103-3 and leads to the sanctuary, which commands a sweeping view of the Minho, over a 1,881-foot mountain pass. Continue on the eastern side of the mountain to the sanctuary of Bom Jesus do Monte, shaded by trees, surrounded by fountains, and known for its magnificent staircase. Braga is 3 miles (5 km) away via N203, but be advised that the hotels around Bom Jesus are superior to those in Braga, and the *Sameiro* restaurant at the Monte Sameiro sanctuary is one of the region's best (see *Braga* in THE CITIES for details).

BRAGA For a detailed report of the city, its sights, hotels, and restaurants, see *Braga* in THE CITIES.

En Route from Braga Take N201 north and stop at Real to inspect the neo-Byzantine Chapel of São Frutuoso de Montélios, 2½ miles (4 km) from Braga. Farther along, at Prado, cross the Cávado River via the elegant 17th-century bridge, said to have been built by a rich Spanish grandee to allow him to visit his Portuguese lover. The road then begins to climb and, after cresting the pass at Queijada, enters the heart of the Minho. Tiny wood and stone villages and large manor houses dot the landscape, and grape vines on granite crosses follow the contours of the road as it winds down to the valley of the Lima River and the town of Ponte de Lima, 20 miles (32 km) from Braga.

PONTE DE LIMA When the Roman legions first came upon the Lima, they were so enchanted by its beauty that they mistook it for the Lethe, the mythical river of forgetfulness, and refused to budge until one of their braver generals swam across. Eventually they built a bridge and included the Celtic town on its south bank in the network of roads between Braga and Rome. During the 12th century, the town was an important stronghold against the Moorish-dominated south and it strongly supported young Afonso Henriques when he revolted against León and Castile to establish the Portuguese nation. Today, the river is as enchanting as ever, as is the pedestrians-only Roman bridge. The charming medieval town's martial bent is gone — one of the two medieval towers that used to be a prison is now the town archives, and the 15th-century fortress-palace of the Marquis of Ponte de Lima serves as the Town Hall. The Igreja Matriz (Parish Church), a 14th-century building with 18th-century additions, has an interesting Romanesque doorway, while the 18th-century church of São Francisco, at the eastern end of town facing the river, has been turned into the *Museu dos Terceiros,* a museum of sacred art, containing beautifully carved wood pulpits and altarpieces (open from 10 AM to noon and 2 to 6 PM; closed Tuesdays; no admission charge).

The main square, with its ornate baroque fountain, is the town's sitting room, a good place from which to admire the river, the bridge, and the church and tower of Santo António da Torre Velha on the opposite bank. (The tiny Chapel of São Miguel beside it was used as a stopover by pilgrims on their way to the shrine of Santiago de Compostela in Spain.) Every other Monday, the riverbanks are transformed into the most picturesque of markets, selling produce, animals, and local crafts such as linen, wooden furniture, wickerwork, tin lamps, rugs, pottery, and colorful wool blankets. Other good times to be here are during the *Festas de São João* (Feast of St. John), June 23 and 24, and during the *Feiras Novas* (New Fairs), the third weekend (Saturday through Monday) in September. At these times, the town's monuments shimmer in the sparkle of thousands of decorative lights, while the night sky is streaked by lavish firework displays. Several parades provide medieval pageantry and costumes, and gigantic floats display the wares and crafts of the region. Other attractions are folk dancing and singing by the river, and nocturnal cornhusking parties at nearby manor houses. Many of these private properties in the vicinity take in guests, and the headquarters of *Turihab,* the manor house owners' association (phone: 58-942729; fax: 58-741444), is in the same building as the local tourist office (Praça da República; phone: 58-942335 or 58-943327).

CHECKING IN

Paço de Calheiros An impressive 18th-century manor house (a member of *Turismo de Habitação*) perched high amid vineyards a few miles northeast of Ponte de Lima. In the main house, 4 rooms with private baths face a courtyard and garden; 6 apartments with kitchenettes are in a newer addition. A tennis court and a sleek pool with sweeping views of the valley are added attractions. The Count of Calheiros, whose family traces its ancestry back to the founding of the nation, is a charming host who may invite guests to dinner or to visit his textile factory. Calheiros (phone: 58-947164; fax: 58-947297). Expensive.

Casa do Arrabalde A spacious townhouse, it has 4 guestrooms (shared baths) and a large lounge, complete with a fireplace. Ask for a room that faces the courtyard, which is graced by the family chapel and ablaze with camellias. On a quiet residential street across from the handsome Roman pedestrian bridge. Arcozelo, Ponte de Lima (phone: 58-941702). Moderate.

Casa do Crasto A pleasant 17th-century manor house (a *Turismo de Habitação* participant) ideally located on a hill to the west of the town center. The property includes a vineyard, a rose garden, and a long verandah with sweeping views of Ponte de Lima and the valley. Its 5 guestrooms (some with private baths) are spacious and decorated with all the proper patrician trimmings, including fresh flowers from the garden. Guests are given the run of the restored house, including the baronial kitchen with its huge granite chimney, where whole oxen once were roasted. Ribeira, Ponte de Lima (phone: 58-941156). Moderate.

Casa do Outeiro A baronial 16th-century manor house (a member of *Turismo de Habitação*) with appropriately aristocratic touches, including a crenelated entrance, a ceremonial, tree-lined courtyard, rich family heirlooms, and a stately dining room and parlors. Eating breakfast in the huge Renaissance kitchen with wood-fired stoves and a large granite chimney is like taking a trip back to a grander era. It has 2 guestrooms with private baths and views of the courtyard and fountain. Arcozelo, Ponte de Lima (phone: 58-941206). Moderate.

Casa do Pomarchão Guests can look at the manor house, but they stay in a more modest 2-story house surrounded by orchards and vines. The upper floor (2 rooms, a fireplace, and a kitchen) is ideal for a family; downstairs is more rustic and suitable for a couple (both have private baths). A *Turismo Rural* participant, it's located 1¼ miles (2 km) north of town on N201. Arcozelo, Ponte de Lima (phone: 58-941139). Moderate.

Moinho de Estorãos Another participant in the *Turismo Rural* program, this is a converted 17th-century water mill beside a Roman bridge on a peaceful river nearly 4 miles (6 km) west of Ponte de Lima. It has 1 guestroom, a small kitchen, bath, and a living room with a fireplace. Estorãos (phone: 58-942372). Moderate.

Quinta de Sabadão A typical Minho manor house (a *Turismo de Habitação* participant) with an impressive crenelated entrance bearing the family crest. It's just short of a mile (1.6 km) northeast of Ponte de Lima, with 3 large rooms (2 rooms share a bath, the other has its own) in the main house. Arcozelo, Ponte de Lima (phone: 58-941963). Moderate.

Solar de Cortegaça A member of the *Promoções e Ideias Turisticas* (*PIT*) program, this stately manor with 3 guestrooms (all with private baths) provides all the comforts enjoyed by the rural aristocracy. For additional details, see *Pousadas and Manor Houses* in DIVERSIONS. Closed November through February. Situated on the right bank of the river, 5½ miles (9 km) east of Ponte de Lima on EN202. Subportela, Viana do Castelo (phone: 58-971639). Moderate.

EATING OUT

Churrasqueria Tulha Pleasant and welcoming, it specializes in grilled meat and fish. It's set up in a former grain storage barn, and guests can see the food cooking over a wood fire in the open kitchen. Try the paço do cardido, a fine estate-bottled *vinho verde* from the area. Closed Tuesdays. Reservations unnecessary. Visa accepted. Rua Formosa, Ponte de Lima (phone: 58-942879). Moderate.

Monte da Madalena A great view, classical elegance, gracious service, and well-prepared regional dishes make this a favorite with local dignitaries and aristocrats. Trout with ham and *coelho à caçador* (wine-stewed rabbit) are specialties. It's located on N307 about 2½ miles (4 km) south of town at the summit of a hill overlooking the Lima Valley. Closed Wednesdays. Reservations unnecessary. Visa accepted. Monte de Santa Maria Madalena (phone: 58-941239). Moderate.

En Route from Ponte de Lima Take N203 east toward Ponte da Barca, 10½ miles (17 km) away, passing impressive Minho estates, old water mills, rococo monasteries, Romanesque churches, and typical granite farmhouses. At Bravães, 9½ miles (15 km) from Ponte de Lima, is the lovely São Salvador, an intriguing church in a mixture of Romanesque, Moorish, Gothic, and local styles (although the predominant note is 12th- to 13th-century Romanesque). Human and animal motifs are carved in its doorways, and the interior walls show vestiges of Renaissance frescoes.

CHECKING IN

Casa do Barreiro This participant in the *Turismo de Habitação* program, a lovely estate overlooking the Lima 3 miles (5 km) east of Ponte de Lima on N203, is a particularly fine example of a traditional Minho *solar*. It's complete with a colonnaded courtyard, a quaint garden with tiles, flowerpots, roses, and geese, and an adjoining terraced vineyard. There are 7 guestrooms with private baths, common rooms, a small bar furnished with Portuguese antiques, and a swimming pool. Gemieira (phone: 58-941937). Moderate.

PONTE DA BARCA The town where the explorer Fernão de Magalhães — more commonly known as Ferdinand Magellan — is said to have been born lies on both banks of the Lima. At the entrance to the town, beside an 18th-century bridge, is a pleasant square with a covered market and a *pelourinho* (pillory — a decorative column that served, from the Middle Ages to about the 18th century, as both a symbol of municipal power and a place of punishment). Nearby is the Garden of the Poets, paying tribute to two of the region's most famous men of letters, Diogo Bernardes and Father Agostinho da Cruz. It's said that baptisms used to be performed at midnight under the bridge, with the first passerby acting as the godparent. The tourist information office (Largo de Misericórdia; phone: 58-42899) hands out maps with detailed walking tours of the region. Every other Wednesday, the town holds a large crafts fair (on the alternate Wednesdays, the fair takes place in Arcos de Valdevez, a few miles north — see below). The *Festas de São Bartolomeu,* August 23 and 24, is a lively event with music, dancing, and fireworks.

CHECKING IN

Paço Vedro de Magalhães This baronial 18th-century manor house (a member of *Turismo de Habitação*) belongs to one of Portugal's oldest families. The sprawling grounds — 1¼ miles (2 km) southeast of town off N101 — have views of the surrounding mountains, and the 3 rooms and 2 suites are furnished with antiques (all have private baths). The imposing baronial hall of the estate is lined with heraldic standards and portraits of family members, among them famous Portuguese explorers and statesmen. Ponte de Barca (phone: 58-42117). Expensive.

Casa da Agrela Another handsome 18th-century manor house, this one has a garden and panoramic views of the Amarela mountains. A *Turismo de Habitação* property, it has 1 suite and 2 guestrooms, and private baths. Located 4 miles (6 km) south of Ponte da Barca off N101. São Pedro do Vade (phone: 58-42313). Moderate.

EATING OUT

Varanda do Lima A pleasant spot near the bridge over the Lima, it's very popular during the summer. Regional specialties include *rojões com arroz de sarrabulho,* a pork and rice dish. Open daily. Reservations advised. No credit cards accepted. Largo do Corro, Ponte da Barca (phone: 58-43469). Moderate.

En Route from Ponte da Barca Travelers in a hurry should take N101 north 24¼ miles (39 km) to the spa town of Monção. Otherwise, take a 50-mile (80-km) day tour through the Parque Nacional da Peneda-Gerês. The national park, hard by the Spanish border and roughly horseshoe-shaped as it follows the outlines of the Serra da Peneda to the north and the Serra do Gerês to the south, with the Lima River between, contains some of the wildest mountain country in Portugal. Head east out of Ponte da Barca along N203, which accompanies the wooded banks of the Lima, and in 10 miles (16 km) arrive at the park entrance at Entre Ambos-os-

Rios. (Since there are no recommendable restaurants along the park route, it's a good idea to pack a picnic lunch for the trip; also, although the road has been widened, night driving should be avoided.) Take the river road into the park toward Lindoso; as it climbs, the terrain becomes rockier — all available land, which is not much, is planted with corn, and cattle graze along the steep slopes. Before Lindoso, about 6 miles (10 km) east of Ponte da Barca, there is a turnoff to the right for Ermida, the site of several prehistoric dolmens.

LINDOSO The 13th-century castle of this tiny frontier village guards a pass where the Lima River enters Portugal from Spain. Its moat, walls, and towers are well preserved, and some of the original soldiers' quarters have been restored (open daily from 10 AM to sunset from May through September; no admission charge). Look down from the southern end of the castle walls toward the village to see a large concentration of granite *espigueiros* (grain storage huts) on stilts. In the fall, villagers help each other husk corn, and the mountain echoes with their singing.

En Route from Lindoso To cross the Lima, backtrack 7 miles (11 km) to Parada do Monte, cross the river, and take the N304 2 miles (3 km) to Soajo. This tiny village sits at the edge of the park atop a mountain overlooking the barren peaks of the Serra da Peneda as they stretch northeast to form a natural border with Spain. Its inhabitants, called *monteiros* (hunters), are known for their independent character, derived from centuries of earning their living by hunting for themselves and the royal house. In turn, they were allowed to govern themselves. King Dinis (1261–1325) went so far as to prohibit the nobility from living here, by ruling that they could not spend more time in the village than it took for a piece of bread to cool down on a spear. This may explain the unusual pillory in the main square, shaped like a spear with a triangle, presumably bread, perched on top. At the eastern end of town, on a large, smooth granite rock, is a large group of *espigueiros*. Cornhusking parties, with singing and dancing, take place on the spot during the fall harvest.

Leave Soajo and the park by heading for Arcos de Valdevez, about 10 miles (16 km) away, either by taking N202 directly west or by taking the more scenic route along the Lima. For the latter, leave Soajo by the same road used to reach it and turn toward Ermelo. The cluster of crude, round stone houses seen at the edge of the mountain along the way are *brando* (soft) houses — improvised rock shelters used by shepherds in the summer months. Ermelo itself is a quaint village perched on the steep banks of the river, with a pretty Romanesque church. (To visit the town, park the car on the road and walk several hundred yards on a narrow stone path.) Continue to São Jorge, where the road curves north to Vale and Arcos de Valdevez, leaving the river behind.

CHECKING IN/EATING OUT

Casa do Adro A participant in the *Turismo Rural* program, there are 6 rooms and suites in this renovated 18th-century townhouse beside the town square. Guests have breakfast in the old, rustic kitchen; two cafés next door serve simple meals. Soajo (phone: 58-67327). Moderate to inexpensive.

ARCOS DE VALDEVEZ The town, dating from the 10th century, takes its name from the calm Rio Vez, whose banks it graces. It has known better days, but there are several monuments of note, including a Romanesque chapel and a Manueline pillory in the center and the Paço de Giela, a fine example of a medieval baronial house with crenelated tower, about 1¼ miles (2 km) northeast. Arcos de Valdevez can be used as a base to explore the river valley or the mountains (short hikes will turn up a variety of rustic farmhouses, water mills, and *canastros* — wicker containers with thatch covers used to store and dry corn). The tourist office, located at the southern end of town (Av. Tílias; phone: 58-66001), provides maps and tour information. A crafts fair takes place every other Wednesday in Arcos, alternating with the one in Ponte da Barca, a few miles south.

CHECKING IN

Casa de Requeijo The terraced gardens of this 17th-century manor house (a *Turismo de Habitação* property) have been replaced by a concrete tennis court, a swimming pool, and an outdoor grill, and all available space in the house has been turned into guest quarters, furnished in less than baronial style. The riverside location and sports facilities (including several rowboats and bicycles), however, are an attraction. There are 2 apartments with kitchenettes and 2 suites on the main floor, plus 2 rustic and slightly cramped suites in the garden. A minimum stay of 5 days may be required from mid-June through September. Arcos de Valdevez (phone: 58-656530). Expensive.

EATING OUT

Adega Regional Dine in a rustic courtyard covered with vines or in a pleasant room decorated with farm implements at this converted farmhouse in the northern outskirts of town beside the Rio Vez. The restaurant's grill draws a large clientele — meat and fish are brought in fresh from nearby farms and the river. Closed Mondays. Reservations advised. Major credit cards accepted. Located off N101 toward Monção. Silvares (phone: 58-66122). Moderate.

En Route from Arcos de Valdevez About 9½ miles (15 km) north (N101), the winding but well-paved road begins to climb the Serra de Boulhosa, via a spectacular pass onto whose slopes villages, churches, and vines cling precariously. Once over the top, the valley of the Minho suddenly comes in view and the road descends into the Pinheiros district. It is here that alvarinho, the king of *vinho verde* grapes, grows best, particularly on the estate surrounding the sumptuous 19th-century Palácio de Brejoeira, whose *vinho verde* is the most famous and most expensive of the "green wines." (The estate's *aguardentes* — rough brandies — are also prized.) Peer through the wrought-iron gate into the sprawling grounds; the last King of Portugal spent his final night before exile here.

MONÇÃO The Minho forms Portugal's northwestern border with Spain, and this small town on the river's south bank — a spa noted for its hot mineral springs — is one of a string of fortified towns that have for centuries guarded the Portuguese frontier. Legend has it that during the 14th century, a young noblewoman, Deu-la-Deu Martins, saved Monção from a Castilian siege by throwing what was left of the town's bread over the walls, to make the Spanish believe there was bread enough to last a long time. The invaders swallowed the ruse and lifted their siege, and today, a statue of the heroine stands in the town square. Some of Monção's medieval walls and parts of a 17th-century fortress are still standing, and the Romanesque parish church has an elegant 12th-century door. In May or June, the *Feast of Corpus Christi* is celebrated with a colorful bout between a dragon and a brilliantly clad St. George mounted on a white steed. The tourist office is in the center at Largo do Loreto (phone: 51-652757).

CHECKING IN/EATING OUT

Casa de Rodas This elegant 18th-century manor house (a member of *Turismo de Habitação*) surrounded by woods and vineyards is about 1¼ miles (2 km) southeast of Monção. Guests have access to most of the house, which has several drawing rooms furnished with Portuguese antiques, a turn-of-the-century billiards room, and a dining room dripping with chandeliers. There are 4 guestrooms with views and shared baths. Lugar de Rodas, Monção (phone: 51-52105). Moderate.

Mané A simple, clean *pensão* with 8 rooms and private baths in the historic center near the river, suitable for an overnight stay. There is a modern restaurant and snack bar serving tasty food. Open April through September. 5 Rua General Pimenta de Castro, Monção (phone: 51-652490; fax: 51-652376). Moderate.

En Route from Monção The road southwest (N101) meanders through hills and farm country, playing hide-and-seek with the river. Before entering Valença do Minho, 12 miles (19 km) from Monção, turn left onto N101-1 for a short detour to Monte do Faro, whose 1,865-foot summit provides an impressive view. The Minho Valley and Spain stretch to the north and west, coastal towns and the Minho estuary to the southwest, and the mountains of the Peneda-Gerês National Park to the east.

EATING OUT

Monte do Faro This fine restaurant serving regional fare has sweeping views of the surrounding countryside. Open daily. No reservations. Major credit cards accepted. Monte do Faro (phone: 51-22411). Moderate to inexpensive.

VALENÇA DO MINHO Perched on a hillock overlooking the Minho and, on the opposite bank, the Galician town of Túy, this walled fortress town is another in the series of fortified settlements that have guarded Portugal's northern border. Today, the impregnable garrison has become a bazaar, which the Spanish are welcome to plunder as long as they leave their valuable pesetas behind. The old fortified town consists of two 17th-century double-walled forts that are linked to each other by a bridge and a manmade vaulted passage and are lined with two sets of walls, a moat, and trenches. Inside are two quaint quarters with narrow, cobbled streets, whitewashed churches, crenelated townhouses, and loads of shops selling linens, leatherware, pottery, wicker, and Portuguese scarves and sweaters. From the ramparts on the northern side of one of the forts, a 19th-century bridge across the Minho, designed by Alexandre-Gustave Eiffel, is visible.

Outside the walls, to the south, is the new town of Valença, devoid of the charm of the old one except for the vintage train museum in the railroad station. On display are a British steam engine built in Manchester in 1875 and an elegant salon car built in France for the Portuguese royal family. (Ask permission from the stationmaster to visit.) The tourist office (Av. Espanha; phone: 51-23374/5/6) is at the border post by the bridge.

A word of caution: Valença is on the main road (N13) between Porto and Santiago de Compostela in Spain — a road that becomes congested during the high summer season and on weekends, particularly during July and August.

CHECKING IN

Pousada de São Teotónio An elegant inn at the northern end of Valença's fortifications, it boasts a gorgeous view of the Minho and Spain. Although this is a contemporary structure, the architects cleverly incorporated its courtyard and garden into one of the bastions and ramparts of the fortress. There are 16 rooms, a bar, and a restaurant, where tasty regional dishes and Portuguese nouvelle cuisine are served by a courteous staff. Baluarte Socorro, Valença do Minho (phone: 51-824242 or 51-824252; 212-686-9213 in the US). Expensive.

Lara Outside the old fortified town, this modern 54-room property with a reasonable restaurant is suitable for a night if the *pousada* is booked. Rua São Sebastião, Valença do Minho (phone: 51-824348 or 51-824349). Moderate.

EATING OUT

Parque A cozy, family-run establishment in the Old Town, decorated with tiles and peasant pottery and offering a view of the western battlements. Grilled dishes, particularly chicken, are its forte. Closed Fridays. Reservations unnecessary. No credit cards accepted. Rua Oliveira, Valença do Minho (phone: 51-23131). Moderate.

Monumental A typical, bustling Minho bistro housed inside the stone walls of the fortress, in the former guardhouse that overlooks the town's main entrance. Surrounded by pine, stone, and folk art, customers dine informally on grilled specialties. Open daily. No reservations. No credit cards accepted. Valença do Minho (phone: 51-23557). Inexpensive.

En Route from Valença As N13 leads southwest 17 miles (27 km) to Caminha, the rough forested terrain softens. The river begins to widen and a patchwork of orchards and fields of grain, vines, and vegetables spreads quilt-like along its flat embankment. Two tiny islands, Boega and Amores, appear in front of the ancient town of Vila Nova de Cerveira. This is an ideal place to stop and explore the river and surrounding hills, which abound in legends of hidden Moorish treasures and echo with the romantic song of nightingales. Patrician northerners — and wealth from Portugal's colonies — built splendid estates on the banks of this section of the Lima.

CHECKING IN

Pousada de Dom Dinis Built within the ruins of a 14th-century castle overlooking the Minho, it has 29 rooms and apartments with kitchenettes, terraces and patios, several bars, and a glass-enclosed restaurant specializing in fish. Praça da Liberdade, Vila Nova de Cerveira (phone: 51-795601, 51-795602, or 51-795603; 212-686-9213 in the US; fax: 51-795604). Expensive.

Da Boega An *estalagem* (inn) of 48 rooms perched on terraced slopes above the quaint town of Vila Nova de Cerveira. Guests have a choice of motel-style accommodations or more gentrified rooms in the main ivy-covered house. There is a good restaurant (see *Eating Out*), a swimming pool fed by spring water, a garden, and a tennis court. Quinta do Outeiral, Gondarém (phone: 51-95231). Moderate.

EATING OUT

Da Boega Lodged in the inn of the same name, this aristocratic, baroquely furnished dining room evokes the charm of patrician Portugal. The fixed-price menu of the day usually features regional lamb or pork dishes, served with decorum. There's even a mistress of ceremonies who, in accordance with tradition, presides over the dining room, banging a gong in between courses and ensuring that all the guests are satisfied with their meals. The house wine — a *vinho verde* — is quite good. Open daily. Reservations necessary. Major credit cards accepted. Quinta do Outeiral, Gondarém (phone: 51-95231). Expensive to moderate.

Kalunga Perched on the crest of the mountain above *Da Boega,* this homey place boasts the best views of the region's vineyards and tiny farms, as well as of the Minho River. Guests can dine on regional fare in the pub-like indoor area or alfresco on the terrace. Open daily. No reservations. No credit cards accepted. The signposted restaurant is off the road to Gondarém, on a cobbled lane across from a diminutive country chapel. Calvar, Gondarém (phone: 51-795886). Moderate.

CAMINHA This ancient fortified town guards Portugal's northern border at the mouth of the Minho, at a point where a lesser river, the Coura, flows into the larger one. The tiny Portuguese fortress island of Insua and the Spanish town of Santa Tecla face it. Caminha's whitewashed town square still retains some of its medieval flavor: Of interest here are the loggia and coffered ceilings of the 17th-century Town Hall; the crenelated clock tower; the 15th-century Gothic Pitas Palace, with its neo-Manueline windows; and the parish church, with its beautifully carved Mudéjar ceiling. Inspect the northern exterior of the church to see an amusing gargoyle of a man relieving himself, with his backside facing Spain.

CHECKING IN

Casa do Esteiro This pleasant country house, a *Turismo Rural* property, is surrounded by gardens and vineyards in the southeastern suburbs of Caminha. There is 1 guestroom and 1 suite, both with private baths. Caminha (phone: 58-921356). Moderate.

Quinta da Graça A member of *Promoções e Ideias Turisticas,* this blue-blooded estate occupies the slopes to the southeast of Caminha, offering breathtaking views of the Atlantic Ocean and the Minho and Coura rivers. There are 3 antiques-filled rooms (with private baths) in the main house, plus 3 apartments with kitchenettes and terraces. Guests can lounge beside the tree-lined pool or meander down to the bucolic Coura river. Vilarinho, Caminha (phone: 58-828637). Moderate.

Ideal A clean and simple, 30-room *pensão* with private baths on a hill overlooking Caminha, about 2 miles (3 km) from town. 125 Rua Engenheiro Sousa Rego, Moledo do Minho (phone: 58-922605). Moderate to inexpensive.

EATING OUT

Adega Machado The coziest and most hospitable eatery in town is located on a secluded street southwest of the main square. Discreetly decorated with tiles and wood, it offers a wide selection of typical regional dishes, including *tainha assada no forno* (oven-baked mullet), cold and pickled *sável* (shad), and shellfish. Closed Mondays for dinner. Reservations unnecessary. No credit cards accepted. 85 Rua Visconde Sousa Rego, Caminha (phone: 58-922794). Moderate.

Remo A modern restaurant sitting on stilts on the wharf of the Caminha sailing club, facing Spain. Although its decor has seen better days, its view of Spain and the river, and its food, have secured a loyal clientele. Both Spanish and Portuguese dishes are served; *arroz de marisco,* Portugal's version of Spain's paella, is a specialty. Closed Tuesdays. Reservations advised. Major credit cards accepted. *Pôsto Náutico do Sporting Clube Caminhense,* Caminha (phone: 58-921459). Moderate.

Confeitaria Docelandia This immaculate Old World sweet shop is the area's best. Cakes, cookies, deli sandwiches, and port and tea are all served; they also do a respectable take-out business. Open daily. No reservations. No credit cards accepted. 32 Rua de São João, Caminha (phone: 58-921144). Moderate to inexpensive.

En Route from Caminha The road (N13) to Viana do Castelo, 15 miles (24 km) from Caminha, heads south along the Atlantic coast past fishing villages and tourist resorts. The crème de la crème of northern Portugal's elite own homes in the pine woods here, about 1 mile (1.6 km) south of Caminha, where wide, uncluttered Modelo beach stretches south from where the Minho meets the Atlantic. Vila Praia de Ancora, set at the mouth of the Rio Ancora, has a small castle, secluded beaches, and good fish restaurants. The river and town apparently received their name after the wife of a local patrician ran away with a Moorish emir, was brought back in chains, and was dropped into the river strapped to an *âncora* (anchor). Afife, nearby, is another small beach resort, with a strange (and sexist) *Lenten* custom: The townspeople burn one of the town's older women in effigy as part of a cleansing ritual. After Afife, the road crosses a flat, windswept marshland and enters Viana do Castelo.

VIANA DO CASTELO This holiday resort lies at the mouth of the Lima River, with a basilica-topped hill, Monte de Santa Luzia, looming behind it. Legend has it that Viana takes its name from a beautiful woman, Ana, who lived here. Her fiancé, a boatman on the Lima, was so persistent in asking acquaintances encountered on his run whether they had seen Ana — to which they would answer "Vi Ana" ("I saw Ana") — that the name stuck. (Others say the name has something to do with the Greek goddess Diana.)

The small city's Manueline and Renaissance houses attest to its prominence during the 16th century, when it played a major role in Portugal's maritime discoveries, providing boats, seamen, and explorers such as Alvares Fagundes, who charted the waters of Newfoundland for Portuguese fishermen. Gold from Brazil and an early prominence in the port wine trade with England contributed to a baroque building boom in the 18th century.

The Praça da República and its environs hold some of the city's most impressive architecture. An ornate 16th-century fountain by Viana's master stonemason, João Lopes the Elder, stands in the middle of the cobbled square. Facing it, to the east, is the crenelated Paços do Conselho, the former town hall, a late-16th-century Gothic structure. Next door is one of Viana's most delightful buildings, the Misericórdia; the façade of this 16th-century Renaissance hospice, designed by João Lopes the Younger, is alive with nubile atlantes and caryatids. The adjoining church contains important 18th-century *azulejos*. South of the square, medieval tradesmen and merchants can be seen resting on the shoulders of the Apostles in the carved portal of the Gothic parish church, which faces a lovely Renaissance house reputed to have belonged to João Lopes the Elder. More contemporary artwork created by regional and city artists can be appreciated and purchased nearby at the *Instituto da Juventude Viana do Castelo* (Rua do Poço). The center's café-bar is open at night and is a popular haunt of Viana's artistic community. On the west side of town, the *Museu Municipal* (Largo de São Domingos; phone: 58-24223), housed in an 18th-century palace, contains many treasures, including a valuable collection of 18th-century glazed pottery from Coimbra and a handsome, pre-Roman statue of a Lusitanian warrior. The museum is open for guided tours from 9:30 AM to noon and 2 to 5:30 PM; closed Mondays; admission charge.

Walking tours (in Portuguese only) of Viana depart from the tourist office, lodged in a handsome 15th-century palace (Rua do Hospital Velho; phone: 58-822620; fax: 58-829798). Regional crafts are on display here, as well as in several shops around the colonnaded courtyard. Viana is known for its blue-and-white ceramics, table linen, copper goods, gold and silver filigree work, regional costumes and dolls, peasant scarves, and sprays of artificial flowers called *palmitos*. Most conspicuous are the handkerchiefs decorated with hearts that young women traditionally give to their boyfriends.

Tradition is indeed strong in this city, which has been called the capital of Portuguese folklore because of the flair and the sheer number of the *festas* (feast days) and *romarias* (pilgrimages) that occur in and around it. The tiny baroque Igreja Nossa Senhora da Agonia (Church of Our Lady of Suffering) is famous throughout Portugal for its annual pilgrimage that takes place in August, probably the most spectacular and lively event of its kind in the north. For additional details, see *Best Festivals* in DIVERSIONS.

Another special event is the *Festas de Santa Cristina,* which takes place the first weekend (Friday through Sunday) in August in the suburb of Meadela. It features lively folk music and dancing, floats, and religious pageantry — the regional costumes worn by the women are a big part of the attraction. In May there are lavish flower festivals in Viana and its environs. For the *Festas da Senhora das Rosas* (Festival of Our Lady of the Roses), held in early May in Vila Franca do Lima, young women carry large baskets woven with intricate rose petal designs of their own making; during the *Festa dos Andores Floridos,* late May in Alvarães, floats covered with roses ride over a carpet of flowers.

Before leaving Viana, be sure to visit the Basílica de Santa Luzia, on Monte de Santa Luzia (Mount St. Lucy), roughly 2½ miles (4 km) north of town on a well-marked road. It also can be reached by funicular from Av. 25 de Abril; it runs every hour from 9 AM to noon, then every half hour from 12:30 to 6 PM (from April through September, it also operates at 6:30 and 7 PM). In times of plague or invasion, the people of Viana have always taken refuge in the woods here, and the neo-Byzantine basilica on top of the mountain — a 20th-century copy of the Sacré-Coeur in Paris — is an important pilgrimage church. Those who don't mind narrow passages and a climb of 142 steps will be rewarded at the top of the lantern tower with a panoramic view of the city and its environs.

CHECKING IN

Paço d'Anha One of the most attractive manor houses in the north of Portugal, it's part of the *Agroturismo* program and is located on a large *vinho verde*-producing estate near the beach 3 miles (5 km) south of town. Guests stay in farm buildings converted into 4 apartments (each with 2 bedrooms, living room, bath, and kitchen). Horseback riding and meals can be arranged; the estate wine is highly recommended. While a guest here in 1580, the Prior of Crato received the news that he had been proclaimed King of Portugal. Anha (phone: 58-322459). Expensive.

Santa Luzia A turn-of-the-century luxury hotel on Monte de Santa Luzia, it commands a sweeping view of the region. Refurbished in a 1930s style, it has an elegant dining room, salon, and terrace, plus 52 rooms and 3 suites, an outdoor swimming pool, and a tennis court. Monte de Santa Luzia (phone: 58-828889). Expensive.

Casa do Ameal This *Turismo Rural* program participant is a pleasant townhouse on the Lima River in suburban Meadela; it has 4 rooms and 2 apartments, all with private baths. For additional details, see *Pousadas and Manor Houses* in DIVERSIONS. Meadela (phone: 58-22403). Moderate.

Casa Grande da Bandeira A *Turismo de Habitação* property, it offers 2 guest-rooms with shared baths in a large 18th-century townhouse near the center. 488 Rua da Bandeira, Viana do Castelo (phone: 58-823169). Moderate.

Jardim This quaint inn with 20 tastefully furnished rooms (some with private baths) faces the river and an esplanade near the center of town. There's no restaurant. 68 Largo 5 de Outubro, Viana do Castelo (phone: 58-828915). Moderate.

Viana Sol Pleasant and hospitable, it's near the city center, with 72 rooms with private baths, a cozy bar, a discotheque, a sauna, a squash court, and an indoor pool. The only weak point is a rather staid indoor restaurant. Largo Vasco da Gama, Viana do Castelo (phone: 58-828995). Moderate.

Calatrava This tiny *albergaria* (inn) offers guests plenty of rustic charm, including shared baths. The 15 rooms feature pinewood decor and colorful folkloric pottery and handicrafts; ask for one with a view of the Lima River. An intimate bar and lounge (no restaurant) with soft lighting provide a romantic touch. In the east part of town, at 157 Rua M. Fiúza Junior, Viana do Castelo (phone: 58-828911 or 58-828912; fax: 58-828637). Moderate to inexpensive.

Alambique A simple *pensão* of 24 rooms (some with private baths) on a quiet side street near the center, it has an adjoining restaurant serving good traditional fare (see *Eating Out*). 86 Rua Manuel Espregueira, Viana do Castelo (phone: 58-823894). Inexpensive.

Dolce Vita Another little *pensão,* in the center of town across from the tourist office. The 7 rooms are basic (shared baths) and clean; some look out onto medieval streets and Renaissance houses. There is an adjoining restaurant (see *Eating Out*). This is only for those who don't mind kitchen sounds and don't need parking in the immediate vicinity. 44 Rua do Poço, Viana do Castelo (phone: 58-24860). Inexpensive.

EATING OUT

Cozinha das Malheiras The fanciest dining place in Viana has a nouvelle Portuguese decor. It is lodged in the stable of an adjoining palace behind the former Town Hall. *Arroz de marisco* (shellfish stew) is a house specialty. Try the Paço d'Anha, a white *vinho verde* from a neighboring estate. Open daily. Reservations advised. Major credit cards accepted. 19 Rua Gago Coutinho, Viana do Castelo (phone: 58-823680). Expensive.

Casa d'Armas A waterfront restaurant in an old armory. The medieval decor may be slightly stiff, but the food is good and served by a courteous staff. Try the river salmon or the veal with mushrooms for a main course, and the rich *torta de amêndoa* (almond tart) for dessert. Closed Mondays. Reservations advised. Major credit cards accepted. 30 Largo 5 de Outubro, Viana do Castelo (phone: 58-24999). Expensive to moderate.

Alambique This bistro has good regional food and lively decor. The *carro de caranguejo* (crab stuffed with onions, olives, and egg), lobster with rice, and *cabrito no forno* (roast kid) are recommended. Closed Tuesdays.

Reservations unnecessary. Major credit cards accepted. 86 Rua Manuel Espregueira, Viana do Castelo (phone: 58-823894). Moderate.

O Espigueiro The regular clientele keeps coming back for the fine cooking and the outdoor vine-covered courtyard of this regional restaurant 3 miles (5 km) out of Viana, off the road to Porto. Open daily. Reservations necessary. Major credit cards accepted. Lugar do Santoinho, Darque (phone: 58-322156). Moderate.

Os Tres Portes The city's most typical Minho restaurant, in an old bakery near the town center, features soft lighting, rustic decor, waitresses in traditional dress, and regional cooking. It's also the place to see and hear folk dancing and singing on Friday and Saturday nights from June through September (Saturdays only during the rest of the year). A fixed-price menu gives guests a sampling of various dishes, including baked kid and *rojões* (pork cooked with pigs' blood). The English owner makes sure the Irish coffee is up to par. Closed Mondays. Reservations necessary in summer. Major credit cards accepted. 7 Beco dos Fornos, Viana do Castelo (phone: 58-829928). Moderate.

Dolce Vita This rustic Italian bistro done up with checkered tablecloths is across from the tourist office. The Italian specialties, including pizza baked in a large adobe oven, are a nice change of pace from the sometimes heavy Minho diet — and they go well with white *vinho verde*. Open daily. Reservations unnecessary. No credit cards accepted. 44 Rua do Poço, Viana do Castelo (phone: 58-24860). Inexpensive.

Quinta do Santoinho To experience an *arraial,* the Minho's version of a barn party, head for this lively and colorful barn-like locale where the folk music and dancing go on until late, with fireworks and *gigantones* to fuel the excitement. For a fixed price, guests feast on grilled pork, sardines, and chicken, and drink to their heart's content out of barrels of wine. Those who last until morning are served a *champorreão* — a powerful punch. The *arraial* takes place at 8 PM on Tuesdays, Thursdays, and Saturdays in August; on Thursdays and Saturdays in July and September (the last two Thursdays of September excluded); and on Saturdays in May, June, and October. The location is 3 miles (5 km) out of town, at Lugar do Santoinho, Darque, but the necessary reservations can be made in Viana at the *AVIC* travel agency, 206 Av. dos Combatentes (phone: 58-829705), or at the *Quinta* (phone: 58-322156). Inexpensive.

En Route from Viana do Castelo The main road (N13) toward Porto crosses the Lima on a bridge designed by Alexandre-Gustave Eiffel. Stay on the road for 6 miles (10 km), then turn left onto N103 to Barcelos.

BARCELOS The home of the Portuguese symbol of good luck, the rooster, lies inland 19 miles (30 km) southeast of Viana do Castelo on the Rio Cávado.

According to the story, a Galician on his way to Santiago de Compostela was accused of stealing from a wealthy landowner and was sentenced to death by hanging. As his last wish, he requested an audience with the judge, who happened to be sitting down to a meal of roast cockerel when the condemned man was brought before him. The accused pointed to the bird and cried out that as proof of his innocence the cock would get up and crow. The judge laughed and sent the Galician off to his death, but did not touch his meal. Just as the man was being hanged, the cock stood, crowed, then fell back dead again. The judge rushed to the gallows and found the man alive because the knot around the noose had not tightened. A 15th-century monumental cross documenting the miracle, the Cruzeiro do Senhor do Galo (Cross of the Gentleman of the Cock), can be seen in the ruins of the 15th-century Paço dos Duques de Bragança (Palace of the Dukes of Bragança), which has been turned into an open-air archaeological museum (open daily from 9:30 AM to 5:30 PM; no admission charge). The Solar dos Pinheiros, a 15th-century mansion facing the palace on the northeast side of the square, is also known as Casa do Barbadão (bearded one). The nickname comes from a Jewish occupant who vowed never to shave following his daughter's shameful affair with a gentile. The gentile happened to be King João I, who later made the son the woman bore him out of wedlock the first Duke of Bragança. Up the street from the house, on Largo do Município, is the parish church, which has some interesting capitals and rich interiors, while the Igreja do Terço (Av. dos Combatentes da Grande Guerra), to the east, is covered with 18th-century *azulejos.*

Most visitors to Barcelos, however, are drawn by its weekly fair, one of the biggest and most colorful in the country, held on Thursdays in Campo da República. Handloomed rugs, colorful straw bags and hats, lace, and other regional crafts are sold, but the main attraction is the pottery — literally tons of it, decorative and utilitarian, in every size and color, made in small cottages and factories in the surrounding countryside. The anthropomorphic animals and large-headed devils playing musical instruments are amusing buys, holdovers of an earlier pagan tradition. The foremost artist of this genre, Rosa Ramalho, who made delightful pregnant goat figures that are said to have inspired Picasso, is no longer living, but her granddaughter continues the family trade. Those who miss the fair can take heart, because many of the goods can be purchased at the *Centro de Artesanato* (phone: 53-812135), the handicrafts shop in the same building as the tourist office (Largo da Porta Nova; phone: 53-811882; fax: 822405).

Barcelos is also known for its elegant sweets. The top tasting establishment is the *Confeitaria Salvação,* which sits on the pedestrian mall just a few minutes' walk west of the tourist office. A front parlor exhibits award-winning pastries fashioned by its fifth-generation owner and master confectioner, Dona Alice, while a more intimate tearoom in the back exhibits her trophies and antique pastry shop wares. Dona Alice's creations include the rich *Barca Cellus,* an almond, egg, and pumpkin treat named after the original river boat that ferried people across the Cavado River and from which Barcelos derived its name. Dona Alice also runs a tiny curio shop that stocks Barcelos pottery and other regional crafts (137-43 Rua Dom António Barroso; phone: 53-811305).

CHECKING IN

Casa dos Assentos The main house of this *Turismo de Habitação* member is an 18th-century mansion with ivy-covered walls amid manicured lawns; it has 1 large guestroom (with a private bath) filled with family heirlooms and antiques. There also are 4 apartments in converted granite-and-wood storage houses that are more rustic. Closed *Christmas* week. About 7½ miles (12 km) north of Barcelos off N204, Quintiães, Barcelos (phone: 53-881160). Expensive.

Casa do Monte An *Agroturismo* participant, it is a large, 2-story house with ivy-covered walls and manicured lawns overlooking a valley, a pool, and a tennis court. There are 3 guestrooms, a large suite with 2 adjoining bedrooms, and another smaller suite with a parlor in the main house (all have private baths). The look and feel fit the gentrified country background of its owners. About 2 miles (3 km) north of Barcelos off N103, Abade de Neiva, Barcelos (phone: 53-811519). Moderate.

Quinta do Convento da Franqueira Now the residence of an English family, this former 16th-century Franciscan monastery stands on 35 acres of pines and vineyards. A participant in *Turismo de Habitação,* it offers a suite and 2 guestrooms with private baths looking onto attractive gardens, and a swimming pool. Meals can be arranged (the *quinta* produces its own estate-bottled *vinho verde*). Open April through September. 2½ miles (4 km) southwest of town off N205, Lugar de Pedrego, Barcelos (phone: 53-815606). Moderate.

Arantes Clean and simple, this 12-room bed-and-breakfast establishment (no private baths) is in the center of town, across from the park where the weekly crafts fair is held. 35 Av. da Liberdade, Barcelos (phone: 53-811326). Inexpensive.

Dom Nuno Another *pensão,* with 27 rooms and shared baths near the center of town. 76 Av. Dom Nuno Alvares Pereira, Barcelos (phone: 53-815084). Inexpensive.

EATING OUT

Bagoeira One of the oldest eating places in town. Wholesome traditional cooking and good service make it a favorite of the old guard. Open daily. Reservations unnecessary. Major credit cards accepted. 53 Av. Dr. Sidónio Pais, Barcelos (phone: 53-811236). Moderate.

Casa dos Arcos It's cozy and charming, with tasty, authentic Minho cuisine. Ancient stone walls, wood beams, and soft lights create a medieval ambience. Closed Saturdays. Reservations unnecessary. Major credit cards accepted. 185 Rua Duques de Bragança, Barcelos (phone: 53-811975). Moderate.

Pérola da Avenida A modern Portuguese bistro with fine regional cooking and a gracious staff. It faces the park where the weekly crafts fair is held. Open daily. Reservations unnecessary. Major credit cards accepted. 66 Av. dos Combatentes da Grande Guerra, Barcelos (phone: 53-821363). Moderate.

Muralha Basic regional fare served in a simple, rustic setting beside the tourist office. Open daily. Reservations unnecessary. No credit cards accepted. 1 Largo da Porta Nova, Barcelos (phone: 53-812042). Inexpensive.

En Route from Barcelos Take N205 southwest 12½ miles (20 km) to the beach town of Póvoa de Varzim, a popular resort with Porto locals. It is noted for the *Festas da Senhora da Assunção* (Feast of Our Lady of the Assumption), August 14 and 15, when a large procession of fishermen carries a life-size statue of their patron saint to bless the boats. Continue on N13 another 2 miles (3 km) south to the neighboring resort of Vila do Conde. Anyone in a hurry to return to Porto, however, can skip Póvoa and Vila do Conde and take a bypass that begins about 3 miles (5 km) north of Póvoa and continues for 11 miles (18 km) before connecting again with the main road south (N13).

VILA DO CONDE The picturesque Old Quarter of this resort and fishing town retains some of its earlier flavor and architectural beauty. Set on the north bank of the Rio Ave, Vila do Conde was one of Portugal's major shipbuilding and commercial centers during the voyages of discovery, and the shipyards continue to make handsome wooden boats for the country's cod fleet. The cod is still dried in the traditional way on stilts by the river. A tradition of lace making going back to the 17th century also endures. Visitors are welcome at the Escola de Rendas (Lace School; 70 Rua Joaquim Maria de Melo), where they can buy *rendas de bilros* (bobbin lace) on the spot. The town's annual crafts fair, beginning on the Saturday of the third week of July and running through the first weekend in August, is another attraction. One of the largest of its kind in Portugal, it features artisans at work, along with folk singing and dancing. The *Festas de São João* (Feast of St. John) on June 23 and 24, another occasion for singing, dancing, feasting, and fireworks, ends with a floodlit procession to the beach.

The Praça Vasco da Gama is the heart and architectural pearl of the Old Quarter. At the center of the square is an unusual carved *picota* (pillory), where the hand of justice is personified by a sword pointed menacingly at several heads above it. On the eastern end of the square lies the handsome 16th-century Igreja Matriz (Parish Church) with a sumptuous Plateresque doorway carved by Biscayan stonemasons. The elegant Manueline carvings of some of the houses and windows of the tiny, stone-paved Rua da Igreja, running north from the square, reflect some of the Renaissance wealth of the town. The Mosteiro de Santa Clara (Convent of St. Clare), founded during the 14th century but rebuilt during the 18th, has a Gothic church with beautifully carved Renaissance tombs. Note the 18th-century fountain in the cloister — it's fed by an aqueduct that runs from Póvoa de Varzim and was built with 999 arches. (The builders thought that 1,000 would have been too grandiose and might have offended God.) Apply at the convent (it is now a juvenile rehabilitation center) to visit the church and climb the parvis before the church for a view of Vila do Conde and the surrounding countryside. From the southwestern corner of the monastery, you can gaze down at the river at low tide and see the top half of an artificial tunnel stretching across the Ave River to a watermill on the left bank. This was the escape hatch for the nuns in times of trouble. The tourist office (103 Rua 25 de Abril; phone: 52-642700) can provide further information on the town and its environs, and when the tourist office is closed, the *Centro de Artesanato* (Handicrafts Shop; 207 Rua 5 de Outubro; phone: 52-642700) provides information.

CHECKING IN/EATING OUT

Do Brasão A comfortable, centrally located *estalagem* (inn) with 30 rooms (all with private baths), with a lived-in feeling and small-town touch to it. It is ideally located in the center of the old town, a few paces away from the Praça Vasco da Gama. The restaurant serves good fish dishes such as river trout and shad. Order the *doce de ovos* for a final dose of eggs and sugar. Restaurant closed in September. Major credit cards accepted. 144 Av. Dr. João Canavarro, Vila do Conde (phone: 52-642016; fax: 52-632028). Moderate.

En Route from Vila do Conde Stop off at Azurara, across the river from Vila do Conde, to inspect the Manueline parish church or do some last-minute shopping. (The town is known for its wool fishermen's shirts, hats, and socks.) Then continue down N13 to Porto, 17 miles (27 km) from Vila do Conde. For a full report on Portugal's second-largest city, the home of port wine, see *Porto* in THE CITIES.

EATING OUT

Sant'Ana The view of Vila do Conde and the monastery from the restaurant at the *Sant'Ana* motel make it a favorite dining venue in the area, as do the aroma and sizzling sounds of its dining room grill. Open daily. No reservations. Major credit cards accepted. Monte de Sant'Ana, Azurara (phone: 52-631994).

Douro and Trás-os-Montes

Until fairly recently, the spectacular, rugged scenery of the Douro and Trás-os-Montes regions of northern Portugal eluded most visitors. The natural urge to peer behind the massive mountain ranges east of the country's northern coastal areas was tempered by a lack of suitable accommodations and other facilities for tourists. The situation has improved, however, and now intrepid travelers in search of a scenic vacation free of crowds and noise can venture into this remote hinterland. The reward is a look at Portugal's last frontier.

The Douro River flows from Spain across the north of Portugal into the Atlantic Ocean at Porto. For some 70 miles, the river is the natural border between the two countries. Its namesake region consists of the Douro Litoral (Coastal, or Lower, Douro), which stretches from Porto and its industrial environs east to the Marão mountain range, and, farther upriver, the Alto Douro (Upper Douro), a dramatic, vine-covered river valley hemmed in by mountains, which is actually part of Portugal's Trás-os-Montes province. The river is the backbone of the region, and, before roads, railroad tracks, and dams, it was the region's major highway — called the Rio do Ouro (River of Gold) because of its golden tones in certain kinds of light. The real gold mines, however, are the grapevines that grow on its banks and those of its tributaries, which produce Portugal's famous port wine.

The port wine region begins at Peso da Régua, 75 miles upstream from Porto, and fans out from there to the richest areas in the vicinity of Pinhão, 20 miles farther east. The countryside here is one huge mantle of green and yellow leaves, punctuated occasionally by the white manor house of a grower or shipper. The vines are cultivated on terraces that follow the contours of granite and schist hills, making the riverbanks appear to be edged by gigantic pyramids. There are 85,000 vineyards and 25,000 growers in the port wine zone, the limits of which were set in 1756, making it the world's oldest demarcated zone for wine production. Thanks to the mountains that keep out cold Atlantic winds and rains, this part of the Douro Valley enjoys a semi-Mediterranean climate that is heaven for grapes. It also allows the cultivation of olive, almond, and fruit trees wherever the terrain permits.

In the summer, the Alto Douro is scorched by temperatures up to 104F (40C). A good time to visit is during the *vindima* (vintage, or grape harvest) in September and October, when the region bustles with life and the songs of grape pickers echo throughout the valley. The sheer bravado of the men, women, and children who carry heavy baskets up and down steep slopes adds to a visitor's appreciation of the labor behind a glass of port.

The Trás-os-Montes province stretches far beyond the river, the Alto Douro, and the port wine region into the northeastern corner of the country. Its name means "behind the mountains," and much of this land — a plateau sloping up to Spain, surmounted by rocky heights and cut through by deep river valleys — is indeed remote. Roads and electricity are fairly new to some of the tiny villages tucked away in its fertile valleys, so its air remains pure, its waters fresh and clean. Cold, blistering winters and blazing hot summers are the norm, but oases can be found in the valleys where corn, almonds, olives, and citrus fruits thrive. On its high pasturelands, sheep and cattle graze, producing some of the country's best meat.

The area has been inhabited for thousands of years. There are vestiges of Celtic and pre-Celtic habitation in stone *castros* (fortified hamlets), in dolmens, and in the customs and dances of the people. Ancient beliefs such as devil worship persist, and *bruxas* (witches) and *curandeiros* (medicine men) are consulted regularly. Some villages continue to be self-sufficient, leading a communal life. Their inhabitants are friendly and may invite visitors into their granite houses for a taste of rich corn bread, smoked ham, and homemade wine.

Today, Trás-os-Montes and the Douro Valley are maturing like an ancient bottle of port. A major highway linking Porto and Spain is under construction, and part of it is already in use. There are also large iron and coal deposits under the soil of Trás-os-Montes, waiting to be exploited. The Douro Valley has been transformed by hydroelectric dams and the river is now navigable to the Spanish border, using a system of locks at each dam.

The route outlined below takes travelers east from the Douro capital of Porto, Portugal's second-largest city, to the picturesque town of Amarante. From there, it dips south to Lamego and follows the south bank of the Douro through the port wine region. It returns to the river's north bank at Pinhão and climbs vine-covered mountains to Vila Real, the capital of southwestern Trás-os-Montes. Some 50 miles (80 km) east of Vila Real, a decision must be made either to continue directly to the fortified town of Bragança, at the northeastern tip of Portugal, or to reach the same goal via a less direct swing through the rarely visited southeastern part of Trás-os-Montes, which offers almond-studded valleys, a final view of the Douro before it turns into Spain, and tiny border towns such as Miranda do Douro, renowned for its ancient stick dances and unique dialect. After Bragança, the route turns west, skirting the Montezinho Natural Park on its way to the spa town of Chaves, graced with a Roman bridge and picturesque wood-balconied houses. Several short excursions are suggested as the route continues west to the spectacular lake region in and around the Peneda-Gerês National Park and into the spa town of Caldas do Gerês. The itinerary ends in Portugal's Minho region, at Braga.

Along the way, dine heartily on veal, lamb, kid, ham, and sausages, on dairy products such as goat cheese, and on thick vegetable soups such as *caldo verde*. Fish lovers can order trout stuffed with ham in Lamego and Chaves. Wine drinkers will savor real port — now officially known as Porto to distinguish it from port-like wines made elsewhere. The Douro Valley also produces dry red and white wines, and rosés from the Vila Real area and reds from Valpaços in central Trás-os-Montes are other popular choices.

Hotels and good restaurants in the area are limited, but the dearth of accommodations is relieved by the existence of private homes taking in paying guests under the auspices of Portugal's *Turismo no Espaço Rural* (Tourism in the Country) program, whose participants range from the manor houses of *Turismo de Habitação* to the simpler houses of *Turismo Rural* and *Agroturismo* (for additional information, see *Pousadas and Manor Houses* in DIVERSIONS). Reservations for all accommodations in summer (June through September) should be made well in advance. Expect to pay $75 or more for a double room in hotels listed below as expensive ($100 and higher for a *pousada*), between $55 and $70 for accommodations in the moderate category, and less than $50 in inexpensive ones. A dinner for two runs from about $45 to $50 or more in restaurants listed as expensive, from $25 to $40 in those listed as moderate, and less than $25 in those listed as inexpensive. For each location, hotels and restaurants are listed alphabetically by price category.

AMARANTE This old town lies on the banks of the Tâmega River at the foot of the Serra do Marão, 45 miles (72 km) east of Porto via the IP4 highway. At sundown or in the morning mist, with the wooden balconies of its picturesque houses leaning over the river, there is a dreamy enchantment to the scene. The town is known for its patron saint, São Gonçalo, a 13th-century priest who gained a reputation for helping women find husbands. The colorful saint is remembered on June 1 and 2, when, for the semi-religious *Romaria de São Gonçalo* (St. Gonçalo Pilgrimage), single women take red carnations to the Igreja de São Gonçalo, kiss the statue of him there, pull the red cord of his habit, and pray for a good husband. The lovely 16th-century church, part of the Convento de São Gonçalo, stands by the 18th-century São Gonçalo bridge and contains, besides the remains of the saint, an attractive 17th-century organ case. The *Museu Municipal Amadeu de Sousa Cardoso* (phone: 55-432663), in the cloister of the church, contains an extensive art gallery, as well as the town's *demônios,* a pair of devils that are holdovers from the devil worship that once was practiced in the area. A Bishop of Braga took a dim view of this practice and sold the pair to England — causing such a furor that they had to be returned. The museum is open from 10 AM to 12:30 PM and 2 to 5:30 PM; closed Mondays; no admission charge.

Also to be seen in the town is the 18th-century Igreja de São Pedro, which has a baroque façade and an unusual nave decorated with 17th-century *azulejos*. Leisurely repasts on the balconies of the tea houses overlooking the river, scenic walks on paths in the wooded park above the town, and swimming, trout fishing, and boating on the Tâmega are popular local pastimes.

Ask at the Amarante Tourist Office, located in the museum (Alameda Teixeira Pascoais; phone: 55-432259), for information on excursions in the vicinity; it's open daily from 9:30 AM to 7 PM from July through September; closed Sundays and open from 9:30 AM to 12:30 PM and 2 to 5 PM from October through June. The area is rich in *solares* (manor houses), Romanesque churches, dolmens, Iron Age *castros,* and strange rock formations called *pedras baloiçantes* (balancing rocks). Drive north along N210 and the banks of the Tâmega for 14½ miles (23 km) to visit Celorico de Basto, a medieval earldom with fine country houses and an 18th-century castle.

CHECKING IN

Casa Zé da Calçada This is a pleasant townhouse overlooking the Tâmega, a short walk from the town center. A participant in *Turismo de Habitação,* it offers 7 rooms with private baths, and the owner runs the town's best restaurant, opposite the townhouse (see *Eating Out,* below). 83 Rua 31 de Janeiro, Amarante (phone: 55-422023). Expensive.

Navarras A few minutes' drive from the center, this place is modern, with 61 air conditioned rooms, a heated indoor pool, and a large restaurant with a verandah. Rua António Carneiro, Amarante (phone: 55-431036). Expensive to moderate.

Amaranto Modest, it has 35 rooms (all with private baths), a panoramic view of the town monuments, and a restaurant serving regional fare. Rua Madalena, Amarante (phone: 55-422106). Inexpensive.

EATING OUT

Zé da Calçada This restaurant has an old-fashioned look and serves tasty local dishes. House specialties include cod *Zé da Calçada*-style, *cabrito assado no forno* (roast kid), and a variety of fancifully named sweets made with eggs, sugar, and almonds. Several local *vinho verde* wines, such as caves moura bastos and quinta do outeiro, are on the wine list. Open daily. Reservations advised. Major credit cards accepted. 72 Rua 31 de Janeiro, Amarante (phone: 55-422023). Expensive.

Adega Regional de Amarante This is a favorite pre-dinner haunt for tasting regional snacks, including the hams and spicy sausages hanging from the ceiling. The *salpicão* (sausage cured in red wine and smoked) is a favorite with locals. Open daily. Reservations unnecessary. No credit cards accepted. 57 Rua António Carneiro, Amarante (phone: 55-424581). Inexpensive.

A Tasquinha Set in an old cottage, this traditional *tasca* features a rustic ambience — farming tools hang on the walls, and diners sit on wooden benches. Hearty regional fare is prepared in the wood-burning oven. Try the local red wine, which is served here in white china tankards. Open daily. No reservations. No credit cards accepted. Campo de Feira, Amarante (phone: 55-422450). Inexpensive.

En Route from Amarante Head southeast toward Lamego on N15 and N101, stopping at Mesão Frio, 14½ miles (23 km) from Amarante, to admire the elegant churches and manor houses in its tree-lined center. At Mesão Frio, take N108 8½ miles (14 km) east to Peso da Régua, at the confluence of the Douro and Corgo rivers. The best port wine vineyards begin here and spread eastward along the Douro and its tributaries. Peso da Régua, also known simply as Régua, is the industry's main administrative and storage center in the Alto Douro, and although the town lacks charm, the surrounding countryside is starkly beautiful. In fact, Régua is the junction of several scenic train routes, including the "Linha do Douro," which runs from Porto up to Pocinho, about 19 miles (30 km) short of Barca d'Alva on the Spanish border. For details, contact the tourist office opposite the Régua train station (Largo da Estação; phone: 54-22846). It is open daily from 9 AM to 6 PM from May through October; weekdays from 9 AM to 12:30 PM and 2 to 6 PM from November through April.

Cross the Douro at Régua; just past the bridge is *Garrafeira e Artesanato Duriense* (phone: 54-23504), an interesting shop that carries a wide variety of local wines and handicrafts. Drive south on the N2 8 miles (13 km) to Lamego. The well-paved but winding road climbs mountain slopes covered with terraced vineyards and whitewashed manor houses.

LAMEGO The location of this attractive and peaceful agricultural town — at the edge of a valley surrounded by mountains, vineyards, and orchards — made it an important commercial center in the Middle Ages. Portugal's first *cortes,* a representative assembly of nobles, met here in 1143 to recognize Dom Afonso Henriques as the country's first king. On a hill northeast of town are the partially restored ruins of a 12th-century castle, while the baroque Santuário da Nossa Senhora dos Remédios (Sanctuary of Our Lady of the Remedies) occupies a hill to the south of town. The sanctuary can be reached by car, 2½ miles (4 km) through a lovely wooded forest, or, more dramatically, by climbing an impressive granite staircase decorated with *azulejos* and bristling with pinnacles. During the *Festas da Nossa Senhora dos Remédios,* the largest cultural and religious event in the region and one of the country's biggest fairs, pilgrims can be seen crawling up the steps on their knees. Held from late August to mid-September, the fair also features folk dancing and singing and religious processions with dazzling floats pulled by oxen.

In town, the Sé (Cathedral) has a fine Gothic entrance in which an amusing scene of animal eroticism appears to have eluded the censors of the time. The 18th-century Paço Episcopal (Bishop's Palace) next door now houses the *Museu de Lamego* (Largo de Camões; phone: 54-62008), where priceless 16th-century tapestries from Brussels and an early-16th-century painting of the Visitation by the Portuguese master Grão Vasco can be seen. It's open from 10 AM to 12:30 PM and 2 to 5 PM; closed Mondays; admission charge, except on Sundays from 10 AM to 12:30 PM. Also of interest is the Capela do Dêsterro (Chapel of the Exile), with its sumptuous coffered ceiling depicting scenes from the life of Christ. (Ask at 126 Rua da Calçada for the key to visit.) Lamego produces Raposeira, one of Portugal's best sparkling wines. For a taste, visit the Raposeira company's cool cellars carved into the mountainside south of town, reachable via N2. There are tours weekdays at 10 AM, 11 AM, 2 PM, 3 PM, and 4 PM, but it's best to call *Caves de Raposeira* for an appointment first (phone: 54-65503).

Among the sights in the vicinity of Lamego is the 7th-century Visigothic Igreja de São Pedro de Balsemão, 9 miles (14 km) east on the banks of the Balsemão River. Besides the elaborate granite tomb of the bishop who remodeled the church during the 14th century, it contains a 15th-century stone statue of Nossa Senhora de O (Our Lady of O), depicting a pregnant Virgin. To reach the church, leave Lamego via the popular Bairro da Fonte quarter, where women still bake bread in old-fashioned ovens and blacksmiths still work at open forges. Turn left at the bridge and follow a narrow road running north along the banks of the river.

The 12th-century Mosteiro de São João de Tarouca, a former Cistercian monastery (Portugal's first), lies 10 miles (16 km) southeast of town off N226. The impressive church, which was later given a baroque interior, contains exquisite paintings by the 16th-century master Gaspar Vaz, as well as the granite tomb of Dom Pedro, Count of Barcelos and bastard son of King Dinis. (His wife's tomb was taken by a local farmer and used as a wine press before it was recovered and put in the museum in Lamego.) The sacristy has 4,709 tiles, no two alike, and its ceiling has a series of paintings depicting the life of St. Bernard. The church is open daily from 9 AM to 12:30 PM and 2 to 5 PM. For information on other sights, contact Lamego's Tourist Office (Av. Visconde Guedes Teixeira; phone: 54-62005).

CHECKING IN

Do Cerrado A pleasant *albergaria* (inn) at the entrance to Lamego, it has 30 air conditioned, balconied rooms with private baths. Regional furniture and handmade rugs decorate the common room. Breakfast and snacks are served on a terrace with views of the town and the surrounding countryside, but there's no restaurant. Lugar do Cerrado, Lamego (phone: 54-63164). Expensive.

Vila Hostilina This restored farmhouse, a *Turismo Rural* participant, sits on a hill overlooking the town and the valley, surrounded by gardens and vineyards. Guests are invited to help with the *vindima* (grape harvest) in the fall and to crush grapes the old-fashioned way — by foot. There are 7 rooms with private baths, a rustic bar, a tennis court, and a large swimming pool, plus a health club with a gym, exercise machines, and a sauna. Meals are served on request; reservations are a must in summer. Contact Joaquim Brandão dos Santos, *Vila Hostilina,* Lamego (phone: 54-62394). Expensive.

Parque A simple, turn-of-the-century hotel, it has 40 rooms with private baths. It's known for its fine restaurant (see *Eating Out*) and ideal location in the gardens beside the Nossa Senhora dos Remédios sanctuary. Nossa Senhora dos Remédios, Lamego (phone: 54-62105; fax: 54-65203). Moderate.

Solar A small and comfortable *pensão* with 25 rooms (with baths) in front of the tourist office. There's no restaurant. 9 Av. Visconde Guedes Teixeira, Lamego (phone: 54-62060). Moderate.

Império Simple but quaint, this *pensão* is beside the town's main street and monuments. The look is small-town Portugal; there are 14 rooms with baths, no restaurant. 6 Travessa dos Loureiros, Lamego (phone: 54-62742). Inexpensive.

Solar do Espírito Santo Lamego's newest hotel — with 28 rooms — offers comfort, dependable service, and a central location. There is private parking, plus a good restaurant that's just across the road (see *Eating Out*). Rua Alexandre Herculano, Lamego (phone: 54-63450). Inexpensive.

EATING OUT

Parque By far the best place to eat in Lamego, it has a varied regional menu that includes river trout baked with ham and the chef's award-winning cod dish. Courteous service, an austere old Portugal ambience, and garden views enhance the repast. Raposeira sparkling wines are stocked; have a *bruto* (brut) with the meal and a *meio-seco* (semisweet) with dessert. Open daily. Reservations unnecessary. Major credit cards accepted. *Hotel Parque,* Nossa Senhora dos Remédios, Lamego (phone: 54-62105). Moderate.

Turiserra The reward for a 20-minute drive into the mountains north of Lamego is a modern restaurant serving regional fare, with a spectacular view of the Douro Valley and the atmosphere of a mountain lodge. To reach it, take Avenida 5 de Outubro, turn left onto Avenida Marquês de Pombal, and follow the signs for the Parque de Campismo Turiserra. Closed Mondays and 1 month each year. Reservations necessary on Sundays. Major credit cards accepted. Serra das Meadas (phone: 54-63380). Moderate.

Mina A rustic, family-run spot with a wholesome regional menu, near the town center, beside the charming Capela do Espírito Santo. The specialty, *cordeiro assado* (roast lamb), is cooked and served in unglazed black pottery from the region. This is also a good place to try *bôlo de Lamego* (ham pie). Closed Mondays. Reservations unnecessary. Major credit cards accepted. 5 Rua Alexandre Herculano, Lamego (phone: 54-63353). Inexpensive.

Solar do Espírito Santo This wood-paneled eatery gets high marks for its renditions of local specialties such as *vitela assado* (roast veal) and *cozida portuguesa* (pork stew). Closed Tuesdays. Reservations unnecessary. Major credit cards accepted. Rua Alexandre Herculano, Lamego (phone: 54-64470). Inexpensive.

En Route from Lamego To reach Vila Real by the shortest route (3½ miles/38 km), return to Peso da Régua and cut north through the impressive gorge of the Corgo River. To take the longer (43½ miles/73 km), more scenic route through the epicenter of the port wine zone, return to the Douro and take N222 east along its south bank, crossing to the north bank at Pinhão. The road passes some of the larger wine estates along the way; one open to visitors is the Quinta de Penascal, a Fonseca Guimaraens port wine property (phone: 54-72321). It provides an audio tour in English; open weekdays from 10 AM to 7 PM; no admission charge. In Pinhão there is a lovely train station with *azulejos* depicting the history of wine making in the area. From Pinhão, take N323 north for 9 miles (14 km) to Sabrosa, climbing steep mountain slopes streaked with terraces and vines and punctuated only occasionally by a lone tree or a white manor house. At Sabrosa, a suitable watering hole with a Luso-Roman cemetery, head west 13 miles (21 km) on N322 to Vila Real.

About 1¼ miles (2 km) short of Vila Real, the 18th-century Palace of Mateus appears on the left. It may look familiar, because the façade graces the label of the famous Mateus rosé wine. The palace is one of the most elegant examples of the baroque style in Portugal. Although it's a private residence, parts of it, along with the grounds, are open to the public daily from 9 AM to 1 PM and 2 to 6 PM from April through September, and from 10 AM to 1 PM and 2 to 5 PM the rest of the year; admission charge. A museum in the palace contains, among other things, a precious collection of fans and letters from 19th-century personalities. Classical music concerts and opera, guitar, and other music courses are given on the premises in August and September. For information, contact the Fundação da Casa de Mateus (Vila Real; phone: 59-23121). Wine tasting takes place at the Sogrape bottling plant nearby; it's open weekdays by appointment only from 9 AM to noon and 2 to 5:30 PM. Contact *Sogrape-Vinhos de Portugal*, 1159 Av. da Boavista, Porto (phone: 2-695751).

VILA REAL The administrative capital of the southwest Trás-os-Montes is a thriving agricultural town on a plateau at the foot of the Marão and Alvão mountain ranges and at the confluence of the Cabril and Corgo rivers. The major road from Porto to the northeast Trás-os-Montes capital of Bragança passes through here, and the scenic "Linha do Corgo" train line arrives here from Peso da Régua. There are also air links with Porto and Lisbon. The main sights are in the town center along the Avenida Carvalho Araújo, where the tourist office is located (No. 94; phone: 59-322819). The cathedral, a former Dominican monastery with Romanesque and Gothic touches, has an interesting statue of the Virgin. Beside the church, at No. 19, is the Renaissance façade of the house of Diogo Cão, the Portuguese explorer of the Congo basin. Just off Avenida Carvalho Araújo, on Rua Central, is the lovely baroque 17th-century Capela Nova (New Chapel), which features beautiful tilework. At the western end of the avenue is the monumental double staircase of the 19th-century Câmara Municipal (Town Hall). The Old Town behind it has an esplanade encircling the 14th-century Igreja de São Dinis and a commanding view of the Corgo ravine. Vila Real is a good base from which to explore the Parque Nacional do Alvão, which lies to the northwest and is endowed with stone and shale houses, ancient water mills, tumbling waterfalls, ravines, and valleys carpeted with flowers. To reach the park, take the 1P4 west for 6 miles (10 km); then turn right onto the N304 for Mondim de Basto and Campeã. Along this stretch, the Alto do Velão pass affords a breathtaking view of the environs.

CHECKING IN

Cabanas A modern hotel near the center, it has 24 well-appointed rooms, a restaurant, and a bar. Rua D. Pedro de Castro, Vila Real (phone: 59-323153; fax: 59-74181). Expensive.

Casa das Quartas A handsome, 16th-century manor house, this *Turismo de Habitação* property is surrounded by orchards and flower beds in a southeastern suburb. The sprawling estate, which even has its own private chapel, offers 3 rooms with private baths and mountain views. Abambres (phone: 59-22976). Expensive.

Mira Corgo Modern, it has 76 air conditioned rooms, a bar (but no restaurant), an indoor swimming pool, and a disco. It overlooks the Corgo River gorge. 76-78 Av. 1 de Maio, Vila Real (phone: 59-25001). Moderate.

Tocaio This aging hostelry in the center of town has 52 rooms and simple country charm. No restaurant. 45 Av. Carvalho Araújo, Vila Real (phone: 59-323106). Moderate.

Casa da Cruz Near the Alvão National Park, this typical 18th-century Trás-os-Montes house (a *Turismo Rural* property) offers 6 guestrooms with private baths. Vila Real (phone: 59-72995). Inexpensive.

EATING OUT

Espadeiro There's a classic dining room, endowed with a fireplace, and in summer an adjacent smaller room with a terrace overlooking the Corgo River.

This is a sophisticated restaurant, well known for regional dishes such as *truta com presunto* (grilled trout with ham) and *cabrito assado com arroz* (roast kid with rice). Open daily. Reservations unnecessary. Major credit cards accepted. Av. Almeida Lucena, Vila Real (phone: 59-22302). Expensive.

Maranus Light, airy, and modern, this establishment boasts regional specialties — try the *bife à Maranus,* a mouth-watering beefsteak. Open daily. Reservations unnecessary. Major credit cards accepted. In the suburb of Quinta do Seixo, Lote 2, Loja 5 (phone: 59-321521). Expensive to moderate.

Nevada The regional menu here features Vila Real's very own *bôlo de carne* (a spicy meat loaf). Modern, with a relaxed atmosphere and simple decor, it's beside the *Mira Corgo* hotel. Try a table wine from the Adega Cooperativa de Vila Real. Open daily. Reservations unnecessary. Major credit cards accepted. Av. 1 de Maio, Vila Real (phone: 59-72828). Moderate.

22 In the center of town, this new restaurant has rustic decor, friendly service, and traditional dishes. Try the *cozido portuguesa* (pork stew) and *bacalhau 22* (oven-baked salt cod). Closed Mondays. Reservations unnecessary. Major credit cards accepted. Praça Luis de Camões, Vila Real (phone: 59-321296). Moderate to inexpensive.

Churrasco A medium-size eatery decorated in local traditional style. Grilled meats are the specialty. Closed Sunday evenings. Reservations unnecessary. Major credit cards accepted. 24 Rua António Azevedo, Vila Real (phone: 59-322313). Inexpensive.

En Route from Vila Real As N15 leads northeast toward Bragança, pine trees begin to alternate with vineyards, olive groves, and fields of grain. The town of Murça, on high slopes above the Tinhela River 25 miles (40 km) out of Vila Real, has an interesting Iron Age granite boar (Porca de Murça) in its main square, one of many such peculiar statues found throughout the region. The agricultural town of Mirandela, known for its 16th-century bridge and a lively fair that runs from the end of July to early August, lies another 19 miles (31 km) east on the banks of the Tua River. The rolling hills around Jerusalem do Romeu, 7 miles (11 km) farther east, are covered with olive and cork oak trees. Turn right at Jerusalem do Romeu and go about 2 miles (3 km) to Romeu, a typical Trás-os-Montes village that has been restored. The tiny hamlet and its *Maria Rita* restaurant (see *Eating Out*) are owned by a patrician Portuguese family, as is the interesting *Museu das Curiosidades* (Museum of Curiosities; phone: 78-22526), which contains family memorabilia such as old sewing machines, photographic and musical equipment, four Model Ts, and 19th-century fire trucks. It's open daily (the caretaker lives on the premises); admission charge.

Return to N15 and continue east 5½ miles (9 km) to the junction with N216. Here a decision must be made. Either continue on N15 28½ miles (46 km) directly to Bragança (through some of the most barren and thinly populated countryside in southern Europe), or take a more circuitous route via a string of old fortress towns running along the Douro and the Spanish border. To follow the latter course, turn southeast onto N216 and drive the few miles to Macedo de Cavaleiros, a neat farming town and favorite hunting spot for northern aristocrats. Continue on N216 toward Mogadouro; in about 7 miles (12 km), take a short detour left to the Santuário Nossa Senhora de Balsamão. Perched atop a small hill, the hermitage is now run by Polish Marianist brothers; the structure dates back to the early 13th century. The chapel, added in the 18th century, features a beautiful painted ceiling and a statue representing the Immaculate Conception.

Return to N216 to Mogadouro, 26 miles (44 km) away, known for its woodcrafts and silk, wool, and leather goods. There's also a ruined 12th-century fortress and the 17th-century Igreja de São Francisco (Church of St. Francis), which has one of the finest carved and gilded-wood altars in the region. Near the Old Town center is a small archaeological museum (no phone) that displays excavated artifacts from the area's *castros* (fortified villages). It's open Tuesdays through Fridays from 10 AM to 12:30 PM and 2 to 5 PM; no admission charge. If it's spring, drive up to the nearby Serra da Castanheira and see the countryside covered by a mantle of white from thousands of blossoming almond trees. Seventeen miles (27 km) east of Mogadouro on N221 is the tiny town of Sendim, whose main square is the site of a well-preserved 17th-century church in which traditional *capas de honra* are still made. (These "capes of honor," made from a local coarse woven-wool fabric, are worn by landowners and farmers on market days and special occasions. The degree of detail on the front of the cape denotes the wealth of the owner; capes are often passed down in families for generations.) Surprisingly, Sendim also boasts one of the better restaurants in Trás-os-Montes (*Gabriela's;* see *Eating Out*). The border town of Miranda do Douro is another 13 miles (20 km) beyond Sendim.

CHECKING IN

Do Caçador A splendid *estalagem* (inn) and hunting lodge in the former Town Hall of Macedo de Cavaleiros. The 25 rooms (all with private baths) are furnished with antiques, the public rooms are rife with wood and leather, and the bar, filled with wicker furniture and hunting trophies, looks like a set out of colonial Africa. Specialties in the dining room include steaks stuffed with ham and, during hunting season (mid-October through December), game dishes such as partridge and hare. Guests can stroll around a tiny rose garden and swim in a marble-lined pool. Largo Manuel Pinto de Azevedo, Macedo de Cavaleiros (phone: 78-421354; fax: 78-421381). Expensive.

EATING OUT

Gabriela's Almost a century old, this restaurant is the culinary pride and joy of Trás-os-Montes. Adelaide Gabriela, the third-generation owner, prepares the famous traditional dishes for which her late mother won many awards. Try the *posta à mirandesa à Gabriela* (a large veal steak cooked over a fire of grape vines or olive branches). The sauces are a professional secret. Open daily. Reservations advised on Sundays. Major credit cards accepted. 28 Largo da Praça, Sendim (phone: 73-73180). Moderate.

Maria Rita One of the best restaurants in the region, lodged in a typical Trás-os-Montes house in a tiny village. The large stone fireplaces, antiques, and heavy oak tables set with china and silver add up to an elegantly rustic setting. The menu features regional fare such as *sopa da pedra* (a thick and spicy garlic soup), and *espargos bravos* (wild asparagus) — not to mention whole turkeys, baby pigs, and lambs for parties calling in advance. Closed Mondays. Reservations advised. No credit cards accepted. Rua da Capela, Romeu (phone: 78-93134). Moderate to inexpensive.

MIRANDA DO DOURO This ancient town perches atop the narrow rocky canyon of the Douro that here forms a natural border between Portugal and Spain. It is remote enough to have its own dialect, Mirandes, a mixture of Galician Spanish, Portuguese, and Hebrew, yet during the 16th century it was the cultural center of Trás-os-Montes and the seat of an important bishopric. After several military catastrophes and the loss of its bishop's seat, the town fell into obscurity during the 18th century and has only recently come out of its isolation with the completion of a dam (the northernmost of five on the Douro) and the opening of a border road with Spain. Among the sights to see is the former cathedral, a 16th-century building rich in carved and gilded wood and graced with an unusual little statue — Menino Jesus da Cartolinha — of the baby Jesus sporting a top hat. (It's said to represent a boy who appeared miraculously to help the townspeople resist a Spanish invasion in the 18th century.) The *Museu da Terra de Miranda* (Museum of the Land of Miranda, Plaza Dom João III; phone: 73-42164) has costumes of the area, rustic furniture, archaeological artifacts, and carved stones from an old synagogue. It's open from 10 AM to 12:15 PM and 2 to 4:45 PM; closed Mondays; admission charge.

The *Festas de Santa Bárbara,* on the third Sunday in August, and the *Romaria de Nossa Senhora de Nazaré,* in early September, are two occasions on which the town's *pauliteiros,* or stick dancers, perform. Although other ancient and colorful folk dances, such as the *pingacho* (rough ballet), the *geribalda* (a round dance), and the *mira-me-Miguel* (a square dance), are still performed here, the stick dance is the one for which the town is best known. It's a sort of ritual sword dance performed by men in white flannel skirts, aprons, and flower-covered hats, who clash their *paulitos* (sticks) to the tune of a bagpipe, cymbals, and drums. Other unique aspects of the local culture are the coarse wool capes and waistcoats worn by the people of the region and the *facas de palacoulo* — knives with forks attached to them — used traditionally by the shepherds of the area.

CHECKING IN

Pousada de Santa Catarina This simple, modern, 12-room *pousada* (with private baths) sits on a hill overlooking a dam on the Douro about 2 miles (3 km) east of town. The restaurant, which has a fine view of the water and the Spanish plain of Zamora, serves regional dishes such as wood-fired *posta à mirandesa* (veal steaks), *fumeiro* (smoked sausage), river trout, and small game. Estrada da Barragem, Miranda do Douro (phone: 73-42255; 212-686-9213 in the US). Expensive.

Santa Cruz A family-run *pensão* on a quiet street off the Praça do Castelo. There are 17 simple rooms (all with private baths) plus a restaurant offering typical local fare such as *posta à mirandesa* and *bacalhau à sargento* (oven-baked salt cod). 61 Rua Abade de Baçal, Miranda do Douro (phone: 73-42474). Inexpensive.

EATING OUT

Buteko This air conditioned eatery affords diners a nice view of the main square, and serves dishes typical of the region. Open daily. Reservations unnecessary. Major credit cards accepted. Largo Dom João III, Miranda do Douro (phone: 73-42150). Moderate.

Mirandes A rustic, family-run restaurant in the heart of town, it offers a range of regional specialties. The *folares de Páscoa* (sweet *Easter* cakes) are a local dessert. Closed Mondays. Reservations unnecessary. Major credit cards accepted. Largo da Moagem, Miranda do Douro (phone: 73-42418). Moderate to inexpensive.

En Route from Miranda do Douro Head north on N218 toward Bragança. Outeiro, 32½ miles (52 km) up the road, has a large church with an ornate Manueline doorway and a Gothic rose window. Bragança is another 20½ miles (33 km) ahead.

BRAGANÇA The medieval walls and castle that dominate this fortified town at Portugal's extreme northeastern corner are the best preserved in the country. Bragança, which occupies a high hill in the Serra da Nogueira, was known to the Celts as Brigantia and to the Romans as Juliobriga. During the 15th century, it was made a fiefdom of the powerful Dukes of Bragança, who became Portugal's royal family in 1640 and ruled until the end of the monarchy in 1910. The town was a major silk center during the 15th century, thanks largely to a thriving Jewish merchant community (which dispersed with the Inquisition, although the area's remoteness allowed some Jews to stay and practice their religion in secret). Today, copper and leather goods and baskets replace silks in the shops around the main square, Praça da Sé, which is outside the walls in the newer (but still old) part of town — Bragança had already begun to expand beyond its medieval walls during the 15th century.

The old walled town contains the 12th-century castle and its tall, square keep, which serves as a military museum. Beside it is the Torre da Princesa (Princess Tower), where the fourth duke locked up his lovely wife, Dona Leonor, to keep men from looking at her; later, when he moved his court south, he murdered her. In front of the castle is a medieval *pelourinho* (pillory), its shaft driven through a granite statue of a boar said to date from the Iron Age (as does the boar in Murça). The 12th-century Domus Municipalis (Town Hall) is one of the few remaining Romanesque civic buildings in Portugal (to visit, apply at the house in front); it stands next to the 16th-century Igreja da Santa Maria. The interesting *Museu do Abade de Baçal* (27 Rua Conselheiro Abilio Beça; phone: 73-23242) is outside the walls in the 18th-century Paço Episcopal (Bishop's Palace). Named for the Abbot of Baçal (1865–1945), who spent years recording the history and customs of the region in an 11-volume series, it houses archaeological artifacts, furniture, tools, ancient coins, church plates and vestments, and paintings. The museum is open from 10 AM to 12:30 PM and 2 to 5 PM; closed Mondays. There's an admission charge, except on Sunday mornings.

Bragança is the ideal spot from which to explore the Parque Natural de Montezinho, whose high plateaus and mountains stretch northeast and northwest of town and contain some of the wildest country in Portugal. Populated with wild boar, wolves, foxes, and other small game, the park is also dotted with tiny, self-sufficient villages where communal life and pre-Christian rituals and superstitions endure. The town of Rio de Onor, straddling the border 16½ miles (26 km) northeast of Bragança, has a communal system of ownership and a democratic electoral system that has piqued the interest of sociologists. Half of the village lies in Portugal and the other in Spain, and the inhabitants, who cross freely from one to the other, have intermarried for centuries. For more information on the area, and a map of the park, visit the main tourist office (in the Edifício do Principal; phone: 73-23078; open weekdays from 9 AM to 12:30 PM and 2 to 5:30 PM); the small tourism booth at the entrance to town from N218; or the park's administrative office in Bragança (past the entrance to town from N218, take a right into the signposted housing estate; phone: 73-28734).

CHECKING IN

Pousada de São Bartolomeu A 16-room inn with private baths perched on a hill facing the walled town, its castle, and the surrounding mountains. Guests have a choice of regional or international dishes in the posh restaurant.

Estrada do Turismo, Bragança (phone: 73-22493; 212-686-9213 in the US). Expensive.

Bragança Simple, near the town center, with 42 rooms facing the battlements and castle. There is a restaurant serving a range of regional dishes. Av. Dr. Francisco Sá Carneiro, Bragança (phone: 73-22579). Moderate.

Tulipa A modern *residencia* with 33 rooms (all with private baths) and a good restaurant, conveniently close to the center of town. 8-10 Rua Dr. Francisco Felgueiras, Bragança (phone: 73-23675; fax: 73-27814). Moderate.

Cruzeiro A no-frills *pensão* with 31 rooms and private baths near the town center. No restaurant. Travessa do Hospital, Bragança (phone: 73-22634). Inexpensive.

EATING OUT

O Geadas An air conditioned dining spot specializing in local fare. Highlights of the unusually extensive menu include *butelo com feijão* (smoked sausage with beans) and *arroz de lebre* (hare with rice). Open daily. Major credit cards accepted. Reservations unnecessary. 4 Rua do Laureto, Bragança (phone: 73-24413). Expensive.

Solar Bragançano This pleasant, old-fashioned restaurant occupies a palatial townhouse in the main square. A tiled entrance and staircase lead to the formal dining room with wood ceilings, chandeliers, and handwoven rugs. Specialties of the house are *cabrito branco à Montezinho* (white Montezinho kid), cod, and *posta mirandesa a Solar* (veal steak with wine sauce). Try the semisweet favaios wine as an aperitif, with *alheiras* (spiced sausages) or some goat cheese. Open daily. Reservations unnecessary. Major credit cards accepted. 34 Praça da Sé, Bragança (phone: 73-23875). Moderate.

Lá em Casa A modern, airy restaurant with pine-paneled walls and rustic regional decor and fare. Open daily. Reservations unnecessary. Major credit cards accepted. 7 Rua Marquês de Pombal, Bragança (phone: 73-22111). Moderate to inexpensive.

En Route from Bragança The road (N103) to Chaves, 60 miles (96 km) west, sets out running along the edge of and sometimes into the Parque Natural de Montezinho. Only 3 miles (5 km) beyond Bragança, the Benedictine Monastery of Castro de Avelãs, a handsome building with Romanesque and Moorish touches, sits beside the road; once flourishing, it was abandoned when religious orders were banned during the 19th century. Moving westward, as the high peaks of the Serra de Montezinho and the Serra da Coroa begin to loom majestically, the traveler passes chestnut and oak trees, whitewashed *pombaias* (pigeon houses), trout farms, and grazing cattle. Vinhais, overlooking a valley 19½ miles (31 km) from Bragança, is worth a stop for its large market held on the 9th and 23rd days of the month. If your car can endure a bumpy dirt road, take the turnoff, 8½ miles (14 km) short of Chaves, to the Castelo de Montorte, about half a mile (1 km) away. The impressive 14th-century castle sits on a high, windswept hill with views of Spain to the north. Surrounding it are the remains of what is believed to be a Lusitanian *castro* (fortified village) with Roman additions. The castle can be visited daily from 3 to 6 PM (tip the guard).

CHAVES The spa capital of Portugal, Chaves is on the banks of the Tâmega River in the center of a fertile valley near the Spanish border. The Romans took advantage of this breach in Portugal's northern mountains during the 1st century, when they captured the site, exploited its rich gold and mineral deposits, and built a town called Aquae Flaviae — so named for its warm thermal springs, which are said to cure rheumatism and liver and stomach disorders. When they built Trajan's Bridge over the Tâmega, the town became an important stopover on the Roman road between Braga and Astorga, Spain. The bridge is still in use, but most of the Roman town lies beneath the medieval and modern town. Agriculture and textiles are the economic mainstays today, and Chaves is particularly known for its *presunto* (ham).

Most of the sights are found in and around Praça de Camões, the main square. The *Museu da Região Flaviense* (Museum of the Flaviae Region), housed in the former palace of the Dukes of Bragança, contains archaeological and ethnographic exhibits, including Roman and pre-Roman relics and old coins. The *Museu Militar* (Military Museum), in the adjacent 12th-century keep, has 4 floors of uniforms and weapons from various periods of Portuguese history, while the view from the platform at the top embraces the town and the surrounding countryside. Both museums (phone: 76-332965) are open Tuesdays through Fridays from 9:30 AM to 12:30 PM and 2 to 5 PM; weekends from 2 to 5 PM; admission charge. The manicured keep gardens contain archaeological remains, and its ramparts provide a sweeping view of the river.

Also on the Praça de Camões is the baroque Misericórdia church, its interior embellished with 18th-century *azulejos* depicting the life of Christ; the parish church with a lovely Romanesque doorway; and an ornate Manueline pillory. Note the houses on the eastern side of the square and on the neighboring Rua Direita — they have lovely painted wood verandahs. Nearby, on Rua General Sousa Machado, is the former Jewish Quarter (the chapel at No. 63 is thought to have been a synagogue). Other points of interest in town are two 17th-century fortresses, São Francisco and São Neutal, and the 13th-century Romanesque chapel of Nossa Senhora de Azinheira (Estrada de Outeiro Seco).

For more information and maps of the Chaves area, contact the tourist office (Terreiro da Cavalaria; phone: 76-21029); it's open daily from 9 AM to 7 PM. Two neighboring spa towns, Vidago and Pedras Salgadas, respectively 10½ miles (17 km) and 18½ miles (30 km) south of Chaves on N2 toward Vila Real, provide most of the region's recreational facilities (swimming, golf, and other sports).

CHECKING IN

Aquae Flaviae Located near the 12th-century keep, overlooking the Tâmega, this hostelry has 170 rooms, 3 restaurants, a bar, a health club, a swimming pool, tennis courts, miniature golf, and conference facilities. Praça do Brasil, Chaves (phone: 76-26711; fax: 76-26497). Expensive.

Vidago Palace Set in a lush park and surrounded by gardens, ponds, and fountains, this pink Belle Epoque building offers guests a taste of royal Portugal. The hotel was inaugurated by King Dom Luís in 1910. The "palace" was recently restored to its former splendor and the 94 guestrooms were modernized. There also are 9 rooms and a restaurant in an annex, a discotheque behind the hotel, and a swimming pool, tennis, and rowing on the sprawling grounds. A picturesque 9-hole golf course is nearby. Parque, Vidago (phone: 76-97356; fax: 76-97359). Expensive.

Trajano On a quiet cobbled street near the center of town, this recently redecorated 39-room hostelry stands on top of a Roman bathhouse, discovered while the newer foundations were being laid. The dining room is somewhat dim, but the food, particularly the desserts, brightens things up. Travessa Cândido dos Reis, Chaves (phone: 76-22415). Moderate.

São Neutel A modern, family-run *residencia* near the stadium, with 31 rooms and private baths, but no restaurant. Av. 5 de Outubro, Chaves (phone: 76-25632; fax: 76-27620). Inexpensive.

EATING OUT

Carvalho Subtly lit and decorated, this first class restaurant serves many regional dishes, including *cabrito assado* (roast kid) and *arrozo de salpicão* (spicy sausage and rice); fresh fish is always on the menu. Closed Thursdays. Reservations unnecessary. Major credit cards accepted. Largo das Caldas, Chaves (phone: 76-21727). Expensive to moderate.

Adega Faustino An 80-year-old inn with cobbled floors and high, rafted ceilings, this is the last authentic tavern in Chaves. Regional snacks such as smoked eel and cod fritters are the specialities. Open daily. Reservations unnecessary. Major credit cards accepted. Travessa do Olival, Chaves (phone: 76-22142). Moderate.

Cubata II The *bacalhau à Cubata* (salt cod with Chaves ham) is especially good at this small eatery specializing in seafood. Open daily. Reservations necessary. Major credit cards accepted. Av. Nuno Alvares, Chaves (phone: 76-25499). Moderate.

O Pote Busy and popular, this spot on the outskirts of town offers a large regional menu. Closed Mondays. Reservations unnecessary. No credit cards accepted. Casa Azul, on the road to Spain, Av. Duarte Pacheco, Chaves (phone: 76-21226). Moderate to inexpensive.

En Route from Chaves The goal is Caldas do Gerês, 71 miles (114 km) away in the Peneda-Gerês National Park. Take N103 west into countryside littered with ancient *castros* and dolmens, as well as primitive granite villages known for their dairy products and handsome, long-horned oxen. At Sapiãos, 12 miles (19 km) from Chaves, take a short side trip via N312 to Boticas, 2½ miles (4 km) away, and then via N311 to Carvalhelhos, another 5 miles (8 km) away. Carvalhelhos is known for its spa waters and solitude, Boticas for its wine, which is buried for a year before it is drunk. The practice developed during the Napoleonic invasions, when the villagers hid their wine from French soldiers. Later, when the bottles were dug up, the wine was found to be much improved — and wine bottles ever after have been called *mortos* (dead ones). In summer, tiny villages around Boticas pit their best bulls against each other in the *Chegas de Touros*. The bull that manages to kill its opponent or force it to retreat is led away triumphantly, a source of great pride to its village. At the end of the season, the champion is rewarded by being put to pasture with the region's cows.

Return to N103 and, some 10½ miles (17 km) farther along, make another short detour, to the town of Montalegre, 5½ miles (9 km) away on N308. The small town is crowned by a 14th-century castle facing the peaks of the Serra do Larouco and an ancient *castro* to the north. To return to the route, follow signs to Vila Nova da Chá and then, back on N103, continue westward along the rocky north bank of the huge artificial lake formed by the Barragem do Alto Rabagão, a dam on the Rabagão River. Beyond the dam, the road crosses the river itself and proceeds along its south bank to another lake, the reservoir of the Barragem de Venda Nova, an ideal place for picnics and swimming.

After the Venda Nova Dam, the Rabagão River flows into the Rio Cávado, and the road weaves along the steep slopes above the latter, passing stone houses, water mills, and churches, with the majestic peaks of the Serra do Gerês looming to the north. About 15 miles (24 km) west of Venda Nova, just before Cerdeirinhas, turn right onto N304; as the road descends past heather and pine trees, the steep Cávado gorge appears, offering one of the most spectacular natural sights in Portugal. (Farther to the west, the power of the Cávado and its tributary, the Caldo, have been harnessed by the Barragem da Caniçada.) After passing Caniçada itself (really only a cluster of houses) and crossing a bridge, turn right onto N308-1, cross a second bridge, and drive along the wooded banks of the

Caldo River past the village of Vilar de Veigas and into the spa town of Caldas do Gerês, in the Peneda-Gerês National Park.

CHECKING IN

Pousada de São Bento This establishment has 30 rooms with private baths and a dining room with spectacular views. For additional details, see *Pousadas and Manor Houses* in DIVERSIONS. Caniçada (phone: 53-647190; 212-686-9213 in the US; fax: 53-647867). Expensive.

De Carvalhelhos A simply decorated *estalagem* (inn) with 19 rooms (all with private baths) surrounded by gardens and forested hills, it is a pleasant retreat for those in search of something quiet and off the beaten track. Other attributes are the courteous service and the tasty regional and international dishes available in the dining room. Carvalhelhos (phone: 76-42116). Moderate.

CALDAS DO GERÊS This small resort town, whose mineral springs were known to the Romans, was a fashionable spa in the 18th century and still has several quaint, turn-of-the-century hotels, many of which have been restored, thanks to an EEC grant. Tennis, lake and pool swimming, boating, and horseback riding are all available in the area, but since the town lies at the base of a deep wooded gorge just inside the boundary of the Parque Nacional da Peneda-Gerês, it is an important base for park excursions. The 178,000-acre park, shaped like a horseshoe to encompass the Serra do Gerês on its southeastern side and the Serra da Peneda on its northwestern side, runs beyond Caldas up to the Spanish border and contains a wealth of archaeological vestiges — such as milestones and sections of Roman road — as well as waterfalls, wild ponies, rare birds, and 18 species of plants unique to the area. Hiking on marked trails, alone or with a guide, camping, fishing for trout in rivers and lakes, and going on organized day-long or week-long tours by bus or horseback are all possible. The *Museu Etnológico* (Museum of Ethnology; phone: 53-35888), outside São João do Campo, offers a look at the area's crafts, home furnishings, and farm implements. It's open weekdays from 8 AM to noon and 1 to 7 PM, and weekends from 9 AM to 12:30 PM and 1:30 to 6:30 PM from May through September; weekdays from 8 AM to noon and 1 to 5 PM, and weekends from 9 AM to 12:30 PM and 1:30 to 6 PM from October through April; admission charge.

Maps of the park are available at the park's cabin (phone: 53-391181) at the entrance to town or at the local tourist office (Av. Manuel Francisco da Costa; phone: 53-391133), which is open daily from 9:30 AM to 12:30 PM and 2 to 5:30 PM from May through October. For advance tour reservations and brochures, contact Paulo Pires, *Trote-Gerês* (Cavalos Cabril, Borralha 5495; phone: 53-659292). The park headquarters, Sede do

Parque Nacional (Quinta de Parretas, Braga 4700; phone: 53-613166), or their branch office (29 Rua de São Geraldo, Braga 4700; no phone) also can mail information on the park.

CHECKING IN

Termas On the main street, this fin de siècle establishment has 31 rooms with private baths; the outdoor tables of the busy bar-café face the passing street scene. Av. Manuel Francisco da Costa, Caldas do Gerês (phone: 53-391143). Expensive.

Universal These nicely restored turn-of-the century lodgings are right on the tree-lined main street. There are 50 air conditioned rooms with TV sets and radios, plus a quiet restaurant, a bar (with a fireplace) in the glass-enclosed patio, and a café that opens onto the street. Open year-round. Av. Manuel Francisco da Costa, Caldas do Gerês (phone: 53-391135). Expensive.

Jardim A *pensão* popular with travelers in search of modest accommodations (some of the 57 rooms have TV sets and VCRs, however) and wholesome home cooking. Open year-round. Av. Manuel Francisco da Costa, Caldas do Gerês (phone and fax: 53-391132). Moderate.

Carvalho Araujo Perched on the north side of the valley, this family-run *pensão* has a log-cabin-style design. There are 20 rooms with private baths, all facing south. On the premises are a bar and a worthy restaurant specializing in *bacalhau no forno* (oven-baked salt cod). Open year-round. Termas do Gerês (phone: 53-391185; fax: 53-391225). Inexpensive.

En Route from Caldas do Gerês Return to N103 and head southwest toward Braga, 26½ miles (43 km) from Caldas. Beyond Cerdeirinhas, the landscape becomes barren, with round boulders, smoothed by time, teetering precariously on rocky crests. If you have time, take the dirt road that begins about 4 miles (6 km) beyond Cerdeirinhas, barely a mile (1 km) up to the sanctuary of São Mamede. At the summit, there's a tiny chapel and a panoramic view of the region that extends, on a clear day, as far as Monte Sameiro, outside Braga. Return to N103; soon the barren landscape gives way to the fertile valley of the Ave River, rich in vines and dotted with tiny hamlets. At Pinheiro, turn left to visit the castle at Póvoa de Lanhoso, about 1¼ miles (2 km) off N103. It was here that the first King of Portugal, Afonso Henriques, imprisoned his mother after defeating her forces in 1128, and here that the wife and father confessor/lover of an enraged Póvoa mayor were later burned. Póvoa de Lanhoso is also known for its goldsmiths and silversmiths who fashion some of Portugal's famous filigree.

Braga is 10 miles (16 km) beyond Pinheiro on N103, and Porto is 33 miles (54 km) beyond Braga. For full details on these cities, see *Braga* and *Porto* in THE CITIES.

The Beiras

Occupying a roughly horizontal strip of Portugal slightly north of the center, between the Douro and Tagus rivers, the Beiras region unfolds before visitors like the pages of an age-old romance. Ancient crafts endure in picturesque villages that reverberate with the clang of smithies' anvils and the whir of potters' wheels. Shepherds draped in long woolen blankets as protection from the mist and cold watch over their flocks. Medieval castles wreathed in legend cling to the mountains, where visitors can toboggan down a snow-covered slope or hook a trout from a tumbling river. Even the air, scented with the fragrance of almond blossoms, holds a touch of magic.

The region's inspiring beauty and historical fascination have not yet been undone by mass tourism. Yet the traditional country cooking and fine local wines found in its pleasant hotels and restaurants often rival those of more sophisticated locations, and the friendly welcome surpasses them. Visitors from abroad are usually surprised by the low prices and happy to find themselves far from the madding crowd — although hotels are often fully booked during the peak *Christmas, New Year, Easter,* and summer holiday weeks.

The name Beira, meaning "edge," is thought to derive from the region's position on the edge of the central Spanish mountain range that spills over into Portugal as the Serra da Estrela. There are three Beiras. Beira Alta (Upper Beira), in the northeast, is a high plateau capped by the Serra da Estrela range, with the country's highest peaks. Beira Baixa (Lower Beira) drops in altitude as it slopes southward to the highlands of the Alentejo. Beira Litoral (Coastal Beira), to the west of both of these, is a lower-lying region reaching down past the city of Coimbra to the Atlantic coast.

The mountains of the Beiras ripple throughout the region. Their granite and schist rocks can be seen in the sturdy village houses and monuments that have withstood the weathering of centuries. Two main rivers, the Mondego and the Zêzere, rise in the Serra da Estrela, cutting deep valleys in the mountains on their way to the sea. High in the *serra,* gorges, glacial basins, and artificial lakes spreading out behind hydroelectric dams provide dramatic vistas; lower down, the contrast between fertile, green river valleys and craggy uplands is striking. The region's climate is relatively temperate. Winter temperatures in the Serra da Estrela are the lowest in Portugal, dropping to between 23 and 59F; in summer, they range from 50 to 68F. Elsewhere in the Beiras, winters are milder and summers hotter, but there are always cooling breezes from the river valleys. Rainfall is considerable in the mountains.

Castles, ramparts, forts, and city walls scattered across the Beiras attest to a history of invasion. Viriatus (Viriato in Portuguese), a shepherd-

warrior from the Serra da Estrela, valiantly led a Celtic people known as
the Lusitanians in fighting off Roman domination until his assassination
(ca. 140 BC). Barbarian tribes — the Suevians and the Visigoths — later
overran the province, and the Moorish invasion of Portugal and the subsequent Christian reconquest also brought heavy fighting. The next wave of
invaders came from across the border, when Philip II of Spain seized
Portugal in 1580; an uprising in Lisbon in 1640 restored the country's
independence, but before Spain formally recognized it in 1668, Portuguese
troops had made several stands along the frontier.

Portugal's alliance with Britain against Napoleonic France led to the
Peninsular War of 1807–10. Although Portugal emerged the winner, the
war ravaged the country. Traces of the military campaigns abound in the
region, particularly around the ancient forest of Buçaco, where the leader
of the Anglo-Portuguese forces, Sir Arthur Wellesley (later the Duke of
Wellington), achieved his most significant victory.

Today the Beiras region is very much a rural world, where the earth is
often tilled by hand and where donkeys and oxen have not yet been totally
replaced by mechanical beasts of burden. Life is still dominated by the
seasons, and many of the local festivals, while related to the Roman
Catholic calendar, have their roots in pre-Christian beliefs. Spring flower
festivals echo pagan fertility rites, and some *Christmas* customs, such as
dances around burning *Yule* logs, hark back to winter solstice celebrations. Almost every town and village has its patron saint, and the many
pilgrimage festivals, or *romarias,* held every year to honor local saints
provide congenial ways of discovering the region's heart.

Beiras farmers cultivate corn and rye in the arable land of the valleys;
orchards and olive groves occupy the lower slopes and spill over onto
terraces supported by granite stones as the hillsides grow steeper. Livestock is raised in the rich upper valley of the Zêzere. But the true wealth
of the region is in trees. One-third of Portugal is covered with trees, with
the Beiras among the most prominent of the forested areas. The scents of
pine, eucalyptus, resin, and wood smoke are pervasive. Forests, from
productive extents of oaks and Aleppo and umbrella pines to the hundreds
of exotic varieties at Buçaco, form the backdrop to all the area's breathtaking panoramas. Wood pulp, used to make paper and cardboard, is the
main product of the forests, as well as Portugal's biggest foreign currency
earner after tourism and textiles.

Above the forests rise the mountains, the other key to the soul of the
Beiras. Where the craggy terrain can no longer support crops, sheep and
goats are the mainstay of Portugal's mountain communities. The animals
provide wool, milk, and *queijo da serra,* one of Portugal's most sought
after delicacies. For hundreds of years, between December and May, this
oozy ewe's milk cheese has been made by hand in the farmhouse dairies of
the Serra da Estrela — an area of production that is now strictly limited
by law. Every restaurant in the region serves *queijo da serra,* and shopkeepers will be happy to help buyers choose a properly ripe one.

The Beiras also produce what many consider to be Portugal's finest wines — the smooth, strong dão reds and crisp dão whites, which take their name from the Dão River, a tributary of the Mondego. The demarcated zone centers on the town of Viseu and includes some 1,200 square miles, although vines can be grown on little more than 5% of the land. The zone's high, forested terrain, rocky granite soil, and climate of hot summers and cold, wet winters give dão reds their distinctive flavor — silky with a slight earthy tang — and their strength, averaging 12% alcohol. The whites have a clean, fresh taste. The best age for a good dão red is 7 to 10 years, but whites get no better after 3 years, the experts say.

This route, focusing on the heart of the region where the three Beiras meet, begins in the historic university city of Coimbra and winds eastward into the Serra da Estrela mountains (encompassed since 1976 by the Serra da Estrela Natural Park, which seeks to protect the plant and animal life, as well as the environment, culture, and traditions of Portugal's most extensive and highest mountain range). It dips south across the *serra* — detouring toward the summit of the 6,532-foot-high Torre, Portugal's highest peak, if desired — to the wool town of Covilhã and then travels along the verdant valley of the Zêzere River to the *serra*'s northeastern tip at Guarda, the country's highest town. A modern highway leads westward to Viseu in the heart of the Dão wine region, from where the route descends through the forested *serras* of Caramulo and Buçaco back to Coimbra.

The round-trip distance, about 550 miles (878 km), can be covered comfortably in 5 to 7 days. Distances between possible overnight stops are short, which allows for leisurely detours to villages and other sights along the way, since many attractions lie off the principal roads. Nevertheless, drivers should be cautious and allow plenty of time for traveling; driving in the Beiras is enjoyable, but it can be taxing. Many of the roads are steep and narrow, twisting up hillsides in sharp hairpin bends, and some are in poor repair. Stop at the designated viewing points (signposted *miradouros*) to enjoy the magnificent views. In winter, the roads can be treacherously icy and snow occasionally makes it impossible to cross the Serra da Estrela.

Although the region has not been commercialized by tourism, it does not lack comfortable accommodations, which include the luxury of the *Palace Hotel do Buçaco* — among the finest in Europe — and other pleasant hotels, plus government-owned *pousadas* and small, welcoming inns and *pensões*. Also available, under Portugal's *Turismo no Espaço Rural* (Tourism in the Country) program, are rooms in privately owned houses, including the manor houses and other stately country homes that are part of the *Turismo de Habitação* network and the simpler rural houses and farmhouses categorized as *Turismo Rural* and *Agroturismo* (for additional information, see *Pousadas and Manor Houses* in DIVERSIONS). Most hotels are small, and booking ahead is essential for the peak summer and winter seasons, particularly at the *pousadas*. Expect to pay $150 or more for a double room at the very expensive *Palácio de Buçaco,* $100 to $150 in establishments listed as expensive, $50 to $100 in moderate places, and less than $50 in inexpensive ones.

Excellent country fare — such as roast mountain kid, trout, and a delicious variety of sausages — is offered at even the simplest of restaurants. The majority of the best restaurants belong to hotels or pensions, leaving relatively few independent places in the listings. Most restaurant meals, including wine, will be in the moderate range, meaning from $30 to $50 for two, but there are many small places where an inexpensive meal for two will cost under $25.

For each location, hotels and restaurants are listed alphabetically by price category.

COIMBRA For a detailed report on the city, its sights, hotels, and restaurants, see *Coimbra,* THE CITIES.

En Route from Coimbra Take N17, which leads northeast out of the city to the edge of the Serra da Estrela. You'll soon be climbing steep hills clothed in tall pine trees. Black-clad women balancing baskets on their heads, heavily laden donkey carts, and terraced plots of vines and fruit trees high on the hillsides are an indication of how the people of the Beiras earn their livelihoods. After about 9½ miles (15 km), turn right onto N236 to Lousã, crossing the Arouce River, which was named after an early king, Arunce, whose court was at Conímbriga. Arouce Castle, with an imposing square watchtower and a brook winding around its base, dominates a nearby hillside. Historians date the fortress to the 11th century, but according to legend, it was built during the 1st century BC for the protection of King Arunce's daughter when the king fled to the forests below to escape pirate attacks. Most of the present structure is from the 14th century, although it has been heavily damaged by hunters searching for the treasure the king reputedly buried somewhere inside. Ancient hermitages lie on a ridge below.

LOUSÃ This small, busy town is deep in the Arouce Valley, 5 miles (8 km) from the turnoff from N17. Here, wood from the dense forests of the Beiras is still turned into paper at the country's oldest paper mill, founded in 1718. The town has some fine 18th-century houses, former residences of aristocrats. Note those on Rua Norton de Matos, as well as the white-walled Casa da Viscondessa (Rua do Visconde), whose neo-classical frontage and door were added in 1818. The green wooded hills and bare purple crests of the Serra da Lousã sweep southeast from the town, with small villages and farms dotting the forests. At the western end of the range, not far outside Lousã, is its highest peak, the 3,942-foot-high Alto do Trevim, which rewards climbers with spectacular views over much of central Portugal. Close by the peak are the Real Neveiro, or "royal snow caves," where ice used to be dug out for the court in Lisbon, and the Chapel of Santo António da Neve (St. Anthony of the Snow).

En Route from Lousã One road from Lousã leads south across the Serra da Lousã to Castelo Branco. But it is a long haul over difficult mountain roads and, despite breathtaking views, offers too few interesting stopping places to make the journey worthwhile. Instead, return to N17, turn right, and continue eastward toward Seia. After about 25 miles (40 km), a turn to the right leads to Lourosa, an ancient village noted for its pre-Romanesque church; built in the form of a basilica in 912, it is one of the rare religious monuments of its era to survive in Portugal. Continue on N17 another few miles to Venda de Galizes, turning right there onto N230 to visit some particularly picturesque Beiras villages. Follow the narrow road 4 miles (6 km) as it winds through terraced orchards and vineyards amid magnificent mountain views and turn right at the first crossroads, where the tiered granite houses of the village of Avô, rising from the far side of the banks of the Alva River, can be glimpsed below.

AVÔ One of the most attractive of the Beiras' many pleasant villages, Avô has a quiet rural charm that belies its somewhat turbulent past. The village, dating back to the 12th century, was part of a line of defense during the reconquest of Portugal from the Moors, and in the early years of this century, when the country became a republic, it was at the center of a short-lived effort to restore the monarchy. Before crossing the narrow bridge that leads into the village, stop in the courtyard beside the Igreja Matriz (Parish Church). The restored 18th-century church, of medieval origin, has a distinctive entrance with round bell towers rising on each side, linked by a crowning arch; inside is a precious baroque altarpiece. Across the bridge, narrow cobblestone steets, steep alleys, and mossy stone steps weave around Avô's ancient houses, some dating from the 16th and 17th centuries. The sadly dilapidated house of Brás Garcia de Mascarenhas, an early-17th-century poet and adventurer, stands by the water (to the left of the bridge when leaving the village). Modified during the 18th century, it has a beautiful Manueline window at the rear.

En Route from Avô Return to the crossroads and N230, taking it east about a mile to the curious Ponte das Três Entradas (Bridge of the Three Entrances). Three roads meet here, simultaneously crossing the Alvoco and Alva rivers at their junction. Turn right from the bridge to climb a few miles up the steep, narrow, winding road up the Serra do Colcorinho to Aldeia das Dez. Before reaching the village, stop at the Miradouro (Lookout) Penedo da Saudade to take in the exhilarating view.

ALDEIA DAS DEZ The name, meaning Village of the Ten, derives from the ten houses that gave the settlement its start during the 12th century. Set in the folds of the *serra*, Aldeia das Dez is banked too steeply to be traversed easily by streets and is consequently threaded through with cobblestone steps. The stone pillory, a symbol of municipal authority found in towns throughout Portugal, is dated 1661. Most of the village's dwellings are in traditional Beiras style, the lower part built solidly of granite, with wooden balconies sheltered by the roof eaves. Similarly, the lifestyle here is typical of a Beiras farming village — witness the goatskins hung out to dry, the stacks of pine logs dotted about the streets, and the men returning from the fields with hoes on their shoulders. After stopping here, continue another 4 miles (6 km) on the unnamed road to Piodão, a yet more remote and untouched village, built almost entirely of dark schist into the Serra d'Acor mountainside.

CHECKING IN/EATING OUT

Italva The owners of this restaurant, in a large shady square facing the Ponte das Três Entradas, also have 11 comfortable, simply furnished rooms with private baths in the same building, as well as camping facilities across the road. Regional dishes and homemade desserts are served in an airy salon, with nice touches like chrysanthemums on the tables. The house pudding is made of milk, almonds, and cinnamon. Open daily. No reservations. Major credit cards accepted. Ponte das Três Entradas, Avô (phone: 38-57283; fax: 38-57685). Moderate.

En Route from Aldeia das Dez Return to N17 at Venda de Galizes and continue northeast 10½ miles (17 km), skirting the edge of the Parque Natural da Serra da Estrela (Serra da Estrela Natural Park). Turn right onto N231 at the crossroads signposted Seia. The town is 2 miles (3 km) farther along, inside the park at the foot of the mountains. The parish church, of Romanesque origin but rebuilt after the Napoleonic wars of the early 19th century, dominates the town from a hilltop. Shops in the streets around the main square are a good place to buy *queijo da serra,* the ewe's-milk cheese that is justly famed among Portugal's cheeses.

Before penetrating the Serra da Estrela, check whether the roads across the mountain — which are sometimes blocked by snow for short periods from November through May — are passable. If the weather is poor, or time is short, return to N17 and continue north 8 miles (13 km) to the turnoff for Gouveia. If the route is clear, take N339 and climb 7 miles (11 km) to the junction of N339-1 (be sure to avoid the detour to Sabugueiro, the highest village in Portugal, now crowded with souvenir stalls and shops); turn left and continue 2½ miles (4 km) to N232. Continue another 10 miles (16 km) to Gouveia. The road climbs into a desolate landscape where granite crags are strewn with massive boulders, some whipped into strange shapes by the wind and snow. Serpentine roads offer breathless vistas from the plateau, and mountain flowers blossom among the scrub of grass, heather, and *zimbro* (juniper) — the latter used to brew the fiery white brandy, *aguardente de zimbro,* found all over the Beiras.

CHECKING IN

Pousada de Santa Bárbara This modern member of the government-run *pousada* chain was built in the 1970s. It's set among pines on the western edge of the Serra da Estrela, 2 miles (3 km) along N17 from the Oliveira do Hospital turnoff. There are 16 secluded rooms with private baths, plus tennis courts and a swimming pool. Visitors can warm themselves in front of a log fire in the wood-paneled interior and enjoy the view across the hills from the excellent restaurant. Regional specialties include roast kid and trout. Póvoa das Quartas (phone: 38-52252; 212-686-9213 in the US; fax: 38-50545). Expensive.

Camelo Highly regarded and decorated with antiques, this hostelry has 65 rooms and suites with wood-paneled ceilings, pink marble bathrooms, and TV sets. The restaurant is one of only five in the country distinguished by an award from the Portuguese government; specialties include *sopa à nossa moda* (vegetable and veal soup), *bacalhau com broa* (codfish with corn bread and almonds), and *requeijão,* a farmer cheese served as dessert. *Bacalhau* is served at Thursday and Sunday lunch; at other times it has to be ordered in advance. 16 Av. Primeiro de Maio, Seia (phone: 38-22530; fax: 38-23031). Moderate.

Casa do Boco A participant in *Turismo Rural,* this is a large Beiras house in the village of Meruge, on the Cobral River 5 miles (8 km) north of Oliveira do Hospital. Two apartments with double bedrooms are available, for a minimum of 2 nights. Meruge, Lagares da Beira (phone: 38-53318). Moderate.

Seia This elegantly renovated old granite *estalagem* (inn) has 35 rooms with private baths (those in the old section are cozier) and a restaurant; a swimming pool was being built at press time. Av. Afonso Costa, Seia (phone: 38-25866; fax: 38-25538). Moderate.

GOUVEIA An attractive, ancient town in the hills rising from the Mondego Valley, Gouveia is filled with tiny parks, gardens, and lookout points. The town (pop. 4,000) reputedly dates back to the 6th century BC. Just outside of town, it's possible to climb to a pre-Roman fortification, the *castro* of Alfátima, where Julius Caesar is said to have stayed in 38 BC. One of the most attractive buildings in town is the Casa da Torre, a late-17th-century manor house with the sculpted ropes of the Manueline style wreathing its windows. It now houses an information center for the Parque Natural de Serra da Estrela (phone: 38-42158; open daily from 9 AM to 12:30 PM and 2 to 5:30 PM). Branching down from here is the Bairro da Biqueira — a tiny, ancient quarter of winding alleys and carefully tended houses that overlooks the town's southern entrance. The center of 14th-century Gouveia's Jewish community, it can be entered by any of the small streets directly in front of the Casa da Torre. The imposing *paço* (palace) was built during the 18th century, originally as a Jesuit school, although the Jesuits were able to use it for only a few years before they were expelled from Portugal by the Marquês de Pombal. Directly uphill from the *paço,* an esplanade leading off the small baroque Calvário chapel affords splendid views of the Mondego Valley. Farther along is the Jardim Infantil, a children's park with animal and bird topiaries, swings and slides, an aviary, and a merry-go-round.

In March, a fair dedicated to *queijo da serra* takes place in Gouveia, but all of the rural trades and crafts around which local life revolves are on display during the *Festas do Senhor do Calvário,* a summer festival held on the second Sunday of August. A religious procession and folk dances are the highlights of the festival, but parts of the event are devoted to the dark honey of the Beiras — which owes its special flavor to the mountain flowers the bees feed on — and to a competition for Serra da Estrela sheepdogs.

CHECKING IN

Casa Grande Three apartments with double bedrooms are available in a 16th-century manor house (with a façade, entrance hall, and upper quarter added in the 18th century) at this *Turismo Rural* participant in Paços da Serra, 5 miles (8 km) south of Gouveia on N330. All the apartments have log fireplaces. Extra rooms can be provided for larger families. There also are 3 cottages, each with a double bedroom and kitchenette. Breakfast and firewood in the winter are included. Paços da Serra (phone: 38-43341; reservations in Vilamoura: 89-314867; reservations in Porto: 2-816587). Moderate.

Gouveia In the center of town, this hostelry has 27 rooms and 4 suites, all with private baths, central heating, radios, TV sets, telephones, and a restaurant. Guests have access to the municipal swimming pool and tennis courts. Av. Primeiro de Maio, Gouveia (phone: 38-42890). Moderate.

Estrela A 20-room *pensão* (some with private baths) with a small, highly regarded restaurant, looking out over the Mondego Valley. Ask for No. 205 — it has a wraparound balcony with the same vista. 36 Av. da República, Gouveia (phone: 38-42171). Inexpensive.

EATING OUT

O Julio A few hundred yards beyond the Casa da Torre, this regionally known restaurant offers specialities using *chouriço* and *morcela* (pork and blood sausage), and *bacalhau* (cod). Closed Tuesdays. No reservations. No credit cards accepted. Travessa do Loureiro, Gouveia (phone: 38-42142). Moderate.

En Route from Gouveia Follow signs out of Gouveia toward Guarda and Viseu, turning right onto N17 and heading north for about 7 miles (11 km) through a beautiful stretch of pink-granite hills and scrub, punctuated with isolated, leaning pine trees. At the sign for Carrapichana take the right-hand exit heading east and continue for 4 miles (6 km), following signs for Linhares, one of the loveliest and least spoiled of the ancient fortress-villages in the Serra da Estrela region. The road twists slowly up the mountainside, offering wide vistas of the valley below.

LINHARES Established by King Dinis I in 1169, but inhabited since pre-Roman times, Linhares (pop. 463) was at different times named Lenio and Leniobriga. Its castle at the north end of the main square is thought to have been built by the Romans to guard the imperial road from Conímbriga to Guarda. The castle was destroyed by the Moors in the 8th century, later rebuilt, then taken and retaken by Moors and Christians until the 12th-century reign of Dom Afonso Henriques. The village was once entirely enclosed within the castle keep. If the castle is locked, ask for the key at the café on the southwest side of the square; they also serve excellent cheese sandwiches on homemade bread. Weekday afternoons, women scrub laundry on the rocks at the fountain in front of the castle.

On a small, granite terrace opposite the castle is a *tribuna* (pulpit), the ancient forum for the town's tribunal meetings. Many of the houses near the forum have 15th-century carved-stone windows. The most elaborate examples can be seen in two former manor houses, the Casa das Pinas and the Casa Corte Real. By the side of the Igreja da Misericórdia (at the east end of the square), a shady country lane lined with chestnut and pine trees ambles downhill past the village cemetery. Footpaths off it lead to meadows and streams.

En Route from Linhares Return to N17 and head south. At the Gouveia exit, take N232 toward Manteigas and Covilha. The road climbs for 2 miles (3 km) to a magnificent view of the Penhas Douradas, a line of three peaks called "golden crests" because they glow in the setting sun. They rise up to 5,471 feet and, like other Serra da Estrela summits, remain capped with snow for all but the three hottest summer months. Continuing to Manteigas, the road begins to descend through 9 miles (14 km) of tortuous bends to the town, which lies at an altitude of 2,362 feet. The scenery is superb: Small waterfalls cascade down the mossy rocks, tumbling through tunnels under the road or freezing into a wild filigree of ice in winter. Tall pines provide green, leafy shade, while ferns, golden and red in the fall, light up the slopes.

MANTEIGAS This picturesque town of 5,000 is deep in the valley of the Zêzere River. Its white, pink, and beige houses reflect the bright mountain light; the air is crisp and invigorating, the tranquillity refreshing. Viriatus and his Lusitanian warriors are reputed to have used it as one of their last refuges from the Romans during the 2nd century BC. The square beside the church has a charming bandstand and offers engaging views over the town's steep, tiled rooftops.

Manteigas is a good place to gather information about the scenic road just ahead — some of the most striking sites are in the immediate vicinity southeast of the town, with good hiking trails and resting spots. There is an excellent Posto de Turismo in the main square (2 Praça Dr. Jose Caro; phone: 75-981129). Just down the street is a local branch of the Serra da Estrela Park Service (Rua Primeiro de Maio; phone: 75-98282; open daily from 9 AM to 12:30 PM and 2 to 5:30 PM), which sells the most detailed map and an English-language hiking guide — *Discovering Estrela*. The book includes information about hikes in the region, including times, distances, geographic profiles, and descriptions of flora and fauna, landmarks, villages, and towns along the way.

CHECKING IN

Casa de São Roque There are 5 rooms (some with private baths) and 1 suite in this 19th-century townhouse that is a *Turismo de Habitação* participant. The vine-covered terrace above a courtyard garden is ideal for eating breakfast or sunbathing while looking out on the valley. Two of the guestrooms face the garden, which blooms well into winter. A downstairs lounge has a fireplace, wing chairs, and a kitchenette. 67 Rua de António, Manteigas (phone: 75-981125; in Lisbon: 1-848-8230). Moderate.

Pousada de São Lourenço A 20-room *pousada* of modern vintage, but built of granite high in the hills along the descent to Manteigas from the Penhas Douradas, 8 miles (13 km) north of town. It has private baths, wooden paneling, roaring fireplaces, and marvelous views from its balconies and terraces. The restaurant serves a wealth of excellent regional dishes such as *batatas à caçoila* (pork and potatoes), and regional wines. Estrada de Gouveia, Manteigas (phone: 75-982450; 212-686-9213 in the US; fax: 75-982453). Moderate.

EATING OUT

Serradalto Picture windows overlooking the valley and stuffed heads of mountain game on the walls are just two of the most prominent features of this large eatery on the town's main street. The other is the local fare; specialties include *truta* (trout grilled with oil and herbs) and *cabrito no forno* (stuffed baked kid). There are also 17 guestrooms. Rua Primeiro de Maio, Manteigas (phone: 75-981151). Moderate.

En Route from Manteigas Leave town heading south on N338, passing through Caldas de Manteigas, a small spa town with Alpine-style houses. Cross the bridge over the Zêzere River. Here it's possible to visit a fish farm, the Pôsto Aquícola da Fonte Santa, to see trout gleaming in the clear water before they are released into mountain lakes and rivers. It's open daily from 9:30 to 11 AM and 1 to 5 PM; no admission charge. A narrow, poorly surfaced road turns off to the left, leading about 4 miles (6 km) up through stirring views to the Poço de Inferno (Well of Hell), where a cataract crashes from wooded heights into a limpid pool below. (In winter, it freezes into a wild weave of ice.)

Continue on N338 as it follows the upper valley of the Zêzere — actually a deep trough formed by an Ice Age glacier. Springs and waterfalls tumble down the slopes into the river, and cabins of rough stone, some built in crevices beneath huge boulders, dot the hillsides. Stop at Covão de Ametade, a mountain glade within a steep-walled valley. There are white birch and pine trees, meadows, brooks, and looming granite crags. A tourist post (open daily from 9 AM to 5 PM; closed in winter) orients visitors to the trail markings leading to Lagoa dos Cantaros, a mountain lake.

As the route climbs toward Torre, the highest point in Portugal (its name, in fact, means tower), snow-covered peaks emerge. At the first crossroads, with N339, a left turn leads to Covilhã; but turn to the right and head 5 miles (8 km) toward the Torre summit and Lagoa Comprida. Pale green moss and lichen lend the strangely shaped rocks an otherworldly appearance as the road rises higher and higher, with the lake of the Covão do Ferro dam below on the left. A little farther on, to the right, a statue of Nossa Senhora da Boa Estrela (Our Lady of the Holy Star) has been carved in relief in the black granite. Stone steps lead up to this sanctuary, where a religious festival marked by a long procession is held each year on the second Sunday in August.

The road continues, well surfaced, sufficiently broad, and not too steep; drivers who branch off left at the signpost can drive half a mile right onto the Torre summit, 6,532 feet above sea level. Continue past the Torre signs (passing some tourist shops), through the rocky, lunar-like landscape to Lagoa Comprida, an ancient glacial lake.

Return to N339 and head east for the steep descent to Covilhã, a town tucked into the folds of the mountains at the southeastern edge of the Serra da Estrela Natural Park. The road passes through pine, oak, and chestnut woods along the way, and through Penhas da Saúde, a base for skiers that's in full swing from December through May. There are six ski runs on the 2,590-foot Covão de Loriga slope, which falls away westward from the summit of Torre itself. Ski lessons are available, equipment can be rented, and other activities, such as hiking, climbing, fishing, and camping, are also possible in season. For further information on skiing, contact the *Clube Nacional de Montanhismo* (5 Rua Pedro Alvares Cabral, Covilhã; phone: 75-323364), the *Sede da Região de Turismo da Serra da Estrela* (Praça do Município, Covilhã; phone: 75-322170; fax: 75-313364), or *Turistrela* (111 Rua Rui Faleiro, Covilhã; phone: 75-24933; fax: 75-25213), the company that runs the ski lifts.

CHECKING IN/EATING OUT

O Pastor A small, 9-room *pensão* with ski equipment and toboggans for rent, and a log fire in the lounge for warmth and atmosphere; there's also central heating and some guestrooms have private baths. Specialties of the restaurant include *feijoada serrada* (the traditional Portuguese bean-and-pork stew) and *bacalhau à Pastor* (dried codfish made with grated cheese and cream). Restaurant open daily in the winter and summer peak seasons and closed 1 day weekly (variable) the rest of the year. Major credit cards accepted. Penhas da Saúde (phone: 75-322180; fax: 75-314035). Moderate.

COVILHÃ From Torre to this congenial town (pop. 22,000) on the southeastern slopes of the *serra,* the road drops from 6,532 feet to 2,296 feet in only 12½ miles (20 km). Covilhã is an ancient town, thought to have been founded by the Romans in 41 BC. For centuries, its life has revolved around the flocks of sheep that graze on the mountains, providing raw materials for the town's main industries: dairy products such as *queijo da serra* and wool. But today, much of its livelihood also derives from the winter sports enthusiasts who flock to the area. The intimate relationship with the Serra da Estrela comes as no surprise — almost every street in town offers a stirring panorama of the mountains above and the plains to the south and east.

The earthquake that devastated Lisbon in 1755 also destroyed many of Covilhã's houses and most of the town walls, with their five gates. But what is left is well worth a visit. The stairs behind the municipal building on Praça do Município lead to the Old Town, where houses with 17th-century carved-stone, pillared verandahs line narrow streets, such as Rua da Assunção. The orange roof tiles of other houses extend down over their sides, in typical Beiras style. Other sights include the Praça das Flores, an airy, carefully manicured *jardim publico* (city park) along the tree-lined Avenida Frei Heitor Pinto. The Capela de São Martinho e Calvário, in the lower part of town, is a simple Romanesque chapel of rough stone housing an 18th-century painting of the Crucifixion and two primitive representations of saints.

CHECKING IN

Montalto A comfortable, family-run *residencial* on a quiet corner of the main square, it has 14 rooms, all with baths, TV sets, telephones, and heat. Rooms on the first floor have plant-covered balconies. There's no restaurant, but breakfast is served. Praça do Município, Covilhã (phone: 75-327609). Moderate.

EATING OUT

Solneve Regional dishes, including *truta do paul* (grilled trout with lemon and butter sauce) and roast mountain kid, are the specialties here. Open daily.

No reservations. Major credit cards accepted. 126 Av. Visconde da Coriscada, Covilhã (phone: 75-323001). Moderate.

Café Regional Although this is a good, modest *pensão* in the center, with 20 rooms and shared baths, it is especially recommended for its restaurant, which serves regional specialties such as *panela no forno* (baked rice with pork). Closed Sundays for dinner, Mondays, and the first 2 weeks of September. Reservations unnecessary. Major credit cards accepted. 4-6 Rua das Flores, Covilhã (phone: 75-322596). Inexpensive.

En Route from Covilhã Take N18 north out of town. The road winds through the green, fertile valley of the Zêzere — the river basin here is a rich farming region known as the Cova da Beira — up to Guarda, 24 miles (38 km) from Covilhã. Go 4 miles (7 km) north, exiting at signs for Caria and Sabugal; then head east about 10½ miles (17 km) on N18-3. Turn left at a small sign for Sortelha, and follow signs up the hillside to a Gothic gate in the village's intact walls, which were built in 1187. Its castle (always open) is perched on a steep, craggy outcrop, high over a wooded valley. This ancient fortress village and the surrounding countryside, virtually unaltered over centuries, has long been cloaked in legends of witches, warriors, and werewolves.

Take N18 north for 7 miles (11 km), and make a short detour to the right onto N345, signposted Belmonte. This hilltop town, commanded by a medieval castle, was the birthplace of Pedro Alvares Cabral, who discovered Brazil in 1500; the Romanesque São Tiago church, where he is buried, can be seen.

GUARDA High on an exposed hilltop overlooking Spain (the border is only 29½ miles/47 km away), this town (pop. 15,000) of granite buildings, lantern-lit alleys, and pillared balconies breathes a medieval atmosphere that brings its history vividly to life. Buffeted by rough winds and winter snow, Guarda, at 3,281 feet, is the highest town in Portugal, and its hardy, hearty character reflects its historic role as the first stronghold against successive invasions from across the frontier.

Guarda has been inhabited since prehistoric times, and Julius Caesar is thought to have used it as a military base. The Visigoths and then the Moors took it; after Afonso Henriques, the first King of Portugal, recaptured it, the town was enlarged, fortified, and officially founded by King Sancho I, in 1199. A statue of Sancho stands in the main square, the Praça da Sé (also known as Praça Luís de Camões), to the north of which stands the Sé itself, a magnificent cathedral whose granite stones look almost as pristine as the day they were cut from the surrounding hills more than 500 years ago. To the right is the Paço de Concelho (Town Hall), and to the left is the charming building housing the tourist office (phone: 71-222251). The cathedral was begun in 1390 and completed in 1540, a passage of time that resulted in a mixture of Renaissance and Manueline styles with the original Gothic. The flying buttresses, pinnacles, and gargoyles of the exterior are reminiscent of the monastery at Batalha. (The two buildings both feature work by the master architect Boytac and the Mateus Fernandes family.) The cathedral's main doorway, flanked by two octagonal bell towers, is Manueline; inside is a vaulted interior containing a Renaissance altarpiece by Jean de Rouen. It consists of more than 100 figures, sculpted in high relief and painted in gold and white, depicting scenes from the life of Christ on panels that rise to the arched windows. Through a magnificent Renaissance doorway is the Capela dos Pinas, which holds the late Gothic tomb of a cathedral founder. He is said to have thrown himself from the roof after he asked the people if the building had any defects — and an old lady replied that the door was too small. The cathedral is open from 9 AM to 12:30 PM and 2 to 5:30 PM; closed Mondays. There is a charge to climb to the top of the towers.

From the Praça da Sé, walk through an ancient alleyway to the Torre dos Ferreiros (Blacksmiths' Tower), one of three of the original six gates still standing amid the ruins of the 12th- and 13th-century town walls. (The other two are the Porta da Estrela and the Porta do Rei; the castle keep, or Torre de Menagem, also remains from the original fortifications.) Cross the tree-lined street to the restored 17th-century Misericórdia church, with its attractive white pediment between two pinnacled bell towers; it has a carved wooden ceiling and a baroque altar and pulpits. Farther along the same street is the *Museu da Guarda* (phone: 71-213460), housed in the 17th-century Bishop's Palace, which has been elegantly modernized and extended. Primitive paintings, sculptures, and ancient town manuscripts are on the ground floor; upstairs are examples of the trades and handicrafts of the region, ranging from linen weaving and silk making to basketry, pottery, and ironwork. The museum is open from 10 AM to 12:30 PM and 2 to 5:30 PM; closed Mondays; admission charge.

CHECKING IN

Solar de Alarcão Spending a night at this 17th-century manor house, within yards of the cathedral, is a delightful way to experience Guarda. A *Turismo de Habitação* property, it has a covered terrace, a private chapel, and a garden with a belvedere offering views over the Spanish plains. The 3 rooms with private baths and 1 suite are beautifully decorated with antiques and tapestries. 25-27 Largo Dom Miguel Alarcão, Guarda (phone: 71-211275). Expensive.

De Turismo A sprawling hotel built in the style of a manor house, this *Best Western* member has views across the plains. It has 105 rooms and suites, all with private baths, TV sets, and mini-bars. There are 3 bars, a private discotheque, a pool, a sizable conference room, and a garage. The large restaurant serves Portuguese and international fare. Av. Coronel Orlindo de Carvalho, Guarda (phone: 71-212205; 800-528-1234 in the US; fax: 71-212204). Moderate.

Filipe In the town center, this is a comfortable *pensão* with 40 rooms (not all with private baths) and a restaurant. 9 Rua Vasco da Gama, Guarda (phone: 71-212658; fax: 71-221402). Moderate.

Quinta da Ponte An 18th-century manor house, it stands on grounds in a quiet river valley. There are 12 rooms with private baths and a suite. For additional details, see *Pousadas and Manor Houses* in DIVERSIONS. 16 Estrada Nacional, Faia, Guarda (phone: 71-96126; in Lisbon, phone and fax: 1-691508). Moderate.

EATING OUT

A Mexicana Right outside town on the road to Spain, this is a good restaurant whose specialties include *tornedós à mexicana* (tournedos of beef), *lombinho à Beira Alta* (pork loin), *garoupa com môlho de camarão* (grouper with shrimp sauce), and shellfish. Closed every other Wednesday (market day) for lunch, and for 2 weeks' annual vacation (variable). Reservations unnecessary except for large parties. Major credit cards accepted. Estrada Nacional 16, Guarda (phone: 71-211512). Moderate.

O Telheiro A bit farther (about a mile/1 km) from the town center on the road to Spain, this large dining room offers panoramic views and good regional cooking, as well as French and Italian dishes. Meals can be served on the terrace in fine weather, or visitors can recover from the winter cold in a bar with deep leather armchairs and a log fire. Open daily. Reservations unnecessary. Major credit cards accepted. Estrada Nacional 16, Guarda (phone: 71-211356). Moderate.

Casa Reduto Good home cooking in a small friendly place in the town center. Specialties include kid and *choriçada,* based on a variety of homemade sausages. Open daily. Reservations unnecessary. Major credit cards accepted. 36 Rua Francisco de Passos, Guarda (phone: 71-211879). Inexpensive.

En Route from Guarda Following signs out of Guarda for Viseu will lead to the modern highway, IP5, that cuts across the northern tip of the Serra da Estrela some 55 miles (88 km) west to Viseu. About halfway there, in the town of Mangualde, just off the highway to the left, is a 17th-century aristocratic estate, the Palácio dos Condes de Anadia, with some fine 17th- and 18th-century *azulejos.* It's open daily from 2 to 6 PM, and occasionally also in the morning; admission charge.

VISEU A fresh-faced country town set among vineyards, orchards, and pine-forested hills, Viseu exudes life and a long, cultured history. Every Tuesday, crowds jostle amid the colorful stalls of the weekly market on the narrow, medieval streets of the Old Town. In August and September, people from across the Beiras flock to the annual *São Mateus* fair (black pottery, lace, and carpets are among the traditional crafts to look for). And every June 24, a procession of horseback riders and floats from outlying Vil de Moinhos (Village of the Water Mills) winds through town to the Chapel of São João de Carreira. According to tradition, the annual procession began in 1652 as a gesture of thanks from the millers of Vil de Moinhos to their patron saint, John the Baptist, after a dispute with local farmers over the use of water from the Paiva River was decided in their favor. Rich corn bread, or *broa,* baked from flour milled in Vil de Moinhos can still be bought in Viseu's market, while the cakes and sweetmeats found in the local cafés — *papos de anjo* (angel's cheeks) and *doces d'ovos* (made from eggs, almonds, and lots of sugar) — come from old convent recipes. *Pasteleria Horta* (22 Rua Formosa; phone: 32-22060) is one of the city's grand old cafés, and a good place to sample homemade pastries and regional sweets.

Walk up the hill from the tree-lined main square, Praça da República or Rossio, through the Porta do Soar, a 15th-century gate that leads into the Old Town, and turn right to the Adro da Sé (Cathedral Square), the historical heart of Viseu. On the left, strikingly silhouetted against the sky, is the white façade of the Igreja da Misericórdia, a pure baroque church with twin bell towers, a delicate doorway topped by a balcony, and a magnificent organ. Across the square are the weathered granite towers of the Sé (Cathedral), which dates from the 13th century but was extensively restored between the 16th and 18th centuries. Inside, its graceful vaulting of knotted ropes reflects the seafaring themes of the 16th-century Manueline style, while its gilded wood altarpiece is baroque. The sacristy has 18th-century tiled walls and a wooden ceiling painted with plants and animals; from the Renaissance cloister, a beautiful late-Gothic doorway leads back into the church.

The *Museu de Grão Vasco* (phone: 32-26249), perhaps Viseu's greatest treasure, is housed in the former 16th-century Paço Episcopal (Bishop's Palace) next to the cathedral. Grão Vasco — the Great Vasco — is the name given to Vasco Fernandes (1480–ca. 1543), the founder of a notable school of painting that flourished in Viseu during the 16th century. Two of his masterpieces, *Calvary* and *St. Peter on His Throne,* are on display in the museum, along with a series of 14 panels, originally from the cathedral altarpiece, painted by him and his collaborators. (One of the kings in the *Adoration of the Magi* panel is depicted as Indian from newly discovered Brazil.) The collection also contains two paintings — *The Last Supper* and *Christ in the House of Martha* — by Gaspar Vaz, another master of the Viseu school. The museum is open from 10 AM to 12:30 PM and 2 to 5 PM; closed Mondays; admission charge. Streets off the Praça do Sé, such as Rua Senhora de Boa Morte and Rua Augusto Hilario, wind through the heart of the Old Town to Rua Direita.

CHECKING IN

Avenida Comfortable and overlooking the main square, it has 40 rooms. The restaurant serves regional dishes. 1 Av. Alberto Sampaio, Viseu (phone: 32-423432; fax: 32-25643). Moderate.

Grão Vasco Set in attractive gardens in the town center, this spacious hostelry has 110 rooms, an outdoor pool, a discotheque, and central heating. The restaurant serves meals on the garden terrace in good weather. Rua Gaspar Barreiros, Viseu (phone: 32-423511; 800-528-1234 in the US; fax: 32-27047). Moderate.

Quinta do Vale do Chão This fine 17th-century house, a *Turismo Rural* participant, offers 2 suites, each with a large living room (only one has a private bathroom) — and the run of the rest of the house. Children are welcome. It's located 10 miles (16 km) south of Viseu on N231 at Santar, the birthplace of Dom Duarte de Bragança, the man who would be king if Portugal were still a monarchy. The small village has many attractive 18th-century houses. Santar (phone: 32-944319; in Lisbon: 1-765974). Moderate.

EATING OUT

O Cortiço An excellent restaurant in the medieval part of town, it serves dishes based on old local recipes, whose details are kept secret. Some of the many specialties include *arroz caqueirado* (veal with rice), *coelho bêbado* (stewed rabbit in wine sauce), and *bacalhau podre* (cod steaks in tomato and wine sauce). Closed *Christmas*. Reservations unnecessary. Major credit cards accepted. 43 Rua Augusto Hilário, Viseu (phone: 32-423853). Moderate.

Trave Negra Also in the Old Town, it specializes in traditional dishes, including kid and *espetadas* (kebab-style meat or fish on a skewer). Closed Mondays. Reservations advised. Major credit cards accepted. 36 Rua dos Loureiros, Viseu (phone: 32-26130). Moderate.

En Route from Viseu Take N3 south 15 miles (24 km) through wooded hills to Tondela, then turn right onto N230, following signs for Caramulo, another 12 miles (19 km) away. The N230 highway winds up through the wild pine, oak, and chestnut woods of the Serra do Caramulo, dense with ferns and brambles and interspersed with terraces of olive and other fruit trees and vines.

CARAMULO This small, well-groomed health resort, full of cypress trees and box hedges, stands at an altitude of 2,500 feet, basking in crisp air and exhilarating views. The *Museu de Caramulo* (phone: 32-861270) features an unexpected mixture of vintage cars and fine art. The automobiles, all in pristine condition, include a 1911 Rolls-Royce, classic 1930s Bugattis, a 1924 Hispano-Suiza, and the suitably sober 1937 armored Mercedes used by António de Oliveira Salazar, Portugal's late dictator. Upstairs, the art collection includes a few lesser-known works by Picasso, Dalí, and Chagall, some fine Portuguese primitives, and 16th-century tapestries. The museum is open daily from 10 AM to 6 PM; admission charge.

Several imposing panoramas are within easy reach of Caramulo. Drive 5 miles (8 km) west along Avenida Abel de Lacerda, which becomes N230-3, to reach the foot of Caramulinho, the highest peak of the Serra do Caramulo. It's possible to climb a steep, rocky path to the summit, 3,527 feet high, for an impressive view. Returning toward Caramulo, branch right to Cabeço da Neve, a 3,264-foot-high peak with a view south over the villages of the Mondego River Valley. Pinoucas, a 3,481-foot-high peak offering a magnificent panorama over the *serra,* is 2 miles (3 km) north of Caramulo, via N230 and then a dirt road.

CHECKING IN/EATING OUT

Pousada de São Jerónimo A modern, government-owned inn with spectacular views from the 6 guestrooms (all with private baths) and the dining room. Roaring fires, wooden beams, and an elegant restaurant make this an excellent setting in which to enjoy mountain walks, trout fishing, and seclusion. There also is a badminton court and an outdoor pool. Estrada Nacional 230, Caramulo (phone: 32-861291; 212-686-9213 in the US; fax: 32-861640). Moderate.

En Route from Caramulo Follow N230 back toward Tondela and turn right onto N2. Santa Comba Dão, a pretty village where the Dão flows into the Mondego, is 10 miles (16 km) farther south. It is best known as Salazar's birthplace, but no statue remains of the dictator, and his abandoned family house has fallen into disrepair. Turn right at Santa Comba Dão onto N234, passing the lovely village of Mortágua on the 16-mile (26-km) journey to the Mata do Buçaco — the ancient forest of Buçaco — and the famed spa of Luso.

BUÇACO A secluded forest that was tended by monks for more than 1,000 years, the stirring history of a decisive battle, and a romantic summer palace built by a king are all woven into the magic of Buçaco, a 2-square-mile national park atop the northernmost peak of the Serra do Buçaco. Benedictine monks first built a refuge in the primitive forest during the 6th century, and priests from Coimbra cared for the woodland from the 11th to the early 17th century. In 1628, barefoot Carmelite monks began erecting a monastery, ringing the forest with a wall to keep the outside world at bay. The monks carefully tended their domain, adding maples, laurels, Mexican cedars, and many exotic varieties from seeds gathered by their missions around the globe. Earlier, in 1622, a papal bull banned women from the forest, and in 1643, a second bull prohibited damage to the trees — punishment for either offense was excommunication. When religious orders were suppressed in Portugal in 1834, the care of Buçaco passed to the state. There are now some 400 native tree varieties and 300 exotic ones, from eucalyptus and oaks to sequoias and evergreen thujas.

In 1888, King Carlos commissioned Luigi Manini, an Italian architect and a set painter at the *Teatro Nacional de São Carlos* in Lisbon, to build a summer palace and hunting lodge in the midst of the forest. Much of the Carmelite monastery, including the library, was demolished to make way for it, leaving only a small church and a cloister. The building that emerged is a marvelously extravagant pastiche of the Manueline style, with pinnacles, battlements, towers, arched windows, and a magnificent gallery of 12 double arches in the style of the cloister at the Mosteiro dos Jerónimos in Lisbon. Panels of *azulejos* by renowned Portuguese artists depict scenes from the 16th-century epic *Os Lusíadas,* by Portugal's national poet Luís de Camões, on the outside walls, and famous battle scenes in the interior. The palace was completed in 1907, but King Carlos, who was assassinated in 1908, never occupied it, although his son and successor, King Manuel II, stayed in Buçaco in 1910 — reputedly with a mistress — before seeking exile in England. The palace then became a hotel (see *Checking In*), which is well worth a visit.

Buçaco was the scene of a decisive battle of the Peninsular War, when in 1810 the British general Sir Arthur Wellesley, the future Duke of Wellington, commanding 50,000 Portuguese and British troops, defeated Napoleon's army. Processions on the anniversary of the battle are still held today.

A walk anywhere in Buçaco is enjoyable, particularly if crowded weekends and holidays are avoided. Among the loveliest features is the Fonte Fria (Cold Fountain), where waters that spring from a cave cascade down 144 stone steps into a pool. The path from here leads past a small lake to the Rua dos Fetos (Fern Lane), a 250-yard pathway lined with tall cypresses. The Via Sacra, or Way of the Cross, is a series of 20 small 18th-century chapels in which scenes leading up to the Crucifixion are depicted by terra cotta figures (fashioned in 1938 — sadly, many of them have since been damaged). A few hundred yards outside the Portas de Sula, at the park's southeastern corner, an obelisk topped by a glass star commemorates the Battle of Buçaco and other engagements of the Luso-Britannic campaigns, and offers magnificent views of the Estrela and Caramulo *serras.* Down the hill toward the Portas da Rainha is the interesting *Museu Militar do Buçaco* (phone: 31-939310), a military museum featuring maps, weapons, uniforms, and models from the battle and related campaigns. It's open Tuesdays through Saturdays from 9 AM to 5:30 PM from March through November; from 10 AM to 5 PM the rest of the year. The museum keeper, who lives next door, will open the museum to after-hours visitors; there's an admission charge. One of the trees in Buçaco is an olive tree, the symbol of peace, planted by Wellington after the heavy fighting that led to his victory.

CHECKING IN/EATING OUT

Palace Hotel do Buçaco One of the finest hotels in Portugal, it was built by a king as his summer palace, and it immerses present-day guests in an atmosphere of turn-of-the-century romance and royal luxury. Many of the 60 sumptuous rooms open onto broad terraces, from which guests can watch the stars over the deep green forest. Fine international cooking and local dishes are served under a vaulted, Renaissance-style cupola in good weather, with wine from the hotel's famed cellars, which guests can visit on request. The elegant period charm of the palace and its wonderful setting make it one of the most pleasurable places to stay in the entire country. Mata do Buçaco, Buçaco (phone: 31-930101; in Lisbon: 1-793-1024; fax: 31-930509). Very expensive.

En Route from Buçaco From the gate at the northern tip of Buçaco National Park, head 2 miles (3 km) south to Luso.

LUSO This attractive, bustling spa town on the northwest slope of the Serra do Buçaco is famed for the curative properties of its waters, which rise at a temperature of 80F from a spring in the town center. Bottled Luso, one of the country's most famous mineral waters, is sold all over Portugal. Here, a pavilion given over to physiotherapy has a heated swimming pool, gyms, mud baths, and other specialized installations, where treatment is given under medical supervision. But Luso is a relaxing and enjoyable place to visit even for those not "taking the waters," and it's a less expensive base for visiting Buçaco than the *Palace* hotel. The town has a splendid outdoor swimming pool and visitors can row on a lake, play tennis, or jog around a special circuit; in addition, there's a cinema, a nightclub, and a discotheque, as well as several hotels and small pensions.

CHECKING IN

Grande Hotel das Termas Large and comfortable, it adjoins the thermal baths and is run by the same company that operates them. It offers 173 rooms, a restaurant, indoor and outdoor swimming pools, tennis, squash, miniature golf, and a disco. Some rooms have satellite TV sets. Rua dos Banhos, Luso (phone: 31-930450; fax: 31-930350). Moderate.

Vila Duparchy On a hill above Luso, this large 19th-century house was built by a French engineer engaged in the construction of the Beiras railroad. A *Turismo de Habitação* participant, it has 6 comfortable guestrooms with modern bathrooms, central heating, 4 living rooms, and a dining room. There is a swimming pool in the spacious garden, which offers a view over the town. Rua José Duarte Figueredo, Luso (phone: 31-939120). Moderate.

Alegre This *pensão* of 21 rooms, all with baths, is a former noble's house and offers a splendid view over the town. It has a good restaurant. Rua Emídio Navarro, Luso (phone: 31-939251). Inexpensive.

Astória A pleasant 12-room *pensão* (some with private baths) with an English country touch. The amenities include a pub. Rua Emídio Navarro, Luso (phone: 31-939182). Inexpensive.

EATING OUT

O Cesteiro This modern eatery offers regional cooking including *chanfana* (kid cooked with red wine) and *leitão* (roast suckling pig) — one of the delicacies of this part of the Beiras. Open daily. Reservations unnecessary. Major credit cards accepted. Rua Monsenhor Raúl Mira, Luso (phone: 31-939360). Inexpensive.

En Route from Luso Drive west 4½ miles (7 km) along N234, a mountain road, past Mealhada to join the main N1, which leads south another 13 miles (21 km) to Coimbra or north 60½ miles (97 km) to Porto. Alternatively, return to Coimbra via the smaller N334.

Central Portugal

The Tagus River is Portugal's Mason-Dixon Line — everything above it is considered "The North" and everything below it, "The South." Crossing Portugal's biggest river heading south is indeed like crossing a frontier. In the space of a few miles the granite of the Beiras fades and a radically different landscape takes its place: terra cotta in color, brilliantly lit, studded with olive, cork, and holm oak trees — unmistakably the landscape of southern Europe.

The two Portuguese provinces where this intriguing transformation occurs are the Ribatejo and its eastern neighbor, the Alto (Upper) Alentejo. The latter is the northern half of a region that is not only by far the largest in the country, but also the least densely populated, the hottest, and the driest. It also produces more cork than anywhere else in the world and has what must be the most readily recognized landscape in Portugal. Apart from the São Mamede range in the northeast, reaching up to 3,382 feet high, and the Ossa range near Evora, with peaks up to 2,154 feet, there are few outcrops in the Alentejo high enough or rocky enough to be called mountains. The whole region unfolds southward from the Tagus River to the Algarve in a practically unbroken succession of low, rolling hills, bright with wildflowers in the spring, ocher in summer. Providing the car's suspension is youthful enough to handle the sometimes rough roads, it is good driving country — the landscape uncluttered, the roads relatively uncrowded.

The topography of the Ribatejo is also distinctive. The area near the town of Santarém is the quintessential Ribatejo — lonely expanses of grassland where egrets and other wild fowl congregate and where horsemen with long wooden lances herd black fighting bulls. The Tagus spreads out here and threads through wide alluvial flats before finally flowing into the estuary above Lisbon. The area has an almost mystical appeal for romantics and aficionados of Portuguese bullfighting and the equestrian arts, but it also has a more prosaic side, as Lisbon's breadbasket and kitchen garden. The big riverside fields, the *lezirias,* produce large quantities of grain and vegetables, and vineyards in the drier zones away from the river produce much of the country's staple table wine.

Both the Alentejo and the Ribatejo are legendary places: lands of giants, heroic deeds, battles, and chivalry. In some places, the traces of human occupation reach back to the Stone Age. During the Iron Age, various Indo-European tribes, probably mostly Celts, drifted across the *mesetas* from Spain, some of them — the ones who were later to become known as Lusitanians — settling the highlands north of the Tagus and elbowing their way into a position of dominance over the whole of the central region. When the Romans turned up during the 2nd century BC, these hillsmen put up fierce resistance under the leadership of Portugal's first truly national hero, the Lusitanian chieftain Viriatus. His death in 139 BC opened the way for the Roman troops and marked the beginning of an occupation of the Ribatejo and Alentejo that lasted some 400 years.

The Roman period was followed by centuries of invasion and settlement by tribes from northern Europe and ultimately by the Visigoths, who ruled until the arrival of the Moors during the 8th century. Little is left of the Visigothic presence, apart from architectural traces in fortifications, but the influence of their Muslim successors, while almost as fugitive in terms of architecture, was more pervasive, and it is detectable today in such things as place-names (many that begin with "al" are Moorish in origin), language, and local tradition.

Moorish dominance lasted until nearly the end of the 12th century. In 1139, Portugal's first king, Afonso Henriques, won a decisive victory at Oric, which may or may not have been the present-day Chã de Ourique, near Santarém; later, he took Santarém itself and, in 1159, the Muslim strongholds of Evora and Beja. By 1190, the area was in Christian hands, its defense largely entrusted to military orders — the Knights Templars in the Ribatejo and the Knights of Avis in the Alentejo — and the Portuguese turned their attention toward their Spanish neighbors. Both the Ribatejo and the Alentejo lay in the path of any army bent on Lisbon, so fortifications became a major preoccupation. One of the legendary figures of the new nation, King Dinis, who ruled from 1279 to 1325, was a prodigious builder: He had a hand in the creation of most of the castles encountered along this route.

Spain, France, Great Britain, and Portugal played their martial chess games until well into the 19th century. Throughout the military maneuvering, however, the Alentejo retained the distinctive social structure it had acquired from the Romans and the Moors. North of the Tagus, inheritance laws and custom turned the countryside into a mosaic of tiny properties. The Alentejo, on the other hand, is the land of the *latifúndio:* the big landed estate where workers are hired (and fired) seasonally and conditions are sometimes close to feudal. An attempt to change the system was made after the April 25 revolution in 1974. Nearly 3 million acres were confiscated in an agrarian reform program, and many of the big estates were turned into collective farms.

The route outlined below, beginning at Lisbon, follows the Tagus up through the Ribatejo, with stops at two towns of great touristic interest: Santarém and Tomar. It then turns inland in the direction of the Spanish border, crossing into the Upper Alentejo. At the spa town of Castelo de Vide, it turns south into the heart of the region, visiting Portalegre, Estremoz, and Evora, one of the most picturesque old cities in Portugal. The route proceeds due west from Evora to Setúbal and the Arrábida Peninsula, which actually fall within the boundaries of a third region, Estremadura, although its cultural and geographic affinity with the Alentejo is so close that travelers will hardly note a difference. After a Setúbal-to-Sesimbra-to-Palmela loop around the peninsula, the route heads back to Lisbon.

Apart from two stretches of toll highway, the route follows the regular main highway system, and the roads are good, with two lanes in either direction. Leave the highway to take one of the secondary roads, however, and be prepared for rougher conditions. Even on main roads, in addition to such rustic hazards as slow-moving tractors, herds of animals, and horse-drawn carts, watch out for locals rattling along at night on little motorcycles. Quite often they don't bother about lights — particularly tail-lights. Finally, try to avoid approaching Lisbon from the south on a Saturday or Sunday evening in summer. That is precisely when everybody else will be trying to get back after a day at the beach, and the lineup before the bridge sometimes stretches for miles.

Regional cooking is served in most dining spots on this itinerary. Meat dishes such as the typical *ensopado de cabrito* or *ensopado de borrego* (kid or lamb stew) are more prevalent than fish dishes in these inland areas, although the rare and pricey *lampréia* (lamprey eel) and *sável* (river shad) are Ribatejo delicacies. Even in the dry Alentejo, *bacalhau* (dried salt cod) dishes are popular, and one of the Alentejo's better-known dishes is *carne de porco à alentejana* (a mixture of clams and pork). A superb ewes' milk cheese is made at Serpa, in the Alentejo, and another at Azeitão on the Arrábida Peninsula. The latter is becoming regrettably hard to find, but it's worth the search. Try both with fresh bread cut from one of the huge, crusty *alentejano* loaves and some of the strong-bodied wine made in the Reguengos or Borba areas.

Predominantly agricultural regions, neither the Ribatejo nor the Alentejo has a highly developed tourist industry. This means that their paths are still relatively untrodden, but it also makes advance planning advisable, because good hotels are not plentiful. Nonetheless, some of the most interesting accommodations in Portugal are to be found along this route. Expect to pay from $125 to $175 for a double room with bath at hotels listed below as expensive; from $80 to $125 at places described as moderate; and less than $80 at inexpensive hostelries. Dinner for two with wine and coffee will cost $70 or more in one of the few expensive restaurants listed, from $45 to $60 in the more common regional places described as moderate, and less than $40 in inexpensive eateries. For each location, hotels and restaurants are listed alphabetically by price category.

En Route from Lisbon Pick up the A1 toll highway on the northern outskirts of town, just past the airport (from downtown, follow signs for the *aeroporto* and the city of Porto). The exit for Santarém, the first major sightseeing stop on this route, is at Km 65. However, if you don't feel like an extended amount of uninterrupted highway driving, an attractive alternative is to drive to Santarém on EN118 on the other side of the river. EN118 is a secondary road, but it provides a closer look at the Ribatejo region. Turn off the A1 at the Vila Franca de Xira exit (follow signs for *Espanha* — Spain), drive across the bridge, and turn onto EN118 6 miles (10 km) down the road at Porto Alto. The road passes through typical Ribatejo wine and cattle country all the way to Almeirim, where you cross the river again into Santarém. Several of the little towns along the way are worth stopping in, perhaps to sample some of the full-bodied red cartaxo wines from this region, found at their simple best in local taverns. The whole area was once a preserve of royalty and the Lisbon aristocracy. At Salvaterra de Magos, for instance, there are the remnants of the once famed palace of the Bragança dynasty. At the height of its glory in the 17th and 18th centuries, the palace boasted its own opera house. Today, all that remains are the Capela Royal (Royal Chapel) and an interesting *falcoaria* (falcon house) with perches for over 300 hawks; both are worth seeing.

SANTARÉM The administrative capital of the Ribatejo and an important market town, Santarém hosts one of Europe's leading agricultural fairs, the *Feira Nacional de Agricultura* (10 days in June, beginning the first Friday of the month), which is accompanied by bullfights and other festivities, as well as the *Festival Nacional de Gastronomia,* a national culinary and handicrafts fair held every November. The city is assumed to stand on or close to the site of the Roman city of Scallabis, an important provincial capital in ancient times that has since disappeared without leaving a physical trace. The city's present name comes from Santa Iria (St. Irene), a 7th-century nun who was martyred in Tomar — according to tradition, her body was thrown into the river and washed ashore here. A statue of the saint stands in a riverside shrine on the edge of town, and it is said that if the river ever rises to touch her feet, the final deluge will have come. Winter flooding is a common scourge here and may even have accounted for the disappearance of Scallabis.

Santarém was conquered by the Moors during the 8th century and reconquered by Portugal's first king, Afonso Henriques, during the 12th century. After that, it grew into a town of considerable strategic importance. King Dinis died here in 1325, and it was here, in 1360, that King Pedro I staged the final act in one of history's great tragic love stories by exacting bloodthirsty revenge on the murderers of his former mistress, Inês de Castro. Several monarchs held court in the city at one time or another, a fact that contributed to its architectural heritage.

In the oldest part of the city, which was once walled and fortified, is the 14th-century Graça church. It has an ornate Portuguese Gothic doorway, but its outstanding feature is a superb rose window above the door, with tracery carved out of a single piece of stone — possibly the finest example of such work in Portugal. Inside is a plain tomb said to hold the remains of the discoverer of Brazil, Pedro Alvares de Cabral. The charming little

13th-century Igreja de São João de Alporão nearby functions as a somewhat disorganized *Museu Arqueológico* (no phone). Its collection includes several Roman pieces, Moorish architectural fragments, and, notably, the beautiful Gothic tomb of Dom Duarte de Meneses, a knight who died in battle against the Moors in 1465. The tomb contains just one tooth — all that could be found after the ferocious contest. The church's original Romanesque bell tower was knocked down to make way for the royal coach of Queen Maria during a visit in 1815, but the 15th-century Torre das Cabaças — so called because of the *cabaças* (gourd-shaped pots) placed around the bell on top to give it greater resonance — still stands. The museum is open from 9 AM to noon and 2 to 5 PM; closed Mondays; no admission charge.

A short distance beyond is the little tree-lined Avenida 5 de Outubro, which leads to an ornamental garden, Portas do Sol, set within the old castle walls. From here, there are panoramic views of the Ribatejo countryside, with the Tagus River and the 4,000-foot-long 19th-century Dom Luís Bridge in the foreground. On the way back to the center, stop in at the Igreja da Marvila, founded by the Knights Templars during the 12th century after Afonso Henriques retook the city from the Moors. This church has a wonderfully ornate Portuguese Gothic porch and, inside, three lofty aisles covered with fine 16th-century *azulejos.* Two more churches, Santa Clara and Santa Cruz, can be seen as the road winds down to the river on the way out of Santarém. Santa Clara, its interior stripped down to its 13th-century bones, is a fine example of early Gothic, with another superb rose window. The early Gothic doorway of Santa Cruz, also founded during the 13th century (by King Dinis), was uncovered during restoration work in the 1960s.

The regional tourist office is at 102 Rua Pedro de Santarém (phone: 43-333318).

CHECKING IN

Alcageme All 67 rooms in this new, modern hostelry have baths and TV sets. There's a bar, but no restaurant. 38 Av. Bernardo Santareno, Santarém (phone: 43-370870 or 43-370870; fax: 43-370850). Moderate.

EATING OUT

Pateo d'Al-Meirim This restaurant, in an old Ribatejo house on the outskirts of the town of Almeirim, 4½ miles (7 km) southeast of Santarém, is famed for its *borrego assado no forno de lenha* (lamb roasted in a wood oven), but it's also a good place to try any of the regional specialties. Closed Mondays. Reservations advised. Major credit cards accepted. 10 Rua das Cancelas, Almeirim (phone: 43-52836). Moderate.

Castiço A popular, regional-style dining spot at the cattle fairground on the outskirts of Santarém. The decor is heavily rustic — the chairs are tree trunks — but the food is good. Try the *magosto de bacalhau* (baked codfish) and the grilled steaks. Open daily. Reservations advised. Major credit cards accepted. Campo da Feira, Santarém (phone: 43-23891). Inexpensive.

O Mal Cozinhado One of Santarém's most popular eateries, and the one with perhaps the strongest regional flavor. It has wooden walls, bullfight posters, a bull's head over the bar, and a husband-and-wife team running a kitchen that produces some of the best dishes in town, including *lombinho com coentros* (pork tenderloin with coriander) and *magosto de bacalhau*. Open daily. No reservations. Major credit cards accepted. Campo da Feira, Santarém (phone: 43-23584). Inexpensive.

Portas do Sol Unpretentious but good regional cooking is served in this small place, which has an outdoor terrace for summer dining. It's inside the Portas do Sol garden, so the surroundings and view are attractive. Closed Mondays. Reservations advised. No credit cards accepted. Jardim das Portas do Sol, Santarém (phone: 43-29520). Inexpensive.

Toucinho A favorite of Ribatejo cooking fans in search of authenticity rather than comfort. Helia, the owner, presides over her open country kitchen and the brick oven where the restaurant's famed bread is baked. Try the various grills or the local specialty, *sopa de pedra* (stone soup, literally), a soup made of beans and a variety of meats and vegetables, and served with a small stone in the bowl. (It doesn't taste the same without it, they say.) Closed Thursdays and August. No reservations. No credit cards accepted. Rua Macau, Almeirim (phone: 43-52237). Inexpensive.

En Route from Santarém Those who haven't already driven over to Almeirim should take N114 across the Dom Luís Bridge and, about 1¼ miles (2 km) beyond it, turn left onto N368 for 6 miles (10 km) to Alpiarça. (Those already in Almeirim should take N118 north 4 miles/7 km to Alpiarça.) Both Almeirim and Alpiarça are little towns that have been favorite country haunts of Portuguese royalty at one time or another — an abundance of game and excellent wines were the attractions. In Alpiarça, stop at the *Casa dos Patudos* (phone: 43-54321), on the left side of the road as you enter the town. This was once the country residence of José Relvas, a prominent political figure and patron of the arts at the beginning of the century. When he died in 1929, he left his house and his sizable art collection to the town as a museum. The Oriental rugs, porcelains, and tiles are outstanding. The museum is open Wednesdays through Sundays from 10 AM to 12:30 PM and 2 to 5 PM; admission charge. Then take N118 north 11 miles (18 km) to Chamusca.

CHAMUSCA Scarcely anything remains from medieval times, when this town was an important port on the busy thoroughfare of the Tagus, but Chamusca still has a few sights worth seeing, and the old part, with its typical Ribatejo houses, is a pleasant place to stroll. Those who appreciate early Portuguese tiles should not miss the 17th-century interior of the parish church of São Brás or the charming little Igreja da Nossa Senhora do Pranto, from which there is also a magnificent view of the surrounding countryside. The *Casa Rural Tradicional* (Largo 25 do Abril; no phone; no admission charge) is an interesting reconstruction of a typical Ribatejo farmhouse of about 50 years ago, with some fine pieces of rustic furniture and other household items. To visit, ask for the keys at the Câmara Municipal (Town Hall; Rua Direita; phone: 49-760566), which is open weekdays from 9 AM to 12:30 PM and 2 to 5:30 PM.

En Route from Chamusca Continue north about 2½ miles (4 km) and take N243 across the river — those with an eye for engineering will like the iron bridge the French built in 1905 — and another 3 miles (5 km) into Golegã.

GOLEGÃ For the first 2 weeks of November each year, when one of Europe's most important horse fairs, the *Feira Nacional do Cavalo* (also known as the *Feira de São Martinho*), takes place here, this town becomes horse lovers' heaven. The event attracts breeders and dealers from all over the world, principally because of the high-stepping Lusitanian and Andalusian breeds for which the Ribatejo is famous. (If you happen to come here during the fair, be prepared for jam-packed, narrow streets; it's advisable to leave your car on the outskirts of town.) At other times of the year, the main attraction is the Igreja Matriz (Parish Church), toward the center of town on the road from Chamusca. Founded by King Manuel I during the 16th century, the church has a magnificent doorway in the Manueline style (the Gothic-to-Renaissance transitional style named after the king). In front of it stands the town's *pelourinho*, or pillory (in the old days, both a symbol of municipal power and a whipping post). A block away, off Largo Dom Manuel I, is the *Museu Municipal de Fotografia Carlos Relvas* (phone: 49-94387), which is well worth a visit even for those who are not photography buffs. Carlos Relvas, the father of José Relvas (responsible for the *Casa dos Patudos* in Alpiarça), was a wealthy landowner, art collector, and statesman, as well as a passionate amateur photographer, and his studio and splendid Victorian house have been preserved as a museum. It's open from 11 AM to 12:30 PM and 2:30 to 6 PM; closed Mondays; admission charge.

EATING OUT

Central This restaurant is in the restored house of one of Portugal's best-known bullfighters, Manuel dos Santos. No great flights of fancy, but the regional fare is good, including the specialty, *açorda de sável* (shad soup with bread and other ingredients). Open daily. Reservations advised. Major credit cards accepted. Largo da Imaculada Conceição, Golegã (phone: 49-94345). Inexpensive.

En Route from Golegã Take N365 north to the junction with N3, 4½ miles (7 km) away, then turn onto N110, following signs for Tomar, 12 miles (19 km) from the crossing. About 1¼ miles (2 km) along, the road passes the church of Nossa Senhora da Assunção (Our Lady of the Assumption) in Atalaia. The church is an interesting example of Renaissance architecture, with an impressive portal at the center of a very imposing but oddly shaped façade; its most beautiful feature is the yellow-and-blue-tiled interior — a must-see for tile fans. Another 4 miles (6 km) along, off the road to the right, is the village of Asseiceira, the center of a once-important earthenware pottery industry. Though the use of these traditional pots has declined, some of the family potteries are still in business after 200 years or more. Asseiceira is also known for its cast-metal cowbells, *chocalhos,* considered by some collectors to be the best in the country.

TOMAR Founded during the early 12th century on the Nabão River, near the site of a Roman town and a later Visigothic and Moorish settlement, Tomar is intimately linked with what is often termed the heroic period in Portuguese history — encompassing the founding of the nation during the 12th century, the Christian reconquest, and then the great maritime expansion of the 15th century. The first sight to see is the Convento de Cristo (Convent of Christ; no phone), the extraordinary convent-castle of the two military orders that made Tomar their headquarters. Begun by the Knights Templars on a hilltop overlooking the town during the 12th century, the construction was continued by the Order of Christ, who replaced the disbanded Templars during the 14th century, and was finished only during the 17th century. The Templars had been entrusted with the defense of the Tagus Valley after the recapture of Lisbon from the Moors in 1147, and they used their crusaders' knowledge of the military architecture of the Holy Land to build a state-of-the-art castle, with double walls protecting a towering keep. The design proved its value in 1190 when Moors attacking the castle breached the south gate, only to be trapped between the two lines of defense and massacred. To commemorate the carnage, the gate became known as the Porta do Sangue (Gate of Blood).

The Charola — a circular oratory, modeled after the Holy Sepulcher in Jerusalem — is also part of the convent's 12th-century nucleus (the painted decorations and figures in it are from a later period, however). It is said that when the knights were at prayer, they would leave their horses standing behind them in the passage surrounding the altar. The early-16th-century Manueline nave attached to the oratory is one of many additions to the original convent. Its exterior is decorated with splendidly ornate tracery full of allusions to Portugal's seafaring past — not surprising, since the Convento de Cristo had been closely linked to the epic voyages of the 15th century, and the square cross that Prince Henry the Navigator's caravels bore on their sails was in fact the emblem of the Order of Christ, of which Prince Henry himself was a Grand Master. Among other buildings, the labyrinthine complex contains seven cloisters, including a magnificent mid-16th-century Palladian structure, the Claustro dos Filipes (Cloister of the Philips), in which King Philip II of Spain is said to have been proclaimed King Philip I of Portugal. The convent was sacked and pillaged by the French during the 19th-century Peninsular War, but it remains one of Europe's great historical sites. It's open daily from 9:30 AM to 12:30 PM and 2 to 6 PM, to 5 PM in winter; admission charge.

Also to be seen in Tomar is the little church of Nossa Senhora da Conceição, perhaps the best example of early Renaissance architecture in Portugal. It's on the way down the hill from the convent, but arrange the visit with the tourist office in town (address and phone below), because the church has been stripped practically bare by thieves and is now kept locked. In the Old Town between the foot of the hill and the river is the country's oldest surviving synagogue (73 Rua Dr. Joaquim Jacinto; no phone). Built during the 15th century (although excavations next door have revealed a *mikvah* — a Hebrew ritual bath — from the 13th century), it was probably used only briefly before the Inquisition was introduced into Portugal (by a monk named Baltazar de Faria, who is entombed in one of the cloisters in the convent). Once again a practicing synagogue, it is open from 9:30 AM to 12:30 PM and 2 to 6 PM (to 5 PM in winter); closed Wednesdays.

Just across the river is the lovely and historic Santa Maria do Olival (St. Mary of the Olive Grove), once the mother church for all of Portugal's churches overseas. Historians date it to the mid-13th century, but popular tradition holds that it was founded a century earlier by the celebrated Grand Master of Portuguese Templars, Gualdim Pais, whose bones are interred here along with those of other Templar worthies. Restoration has ruthlessly stripped away the decorative accretion of centuries, but two little stone images of the Virgin and some very pretty tiles relieve the starkness inside. Another church worth a visit is São João Baptista, the parish church with an imposing bell tower and Manueline doorway that dominates Praça da República, the main square in the center of town. The pulpit in the central nave is a masterpiece of Gothic stone carving.

Near the weir in the town's lovely riverside gardens is a huge waterwheel, of the sort once used for irrigation purposes in the Tomar region. The Aqueduto dos Pegões, built between 1593 and 1616 to bring water to the convent, is about 3 miles (5 km) out of town (almost 2 miles/3 km on the N113 in the direction of Fátima and Leiria, then left onto the road for Pegões). Over 3 miles long, with 180 arches, the structure was a remarkable piece of engineering for its time and is impressive even now. It is also fairly close to one of Tomar's best restaurants, *Chico Elias* (see *Eating Out*).

The 17th-century Convento de São Francisco just off the Praça Varzea Grande near the railway station is not in itself particularly interesting, but its ground floor cloisters house a small pottery studio (on the right as you enter; no phone) where artisans turn out reproductions of regional tiles and ceramics. The studio is open weekdays from 9 AM to 1 PM and 2 to 6 PM. On the opposite side of the same cloisters is the *Museu dos Fosforos* (Matchbox Museum; no phone); it reportedly has the largest collection of matchboxes in Europe from all over the world (open from 2 to 5 PM; closed Saturdays; no admission charge).

One of Portugal's most spectacular traditional festivals, the *Festa dos Tabuleiros,* takes place in Tomar. During the festivities, which were probably pagan in origin but later became associated with the alms-giving activities of the saintly Queen Isabel, young girls in white parade through the streets, balancing *tabuleiros* — enormous crown-like contraptions made of loaves of bread interwoven with flowers — on their heads. The celebration takes place 50 days after *Easter,* but it is not a regular event (at one time it was held more or less biennially), so check with either the main tourist office on Avenida Dr. Cândido Madureira (phone: 49-313237) or the branch at Rua Serpa Pinto (phone: 49-313095).

CHECKING IN

Ilha do Lombo This exceptionally pretty *estalagem* (inn) is located about 10 miles (16 km) east of Tomar, on an island in the reservoir upstream from the Castelo de Bode dam (Portugal's biggest dam). There are 17 rooms with private baths and tiled terraces looking onto the water. There is also an outdoor pool, and boating and fishing are available. To reach the inn, take N110 north for about half a mile (1 km), then turn right onto the road to Serra and Barreira for the remaining 9½ miles (15 km). The road is narrow and poorly paved, but it winds through pleasant scenery; from Barreira, a small, closed cabin boat called the *Zêzere* ferries guests out to the island — about a 5-minute trip. Reserve at least 2 weeks in advance for the summer. Ilha do Lombo, Serra de Tomar (phone: 49-371128 or 371108). Moderate.

Lago Azul Handsome and modern, this *estalagem* boasts 20 air conditioned rooms with private baths, telephones, radios, and panoramic views of the Zêzere River. The management also runs *Templários* (see below). The restaurant focuses on regional fare; when it's in season, order the *lampréia* (eel). Located 12½ miles (20 km) northeast of Tomar in Lago Azul, Ferreira do Zêzere (phone: 49-361445 or 49-361654; fax: 49-361664). Moderate.

Pousada de São Pedro A quiet and comfortable 25-room government-run inn, with private baths, genuine antique furnishings, and old prints on the walls. The picture window in the air conditioned restaurant looks out onto the dam. On the Zêzere River, right beside the Castelo de Bode dam, 8 miles (13 km) southeast of Tomar. Take N110 south for 4½ miles (7 km), then turn left onto N358. Castelo de Bode (phone: 49-381159; 212-686-9213 in the US). Moderate.

Santa Iria This riverside *estalagem* (inn) successfully combines rustic charm with modern amenities like private baths, air conditioning, TV sets, and tennis facilities. There are 13 rooms, plus 1 elegant suite. The restaurant serves good regional dishes and wines. Right in the center of town, in the delightful Mouchão Park. Parque do Mouchão, Tomar (phone: 49-313326; fax: 49-321082). Moderate.

Templários A regional favorite combining modern comforts with small-town tranquillity, it's set in a pleasant garden by the river and has 84 rooms, an excellent restaurant, an outdoor pool, and tennis courts. From the balconies of many of the upper rooms, guests can look across to the convent on the hill. The hotel organizes all-day boat excursions on the Zêzere River. 1 Largo Cândido dos Reis, Tomar (phone: 49-321730; fax: 49-322191). Moderate.

Sinagoga Also modern and in the old part of town, this 23-room *pensão* is in a converted house. All guestrooms have baths, air conditioning, satellite TV, mini-bars, and direct dial telephones. There's a small bar and breakfast room, but no restaurant. 32 Rua Gil Avo, Tomar (phone: 49-316783; fax: 49-322196). Inexpensive.

Trovador One of Tomar's best economical hostelries, it's modern, clean, and located in the newer part of town, near the bus station. The 30 rooms all have private baths and TV sets. No restaurant, but there is a breakfast room and a small bar that's open at night. Rua Dr. Joaquim Ribeiro, Tomar (phone: 49-322567; fax: 49-322194). Inexpensive.

EATING OUT

Bela Vista One of the oldest restaurants in Tomar and regarded as the most traditional in culinary terms. The combination of old-fashioned decor and good home cooking — including an excellent *cabrito no forno* (roast kid) — plus a nice riverside location next to the old bridge, have turned it into an obligatory port of call. Closed Mondays at lunch and Tuesdays. Reservations advised. No credit cards accepted. 6 Fonte do Choupo, Tomar (phone: 49-312870). Moderate.

Chez Nous It has a French bias, but it's also noted for excellent local fare — *bacalhau com natas* (dried cod with a cream sauce), for example. In the old part of town, with an agreeably cozy ambience, it's a popular place and seats only 30, so reserve before going. Closed Saturdays. Reservations advised. Major credit cards accepted. 31 Rua Dr. Joaquim Jacinto, Tomar (phone: 49-314743). Moderate.

Chico Elias This stands apart among the handful of top restaurants in Tomar because the excellent food is cooked to order. Call first and tell them what you want to eat. Among the choices — prepared by Dona Ceu, wife of the owner — are *coelho na abóbora* (rabbit served in a pumpkin), *bacalhau* *assado com carne de porco* (dried cod baked with pork), *couves a Dom Prior* (a spicy cabbage dish), and *leite creme* (a creamy milk-based dessert that Dona Ceu is reputed to make better than anyone else). The decor is not entirely successful pseudo-rustic, but the fare makes up for it. Closed Tuesdays. Reservations necessary. No credit cards accepted. The restaurant is in a small village about 1¼ miles (2 km) beyond Tomar. Estrada de Torres Novas, Algarvias (phone: 49-311067). Moderate.

Marisqueira de Tomar Large, air conditioned, and pleasantly decorated with rural scenes painted on glass, this is the place to sample the famous Nabão River lamprey. Try the *arroz de lampréia,* a Ribatejo specialty in which the eel is cooked with rice, wine, and garlic, and served in a black earthenware pot. The restaurant also has a good seafood bar next door. Closed Mondays. Reservations unnecessary. Major credit cards accepted. 9 Av. Norton de Matos, Tomar (phone: 49-313903). Moderate.

En Route from Tomar Take N110 south 4½ miles (7 km) and turn left onto N358. The pleasant country road winds through hills and woods for 10 miles (16 km), crossing the Zêzere River via Portugal's biggest dam, at Castelo de Bode, until it reaches Constância. A pretty, quiet little town nowadays, Constância has known busier times, thanks to its strategic position at the confluence of the Tagus and Zêzere rivers. During the Peninsular War in the early 19th century, the future Duke of Wellington mustered his troops here before marching against the French at Talavera, Spain. The town can even boast the not very impressive ruins of a house where Portugal's greatest poet, Luís de Camões, is said to have written some of his verses in 1546. The steps beside the ruined house afford views of Constância's narrow, whitewashed streets as they climb up to the 18th-century parish church that sits atop everything.

Almost 3 miles (5 km) west of town, and definitely worth the short backtrack, is the Castelo de Almourol. The castle hasn't seen much real action since the Knights Templars built it on top of earlier fortifications in 1171, but it has made up for that by accumulating legends — a process to which its remarkably romantic appearance on an island in the Tagus has contributed enormously. A boatman will row travelers across during visiting hours, daily from 9:30 AM to 5 PM (no admission charge, but pay the boatman). East of town, N3 leads away from the river through wooded countryside and then back to it again at the old town of Abrantes, 10 miles (16 km) from Constância.

ABRANTES The town stands on the north bank of the Tagus, and its castle commands a wide circle of the surrounding land. Abrantes has been fought over repeatedly during its long history. King Afonso Henriques took it from the Moors in 1148 and then successfully fought off a recapture attempt in 1179. The castle was restored and enlarged, most notably by

King Dinis, who finished the walls in 1279. Afterward, it was frequently used as a royal residence; several Portuguese princes were born in it. (Some of the halls that once formed part of the residential quarters have been restored to reveal their fine brickwork vaults.) It was here, too, that King João I assembled the army that won the celebrated battle of Aljubarrota against the forces of Castile on August 14, 1385, thus assuring Portugal's continued independence. In 1807, during the Peninsular War, the French took Abrantes for Napoleon, only to be chased out shortly after by the British. (The French general was named Duke of Abrantes for his pains, however.) The castle is open daily from 9 AM to 6 PM; no admission charge.

On the hilltop with the castle is the 13th-century Igreja da Santa Maria do Castelo, inside which is installed the *Museu Regional de Dom Lopo de Almeida*. It contains an interesting collection of Roman statuary, 15th- and 16th-century church carvings, and some very fine early Mozarabic tiles from Seville, Spain. The church was badly damaged by an earthquake in 1492 and was then reconstructed as the pantheon of the Almeida family, counts of Abrantes, whose elegant Gothic tombs are part of the collection. The museum is open from 10 AM to 12:30 PM and 2 to 5 PM; closed Mondays; no admission charge. Information on other sights in town is available at the tourist office on Largo da Feira (phone: 41-22555).

CHECKING IN

Abrantur A brand-new hotel with 54 air conditioned rooms with baths, satellite TV, and direct-dial telephones. It has a large swimming pool set in the lawn, floodlit tennis courts, mini-golf, a large, glass-enclosed restaurant, a self-service restaurant, a bar, and a discotheque. About a half mile (1 km) from the center of town on EN118 at Pego (phone: 41-93464; fax: 41-93287). Moderate.

Casa do Pastor This old manor house on a huge estate is a 7½-mile (12-km) drive away, but well worth the detour. There are 6 guestrooms with private baths. The rustic-style restaurant serves regional dishes such as *ensopado de borrego* (lamb stew), as well as international standbys including steaks. Before noon it doubles as a cafeteria for snacks, and after 10 PM as a pub. Take N244-3 north of Abrantes for 5 miles (8 km), then turn right onto N358 for Mouriscas. The house is about 2 miles (3 km) down this road on the right, between Cabeça das Mos and Mouriscas (phone: 41-95255). Hotel, inexpensive; restaurant, moderate.

Turismo A modern, comfortable hostelry of a standard not usually found in the provinces, it has a privileged and convenient hilltop site on the edge of town, gardens, use of a nearby swimming pool, and tennis courts. Most of the 50 rooms and suites are air conditioned. The restaurant is the best in town, serving very good local and regional dishes in addition to more standard hotel fare. It also offers pleasantly panoramic views from its big picture windows. Largo de Santo António, Abrantes (phone: 41-21261 or 41-21271; 800-528-1234 in the US; fax: 41-25218). Moderate.

EATING OUT

Cascata Decorated in typical Abrantes style, this large air conditioned eatery serves regional fare. One of its specialties is *maranos* (stuffed sheep's belly). Closed Mondays. Reservations unnecessary. Visa accepted. Rua Dom Tatado, Abrantes (phone: 41-21011). Moderate.

En Route from Abrantes At Rossio, just after crossing the bridge going south (note the ruins of an old Roman bridge over the Tagus), turn east at the signposted crossing onto N118 for Portalegre. The road climbs away from the river as it moves toward the Alto Alentejo. At Alpalhão, 37 miles (59 km) from Abrantes, turn left onto N246 in the direction of the Spanish frontier and drive the 10 miles (16 km) to Castelo de Vide.

CASTELO DE VIDE This spa town on the slopes of the Serra de São Mamede is of considerable historical interest and one of the prettiest towns in the region. Its waters are said to do wonders for sluggish digestive systems, and for this reason, as well as because it escapes the fierce Alentejo heat, Castelo de Vide has long been a popular summer resort for the Portuguese. Like virtually all Alentejo border towns of any size, it grew up around a castle — in fact, 60 families still live within the walls of this one. Portuguese occupation of the site, originally fortified by the Romans, dates from the beginning of the 13th century; early in the following century, King Dinis strengthened it. Since then, the castle has been the object of numerous sieges; one of the worst (and last) was in 1704 when it was badly damaged by the Spanish when they tried to wrest the castle from its Portuguese and English defenders.

Most of this small town can be seen on a morning's stroll. Begin in the central square, Praça Dom Pedro V, which is bordered by two fine 18th-century buildings — the Town Hall and the big Igreja da Santa Maria da Devesa — and by several handsome 17th-century mansions. Head down from the northwest corner of the square to the 16th-century *fonte da vila* (village fountain), in a square at the foot of the oldest part of town. The fountain, one of the prettiest in Portugal, consists of four marble columns supporting a pyramidal roof set over basins that have been worn into undulating curves by centuries of use. From the square, walk up to the castle through the enchanting medieval alleys of the old Jewish Quarter. On the way up, don't miss the tiny 16th-century synagogue on Rua da Judiaria, which is partly restored and open to the public daily. Also note the original medieval details, such as doorways and windows, on the houses on the same street. Not to be missed in the castle itself are the superbly vaulted Gothic hall in the tower and the fine main hall with its brick tunnel vault ceiling. There are stunning views of the surrounding countryside from the ramparts. The castle can be visited at any time — a caretaker will open sections that are closed off. Castelo de Vide's tourist office is at 81 Rua Bartolomeu Alvares da Santa (phone: 45-91361).

CHECKING IN

Sol e Serra Modern, comfortable, and conveniently situated near a park at the edge of town, it has 51 rooms with balconies, most with an agreeable view, and a swimming pool. The restaurant specializes in Alentejo dishes (try the *cachafrito de cabrito,* a casserole of kid), and — in keeping with the town's Jewish heritage — kosher fare is offered as well. Estrada de São Vicente, Castelo de Vide (phone and fax: 45-91337). Moderate.

Casa do Parque A charming old mansion in the center of town that has been converted into a 24-room hostelry, all with baths. Its cheery, attractive restaurant serves good regional fare without putting on any airs. On the menu are *ensopado de cabrito* (kid stew), a regional and house specialty, and *pezinhos coentradas* (pigs' trotters cooked with fresh coriander). 37 Av. de Aramanhã, Castelo de Vide (phone: 45-91250). Inexpensive.

Quinta da Bela Vista Just 9 miles (14 km) from Castelo de Vide, this lovely old manor house offers 4 rooms with baths, 2 apartments, a TV room, a swimming pool, and a tennis court. On EN2 between Povoa and Miudas (phone: 45-98125). Inexpensive.

EATING OUT

Dom Pedro V On the central square, it serves excellent, classic Portuguese dishes, as well as some regional ones. Apart from those attached to hotels, it's considered the best restaurant in the area. Closed Mondays. Reservations advised. Major credit cards accepted. Praça Dom Pedro V, Castelo de Vide (phone: 45-91236). Moderate.

En Route from Castelo de Vide Continue on N246 another 5½ miles (9 km) to the turnoff (left) to Marvão. The road winds up another 2½ miles (4 km) into the mountains right to the town walls; squeeze through the gate and find a parking space — driving is limited along the town's tortuous cobbled streets.

MARVÃO This beautiful little walled town perches on a mountaintop overlooking the Spanish border, only 5 miles (8 km) away. Because of its strategic position, Marvão has played a part in a great many wars. Afonso Henriques captured the town in 1116, and at the end of the 13th century King Dinis fortified it, building up the walls and the tall castle keep. From then on, it was a vital piece in the military chess game played out on the Iberian Peninsula. The views from the castle, which can be visited at any time, are surely the most impressive in the Alentejo — the only place where "you can look down on eagles," as one Portuguese poet put it. The tourist office is on Rua Dr. Matos Magalhães (phone: 45-93226).

CHECKING IN

Pousada de Santa Maria A state-owned inn housed in two converted 17th-century mansions. Very comfortable, very popular, and the best in town, it's in a beautiful spot above the high walls. There are 24 rooms with baths (it's a good idea to book well ahead). Its restaurant has a spectacular view of the surrounding countryside. The house specialties are regional ones such as *sopa de sarapatel* (richly flavored, heavy, gruel-like soup of giblets) and *robalo com amêijoas* (turbot cooked with clams and flavored with fresh coriander). 7 Rua 24 de Janeiro, Marvão (phone: 45-93201; 212-686-9213 in the US; fax: 45-93440). Expensive.

Dom Dinis The 8 guestrooms in this *pensão* are tiny, but they're attractive; some have delightful views, and all have private bathrooms. The restaurant serves plain, regional home cooking. Rua Dr. Matos Magalhães, Marvão (phone: 45-93236). Inexpensive.

EATING OUT

Varanda do Alentejo This air conditioned restaurant is located in the central square by the old pillory, and is a good place to try regional dishes such as *carne de porco Alentejano* (pork with clams) and *perdiz estofada* (partridge casserole). Open daily. Reservations unnecessary. Major credit cards accepted. 1 Praça do Pelourinho (phone: 45-93272). Moderate.

En Route from Marvão Heading 13 miles (21 km) south to Portalegre, N359 crosses the Serra de São Mamede, which contains the highest peak (3,382 feet) in the Alentejo plain. The landscape is pretty, with cork and olive trees beginning to predominate and small farms disappearing as the route enters the domain of the large estate.

PORTALEGRE The capital of the Alto Alentejo is a busy city and one of the few centers of industry in the region. The cathedral, in the old part of town, is an impressively large edifice, mostly from the 18th century, although it was founded 200 years earlier. It has three vast naves, a wonderfully elegant dome crowning the transept crossing, and some fine 17th-century *azulejos*. Also worth visiting is the church of the Convento de São Bernardo. Founded for the St. Bernard sisters in 1530, the convent is now a barracks, but visitors are escorted in to see the church. Worth noting are the fountain in the courtyard and the superb 16th-century carved doorway, in marble quarried in nearby Estremoz. The history of the order up to its dissolution by the Marquês de Pombal during the 18th century has been poignantly recorded by the nuns on the backs of the stalls in the upper choir.

Portalegre has a famous tapestry factory, located in the center of town in a 16th-century Jesuit convent on Rua Guilherme Gomes Fernandes. Founded in 1947, it specializes in tapestries designed by Portugal's leading artists. All are handwoven, by women who sit at two long looms running the length of the workshop, surrounded by beautifully dyed wools. The factory can be visited weekdays from 9 to 11 AM and 2 to 4:30 PM. Information on other sights in town can be obtained from the tourist office in the Convento de Santa Clara near the cathedral (Rua de Elvas; phone: 45-21815).

CHECKING IN

Dom João III This modern hotel near the town center has 56 rooms with baths, a bar, and a swimming pool. The restaurant serves good regional food; its specialty is *bife a Dom João III* (grilled steak). Av. da Liberdade, Portalegre (phone: 45-21192). Moderate.

EATING OUT

Alpendre An air conditioned restaurant in the center of town, it offers local dishes such as *carne de porco Alentanjo* (pork with clams) as well as international fare. Closed Mondays. No reservations. Major credit cards accepted. 21 Rua 31 de Janeiro, Portalegre (phone: 45-21611). Moderate.

En Route from Portalegre Take N18 south through a characteristic Alentejo landscape of dry, open expanses, cork trees, and distant clusters of low, white houses. About halfway to Estremoz, which is 36 miles (58 km) from Portalegre, is the village of Monforte, with Roman excavations nearby and several fine old country houses.

ESTREMOZ A magnificent 13th-century fortified tower, surrounded by battlements and 18th-century palace buildings, looms majestically over the medieval summit of this attractive and interesting old town. A full 89 feet high, with corner balconies from which boiling oil could be conveniently poured on attackers, the tower was the main defensive feature of what was once one of the Alentejo's most formidable castles, and it is generally considered to be among the finest surviving pieces of medieval military architecture on the Iberian Peninsula. The imposing structure is known as the Torre das Tres Coroas (Tower of the Three Crowns), because three kings are said to have had a hand in its construction. However, it seems to have been mostly the work of King Dinis, who finished it shortly before the end of the 13th century. Dinis also added a royal palace to the fortifications, and this became one of the favorite residences of his wife, Queen Isabel. Unfortunately, most of the original palace was destroyed in 1698 in the explosion of a powder magazine. The present palace, which adjoins Dinis's tower and is now a state *pousada* (see *Checking In*), was built on the same site during the 18th century by King João V. All that is left of the royal residence of Dinis and Isabel is a lovely little arcade of Gothic arches, known as the Gallery of the Audience Hall, as well as the room where the sainted queen died in 1336, which was later turned into a chapel decorated with scenes from her life. Access to the chapel, the tower, and the gallery is through the *pousada* (all three are open to non-guests).

In the Lower Town, which is partially enclosed by a second set of walls (17th-century), the focal point is the great central square, the Rossio (in full, the Rossio do Marquês de Pombal). Among the interesting buildings surrounding it is the Câmara Municipal (Town Hall), built during the 17th century as a convent; inside is a superb marble staircase decorated with 18th-century tiled panels depicting the life of St. Philip Neri. Another is the Misericórdia Church, with lovely Gothic cloisters. The *Museu Rural da Casa do Povo de Santa Maria* (Santa Maria Rural Museum; also on the square; no phone) contains a small but extremely interesting collection of local crafts and costumes. It's open from 9:30 AM to 12:30 PM and 2:30 to 5:30 PM; closed Mondays; admission charge. The market held on the Rossio every Saturday is a good opportunity to see the earthenware pottery for which Estremoz has been famous for centuries. The traditionally shaped jugs and cooking pots and the charming little painted figures have become collectors' items, although they remain inexpensively priced here. Estremoz's tourist office is on Largo da República, south of the Rossio (phone: 68-22538).

CHECKING IN

Pousada da Rainha Santa Isabel One of the most highly rated of Portugal's string of state-owned *pousadas,* it's installed in the former palace of King João V, adjoining the Tower of the Three Crowns, and the views are spectacular. The 29 rooms and 4 suites (all air conditioned and with private baths) are beautifully furnished with genuine 17th- and 18th-century antiques; there is a swimming pool in the garden. The restaurant is the best choice in town — in addition to the food (regional cooking, with particularly noteworthy game dishes in season), there are panoramic views from the dining room windows. Try the various *borrego* (lamb) dishes or, during hunting season, the *javali assado* (roast wild boar) or *coelho ao caçador* (richly flavored rabbit casserole). Largo Dom Dinis, Estremoz (phone: 68-22618 or 68-23982; 212-686-9213 in the US). Expensive.

EATING OUT

Aguias d'Ouro A comfortable, air conditioned restaurant on the main square. The *borrego assado no forno* (roast lamb with onions and bay leaves) is reputed to be the best in the area. Open daily. Reservations advised. Major credit cards accepted. 27 Rossio do Marquês de Pombal, Estremoz (phone: 68-22196). Moderate to inexpensive.

En Route from Estremoz To go directly to Evora, 28½ miles (46 km) from Estremoz, drive west on N4 for about 4 miles (6 km) and then pick up the southbound N18. Or first make a short but worthwhile detour to the lovely royal town of Vila Viçosa, 11 miles (18 km) from Estremoz, by taking N4 east for 9 miles (14 km) and then turning right onto N255.

VILA VIÇOSA During the 15th and 16th centuries, this town was the seat of the Dukes of Bragança, who continued to maintain a residence here even after the family became Portugal's last ruling dynasty in 1640. Be sure to visit the Paço Ducal (Ducal Palace), whose gorgeous marble façade fills one side of the Terreiro do Paço, the spacious main square. Begun during the 16th century, although dating mainly from the 17th century, the palace has been turned into a museum — the *Museu Biblioteca da Casa de Bragança* — containing furniture, tapestries, paintings, ceramics, and other works of art, as well as many of the possessions of the last Portuguese king, Manuel II, who died in exile in England in 1932 and left behind an important library of 15th- and 16th-century Portuguese books. There is also a small *Museu dos Coches* (Coach Museum). The palace is open for guided tours (in Portuguese) from 9:30 AM to 1 PM and 2 to 6 PM (to 5 PM in winter); closed Mondays; admission charge.

In the same square is another fine 16th-century Renaissance building, the Convento das Chagas, where the duchesses of Bragança are buried. The Bragança dukes are buried apart from the women, in the nearby Igreja de Santo Agostinho. The *tapada,* the family's walled hunting preserve, the largest in Portugal, has remained intact and is now a nature reserve. For additional information, contact the tourist office on Praça da República (phone: 68-98584).

CHECKING IN

Casa dos Arcos Near the Ducal Palace, this manor house built in 1599 is filled with valuable antiques and artwork, including 18th-century paintings. There are 8 guestrooms and 1 suite (all with baths). 16 Largo Afonso, Vila Viçosa (phone: 68-98518). Moderate.

EATING OUT

Ouro Branco This large, regional restaurant in the center of town is air conditioned in summer and warmed by a big fireplace in winter. Specialties include *borrego na churrasco* (barbecued lamb) and *arroz de tamboril* (rice with monkfish). Closed Mondays. Reservations unnecessary. Major credit cards accepted. 44 Campo da Restauração, Vila Viçosa (phone: 68-98556). Moderate.

EVORA For a complete description of sights, hotels, and restaurants in this historic city, see *Evora,* THE CITIES.

Before going on to Arriaolos, take a detour to Monsaraz, a lovely little town near the Spanish border. Head east 31 miles (50 km) on N256. At the junction with N139, go north 4½ miles (7 km).

MONSARAZ Set on a high hill above the Guadiana River, Monsaraz's church spires, castle towers, and houses stand out dramatically against the skyline. Dusk is the best time to be here, when the rose and orange tones bounce off the whitewashed buildings and the sun goes down over the sere hills. The town seems to have been preserved almost intact since the Middle Ages; originally a prehistoric *castro,* it subsequently belonged to the Knights Templars and later to the Order of Christ. The castle, its walls and square tower still standing, dates from the 14th century. No cars are allowed inside the walls, which only adds to the sense of peace in this idyllic setting. The only thing to do in this tiny hamlet is watch the sunset from the castle (always open) and enjoy the stillness — a welcome respite from a day's sightseeing in Evora or driving through the Alentejo.

CHECKING IN

Estalagem de Monsaraz A charming inn in a totally modernized, whitewashed manor house set amidst gardens in a valley outside the town walls. It has 8 rooms with baths, a bar, and a restaurant where the specialty is roast lamb. Largo de São Bartolomeu, Monsaraz (phone: 66-55112). Moderate.

Casa Dom Nuno There are 8 rooms with baths in this beautifully restored, centuries-old mansion built on several levels inside the old walls. 6 Rua do Castelo, Monsaraz (phone: 66-55146). Inexpensive.

EATING OUT

Alcaide The decor is regional, and on one side there are windows offering a panoramic view of the countryside below the town. The featured dishes center around lamb. Closed Thursdays. Reservations advised. Visa accepted. 18 Rua de Santiago, Monsaraz (phone: 66-55168). Moderate.

En Route from Evora Heading west, N114 leads back to the N4 at Montemor-o-Novo, 20 miles (32 km) from Evora. Anyone who has admired the Arraiolos carpets seen in shops, museums, and some of the better hotels throughout Portugal, however, is advised to take a short detour to the town where they are made, 10 miles (16 km) north of Evora on N370. Arraiolos has been producing these famed woolen carpets since the beginning of the 18th century, and while there is actually no price advantage in buying straight from one of the factories, it is possible to ask to see the workshops and watch the carpets being made. The oldest factory, as well as one of the most highly regarded, is *Kalifa* (44-46 Rua Alexandre Herculano; phone: 66-42117). Others recommended include *Tapetes Calantica* (20 Rua Alexandre Herculano; phone: 66-42356), with a wide variety of tapestries and rugs; *Fracoop* (Praça Lima Brito; phone: 66-42277), a cooperative that carries items from a number of different workshops; and the long-established *Condestavel* (Av. Bombeiros Voluntarios; phone: 66-42423), offering many designs.

Montemor-o-Novo, 15½ miles (25 km) west of Arraiolos on N4, has the picturesque remains of a Moorish castle at the top of the Old Town, but it's notable mainly as the birthplace of João de Deus (John of God), the founder of the Order of Charity, who was declared patron saint of hospitals throughout the Christian world 350 years after his death in 1550. Continue 23 miles (37 km) west of Montemor to Pegões, where there is a crossroads with two possible routes to Lisbon. Be sure to take the one going left, toward Setúbal, for 20 miles (32 km).

SETÚBAL This busy, ancient port town sits on the estuary of the Sado River, at the edge of the range of hills known as the Serra da Arrábida. Hans Christian Andersen, who visited Setúbal in 1866, called it a terrestrial paradise. It is now the hub of the most important industrial area in the south of Portugal, with shipbuilding, chemical manufacturing, automobile assembly, and fishing its major activities, but it has nevertheless retained a lot of the charm that delighted Andersen over a century ago. On Praça Miguel de Bombarda is the pretty little Igreja de Jesus, built in the late 15th century and the earliest example of the Manueline style of architecture. The main street, Avenida Luisa Todi, is lined with charming outdoor cafés, restaurants, and bars.

Across the river on the Tróia Peninsula — a dune- and pine-backed sandbar blocking the estuary — is the big Torralta tourism development, with apartment-hotels, a golf course, and miles of good white sand. In a quiet creek near the apartment complex are the excavated ruins of a Roman fish processing factory (which may have been part of the once important Roman town of Cetóbriga) and a fascinating little 8th-century church. The site is open to visitors daily from 9:30 AM to 5:30 PM from June through September; no admission charge. Regular car ferry service connects Setúbal to Tróia. Information is available from the tourist office on Largo do Corpo Santo (phone: 65-524284) in Setúbal.

CHECKING IN

Pousada de São Filipe This government-run inn is about half a mile (1 km) west of town, overlooking the Sado estuary. There are 14 rooms with private baths (ask for one on the waterfront) and a panoramic restaurant (see *Eating Out*). For additional details, see *Pousadas and Manor Houses* in DIVERSIONS. Castelo de São Filipe, Setúbal (phone: 65-523844; 212-686-9213 in the US; fax: 65-532538). Expensive.

Apartamentos Turísticos Torralta There are three high-rise apartment-hotels in this development: the *Magnóliamar,* the *Rosamar,* and the *Tulipamar.* On the Tróia Peninsula, a 20-minute ferry ride across the Sado River estuary from Setúbal, they're worth considering as an alternative to something in town, because guests have access to all the facilities of the residential resort complex — a golf course, tennis courts, seawater pools, a supermarket, restaurants, and a disco. The three buildings, each with 129 spacious rooms and suites with kitchenettes, stand close to the beach, surrounded by lawns and flowerbeds; views from the upper-floor balconies are superb. Each hotel has its own telephone number (*Magnóliamar:* 65-44361; fax: 65-44162; *Rosamar:* 65-44151; *Tulipamar:* 65-44201). There also is a central booking office for information and reservations (phone: 65-44221; fax: 65-44256). Expensive to moderate, depending on the season.

Ibis This 102-room hotel, a member of the international chain, provides a full range of basic amenities — private baths, satellite TV, telephones, air conditioning, automatic wake-up service — at extremely reasonable rates. The convenient location is another plus. Located 2½ miles (4 km) east of Setúbal, on N10 (phone: 65-772927; 800-221-4542 in the US; fax: 65-772447). Inexpensive.

Solaris A centrally located *albergaria* (inn) lodged in a converted 18th-century home. There are 24 nicely furnished, air conditioned rooms, all with private baths, TV sets, and telephones. The restaurant features hearty regional fare; the 18th-century pillory in the square on which the inn is situated is a national monument. Praça Marquês de Pombal, Setúbal (phone: 65-525914; fax: 65-522070). Inexpensive.

EATING OUT

Pousada de São Filipe The inn's dining room offers very good regional dishes, along with a good view. The fish is especially recommended: Try the *cherne grelhado com frutas do mar* (grilled turbot with a seafood sauce) or *amêijoas na cataplana* (clams with tomatoes and onions, steamed quickly in a covered copper pan — the *cataplana*). Open daily. Reservations necessary. Major credit cards accepted. Castelo de São Filipe, Setúbal (phone: 65-523844). Expensive.

Rio Azul Big, with an open kitchen, this is a prime place for lovers of seafood — fresh crab, lobster, shrimp, and prawns. Remember, however, that seafood can be astronomically expensive by local standards (although it's sold by weight, so diners can control what they spend). Try the *sapateira* (sea spider) — it's cheaper than crab or lobster, and just as good. Closed Wednesdays. Reservations advised. Major credit cards accepted. 44 Rua Guilherme Fernandes, Setúbal (phone: 65-522828). Expensive to moderate.

A Roda This small place produces some of the best regional cooking in Setúbal and serves it up with a certain amount of cosmopolitan dash. Like most of the local restaurants, it specializes in fish dishes, but the *lombinho de vaca ao moscatel* (filets of beef braised in wine from nearby Azeitão) is a good non-marine alternative. Or try the *espadarte na cataplana* (swordfish cooked in a covered copper pan). The house wine is the local pedras negras. Closed Sundays. Reservations advised. Major credit cards accepted. Near the ferryboat station for Tróia. 7 Travessa Postigo do Cais, Setúbal (phone: 65-29264). Moderate.

Retiro da Algodeia No frills, and they aren't needed. Big, informal, noisy, and very enjoyable, this is the destination of fish lovers for miles around. *Caldeiradas* (fish stews) and open-fire grills are the specialty. Try the *salmonete* (red mullet) or the *peixe espada* (blade, or scabbard, fish), both of which lend themselves wonderfully to grilling. The local pedras negras wine is a good accompaniment. Closed Mondays. Reservations advised. No credit cards accepted. 30 Estrada de Algodeia, Setúbal (phone: 65-527090). Moderate to inexpensive.

Bocage A popular dining spot where the traditional regional food is prepared simply but well. The establishment doesn't aspire to gastronomic heights or surprises, but it does offer good value. The *costeletas de vitela ao moscatel* (veal cutlets braised in wine with potatoes and onions) are a good choice. Closed Mondays for dinner and Tuesdays. Reservations advised. Major credit cards accepted. 5-8 Rua Marquesa de Faial, Setúbal (phone: 65-522513). Inexpensive.

En Route from Setúbal The Serra da Arrábida, on the Arrábida (or Setúbal) Peninsula, is one of Portugal's loveliest and most distinctive regions. This range of hills rises out of the Sado River estuary west of Setúbal and forms a high ridge of limestone along the peninsula's southern coast. The whole area, comprising the *serra,* which is a national park, and the region around it, has a character of its own, with its own wines, its own cheeses, its own microclimate, and its own flora and fauna. Because of its unique geography, plants survive here that long ago disappeared from the rest of the Iberian Peninsula. Two roads lead west from Setúbal through the range: N10-4 follows the coastline, while the more spectacular N379-1 traverses the spine of the hills, offering stunning views along the way. About 7½ miles (12 km) from Setúbal along N379-1, a signposted left turn winds down to a little harbor, Portinho da Arrábida, where there is a marvelous, crescent-shaped beach protected by a high escarpment. (Lack of space makes parking formidable in summer.) High on the mountainside above the harbor is the Convento de Arrábida, a Franciscan monastery founded in 1542. A close view of the lovely old monastic building, rising in cellular form like a terraced wasp's nest, can be had by driving a little way along N10-4 from the road leading down into Portinho. About 4½ miles (7 km) beyond the Portinho turnoff from N379-1, the road branches left to the fishing town of Sesimbra.

SESIMBRA A popular holiday resort and consequently very crowded in summer, Sesimbra is a center for big-game fishing. Tuna, shark, and swordfish are all caught here. Unfortunately, uncontrolled development has blighted the outskirts of what was once an attractive little fishing village, but there is some charm left in the old village core. The remains of a fine 13th-century castle stand guard over the town from a high hilltop (the castle is empty now, but visitors can walk around it for the superb view). Sesimbra has plenty of fish restaurants where it is easy to get a good meal — although there is no really outstanding dining spot. The fish to order here is swordfish, because it's difficult to find on menus elsewhere; it's usually prepared as a steak (*bife de espadarte*). Also a delicacy is *peixe espada,* which translates literally as "swordfish" but is, in fact, blade, or scabbard, fish. Sesimbra's *caldeiradas* (fish stews made with six or seven varieties of fish) are also particularly good. The tourist office is at 26-27 Largo da Marinha (phone: 1-223-5743).

CHECKING IN

Villas de Sesimbra An apartment-hotel complex set back in the hills, it boasts a full complement of resort-type facilities, including heated outdoor pools, a health club (with a gym and a sauna), tennis and squash courts, bars, restaurants, and even a children's play area. The 207 units — all equipped with kitchenettes, telephones, satellite TV, 4-channel video, and private baths — range in size from studios to penthouse suites, and are set around gardens and panoramic terraces. About 1¼ miles (2 km) from the ocean, on Altinho de São João, Sesimbra (phone: 1-223-2775; fax: 1-223-1533). Expensive to moderate.

Mar In a good position overlooking the sea, this is an excellent, modern hostelry offering 120 rooms with private baths and balconies, as well as a restaurant, a disco, and a swimming pool. 10 Rua General Humberto Delgado, Sesimbra (phone: 1-223-3326; fax: 1-223-3888). Moderate.

Residencial Nautico Just a short distance from the sea, this charming little hotel has 15 rooms and 2 suites (all with baths), and a bar, but no restaurant. Bairro Infante Dom Henrique, Sesimbra (phone: 1-223-3233). Moderate.

EATING OUT

Algamar Very close to the beach, it specializes (not surprisingly) in seafood, such as *feijoada de gambas* (shrimp with beans). Closed Mondays. Reservations unnecessary. Major credit cards accepted. Av. dos Naufragos, Sesimbra (phone: 1-223-4214). Moderate.

Ribamar There is no "best" seafood restaurant in town, but this is typical of the better eateries. Try any of the Sesimbra specialties. Closed Mondays. Reservations advised. No credit cards accepted. 29 Av. dos Naufragos, Sesimbra (phone: 1-223-4853). Moderate to inexpensive.

En Route from Sesimbra Returning eastward, a 9-mile (14-km) drive along N379 leads to Vila Nogueira de Azeitão, at the foot of the Serra da

Arrábida. The most notable of several fine buildings in this attractive old village is the early-16th-century palace of the dukes of Aveiro, still used as a family residence. Here also are two wineries that should be visited. On the main street of town are the old cellars of *José Maria da Fonseca* (phone: 1-208-0002), where the once widely appreciated moscatel de Setúbal is made. Little known outside of Portugal, it is nevertheless a superb dessert wine that many experts place among the finest of Europe's sweet wines. The cellars are open weekdays from 9 AM to noon and 2 to 5 PM; members of small groups can ask to see the small wine museum that the firm maintains here. Around the corner, on the main Lisbon–Setúbal road, is the big, ultramodern winery belonging to *J. M. da Fonseca International* (phone: 1-208-0227), which makes several classic table wines that are highly regarded in Portugal, but is best known abroad for Lancers Rosé. Visiting hours are the same as those of the *José Maria da Fonseca* cellars.

Continue eastward from Azeitão, taking N10 in the direction of Setúbal for about 1¼ miles (2 km); then branch left onto N379 and follow the signs for Cabanas, Quinta do Anjo, and Palmela; the latter is 7 miles (12 km) from the turnoff.

CHECKING IN/EATING OUT

Quinta das Torres This very comfortable *estalagem* is in a 16th-century mansion, approached by a tree-lined driveway and surrounded by delightful gardens. A natural pool for swimming graces the grounds, as does a fine ornamental irrigation pond with a little classical pavilion in its center. There are 8 rooms with baths, 2 suites, and 2 bungalows. The style of an old country house extends to the dining room, which serves simple but good Portuguese fare, and to the service. Two dishes to try are the *bacalhau dourado* (fried dried cod) and the *carril de gambas* (curried shrimp). This is also one of the few places where the exquisite and increasingly rare azeitão cheeses — small, creamy sheep's milk cheese with a flavor rather like good brie — can still be found. Restaurant closed Saturdays. The entrance to the inn's driveway is on the right side of N10 just after leaving Vila Nogueira de Azeitão in the direction of Setúbal (phone: 1-208-0001). Expensive.

PALMELA The massive castle towering over this little town, at the northeastern end of the Serra da Arrábida, is worth the climb for the views alone. Constructed by the Moors, it was reconstructed after the 12th-century reconquest, but was partially demolished by the 1755 earthquake that laid waste to Lisbon. Many of the 18th-century houses in the narrow streets below the walls were built with stones salvaged from the disaster.

CHECKING IN/EATING OUT

Pousada de Palmela This 27-room, air conditioned inn is installed in a monastery (Convento de São Tiago) that was built within the castle precincts during the 15th century. The marvelous location and handsome appointments make it one of the flagships of the state-owned *pousada* chain, and the restaurant, occupying the old refectory, offers not only delightful decor, but also the best cooking to be found around Palmela. When game is in season in the fall and around *Christmas,* this is a good place to try *perdiz* or *codorniz estufado* (partridge or quail casseroles in red wine). At other times, try the various lamb dishes, especially *borrego assado no forno* (oven roast with onions, garlic, and bay leaves). This is another of the few remaining places where azeitão cheeses can be found. Castelo de Palmela, Palmela (phone: 1-235-1395; 212-686-9213 in the US; fax: 65-235-0410). Expensive.

En Route from Palmela The signposted access to the A2 toll highway is about 1¼ miles (2 km) away. From there, it is a 20-mile (32-km) drive to the Tagus bridge — the Ponte 25 de Abril — which leads into Lisbon. The world's third-longest suspension bridge, it offers what is probably the finest view of the capital.

The Algarve

From the wild and windy headlands of Cabo de São Vicente (Cape St. Vincent) to the tranquil estuary of the Guadiana River on the Spanish border, the natural setting of Portugal's Algarve coast is markedly different from that of the rest of the country. While the Alentejo region, just to the north, shares the Algarve's sunny disposition, its undulating landscape is sparsely vegetated. By contrast, the Algarve has distinctive vegetation, including almond trees (a delight when they blossom in early spring), lush spreading fig trees, olive trees, and the *alfarrobeira* (carob bean tree), which is the basis of a thriving local industry. Unfortunately, development for the tourism industry has destroyed much of this natural growth on the main highway that traverses the coast for about 100 miles, but the back roads of the Algarve open up another world. Here the traveler may share the road with only a plodding mule cart and breathe in the beauty of a landscape uncorrupted by neon signs.

There are wide variations in the landscape even within this relatively small coastal province of Portugal. The area between Sagres and Lagos — known as the Costa Vicentina, at the western end of the Algarve — is characterized by dramatic bluffs and promontories and has been declared a protected zone because of the special value of its flora and fauna. To the east, near Faro, is the Ria Formosa marshland, where the coast is paralleled by long sandbanks enclosing seawater lagoons, considered unique in Europe, that are teeming with interesting birds and marine creatures.

Its Moorish past also distinguishes the Algarve from the rest of mainland Portugal. The marked Arabic character derives from the sheer duration of the Islamic occupation, which lasted longer here than it did elsewhere in the country. Before the coming of the Moors, however, the Algarve shared with the rest of Portugal a history of invasion by Phoenicians, Romans, and barbarians. The original inhabitants of the area — known to the ancient Greeks as the Cunete tribe — played host first to the Phoenicians, who, around 1300 BC, founded cities at Tavira, Faro, Portimão, and Lagos. Their influence can be seen in the exotic form of the local fishing boats, which are graced with sweeping Asian prows and sometimes have a mystical-looking eye painted on either side. (They can still be seen in Albufeira, Portimão, and Faro.)

The Romans then had their turn. Their road system ran south from Lisbon through Alcácer do Sal to Beja (which was their southern capital) in the Alentejo, then on through Mértola to emerge in the Algarve at Castro Marim, just north of Vila Real de Santo António on the Spanish border. Castro Marim, a fortress town of humble, whitewashed houses that commands a view into Spain over the Guadiana River, imparts a sense of this history. The salt pans that lie below the battlements were worked by the Romans, too.

The Moors conquered the Iberian Peninsula in 711. While the crusaders managed to recapture most of it for Christianity by 1139, the Algarve did not come back into the fold until 1249. The inland city of Silves, on the Arade River, was then known as Xelb and was the capital of Moorish Algarve. At its apogee, it was an Arab city of great luxury and nobility, a place where fleets loaded oranges, figs, and olives for export to distant lands. The river has long since silted up, but the rich orange groves and an imposing castle testify to its role in this period. Many Algarve towns have Moorish names — Faro, Tunes, Odeleite, Odeceixe, Odeáxere, Odelouca, Alcoutim, Aljezur, Alvor — as does the region itself; "Algarve" comes from the Arabic *Al-Gharb,* meaning "the West," referring to the land west of their territory in Andalusia.

The Algarve has been attracting European vacationers for years, but only fairly recently have Americans begun to discover its beaches — fine, pale sand in long stretches and tiny coves — and year-round sunshine (the best weather is from the end of January through October; from mid-May to the beginning of October for swimming). Luxury and lesser hotels and resort complexes abound in the more developed parts of the coast, offering excellent opportunities for fishing, boating, water skiing, windsurfing, golf, tennis, and riding. Yet development notwithstanding, there are also simple towns and small fishing villages.

Seafood is, naturally, the basis of traditional Algarve cooking. *Amêijoas* (clams) are the prize coastal produce, and they are presented at their best as *amêijoas na cataplana,* a dish of clams, ham, local salami, garlic, and coriander, named after the Moorish copper pressure cooker in which it is prepared. *Lavagante, lagosta,* and *caranguejo* (lobster, crayfish, and crab, respectively) are also featured, as is *lula* (squid), cooked in a variety of ways. No visit to Portugal would be complete without trying the humble but tasty sardine, and the recommended place to do this in the Algarve is at the *Portimão Sardine Festival,* held in August on the waterfront, under the town's picturesque iron bridge.

The town of Sagres, at Portugal's southwesternmost point, is a logical starting place for a visit to the Algarve, although reaching it may involve retracing steps, because the main road from Lisbon meets the coast's two main arteries near Albufeira, 50 miles (80 km) east. An alternative is to take the coastal road from Lisbon, passing through Odemira and Aljezur and picking up N125 at Vila do Bispo, a few miles north of Sagres. Because the Algarve's coastal road, N125, is only 100 miles (160 km) long, however, repeating any part of it is easily done. In addition, the recently inaugurated Via do Infante Highway (IP1), running from Albufeira to Vila Real do Santo António, is a wider, speedier alternative to N125, and a way to avoid the most heavily touristed coastal region between Albufeira and Faro when traveling to points east or west. N125, however, runs closer to the coast, with connecting roads to the quieter, less-trafficked beaches.

Those arriving by plane at Faro, toward the Spanish border, can either reverse the route, working their way east to west, or go directly to Sagres, and then follow the route west to east as outlined below. One possibility for those choosing the latter option would be to take the back road to Silves from Faro, through the Algarve's rural hinterland. Leave the main highway 5 miles (8 km) west of Faro and go to Loulé, turning left at the main city square, near the bus terminal, and heading north to Salir, 9½ miles (15 km) away. Turn left there and go another 9½ miles (15 km) to the delightful town of Alte, immortalized by James Michener in his book *The Drifters*. Continue in the same direction, through São Bartolomeu de Messines, to Silves. When returning east from Sagres, proceed straight on N125, dispensing with the detour to Silves and Loulé described below.

Expect to pay $175 to $300 for a double room in a hotel listed below as very expensive, $100 to $175 at an expensive establishment, and $50 to $100 at a moderate place. Inexpensive hotels and pensions can cost less than $50 — much less in the low season — but none has been included below, because such establishments are generally not up to the standards of the foreign pleasure traveler. All hotels listed have air conditioning and most are open year-round; for accommodations in July through September, it is advisable to book well in advance. Eating out needn't be costly. A good meal for two with wine at the inexpensive end of the spectrum will cost from $20 to $30. Expect to pay $30 to $70 for two at a place described as moderate; at restaurants listed as expensive, allow $70 to $100. For each location, hotels and restaurants are listed alphabetically by price category.

SAGRES This dramatic promontory, known as Ponta de Sagres in Portuguese, and Cabo de São Vicente (Cape St. Vincent), 4 miles (6 km) away, form the southwestern tip of Europe, a wild landscape where rugged cliffs plunge down to clear blue waters. A popular belief stemming from prehistoric times held that the gods met here, and to the ancients, this was the end of the known world, beyond which the setting sun fell off the face of the earth. The gods aside, the area has played an important role in Portuguese history. It was here during the early 15th century that Prince Henry the Navigator, son of João I of Portugal and his English wife, Philippa of Lancaster, established a school of geography and navigation — a community of scholars who pooled their knowledge of mapmaking, shipbuilding, and mathematics. Under his leadership, Portugal's first voyages of discovery were planned and undertaken, preparing the way for the epic voyages of later men such as Vasco da Gama, Bartholomeu Dias, and Christopher Columbus (the latter — an Italian — sailed under the Spanish flag after being snubbed by the Portuguese). Although Prince Henry, known in Portuguese as Infante Dom Henrique, did not sail himself, the contributions he made to the advancement of navigation and exploration provided the basis for the rise of the Portuguese colonial empire and allowed the country to maintain naval supremacy for almost 2 centuries.

The village of Sagres, set on the cliffs, was razed in 1597 by the British fleet under Sir Francis Drake, then at war with the Spanish (Portugal was subordinated to the Spanish throne at this time). Today it is a bit of an eyesore, but redeemed by the area's spectacular views. Within walking distance of the village is Cabo de São Vicente, where the lighthouse can be inspected at the keeper's discretion daily between 10 AM and noon and 2 and 5:30 PM (a tip is expected). Between the two villages, on a windswept bluff, is the Fortaleza do Beliche, dating from the 15th century, but largely reconstructed during the 18th century. An enormous mariner's compass etched into the ground here was presumably designed by Prince Henry. The fort (closed January through March; no admission charge) has climbable ramparts, and its main building houses a restaurant and a *pousada* (see *Checking In*). Also within the walls is the Sagres Tourist Office (phone: 82-64125). Six miles (10 km) north of Sagres, near Vila do Bispo, is Praia de Cordoama — one of the least spoiled beaches on the west end of the Algarve.

CHECKING IN

Pousada do Infante Set on a cliff top, this government-owned inn has 23 rooms with private terraces overlooking the sea; there also are 16 guestrooms in an annex (all have private baths). For additional details, see *Pousadas and Manor Houses* in DIVERSIONS. Sagres (phone: 82-64222; 212-686-9213 in the US; fax: 82-64225). Expensive.

Baleeira Also on the cliffs, it offers quality service and a tasteful, well-maintained interior. Dining here at sunset as migratory swallows swoop around the bluff is an experience in itself; the 120-room hotel also has its own tennis court, swimming pool, and bicycles for hire. Fishing excursions can be arranged. Sitó da Baleeira, Sagres (phone: 82-64212; fax: 82-64425). Moderate.

Casa da Chá Fortaleza do Beliche Under the same management as *Pousada do Infante,* this *pousada* has 4 guestrooms with private baths within the Beliche fortress. All are furnished in simple, regional style, and overlook either the sea or a garden courtyard. The terraced restaurant serves good local fare. Fortaleza do Beliche, Sagres (phone: 82-64124). Moderate.

EATING OUT

Tasca Set on a cliffside beneath the *Baleeira,* this is a wonderful place to dine alfresco on a summer day. Shellfish is the specialty (the restaurant has its own lobster pools), the salads are fresh, and the wine list is good. In addition, the service is quietly efficient and prices are very reasonable. (Guests at the *Baleeira* receive a 10% discount upon presentation of their check-in card.) Closed Saturdays and from mid-December to mid-January. Reservations unnecessary. Major credit cards accepted. Sagres (phone: 82-64177). Inexpensive.

En Route from Sagres The road to Lagos (N125), 20½ miles (33 km) east, has little traffic, heightening the feeling of otherworldliness at the Algarve's western tip. The road runs inland from the coast — here called the Costa Vicentina — but a series of good *praias* (beaches) can be reached by turning off N125. All signposted, they include Praia do Martinhal (the sign reads *Martinhal Motel Restaurant*), Praia da Salema, Praia do Burgau, and Praia da Luz, a popular resort center.

LAGOS An attractive harbor town, this, too, holds memories of Henry the Navigator. It was from this port in the mid-15th century that the ships sailing under Prince Henry's authority actually embarked, setting their course south to explore the west coast of Africa. It was also from Lagos that the doomed, fanatically religious King Sebastian sailed in 1578 to fight the Moors at the historic battle of Alcázarquivir in Morocco. He died on the battlefield, leaving the throne to his elderly uncle, the childless Cardinal-King Henrique, who reigned for 2 years. An illegitimate member of the royal family, the Prior of Crato, claimed the throne next but was bested by the superior force of another claimant, Philip of Spain. Because Sebastian's death in North Africa had not been confirmed, his subjects persisted in the belief that he would one day return to rule again. In the centuries since, fake Sebastians have "returned" to Portugal — even today claimants show up in small villages — and the term Sebastianism came to be used to describe the belief in a returning redeemer. The legend is commemorated in Lagos with a controversial statue by modern sculptor João Cutileiro, who depicts Sebastian as a visionary adolescent gazing out to sea. The statue is in the central Praça de Gil Eanes (named after one of Prince Henry's explorers, born in Lagos), where young travelers with backpacks congregate nowadays.

As a result of the voyages to Africa, Lagos had the dubious privilege of being the site of Europe's first slave auctions. The arcaded building where they were held, the Mercado de Escravos (Slave Market), still stands near the waterfront in the Praça da República, opposite the Igreja de Santa Maria, although there is no plaque to mark its significance. Another of the town's interesting sites is the 18th-century baroque Igreja de Santo António (Rua General Alberto da Silveira), with a breathtaking ornate altarpiece, gilt cherubs, and antique tiled surfaces. The *Museu Regional* (adjoining the church; phone: 82-762301) contains a strange mix of works, from local handicrafts to Roman statuary and a mid-16th-century diptych showing the Annunciation and the Presentation in the Temple, attributed to Francisco de Campos. The museum is open from 9:30 AM to 12:30 PM and 2 to 5 PM; closed Mondays; admission charge. Parts of the Old City walls remain; built by the Moors and fortified by their Christian successors, they were largely destroyed by the 1755 earthquake that devastated most of Lagos. Outside the walls is the 17th-century Forte do Pau da

Bandeira, built as a defense against pirates. For more information on this historic city, capital of the Algarve from the late 16th to the mid-18th century, stop in at the Lagos Tourist Office (Largo Marquês de Pombal; phone: 82-763031).

CHECKING IN

De Lagos Gardens, patios, pools, and villas with orange-tiled roofs surround the main building of the best property in town. There are 300 balconied rooms, tennis courts, and a restaurant. Rua Nova da Aldeia (phone: 82-769967; fax: 82-769920). Expensive.

Casa de São Gonzalo An 18th-century manor house in the center of town, with a flower-filled patio, a stone fountain, and 10 rooms with private baths. Closed November through March. 73 Rua Candide dos Reis (phone: 82-762171). Moderate.

Meia Praia Located over 2½ miles (4 km) east of Lagos, this modest hotel has 66 rooms with a sea view, a restaurant, a pool, gardens, and tennis courts. Closed November through March. Meia Praia (phone: 82-762001; fax: 82-459171). Moderate.

EATING OUT

Alpendre A stop in Lagos would be worthwhile for this restaurant alone. Classic Portuguese cooking and service have made it a legend — the best dishes are distinctively local. Try the *amêijoas na cataplana* or the *amêijoas à bulhão pato* (clams cooked in a garlic and coriander sauce). For dessert, the crêpes suzette are a rich delight — the restaurant uses a rare, expensive, aged brandy, adega velha, for the flambé process. There is also an impressive list of the best Portuguese wines. Open daily. Reservations advised. Major credit cards accepted. 17 Rua António Barbosa Viana, Lagos (phone: 82-762705). Expensive.

Dom Sebastião Specialties at this rustic inn include *cabrito* (kid) in wine sauce, and *amêijoas na cataplana.* Closed 2 weeks in December. Reservations advised. Major credit cards accepted. 20-22 Rua 25 de Abril, Lagos (phone: 82-762795). Moderate.

En Route from Lagos There are several good beaches and rocky coves off N125 between Lagos and Portimão, 11 miles (18 km) away, including Praia da Dona Ana, Meia Praia, and Praia dos Três Irmãos.

PORTIMÃO This is one of the fishing capitals of the Algarve — but it's a modern commercial fishing center rather than a picturesque village. Set on the estuary of the Arade River, Portimão was largely destroyed by the 1755 earthquake, but it is now the second-largest town along the coast (after Faro). It has a relaxed Mediterranean atmosphere and a host of sidewalk cafés, bars, restaurants, and shops; its August sardine festival is an optimal occasion to sample the Algarve's *sardinha assada* straight from the charcoal grill. A little over a mile south of town, on the western side of the river's mouth, is Praia da Rocha, a seaside resort on one of the best (but unfortunately overcommercialized) beaches on the coast, noted for its majestic rock formations. On the opposite side of the river is Ferragudo, a small waterfront hamlet with a ruined 16th-century castle. The tourist office is at Largo Primeiro de Dezembro (phone: 82-23695).

CHECKING IN

Golfe da Penina A long-established luxury property, this hotel — set amid 3 golf courses — features 192 rooms and suites, several restaurants, tennis, horseback riding, a swimming pool, transportation to the beach, water sports, and a conference room. Three miles (5 km) west of Portimão. Montes do Alvor (phone: 82-458900; fax: 82-458999). Very expensive.

Bela Vista At Praia da Rocha, this is an oasis of quality in a desert of tourist hype. An old-fashioned hotel with 14 rooms (all with private baths) in a former mansion, it is something of a Victorian folly, with spires, dark woodwork, and stained glass windows. There is direct access to the beach. Av. Tomás Cabreira, Praia da Rocha (phone: 82-24055; fax: 82-415369). Expensive.

EATING OUT

A Lanterna This eatery on the road to Ferragudo, near the bridge over the Arade, serves fish and seafood, as well as the house specialty — duck. Closed Sundays and early December through late January. Reservations unnecessary. Major credit cards accepted. N125, Cruzamento de Ferragudo, Portimão (phone: 82-23948). Expensive.

Safari An unpretentious place with good, fresh seafood and a beachfront view. Some Angolan cuisine also is served; there is Brazilian and African music on summer weekends. Open daily, except for a few weeks in January or February. Reservations unnecessary. Major credit cards accepted. Rua António Feu, Praia da Rocha (phone: 82-23540). Moderate.

En Route from Portimão Drive north on N124 and N266 for 13 miles (22 km) to the Monchique mountain range.

MONCHIQUE The eucalyptus-scented and lushly wooded heights of the Monchique Mountains are a pleasant change from the landscape of the coast. The Serra de Monchique, along with the Serra do Caldeirão to the east, forms a natural barrier between the Algarve and the rest of Portugal — which explains not only the coastline's flawless weather, but also why the Moors were able to hold out longer here than elsewhere in the face of advancing Christian armies. In bygone days, the Monchique hills were also a fashionable retreat from the Algarve's searing heat, the medicinal springs bursting from volcanic rock deemed beneficial for a variety of ailments. The springs, located at Caldas de Monchique, a leafy spa town about 10 miles (16 km) north of Portimão, were known to the Romans; King João II, who reigned from 1481 to 1495, was said to have been treated for dropsy here (to no avail — he died soon after). The spa's more recent heyday was around the turn of this century, when the *Grand* hotel and its casino were in full swing. Today, the charm of Caldas still lies in its old-fashioned cafés banked with potted palms, its walks and views, and the cool town square, where the old hotel (but not the casino) has been restored. The town of Monchique proper, 4 miles (6 km) north of Caldas, has a parish church with a Manueline doorway, but the town itself is less an attraction than the drive to the summit of the nearly 3,000-foot Fóia, the highest point of the Serra de Monchique. Take N266-3 west out of Monchique, and in a few miles the view opens up to the coast and the sea and seems to stretch almost to Africa. The whole Monchique area is known for its handicrafts, including colorful rugs and furniture — the folding wooden Monchique stools are derived from a Roman design and are a good bargain.

CHECKING IN

Abrigo da Montanha A recently enlarged *estalagem* (inn) of 27 rooms and 5 suites, it sits a mile or so southwest of Monchique, along the way to Fóia. Even if you're not staying here, sit under the umbrellas amid the cool hydrangeas of the terrace restaurant and supplement the famous Fóia view with good food and wine — specialties are meat and fish dishes prepared with cilantro, garlic, olive oil, and lemon. Estrada de Fóia, Monchique (phone: 82-92131; fax: 82-93660). Moderate.

Mons-Cicus Above Monchique, this former private house has 3 rooms opening onto a terrace overlooking the hills to the ocean, and 6 other guestrooms in the back, all with private baths. There are 2 pools and a tennis court, as well as a restaurant and bar with several fireplaces. Estrada da Fóia, Monchique (phone: 82-92650). Moderate.

EATING OUT

1692 The restaurant's name comes from the date the stone building it occupies was constructed. At first owned by the Catholic church, then converted into a hotel — the *Grand* — the building has been restored. Local dishes are served in a wonderfully green, shady setting. Be sure to try the traditional hot bread, baked with *chouriço,* the spicy Portuguese sausage; it comes from the village's restored bread oven. Open daily. Reservations unnecessary. Major credit cards accepted. Caldas de Monchique (phone: 82-92205). Inexpensive.

En Route from Monchique Return to Portimão and take N125 east 5 miles (8 km) to Lagoa, a market town with a well-known crafts fair, *Fatacil,* held every August. This is the junction for the road to Silves, 4½ miles (7 km) north, and Carvoeiro, 3 miles (5 km) south.

CHECKING IN

Almansor Built in a low, semicircular shape to mirror the curving, jagged cliffs and hidden cove that it overlooks, this hotel has 290 rooms with sea views. An excellent restaurant, a pool, tennis, horseback riding, conference facilities, and the nearby 9-hole *Quinta do Gramacho* golf course round out the amenities. It's also within walking distance of Carvoeiro. Vale de Covo, Praia de Carvoeiro, Lagoa (phone: 82-358026; fax: 82-358770). Expensive.

SILVES The sleepy, sunny inland town gives few clues to its former importance as the capital of the Moorish kingdom of the Algarve, although its combination of cypresses, orange groves, and the red stone Moorish castle do impart the flavor of an Arab city. Known as Xelb in Moorish times, Silves sits on the north bank of the Arade River, which is now silted up but at one time made the town a flourishing river port. The castle (open daily from 8 AM to 7 PM, to 5:30 PM in winter; no admission charge) has enormous underground cisterns and provides a sweeping view of the Algarve coast. Next to it is the 13th-century Gothic cathedral, the Sé, built on the site of the former mosque. With its gargoyles and cleft windows offset by the same rich, reddish local stone as the castle, the church holds considerable architectural interest. The Cruz de Portugal, an unusual 15th-century limestone sculpture about 10 feet high showing Christ crucified on one side and in the arms of the Virgin Mary on the other, is at the town's eastern exit (on N124 toward São Bartolomeu de Messines). The tourist office in Silves is on Rua 25 de Abril (phone: 82-442255).

CARVOEIRO This little fishing village has become the favored Algarve playground of northern Europeans — Germans, Dutch, and Scandinavians (and British, too, although their stamping ground tends to be the zone farther east, from Albufeira to Faro). Fishermen's white houses on the cliff tops set the tone, and Carvoeiro remains picturesque, despite the modern resort villa complexes that encircle it, with tennis courts, pools, and their own bar and restaurant facilities. The town has a small but pretty beach.

En Route from Carvoeiro Pick up N125 east once again and continue to Ferreiras, where a right turn onto N395 leads to Albufeira, 16 miles (26 km) from Lagoa. A few miles beyond Lagoa, on the right side of the road, is *Porches Pottery,* just before the village of the same name. Founded by the late Irish artist Patrick Swift, who was well known in Portugal as an illustrator, the pottery sells hand-painted ceramics, many bearing his distinctive designs. The pieces are not as authentically Portuguese as other local products, but traditional Portuguese techniques have been used in making them, and their superior glazes make them less likely to chip.

CHECKING IN

Vilalara Set in a lush, dream-like garden landscape, this resort village on the way to Albufeira has 50 suites and 152 beautifully furnished villas. There is an indoor and an outdoor restaurant, 5 swimming pools, and a private beach. Armação da Pera (phone: 82-314910; fax: 82-314956). Very expensive.

ALBUFEIRA This large resort town was the last Moorish stronghold in the Algarve. At one time, it was a picturesque fishing village, but in recent years it has suffered from the onslaught of development and become the heart of the tourist's Algarve. Set on a cliff, it has steep, cobbled streets that are thronged in summer, and its main beach, reached via a tunnel carved through rock, is wall-to-wall flesh at the height of the season. (There are beaches nearby where it is possible to find space, however — just walk along in either direction.) Little of historical value remains in Albufeira, but a walk through town is a pleasant experience, since there are multitudes of shops, small bars, and restaurants to suit every taste. Albufeira's tourist office (phone: 89-512144) is on Rua 5 de Outubro, the main street.

CHECKING IN

Sheraton Algarve Situated on a low cliff above a good swimming beach outside Albufeira and set amid pine groves and Japanese gardens, this new luxury hotel in an elegant Moorish-style building has 215 rooms, most with a sea view. The decor is inspired by regional styles — the guestrooms have marble surfaces, orange-tile floors, and white, stone-carved ornamentation. Facilities include 2 restaurants, a private beach, tennis, a 9-hole golf course, 3 pools, a health club with a gym and sauna, and conference rooms. Praia de Falésia, Albufeira (phone: 89-501999; fax: 89-501950). Very expensive.

Boa Vista A cut above average in the Albufeira area, mainly because of its tasteful decor and its site on the cliff, which faces a little away from the center of town. It has 93 rooms and a swimming pool, plus a restaurant. 20 Rua Samora Barros, Albufeira (phone: 89-589175; fax: 89-588836). Expensive.

EATING OUT

A Ruína Good fish and seafood are served in the pleasant setting of an old fort overlooking the main beach. Open daily. Reservations unnecessary. No credit cards accepted. Cais Herculano, Albufeira (phone: 89-512094). Moderate.

En Route from Albufeira Return to N125 and continue east to Almansil, where roads lead north to the town of Loulé, and south to the hotel, resort villa, and golf course complexes of Vale do Lobo and Quinta do Lago, while the main road presses on to Faro. A must stop in the vicinity is the Igreja de São Lourenço, in the village of São Lourenço, a mile (1.6 km) beyond Almansil. A small church, this is nevertheless one of the most noteworthy in the Algarve, because its walls and barrel-vaulted ceiling — even the underside of the dome — are entirely covered with blue-and-white 18th-century *azulejos* depicting the life of St. Lawrence. The nearby *Centro Cultural São Lourenço,* set up in restored, 200-year-old buildings, is a privately run establishment that maintains its own art gallery and sponsors classical music concerts in summer. Among the regular exhibitors at the gallery are Portuguese artists José Guimarães and João Cutileiro (creator of the statue of King Sebastian in Lagos), whose works can be bought here for prices that are reasonable by the standards of the international art market.

CHECKING IN

Quinta do Lago The luxury hotel of the Quinta do Lago resort offers 132 rooms and 9 suites on an extensive, pine-covered, beachfront property. All rooms have oceanview balconies; there are 2 swimming pools (3 if you count the private pool that goes with the presidential suite), 2 tennis courts, and a health club, in addition to the resort's four 18-hole golf courses. There's also the *T Club* restaurant (see *Eating Out*). Quinta do Lago, Almansil (phone: 89-396666; 212-838-3110 or 800-223-6800 in the US; fax: 89-396393). Very expensive.

EATING OUT

Pequeno Mundo One of the better-known nouvelle cuisine restaurants in the Algarve, it's set in a restored typically Algarvean farmhouse. Closed Mondays. Reservations necessary. Major credit cards accepted. Almansil (phone: 89-399866). Expensive.

T Club One of the most luxurious culinary spots in the Algarve, set on the grounds of the exclusive, posh *Quinta do Lago* resort. Owner José Manuel Trigo learned his trade from Régine, the queen of clubs, managing her establishments in Brazil. Marbled wood, velour curtains, impeccably set tables, and soft lighting set the tone in this elegant place, where international nouvelle cuisine and traditional dishes from Portugal and Europe share the menu. A Central European flavor is added in the summer with the arrival of a French cook. Guests can dance their calories away in the adjoining *boîte,* or adjourn to the plush bar for a glass of port. Closed Sundays. Reservations necessary. Major credit cards accepted. Quinta do Lago, Almansil (phone: 89-396588). Expensive.

LOULÉ This old market center with tree-lined streets is in the hills only 3 miles (5 km) up a back road from Almansil. The market in the center of town (open every morning except Sundays) used to be the place to buy traditional, hand-crafted wooden toys. Alas, they've given way to the plastic variety, but there are other bargains to be had: rough terra cotta plates hand-painted with exuberant peasant designs; figs, almonds, mountain cheeses, and juicy local oranges; and, in the surrounding shops, excellent baskets and raffia hats at ridiculously low prices. Decorative bridles and cattle bells that make good wall hangings can also be bought at local saddleries. The tourist office is in the Edificio do Castelo (phone: 89-63900).

CHECKING IN

Loulé Jardim A charming small hostelry in Loulé's town center, set on an old-fashioned square. It has 52 rooms and a rooftop swimming pool, but no restaurant. Praça Manuel de Arriaga, Loulé (phone: 89-413094 or 89-413095; fax: 89-63177). Moderate.

EATING OUT

Aux Bons Enfants French provincial fare is served at this small establishment. Closed Sundays. Reservations necessary. Major credit cards accepted. 116 Rua Eng. Duarte Pacheco, Loulé (phone: 89-62096). Moderate.

En Route from Loulé Take the road to Faro, 10 miles (16 km) southeast of Loulé.

CHECKING IN/EATING OUT

La Réserve Off the road between Loulé and Faro, this is an elegant, modern, and luxurious establishment (the only member of the prestigious Relais & Châteaux group in Portugal). It offers 20 suites (each with a bedroom, bath, and living room, plus a verandah with a sea view) and 12 rooms; grounds that include a swimming pool and a tennis court; and a highly praised restaurant that has earned a Michelin star. Open year-round (restaurant closed Tuesdays). Santa Bárbara de Nexe (phone: 89-899-0474; 800-677-3524 in the US; fax: 89-90402). Expensive.

Quinta da Benatrite About 11 miles (18 km) northwest of Faro, this *Turismo de Habitação* participant is housed in a 300-year-old farm manor with carved-stone windows and doors, and is warmly furnished in a combination of 18th- and 19th-century Portuguese and English styles. The 2 guest-rooms have bamboo-lined ceilings. There also are 2 suites and a separate garden house, with a terrace leading down to the garden. All have private baths. Sports options include a pool, tennis, and horseback riding. Dinner is prepared on request. Santa Bárbara de Nexe, Faro (phone and fax: 89-90450). Moderate.

FARO Although the airport for the Algarve is located here and the city teems with tourists, there is nevertheless a very attractive quality about Faro, which is the modern-day capital of the Algarve and, with about 50,000 inhabitants, the largest town on the coast. It has streets paved with white cobblestones, cafés set in parkland, and, despite having been reduced to nearly total rubble in the earthquakes of 1722 and 1755, an Old Town partly enclosed by 13th-century defensive walls. Enter the old section, São Pedro, through the 18th-century Arco da Vila, an archway just south of the Manuel Bivar Gardens bordering the *doca* (harbor). Not far away is the Sé (Cathedral), in Largo da Sé, a square noteworthy for its harmonious lines. Little of the original cathedral remains — just a 13th-century Gothic tower — but its main body is lined with 17th-century *azulejos*. The *Museu Arqueológico* (Archaeological Museum; phone: 89-822042), near the cathedral in the 16th-century Convento de Nossa Senhora da Assunção (which has a very fine cloister), is made up of two sections: an archaeological collection containing rare Roman objects unearthed in the area, and the Ferreira do Almeida collection of sculpture and painting, including 14th-century jasper statues. It's open weekdays from 9:30 AM to 12:30 PM and 2 to 5 PM; admission charge. Faro's tourist office (8-12 Rua da Misericórdia; phone: 89-803604) is near the Arco da Vila. Several blocks north is the interesting Igreja do Carmo. A baroque church of some beauty, it has a gruesome Capela dos Ossos — a chapel delicately paneled in bones and skulls dug up in the adjacent cemetery. Also in the Old Town are the *Museu da Marinha* (Seafaring Museum; Av. da República; phone: 89-803601; open weekdays from 9 AM to 12:30 PM and 2 to 5:30 PM; admission charge); and the *Museu Etnográfico Regional* (Museum of Regional Culture; Praça de Liberdade; phone: 89-27610; open weekdays from 9 AM to 12:30 PM and 2 to 6 PM; admission charge).

A completely different Faro can be discovered by taking a hiking tour through the rare Ria Formosa marshlands, which form a sort of coastal apron of dunes, inlets, and islands south of the city. As planes drone regularly overhead to and from the airport runway nearby, it is possible to see — with the help of a guide — fiddler crabs, gray herons, egrets, storks, gannets, plover, terns, oystercatchers, and, on a good day, the rare purple gallinule. Guided English-language tours are offered daily at 9 AM and 2:30 PM, starting from the Parque Natural da Ria Formosa in Olhão (Quinta de Marim; phone: 89-704134), about 7 miles (12 km) from Faro. The town's beach, Praia de Faro, also occupies an island, Ilha de Faro; this long and narrow coastal sandbank, about 3 miles (5 km) south of the center, is connected to the mainland by a bridge and also by a ferry from the harbor.

CHECKING IN

Casa da Lumena There are 12 rooms with baths in this 150-year-old manor house in town, also a quiet stone courtyard with a vine-covered bar, and an excellent restaurant. 27 Praça Alexandre Herculano, Faro (phone: 89-801990; fax: 89-804019). Moderate.

Eva A modest hotel on the marina, with 150 rooms, some overlooking the Old Town, others with terraces with views of the boats and the ocean. Two rooftop pools, and an outdoor café and dining area, round out the amenities. Av. da República, Faro (phone: 89-803354; fax: 89-802304). Moderate.

Pousada de São Brás About 14 miles (22 km) north of Faro, this whitewashed country inn has 29 rooms, all with verandahs facing the hills above town and private baths. There is a pool, a tennis court, and a restaurant over a garden terrace. N2, São Brás de Alportel (phone: 89-842306; fax: 89-842305). Moderate.

EATING OUT

Roque Popular with the locals for its fresh sea fare and low prices, it is on the Ilha de Faro, a short drive from town on the airport road and then across a long, low bridge. The restaurant faces the beach on the marshland side of the island, with a large area for dining outside. Closed Wednesdays in winter. Reservations unnecessary. Major credit cards accepted. Ilha de Faro, Faro (phone: 89-817868). Inexpensive.

En Route from Faro From here to the east, almost to the Spanish border, the coast is paralleled by a series of sandbars. Like the Costa Vicentina of the western Algarve, the eastern extremity has special charms — it is less spoiled by development, and less crowded in summer. Take N125 about 5 miles (8 km) to Olhão and then another 14 miles (22 km) to Tavira.

OLHÃO A pretty fishing port, Olhão is known as the "Cubist" village, because of its cube-shape white houses with terraced roofs. The peculiarity of its architecture gives it a Moorish appearance, although the town was founded during the 18th century, long after the Moors departed the Algarve. A good local market sells fresh produce and some handicrafts. The tourist office is at the Largo da Lagoa (phone: 89-713936).

TAVIRA A leading Portuguese weekly has described this as "one of the few places in the Algarve that tourism hasn't corrupted and urban development hasn't disfigured." Happily, the town council has banned construction that might affect the historic qualities of the Old Town center, which is well worth a stroll. Another fishing port, straddling the Gilão River, Tavira is of ancient origin — the foundations of the bridge across the river date from Roman times. There are remains of an old Moorish castle, and the houses have an Eastern touch to them, with Moorish-influenced roofs. Tavira's tourist office is at Praça da República (phone: 81-22511).

En Route from Tavira Continue east on N125; after Conceição there is a turnoff for Cacela Velha, a small village reconquered by the Moors in 1240 and featuring an 18th-century fort. Another tiny coastal settlement, almost within sight of Cacela Velha, is Fabrica, reached from a road leading off from the Cacela Velha turnoff. Both places have restaurants — little more than local taverns — that are good places to stop for a meal. Or stop for a swim or a meal at Praia da Manta Rota (reached by another turnoff from N125), a beach offering a long stretch of white sand (although it is pretty packed in summer). Alternatively, press on 14 miles (22 km) along N125 past Monte Gordo — a fishing village turned overdeveloped resort, with pale blue houses and a wide, pine-backed beach — to Vila Real de Santo António, where the Algarve coast comes to an end at the Spanish border.

EATING OUT

O Estábulo On Manta Rota Beach, it offers a cross section of traditional Algarve seafood dishes and a good wine list. Closed Mondays. Reservations unnecessary. Major credit cards accepted. Praia da Manta Rota (phone: 81-951246). Moderate.

Costa Another very simple place, with a large rush verandah providing an outdoor dining area facing a lagoon-like strip of water busy with swimmers, boaters, and windsurfers. The menu includes *caldeirada* (seafood stew), *frango com amêijoas* (chicken with clams), *ensopado de enguia* (stewed eels), and *arroz de marisco* (rice with shellfish), as well as fresh, steamed oysters. Closed Mondays, and weekdays from December through March. No reservations. No credit cards accepted. Sitió da Fabrica, Vila Nova de Cacela (phone: 81-951467). Inexpensive.

VILA REAL DE SANTO ANTÓNIO This town provides a fitting farewell to the Algarve. When Lisbon was destroyed by an earthquake in 1755, much of the Algarve also was affected, and Vila Real de Santo António was razed. It benefited from the national reconstruction plan drawn up by the Marquês de Pombal, whose classical buildings with minimal exterior decoration were laid out in an austere grid pattern. The old center, an example of a pure Pombaline town, imparts the sense of harmony inherent in this style, but the town's unique flavor also comes from the strong Gypsy influence here. Vila Real looks out on the great expanse of the Guadiana River, across which is Ayamonte, Spain, reached by a bridge. A whimsical but interesting museum, the *Museu Manuel Cabanas* (Praça Marquês de Pombal) specializes in wood engravings, but it also has material on the history of the town. It's open from 4 to 6 PM and 9 to 11 PM from July through September; from 11:30 AM to 12:30 PM and 2 to 7 PM the rest of the year; closed Mondays year-round; no admission charge. The Vila Real de Santo António Tourist Office is on the riverside Avenida da República (phone: 81-43272).

CHECKING IN/EATING OUT

Vasco da Gama One of the better places to stay at this far eastern end of the Algarve, it's set among pine trees in the seaside resort of Monte Gordo, a bit less than 2 miles (3 km) west of Vila Real. It has 164 rooms, a restaurant, a bar, tennis courts, and its own swimming pool, as well as access to a long strip of sandy beach. Av. Infante Dom Henrique, Monte Gordo (phone: 81-511321; fax: 81-511622). Moderate.

En Route from Vila Real de Santo António Travelers can either cut roughly 125 miles (200 km) north across the Alentejo via Beja to Evora (see *Evora* in THE CITIES) and from there return to Lisbon, or they can retrace their path along the Algarve coast (or take the new IP1 highway) to Albufeira and pick up the trunk road back to Lisbon. Before leaving Vila Real, however, one last Algarve excursion can be made to the historic fortress town of Castro Marim, 2½ miles (4 km) north on N122.

CASTRO MARIM Possibly Portugal's oldest town, it has an unbroken history of settlement going back many centuries before the birth of Christ — Neolithic implements found here are believed to have been hewn by the original Portuguese tribes. The Phoenicians arrived during the 9th century BC, and the Romans and the Moors followed centuries later, until the Christian reconquest in 1242. Most of the walls of the original castle-fortress, an accretion of centuries of building, have collapsed, but at one time the whitewashed houses that now constitute the town all nestled within them. The castle ramparts provide a wonderful view of the Guadiana and the Spanish town of Ayamonte, as well as the Castro Marim salt pans (worked since Roman times) and Vila Real de Santo António.

The Azores

Dreamers and rebels quickly appreciate places like the Azores, which continue to resist the inevitability of progress as the developed world has come to know it. Rising from the depths of the mid-Atlantic (Lisbon lies about 900 miles to the east, New York 2,300 miles to the west), they are a land apart in pace and setting. Although there has been substantial economic evolution during the past decade or so, the nine volcanic islands of the archipelago retain a simplicity and cohesiveness that exist in very few places.

Of the nine islands in the Azores chain, São Miguel, the largest, and neighboring Santa Maria are easternmost. Between 90 and 160 miles to the west are Terceira, Graciosa, São Jorge, Pico, and Faial, clustered in a central island grouping. Flores and its tiny companion, Corvo, are approximately another 150 miles to the west. That the islands are today an autonomous region of Portugal (linked to the mainland, but fiscally and operationally independent) is a result of agreements established soon after Portuguese explorers came upon them in 1427 or 1431, 8 decades or so after the islands first appeared, misplaced by several hundred miles, on a Genoese map of 1351. While Italians (or Italians sailing for Portugal) may have preceded the Portuguese in finding the islands, it is thought that the Carthaginians, consummate seafarers of ancient times, may have preceded them both by nearly 2,000 years, although no remains of Carthaginian settlements have been found.

The Portuguese, who named the islands after what they thought were *açores* (goshawks), but which were actually kites, proved more committed to these mid-ocean outposts than their possible Carthaginian predecessors. In the century following the Azores' discovery, the Portuguese empire extended to Africa, Asia, and South America, and the islands provided an anchorage and resupply point for voyages of exploration, settlement, trade, plunder, and conquest. Colonization of the Azores themselves began almost immediately, in 1439, with farmers and herdsmen the first settlers. Where soil was ample, large pastures soon replaced the native forest. Where the land was more rock than soil, rock removal followed the cutting away of trees and brush, and the rocks became the walls that today etch the landscape. Towns developed both in the countryside and along the coasts. Wealth flowed through the ports, where merchants reprovisioned ships or exported barley and maize. By the 18th century, Ponta Delgada (on São Miguel), Angra do Heroísmo (on Terceira), and Horta (on Faial) were large and architecturally distinguished townships.

Land grants provided a basis of wealth for missions established by Jesuits, Franciscans, and other Catholic religious orders. Beautiful churches and chapels were built in thanks for safe passage or for profits anticipated or gained. Their interiors were gilded and richly detailed, their treasuries stocked with valuable gifts. Although the religious orders are long gone (expelled during the 19th century for religious, political, and economic reasons), the churches they left behind are still in use. Easily accessible and remarkably well preserved, they are a fundamental element of the Azorean lifestyle.

In the late 1700s, after the fortunes of empire had waned, a new armada — American whaling ships — discovered the Azores. Many of the thousands of Azorean men who signed aboard American vessels during the better part of the following century ultimately settled in the United States, forming sizable communities in New England, California, and Hawaii. Others headed to Canada, South Africa, and South America. By local reckoning, today's quarter million Azoreans are outnumbered by emigrants and their descendants around the world four to one.

During World War II, the islands served as a staging area for Europe-bound American forces, a factor that strengthened the already existing commercial and family links to the United States. (The American presence continues today with an airfield at Lajes, Terceira.) After the war, but before the advent of the jet plane, the Azores served as a refueling point for airplanes crossing the Atlantic. But with whaling, treasure seeking, and the discovery of new worlds all in the past, the 20th century saw the islands settle into the time warp that today is their greatest asset. Outside of Ponta Delgada on São Miguel, the largest city in the islands, there are no traffic jams in the Azores, no contemporary chic, no franchised homogeneity. There is also no mass tourism to thwart authenticity and clutter the landscape with high-rise hotels (though some building projects recently have been undertaken). Few cruise ships come to call, although several hundred sailboats in transatlantic runs between the Caribbean and the Mediterranean drop anchor off Faial and Flores.

In the villages, where donkeys and horses share the road with cars and pickup trucks, it is the former that set the pace. Even in Ponta Delgada, and in the archipelago's other large town, Angra do Heroísmo on Terceiro, the scale remains human, with buildings rarely more than 4 stories high. And on these two most heavily populated islands, windmills and church towers still dominate the rural skyline. Surrounding them is an intricate web of fields that provide most Azoreans with a livelihood. Farmland — maize and tobacco are the main crops — and dairy pastures occupy the lowlands and foothills. Higher up on the mountains are remnants of the original forests; lumber is one of the Azores' leading exports. Tuna fishing is also a major industry.

The landscape attests to the volcanic origin of the Azores, although once-fiery craters and cinder cones are now dressed in a carpet of green. On most of the islands, the largest craters house lovely, steep-walled lakes, and steam vents and hot springs evince molten fires that still burn beneath the surface calm. Almost all of the islands have experienced either volcanic eruptions or major earthquakes within the past decade.

Wrestling with nature in mid-ocean isolation has made pioneering self-reliance a definitive part of the temperament of the 254,000 Azorean residents. The climate may be benevolent, avoiding extremes of hot and cold and the worst of the earth's storms, but life still exacts its toll, as the weatherworn features of the old reveal.

Yet because many Azoreans have spent time overseas or have family elsewhere, there's a casual sophistication, an awareness of the world that seems incongruous with their rural isolation. English is widely spoken, even in remote villages. Some expatriates return to the islands at retirement, when there's an American pension or savings to bankroll land, a house, and the good life. Like mainland Portugal, the Azores are relatively inexpensive, a feature attractive to visitors, too.

The Catholic church plays a crucial role in communal life, dominating the spiritual as well as the terrestrial landscape. Baroque churches grace every village, their bells chiming the passing hours to those at home or in the field. The full measure of belief surfaces during the long festival season that runs from spring through early fall, with the largest, most impressive processions and displays held soon after *Easter*. Week after week, different villages celebrate and affirm family bonds and religious fraternity, some villages creating giant street tapestries made of countless flower petals in extravagant design. On Terceira, the festival season ends with the running of rope-tethered bulls through the narrow streets of the larger towns.

Some people believe the Azores are all that remain of the lost continent of Atlantis. Certainly few places offer such easy access to their magic, which makes them both wonderful to explore and vulnerable to the impact of discovery. Winding two-lane roads circle the islands and challenge their volcanic heights. Sometimes views are panoramas, encompassing the mountains, cliffs, and sea. At other times, the attention is drawn by details: the sweet smell of native cedar, the pink brilliance of roadside lilies, the harmony of forest birds. Island to island, nature runs rampant, providing justification for hyperbole and the real opportunity to get away from it all.

Sources and Resources

TOURIST INFORMATION

The Regional Tourism Board for the Azores is headquartered on the island of Faial (Edificio do Relogio, Colonia Alema, Horta; phone: 92-23801; fax: 92-31496). Branch tourist offices are found in Horta, Faial (Rua Vasco da Gama; phone: 92-22237); in Ponta Delgada, São Miguel (Av. Infante Dom Henrique; phone: 96-25743; fax: 96-22211); in Angra do Heroísmo, Terceira (47A Carreira dos Cavalos; phone: 95-23393); and at Santa Maria Airport (on the island of Santa Maria; phone: 96-86355). There is also a tourist office representative at the *Aparthotel Caravelas* (Rua Conselheiro Terra Pinheiro, Madalena, Pico; phone: 92-622500). Note: It is 1 hour earlier in the islands than on mainland Portugal all year long.

LOCAL COVERAGE An English-language booklet, *Azores: Guide for Tourists,* revised annually and distributed free at tourist offices, provides excellent information on all the islands. Also worth reading and available in English editions are pamphlets on the individual islands, each containing useful maps of the island and its main town. The Azorean Emigration Center (71 *Centro Comercial Sol-Mar,* Av. Infante Dom Henrique, Ponta Delgada, São Miguel; phone: 96-27486) produces a monthly tabloid that includes some features in English. It is available at the center or at the tourist office in Ponta Delgada.

TELEPHONE The area code for the islands of São Miguel and Santa Maria is 96; for Terceira, Graciosa, and São Jorge, 95; for Pico, Faial, Flores, and Corvo, 92. If calling from a different area code within the Azores, or from mainland Portugal, dial 0 plus the appropriate area code before the local number.

CLIMATE

The Azores are not tropical isles. Neither palm trees or beaches are abundant. The waters of the Gulf Stream modify the islands' maritime climate, and temperatures average a very comfortable 55 to 77F from the coldest to the hottest months. There are, nevertheless, four distinct seasons, with a change of flowers from spring through autumn. At times, the air can be quite humid, exaggerating summer's warmth or winter's chill. Because the islands lie beneath a mid-ocean convergence of high altitude winds, they have earned a reputation for quickly changing weather and frequent rains. The rainfall that keeps them green occurs mostly from October through April, but weather can be changeable in any season.

GETTING THERE

AIRPLANE *TAP Air Portugal* flies to the islands from the United States and from points on mainland Portugual. Inter-island service for all islands except Corvo is provided by *Serviço Açoreano de Transportes Aéreos (SATA).* *TAP* offices can provide ticketing and information for *SATA* flights. *Ocean Air* (Terceira; phone: 96-27281; fax: 96-26382) operates plane service to Corvo and Flores from Terceira. Local weather conditions may result in flight delays or cancellations, and it is advisable to travel to remote islands such as Flores and Corvo only if there's time to absorb a possible delay of several days or longer. Advance reservations and early arrival at the airport are suggested as flights are often sold out, particularly during winter, when frequency is reduced substantially. For additional details, see *Getting Around* in the individual island entries.

FERRY Although no ferries connect mainland Portugal with the islands, there is inter-island ferry service among the islands of the central group (Terceira, Graciosa, São Jorge, Pico, and Faial). The service is operated by *Transma-*

çor (29 Rua Nova das Angústias, Horta, Faial; phone: 92-23334; fax: 92-22585), and if the ferry schedule fits your itinerary, it's a relaxing, scenic, and inexpensive way to travel. The shortest run links Faial to Pico in about a half hour. Faial to São Jorge takes about 2 hours, São Jorge to Terceira about 4 hours, and Terceira to Graciosa about 4 hours. For travel between Flores and Corvo, it's possible to rent a boat, with or without a captain. For additional details, see *Getting Around* in the individual island entries.

SPECIAL EVENTS

Religious festivals held in one village or another fill the calendar year, but are most concentrated from *Easter* through August, so it's worth planning an itinerary to include one. The largest include elaborate processions and tapestries, or mosaics, of flowers laid down in the streets. Particularly noteworthy are the *Festas do Senhor Santo Cristo* (Lord Christ Festivities), the largest religious festival in the islands, held on São Miguel the weekend of the fifth Sunday after *Easter*. Beginning on *Whitsunday* (7 Sundays after *Easter*), all the islands hold *festas* in honor of the Holy Spirit. These go on for successive Sundays as village after village puts on its own version of a celebration that goes back to the Middle Ages. The festivals last throughout the summer on Terceira, where offerings are collected in little chapels called *impérios* and where *touradas à corda* — bullfights in which the bull is tied to a rope and teased but not killed — and the running of bulls through the streets mark the end of the season. The same type of bullfight, as well as folk singing and dancing, are part of the colorful *Festas de São Joaninhos* (St. John's Festivals), held in June on Terceira. From the first to the second Sunday in August, the island of Faial celebrates *Semana do Mar* (Sea Week), a secular event stressing water sports and other water-related activities, with accompanying folk music, band concerts, and parades. Another ocean-related event is the *Festa dos Baleeiros* (Whalers' Festival), the last week in August on Pico; although whaling is a thing of the past in the Azores, this religious procession, followed by music and dancing, fulfills a vow made by local whalers in the 19th century. Also during August, Santa Maria holds the *Maré do Agosto* (August Tide), a music festival of contemporary artists that often features international names.

SPORTS AND FITNESS

In addition to the options below, tours with a focus on sports (fishing, golfing, hunting, and others) can be arranged through *João Freitas Martins,* 14 Rua Açoreano Oriental, Ponta Delgada, São Miguel (phone: 96-27415; fax: 96-27532).

DEEP-SEA FISHING Local waters provide not just sustenance but big-game sport fishing and some world records. From August through October, the catch is marlin; from September through November, swordfish and tuna; shark, barracuda, bonito, and others are in season all year. Contact *Pescatur* (1 Largo Francisco Tavares, Ponta Delgada, São Miguel; phone: 96-629225; fax: 96-24757). Inland waters on São Miguel and Flores offer a limited season on black bass, pike, perch, and trout. The required licenses can be obtained from *Direcção dos Serviços Florestais* (38 Largo de Camões, Ponta Delgada, São Miguel; phone: 96-26288; fax: 96-26745). Also see *Gone Fishing* in DIVERSIONS.

GOLF The *Clube de Golfe da Ilha Terceira* (Fajãs Agualva; phone: 95-25847) has an 18-hole course, clubs and caddies for hire, a clubhouse bar and snack shop, and 2 tennis courts. It's closed Mondays except when they fall on holidays (including American holidays, thanks to the air base nearby). São Miguel has a beautiful 18-hole course at the *Clube de Golfe de São Miguel* (near Furnas; phone: 96-54141), 45 minutes to an hour from Ponta Delgada.

HIKING Hikers can set out on scores of walks in the countryside with no cause for concern. Information about sightseeing hikes can be obtained at the local tourist offices. On Pico, the hike to the summit comes with some precautions (see *Special Places* in the Pico section).

SNORKELING AND SCUBA On Terceira, contact the *Clube Náutico de Angra do Heroísmo* (Estrada Gaspar Côrte Real, Angra do Heroísmo; phone: 95-23300) and rent a boat and driver for a run to the nearest reefs. On Faial, contact *Clube Naval da Horta* (Cais de Santa Cruz, Horta; phone: 92-22331). The *Estalagem de Santa Cruz* (Rua Vasco da Gama, Horta; phone: 92-23021) also handles water sports equipment rentals. On São Miguel, the *Caloura* hotel (Agua de Pau, Lagoa; phone: 96-93240) can provide information regarding equipment, rentals, and locations. Wet suits prevail for much of the year.

SWIMMING Rocky coasts make swimming difficult. Among the few beaches are Praia do Porto Pim, a half-mile stretch of sand on the outskirts of Horta, Faial; the Praia do Populo, near São Roque, and the Praia da Agua d'Alto, both some miles east of Ponta Delgada, São Miguel; and a nice carpet of white sand at São Lourenço Bay, on Santa Maria. In addition, swimming is possible in the freshwater crater lakes of São Miguel, particularly the easily accessible Sete Cidades, although the shoreline entry is muddy and coastal waters shallow. Other natural pools created by volcanic rock formations are popular swimming spots for the locals. Cool winters usually make swimming a summer-only sport.

TENNIS There are courts at the *São Miguel Clube de Tênis* (Av. Cecília Meireles, Fajã de Cima, São Miguel; phone: 96-33647). On Terceira, visitors can play at municipal courts or at the tennis courts of the *Clube de Golfe da Ilha Terceira* (see *Golf*, above). There are 2 courts at Horta's *Clube de Tênis* (at the *Fayal* hotel; phone: 92-22181), and another 2 at Pico's *Clube de Tênis* (Externato da Madalena; phone: 92-92145).

São Miguel

The largest island of the archipelago and the most heavily populated, São Miguel extends approximately 38 miles from east to west and 10 miles from north to south. It is also widely considered to be the most beautiful Azores island, thanks to luxuriant vegetation, a series of magnificent crater lakes, and a landscape that glows with vibrant color. In the eastern part of the island, at Furnas, the still-active volcanic depths surface in sulfur-fumed steam and boiling water.

With Santa Maria, São Miguel was one of the first of the islands to be colonized, and it has maintained its importance ever since. Ponta Delgada, on the south coast, is the island's capital, the capital of the Ponta Delgada district (one of the three political districts into which the archipelago is divided), and the largest city in the Azores. It's a lively town, with much of architectural note, shops that add a touch of unexpected sophistication, and a distinctive charm. Ribeira Grande, Vila Franca do Campo, Lagoa, and Povoação (the first settlement on the island) are other towns of historical and architectural merit.

It takes a day in the countryside to understand why São Miguel is called the *ilha verde* (green island). The landscape is a rock-veined patchwork of greens, accented with blue-purple hydrangeas, azaleas, and other flowers that scent the air for 8 months of the year. Gently sloping lowlands are punctuated by rows of graceful cinder cones, and dark patches of forest crown the heights. From lookouts atop its tallest mountains, the views are spectacular.

GETTING AROUND

It takes 2 to 3 days to begin to do justice to São Miguel. Excellent roads circle the island, cutting through the mountains at several places.

AIRPORT *TAP Air Portugal* arrives daily from Lisbon and weekly from Boston, Porto, and Funchal, Madeira. *SATA* flies in from the other islands. São Miguel's Aeroporto de Ponta Delgada (also called Nordela) is 3 miles (5 km) from the heart of town. Rental cars are available, and a taxi ride into town costs about $6. Offices of both *TAP Air Portugal* (phone: 96- 629777) and *SATA* (phone: 96-27221 for information, 96-22311 for reservations) are at 52 Av. Infante Dom Henrique in Ponta Delgada.

BICYCLE The countryside provides some excellent biking possibilities, although flat, open stretches alternate with hilly terrain that can prove tiring on cross-country rides. Contact *Logo* (Av. Kopke, Ponta Delgada; phone: 96-25795) for bicycle and motorbike rentals.

BUS Local bus service is available around the island. Sightseeing tours by bus are offered by *Agência de Viagens Ornelas* (Av. Infante Dom Henrique, Ponta

Delgada; phone: 96-25379) and *Agência de Viagens e Turismo Melo* (24 Rua Santa Lucia, Ponta Delgada; phone: 96-25314).

CAR RENTAL The local *Avis* affiliate, *Ilha Verde Rent-a-Car* (19 Praça 5 de Outubro, Ponta Delgada; phone: 96-25200; and at the airport; phone: 96-27301), has the largest fleet. You also can find vehicles at *Autoatlantis* (65 Largo de Santo Andre; phone: 96-23465; and at the airport; phone: 96-22491). As a rule of thumb, here and elsewhere in the archipelago, expect a rental car to cost anywhere from $65 to $100 a day, including gas and taxes. Watch out for traffic jams in Ponta Delgada around 9 AM and between 5:30 and 7 PM. Azoreans can be aggressive drivers, so stay alert on the road.

TAXI Cabs are available, and most offer car-and-driver day rates. As on other islands, hiring a car and driver for a day of touring usually costs less than a rental car, with most taxis available at $60 to $85 for an 8- to 10-hour day. Hotel personnel are usually helpful in securing a car and driver if a taxi is not readily at hand. Be on the lookout for newer, plusher Mercedeses (like the one driven by Vasco Guadencio; phone: 96-97119), if you're going to spend the day touring. They're not necessarily more expensive than some of the more basic models seen around town.

SPECIAL PLACES

PONTA DELGADA Capital of São Miguel since 1546, Ponta Delgada (pop. 21,000) is a flat town that stretches nearly 2 miles along a bay on the island's south coast. The seafront promenade — the Avenida Infante Dom Henrique — is fed by narrow streets that invite wandering. Highlights of any tour of the town are several old churches: The Igreja de São Sebastião, a parish church built in the 16th century and altered in the 18th century, is noted for a Manueline façade and two baroque doorways as well as for a high altar of carved cedar; the Igreja do Colégio, a former Jesuit church, was founded in the 15th century, although the present building, an exercise in baroque geometry, dates from later; and the Igreja de São José is decorated with blue-and white 18th-century *azulejos*. Also of note are the 18th-century town gates. The *Museu Carlos Machado* (Rua João Moreira; phone: 96-25532) is the city's museum of ethnographic interest, art, and natural history; it's open Tuesdays through Fridays from 10 AM to 12:30 PM and 2 to 5:30 PM; weekends from 2 to 5:30 PM; no admission charge. Ponta Delgada began as a fishing village, and boats still unload their catches at sunrise at the western end of the harbor. For those who like sleeping past dawn, an equally colorful sight is the open-air market near Largo São João, open weekdays until 5 PM. The best times for market lovers, however, are Fridays and Saturdays before 1 PM. The market is closed Sundays and holidays.

CALDEIRA DAS SETE CIDADES About 20 minutes by car northwest of Ponta Delgada, this is perhaps the single most spectacular sight in the Azores. In the crater of an extinct volcano lie two lakes, separated by a land bridge only a few yards wide. One lake is green, the other blue, and the panorama from the crater rim is worth several visits, since it shifts dramatically with the quickly changing Azorean weather. Two roads lead to the crater rim and the charming lakeside village of Sete Cidades. According to legend, one of the seven cities of Atlantis is buried in the crater.

VALE DAS FURNAS The island's volcanic past comes to life in the steam vents, hot springs, thermal pools, and boiling mud of the Furnas Valley, about an hour east of Ponta Delgada. Also here are a lake (Lagoa das Furnas), a botanical garden (Parque Terra Nostra), and the spa town of Furnas, whose waters are reputedly effective cures for rheumatism, lumbago, sciatica, skin conditions, and other ailments. For those with adventuresome palates, there are local folk who can help prepare stews or corn on the cob cooked or steamed in the hot thermal springs. Ask at the *Terra Nostra* hotel, Rua Padre José Jacinto Botelho (phone: 96-54304).

RIBEIRA GRANDE Granted a charter in 1507, this town of 5,600 on São Miguel's north coast has many fine 16th- and 17th-century buildings. The church of Nossa Senhora da Estrela, consecrated in 1517, is the oldest; inside, the Santos Reis Magos chapel contains various paintings, including a 16th-century Flemish triptych.

SHOPPING

Ponta Delgada is the island's shopping center. Some very high-style European fashions can be found, but on the whole, the town caters to the local population, meaning more basic clothing, housewares, and other necessary items. Shops of interest to visitors include:

CALECHE DESIGN High-fashion leather goods, some made regionally. Largo da Matriz, Ponta Delgada (phone: 96-22523).

CENTRO COMERCIAL SOL-MAR A centrally located mall with a good selection of shops. 71 Av. Infante Dom Henriques (phone: 96-629096).

RADIANTE An interesting collection of small gold charms. 46-51 Rua Machado dos Santos, Ponta Delgada (phone: 96-24696).

XANDI Antiques and contemporary local craftwork. 22 Largo da Matriz, Ponta Delgada (phone: 96-22410).

NIGHTCLUBS AND NIGHTLIFE

After-dark life is scarce in the Azores, and what action there is can be found mostly in São Miguel. The *Nautilus* (1A Praça Velha, Povoção; phone: 96-65481) is a pub on the island's far southeastern end, with an *esplanada* (patio) and snack bar, plus a discotheque that opens daily except Mondays at 11 PM. *Cheers* (2 Rocha Quebrada, Atalhada, Lagoa; phone: 96-92662) is a refurbished disco that attracts rowdy locals and is open daily from 10 PM to 4 AM; *Pópulo's Inn* (Villa Pann, Livramento, Ponta Delgada; phone: 96-31680), closed Mondays, is one of São Miguel's most popular dance spots. *A Taverna* (42 Rua de São Miguel, Ponta Delgada; phone: 96-24727) is a quiet place with live music nightly, and *fado* on Friday and Saturday evenings.

CHECKING IN

Hotels, pensions, and the occasional *albergaria* and *estalagem* (inn) provide accommodations for visitors. On the whole, on all the islands, even modest rooms are clean and comfortable; at better hotels, they generally come with private baths, telephones, and TV sets. As on the Portuguese mainland, breakfast is almost always included in the price. Advance reservations are suggested, particularly during the summer, when limited space may well sell out. Rates are anywhere from 20% to 30% lower in low season, from November through April, but even at their highest, they are quite reasonable compared with mainland Portugal or other tourist destinations. For that reason, almost all of the hotels below fall into either the moderate or inexpensive categories. Expect to pay $115 and up for a double room in the rare hotel listed as expensive, from $70 to $100 at a moderate place, from $50 to $60 at an inexpensive hotel, and under $50 at a very inexpensive one.

EXPENSIVE

Açores Atlântico A pink marble hostelry on Ponta Delgada's main seafront avenue. Outside, it's an exercise in island-style architecture with modern flair; inside, there are 140 air conditioned rooms and suites with private balconies, plus a restaurant, a heated indoor pool, a sauna, and a gymnasium. Av. Infante Dom Henrique, Ponta Delgada (phone: 96-629300; fax: 96-629380).

MODERATE

Avenida A modern, 80-room hotel in the heart of town, it's clean and well kept, with such up-to-date facilities as a bar, a restaurant, satellite TV, and gift shops. Rua Dr. José Bruno Tavares Carreiro, Ponta Delgada (phone: 96-27331; fax: 96-27698).

Gaivota An apartment hotel, its rooms (27) with kitchen facilities are a prime asset; another is a harborfront setting that offers panoramic views from flower-decked balconies. 103 Av. Marginal, Ponta Delgada (phone: 96-23286; fax: 96-27209).

São Pedro This would be a find anywhere in the world, which makes it all the more exceptional in Ponta Delgada. An elegant, early-19th-century private home — it originally belonged to Thomas Hickling, first American consul in the Azores — has been turned into the finest hotel in the archipelago, with 26 spacious rooms, antique furnishings, excellent service, and a quiet setting just on the edge of downtown. It also has a good restaurant (see *Eating Out*). Largo Almirante Dunn, Ponta Delgada (phone: 96-22223).

Solar do Conde A renovated nobleman's mansion, this apartment hotel has 27 rooms with a traditional atmosphere. Situated a half hour from Ponta Delgada on the north side of the island, it's just yards away from the ocean. There is a restaurant, a bar, a pool, and 2 tennis courts, one of which is covered. 36 Rua do Rosário, Capelas (phone: 96-98887; fax: 96-98623).

Terra Nostra Adjacent to the hot springs in the spa town of Furnas, this place is permeated with the spirit of the 1930s, when it was built. Staying here is a good idea for those who want to explore the eastern part of the island without the hour's drive from Ponta Delgada. Guests can play golf nearby, stroll in the lovely botanical gardens, dine at the restaurant, soak in the outdoor thermal pool or the newer indoor pool, or otherwise take the waters. There are 74 rooms, including 40 in the wing that contains a gymnasium. Rua Padre José Jacinto Botelho, Furnas (phone: 96-54304).

Vinha da Areia An *estalagem* (inn) of 38 rooms, 2 of which are suites facing the sea. Located in Vila Franca do Campo, some 20 miles east of Ponta Delgada, this property has a restaurant, a small private beach, and a natural bathing pool. Vila Franca do Campo (phone: 96-53133; fax: 96-52501).

INEXPENSIVE

Canadiano There are 50 rooms in this modern hostelry not far from the *Museu Carlos Machado*. There's no restaurant, but there is a comfortable bar and video room. 24A Rua do Contador, Ponta Delgada (phone: 96-27421).

Central The oldest *pensão* in Ponta Delgada benefits from charm, a friendly atmosphere, and a central location. Half of the 42 rooms have private baths. There's no restaurant. 82 Rua Machado dos Santos, Ponta Delgada (phone: 96-24491).

EATING OUT

On São Miguel and the other islands, restaurant fare tends to be grilled fish or meat rather than local specialties such as *caldo de nabos* (turnip soup) or *linguiça com inhames* (spiced sausage with yams). Dorado is the most common catch of the day; squid, octopus, shrimp, lobster, and crab may all be on the menu of the better restaurants of Ponta Delgada or Angra do Heroísmo. Cheeses, usually tangy, are made in many rural districts; those of São Jorge are the best known. São Miguel's pineapples, grown in greenhouses, are prized. Verdelho wines from Pico are the islands' finest; those of Graciosa and Terceira are also highly rated. The Azores are not the place for haute cuisine, although a few of the better restaurants come close. Happily, the cost of dining in such restaurants is not a great deal higher than eating in more modest establishments, and because the span from most to least is not great, we do not list any of them as expensive. Expect to pay anywhere from $20 to $35 for dinner for two, with light drinks or fairly good wine, in restaurants listed as moderate, and less than $20 in those listed as inexpensive.

MODERATE

Boavista Seafood specialties range from lobster to barnacles, all prepared to order. This is in the residential part of the city, above the downtown area. Closed Saturdays for lunch, and Sundays. Reservations unnecessary. Visa accepted. 12 Rua Ilha São Miguel (upstairs), Ponta Delgada (phone: 96-24272).

O Fervedouro Regional dishes include *caldeirada de peixe* (fish chowder) and *polvo guisado em vinho* (octopus cooked in wine sauce). This is a good lunch stop for those touring the island. Closed Mondays. Reservations unnecessary. Visa accepted. 3 Rua do Passal, Ribeira Grande (phone: 96-72820).

London Local VIPs like to have dinner here. It has good service, a menu featuring good international fare and some excellent regional specialties (try the Azorean cheeses), and a central location. Closed Sundays. Reservations advised. Major credit cards accepted. 21 Rua Ernesto do Canto, Ponta Delgada (phone: 96-22500).

São Pedro The dining room of the best hotel in the islands. Tables are elegantly laid with linen, the waiters are equally well attired, and the food matches the setting. Grilled dorado, shrimp, and spider crab are all worth a mention. Open daily. Reservations unnecessary. Major credit cards accepted. Largo Almirante Dunn, Ponta Delgada (phone: 96-22223).

Tropicália This dining spot created by the owner of the *London* serves seafood specialties. Open daily. Reservations advised. Major credit cards accepted. Just a few steps from the *São Pedro* hotel, Largo Almirante Dunn, Ponta Delgada (phone: 96-27100).

White Shark A small place with interesting maritime decor on the west side of town, it's run by a German couple who specialize in shark and beefsteaks cooked over a lava stone grill. Open daily except Sundays for dinner. Reservations advised. Major credit cards accepted. 95 Rua de Tavares Resendes, Ponta Delgada (phone: 96-27663).

INEXPENSIVE

A Lota Fresh seafood is the specialty, with a sea view the bonus. Open daily. Reservations unnecessary. No credit cards accepted. 13 Largo do Porto, Lagoa (phone: 96-92595).

São Miguel A typical *restaurante da terra* (local eatery) where you'll often see hardy farmers and noisy fishermen having lunch. Very good fish, and some good, though basic, meat dishes are served. Near the *Mercado da Graça.* Open daily. Reservations unnecessary. No credit cards accepted. 45 Rua do Mercado (phone: 96-25603).

Santa Maria

Probably the first of the Azores sighted by Portuguese explorers, Santa Maria is 55 miles south of São Miguel and is the southernmost island in the archipelago. Along with São Miguel, it was also one of the first to be settled, and by 1472 its main town, Vila do Porto — but then known simply as Porto — became the first town in the islands to receive a charter. Christopher Columbus dropped anchor here in 1493 on his return from the West Indies; members of his crew are said to have prayed in a tiny church that still stands at Anjos, on the north coast. The island measures only approximately 77 square miles, yet its terrain ranges from hilly in the northeast to flat in the southwest and encompasses sheer coastal cliffs, deeply indented bays, and pastoral villages. The large airport outside Vila do Porto is a still-used reminder of the role the Azores played during World War II as a forward base for American troops and in Allied antisubmarine efforts. Today, jets occasionally make use of its long runway on flights linking the islands with South America.

GETTING AROUND

AIRPORT *SATA* (phone in Vila do Porto: 96-6501) flies between São Miguel and Santa Maria. The island's Aeroporto de Santa Maria is just short of 2 miles (3 km) northwest of Vila do Porto.

CAR RENTAL Cars are available from *Rent-a-Car Mariense,* at the airport (phone: 96-82880). Two-lane roads crisscross the island, which can easily be seen in a day.

SPECIAL PLACES

VILA DO PORTO Whitewashed walls and red tile roofs define Santa Maria's main town (pop. 2,000), located on a bay in the southwestern corner of the island. Among its landmarks is the 19th-century parish church, built on the site of a ruined 15th-century church, of which a chapel with a Manueline ceiling remains. The Convento de São Francisco, built in the 17th century, then destroyed by pirates and rebuilt in the 18th century, has lovely chapels, including one decorated with 17th-century *azulejos.* Note: At press time, the convent was closed for restoration.

PICO ALTO Santa Maria's highest peak (almost 1,950 feet), in the center of the island, provides wide-angle views.

BAIA DE SÃO LOURENÇO On the northeast coast, São Lourenço has, besides the bay itself, a beach of white sand — a rarity in the Azores. Off the beach is an islet, the Ilhéu do Romeiro, which has an interesting cave and can be reached by boat.

ANJOS CHAPEL This small chapel on the north coast is a beautifully detailed 15th-century gem that is probably the oldest church in the islands. It has associations with Columbus, some of whose crew gave thanks here in 1493 for their safe return from the voyage that resulted in the European discovery of America.

NIGHTCLUBS AND NIGHTLIFE

Nocturnal activities are not the attraction on this island, but late-night drinks and taped music are available at *Chamine,* a discotheque on Rua São Jose, Vila do Porto (phone: 96-84229).

CHECKING IN

Expect to pay from $50 to $60 at one of the inexpensive hotels listed below.

Aeroporto Accommodations are sparse on the island, but luckily, this 73-room hotel at the airport is clean and well run, and has a pretty good restaurant (see below). Estrada do Aeroporto, Vila do Porto (phone: 96-86211 or 96-86215).

Residencial Travassos The only alternative to *Aeroporto* in town, it has 5 rooms, but no private bathrooms. At press time, there were plans to increase the number of guestrooms and to add private baths to all rooms. 108 Rua Dr. Luis Bettencourt, Vila do Porto (phone: 96-82831).

EATING OUT

Expect to pay anywhere from $20 to $35 for dinner for two, with light drinks or fairly good wine, in the moderate restaurants listed below.

Aeroporto This comfortable restaurant with fish, seafood, beef, and chicken specialties is at the *Aeroporto* hotel. Open daily. Reservations unnecessary. Visa accepted. Estrada do Aeroporto, Vila do Porto (phone: 96-82211).

Praia A simple place in a village on a south coast beach; the menu leans toward fish and seafood. Open daily. Reservations unnecessary. Major credit cards accepted. Praia Formosa (phone: 96-82635).

Terceira

The most heavily populated island in the Azores' central group is 90 miles northwest of São Miguel. Measuring approximately 19 miles by 11 miles, Terceira was the third of the islands to be discovered, hence its name. The first settlers, who arrived in 1450, were Flemish — Flanders was linked by marriage to the Portuguese crown. Vasco da Gama made Terceira a port of call on his return from India and buried his brother on the grounds of the Franciscan friary. Thanks to a central location, the port at Angra (the word means "bay") in the middle of the island's south coast soon became the largest in the Azores. Raised to the status of town in 1534, it prospered from the 16th to the 18th centuries and was embellished with beautiful churches, mansions, and government buildings. In the 19th century, Queen Maria II added the honorific *heroísmo* to its name in recognition of the role the island played on behalf of the liberal Regency during the Portuguese civil war. The city is the island's capital and the capital of the Angra do Heroísmo district, the second of the political districts into which the islands are divided.

The Terceiran landscape ranges from starkly volcanic to lushly pastured to meticulously divided into walled fields known as *cerrados*. In contrast to Angra's relative sophistication — and despite the presence of a US air base that also serves as the island's commercial airport — the countryside remains remarkably rural and untouched, much as on the more remote islands.

GETTING AROUND

AIRPORT *TAP Air Portugal* (144 Rua da Sé, Angra; phone: 95-26489 or 95-26490) flies in once a week from Boston and several times weekly from Lisbon. *SATA* (2 Rua da Esperança, Angra; phone: 95-22013 for information, 95-22016 for reservations) flies in from the other islands, and *Ocean Air* (Terceira; phone: 96-27281; fax: 96-26382) offers service to Corvo and Flores. Lajes Airport is 15 miles (24 km) northeast of Angra, about 30 minutes by car (rental cars are available); the local buses that stop near the airport entrance take about an hour.

BUS Public buses provide scheduled, though infrequent, service to outlying villages. Sightseeing tours by bus are arranged by *Empresa de Viação Terceirense (EVT)*, 15 Rua Dr. Sousa Meneses, Angra (phone: 95-24101).

CAR RENTAL Several firms operate, including *Rent-a-Car Angrauto* (14-16 Rua Frei Diogo das Chagas, Angra; phone: 95-25585); *Cruserve-Rent-a-Car* (10 Rua do Cruzeiro, Angra; phone: 95-25242); and *Ilha 3 Rent-a-Car* (22 Rua Direita, Angra; phone: 95-23115), which picks up and delivers anywhere on the island.

FERRY Ferry service connects Terceira with the other islands of the central group: Graciosa, São Jorge, Pico, and Faial.

TAXI Taxis are available for full-day and half-day touring, as well as for point-to-point service.

SPECIAL PLACES

ANGRA DO HEROÍSMO Named for the sheltered bay that made it a commercial port, Angra was planned in the 16th century but built largely in the 17th and 18th centuries. Although it grew to be one of the two largest cities in the Azores (pop. 12,000), the mansions, churches, and residential and commercial core retain their architectural integrity, and the Old Town has been recognized by UNESCO as a historic monument of international significance. Unfortunately, many of the city's oldest buildings collapsed and many others were badly damaged in a 1980 earthquake. Much has been restored, but there still are signs of the quake's damage.

Among Angra's old buildings, which line narrow streets that wind their way uphill from the port, are the 16th-to-17th-century Colégio church, which has an elaborately carved and gilded altar and a collection of 17th-century Dutch glazed tiles (often open only for mass); the 16th-century church of São Gonçalo, also with a carved and gilded altar; and the 17th-century Palácio Bettencourt, a baroque mansion now the repository of extensive archives. The *Museu Angra* (Ladeira de São Francisco; phone: 95-23147), housed in the former Convento de São Francisco (where the remains of Vasco da Gama's brother are supposed to lie), contains paintings, ceramics, coins, and weaponry. It's open weekdays from 9 AM to 12:30 PM and 2 to 5 PM; no admission charge. The 16th-century castle of São João Baptista, at the western edge of town, is still used by the Portuguese military; it stands at the foot of Monte Brasil, an extinct cinder cone that guards the approach to the port and provides panoramic views of the city and surrounding countryside — it's a favorite picnic spot.

BISCOITOS On the island's north coast, this coastal plain is dotted with unusual formations of black volcanic rock with natural pools. Walls of lava rock enclose fields of black soil planted with grapes, which are used to make the local Biscoitos wines. The *Museu do Vinho* (Canada do Caldeira, Biscoitos; no phone) has a collection of wine making equipment, and old labels and bottles. Owned by the local Brum family, it is open daily from 10 AM to 4 PM.

MATA DA SERRATA These forested hillsides on Terceira's west coast, about an hour from Angra, offer expansive views that take in the neighboring islands of São Jorge and Pico. The sight is particularly impressive at sunset.

ALGAR DO CARVÃO AND FURNAS DO ENXOFRE Ten miles (16 km) and approximately 25 minutes from Angra, in the island's central highlands, are caves with stalactites and stalagmites, usually open on weekends only (more frequently during the summer). Nearby are the steam vents known as the Furnas do Enxofre. Check with the tourist office (phone: 95-23393) for hours.

SHOPPING

The best buys are island crafts, particularly embroidered items.

CASA ILHA LILAS Hand-embroidered goods and other regional handicrafts. 40A Rua de Santo Espírito, Angra (phone: 95-22436).

JOÃO PIMENTAL E COMPANHIA Another source of handmade embroidered items and other handicrafts. 107 Rua de Jesus, Angra (phone: 95-24968).

LUÍS BRANDÃO A well-priced selection of handmade embroidery, including appealing children's clothing and high-quality table linen. 84A Rua Rego, Angra (phone: 95-23284).

NIGHTCLUBS AND NIGHTLIFE

Twin's is one of the best-known dance spots in the islands; it's closed Mondays. 54 Rua Dioga Teive, Angra (phone: 95-32999).

CHECKING IN

Expect to pay from $70 to $100 for a double room at a moderate place listed below, from $50 to $60 at an inexpensive hotel, and under $50 at the very inexpensive one.

MODERATE

Angra A popular 86-room hotel in the heart of the Old City — which means both a central location and a noisy stay if your room faces the city's main square. Praça Velha, Angra (phone and fax: 95-27041).

Quinta Nasce-Agua A 5-minute taxi ride from Angra, this country estate has 14 rooms with private baths and offers golf, tennis, a pool, and a sauna. Vinha Brava (phone: 95-628501; fax: 95-628502).

INEXPENSIVE

Beira Mar This 15-room *pensão* in the Old City looks out on the harbor and Monte Brasil. Rooms are comfortable and quiet, with small balconies and modern facilities (but no private baths), while the restaurant on the ground floor (see *Eating Out*) is one of the best in the Azores. 1 Rua São João, Angra (phone: 95-25189).

Cruzeiro A modern *albergaria* (inn) with 47 rooms in a quiet setting only a short walk from the heart of town. There's no restaurant. Praça Dr. Sousa Júnior, Angra (phone: 95-27071).

Monte Brasil In a lovely setting overlooking the harbor in a residential section of Angra, this *pensão* has 32 modern rooms (but those facing the street tend to be noisy on weekends). The dining room offers wide-angle views. 8-10 Alto das Covas, Angra (phone: 95-22440).

VERY INEXPENSIVE

Teresinha A best bet for those who want to stay outside Angra, this residential *pensão* is in smaller Praia da Vitória on the island's east coast, about 10 minutes south of the airport. It offers a homey atmosphere and 27 rooms with private baths, but no restaurant. 45 Praçeta Dr. Teotónio Machado Pires, Praia da Vitória (phone: 95-53032).

EATING OUT

Expect to pay anywhere from $20 to $35 for dinner for two, with light drinks or fairly good wine, in restaurants listed as moderate, and less than $20 in the one listed as inexpensive.

Adega Lusitânia A favorite with local cognoscenti, regional dishes are served in a setting reminiscent of a candlelit wine cellar. Closed Sundays. Reservations unnecessary. Major credit cards accepted. 63 Rua de São Pedro, Angra (phone: 95-22301).

Beira Mar Considered one of the best in the islands, this restaurant offers both continental and regional specialties — fish, seafood, beef, chicken, and pork. The interior is contemporary Portuguese, with plenty of tile to add to the decibel level of a convivial mix of natives and visitors. Closed Mondays. Reservations unnecessary. Major credit cards accepted. 1 Rua São João, Angra (phone: 95-25188).

A Ilha In a village east of Angra, steaks are the specialty of the house. Closed Tuesdays. Reservations unnecessary. Major credit cards accepted. 49 Rua da Igreja, São Sebastião (phone: 95-94166).

Quinta do Martelo About 3 miles (5 km) from Angra, this converted country house offers some of the best regional cooking in the islands. The *alcatra* (beef casserole) is renowned, and the menu is strong on local fish specialties. Closed Wednesdays. Reservations advised in summer. Major credit cards accepted. 24 Canada de Martelos, São Mateus (phone: 95-642842).

Café-Pastelaria Athanasio The best sandwiches and pastries in town. Open for breakfast and lunch only. Reservations unnecessary. No credit cards accepted. 130 Rua da Sé, Angra (phone: 95-23702).

Graciosa

Only 10 miles by 4 miles in size, this island 60 miles northwest of Terceira is the smallest of the central group. Its proper name means "gracious" or "graceful" in Portuguese; it is also often called the *ilha branca*, or "white island," because of numerous place-names derived from that color, from Barro Branco to Serra Branca. Among its first settlers was Pedro da Cunha, brother-in-law of Christopher Columbus. By 1486 a charter had been granted to Santa Cruz da Graciosa, which today is the island's main town. Given its isolation from the other islands of the group to the south, Graciosa attracted few ships and developed a predominantly agricultural economy, exporting barley, wine, and brandy to Portugal via markets on Terceira. It retains its agricultural focus, as is evident in the lowland pastures and fields surrounding centrally located Pico Timão, only about 1,320 feet high but still the highest point on this least mountainous of all the Azores. Windmills, added in the 19th century to grind grain and draw water from subterranean depths, dot the landscape. Some are still in use, for this is also the driest of the Azores.

GETTING AROUND

AIRPORT *SATA* (phone in Santa Cruz: 95-72456) flies in from the other islands several times a week, more frequently in summer than in winter.

BUS There is public bus service on the island.

CAR RENTAL Cars are available from *Medina e Filhos Limitada*, Rua Visconde Almeida Garrett, Santa Cruz (phone: 95-72278).

FERRY Service links the island with Terceira.

TAXI Taxis can be hired for island touring.

SPECIAL PLACES

SANTA CRUZ DA GRACIOSA Set on the northeast coast of the island, this picturesque town (pop. 2,000) of red-roofed white houses is Graciosa's chief port, but it feels like a rural village. The 16th-century parish church and the three small 18th-century chapels at Monte da Ajuda are typically Azorean in style and detail, containing Flemish paintings, carved wood altars, and *azulejos*. The *Ethnographic Museum* (Rua Alexandre Herculano) is a typical old residence displaying artifacts of Graciosa's agricultural past. It's open from 10:30 AM to 12:30 PM and 2 to 5:30 PM; closed Mondays; no admission charge.

PRAIA Narrow streets lined with 16th- and 17th-century homes make for interesting browsing in this small port and fishing village 5 miles (8 km) south of Santa Cruz. A boat takes visitors to nearby Praia islet for views of the town and surrounding countryside.

FURNA DO ENXOFRE This sulfur cave, also called the Furna da Caldeira since it's located inside the island's summit crater, is a rare volcanic phenomenon in the southern part of the island. A 300-foot natural tunnel burrows through rocks into a 250-foot high underground cavern, the roof of which is covered with stalactites that hang over a lake of sulfurous water. Visit between 11 AM and 2 PM, when the sun enters the cave from a narrow opening above and creates dazzling visual effects. Outside, a trail following the crater rim offers sweeping views of the island and, on a clear day, of neighboring, but distant, Terceira, São Jorge, and Pico.

CHECKING IN

Expect to pay from $70 to $100 for a double room at the moderate hotel listed below, and from $50 to $60 at the inexpensive one.

Ilha Graciosa An adaptation of a historic old home, this *pensão* has 15 rooms with baths, and a snack bar. Av. Moniz Albuquerque, Santa Cruz (phone: 95-72675).

Santa Cruz A centrally located *pensão* with 19 comfortable rooms (with private baths) and an at-home ambience. There is a restaurant (see *Eating Out*). Largo Barão de Guadalupe, Santa Cruz (phone: 95-72345).

EATING OUT

Expect to pay anywhere from $20 to $35 for dinner for two, with light drinks or fairly good wine, in the moderate restaurant listed below.

Santa Cruz The dinner menu at this pension dining room includes fish chowder, parrot fish (when available), and chicken and beef dishes. Open daily. Reservations unnecessary. Major credit cards accepted. Largo Barão de Guadalupe, Santa Cruz (phone: 95-72345).

São Jorge

This island is a long, narrow, steep mountain range surrounded by the sea: 33 miles long from end to end, but only 5 miles across at its widest point. Despite its central location, 60 miles west of Terceira, 20 miles north of Pico, and 30 miles east of Faial, it is more often seen from a distance than visited. As was the case with most of the other islands in the archipelago, its fertile lowlands were first settled in the middle of the 15th century; subsequently, aside from an invasion (repelled) of French corsairs in the early 18th century, its history has been uneventful. While farms dominate the lowlands, pasture covers much of a central plateau — São Jorge is particularly noted for its dairy products, especially cheese. The island peaks at the nearly 3,500-foot Pico da Esperança. Up-country views are memorable, encompassing not only broad vistas, but also the sight of blue and purple hydrangeas lining the roads in summer. There are several nature preserves, including the small lagoon of the Caldeira do Santo Cristo and the tiny Ilhéu do Topo, an islet off the village of Topo that attracts masses of seabirds. Topo, at the far southeastern tip of São Jorge, was the island's first settlement, but its two main towns today are Velas (pop. 2,000) and Calheta (pop. 1,300), two ports farther up the south coast.

GETTING AROUND

AIRPORT *SATA* (Rua de Santo André, Velas; phone: 95-42125) flies from the other islands into the airport outside Velas.

CAR RENTAL Cars and automobiles with drivers are available from *J. N. Moura,* Av. do Livramento, Velas (phone: 95-42292). A road runs the length of the island, with several roads climbing upward from it to the central plateau.

FERRY Service links the island with others in the central group.

SPECIAL PLACES

VELAS Houses with whitewashed walls and red tile roofs make up São Jorge's largest village. The church of São Jorge, built in 1460 with funds donated by Prince Henry the Navigator (but rebuilt in the 17th century), was one of the earliest in the Azores. Also of interest are the 17th-century Town Hall and small museums dedicated to religious art and island ethnography.

URZELINA Several miles along the coast south of Velas at Urzelina is an isolated bell tower, all that remains of a church destroyed when Pico da Esperança last erupted in 1808.

BELVEDERES The lookouts at Ribeira do Almeida and Fajã das Almas, both southeast of Velas on the road to Calheta, provide impressive views of Faial and Pico. The lookout at Fajã dos Cubres, on the north coast near Norte Pequeno, takes in the small lakes of the island's summit crater.

NIGHTCLUBS AND NIGHTLIFE

Zodiac is a discreet pub with live music on Tuesdays through Thursdays; it's open from 8 PM to 4 AM; closed Mondays. Av. do Livramento, Velas (phone: 95-42677).

CHECKING IN

Expect to pay from $70 to $100 for a double room at the moderate hotel listed below, and from $50 to $60 at the inexpensive places.

MODERATE

Solmar The best bet for those staying in Calheta, it has 9 clean, comfortable rooms with private baths. No restaurant, but there's a bar. Rua Domingos Oliveira, Calheta (phone: 95-46120).

INEXPENSIVE

Neto A *residencial* offering 16 rooms with private baths and a seawater swimming pool. There's no restaurant. Largo Conselheiro Dr. João Pereira, Velas (phone: 95-42403).

Velas The island's largest hostelry is an *estalagem* (inn) of 24 rooms, featuring private baths and verandahs with views of Velas and of neighboring islands. A restaurant and lounge are on the property. Rua Machado Pires, Velas (phone: 95-42632).

EATING OUT

Expect to pay anywhere from $20 to $35 for dinner for two, with light drinks or fairly good wine, in the moderate restaurant listed, and less than $20 in the one listed as inexpensive.

MODERATE

Beira Mar Seafood specialties include octopus and the catch of the day. Open daily in summer; closed Sundays the rest of the year. Reservations unnecessary. Visa accepted. Largo Conselheiro Dr. João Pereira, Velas (phone: 95-42342).

INEXPENSIVE

Café Central Regional dishes are the menu, with *cozido à portuguesa* (a potluck of various meats and vegetables) topping the list of specialties. Open daily. No reservations. No credit cards accepted. Travessas, Ribeira Seca, Calheta (phone: 95-46178).

Pico

The volcanic peak that dominates the landscape also gives Pico (peak) its name. At just over 7,750 feet, cloud-shrouded Pico Grande is the tallest not only in the Azores, but in all of Portugal. The island is the second-largest in the chain (measuring approximately 30 miles from east to west and 9 miles from north to south). Its northern coast falls to the sea in a series of steep cliffs; its southern coast, where the descent to the sea is more gradual, hosts numerous fishing and farm villages. Pastureland exists, but most of the farming done on rugged Pico is fruit growing and the cultivation of the vine, particularly on the fertile volcanic soil of the western part of the island. Several small lakes are also found on the western side, and throughout there are unusual formations of lava rock, called *mistérios,* caused by 18th-century volcanic eruptions, as well as several caves. Native laurel and cedar line the roads.

Settlement began in 1460 on the island's southern coast, near the village of Lajes do Pico. By the 19th century, Lajes had emerged as a major whaling port. Besides Lajes, Pico has two other main towns: São Roque do Pico, on the island's northern coast, and Madalena, on its northwestern coast, directly across from Horta, Faial. Either Lajes or Madalena can make a good base for touring, although Madalena is better prepared to serve visitors.

GETTING AROUND

AIRPORT *SATA* (phone in Madalena: 92-622411) has daily flights to and from Terceira in summer, less frequently in winter.

BUS Public buses circle the island.

CAR RENTAL Cars can be rented from *Manuel Pereira do Amaral Rent-a-Car* (Largo Cardeal Costa Nunes, Madalena; phone: 92-622253) and from *Colômbis Rent-a-Car* (Av. Machado Serpa, Madalena; phone: 92-622601). The island can be seen in 1 day, although side trips to explore all its villages and caves and perhaps to hike to the summit can easily absorb 3 days.

FERRY Service connects the island with others in the central group.

TAXI Available for car-and-driver hires.

SPECIAL PLACES

PICO GRANDE Pico's summit caldera can be reached by trail. While the hike is not too demanding, it can be dangerous if bad weather suddenly sets in, which frequently happens. During the winter, hiking is complicated by snows that cover the upper slopes. Guides are recommended (check with the tourist office representative at the *Aparthotel Caravelas* in Madalena). The ample reward is a 360° perspective that includes Pico and neighboring Faial, São Jorge, and Terceira.

LAJES DE PICO The focus here is whales, and the town has a small museum, the *Museu dos Baleeiros,* documenting its whaling history (Rua da Pesqueira; phone: 92-97276; open daily from 10:30 AM to 12:30 PM and 2 to 5:30 PM; Sundays afternoons only; no admission charge). The *Festa dos Baleeiros* (Whalers' Festival) takes place the last week in August (see *Special Events*), even though whaling is now a thing of the past in the Azores. *Espace Thalassa* organizes whale-watching excursions in summer — a lookout sends up a flare when a whale is sighted, and rubber boats set out with the watchers. For information and reservations, contact *Museu dos Baleeiros* (see above) or *Agencia Melo* (São Miguel; phone: 92-25314).

CHECKING IN

Expect to pay from $50 to $60 for a double room at one of the inexpensive hotels listed below.

Açor On a quiet street within easy walking distance of both the port and the center of town, this 13-room (with private baths) *residencial* is in a private garden setting. There are wonderful views of the sea; no restaurant. 5A Rua D. João Paulino, Lajes (phone: 92-97243).

Aparthotel Caravelas This modern 67-unit hotel, including 17 apartments with kitchens, is within walking distance of Madalena's small harbor. Rooms have balconies and views of the coast; the hotel has a restaurant, a gymnasium, a sauna, and a solarium. Rua Conselheiro Terra Pinheiro, Madalena (phone: 92-622500).

Montanha A *pensão* in a scenic wooded area that offers a panoramic view over Pico to the island of São Jorge. There are 16 rooms with baths; no restaurant, but there is a snack bar. Rua do Capitão-Mor, São Roque do Pico (phone: 92-642699).

Pico Conveniently located on the outskirts of town, this hotel has 87 modern, comfortable, quiet rooms with private baths, and a friendly and helpful staff. Its restaurants are perhaps the best on the island (see *Eating Out*). Rua dos Biscoitos, Madalena (phone: 92-622500).

EATING OUT

Expect to pay anywhere from $20 to $35 for dinner for two, with light drinks or fairly good wine, in the moderate restaurant listed, and less than $20 in the inexpensive one.

MODERATE

Pico The two restaurants of the *Pico* hotel, one a classic hotel dining room, the other a cozier, regional eatery, offer extensive menus of well-prepared fish and meat specialties, as well as alfresco dining in summer. Open daily. Reservations unnecessary. Major credit cards accepted. Rua dos Biscoitos, Madalena (phone: 92-622500).

INEXPENSIVE

O Cadete Regional dishes and specialties fresh from the sea are served here. Open daily. Reservations unnecessary. No credit cards accepted. Poço, São Roque do Pico (phone 92-642595).

Faial

The westernmost island in the central group, measuring 15 miles by 10 miles, Faial is in part scarred by the eruption of an offshore volcano that took place in 1957, lasted a year, and left the island slightly larger than it had been. Elsewhere, typically flourishing green pastures dominate the landscape, providing a foreground for magnificent views of the towering summit on neighboring Pico, 5 miles away across the Canal do Faial. The island takes its name from the forests of beech that once covered it, although the blue hydrangeas that grow here have earned it the nickname "blue island." Horta, in the southeast corner of the island, is an important port, the island capital, and capital of the third of the Azores' three political districts.

The earliest settlers on Faial were Flemish farmers and herdsmen who arrived in the mid-15th century under the auspices of a Flemish nobleman, Josse de Hurtere. The parish of Flamengos, which lies in a picturesque valley, is a reminder of those times, as is the name of the town of Horta itself. Several centuries later, with the island heavily settled by Portuguese, Faial became a popular port of call for American whalers, who took advantage of Horta's sheltered waters to reprovision their ships. During World War II, the Allies used it as a way station for troops en route to the invasion of Normandy. In 1919, Horta also served as a stopover for the first airplane flight across the Atlantic, and at one time it was the relay point for every cablegram sent across the ocean floor. Today, particularly in April, May, September, and October, it provides refuge for yachts in transit between the Mediterranean and the Caribbean.

GETTING AROUND

AIRPORT *TAP Air Portugal* (28 Rua Vasco da Gama, Horta; phone: 92-22665) flies nonstop from Lisbon 3 days a week year-round. *SATA* (Rua Serpa Pinto, Horta; phone: 92-23911) flies in from the other islands. The island airport, Aeroporto da Horta, is about 6 miles (10 km) west of town, at Castelo Branco.

BUS Local bus service links Horta with other island villages.

CAR RENTAL Contact *Auto Turística Faialense* (12 Rua Conselheiro Medeiros, Horta; phone: 92-22308) or *Ilha Azul* (14 Rua Conselheiro Medeiros, Horta; phone: 92-31150).

FERRY There is direct ferry service between Horta and Madalena, Pico, and between Horta and Velas, São Jorge; service to Terceira and Graciosa is indirect.

TAXI Island taxis are available for touring as well as for individual trips. Try *Fraga* (phone: 92-25575), *João Duarte* (phone: 92-98270), or *Gilberto Dutra* (phone: 92-23921).

SPECIAL PLACES

HORTA This is a tranquil town of 7,000, set on gently sloping land surrounding a sheltered harbor and still graced with the scale and architectural detail of its 16th- and 17th-century origins. It was a battleground in 1583, when the Spanish fleet attacked the Portuguese garrison at the Fort of Santa Cruz; in 1597, Sir Walter Raleigh attacked the same fortress. Horta's harborside jetties are interesting: They're covered with graffiti — signatures, dedications, and hand-painted murals done by sailors throughout the years, their artistic efforts memorializing long journeys and adventures shared. Also see the 17th-century parish Church of São Salvador, with carved choir stalls and two notable panels of *azulejos,* and the 17th-century São Francisco convent, which has a magnificent gilded altar, paintings, and more *azulejos.* The *Museu Horta* (Largo Duque d'Avila e Bolama; phone: 92-23348) includes religious art, wood sculptures, and a collection of intricately carved figwood miniatures that are something of a local tradition. It's open weekdays from 9 AM to 12:30 PM and 2 to 5 PM; weekends from 2 to 5:30 PM; no admission charge. The *Café Sport* (9 Rua Tenente Valadim; phone: 92-22327), also known as "Peter's Café," or simply "Pete's," is the "in" place for the at-anchor yacht crowd and is known in sailing circles far beyond the shores of the Azores. It also attracts its share of locals, which makes for an interesting, high-energy mix when the drinks are flowing, as they usually are after 5 PM. An interesting museum upstairs houses the world's largest collection of scrimshaw; open daily; no admission charge.

Just outside Horta is the Jardim Botânico do Faial (Botanical Garden of Faial; Rua São Lourenço, Flamengos; phone: 92-31119), which features over 100 species of flora. It's open daily from 9 AM to 12:30 PM and 2 to 5 PM; no admission charge.

PONTA DOS CAPELINHOS The lava- and cinder-scarred landscape here at the westernmost point of the island is a result of the 1957 volcanic eruption. Multicolored cinder cones add beauty to a scene of silent devastation, with half-buried houses protruding from hardened ash and the burned-out skeleton of the towering lighthouse that once stood on a coastal cliff now several hundred feet inland. An interesting museum (phone: 92-95165) on the road not far from the lighthouse documents the eruption. It's open from 9 AM to 12:30 PM and 2:30 to 5:30 PM; closed Mondays; admission charge.

CALDEIRA In the center of the island, Faial's summit caldera is more than a mile in diameter and filled with a crater lake. The highest point is reached at 3,500-foot-high Cabeço Gordo, and the road leading up to it provides magnificent views of the islands of São Jorge and Pico. En route, some of the few remaining windmills on the island can also be seen.

CHECKING IN

Expect to pay from $70 to $100 for a double room at a moderate place listed below, and from $50 to $60 at the inexpensive one.

MODERATE

Fayal Set on a hillside overlooking Horta, this is as close as Faial gets to a resort hotel. It offers modern conveniences, 84 comfortable rooms, a nightclub, a restaurant (see *Eating Out*), and a bar, as well as quiet, landscaped grounds that include a swimming pool and tennis courts. Rua Consul Dabney, Horta (phone: 92-22181).

Santa Cruz A contemporary 25-room *estalagem* (inn) built atop the 16th-century fortress of Santa Cruz. It's graced with a historic setting, a central location, Portuguese decor, across-the-harbor views of the summit on Pico, a bar, and a restaurant. Rua Vasco da Gama, Horta (phone: 92-23021).

INEXPENSIVE

São Francisco In the heart of town, this *pensão* offers friendly service, 32 quiet rooms (some with private baths), and something of the feel of a monastery. No restaurant. 13 Rua Conselheiro Medeiros, Horta (phone: 92-22957).

EATING OUT

Expect to pay anywhere from $20 to $35 for dinner for two, with light drinks or fairly good wine, in the moderate restaurants listed below.

O Alfredo A large, attractive place with one of the most extensive menus in town. The grilled swordfish is especially good. Closed Wednesdays, and Thursdays for lunch. Reservations unnecessary. Major credit cards accepted. 81 Rua Pasteleiro, Horta (phone: 92-22580).

Fayal This hotel dining room serves well-prepared dishes such as pork chops "American-style" (grilled) and scallops of beef in madeira wine. Open daily. Reservations unnecessary. Major credit cards accepted. Rua Consul Dabney, Horta (phone: 92-22181).

Vista da Baia American Mary Vargas and her Faial-born husband, Frank, run this restaurant that overlooks the bay at Varadouro, on the island's west coast. Barbecued chicken is the specialty of the house, but it's also a great place to have a drink. Closed Mondays. Reservations unnecessary. Major credit cards accepted. Estrada do Varadouro (phone: 92-95140).

Flores

The remotest islands of the Azores are Flores and Corvo, and of these, Flores, about 150 miles from Faial, is the westernmost island in the archipelago and the westernmost point of Europe. The island (11 miles long and 9 miles wide) offers surprisingly diverse beauty within its modest boundaries: rugged terrain, dramatic shoreline cliffs, lovely crater lakes, waterfalls, and everywhere the abundance of wildflowers that eventually gave it its name. Some visitors consider São Miguel the most beautiful of the Azores, but Flores has equally enthusiastic advocates. After its discovery in 1452, early attempts to colonize the island by Flemish settlers were unsuccessful, so that actual settlement did not begin until 1528, when farmers and herdsmen from northern Portugal arrived. During the 16th and 17th centuries, English privateers encroached on the island's serene isolation by using its waters as a base to attack Spanish galleons returning with treasures from the New World. In 1862, the Confederate privateer *Alabama,* outfitted by the British, used it as a base to attack American ships. Today the island's small population (about 4,350), engaged in agriculture and fishing, lives as peaceably as ever, mainly in two towns: Santa Cruz das Flores, in the middle of the island's east coast, and the smaller Lajes das Flores, in its southeast corner.

GETTING AROUND

AIRPORT The only way to reach the island (except from Corvo) is by plane on *SATA* (phone in Santa Cruz: 92-52425). Infrequent service, however, combined with stormy weather during winter months, makes a quick visit somewhat risky.

CAR RENTAL Available from *Rent-a-Car Turística Flores,* Travessa de São José, Santa Cruz (phone: 92-52190).

TAXI Those in the center of town provide car-and-driver service for sightseeing out of Santa Cruz.

SPECIAL PLACES

SANTA CRUZ DAS FLORES Churches from the 16th through the 19th centuries provide this charming village with architectural significance. Among them are the parish church, Nossa Senhora da Conceição, a 19th-century building with an imposing façade, and São Pedro, an 18th-century rebuilding of a 16th-century structure, notable for its carved and gilded high altar.

ENXARÉUS GROTTO Boats take visitors along the deeply indented, cliff-lined coast to this dramatic sea cave about 3 miles south of Santa Cruz.

VALE DA FAJÃZINHA On the western coast of Flores, this is a valley with lovely waterfalls cascading to the sea and lush vegetation that give it a tropical feel. To get there, take the main road from Santa Cruz to Lajedo. At the Vale da Fajãzinha signpost, turn down the winding road and continue to the valley. The 10-mile (16-km) trip takes about 45 minutes.

LAGOA FUNDA The prettiest of the seven crater lakes on the island is surrounded by hydrangeas. It's about a half-hour drive inland from Santa Cruz.

CHECKING IN

Expect to pay from $70 to $100 for a double room at the moderate place listed below, and from $50 to $60 at the inexpensive one.

MODERATE

Occidental Each of the 36 rooms in this modern hotel has a private bath, TV set, telephone, and ocean views; there's also a good restaurant (see *Eating Out*). Santa Cruz (phone: 92-52142; fax: 92-52199).

INEXPENSIVE

Vila Flores This 9-room *pensão* is clean and comfortable (but no private baths), with a homey atmosphere and a restaurant (see *Eating Out*). Rua Senador André de Freitas, Santa Cruz (phone: 92-52190).

EATING OUT

Expect to pay anywhere from $20 to $35 for dinner for two, with light drinks or fairly good wine, in the moderate restaurants listed below.

Occidental The best choice on the island, this small, pleasant hotel dining room offers regional fare. Open daily. Major credit cards accepted. No reservations. Santa Cruz (phone: 92-52142).

Vila Flores A *pensão* restaurant serving a simple menu of fish, octopus, beef, and pork dishes. Open daily. Reservations unnecessary. Major credit cards accepted. Rua Senador André de Freitas, Santa Cruz (phone: 92-52190).

Corvo

The smallest of the Azores has a population to match its size: Only about 370 people call Corvo home. The island lies 15 miles northeast of Flores and was discovered the same year (1452), although it was settled later (1548). Its name dates back to days when both it and Flores were known jointly by one name, Ilha dos Corvos Marinhos, or "Island of the Sea Crows." Only about 4½ miles long and 3 miles wide, Corvo, like its sister islands, packs a great deal of natural beauty into a very small space. In the north is the Caldeirão, the extinct volcanic crater that formed the island, now carpeted in green and filled with two lovely lakes. From 2,200-foot-high Monte Grosso, atop the crater rim, the panoramic views are magnificent. In the south are the islanders' cultivated fields and pastures, and at the very southern tip, their only settlement, Vila Nova do Corvo, a typically picturesque town of red-roofed white houses laid out along narrow streets called *canadas*. Corvo can be reached by boat or small plane from Santa Cruz das Flores. There are no rental cars, but a few taxis are available — and a taxi should be sufficient, since the island has a single road, about 5 miles long, linking the town in the south to Caldeirão in the north. There are no hotels or other hostelries. Camping out is one possibility; by asking around, you may find someone to rent you a room. As for eating out, you're on your own.

Madeira

Lying nearly 400 miles off Morocco's Atlantic coast and nearly 600 miles southwest of the Portuguese mainland, Madeira rises from the sea in an angular assault of mountains, valleys, ravines, and cliffs, the result of millions of years of volcanic activity and erosion. On coastal lowlands and on steep hillsides, terraced fields and rustic homes replace the anarchy of once primeval forest with the geometry of human settlement. Only in a few places, where mountains and sea cliffs proved too vertical and too inaccessible for even the hardy Madeirans to colonize, can fragments of the dense forest that once dominated the island (Ilha da Madeira means "island of wood" in Portuguese) still be found, along with stark evidence of its volcanic past.

Madeira shares its oceanic isolation with a small fleet of neighboring islands that make up the Madeira archipelago. Porto Santo, 27 miles to the northeast across occasionally choppy seas, is comparatively low lying and the only other inhabited island in the group. It serves as a summer getaway for residents of the main island, thanks to sand dunes, beaches, and some of the islands' sunniest weather. To the southeast lie the rugged, unsettled Ilhas Desertas, often visible from Madeira in sharp-edged silhouette on the southeastern horizon. Still farther south, not far from Spain's Canary Islands, is a cluster of equally barren islets, the wild Selvagens.

Until 1964, when a jet airport was built on Madeira, visitors arrived aboard passenger ships that made Funchal, the only community on Madeira large enough to be called a city, a standard port of call on transatlantic and around-the-world cruises. Cruise ships still drop anchor at Funchal, which is built around a bay along the island's sheltered south coast, but it was the coming of the jets that opened Madeira to the European holidaymakers who have been arriving in increasing numbers ever since. With 115,000 people — more than a third of the island's population — and a year-round flow of visitors, Funchal is a bustling city that also serves as the capital of the archipelago, which is, in turn, an autonomous region of Portugal. Portuguese law applies, although the local legislature plays a significant role in administration, planning, and budgeting.

For winter-weary Europeans, Madeira's climate is its primary attraction. Winter temperatures rarely dip below 50F, and average a comfortable 60F when most of Europe is 20 to 30 degrees colder. Summer temperatures are no more extreme, seldom topping the 70s. Indeed, springtime plots a 12-month course here, with one flower or another — bougainvillea, hibiscus, begonias, birds of paradise, anthuriums, orchids, morning glories, hydrangeas — blooming and one fruit or another — mangos, papayas, figs, oranges, pears, avocados, guavas, passion fruit — ripening throughout the year. Few are indigenous; Madeira's subtropical climate and rich volcanic soil proved a hospitable habitat for plants brought by trading ships from all parts of the globe.

Because the island rises so precipitously from sea level to mountaintop, it has distinct zones of vegetation, and visitors can climb from sugarcane to pines and heather in the course of only a short drive. Madeira's steep rise from the sea is the cause of another peculiarity that may disappoint: its lack of sandy beaches. There are a few stretches of gravel or pebbles along the shoreline, and Porto Santo is well endowed with sand, but in the main, swimming on Madeira is confined to hotel pools or to small coves developed with cabaña facilities. Thus, for an American visitor, it is the charm of Funchal and the dramatic beauty of the landscape, not the lure of a tropical getaway, that makes a visit worthwhile.

Oblong in shape, roughly 35 miles from east to west and 13 miles from north to south, Madeira is traversed by well-maintained, well-marked roads. Panoramic vistas are a part of any drive, even within the confines of Funchal, where city streets climb 2,000 feet or more above sea level before surrendering to farmland, forest, and the jagged mountains seen from lookouts such as that atop 6,104-foot Pico Ruivo, the island's highest point. More than half of Madeira's inhabitants live in the countryside, particularly in the southern part of the island, where their terraced fields — called *poios* — create what seems a vast agricultural suburb extending nearly the full length of the south coast. Funchal itself retains the feel of a large village, with open markets, narrow streets, and a 17th-century scale, while small villages such as Ribeira Brava and Machico, west and northeast of Funchal respectively, and São Vicente, on the north coast, evoke the atmosphere and scale of traditional Madeira, with whitewashed, tile-roofed houses and the distinctive square bell towers of Madeiran churches dominating the skyline. Yet growth has been explosive for the past several decades, fueled by expanding tourism that has left casino gambling, high-rise resort hotels, and condominium apartments in its wake, and by agricultural exports and the money sent back to families by citizens living and working overseas.

Madeirans have been shipping out to parts unknown for several centuries, first drawn aboard as sailors and later enticed by opportunities offered in places as far afield as New England, Hawaii, South Africa, and Australia. Although legend credits the shipwrecked English adventurer Robert McKean (also spelled Machim) with the island's discovery in 1346, better-documented evidence reserves that honor for João Gonçalves Zarco, a Portuguese explorer who, with his fellow sailor Tristão Vaz Teixeira, first spotted the island of Porto Santo (in 1418) and then Madeira (in 1419), and claimed them on behalf of Prince Henry the Navigator, who had sponsored the expeditions.

Many other explorers followed, along with settlers, as Madeira became the first of a string of colonies that would make tiny Portugal a major world power by the mid-16th century, and a popular port for ships heading off across the mysterious Atlantic during the age of exploration. What had been a wilderness was soon home to tens of thousands of Portuguese sailors, fishermen, farmers, herdsmen, and tradesmen. They established ports, cleared most of the forest, and built the extensive network of irrigation ditches (called *levadas*) that still carry water from the cloud-banked interior and the rainy north coast to the drier south, where settlement was heaviest.

Although Spain controlled Madeira from 1580 to 1640 (when Spanish kings sat on the Portuguese throne), it was the British who ultimately provided a more lasting influence. Links to Britain were forged in 1662, when Catherine of Bragança married King Charles II of England and granted favored status to English settlers on Madeira. British traders strengthened those links, shipping large quantities of sugar, the crop that had brought the island its first taste of prosperity, and wine, which still contributes to Madeira's wealth. The British then took advantage of the commercial links when, in the guise of protector during the Napoleonic era, they sent troops to occupy the island, first in 1801, and then again from 1807 to 1814. Napoleon himself anchored off Funchal in 1815 — as a prisoner en route to exile on the isolated south Atlantic island of St. Helena. The British consul in Madeira, the only visitor allowed the emperor, presented Napoleon with a gift of madeira wine.

Sugarcane, imported from Sicily early in the 15th century, was Madeira's original cash crop. Today, bananas and grapes dominate, the former exported fresh, the other fermented to produce the distinctively rich-flavored wines that have a centuries-long reputation. The first vines, brought to Madeira from Crete during the 15th century, produced sweet wines of the *malvazia,* or, to the British, malmsey type. They were known early and well in England; madeira wine is mentioned in Shakespeare's plays. English wine merchants soon set up shop on the island, and began to export wine to the mother country and the colonies so extensively that by the 18th and 19th centuries, the English, with the Americans, were Madeira's major customers.

George Washington, John Adams, and Thomas Jefferson were all madeira enthusiasts, but the wine they drank was not like the earliest madeira. Over the years, it was discovered that fortifying the local wine with brandy not only increased its alcoholic content, but also made it less likely to spoil during long ocean voyages. Then it was noticed that the heat to which the wine was unavoidably subjected during long months at sea resulted in added body and shelf life. Eventually, the heating stage (called *estufagem*) was made a part of the basic fermentation process. Today, the results can be tasted at the *São Francisco Wine Lodge* in Funchal, where the four classic types of madeira, named for the grape variety used to produce each — dry sercials, semidry verdelhos, semisweet boals, and sweet malmseys — are fermented and stored. Madeiras are among the longest lasting of all wines, and storage racks here hold bottles dating from the 1830s, their contents still drinkable.

The British also are credited with creating a market for Madeiran embroidery. In 1856, Elizabeth Phelps, daughter of a British wine merchant, set up a workroom on the island to turn out the embroideries that were so prized by the ladies of the Victorian era. The enthusiastic British response soon had thousands of Madeiran women embroidering for export. An estimated 38,000 still carry on the craft today, as the abundance of embroidered tablecloths, napkins, nightgowns, and other clothing in Funchal's well-stocked shops confirms.

And it was the British, late in the 19th century, who first made Madeira a favorite getaway for sun seekers. That was the era when the legendary *Reid's* hotel, built by a Scot, opened, bringing a touch of Victorian Britain to Funchal. Wealthy British, particularly those in search of a salubrious climate to nurse frail health, soon turned Madeira into something of a private country club, an outpost of the British Empire rather than of the Portuguese. Today, the hotel, which hosted Edward VII while he was Prince of Wales, Winston Churchill, and others, remains the quintessence of British gentility (and still serves afternoon tea), though dozens of other hotels and rental condominiums have opened their doors over the years to accommodate the sharp increase in visitors.

Luckily, the island seems to have absorbed the growth in the number of visitors while maintaining its authenticity. This is due largely to the fact that most Madeirans retain ties to the land, still hand-tending the beautiful green, terraced fields that have been expanded over the centuries as the population has grown.

Other images of this amply flowered island complete a picture of great serenity: the brilliant afternoon light on the boats and harbor at the fishing village of Câmara de Lobos; a misty afternoon in the forest near the highland village of Camacha; Funchal at dusk, with city lights serving as a glowing highlight against the sun's last traces. Madeira is a rare travel fantasy come true, and it lingers in the memory like the sweet aftertaste of a sip of its famous wine.

Sources and Resources

TOURIST INFORMATION

The Regional Tourist Office of Madeira has its headquarters (and a well-supplied street-level office) in the heart of town (18 Av. Arriaga, Funchal; phone: 91-225658); smaller branches on the island are in Machico (Edifício Paz; phone: 91-965712) and at the airport (phone: 91-524933). Several informative tourist publications in English are available, including the *Madeira Tourist Guide, Madeira: Somewhere Special,* and *Madeira Tourist Information,* in addition to maps of Funchal and Madeira. Free visitor publications, including the *Madeira Island Bulletin,* a monthly tabloid, are also available at most hotels. Madeira Tourist Radio broadcasts in English between 5:45 and 6:30 PM daily except Saturdays (1485 on the AM dial).

Porto Santo's Tourism Office is in Vila Baleira, the island's main town (Av. Vieira de Castro; phone: 91-982361). Maps of the island and town are available; in addition, most guides to Madeira include a few pages about Porto Santo.

LOCAL COVERAGE The *Diário de Notícias,* Madeira's daily newspaper, provides a sense of local concerns, as well as information on special events.

TELEPHONE The area code for all of Madeira (including the island of Porto Santo) is 91. If calling from mainland Portugal, dial 091 before the local number.

CLIMATE

A spring-like climate makes Madeira a year-round destination. Fahrenheit temperatures range from the 50s and 60s in winter (November through April) to the 60s and 70s in summer, with warm periods pushing up into the 80s. December through February are the coolest and rainiest months. July and August are the "season," drawing large crowds of vacationing Europeans.

GETTING THERE

AIRPLANE *TAP Air Portugal* flies nonstop daily from Lisbon, and less frequently from Porto, the Azores (São Miguel and Terceira), Spain's Grand Canary, and several European capitals. Once a week, the *TAP* flight from Lisbon to Funchal continues to the island of Porto Santo, 20 minutes away. Porto Santo is also served by daily flights from Funchal aboard the smaller, non-jet planes of *Linhas Aéreas Regionais* (*LAR*), a domestic carrier whose flights can be booked through *TAP* offices. *TAP*'s main office is in Lisbon (3A Praça Marquês de Pombal; phone: 1-544080); they also have an office in Funchal (8-10 Av. das Comunidades Madeirenses; phone: 91-230151 or 91-239210).

FERRY While there is no scheduled boat service to Madeira, numerous cruise ships make calls at Funchal. Porto Santo can be reached by ferry from Funchal, but during the winter, when the seas around these islands are prone to be rough, boat service may be canceled.

SPECIAL EVENTS

Funchal is the prime focus of the special events calendar, setting things going with a magnificent fireworks display over the city on *New Year's Eve.* See the spectacle from land or head out to sea for a deck-top view. From mid-December through the beginning of January, most of the city center's trees and streets are lit up by thousands of colored lights. *Carnaval* features several parades complete with extravagant floats, musicians, and dancers in costume. The *Festa da Flor* (Flower Festival), lasting 3 days in April, celebrates the island's botanic abundance with flower-decked floats and a parade of 2,000 children carrying blossoms pieced together as a floral Wall of Hope. The festivities have a heavy folk flavor, with plenty of Madeiran music, singing, and dancing. The grape harvest begins in late August, and late September sees the *Festa do Vinho* (Wine Festival), when local wine cellars are open, *fados* are sung, folk dances are performed, and traditional Madeiran foods are served. The *Festival de Bandas* comes in late October when brass bands from villages all around the island hold forth in a good-natured competition — with a parade that is an important part of the revelry.

SPORTS AND FITNESS

DEEP-SEA FISHING Blue marlin, tuna, bonito, and barracuda can be caught in Madeiran waters, where world records have been set. The *Madeira Game Fishing Centre–Turipesca* offers charter services for up to four anglers. Prices, including crew, insurance, tackle, and bait, vary between $500 and $565 per charter, depending on the season. Inquire at the entrance to the town pier (Marina) or call 91-231063 or 91-742468. In Machico, contact *Turipesca* at the *Dom Pedro Machico* hotel (Estrada São Roque; phone: 91-965751). Big-game fishing excursions aboard the *Missil* are another possibility; capacity is four to five people, and the price is about $140 per person for the day. Contact Captain Laquai (phone: 91-933414).

GOLF The *Clube de Golfe do Santo da Serra* (Santo da Serra; phone: 91-552139) offers spectacular views over Zarco's Bay. Designed by Robert Trent Jones, Sr., the 18-hole course is near the airport (about a 30-minute drive from Funchal). The clubhouse has a restaurant, a bar, a lounge, and a changing room; golf club rentals and caddies are available. Madeira's second and newest golf course, *Palheiro Golf* (next to the famous Quinta do Palheiro Ferreiro gardens; phone: 91-792116) opened late last year. Just 5 miles (8 km) east of Funchal, it is an 18-hole, par-71 layout designed by British architect Cabell Robinson.

HIKING The tourist office can supply information on a number of recommended trails, which range in difficulty from relatively flat walks following the course of the island's *levadas* (irrigation canals), suitable for almost anyone, to strenuous walks in the vicinity of Pico Ruivo, suitable only for very experienced walkers accustomed to heights. Note that it takes only about half an hour for total darkness to fall, so walks should be timed accordingly. *Savoy Travel,* at the *Savoy* hotel in Funchal (108 Av. do Infante; phone: 91-231151), offers a half-day *levada* walking tour.

HORSEBACK RIDING The facilities of the *Associação Hípica da Madeira* are 5½ miles (9 km) from the center of Funchal at Quinta Vale Pires, accessible via Caminho dos Pretos. There are 50 horses, as well as two open riding areas and a covered one. Horses can be rented for rides through the countryside at about $17 per hour, including insurance. Make reservations through the *Estreliçia* (Caminho Velho da Ajuda; phone: 91-765658) or *Buganvilia* (Caminho Velho da Ajuda; phone: 91-765024) hotels.

SNORKELING AND SCUBA DIVING Equipment is available from *Manta Raener Madeira* (phone: 91-934410) at the Tourist Center Galomar in Caniço de Baixo, several miles east of Funchal; from the *Madeira Carlton* hotel (see *Checking In*); and from *Madeira Dive* (at the *Savoy* hotel; phone: 91-222031, ext. 250).

SWIMMING Except for a small one at the eastern tip of the island, sand beaches are lacking on Madeira, and since the coast is generally too rocky for easy ocean access, most swimming is done in hotel pools or in one of several rock-sheltered, artificial pools just to the west of Funchal. These offer cabañas, lounge chairs, food, and drink. The *Lido* (Rua do Gorgulho; phone: 91-762217), the *Clube Naval* (235 Estrada Monumental; phone: 91-762253), and the *Clube de Turismo* (179 Estrada Monumental; phone: 91-762559) attract a mix of Madeirans and visitors. Both guests and non-guests can rent cabañas at the *Savoy* hotel's swimming pools (see *Checking In*). The island of Porto Santo makes up for the lack of beaches on Madeira with its 4-mile-long strand.

TENNIS The best public facility is at the *Quinta Magnólia* (23 Rua do Dr. Pita; phone: 91-764013), where the courts have been placed in a garden setting swept by cool breezes. In addition, the *Duas Torres* hotel (239 Estrada Monumental; phone: 91-762064), and the *Madeira Palácio, Reid's, the Savoy,* and *Casino Park* hotels (see *Checking In*) all have tennis facilities, and most provide court time for non-guests. Few are equipped for night play.

WINDSURFING Lessons and equipment can be obtained in Funchal at the *Savoy* hotel and in Machico at the *Dom Pedro Machico* hotel (see *Checking In*).

Madeira

Funchal, the island capital, is set on a bay on Madeira's south coast, and attracts by far the greatest number of visitors, although Machico, east of Funchal on another bay, is fast becoming a second tourist center. A chain of mountains stretching across the island — from Ponta de São Lourenço, a low, rocky spit of land at its easternmost tip, to Ponta do Tristão at its northwestern corner — effectively divides Madeira in two. The mountains slope more gently to the sea in the south than in the north, although there are some stunning exceptions, as at Cabo Girão, a headland just west of Funchal. In the more rugged northern half of the island, the mountains come to an abrupt, cliff-hanging halt high above the surf. At points, the road west from São Vicente to Porto Moniz, Madeira's most northwesterly town, follows a narrow shelf that was picked out of the rock by workers who were lowered in baskets from the cliff tops above. Dark tunnels alternate with stunning views, making for a spectacular ride. The northern half of the island is also windier and wetter than the south, since the chain of mountains blocks northerly winds and traps the clouds and rain — providing the sheltered south coast, Funchal included, with generally sunny skies.

There is much for visitors to Madeira to see around the island. Besides Funchal's museums, churches, and gardens, there are coastal and highland villages and a wealth of spectacular scenery, visible along the road or from lookout points set on the island's highest peaks and at other beautiful spots. With either Funchal or Machico as a base, a week's worth of day trips should be enough to see it all, although it is possible to see the highlights in even less time.

GETTING AROUND

Madeira may look small on the map, but narrow, winding roads make for slow going. Most roads consist of only one lane each way, and pedestrian traffic and carts occasionally reduce even these to just a single lane for both directions. Fortunately, roads are well maintained and well marked. Route 101 circles the island; although segments of it follow the coast, much of the time the road runs anywhere from a few hundred to a couple of thousand feet above the seashore, with panoramic views all the way. Similarly picturesque main roads cross the island from south to north. Driving in Funchal, while equally scenic, is complicated by a maze of narrow, slippery, cobblestone, one-way streets. The city cannot be seen entirely on foot, however, although the downtown area is walkable.

AIRPORT Flights land at the island's Aeroporto de Santa Catarina, at Santa Cruz, 14 miles (23 km) northeast of Funchal. Several car rental firms have offices at the airport (see below). The airport-to-hotel taxi fare usually comes to about $20 to $30.

BUS Most city buses travel along Avenida do Mar, and intercity buses heading to all parts of the island leave from curbside locations (signposted *paragem*) along the same avenue. Detailed information on routes and schedules is in the *Madeira by Bus* brochure, available at the tourist office.

CAR RENTAL Cars are readily available at unlimited-kilometer rates averaging $75 a day (including tax), depending on the model. Local firms charge about the same rates as the major ones; advance booking is recommended, particularly during the summer crush. Firms with airport locations include *Hertz* (12 Rua Ivens; phone: 91-223332; and at the airport; phone: 91-524360), *Avis* (164 Largo António Nobre; phone: 91-764546; and at the airport; phone: 91-524392), and *Rodavante* (Edifício Baía, 187 Estrada Monumental; phone: 91-66020; and at the airport; phone: 91-524718). Also try *Atlantic Rent-a-Car* at the *Duas Torres* hotel (239 Estrada Monumental; phone: 91-761711) or *Europcar* (306 Estrada Monumental; phone: 91-765116).

TAXI Metered taxis can be hailed while they are cruising or picked up at hotels or at designated cabstands in town, including a convenient one near the tourist office (18 Av. Arriaga; phone: 91-222500). There is a base rate, after which fares increase by the kilometer, with a typical 10-minute trip costing from $2.50 to $5. (Add a 5 to 10% tip.) Fares for travel outside Funchal are determined by distance, and there is a published list of rates. Many drivers provide day-tour service at prices (about $75) likely to be less than the daily tab for a rental car.

TOBOGGAN Once upon a time, this was a major means of transportation on Madeira, used for carrying both goods and people down the island's steep slopes. Now run primarily for the fun of it, the *carro de cesto* ride down steep, timeworn cobblestone streets from the suburb of Monte (see below) to Funchal is Madeira's most distinctive activity. The vehicle is a wicker-sided sled on wooden runners, powered by gravity and guided and steadied by a team of two people working ropes. From Monte's Nossa Senhora church, the starting point of this one-way trip, the ride takes about 10 to 15 minutes; the cost is about $15 per person plus a small tip (each sled holds up to three).

TOURS Half- and full-day motorcoach tours of the island depart from Funchal and Machico, picking up and dropping off participants at their hotels; most guides speak some English. Tour desks and travel agents in the larger hotels can handle bookings. Among the itineraries are a half-day excursion to Monte and Eira do Serrado or to Camacha and Pico do Arieiro, a full-day visit to Porto Moniz and Cabo Girão, and a "Madeira by Night" tour including dinner and a show, all offered by *Companhia Automóveis de Turismo* (*CAT;* 52 Av. Arriaga; phone: 91-225294). *AB Tours* (177 Rua dos Ferreiros, Funchal; phone: 91-225134) operates out of both Funchal and Machico and offers a day trip to Porto Santo in addition to Madeira island excursions. *Savoy Travel* (at the *Savoy* hotel, 108 Av. do Infante; phone: 91-231151), *Windsor Travel* (254 Estrada Monumental; phone: 91-763694), and *Abreu* (22 Av. do Infante; phone: 91-231077) also offer tours.

Excursions by boat are offered by *Costa do Sol* (Marina do Funchal; phone: 91-38538), which operates several different day tours visiting the principal ports of Madeira aboard the *Tamisa.* Another possibility is the *Pirata Azul* (Marina do Funchal; phone: 91-227020), a riverboat once used as a passenger ferry between Madeira and Porto Santo and now offering half-day excursions (about $20) from April through October.

SPECIAL PLACES

FUNCHAL Thanks to its fine natural harbor on Madeira's south coast, where hillsides were once covered in wild fennel (*funcho* in Portuguese), Funchal, founded in 1428, quickly became a port of call for Portuguese ships bent on discovery and the acquisition of a prosperous overseas empire. Old engravings show it as a village tightly clustered around its port; today, while the port remains active handling cargo, pleasure craft, and cruise-ship visitors, the modern city surrounds the old one and ranges far into the mountain foothills, bringing a sense of the country to within a short vertical drive of the Old City's commercial bustle. Something of the overall layout can be seen from the belvedere at Pico dos Barcelos (about 2 miles/3 km west of town). Another view, from Monte, a hillside suburb above central Funchal, takes in the 1,800-foot drop down the mountainside to the port below. Still another vantage point, at sea level this time, is the Potinha, the breakwater for Funchal harbor built nearly 2 centuries ago. At the end of the Potinha, climb the steps up the retaining wall (ask permission of the port authorities first); the reward is a panoramic view of the harbor, the towers of the Old City, and a heavily populated mountain-side that ultimately surrenders to wilderness.

The Old City of Funchal is east of the hotel zone, stretching roughly between two forts, São Lourenço to the west and São Tiago to the east. Running along the waterfront between them is the Avenida do Mar, a seaside promenade intersected midway by the small town pier. Funchal's main thoroughfare, Avenida Arriaga, is behind Avenida do Mar and parallel to it, with a statue of the island's discoverer, João Gonçalves Zarco, at one end and the Sé, Funchal's 15th-century cathedral, at the other. This, the heart of the Old City and the first Portuguese cathedral to be built "overseas," combines elements of Manueline and baroque design. The structure is made of lava rock and stucco; its interior highlights include a wonderful ceiling of cedar inlaid with ivory, a 17th-century chancel woodwork, beautiful Flemish paintings above the 16th-century altar, and the gilded wood of the Capela do Santissimo Sacramento (Chapel of the Holy Sacrament).

The city's best shopping streets are near the cathedral, as are alfresco cafés at which to sip richly flavored Brazilian coffee and watch the passing scene. Before taking it easy, however, take a tour of the *São Francisco Wine Lodge* (28 Av. Arriaga; phone: 91-742126), run by the Madeira Wine Company, the largest exporter of madeira wines. After an informative film, the tour visits the lodge's wine cellars and aging rooms, where still-capped 19th-century vintages are to be found, and ends in the tasting room, where numerous brands are sold. The lodge is open weekdays from 10 AM to 1 PM and 2:30 to 6 PM (Saturdays by appointment); 1-hour tours take place at 10:30 AM and at 3:30 PM (bookings are necessary for groups, and there is a charge for the tour). On the same street is the *Museu Cristovão Colombo* (48 Av. Arriaga; phone: 91-36192), a museum and library with nearly 500 titles relating to Columbus and other rare items, including a great number of books on Madeira and a fine collection of old prints. It's open weekdays from 10 AM to 1 PM and 2 to 7 PM; admission charge.

Among several other museums of interest is the *Museu de Arte Sacra*

(Museum of Sacred Art; 21 Rua do Bispo; phone: 91-228900), about 10 minutes on foot from Avenida Arriaga. Housed in the former Bishop's Palace facing Funchal's mosaic-covered Praça do Município, it contains paintings from the 15th to the 18th centuries — Portuguese and Flemish painters are well represented — as well as gold and silver plate, ivory sculpture, and gilded wood ornamentation. Another 10 minutes away is another museum, the *Quinta das Cruzes* (1 Calçada do Pico; phone: 91-741388), a 15th-century country house built by the explorer Zarco, but now dedicated to the decorative arts. Portuguese furniture of the 16th century, Chinese porcelain, and French enamel are displayed in rooms that were once the villa's wine cellar; 1 flight up are French and English furniture and a collection of ivory carvings. The building is surrounded by a botanical garden featuring several acres of tropical and subtropical flowers. Both museums are open from 10 AM to 12:30 PM and 2 to 6 PM; closed Mondays; admission charge. Still another museum, near the *Quinta das Cruzes,* is the *Museu Frederico de Freitas* (Calçada de Santa Clara; phone: 91-220578), displaying art objects, furniture, and a unique collection of Madeiran watercolors in an 18th-century house. It's open from 10 AM to 12:30 PM and 2 to 6:30 PM; closed Mondays; admission charge. The Convento de Santa Clara, founded by two of Zarco's granddaughters on the site of a church he had chosen as a burial place for his family, is on the same street. It's now a kindergarten run by nuns, but visitors are welcomed at the door to the right of the church, whose interior, beautifully covered in *azulejos,* contains Zarco's Gothic tomb. Not far away is the *Museu Vicentes* (43 Rua da Carreira; phone: 91-225050), a repository of over 100,000 glass negatives on the history of Madiera and those who have visited it. It's open weekdays from 2 to 6 PM; no admission charge.

Nothing typifies Funchal better than the *Mercado dos Lavradores* (Farmers' Market) at the western edge of the Old City. It's best in the morning: Arrive between 7 and 11 AM (closed Sundays) and see the market come alive with the animated dealings of farmers, fishermen, and price-conscious Madeirans. Flower vendors stationed at the door wear traditional Madeiran garb (cap, red vest, ruffled white blouse, and full skirt). The produce arrayed inside — everything from carrots, onions, chestnuts, and papayas to scabbard fish, tuna, swordfish, and eel — serves as an introduction to the fare available at local restaurants. Several blocks farther east is the Zona Velha (Old Town), a fishermen's quarter where upscale restaurants provide alfresco dining.

The Jardim Botânico, in the hills at Caminho do Meio in the Bom Sucesso district (about 15 minutes by car from Avenida Arriaga), is another must-see. Just about every flower, plant, or tree that grows on Madeira is represented here, laid out on terraces surrounding an old country house. The views of the city and harbor are an added attraction. The garden is open from 8 AM to 6 PM; closed Sundays; admission charge. Close by, and also well worth seeing, is the Jardim dos Louros, home to more than 500 tropical birds from around the world; it's open daily from 9 AM to 6 PM; admission charge. More of Madeira's floral abundance can be seen in the gardens of the Quinta do Palheiro Ferreiro, a private estate 5 miles (8 km) east of the center, which is open weekdays from 9:30 AM to 12:30 PM; admission charge. Orchids are featured at Quinta Boavista (27 Rua Albuquerque), 5 minutes from the center; it's open from 9 AM to 5:30 PM; closed Mondays; no admission charge.

ELSEWHERE ON THE ISLAND

MONTE This hillside community, nestled amid towering trees and an abundance of flowers, is about 3 miles (5 km) and 1,800 feet above the Old City. Once popular as a country retreat, it is now more a suburb of Funchal, but its cool climate, luxuriant vegetation, and panoramic views still attract visitors. The Nossa Senhora do Monte church, built late in the 18th century, has an unexpectedly sophisticated baroque façade atop a steep staircase. Inside, the silver tabernacle above the main altar houses a small statue of Our Lady of the Mount, found in the 15th century at the very spot in Terreiro da Luta where the Virgin Mary is said to have appeared to a young shepherdess. Since that time, Our Lady of the Mount has been Madeira's patron saint, and the church is the object of pilgrimage every *Assumption Day* (August 15), when some of the faithful climb the stairs on their knees. The church also contains the tomb of Charles I, the last of the Austro-Hungarian emperors, who died here in 1922. The famous toboggan ride (see *Getting Around*) begins near the steps of the church.

CÂMARA DE LOBOS Drive 5½ miles (9 km) west of Funchal along Route 101, passing terraces dense with bananas, to reach this picturesque fishing village of whitewashed, red-tile-roofed houses built around a cliff-sheltered harbor and a rocky beach. Named for the seals once abundant in coastal waters, the village was a favorite of Winston Churchill, who often set up his easel here. A roadside viewpoint overlooks the harbor and its colorful array of fishing boats, with the dramatic sea cliff of Cabo Girão as a backdrop. Arrive by 8 AM and you're likely to see fishing boats being unloaded after a night at sea. By midday, the scene is more tranquil, as fishermen cluster amid their boats, drinking wine and playing cards, and women do their wash in the Ribeira do Vigario. The walk along the harbor breakwater provides additional panoramic views.

CABO GIRÃO The 1,900-foot headland, the second-highest promontory on earth, lies 7 miles (11 km) west of Câmara de Lobos. Follow Route 101, then turn left onto the clearly marked road to the lookout at the summit. The view down the almost sheer drop to the pounding sea is magnificent; several hundred feet below, small patches of terraced fields cling to the cliff edges wherever possible.

SERRA DE AGUA Continue west from Cabo Girão and turn inland at Ribeira Brava. Take Route 104 north 6 miles (10 km) to this rustic riverside village, which benefits from a wonderful setting of sharply eroded mountains rising precipitously from terraced hillsides that are often shrouded in mist and clouds. Bamboo and weeping willows line the river, adding a romantic touch to what is otherwise a workaday farm settlement. The road climbs from Serra de Agua to the 3,304-foot-high Encumeada Pass, where new panoramas take in the descent toward the north coast and São Vicente.

SÃO VICENTE This small town on Madeira's north coast, 9½ miles (15 km) from Serra de Agua, and about an hour's drive from Funchal, is set where a river of the same name meets the sea. The views as the road winds its way down from the mountains into this picturesque town are particularly beautiful. More views are in store as Route 101, which makes a complete circuit of the island, leads west of São Vicente, climbing to cliffside heights and offering sweeping views of Madeira's north coast. Because portions of the road are narrow and unpaved, careful attention to driving is necessary, as is an occasional bit of maneuvering when confronting oncoming traffic.

PORTO MONIZ A sheltered anchorage formed by a narrow peninsula that points toward a picturesque islet, Ilhéu Mole, is the setting for this charming fishing village 11 miles (18 km) west of São Vicente on the northwest coast of Madeira. A further attraction, besides the scenery, is the large natural ocean pool set amid lava rock that attracts swimmers during the summer months. (Winter weather and rough surf can make a swim uninviting and dangerous.) At Porto Moniz, the around-the-island road turns inland to wind its way south and eventually back east to Funchal.

EIRA DO SERRADO This 3,385-foot lookout point is about 8 miles (13 km) northwest of Funchal, reached by taking the Pico dos Barcelos road and driving approximately 20 minutes through countryside rife with eucalyptus trees and native forest. The lookout sits atop the sawtooth crater of one of Madeira's great formative volcanoes, and the view down into the crater encompasses, surprisingly, not only farmland, but also the whitewashed village of Curral das Freiras. The name of the village means "nuns' shelter," because it was to this spot that the sisters of Funchal's Convento de Santa Clara retreated when French pirates attacked the city in the 16th century. At the lookout, vendors sell well-priced handicrafts, and a path leads to additional panoramas.

PICO DO ARIEIRO No place on Madeira reveals its volcanic nature better than its second-highest peak, 14 miles (22 km) north of Funchal on Caminho do Arieiro — on a clear day, that is. Often, while the rest of the island is basking in sunlight, this 5,939-foot peak is covered in clouds, mist, and rain. When skies clear, the summit lookout reveals a landscape covered in volcanic debris and the eroded mountains that have been created in the millions of years since Madeira surfaced from the sea. The road goes right to the top of Pico do Arieiro.

PICO RUIVO At 6,104 feet, this is Madeira's highest peak, a prize to be gained only by those who hike (there is no road access). There is a 4-mile (6-km) trail from Pico do Arieiro that takes about 3 hours of hiking and entails a few treacherous stretches without the benefit of safety rails. Another trail (about 1 mile/2 km) from Parque das Queimadas (at the end of a 3-mile/5-km road from Santana, a village on the island's northeastern coast) leads to the heather-covered summit. From here, Madeira's tallest mountains rise all around, and long-distance views take in the valleys of the island's north coast, Ponta de São Lourenço at its easternmost tip, as well as Santana and the village of São Jorge at its northeastern corner. Provided arrangements have been made with the tourist office in Funchal beforehand, it's possible to spend the night in the rustic refuge — *casa de abrigo* — a few minutes' walk from the top.

CAMACHA The quiet highland village is just 6 miles (10 km) northeast of Funchal on Route 102, at an altitude of almost 2,300 feet. The surrounding groves of willows provide the material for making the wickerware that is the village specialty; the wicker shops are worth a visit even for those who don't intend to buy. Try to visit on a Sunday, when the town's buzzing with residents of the area socializing and promenading.

MACHICO It was here, 16 miles (26 km) northeast of Funchal along Route 101, that the Portuguese explorer João Gonçalves Zarco and his crew made their first landfall on Madeira, in 1419. According to legend, Machico was also the place where the Englishman Robert McKean (or Machim) was shipwrecked with his bride, Ana d'Arfet, in 1346. The young couple died, but the unlikely story has other survivors of the ship taking to sea in a raft, being captured by Arab pirates, and ending up in Morocco. Eventually, word of Madeira's existence is supposed to have reached Portugal, resulting in the voyage of discovery led by Zarco, whose shipmate, Tristão Vaz Teixeira, became governor of this part of the island. Machico's parish church and the Capela São Roque both date from the 15th century. At the Capela dos Milagres (Chapel of Miracles), rebuilt in 1829 after having been destroyed by a flood in 1803, a framed cross is said to be the one originally left on the graves of the ill-fated McKean and his wife.

SHOPPING

Embroidery, wine, and wickerware are Madeira's most distinctive products, but a shopping spree on Madeira (and that, for the most part, means Funchal) can also turn up good prices on tooled leather, handmade shoes, and high-fashion European clothing. The best browsing is along Rua do Aljube and the cluster of streets bordered by Avenida Zarco, Rua 5 de Outubro, and Avenida do Mar. Shops are generally open weekdays from 9 AM to 1 PM and 3 to 7 PM; Saturdays from 9 AM to 1 PM. Outside Funchal, shopping is likely to be limited to wicker. The village of Camacha, about 6 miles (10 km) from Funchal, is the center of this activity.

An Englishwoman established Madeiran embroidery during the Victorian era, and today thousands of Madeiran women embroider under contract to makers and retailers of table linen, children's wear, women's lingerie, and other fashions. Prices vary considerably, so shopping around is warranted, but since Madeirans know what the market will bear, don't expect fantastic bargains. Prices, in fact, can be surprisingly high, with a large, intricately embroidered Irish linen tablecloth (napkins included) topping $2,500. But there are lovely things for far less. Some shops to explore:

AGULHA D'OURO A fine selection of hand-embroidered linens at good prices. 30 Rua dos Murças, Funchal (phone: 91-24885).

ARTE RICAMO Embroidered large tablecloths, sheets, and pillowcases are the specialties here. 34 Rua dos Murças, Funchal (phone: 91-20705).

ARTECOURO LEATHER SHOP The leather is from mainland Portugal, but the bags and belts that are the shop's specialties are made on Madeira with great skill and style; there are also wallets, sandals, and children's boots. 15 Rua da Alfândega, Funchal (phone: 91-37256).

BAZAR DO POVO This commercial center, housing several boutiques, also comprises what appears to be a five-and-dime store from another era, which sells inexpensive odds and ends. 1 Rua do Bettencourt, Funchal (phone: 91-222055).

CAMACHA WICKERWORKS Room after room of things made of wicker, from giraffes and other animals to furniture. Shipping available. Largo da Achada, Camacha (phone: 91-922114). There is also a showroom and shop at the *Centro Comercial do Infante Shopping Center,* 75 Av. Arriaga, Funchal (phone: 91-34586).

CASA DO TURISTA A showcase for Portuguese crafts — crystal, porcelain, ceramics, wickerware, dolls, and more, including embroidery — displayed in an old mansion. 2 Rua Conselheiro José Silvestre Ribeiro, Funchal (phone: 91-224907).

CLOE LEATHER Everything from shoes to bags to high-fashion accessories in calf, mustang, and more exotic skins. 13 Largo do Phelps, Funchal (phone: 91-227711).

HÉLIO The source of well-priced Charles Jourdan shoes — the shop is Madeira's exclusive Jourdan agent. 65 Rua do Aljube, Funchal (phone: 91-223447).

H. STERN Brazil's ubiquitous gemstone jeweler has shops in three Funchal hotels — the *Madeira Carlton* (Largo António Nobre; phone: 91-36605); the *Madeira Palácio* (265 Estrada Monumental; phone: 91-764352); and the *Casino Park* (69 Rua Imperatriz Dona Amélia; phone: 91-225442).

LÃS VOGA An old-fashioned, abundantly stocked yarn shop. 60 Rua Dr. Fernão de Ornelas, Funchal (phone: 91-38228).

MARIA L. KIEKEBEN Manufacturers of Gobelin-style tapestries and tapestry kits, petit point embroidery, needlepoint, and high quality handmade rugs, made to order. The factory is at 194 Rua da Carreira, Funchal (phone: 91-222073; fax: 91-31201); the retail shop, *Madeira Gobelins,* is at 2 Av. do Infante, Funchal (phone: 91-227857).

OLIVEIRAS One of the widest selections of embroidery in town. The workroom on the floors above is one of a couple of dozen such factories in Funchal. Ask to visit, and see what it takes to create a finished tablecloth or negligee (and ask for the 25% factory discount). At two adjoining downtown Funchal locations: 22 Rua dos Murças (phone: 91-229340) and 11 Rua da Alfândega (phone: 91-220245).

PATRÍCIO E. GOUVEIA An extensive stock, featuring every variety of embroidery. 34 Rua do Anadia, Funchal (phone: 91-220801).

SÃO FRANCISCO WINE LODGE Run by the Madeira Wine Company — the place to go for seven of the better-known labels, including Leacocks, Blandys, and Cossart Gordon. 28 Av. Arriaga, Funchal (phone: 91-742121).

TEIXEIRAS Still more Madeiran embroidery. This is the place for something special; the prices are a bit higher, but the quality is a bit better, too. 13 Rua do Aljube, Funchal (phone: 91-224216).

NIGHTCLUBS AND NIGHTLIFE

Fado is popular here, as it is in Lisbon. If you like its soulful sound, head to *Bar Marcelino Pão e Vinho* (22A Travessa das Torres; phone: 91-30834). Also check with the major hotels — *Madeira Carlton, Savoy, Casino Park, Madeira Palácio, Reid's* (see *Checking In*) — to see if *fado* or folk performances are scheduled. The *Savoy* hotel has a rooftop nightclub, *Galaxia,* with panoramic views and its own band (folk dancing on Tuesdays and Thursdays); *Safari* (5 Rua do Favila; phone: 91-220455) follows a disco beat, as does *Baccara* (phone: 91-231121), a dance spot located in the casino (see below). The *Prince Albert* (86 Rua da Imperatriz Dona Amélia; phone: 91-35793), a pub with Victorian ambience, is quieter, allowing conversation. *Joe's Bar* (1 Beco Imperatriz Dona Amélia; phone: 91-229087) is intimate and charming, with nightly piano music and a lovely terrace. Salsa Latina (101 Rua da Imperatriz Dona Amélia; phone: 91-225182) has live (quiet) music and serves light meals; *Berilights* (23 Rua do Gorgulho; phone: 91-762535) is a bar and meeting place for young people.

The *Casino da Madeira,* adjoining the *Casino Park* hotel (Av. do Infante; phone: 91-233111), is open daily from 4 PM to 3 AM (jackets required after 8 PM). Slot machines, craps, blackjack, and American and French roulette are played in the three gaming rooms — an American Room, a

European Room, and a Salle Privée (private room), reserved for the casino's best customers. There is a nominal entrance fee for the gaming rooms, and foreigners are expected to present a passport.

CHECKING IN

Although there are several small hotels in outlying towns such as Ribeira Brava, most visitors stay in either Funchal or Machico. Funchal offers elegant high-rise hotels clustered to the west of the port, a few condominiums, and a range of lovely small hotels and pensions on the narrow streets of the Old City. Machico is Madeira in a resort mode, with a number of large hotels. Also available — under Portugal's *Turismo de Habitação* network — are rooms in privately owned manor houses and stately homes (for details, see *Pousadas and Manor Houses* in DIVERSIONS). Expect to pay $150 or more a night for a double room at properties listed below as very expensive, $75 to $150 in a hotel listed as expensive, from $40 to $70 in a moderate place, and $35 or less in an inexpensive one. As on the mainland, breakfast is included; any establishment designated as "residential" does not have a restaurant and usually serves breakfast only.

FUNCHAL

VERY EXPENSIVE

Casino Park Part of the casino–conference center–hotel complex designed by Oscar Niemeyer, the architect of Brasília, this is ultramodern in style: simple yet elegant. The 400 rooms offer sweeping views of the sea and Funchal's harbor; facilities include a large pool with landscaped lounging areas, a children's pool, a health center, tennis courts, shops, and several dining rooms serving good food. Of the top hotels, this is also the closest to the center of town, a 10-minute walk away. 69 Imperatriz Dona Amélia (phone: 91-233153; fax: 91-33153).

Madeira Carlton Stylish decor, 372 rooms with panoramic ocean views, 2 restaurants, 2 large pools, tennis, a sauna, water sports, and a central location within walking distance of downtown describe this high-rise, the island's largest hotel. Largo António Nobre (phone: 91-231031; fax: 91-27284).

Madeira Palácio On the outskirts of town, this property on a hillside affords beautiful views of the 2,000-foot sea cliffs at Cabo Girão. Friendly service is a major plus, as is the decor in the 260 rooms (comfortably contemporary). There's fine dining, and other facilities include tennis courts, water sports, and an oversize pool with Madeira's dramatic landscape as a backdrop. A free shuttle bus links the hotel to several downtown locations, a 10-minute drive. 265 Estrada Monumental (phone: 91-764229; fax: 91-764479).

Reid's The quintessential colonial hotel, an outpost of 19th-century propriety, where guests still linger in the lounge or parade through the lobby in tuxedos and evening gowns. Built in 1891, the building has been beautifully maintained and, where necessary, modernized. It offers sweeping coastal views from many of its 152 rooms and 21 suites, 10 acres of landscaped grounds, 2 lovely heated oceanside pools, water sports, tennis, some of Madeira's best dining options (*Les Faunes* and *Vila Cliff;* see *Eating Out* for both), and a central location within walking distance of the Old City. The price for such pleasures is the highest on Madeira. 139 Estrada Monumental (phone: 91-763004; fax: 91-764499).

Savoy Kitsch says it all for this 350-room oceanfront property, which is even older than *Reid's* and is its traditional rival. Actually, beyond the garish grandeur of the lobby, it tones down considerably. The place is at its best poolside — there are 2 large pools and plenty of space for lounging. Other amenities include 2 restaurants, water sports, tennis, and miniature golf. 108 Av. do Infante (phone: 91-222031; fax: 91-223103).

EXPENSIVE

Estalagem Quinta da Bela Vista A participant in the government's *Turismo de Habitação* program, this beautiful old house is appointed with antique furniture and offers 36 rooms and 4 suites. There's an attractive garden and a good French restaurant on the premises, too. 4 Caminho Avista Navios (phone: 91-764144; fax: 91-765090).

Estalagem Quinta Perestrelo Another *Turismo de Habitação* property, this modern 28-room inn boasts a pleasant pool, a dining room for guests only, and a central location, across from the *Quinta Magnólia* gardens (see *Eating Out*). 3 Rua do Dr. Pita (phone: 91-763720; fax: 91-763777).

Quinta da Penha de França A large townhouse has been converted into a 40-room inn, with lots of local character, a restaurant and snack bar, gardens, quiet surroundings, and a pool. 2 Rua da Penha de França (phone: 91-229087; fax: 91-229261).

Quinta do Sol Mid-size at 116 rooms, it offers friendly service in a park-like setting within walking distance of downtown Funchal, and a restaurant. It's adjacent to the grounds of the *Quinta Magnólia* (see *Eating Out*), and benefits from easy access to the facilities there. 6 Rua do Dr. Pita (phone: 91-764151; fax: 91-766287).

Windsor A middle-of-the-road choice in more ways than one, since this is neither large nor small (67 rooms), quite nice, fairly priced, and the only one of its category in the center of town. There's a rooftop pool and a restaurant. 4C Rua das Hortas (phone: 91-233083; fax: 91-33080).

MODERATE

Monte Carlo It occupies the crest of a hillside in the Old City, so there are breathtaking views of ocean, mountains, and red tile roofs from the balconies, the dining room, poolside, and many of the 45 rooms — about 20 of which are in the main house, a rococo palace that is something of a landmark in its own right. A friendly atmosphere prevails. 10 Calçada da Saúde (phone: 91-226131; fax: 91-226134).

Reno An apartment-hotel overlooking the heart of the Old City, within a short walk of Funchal's shops. Studios and 1-bedroom units are available, all with kitchenettes. 15-25 Rua das Pretas (phone and fax: 91-226125).

INEXPENSIVE

Santa Clara A wrought-iron gate and a walkway lined with hibiscus lead to this *pensão residencial* with 16 rooms (some with private baths), only a block away from the *Quinta das Cruzes* museum and gardens. Inside, the house has a turn-of-the-century, Victorian feel, which means a bit stuffy, but by no means unfriendly. The view from the dining room, pool, and rooftop solarium is particularly beautiful, embracing sea, city, and mountains. 16B Calçada do Pico (phone: 91-742195; fax: 91-743280).

ELSEWHERE ON THE ISLAND

EXPENSIVE

Atlantis One of the island's top properties, this high-rise has 312 rooms — all with balconies and sea views — and is on Zarco's Bay, about 35 minutes from Funchal by taxi or bus. Guests also appreciate the indoor and outdoor pools, rooftop grill, nightclub, gamerooms, cinema, tennis courts, and shops. Agua de Pena, Machico (phone: 91-965811; fax: 91-965859).

Dom Pedro Machico A self-contained resort overlooking Zarco's Bay. It has 218 rooms, a restaurant, a heated saltwater pool, a discotheque, tennis courts, and other amenities, including the equipment for windsurfing and deep-sea fishing. Estrada São Roque, Machico (phone: 91-965751; fax: 91-966889).

MODERATE

BravaMar Those in the mood to stay in a smaller Madeiran town should try this 36-room hotel. The decor is simple, in fact a bit spartan, but there's privacy, a quiet setting, and plenty of exploring to do in the surrounding countryside. Rooms have ocean views and kitchenettes. There's no restaurant. Rua Gago Coutinho, Ribeira Brava (phone: 91-952220; fax: 91-953132).

Estalagem do Mar Right on the ocean, this rustic *Turismo de Habitação* inn offers guests an impressive view of the breathtaking cliffs and mountains on the island's north coast. There are 45 rooms, plus a restaurant that serves local fare. About an hour from Funchal, in São Vicente (phone: 91-842615; fax: 91-842765).

Oásis-Atlantic This new hotel is located at Caniço, halfway between Funchal and the airport, next to the picturesque fishing village of Reis Magos. There are

55 rooms, 27 suites, 30 studios, and 10 duplexes, as well as a restaurant. Separated from the sea by the Caniço promenade, it offers maximum tranquillity in a place that boasts the best climate in Madeira. Caniço de Baixo (phone: 91-934444; fax: 91-934111).

EATING OUT

There are perfectly acceptable restaurants in all of the large hotels, clusters of restaurants taking advantage of the island's natural beauty spots, and even fast-food restaurants; most of the better places are in Funchal, although there are eating places in many towns around the island. Note that Funchal Marina, to the west of the town quay, offers a string of moderate and inexpensive restaurants within a short distance of each other — the area is pleasant and frequented by people of all ages. Madeiran specialties include *sopa de tomate e cebola* (tomato and onion soup), *caldeirada* (fish soup), *bife de atum e milho frito* (grilled tuna steak with fried corn meal), *espada* (black scabbard fish) prepared a variety of ways, and *espetada* (skewered beef, fragrant with laurel and garlic, grilled over charcoal). Pastries may look better than they taste, but *bôlo de mel* (treacle cake) is an exception. Expect to pay $35 to $45 for a meal for two without drinks at restaurants listed below as expensive, from $20 to $30 at those listed as moderate, and under $15 at inexpensive spots.

FUNCHAL

EXPENSIVE

Arsenio's A favorite with Madeirans and visitors. Fine food (local seafood and continental specialties) is complemented by *fado* singers and Brazilian rhythms. Open daily. Reservations necessary. Major credit cards accepted. 169 Rua de Santa Maria (phone: 91-224007).

Caravela Many Madeirans consider this Funchal's best. The menu is mainly continental, but includes local seafood and fish dishes as well. The setting combines casual, contemporary decor with views of the harbor. Open daily. Reservations necessary. Major credit cards accepted. 15 Av. do Mar (phone: 91-225471).

Casa dos Reis Only a short walk from the *Casino Park, Madeira Carlton,* and *Savoy* hotels, this place offers candlelit dinners in a mahogany- and brass-accented setting that still manages to be warm and friendly. Fish, lamb, and specialties of the charcoal grill are the fare. Open daily. Reservations necessary. Major credit cards accepted. 101 Rua da Imperatriz Dona Amélia (phone: 91-225182).

Casa Velha A 19th-century Madeira residence redone as a restaurant with ceiling fans, lace curtains, and blue tiles. Both local and international dishes are served. Open daily. Reservations necessary. Major credit cards accepted.

By the west entrance of the *Casino Park* hotel. 69 Rua da Imperatriz Dona Amélia (phone: 91-225749).

Don Filet A Brazilian-style charcoal grill makes this place a favorite with locals, who also come for the Wednesday-night *fado* performances. The rest of the week, there's live music at the piano bar. The restaurant provides a free shuttle van to and from nearby hotels. Open daily. Reservations necessary on weekends. Major credit cards accepted. 7 Rua do Favila (phone: 91-764426).

Les Faunes Madeira at its most elegant. Customers pay for swank surroundings (several Picasso lithographs adorn the walls), quality service, delicious continental fare, and an oceanfront view. Open daily for dinner. Reservations necessary. Major credit cards accepted. *Reid's Hotel,* 139 Estrada Monumental (phone: 91-763004).

Gavina's Always crowded, lively, and enjoyable, this oceanfront eating place serves fish and seafood — shrimp, lobster, octopus, sea bass, *espada, sargo* (sea bream), *bodião* (parrot fish), *salmonete* (red mullet), and others are all on the menu. A free shuttle van picks up diners and then drops them off at Funchal's major hotels, just 5 to 10 minutes away. Open daily. Reservations necessary. Major credit cards accepted. Rua do Gorgulho (phone: 91-62918).

Golfinho The nautical decor matches the bill of fare at this restaurant in the Old City: Catch-of-the-day fish and seafood are served. Closed Sundays. Reservations necessary. Major credit cards accepted. 21 Largo do Corpo Santo (phone: 91-226774).

O Jardim One of several good restaurants in the Old City specializing in seafood and continental dishes. Dine alfresco or inside, amid Victorian decor. Open daily. Reservations advised. Major credit cards accepted. 60 Rua Campo Dom Carlos I (phone: 91-222864).

Solar do F Portuguese regional cooking is served in this bar/grill/restaurant, where there's also dining on a garden terrace. The surroundings are pleasant and secluded, only 250 yards from the *Madeira Carlton* hotel. Open daily. Reservations necessary. Major credit cards accepted. 19 Av. Luís de Camões (phone: 91-220212).

Vila Cliff Specialties from the mainland and Madeira served in an eatery overlooking the sea. Open daily. Reservations necessary. Major credit cards accepted. Estrada Monumental, next to the entrance to *Reid's* hotel (phone: 91-763025).

MODERATE

O Almirante A central location, a casual atmosphere, good food, and good prices are the lure. Fish and grilled meat are the specialties. Open daily. Reservations advised. Major credit cards accepted. 1 Largo do Poço (phone: 91-224252).

O Celeiro Madeiran cooking is featured at this pleasant eatery in the middle of town, just off the main street. Open daily. Reservations advised. Major credit cards accepted. 22 Rua dos Aranhas (phone: 91-37322).

Lido Mar Within the *Lido* swimming pool complex west of town, this place offers fish and shellfish specialties and selected meat dishes. Open daily. Reservations advised. Major credit cards accepted. Rua do Gorgulho (phone: 91-762212, ext. 59).

Portuguese Grill Smart, quiet, and near the *Lido* pool complex west of town. Despite its name, mostly international fare is served here. Open daily. Reservations advised. Major credit cards accepted. 21 Caminho da Ajuda (phone: 91-764043).

Quinta Magnólia Don't let its status as a hotel-school restaurant serve as a deterrent. The food is some of the best in Madeira, the service (by a staff in training for coveted jobs in the food and beverage field throughout Portugal) is exceptional, and the setting, an elegant old mansion amid botanical gardens — the former *British Country Club* — is perfect. Since the restaurant serves lunch (a set menu, at 1 PM; bar opens at noon), not dinner, spend the morning at the estate's pool or tennis courts or simply walking the grounds, and make lunch the big meal of the day; reservations necessary. Otherwise, stop by for tea (at 4 PM); reservations unnecessary. Closed Sundays. No credit cards accepted. 10 Rua do Dr. Pita (phone: 91-764013).

São José The menu features local specialties such as *galinha regional* (chicken in tomato sauce), as well as duck *à l'orange* and tournedos Orsini. The decor, with entry via a Moorish arch, is as eclectic as the menu. It offers good value for the money. Open daily. Reservations unnecessary. Major credit cards accepted. 11 Largo do Corpo Santo (phone: 91-223214).

ELSEWHERE ON THE ISLAND

EXPENSIVE

O Galo A coastal restaurant facing the sea in a small village 7 miles (11 km) east of Funchal. The fish specialties make it worth the trip. Closed Mondays. Reservations advised. Major credit cards accepted. Caniço de Baixo (phone: 91-934220).

Lagoa Frequented by locals, this seafood restaurant is near the *Madeira* golf course, half an hour by car from Funchal. Open daily. Reservations necessary. Major credit cards accepted. Santo da Serra (phone: 91-552118).

Montanha This place serves charcoal-grill specialties in a spectacular setting overlooking Funchal Bay, 10 minutes east of the city on the old airport road. Open daily. Reservations advised. Major credit cards accepted. 101 Estrada Regional, Neves (phone: 91-793500).

Orca Set in a picturesque village at the northwest corner of the island where there is bathing in rock pools by the sea, this spot serves Madeiran specialties, as well as international dishes. Open daily. Reservations advised. Major credit cards accepted. Porto Moniz (phone: 91-852359).

A Rede Fresh fish and other seafood, plus rice with lobster, crab, shrimp, limpets, clams, and octopus, are the draw; located on the coast 7 miles (11 km) east of Funchal. Open daily. Reservations necessary. Major credit cards accepted. Caniço de Baixo (phone: 91-934427).

Roca Mar Also on the east coast, this is a country restaurant facing the ocean and serving regional and international specialties. Open daily. Reservations advised. Major credit cards accepted. Caniço de Baixo (phone: 91-934999).

Xadrez The local fare served here makes this place popular with Madeirans; it's a 5-minute drive from the *Dom Pedro Machico* hotel. Closed Mondays. Reservations necessary. Major credit cards accepted. Caramachão Machico (phone: 91-965889).

MODERATE

O Boieiro A unique eatery, 15 minutes east of Funchal on the road to the airport, diners are served both international and regional food while sitting in bullock carts. Open daily. Reservations advised. Major credit cards accepted. Caniço de Baixo (phone: 91-934332).

Café Relógio A great place to stop while touring the eastern part of the island. Those in the mood for a sandwich or a good cup of espresso can stay downstairs, where there's lots of local color on weekends. Upstairs, there's a restaurant serving regional specialties. Open daily. Reservations advised. Major credit cards accepted. Largo da Achada, Camacha (phone: 91-922114).

O Facho Regional cooking, with fish and seafood specialties, make this Machico's best. Open daily. Reservations advised. Major credit cards accepted. Machico (phone: 91-962786).

A Seta Head for the hillside village of Monte for a 7-course meal of regional specialties including *espada, espetada,* roast chicken, cod, and *bôlo do caco,* the delicious Madeiran country bread made with sweet potatoes. Dinner is followed by folk music and dancing that ends with audience participation. Open daily. Reservations advised. Major credit cards accepted. 80 Estrada do Livramento, Monte (phone: 91-743643).

Porto Santo

In contrast to mountainous Madeira, which is 27 miles to the southwest, Porto Santo is a low island — its highest point, Pico do Facho, rises little more than 1,600 feet above sea level. Set in the lee of the clouds attracted to Madeira's higher peaks, it is also far drier and several degrees warmer, on average, than Madeira. The island's limited rainfall and chalky soil result in an additional stark contrast: its sparse vegetation versus Madeira's green exuberance. Within the 16 square miles of Porto Santo, however, there is one topographical feature that Madeira cannot claim: a 4-mile-long sandy beach that attracts not only visitors from abroad but the Madeirans themselves.

Though it may lie low on the horizon, Porto Santo was the first island of the Madeira archipelago to be discovered. That was in 1418, when Zarco and Teixeira, sailing for Prince Henry the Navigator, found refuge here during a raging Atlantic storm. In honor of the sanctuary it provided, they named the island Porto Santo, or "Holy Port." Settlement began the following year, with farmers using windmills to draw water to irrigate sugarcane, grains, and grapes. Christopher Columbus, who married Isabel Moniz, the daughter of the island's governor, lived here for a brief time before heading off on the voyages that would make him famous.

Today, about 5,000 people call Porto Santo home; Vila Baleira, roughly in the middle of the south coast, is both the "capital" and the largest town. Most islanders continue to till the soil, harvesting tomatoes, watermelons, figs, grapes, and grain — the few windmills still to be found are a reminder of the difficulties of island agriculture. Other islanders set out to fish, although fewer than before seem willing to put in the time and effort needed to make fishing a career. Summer brings an influx of visitors, but not enough to crowd the beach. Off-season has its appeal, but with temperatures generally in the 60s, it's a bit chilly for swimming. Some visitors arrive on day trips from Madeira. Others, who appreciate Porto Santo's away-from-it-all pace and mood, stay a while.

GETTING AROUND

The island is small, only 7½ miles long and 4 miles wide, so getting around is easy. For those who prefer to leave the arrangements to others, full-day excursions from Madeira are offered by *De Luxe Tours,* 177 Rua dos Ferreiros, Funchal (phone: 91-225134; fax: 91-220151).

AIRPORT Flights arrive daily from Funchal and land at the Aeroporto de Porto Santo, 2 miles (3 km) from Vila Baleira; taxis are available.

CAR RENTAL In Vila Baleira, rental cars are available from *Atlantic Rent-a-Car* (Av. Vieira de Castro; phone: 91-984630; fax: 91-983434) and *Moínho Rent-a-Car* (Rua Dr. Estêvão Alencastre; phone: 91-982780; fax: 91-762125). If you're staying in Vila Baleira, however, a rental car is not really necessary, because taxis can be hired for sightseeing excursions.

FERRY Service links Funchal and Vila Baleira; in winter, service is frequently canceled because of rough seas.

TAXI There is one taxi stand in the center of town, on Rua Dr. Nuno Teixeira (phone: 91-982334). *Blandy Brothers* (Av. Dr. Manuel Pestana Junior; phone: 91-982114) offers sightseeing tours of the island.

SPECIAL PLACES

VILA BALEIRA Also called simply Porto Santo, the island's main town lies toward the center of the 4-mile-long beach. Besides the beach, several pensions, restaurants, and the local tourist office (on Av. Vieira de Castro; phone: 91-982361), its attractions include the small, white Piedade church and the adjacent town hall. Nearby, on Rua Cristovão Colombo, is the house in which Columbus is said to have lived; open daily; no admission charge.

PORTELA This lookout point, on a hillside north of Vila, offers an island-wide panorama.

PICO DO CASTELO A road lined with cedar trees leads north from Vila almost to the top of this 1,445-foot peak, the island's second highest. The views include most of the island and Madeira's distant mountains.

PONTA DA CALHETA The island's southwestern extremity; a lookout here takes in the desolate Baixo islet.

CHECKING IN

The choices are limited to two hotels and several pensions. Advance bookings are necessary in summer, although those who want to take a chance might be able to find an empty room without one. Prices are a bit lower than on the main island of Madeira. Expect to pay $65 or more for a double room at a hotel in the expensive category, $35 to $60 at a moderate place, and $30 or less at an inexpensive hostelry.

EXPENSIVE

Porto Santo This 2-story hotel, a bit over a mile (1.6 km) southwest of Vila Baleira, offers 100 rooms with private baths, a restaurant, a beachfront setting, a pool, and a tennis court. Campo de Baixo (phone: 91-984380; fax: 91-982611).

MODERATE

Praia Dourada Nicely maintained and well operated, it has 35 rooms, all with private baths, but no restaurant. It's in Vila Baleira, a short walk from the beach. Rua Dr. Pedro Lomelino (phone: 91-982315; fax: 91-982437).

INEXPENSIVE

Zarco A small, homey *pensão residencial* of 22 rooms (some with private baths) within a short walk of the beach in Vila Baleira. Rua João Gonçalves Zarco (phone: 91-982273). Inexpensive.

EATING OUT

Fish and seafood predominate. Although many restaurants open only in summer, there are several to choose from throughout the year. Expect a meal for two without drinks to cost $10 to $20 in the moderate restaurants listed below.

Arsénio A centrally located snack bar and restaurant serving Italian specialities. Open daily. Reservations advised. No credit cards accepted. Av. Dr. Mauel Pestana Júnior (phone: 91-984348).

Asia Mar As its name suggests, this popular eatery specializes in Chinese food; the Peking duck is highly recommended. Closed Tuesdays. Reservations necessary. No credit cards accepted. Off the main road near the beach, in Campo de Baixo (phone: 91-982468).

Baiana A café–snack bar–restaurant in the center of Vila, it serves the catch of the day, plus regional dishes. The covered outdoor patio is a pleasant place to dine alfresco. Open daily. No reservations. No credit cards accepted. Rua Dr. Nuno Teixeira (phone: 91-982209).

O Forno A new eatery by a camping site on the west side of town; it offers snacks and reasonably priced meals. Open daily. Reservations advised. No credit cards accepted. 50 Av. Henrique Vieira de Castro (phone: 91-985141).

Teodorico Traditional *espetada* — skewered and grilled beef — is the specialty. The restaurant is in the hills in scenic Serra de Fora, northeast of Vila. Open daily. Reservations advised. No credit cards accepted. Serra de Fora (phone: 91-982257).

Index